Lecture Notes in Computer Science 15191

Founding Editors

Gerhard Goos
Juris Hartmanis

Editorial Board Members

Elisa Bertino, USA
Wen Gao, China

Bernhard Steffen ⓘ, Germany
Moti Yung ⓘ, USA

Formal Methods

Subline of Lecture Notes in Computer Science

Subline Series Editors

Ana Cavalcanti, *University of York, UK*
Marie-Claude Gaudel, *Université de Paris-Sud, France*

Subline Advisory Board

Manfred Broy, *TU Munich, Germany*
Annabelle McIver, *Macquarie University, Sydney, NSW, Australia*
Peter Müller, *ETH Zurich, Switzerland*
Erik de Vink, *Eindhoven University of Technology, The Netherlands*
Pamela Zave, *AT&T Laboratories Research, Bedminster, NJ, USA*

More information about this series at https://link.springer.com/bookseries/558

Erika Ábrahám · Houssam Abbas
Editors

Runtime Verification

24th International Conference, RV 2024
Istanbul, Turkey, October 15–17, 2024
Proceedings

Editors
Erika Ábrahám
RWTH Aachen University
Aachen, Nordrhein-Westfalen, Germany

Houssam Abbas
Oregon State University
Corvallis, OR, USA

ISSN 0302-9743   ISSN 1611-3349   (electronic)
Lecture Notes in Computer Science
ISBN 978-3-031-74233-0   ISBN 978-3-031-74234-7   (eBook)
https://doi.org/10.1007/978-3-031-74234-7

© The Editor(s) (if applicable) and The Author(s), under exclusive license
to Springer Nature Switzerland AG 2025
Chapter "Approximate Distributed Monitoring under Partial Synchrony: Balancing Speed and Accuracy" is licensed under the terms of the Creative Commons Attribution 4.0 International License (http://creativecommons.org/licenses/by/4.0/). For further details see license information in the chapter.

This work is subject to copyright. All rights are solely and exclusively licensed by the Publisher, whether the whole or part of the material is concerned, specifically the rights of translation, reprinting, reuse of illustrations, recitation, broadcasting, reproduction on microfilms or in any other physical way, and transmission or information storage and retrieval, electronic adaptation, computer software, or by similar or dissimilar methodology now known or hereafter developed.
The use of general descriptive names, registered names, trademarks, service marks, etc. in this publication does not imply, even in the absence of a specific statement, that such names are exempt from the relevant protective laws and regulations and therefore free for general use.
The publisher, the authors and the editors are safe to assume that the advice and information in this book are believed to be true and accurate at the date of publication. Neither the publisher nor the authors or the editors give a warranty, expressed or implied, with respect to the material contained herein or for any errors or omissions that may have been made. The publisher remains neutral with regard to jurisdictional claims in published maps and institutional affiliations.

This Springer imprint is published by the registered company Springer Nature Switzerland AG
The registered company address is: Gewerbestrasse 11, 6330 Cham, Switzerland

If disposing of this product, please recycle the paper.

Preface

This volume contains the refereed proceedings of the 24rd International Conference on Runtime Verification (RV 2024), which was held during October 14–17, 2024, at the Boğaziçi University in Istanbul, Turkey. The RV series is a sequence of annual meetings that bring together scientists from both academia and industry interested in investigating novel lightweight formal methods to monitor, analyze, and guide the runtime behavior of software and hardware systems. Runtime verification techniques are crucial for system correctness, reliability, and robustness; they provide an additional level of rigor and effectiveness compared to conventional testing and are generally more practical than exhaustive formal verification. Runtime verification can be used prior to deployment, for testing, verification, and debugging purposes, and after deployment for ensuring reliability, safety, and security, for providing fault containment and recovery, and for online system repair.

RV started in 2001 as an annual workshop and turned into a conference in 2010. The workshops were organized as satellite events of established forums, including the Conference on Computer-Aided Verification and ETAPS. The proceedings of RV from 2001 to 2005 were published in Electronic Notes in Theoretical Computer Science. Since 2006, the RV proceedings have been published in Springer's Lecture Notes in Computer Science. Previous RV conferences took place in Istanbul, Turkey (2012); Rennes, France (2013); Toronto, Canada (2014); Vienna, Austria (2015); Madrid, Spain (2016); Seattle, USA (2017); Limassol, Cyprus (2018); and Porto, Portugal (2019). The conferences in 2020 and 2021 were held virtually due to COVID-19, whereas in 2022 RV took place in Tbilisi, Georgia, and in 2023 in Thessaloniki, Greece.

This year we received 31 submissions, composed of 21 full papers, 8 short papers, and 2 tool papers. Each of these submissions went through a rigorous double-blind review process with three reviews per paper. The evaluation and selection process involved thorough discussions among the members of the Program Committee and external reviewers through the EasyChair conference manager, before reaching a consensus on the final decisions. The Program Committee selected 18 contributions, 11 regular, 5 short, and 2 tool papers, for presentation during the conference and inclusion in these proceedings.

At the conference, an inspiring keynote was given by Borzoo Bonakdarpour, Michigan State University, USA, with the title "Distributed Runtime Verification with Imperfect Monitors: Challenges and Opportunities". An extended abstract of this talk is also included in these proceedings. The program furthermore included a tool showcase session.

RV 2024 is the result of the combined efforts of many individuals to whom we are deeply grateful. In particular, we thank the PC members and sub-reviewers for their accurate and timely reviewing, all authors for their submissions, and all attendees of the conference for their participation. We are grateful for the generous sponsorships by

Toyota and Springer, supporting this year's Best Paper Award and Best Tool Award. The conference would not have been possible without the enthusiasm and dedication of our Local Chair Doğan Ulus and our Publicity Chair Anna Lukina, and the support of the Boğaziçi University. We also thank Laura Nenzi and Panagiotis Katsaros, chairs of RV 2023, for their help and the RV Steering Committee for their support. For the work of the Program Committee and the compilation of the proceedings, the EasyChair system was employed; it freed us from many technical matters and allowed us to focus on the program, for which we are grateful.

October 2024

Erika Ábrahám
Houssam Abbas

Organization

Program Committee Chairs

Erika Ábrahám	RWTH Aachen University, Germany
Houssam Abbas	Oregon State University, USA

Local Chair

Doğan Ulus	Boğaziçi University, Turkey

Publicity Chair

Anna Lukina	Delft University of Technology, the Netherlands

Steering Committee

Saddek Bensalem	VERIMAG, France
Yliès Falcone	Université Grenoble Alpes, France
Giles Reger	Amazon Web Services and University of Manchester, UK
Oleg Sokolsky	University of Pennsylvania, USA
Klaus Havelund	NASA Jet Propulsion Laboratory, USA
Howard Barringer	University of Manchester, UK
Ezio Bartocci	Technical University of Vienna, Austria
Insup Lee	University of Pennsylvania, USA
Martin Leucker	University of Lübeck, Germany
Grigore Rosu	University of Illinois at Urbana-Champaign, USA

Program Committee

Houssam Abbas	Oregon State University, USA
Erika Ábrahám	RWTH Aachen University, Germany
Davide Ancona	Università di Genova, Italy
Fatma Basak Aydemir	Utrecht University, the Netherlands
Ezio Bartocci	Technical University of Vienna, Austria
Borzoo Bonakdarpour	Michigan State University, USA
Silvia Bonfanti	University of Bergamo, Italy
Francesca Cairoli	University of Trieste, Italy
Michele Chiari	Technical University of Vienna, Austria
Thao Dang	CNRS/VERIMAG, France
Jyotirmoy Deshmukh	University of Southern California, USA
Georgios Fainekos	Toyota NA R&D, USA

Marie Farrell	University of Manchester, UK
Lu Feng	University of Virginia, USA
Adrian Francalanza	University of Malta, Malta
Klaus Havelund	NASA Jet Propulsion Laboratory, USA
Zhihao Jiang	ShanghaiTech University, China
Panagiotis Katsaros	Aristotle University of Thessaloniki, Greece
Martin Leucker	University of Lübeck, Germany
Chung-Wei Lin	National Taiwan University, Taiwan
Anna Lukina	Delft University of Technology, the Netherlands
Isaac Mackey	United States Marine Corps, USA
Konstantinos Mamouras	Rice University, USA
Suha Orhun Mutluergil	Sabanci University, Turkey
Laura Nenzi	University of Trieste, Italy
Dejan Nickovic	Austrian Institute of Technology, Austria
Gordon Pace	University of Malta, Malta
Nicola Paoletti	King's College London, UK
Giulia Pedrielli	Arizona State University, USA
Doron Peled	Bar-Ilan University, Israel
Violet Ka I Pun	Western Norway University of Applied Sciences, Norway
Stefan Ratschan	Czech Academy of Sciences, Czechia
Indranil Saha	Indian Institute of Technology Kanpur, India
Sandhya Saisubramanian	Oregon State University, USA
César Sánchez	IMDEA Software Institute, Spain
Gerardo Schneider	University of Gothenburg, Sweden
Julien Signoles	CEA LIST, France
Oleg Sokolsky	University of Pennsylvania, USA
Hazem Torfah	Chalmers University of Technology, Sweden
Dmitriy Traytel	University of Copenhagen, Denmark
Masaki Waga	Kyoto University, Japan

Additional Reviewers

Hipler, Raik
Hsu, Tzu-Han
Kallwies, Hannes
Koll, Charles
Kuipers, Tom
Mahe, Erwan

Nesterini, Eleonora
Paul, Sheryl
Qin, Xin
Requeno, Jose Ignacio
Saraç, N. Ege
Thibeault, Quinn

Sponsors

Toyota

Springer

Boğaziçi University

Distributed Runtime Verification with Imperfect Monitors: Challenges and Opportunities (Extended Abstract)

Borzoo Bonakdarpour

Department of Computer Science and Engineering, Michigan State University
borzoo@msu.edu

A distributed system consists of a collection of (possibly) geographically separated processes that attempt to solve a problem by means of communication and local computation. Applications of distributed systems range over smallscale networks of deeply embedded systems to monitoring a collection of sensors in smart buildings to large-scale cluster of servers in cloud services. However, design and analysis of such systems has always been a grand challenge due to their inherent complex structure, amplified by nondeterminism and the occurrence of faults. Reasoning about the correctness of distributed systems is a particularly tedious task, as nondeterministic choices of actions result in combinatorial explosion of possible executions. This makes exhaustive model checking techniques not scalable and under-approximate techniques such as testing not so effective in finding complex corner cases. In runtime verification (RV), a monitor typically observes the behavior of a distributed system at run time and verifies its correctness with respect to a temporal logic formula. Distributed RV has to overcome a significantly more challenging problems, as compared to the classic RV problems because of the following challenges:

- **Combinatorial explosion.** Due to lack of a global clock, there may potentially exist events whose order of occurrence cannot be determined by a runtime monitor. Additionally, different orders of events may result in different verification verdicts. Enumerating all possible orders at run time often incurs an exponential blow up, making it impractical. This challenge, of course, is on top of the usual monitoring overhead to evaluate an execution.
- **Occurrence of faults.** We have every reason to believe that distributed monitors are not necessarily perfect and are prone to all types of faults like any other distributed process in the real world.
- **Continuous domain.** In distributed systems that deal with continuoustime real-valued signals (e.g., cyber-physical systems), the absence of a global reference of time creates an infinite number of events that cannot be ordered. This creates a unique situation that has not been fully understood in the literature, as the distributed algorithms community has primarily focusedon discrete-event systems.

In this talk, I will present our results in the past few years on runtime verification of distributed systems These results address the three aforementioned challenges as follows:

- **Partial synchrony and SMT solving [4–7].** In order to deal with the inherent combinotrial explosion, we make a realistic assumption by incorporating a clock synchronization algorithm that ensures a maximum clock skew between every pair of distributed processes. We also employ the power of state-of-the-art SMT solvers for a more efficient implementation of algorithms that search for a specification violation.
- **Fault-tolerant distributed monitors [1–3].** A natural question to ask is whether it is possible to take advantage of well-studied problems in distributed computing, such as crash and Byzantine fault-tolerance to design and implement fault-tolerant distributed monitors. It turns out the answer to this question is not straightforward: in some cases simple distributed algorithms are applicable and in some cases, similar problems have completely different settings and solutions.
- **Distributed signal re-timing [8–11].** We introduced a novel re-timing method that allows reasoning about the correctness of formulas in signal temporal logic (STL) among continuous-time signals that do not share a global view of time. This technique has made it possible to deal with establishing the order of an infinite number of events in the absence of a global time clock.

I will also present real-world case studies and demonstrate that scalable online monitoring of distributed applications is within our reach. Finally, I will discuss a landscape of solved and open problems for different models of distributed computation.

References

1. Bonakdarpour, B., Fraigniaud, P., Rajsbaum, S., Rosenblueth, D.A., Travers, C.: Decentralized asynchronous crash-resilient runtime verification. In: Proceedings of the 27th International Conference on Concurrency Theory (CONCUR), pp. 16:1–16:15 (2016). https://doi.org/10.4230/LIPIcs.CONCUR.2016.16
2. Bonakdarpour, B., Fraigniaud, P., Rajsbaum, S., Rosenblueth, D.A., Travers, C.: Decentralized asynchronous crash-resilient runtime verification. J. ACM **69**(5), 34:1–34:31 (2022)
3. Gangulky, R., Kazemlou, S., Bonakdarpour, B.: Crash-resilient decentralized synchronous runtime verification. IEEE Trans. Dependable Secure. Syst. (TDSC) **21**(3), 1017–1031 (2023)
4. Ganguly, R., Momtaz, A., Bonakdarpour, B.: Distributed runtime verification under partial asynchrony. In: Proceedings of the 24th International Conference on Principles of Distributed Systems (OPODIS), pp. 20:1–20:17 (2020)
5. Ganguly, R., Momtaz, A., Bonakdarpour, B.: Runtime verification of partiallysynchronous distributed system. Formal Meth. Syst. Des. (FMSD) (2024).
6. Ganguly, R., et al.: Distributed runtime verification of metric temporal properties for cross-chain protocols. In: Proceedings of the 42nd IEEE International Conference on Distributed Computing Systems (ICDCS), pp. 23–33 (2022)
7. Ganguly, R., et al.: Distributed runtime verification of metric temporal properties. J. Parallel Distrib. Comput. **185**, 104801 (2024)

8. Koll, C., Momtaz, A., Bonakdarpour, B., Abbas, H.: Decentralized predicate detection over partially synchronous continuous-time signals. In: Katsaros, P., Nenzi, L. (eds.) Runtime Verification. RV 2023. LNCS, vol. 14245, pp. 213–230. Springer, Cham (2023). https://doi.org/10.1007/978-3-031-44267-4_11
9. Momntaz, A., Abbas, H., Bonakdarpour, B.: Monitoring signal temporal logic in distributed cyber-physical systems. In: Proceedings of the 14th ACM/IEEE International Conference on Cyber-Physical Systems (ICCPS) (2013)
10. Momtaz, A., Basnet, N., Abbas, H., Bonakdarpour, B.: Predicate monitoring in distributed cyber-physical systems. In: Feng, L., Fisman, D. (eds.) Runtime Verification. RV 2021. LNCS, vol. 12974, pp. 3–22. Springer, Cham (2021). https://doi.org/10.1007/978-3-030-88494-9_1
11. Momtaz, A., Basnet, N., Abbas, H., Bonakdarpour. B.: Predicate monitoring in distributed cyber-physical systems. Int. J. Softw. Tools Technol. Transf. **25**(4), 541–556 (2023).

Contents

Cyber-physical Systems

A Formal Approach for Safe Reinforcement Learning: A Rate-Adaptive Pacemaker Case Study... 3
   Sai Rohan Harshavardhan Vuppala, Nathan Allen, Srinivas Pinisetty, and Partha Roop

Stream-Based Monitoring Under Measurement Noise 22
   Bernd Finkbeiner, Martin Fränzle, Florian Kohn, and Paul Kröger

Dynamic, Multi-objective Specification and Falsification of Autonomous CPS 40
   Kevin Kai-Chun Chang, Kaifei Xu, Edward Kim, Alberto Sangiovanni-Vincentelli, and Sanjit A. Seshia

Oblivious Monitoring for Discrete-Time STL via Fully Homomorphic Encryption... 59
   Masaki Waga, Kotaro Matsuoka, Takashi Suwa, Naoki Matsumoto, Ryotaro Banno, Song Bian, and Kohei Suenaga

Sampling-Based and Gradient-Based Efficient Scenario Generation 70
   Vidisha Kudalkar, Navid Hashemi, Shilpa Mukhopadhyay, Swapnil Mallick, Christof Budnik, Parinitha Nagaraja, and Jyotirmoy V. Deshmukh

HyperPart-X: Probabilistic Guarantees for Parameter Mining of Signal Temporal Logic Formulas in Cyber-Physical Systems 89
   Tanmay Khandait and Giulia Pedrielli

Temporal Logics

faRM-LTL: A Domain-Specific Architecture for Flexible and Accelerated Runtime Monitoring of LTL Properties 109
   Amrutha Benny, Sandeep Chandran, Rajshekar Kalayappan, Ramchandra Phawade, and Piyush P. Kurur

Efficient Offline Monitoring for Dynamic Metric Temporal Logic........... 128
   Konstantinos Mamouras

TimelyMon: A Streaming Parallel First-Order Monitor........................ 150
   Lennard Reese, Rafael Castro G. Silva, and Dmitriy Traytel

Specification and Visualization

Adding State to Stream Runtime Verification 163
   Manuel Caldeira, Hannes Kallwies, Martin Leucker, and Daniel Thoma

The Complexity of Data-Free Nfer 174
   Sean Kauffman, Kim Guldstrand Larsen, and Martin Zimmermann

RTLolaMo^{3}Vis - A Mobile and Modular Visualization Framework
for Online Monitoring 192
   *Jan Baumeister, Bernd Finkbeiner, Jan Kautenburger,
   and Clara Rubeck*

Deep Neural Networks

Case Study: Runtime Safety Verification of Neural Network Controlled
System 205
   *Frank Yang, Sinong Simon Zhan, Yixuan Wang, Chao Huang,
   and Qi Zhu*

Gaussian-Based and Outside-the-Box Runtime Monitoring Join Forces 218
   *Vahid Hashemi, Jan Křetínský, Sabine Rieder, Torsten Schön,
   and Jan Vorhoff*

Box-Based Monitor Approach for Out-of-Distribution Detection in YOLO:
An Exploratory Study 229
   Weicheng He, Changshun Wu, and Saddek Bensalem

Distributed Systems

Distributed Monitoring of Timed Properties 243
   Léo Henry, Thierry Jéron, Nicolas Markey, and Victor Roussanaly

Towards Efficient Runtime Verified Linearizable Algorithms 262
   Gilde Valeria Rodríguez and Armando Castañeda

Approximate Distributed Monitoring Under Partial Synchrony: Balancing
Speed & Accuracy 282
   Borzoo Bonakdarpour, Anik Momtaz, Dejan Ničković, and N. Ege Saraç

Author Index 303

Cyber-physical Systems

A Formal Approach for Safe Reinforcement Learning: A Rate-Adaptive Pacemaker Case Study

Sai Rohan Harshavardhan Vuppala[1], Nathan Allen[2], Srinivas Pinisetty[1(✉)], and Partha Roop[2]

[1] Indian Institute of Technology Bhubaneswar, Bhubaneswar, India
{shv12,spinisetty}@iitbbs.ac.in
[2] The University of Auckland, Auckland, New Zealand
{nathan.allen,p.roop}@auckland.ac.nz

Abstract. As learning-enabled Cyber-Physical Systems (CPSs) are increasingly used in safety-critical settings, there is a growing need to ensure their safety. For example, to tackle the problem of rate-adaptive pacemakers which correct Sinus Node Dysfunction, a Reinforcement Learning (RL) approach may be used to mimic the natural pacing rhythm of the heart. However, this is currently not done and there are no known approaches to ensure the safety of combining RL with conventional pacing algorithms. While there is growing interest on ensuring the safety of AI-enabled CPS, the issue of safe RL for CPS, using light-weight formal methods, has drawn scant attention.

Therefore, we present an approach which combines Runtime Enforcement with RL. To guarantee safety throughout the RL agent's learning and execution stages, an enforcer is constructed from a set of safety policies expressed using a variant of timed automata. The RL agent's outputs are observed by the enforcer, which ensures that only safe actions are delivered to the environment by correcting the outputs which would violate the safety policies. In order to evaluate the proposed approach, we have implemented a rate-adaptive pacemaker which learns the natural pacing rhythm through an RL agent, allowing it to pace appropriately during disease. This model is executed in closed-loop with a real-time heart model where various diseases can be exhibited in order to test its efficacy. Furthermore, we illustrate the benefits of this system by contrasting it with traditional pacing techniques and RL without the use of an enforcer.

Keywords: Runtime enforcement · Reinforcement learning · Rate adaptive pacemaker

1 Introduction

Pacemakers are used to treat bradycardia, a condition where the heart beats below 60 beats per minute (bpm). Conventional pacemakers are used to ensure normal cardiac rhythm, albeit that the pacing rate is unable to learn and adapt dynamically to mimic the intrinsic heart rate. Such pacing, if developed, could improve complex arrhythmia, such as 2nd Degree Sinoatrial (SA) Block, illustrated in Fig. 1[1], which has no pacing solution as of now [5].

Learning-based controllers have gained prominence with the emergence of RL-based controllers, that can solve many complex optimisation and control problems, including dynamic environments such as the human heart or the environment of an autonomous car. In RL, an agent (the controller) is trained on a reward and punishment system as a result of its generated actions, allowing the agent to learn an optimal policy. Such a policy maps environmental inputs to control outputs to ensure that the cumulative reward is maximised [24].

However, the application of RL to safety critical systems is problematic due to their potential for failures. Hence, safety verification of RL controllers is taking center stage as highlighted in a recent survey [14]. Scalable RL verification, using static analysis, remains challenging albeit that a recent method has shown some promise [3].

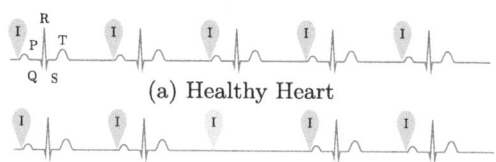

(a) Healthy Heart

(b) 2nd Degree Sinoatrial Block, Type II with one blocked impulse

(c) 2nd Degree Sinoatrial Block, Type II with two blocked impulses

Fig. 1. Electrocardiograms showing a healthy heart, and various instances of 2nd Degree Sinoatrial Block, Type II. In each case, the *I* markers represent Sinoatrial Impulses.

However, ensuring safe operation at all times just using static methods remains a challenging problem [10], especially for CPS involving dynamic environments such as autonomous cars. Therefore, we hypothesise that run-time methods, using Runtime Verification (RV) and Runtime Enforcement (RE) can offer a formal and scalable alternatives for verifying RL controllers. These methods verify the execution of a system, and hence are both scalable and light-weight. RE is especially attractive, since upon verification failure, a suitable evasive action can be taken at run-time to ensure safe operation.

There has been a set of recent RE approaches for RL by extending the concept of shield synthesis [10]. A shield is an enforcer that is suitable for reactive systems and examines the environmental inputs to determine evasive actions that mitigate failures. However, this approach may not be suitable for CPS, which require bidirectional enforcement proposed in [20]. Bidirectional RE for reactive CPSs, which monitors and corrects both inputs and outputs of a controller, is presented in [20], where Discrete Timed Automata (DTAs) are used to formally specify safety policies.

---

[1] The figure is discussed in detailed in Sect. 3.

Problem Discussion: In this paper, we intend to solve the safety assurance problem of RL-based control by applying RE techniques. We specifically consider the case study of an adaptive pacemaker controller for patients suffering from 2nd Degree SA Block, Type II. Standard pacing algorithms, from device companies such as Boston Scientific, provide pacing signals such that a set of pacemaker requirements are satisfied. In 2nd Degree SA Block, Type II, some impulses fail to conduct to the atria as illustrated in Fig. 1. Thus, RL can be a good solution to this problem since it is often used to find optimal control tasks in dynamic environments.

Through a reward mechanism, the RL agent learns to pace the heart according to the intrinsic rhythm of the patient during any disease conditions, rather than at a fixed rate. The use of RE techniques is especially important in this, since pacemakers are inherently safety critical systems where any incorrect operation could have drastic effects on the patient. As such, we express a set of requirements as a set of DTAs, and enforcers based on them guarantee a minimum level of operation for the pacemaker, providing a formal guarantee that the operation of our RL-based controller is safe for the patient, including during the early learning phases.

The approach that we propose is generic and suitable for other reactive CPS, where the controllers are developed using RL-based approaches.

Contributions. The main contributions are: (1) We propose a formal approach for safe RL, specifically where the environment is dynamic in nature, showing how a bidirectional formal RE approach can be combined together with RL-based control, to ensure safety of the overall system. Bidirectional RE approaches for CPS exist [17,20,21], but so far there have been no attempts to utilise them for RL. (2) For synthesis of enforcers in our proposed setting, we generalise an existing DTA based bidirectional RE framework [20] by introducing an additional optimization component within the enforcer that indicates when the training of the agent can be turned ON/OFF to save power. (3) As a case-study, we focus on the SA Block heart condition and discuss why an RL-based approach is useful to handle that condition. As far as we know, there are no techniques that have studied RL approaches in this use-case. (4) We implement the proposed scheme for the considered case-study, and show experiments that clearly illustrate the advantages of combining bidirectional RE for RL-based control of safety-critical systems.

2 Overview of the Proposed Approach

Figure 2 shows the architecture of safe RL using bidirectional RE. Here, the controller is made up of an RL system and an enforcer, where an RL system consists of an agent and a reward generator (R), while there is an additional Optimisation Enforcer which enables or disables the online learning behaviours. Starting from the left, the environment is the physical process which

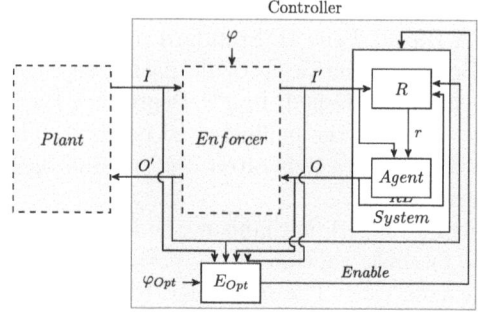

Fig. 2. Safe Reinforcement Learning using Bidirectional Runtime Enforcement

the agent must learn to control. The enforcer, meanwhile, is automatically synthesised using a DTA-based specification of key safety properties (φ), which need to be continually satisfied. The enforcer achieves this by modifying the incoming input signals (I) before reaching the controller and outgoing output signals (O) before reaching the environment.

The agent selects an action to perform (O) based on the observations that it is receiving (I'), in this case from the enforcer. The reward generator (R) takes in the observations passed to the controller (I'), the output of the controller (O), and the enforced outputs of the enforcer (O') and uses this information to compute a *reward* (r) for the agent. In this case, the reward generator can include enforcement actions as part of the reward function, providing a negative reward (i.e. a penalty) if the agent's output (O) does not match that of the enforcer (O'). The agent can then subsequently use this generated reward to learn what are the optimal actions to take at any point in time, and which actions result in negative consequences.

3 Case-Study and Problem Discussion

Here, we introduce our motivating case study in detail—a cardiac pacemaker for SA Block.

3.1 Cardiac Conduction System

Before talking about the heart diseases that our pacemaker will try to correct, we first need to introduce a set of foundational knowledge on the cardiac conduction system itself.

A human heart consists of 4 chambers—left atrium, right atrium, left ventricle and right ventricle—as show in Fig. 3. Each of these chambers are connected through the cardiac conduction system, which conveys electrical signals to coordinate the contraction of each chamber. The SA node is made up of pacemaker cells which have their own intrinsic autorhythmic rate and is located at the top of the heart in the right atrium. This node sets the intrinsic heart rate of the overall system, serving as the "natural pacemaker" of the heart. From here, electrical signals propagate out to each of the two atria to initiate their contractions, as well as down towards ventricles.

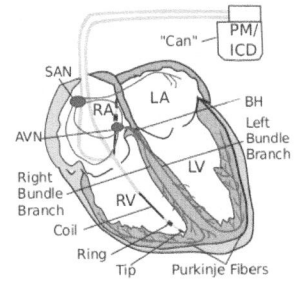

Fig. 3. An overview of the Heart-Pacemaker system (Adapted from [19])

The Atrioventicular (AV) node delays the propagation of pulses to the ventricles to ensure synchronisation between the atria and ventricles. Additionally, this node serves as a low-pass filter which prevents high frequency pulses, such as in cases of Atrial Fibrillation (AF), from reaching the ventricles. After passing through the AV node, propagation proceeds down through the bundle branches before branching out throughout each of the two ventricles, initiating their respective contractions and pumping blood through the body. Electrocardiograms (ECGs) consist of the typical shape which represents one complete heartbeat, made up from a series of subset waves, collectively known as $PQRST$, as shown in Fig. 1a. A brief discussion on this is given in Appendix D at [4].

Sinoatrial Block: Arrhythmias are abnormal rhythms of the heart which can be categorized into two main types—bradyarrhythmias, where the heart is beating slower than normal, and tachyarrhythmias, where the opposite is true. The prevalence of arrhythmias is generally accepted to be between 1.5% and 5% in the general population [7], with AF being the most common form. Sinus Node Dysfunction (SND) is a group of arrhythmias which stem from a malfunction of the sinus node and can affect people of all ages, but most predominantly occurs in older adults. One in 600 cardiac patients older than 65 years has suffers from a form of SND [6]. One key form of SND is known as SA Block, where the tissue surrounding the sinus node fails to conduct the depolarization to the atria and beyond. In the most commonly diagnosed case of SA Block, some depolarizations are successfully conducted, but not all, a case which is called 2nd Degree SA Block and is illustrated in Fig. 1.

The blocked impulses in a case of SA Block result in an overall heart rate which varies, although at all times the P-P intervals remain an exact multiple of the normal P-P intervals. Figure 1b shows an intermittent case where one sinus impulse is blocked, resulting in a one-off "missed beat" of the heart and an associated P-P interval that grows to be twice the normal size. Similarly, Fig. 1c shows the same case but where two impulses are blocked in a row, resulting in a

P-P interval which is three times the normal size and a prolonged period of no cardiac activity.

Without treatment, the yearly mortality rate for patients suffering from SND is 2% [16]. Additionally, each year roughly 5% of patients suffering from SND develop AF with its further risks of heart failure and stroke [16]. Symptomatic SA Block is treated through the use of cardiac pacemakers.

3.2 Pacemakers

A dual chamber pacemaker device is shown connected to the heart in Fig. 3, with one lead connected to each of the right atrium and ventricle. These leads sense the previously described Electrograms (EGMs) on the interior cardiac surface.

The basic timing diagram for a dual chamber pacemaker is shown in Fig. 4. Three types of events are shown on the EGM traces—sensed natural events (Atrial Sense (AS) and Ventricular Sense (VS)), ignored natural events (Atrial Refractory Sense (AR) and Ventricular Refractory Sense (VR)), and artificial pacing events (Atrial Pace (AP) and Ventricular Pace (VP)). Additionally, six timers are used to govern the operation of the device, with Ventricular Refractory Period (VRP) and Post-Ventricular Atrial Refractory Period (PVARP) governing the refractory periods for sensing, Atrioventricular Interval (AVI) and Atrial Escape Interval (AEI) ensuring AV synchronisation, and Lower Rate Interval (LRI) and Upper Rate Interval (URI) determining the overall heart rate of the device. However, such pacemaker designs, while simple and therefore relatively easy to guarantee their operation, may not produce the optimal pacing for a given patient. Traditional pacemakers provide pacing signals such that each of the timing requirements are satisfied, rather than attempting to match the intrinsic pacing rhythm of a patient's SA node. Quality of life can be enhanced by providing pacing signals which more closely align with the intrinsic rates. Instead, by using RL the agent can learn the pacing rhythm of the patient's heart through the reward-punishment mechanism and adapt its pacing rates.

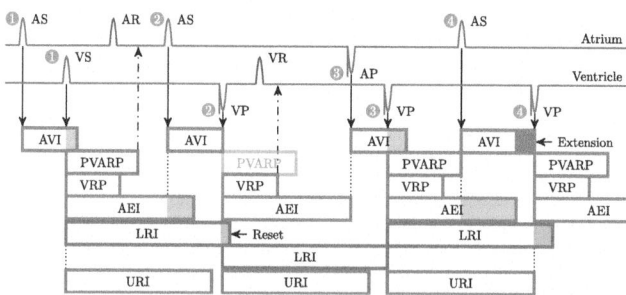

Fig. 4. Timing diagram for a dual chamber pacemaker, adapted from [20]

One drawback of such a learning-based approach is that it becomes practically impossible to guarantee its operation as a result of its dynamic behaviours, which becomes a problem for safety-critical applications such as the pacemaker. Instead, the combination of RE will allow us to guarantee a base set of requirements, and allow the controller full freedom in its attempts to find an optimal strategy. In the event where the RL agent attempts to perform an action which violates one of the requirements, the RE system will step in and override the pacing signals.

3.3 Setup of the Proposed Approach

In this section, we provide the overview for the design of rate adaptive pacemaker where the pacing rate is proportional to the intrinsic rate of the heart. The overall operation of the pacemaker in each iteration of the closed loop is as follows:

- Step 1: Input signals (AS, VS) from heart are sent to the enforcer.
- Step 2: The enforcer modifies them if necessary and sends the correct input signals (cAS, cVS) to the agent.
- Step 3: Agent selects pacing signals (AP, VP) and sends them to enforcer.
- Step 4: These enforcer sends the correct pacing signals (cAP, cVP) (modified in case of violation) to the heart.
- Step 5: The reward generator computes the reward (r) by taking the output signals selected by the agent (AP, VP)and the correct input and output signals (cAS, cAP, cVP, cAP, cVP).

These steps are further discussed with an algorithm in Sect. 6.

For some diseases it may be possible to perform learning using pre-recorded EGMs in an open-loop manner, where the pacemaker does not impact its inputs in real-time. However, in many cases, including SA Block, it is more desirable to use a closed-loop system where the pacemaker's outputs can change the inputs that it will receive in the future. This is achieved using a physiologically-based computational cardiac model containing 33 nodes, where both the cell and conduction dynamics are modelled using Hybrid Automata (HA) [1]. Various heart conditions can be simulated by adjusting the parameters associated with the model, which can also be configured at run-time. Additionally, we introduced variability in the intrinsic pacing rate of the SA node to more accurately capture real cardiac dynamics.

On the enforcer side, we consider the following set of safety properties and requirements based on [11], corresponding to the six timers shown in Fig. 4 along with one additional basic safety property (P_1).

P_1 AP and VP should not occur at the same time step.
P_2 VS or VP should follow an atrial event (AS or AP) within AVI ticks.
P_3 AS or AP should follow a VS or VP within AEI ticks.
P_4 VS or VP should occur within LRI ticks of another VS or VP.
P_5 VS or VP should occur only after URI ticks of another VS or VP.
P_6 A ventricular event (VS or VP) which occurs within VRP ticks from the last accepted ventricular event should be ignored.
P_7 An atrial event which occurs within PVARP ticks from the last accepted ventricular event should be ignored.

4 Properties as Discrete Timed Automata

We focus on systems such as the pacemaker that has Boolean signals as inputs and outputs. We consider a reactive system with a finite ordered sets of Boolean inputs $I = \{i_1, i_2, \cdots, i_n\}$ and Boolean outputs $O = \{o_1, o_2, \cdots, o_n\}$. The input alphabet is $\Sigma_I = 2^I$, and the output alphabet is $\Sigma_O = 2^O$ and the input-output alphabet $\Sigma = \Sigma_I \times \Sigma_O$. Each input (resp. output) event will be denoted as a bit-vector/complete monomial. For example, let $I = \{X, Y\}$. Then, the input $\{X\} \in \Sigma_I$ is denoted as 10, while $\{Y\} \in \Sigma_I$ is denoted as 01 and $\{X, Y\} \in \Sigma_I$ is denoted as 11. A reaction (or input-output event) is of the form (x_i, y_i), where $x_i \in \Sigma_I$ and $y_i \in \Sigma_O$.

We will now introduce DTA that are automata extended with a set of integer variables that are used as discrete clocks for instance to count the number of ticks before a certain event occurs. In this paper, properties that we want to enforce are defined using a variant of DTAs, defined as follows:

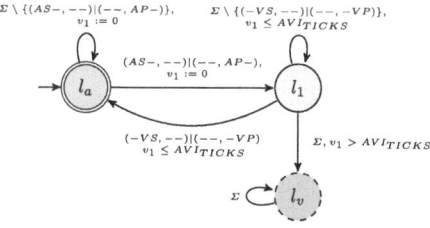

Fig. 5. Property P_2 defined as a DTA $\mathcal{A}_{P_2}$.

Definition 1. (Discrete Timed Automaton). A *Discrete Timed Automaton* is a tuple $\mathcal{A} = (L, l_0, l_v, \Sigma, V, \Delta, F)$ where L is the set of *locations*, $l_0 \in L$ is the initial location, Σ is the alphabet, V is a set of integer clocks, $F \subseteq L$ is the set of accepting locations, and l_v is a unique non-accepting *trap* location. The transition relation Δ is $\Delta \subseteq L \times G(V) \times R \times \Sigma \times L$ where $G(V)$ denotes the set of *guards*, i.e., constraints defined as conjunctions of simple constraints of the form $v \bowtie c$ with $v \in V$, $c \in \mathbb{N}$ and $\bowtie \in \{<, \leq, =, \geq, >\}$, and $R \subseteq V$ is a subset of integer clocks that are reset to 0.

Let $V = \{v_1, \ldots, v_k\}$ be a finite set of integer clocks. A *valuation* for v is an element of $\mathbb{N}$, that is a function from v to $\mathbb{N}$. The set of valuations for the set of clocks V is denoted by χ. For $\chi \in \mathbb{N}^V$, $\chi + 1$ is the valuation assigning $\chi(v) + 1$ to each clock variable v of V. Given a set of clock variables $V' \subseteq V$, $\chi[V' \leftarrow 0]$ is the valuation of clock variables χ where all the clock variables in V' are assigned to 0. Given $g \in G(V)$ and χ, $\chi \models g$ if g holds according to χ.

Example 1. (Example property defined as DTA). The DTA in Fig. 5 defines the property P_2: VS or VP must be true within AVI ticks after an atrial event AS or AP, where the set of integer clocks $V = \{v_1\}$. The set of inputs $I = \{AS, VS\}$, and outputs $O = \{AP, VP\}^2$. Location l_a is the initial location, location l_v is the non-accepting trap location and the set of accepting locations is $\{l_a\}$. Clock v_1 is reset to 0 upon transition from l_a to l_1. The transition from location l_1 to l_1 (self-loop) is taken whenever both VS and VP are not present, and the value

---

[2] For convenience, we use − to indicate either 0 or 1. Thus, $(AS-, --)$ indicates all the events where AS is present and the other input/outputs are present or absent.

of the clock v_1 has not exceeded the AVI timer in terms of synchronous ticks, denoted AVI_{TICKS}.

Further details of the definitions of semantics of a DTA, run, trace of a run, and the language accepted by a DTA can be referred from [20].

5 Discrete Timed Automaton Based Runtime Enforcement for Safe Reinforcement Learning

In this paper, we consider the RE framework for policies specified as DTAs from [20]. The enforcement framework in [20] is bi-directional, respecting constraints such as causality. We extend the framework in [20] with an additional optimization component in the enforcer that takes care of deciding when the training of the agent can be turned off.

This bi-directional RE framework is suitable in our context for safe reinforcement learning as illustrated in Fig. 2. In addition to a set of safety policies (denoted as φ), in our framework, the enforcer also takes an additional optimization policy denoted as φ_{op} as input. The synthesized enforcer will have an additional optimization component which indicates when the training of the agent can be turned ON/OFF.

An enforcer may be viewed as a function that transforms words. An enforcement function for a given safety property $\varphi \subseteq \Sigma^*$, and an optimization property $\varphi_{op} \subseteq (\Sigma \times \Sigma)^*$ is denoted as $E_{\varphi,\varphi_{op}} : \Sigma^* \to (\Sigma, K)^*$ where K in an element from $\{ON, OFF\}$. It takes as input a word over Σ^* and outputs a word of tuples over $(\Sigma, K)^*$, where the second element indicates when the training of the agent should be turned ON/OFF.

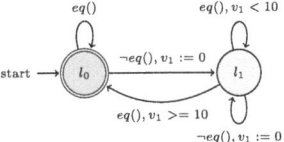

Fig. 6. Optimization Policy: φ_{op}

Optimization Policy — φ_{op}. We consider the following optimization policy defined over the alphabet $\Sigma_{op} = \Sigma \times \Sigma$ where $\Sigma = \Sigma_I \times \Sigma_O$, and $\Sigma_I = 2^I$ and $\Sigma_O = 2^O$. It is defined using the predicate $eq : \Sigma \times \Sigma \to Bool$, which takes as input both the actual and the edited input-output events. It returns **true** if both match and **false** otherwise. The purpose of the optimization policy is to indicate when the training of the agent should be turned ON/OFF by comparing the actual input-output and the enforced input-output produced by the enforcement components.

The optimization policy illustrated in Fig. 6 upon receiving each event compares the actual and the enforced input-output. The set of locations is $\{l_0, l_1\}$, and the set of integer clocks $V = \{v_1\}$. Location l_0 is the initial location which is also an accepting location. When an accepting location is reached it is also an indication that the training of the agent can be turned OFF. It makes use of one discrete clock v_1. When the actual and the enforced I/O do not match, a transition is taken to l_1. A transition back to l_0 can be made only if the actual and enforced I/O match consecutively for 10 time steps.

The only difference compared to the enforcement mechanism that we use here compared to the enforcers proposed in [20] is that we use an additional optimization policy as input, and based on it, the enforcer produces an additional ON/OFF signal as output in every step. If we exclude this optimization policy and the additional ON/OFF signal output, the behavior of the enforcement mechanism should be the same as the enforcement mechanism proposed in [20].

Regarding the verified/corrected input-output word produced by the enforcer, the enforcer should fulfill various constraints as defined in [20].

In our setting, where $E_{\varphi,\varphi_{op}} : \Sigma^* \to (\Sigma, K)^*$, if we consider $\Pi_1(E_{\varphi,\varphi_{op}}(\sigma))$ (which is the stream of input-output events by discarding the ON/OFF signal) released as output by the enforcer, it should satisfy the constraints of the enforcement mechanism proposed in [20].

In Appendix C at [4], we briefly recall some of the key constraints that an enforcer synthesized using the approach proposed in [20] satisfies. We also discuss about the condition for enforceability that is useful to identify whether an enforcer for a given property exists or not.

6 Implementation and Scenarios

In this section, we will briefly describe the different scenarios that we have considered and implemented for the considered case-study in order to analyse the advantages of the proposed approach. Details of how each component in the set-up is implemented is given in Appendix B in the repository at [4].

Scenario 1—Enforcer Only: The first scenario in our comparison is that which is made to mimic a traditional pacemaker with enforcement. Given that the enforcer properties align with those of the pacemaker specification, its operation can be regarded as representative of those achieved by a standard DDD-mode pacemaker. In each iteration, the enforcer runs the input enforcement function and adjusts the input signals if necessary. The enforcer will just enforce pacing at the boundaries of the timing intervals exactly as shown in the diagram (Fig. 4).

Reinforcement Learning Preliminaries: RL agent interacts with environment by taking actions based on a policy, which selects actions given the current state. Agent receives rewards as feedback and aims to maximize cumulative reward over time (return). Q-value estimates expected return for a specific action in a given state, following a particular policy. Q-Learning is a model-free RL algorithm that updates Q-values based on rewards received to learn optimal action-selection policy. The epsilon-greedy strategy balances exploration and exploitation by choosing the best-known action with probability $1-\epsilon$ and random action with probability ϵ. A good introduction of RL concepts can be found at [4,24].

Scenario 2—Reinforcement Learning without an Enforcer: To understand how the safety of the closed loop system is affected in the absence of enforcer, we have implemented a scenario which omits the enforcer. Here, the input signals are directly fed to the RL agent, and the output of the agent is directly sent to the heart. An additional component, taking account of VRP and $PVARP$ intervals is used for the agent to maintain the correct information of the intervals in the history. During the initial stages of learning, without an enforcer present, the agent will generally try to pace over the heart (i.e., agent may pace the atrium before the intrinsic atrial event occurs). Therefore, this setup cannot have a high initial value of epsilon as it would disturb the heart rhythm to a large extent and as such, an initial value of 0.2 is chosen. All other aspects of RL agent are same as for Scenario 1, including the training approach and reward scheme.

Scenario 3—Reinforcement Learning with an Enforcer: This follows our proposed approach (as in Fig. 7) where the overall controller is made up of three components—the RL agent, the reward generator and the enforcer. As discussed earlier, the RL agent requires the state of the environment (heart) to select the action which maximizes the return. As mentioned earlier in Sect. 3.2, the ignored natural events (AR and VR in Fig. 4) will be corrected by the enforcer to (0, 0) due to the safety property specified for $PVARP$, and VRP intervals.

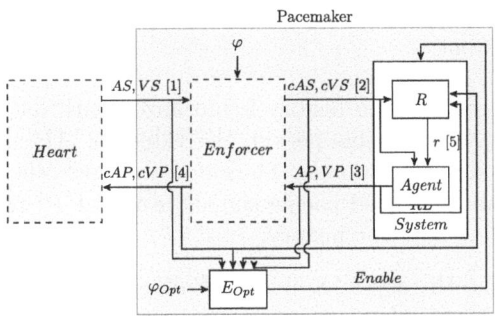

Fig. 7. Schematic of the intrinsic rate based adaptive pacemaker

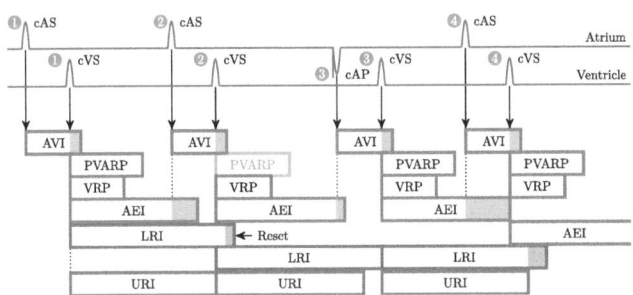

Fig. 8. Timing diagram for a trace with rate adaptive pacemaker

How the state information is represented in the implementation is provided in Appendix B at [4]. Figure 8 shows the timing diagram for a trace with rate adaptive pacemaker. Let us say that the second AS occurred after x milliseconds from the first AS. Then, the Type II SA block occurs after the second heart beat where the agent provides the pacing signals just before the AEI timing cycle finishes and therefore the enforcer accepts it. The agent learns the heart rate variability (hrv) and provides atrial pacing after $x + hrv$ milliseconds from the second AS. Further details about hrv are available in Appendix A at [4].

Training Approach for Reinforcement Learning with an Enforcer: Algorithm 1 outlines the training process for an RL-based adaptive pacemaker controller. Key components include the agent (ag), reward generator ($rGen$), current state (st), new state ($newSt$), and enforcer (enf). Corrected values for the signals ($AS, VS, AP,$ and VP) are denoted as cAS, cVS, cAP, and cVP, respectively. The heart's state is represented using the history of the last 10 beats from the current iteration. This history includes the last 10 A-A and A-V intervals, the latest correct input signals (AS and VS), and the time elapsed since the last atrial event.

Initialization: The history is initialized with data from the first 10 heartbeats (line 6). During this period, the values of AP and VP are both set to 0 and provided to the enforcer. The enforcer adjusts these based on safety policies and sends the corrected pacing signals (cAP, cVP) to the heart. Two functions are used to update the history:

- updateHistory(cAS, cVS, cAP, cVP): Updates the history with new A-A or A-V intervals in case of atrial or ventricular events and adjusts the time elapsed since the last atrial event.
- updateSenseSignalsInHistory(cAS, cVS): Updates the history with the latest correct input signals from the heart (cAS, cVS).

Main Loop: After initializing the history, the MAIN_LOOP (line 17) function starts the RL agent training. The process is as follows:

- **Receive input signals**: The heart provides input signals (AS, VS), which are used to update the correct sense signals (cAS, cVS) in history.
- **Initialize state**: The current history initializes the state.
- **Select action**: The agent selects an action using its Deep Q Network (DQN), which represents the best action for the given state. The action is a vector which represents the three possible actions the agent can take—pace the atria, pace the ventricles, or do nothing.
- **Get pacing signals**: The getPaceFromAction(action) (line 24) method translates the action into the associated pacing signals (AP, VP).
- **Adjust and send pacing signals**: The enforcer may adjust these signals (line 25) before sending correct pacing signals (line 26) to heart.
- **Compute reward and update history**: The reward generator ($rGen$) calculates the reward using the current state, selected pacing signals, and correct pacing signals, then sends it to the agent. The current pairs of input and output signals are updated in the history (line 29).
- **Update history with next input signals**: The new input signals from the heart (line 30) are fed through the enforcer, which modifies them if needed. The agent updates the history with the corrected input signals (line 33) and stores the new history in $newSt$.

Algorithm 1. Training-RL with an Enforcer

```
 1: Parameters:
 2:   N, PacedRewardValue, IterationThreshold, nIter ← 10, 5000, 100, 0
 3:   enf, heart, rGen, ag ← Enforcer(), Heart(), RewardGenerator(), Agent()
 4:   gotPR, history, memory ← False, [], []        ▷ history is initialized with an empty queue
 5:
 6: function INITIALIZE_HISTORY(N)
 7:   for i ← N down to 0 do
 8:     AS, VS ← heart.getSignals()                 ▷ recieve signals from heart
 9:     cAS, cVS ← enf.enforceInputs(AS, VS)        ▷ enforcer corrects the input signals
10:     AP, VP ← 0, 0                               ▷ select dummy output signals
11:     cAP, cVP ← enf.enforceOutputs(AP, VP)       ▷ enforcer corrects the output signals
12:     heart.sendSignals(cAP, cVP)                 ▷ correct output signals are sent to heart
13:     ag.updateHistory(cAS, cVS, cAP, cVP)        ▷ correct i/o signals are updated in history
14:   end for
15: end function
16:
17: function MAIN_LOOP
18:   AS, VS ← heart.getSignals()                   ▷ recieve input signals from heart
19:   cAS, cVS ← enf.enforceInputs(AS, VS)          ▷ enforcer provides correct input signals
20:   ag.updateSenseSignalsInHistory(cAS, cVS)      ▷ cAS and cVS are updated in history
21:   while True do
22:     st ← ag.history                             ▷ initialize state
23:     action ← ag.getAction(st)                   ▷ select action
24:     AP, VP ← ag.getPaceFromAction(action)       ▷ get pacing signals
25:     cAP, cVP ← enf.enforceOutputs(AP, VP)       ▷ enforcer corrects output signals
26:     heart.sendSignals(cAP, cVP)                 ▷ correct pacing signals sent to heart
27:     signals ← (AP, VP, cAS, cVS, cAP, cVP)
28:     reward, done, score ← rGen.getReward(st, signals, score)   ▷ compute reward
29:     ag.updateHistory(cAS, cVS, cAP, cVP)        ▷ update history with the correct i/o
30:     AS, VS ← heart.getSignals()                 ▷ receive input signals for next iteration
31:
32:     cAS, cVS ← enf.enforceInputs(AS, VS)        ▷ correct the input signals from heart
33:     ag.updateSenseSignalsInHistory(cAS, cVS)    ▷ updated history with cAS, cVS
34:     newSt ← ag.history                          ▷ initialize new state with current history
35:     ag.remember(st, action, reward, newSt, done) ▷ store the tuple in replay memory
36:     nIter ← nIter + 1                           ▷ increment nIter
37:     if reward = PacedRewardValue then
38:       gotPR ← True
39:     end if
40:     if gotPR then
41:       ag.trainShortMemory(st, action, reward, newSt, done)  ▷ train on current tuple
42:       if nIter = IterationThreshold then
43:         nIter ← 0
44:         ag.trainLongMemory()                    ▷ train on randomly selected batch of tuples
45:       end if
46:     end if
47:   end while
48: end function
49:
50: Initialize history
51: INITIALIZE_HISTORY(N)
52: Start main loop
53: MAIN_LOOP
```

- **Store Experience**: The remember(st, action, reward, newSt, done) method stores this tuple in the experience replay memory (*memory*).
- **Train DQN**: Deep Q Network (DQN) is an artificial neural network trained on tuples of form (*st, action, reward, newSt, done*) to accurately estimate quality of state-action pairs using a simplified version of bellman equation [24].

$$Q = \text{model.predict}(\text{state}_0) \qquad (1)$$

$$Q_{\text{new}} = R + \gamma \cdot \max(\text{model.predict}(\text{state}_1)) \tag{2}$$

Training Functions: The DQN is trained using two key functions:

- *trainShortMemory()*: Trains model on current iteration's tuple (line 41).
- *trainLongMemory()*: Trains the model on a randomly selected batch of 1000 tuples from the memory (line 44).

Experience Replay Memory: The experience replay memory (*memory*), implemented as a queue with a capacity of 100 000, stores information about tuples from every iteration, including the current state, next state, action taken, reward generated, and episode termination status. An episode ends when the chosen action results in a negative reward. Since the optimal action is often no pacing $(0,0)$, the memory will contain many such actions. To ensure balanced training, *trainLongMemory()* function resamples data to create a uniformly distributed training batch over action types and rewards.

Training Criteria: The agent must pace the atrium correctly at least once (*gotPR*) before training begins, ensuring that each transition type is represented for data resampling. The DQN is trained to determine the Q values of the three actions for the given state. The number of iterations (*nIter*) resets to 0 after reaching 100. Every 100 iterations, if *gotPR* is true, a long memory train is performed on a batch with an equal number of transitions for each action-reward pair.

Reward Scheme: The implemented reward scheme gives a major negative reward (of 5000) whenever the agent fails to pace the atrium when the pause occurs. We discuss two important situations which may occur.

- The agent should learn the current value of heart rate variability (refer Appendix A at [4]) of the person and should pace after that amount of time from the 2nd consecutive AS. If the agent fails to do so, i.e. the SA node pacing rate is increased and the agent paces (which it should not have) and after which the pause occurs causing the enforcer to send a pacing signal when the AEI timer fires, a negative reward is given to the agent.
- If an atrial pace selected by the agent causes the next atrial sense to deviate from the current rhythm (i.e. the previous AS-AS interval).

A reward is given to the agent which is directly proportional to the absolute difference between the duration of the next atrial signal(agent's AP for case-i and AS for case-ii) from AP and the previous AS-AS interval. The reward is negative if the difference is more than 100 and positive if it is less than 100. The signals chosen by the agent are termed as correct if they are not modified by the enforcer.

A positive reward of 5000 is given if the agent paces the atrium correctly. A positive reward of 50 is given if the agent correctly paces the ventricle. A positive reward of 1 is given when no pacing signal is given and it is not modified by the enforcer. A negative reward of 5000 is given for all other cases.

7 Results

In this section, we will briefly analyse the observations of the different scenarios that were presented in Sect. 6.

Firstly, Scenario 1, as in Fig. 9a, we can see that the pacemaker does not try to match the intrinsic rates of the patient, and instead always provides pacing when the AEI timer elapses. On the positive side, this implementation never allows for unsafe conditions to occur in the heart, always meeting the provided safety properties.

For Scenario 2, where we implemented the RL agent without an enforcer, we present the frequency plot of A-A intervals in Fig. 9b. Here, we can see a range of problems with the pacemaker operation, including both instances of pacing too quickly (initiated by the pacemaker on the left of the graph) and uncorrected bradycardia where the A-A intervals exceed 1.6 s. Such a comparison shows the great advantage of using RE to guarantee a minimum level of operation.

Regarding Scenario 3, RL with an enforcer, the agent was trained using epsilon greedy exploration for the first 100 000 iterations where the time step between two iterations is considered as 1 ms. Table 1 depicts a single sequence of events, that can be read row-wise (i.e., events in the first row left to right, followed by second and so on). Table 1 shows the sequence of atrial signals (ASs denoted by $(0, x)$, agent selected APs denoted by $(1, x)$, enforced APs denoted by $(2, x)$ where x is interval after which the atrial event occurred from the previous atrial event) for 100000 iterations with epsilon set to zero after the initial training mentioned above.

Table 1. Sequence of atrial events occurred during simulation

	Col 1	Col 2	Col 3	Col 4	Col 5
Row 1	(0, 810)	(0, 874)	(0, 898)	(0, 898)	(1, 967)
Row 2	(0, 720)	(0, 898)	(0, 898)	(0, 898)	(1, 997)
Row 3	(0, 690)	(0, 898)	(0, 898)	(0, 874)	(0, 874)
Row 4	(1, 901)	(0, 786)	(0, 874)	(0, 788)	(0, 788)
Row 5	(1, 891)	(0, 712)	(0, 788)	(0, 788)	(0, 750)
Row 6	(1, 795)	(0, 732)	(0, 750)	(0, 718)	(1, 743)
Row 7	(0, 720)	(0, 718)	(0, 718)	(0, 686)	(1, 870)
Row 8	(0, 529)	(0, 686)	(1, 823)	(0, 576)	(0, 686)
Row 9	(0, 686)	(0, 686)	(1, 821)	(0, 578)	(0, 686)
Row 10	(0, 655)	(1, 730)	(0, 607)	(0, 655)	(0, 686)
Row 11	(1, 703)	(0, 568)	(0, 622)	(0, 622)	(0, 601)
Row 12	(1, 653)	(0, 576)	(0, 601)	(0, 663)	(1, 811)
Row 13	(0, 542)	(0, 663)	(0, 663)	(0, 699)	(1, 884)
Row 14	(0, 541)	(0, 699)	(0, 699)	(1, 724)	(2, 1122)
Row 15	(0, 386)	(0, 735)	(0, 697)	(1, 742)	(0, 679)
Row 16	(0, 697)	(1, 821)	(0, 600)	(0, 697)	(0, 697)
Row 17	(0, 625)	(1, 779)	(0, 498)	(0, 625)	(1, 761)
Row 18	(0, 516)	(0, 625)	(0, 601)	(1, 662)	(0, 567)
Row 19	(0, 601)	(0, 601)	(1, 616)	(2, 1144)	(0, 863)
Row 20	(0, 649)	(0, 606)	(0, 741)	(0, 605)	(0, 695)
Row 21	(1, 803)	(0, 614)	(0, 695)	(0, 695)	(0, 741)
Row 22	(1, 780)	(0, 729)	(0, 741)	(0, 741)	(1, 895)
Row 23	(0, 614)	(0, 741)	(0, 784)	(1, 954)	(0, 641)
Row 24	(0, 784)	(0, 784)	(0, 839)	(1, 850)	(0, 835)
Row 25	(0, 839)	(0, 839)	(1, 849)	(0, 836)	

In Table 1, after every correct atrial pacing by agent we can observe that the difference between the current AS-AP interval and the previous AS-AS interval had the following values - 178, 208, 88, 76, 18, 2, 157, 110, 108, 48, 54, 25, 121, 158, 82, 18, 109, 34, 1, 81, 12, 127, 143, 4, 3. We can observe that the difference is not decreasing constantly but the maximum value it's reaching is decreasing gradually and moreover there were only two instances (cells (14, 5) and (19, 4)) where the agent paced when the pacing rate was increased which shows that the agent is also learning the heart rate variability. The agent is gradually learning to maintain the intrinsic rhythm and also avoiding to pace over the heart.

The learning graphs and a video of plots of frequency of the different atrial events over the A-A interval over the 100000 iterations were generated for the simulation (available in the repository at [4]).

Results of RL Agent with Optimization: Figure 9c shows the frequency of A-A intervals for the RL agent with enforcer and optimization component. The model initially trained for the 100 000 iterations was trained without optimization for another 100 000 iterations which ran for 120 min whereas the one with optimization as shown in Fig. 9c ran for 90 min. This method yields comparable outcomes to the unoptimized approach but consumes less power. This is evident from the observation that it completed the same number of iterations 30 min faster. The number of incorrect pacing actions were increased but it does not affect the performance as the enforcer corrects them.

Summary of the Observations: Compared to our proposed approach of Scenario 3 (Table 1), each of the other scenarios have their own shortcomings. To start with, while Scenario 2 (Fig. 9b) shows some pacing which matches that of the intrinsic rates, it provides no safety guarantees and shows instances where the pacemaker has both paced too quickly, and failed to pace within an adequate time. In both cases, the effects could be catastrophic for a patient. Conversely, Scenario 1 (Fig. 9a) shows a safe design which never violates the timing constraints or paces too quickly, however it does not attempt to mimic the intrinsic rates of the patient. This clearly demonstrates the advantage of our proposed approach combining RL with RE, at least for the design of pacemakers to treat SA Block.

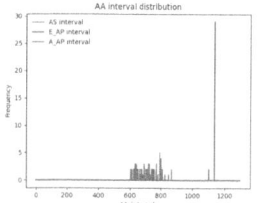 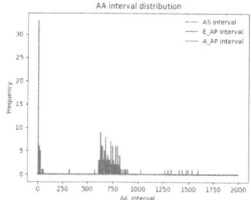 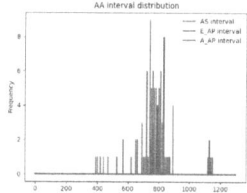

(a) Frequency over A-A interval for traditional pacemaker (b) Frequency over A-A interval for RL-based pacemaker without enforcer (c) Frequency over A-A interval for RL agent with enforcer and optimization

Fig. 9. Results of different scenarios

8 Related Work

Runtime Enforcement and Shielding: Various RE models, such as security automata [23], have been proposed which address the enforcement of safety properties by blocking/halting the execution. The mechanism in [15] enables the enforcer to rectify the input sequence by suppressing and/or introducing events. The RE techniques suggested in [9,18] enable the buffering of events and their release when a sequence that meets the required property is observed. These enforcement approaches however are not suitable for reactive systems such as pacemakers. The work by Bloem et al. [12] presents a framework for the synthesis of enforcers for reactive systems, referred to as *shields*, based on a collection of safety properties specified as automata. The shield described in [12] is a one-way system that receives inputs from the plant and outputs from the controller, and corrects any incorrect outputs.

Runtime Enforcement via Shielding for Safety of Reinforcement Learning: Combining shielding with RL for safety of the system is being explored [2,13]. In one of the methods [2], the shield is constructed using a two-player game approach, a safety game is constructed from the LTL safety specification and a formal model of the environment. Environment is modeled as an MDP. Attempts are made to utilize the safety specification for reward shaping [13], focusing on deriving a state-adaptive reward structure from the specification.

Reinforcement Learning-Based Control for Cardiac Systems: In [22], the authors came up with an adaptive Cardiac Resynchronization Therapy (CRT) device which is used for treating patients suffering from systolic congestive heart failure (insufficient blood supply by ventricles). The architecture of the CRT device consists of Spiking Neuron Processor (SNP), controller and a Pulse Generator and Sense Amp (PGSA). The Spiking Neuron Processor (SNP) provides the AV delay and VV interval parameters to the controller. An RL based approach is used for the adaptation of the SNP synaptic weights. However, the approach does not propose any technique for ensuring the safety of the overall system.

In [8], the authors identified the need for an adaptive pacemaker for patients suffering from 2nd Degree AV block (Mobitz Type II). In 3:2 AV Block, every third atrial signal generated by the SA node is blocked from reaching the ventricles. Traditional pacemakers do not attempt to match the intrinsic heart rhythm of the patient and pace the ventricles at the lower rate limit. The approach in [8] used Durational Calculus (DC)-based specification of the pacemaker requirements. A correct by construction reinforcement learning of adaptive pacemaker is proposed by using a shield (applying the shield synthesis approach) from the DC formal specification.

This Work: Our work is closely related to [8] discussed above. In this work, we also consider a practical scenario related to a cardiac pacemaker where a reinforcement learning based control is more suitable/essential. We specifically focus on the SA block heart condition, whereas [8] focuses on AV block. Dealing with SA block is more challenging than AV block because both the atrial and ventricular rhythms are affected based on the agent's pacing strategy. Also, in our work, for ensuring safety of the overall system, instead of shielding, we apply the bidirectional runtime enforcers in [20], where for the enforcers, both the environment and the plant are black-boxes. Thus our approach, unlike shielding, does not require any formal model of the environment. Moreover, in our case, our enforcer is bi-directional unlike shields where we also correct the inputs (ignoring the atrial and ventricular sense signals when essential as per the specification) which is essential to correctly determine the state of the environment for the agent to choose an optimal action. The enforcer also corrects the pacing signals chosen by the RL agent if violating the pacemaker requirements (before sending

9 Conclusion

RL-based solutions are beneficial to tackle problems considering optimal control, specifically where the environment is dynamic in nature. However applying them to safety-critical systems is a challenge as safety of the overall system cannot be compromised. In this work, we propose a formal approach for ensuring safe execution of the overall system at runtime by combining RL with bi-directional RE. The enforcer is based on the key safety properties specified over the inputs-outputs of the closed-loop system. In this work, we specifically considered the heart-pacemaker system and to condition of 2nd degree SA block Type II. We have discussed why an RL-based approach is essential to handle the SA block condition. From our experiments, we have observed that the agent eventually learns the to pace according to the intrinsic rhythm of the SA node during the block. Our experiments and results clearly illustrate the suitability of the proposed scheme for verifying and enforcing the safety of an RL-based system at runtime.

References

1. Ai, W., Patel, N.D., Roop, P.S., Malik, A., Trew, M.L.: Cardiac electrical modeling for closed-loop validation of implantable devices. IEEE Trans. Biomed. Eng. **67**, 536–544 (2020)
2. Alshiekh, M., Bloem, R., Ehlers, R., Könighofer, B., Niekum, S., Topcu, U.: Safe reinforcement learning via shielding. In: AAAI 18. AAAI'18/IAAI'18/EAAI'18, AAAI Press (2018)
3. Amir, G., Schapira, M., Katz, G.: Towards scalable verification of deep reinforcement learning. In: FMCAD, pp. 193–203. IEEE (2021)
4. Appendix: A Formal Approach for Safe Reinforcement Learning- A Rate-Adaptive Pacemaker Case Study (2024). https://github.com/saferl605/Safe-RL. Accessed August 2024
5. Burkett, D.E.: Chapter 45 - Bradyarrhythmias and Conduction Abnormalities. In: Silverstein, D.C., Hopper, K. (eds.) Small Animal Critical Care Medicine, pp. 189–195. W.B. Saunders, Saint Louis (2009)
6. Dakkak W, D.R.: Sick Sinus Syndrome. StatPearls, StatPearls Publishing, St. Petersburg (2024)
7. Desai, D.S., Hajoul, S.: Arrhythmias. StatPearls, StatPearls Publishing, St. Petersburg (2023)
8. Dole, K., Gupta, A., Komp, J., Krishna, S., Trivedi, A.: Correct-by-construction reinforcement learning of cardiac pacemakers from duration calculus requirements. In: AAAI Conference on Artificial Intelligence (2023)
9. Falcone, Y., Mounier, L., Fernandez, J.C., Richier, J.L.: Runtime enforcement monitors: composition, synthesis, and enforcement abilities. FMSD **38**(3), 223–262 (2011)

10. Ivanov, R., Weimer, J., Alur, R., Pappas, G.J., Lee, I.: Verisig: verifying safety properties of hybrid systems with neural network controllers. In: HSCC, pp. 169–178 (2019)
11. Jiang, Z., Pajic, M., Moarref, S., Alur, R., Mangharam, R.: Modeling and verification of a dual chamber implantable pacemaker. In: Flanagan, C., König, B. (eds.) TACAS 2012. LNCS, vol. 7214, pp. 188–203. Springer, Heidelberg (2012). https://doi.org/10.1007/978-3-642-28756-5_14
12. Könighofer, B., et al.: Shield synthesis. Form. Methods Syst. Des. **51**(2), 332–361 (2017). https://doi.org/10.1007/s10703-017-0276-9
13. Könighofer, B., Bloem, R., Ehlers, R., Pek, C.: Correct-by-construction runtime enforcement in AI - a survey. In: Principles of Systems Design (2022). https://doi.org/10.1007/978-3-031-22337-2_31
14. Landers, M., Doryab, A.: Deep reinforcement learning verification: a survey. ACM Comput. Surv. **55**(14s), 1–31 (2023)
15. Ligatti, J., Bauer, L., Walker, D.: Run-time enforcement of nonsafety policies. ACM Trans. Inf. Syst. Secur. **12**(3), 19:1–19:41 (2009)
16. Mitchell, L.B.: Sinus Node Dysfunction. MSD MANUAL (2023)
17. Pearce, H., Pinisetty, S., Roop, P.S., Kuo, M.M., Ukil, A.: Smart i/o modules for mitigating cyber-physical attacks on industrial control systems. IEEE TII **16**(7), 4659–4669 (2020). https://doi.org/10.1109/TII.2019.2945520
18. Pinisetty, S., Falcone, Y., Jéron, T., Marchand, H., Rollet, A., Nguena Timo, O.: Runtime enforcement of timed properties revisited. FMSD **45**(3), 381–422 (2014). https://doi.org/10.1007/s10703-014-0215-y
19. Pinisetty, S., Roop, P.S., Sawant, V., Schneider, G.: Security of pacemakers using runtime verification. In: MEMOCODE 2018, pp. 51–61. IEEE (2018). https://doi.org/10.1109/MEMCOD.2018.8556922
20. Pinisetty, S., Roop, P.S., Smyth, S., Allen, N., Tripakis, S., von Hanxleden, R.: Runtime enforcement of cyber-physical systems. ACM TECS **16**, 1–25 (2017)
21. Pinisetty, S., Roop, P.S., Smyth, S., Tripakis, S., von Hanxleden, R.: Runtime enforcement of reactive systems using synchronous enforcers. In: Erdogmus, H., Havelund, K. (eds.) SPIN 2017, pp. 80–89. ACM (2017). https://doi.org/10.1145/3092282.3092291
22. Rom, R., et al.: Adaptive cardiac resynchronization therapy device based on spiking neurons architecture and reinforcement learning scheme. IEEE Trans. Neural Netw. **18**, 542–550 (2007)
23. Schneider, F.B.: Enforceable security policies. ACM Trans. Inf. Syst. Secur. **3**(1), 30–50 (2000)
24. Sutton, R.S., Barto, A.G.: Reinforcement Learning - An Introduction. Adaptive Computation and Machine Learning, MIT Press, Cambridge (1998)

Stream-Based Monitoring Under Measurement Noise

Bernd Finkbeiner[1], Martin Fränzle[2], Florian Kohn[1(✉)], and Paul Kröger[2]

[1] CISPA Helmholtz Center for Information Security, Saarbrücken, Germany
{finkbeiner,florian.kohn}@cispa.de
[2] Carl von Ossietzky Universität, Oldenburg, Germany
{martin.fraenzle,paul.kroeger}@uol.de

Abstract. Stream-based monitoring is a runtime verification approach for cyber-physical systems that translates streams of input data, such as sensor readings, into streams of aggregate statistics and verdicts about the safety of the running system. It is usually assumed that the values on the input streams represent fully accurate measurements of the physical world. In reality, however, physical sensors are prone to measurement noise and errors. These errors are further amplified by the processing and aggregation steps within the monitor. This paper introduces RLOLA, a robust extension of the stream-based specification language Lola. RLOLA incorporates the concept of slack variables, which symbolically represent measurement noise while avoiding the aliasing problem of interval arithmetic. With RLOLA, standard sensor error models can be expressed directly in the specification. While the monitoring of RLOLA specifications may, in general, require an unbounded amount of memory, we identify a rich fragment of RLOLA that can automatically be translated into precise monitors with guaranteed constant-memory consumption.

Keywords: Slack Variables · Robust Monitoring · Measurement Noise

1 Introduction

Stream-based monitoring is a successful runtime verification approach for cyber-physical systems. Input streams containing sensor readings and other data are translated into output streams that process and aggregate this data. The resulting values on the output streams are then continuously evaluated against trigger conditions that characterize erroneous or dangerous situations. Tools for stream-based monitoring, like RTLola [4], TeSSLa [6] or Striver [14], are used in safety-critical applications, such as autonomous aircraft [3], where the precision of the monitoring result is vital. But how precise are stream-based monitors?

This work was partially supported by the German Research Foundation (DFG) as part of PreCePT (FI 936/7-1; FR 2715/6-1) and of TRR 248 (No. 389792660), by the State of Lower Saxony within the Zukunftslabor Mobilität, and by the European Research Council (ERC) Grant HYPER (No. 101055412).

© The Author(s), under exclusive license to Springer Nature Switzerland AG 2025
E. Ábrahám and H. Abbas (Eds.): RV 2024, LNCS 15191, pp. 22–39, 2025.
https://doi.org/10.1007/978-3-031-74234-7_2

Most frameworks for stream-based monitoring operate under the assumption that the values on the input streams represent fully accurate measurements of the physical reality. As a result, the values in the output streams are also assumed to be precise, even if they are based on input data that was collected from physical sensors, which are prone to measurement noise and errors, and even if this data has been processed in a way that may have amplified these errors significantly.

A straightforward idea to keep track of the precision of the stream values is to lift the individual values from scalars to intervals, akin to interval-based robust monitoring of Signal Temporal Logic specifications [21]. Input streams then produce intervals centered around the measured value with a width defined by the precision of the sensor. The error in the output streams can be tracked via interval arithmetic: as more errors are combined into individual output values, the intervals of these outputs become larger, and we can determine whether a violation of the trigger conditions is possible, given the precision of the data.

Unfortunately, interval analysis usually leads to an overly pessimistic result. This phenomenon is known as the *aliasing* or *dependency problem*: in situations where errors cancel each other out, for example, because the same input is added and later subtracted from an aggregate value, interval arithmetic will still add, rather than subtract, the errors. In the trivial example, the term $x - x$ should evaluate to 0, independently of the value of x. However, if, because of noise, we assume x to be in the interval $[-10, 10]$, then interval arithmetic produces the even larger interval $[-10, 10] - [-10, 10] = [-20, 20]$.

In this paper, we present a new version of the Lola monitoring language [7], where we explicitly track the precision of the stream values. To avoid the aliasing problem, we introduce explicit *slack variables* that represent measurement noise by symbolically representing the interval $[-1, 1]$, which can be extended to arbitrary intervals through affine arithmetic [11]. Because each variable identifies a particular source of noise, they are not susceptible to the aliasing problem. In the example, the uncertain input is represented as $x + 10\epsilon$, where ϵ is a slack variable. Subtracting the input from itself would then result in $(x + 10\epsilon) - (x + 10\epsilon) = 0$.

The challenge in building a stream-based monitor with slack variables is the unbounded number of input values. If the noise on individual values of some input stream is at least partially independent, then we need a separate slack variable for each point in time. As slack variables are unlikely to resolve to scalar values, the number of slack variables in the equation store of the monitor may grow beyond any bound. In the paper, we demonstrate this phenomenon for the stream-based monitoring language Lola [7]. We define the syntax and semantics of RLOLA (*robust* Lola), the extension of Lola with slack variables.

It turns out, however, that for a large class of practically relevant RLOLA specifications, it is possible to combine multiple slack variables into a single variable without losing precision. For example, the term $x + 5\epsilon_1 + 5\epsilon_2$ is equivalent to $x + 10\epsilon'$ if ϵ_1 and ϵ_2 occurs only there. Suppose now that x is an output stream in which the term 5ϵ, with fresh slack variable ϵ, is added in every step. Then instead of keeping a growing term $5\epsilon_1 + 5\epsilon_2 + \ldots + 5\epsilon_n$ in memory, it suffices to count the number of steps n, and replace the n slack variables with a single slack variable with factor $5n$, resulting in the term $5n\epsilon'$. In fact, we can eliminate the slack variables and use an ordinary Lola specification to track the factor $5n$.

In the paper, we make use of this insight to identify a syntactic fragment of RLOLA for which we can automatically translate the given RLOLA specification into an equivalent Lola specification. The memory consumption of the resulting monitor is guaranteed to be constant.

1.1 Motivating Example

As a motivating example, consider an industrial warehouse robot that autonomously navigates by tracking its position through an unreliable indoor positioning system. To validate these potentially erratic position readings, a runtime monitor compares position measurements to positions computed from the traveled distance and a discrete direction. The movement directions of the robot are visualized in Fig. 1. An RLOLA specification capturing this behavior is given in Example 1 below. Note that for simplicity, the computation of the y position is omitted as it follows analogously.

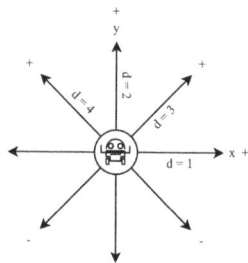

Fig. 1. Movement Directions in Example 1

Example 1 (Warehouse Robot).

```
input direction: Int
input raw_distance, position_x, position_y: Float
constant cos_45: Float := (1/2) * sqrt(2)

constant delta: Variable
output e: Variable
output distance := raw_distance + e + 5*delta

output computed_pos_x := if direction = 1 then
                    computed_pos_x.offset(by: -1, or: 0) + distance
                else if direction = -1 then
                    computed_pos_x.offset(by: -1, or: 0) - distance
                else if direction = 3 then
                    computed_pos_x.offset(by: -1, or: 0) + cos_45 * distance
                else if direction = -3 then
                    computed_pos_x.offset(by: -1, or: 0) - cos_45 * distance
                else if direction = 4 then
                    computed_pos_x.offset(by: -1, or: 0) - cos_45 * distance
                else if direction = -4 then
                    computed_pos_x.offset(by: -1, or: 0) + cos_45 * distance
                else
                    computed_pos_x.offset(by: -1, or: 0)

trigger position_x >_{0.5} computed_pos_x || position_x <_{0.5} computed_pos_x
```

Intuitively, slack variables extend the value domain of streams such that a stream of type Variable produces a fresh slack variable every time it is computed. As the precise value of the slack variables cannot be computed, such streams do not require a defining stream equation. Similarly, a constant of type Variable represents a single slack variable. In the above example, we define a stream of slack variables e and a single slack variable delta that are added to the raw_distance in the distance output stream to capture the measurement noise of the distance measurements. A more detailed description of this measurement error model is given in Sect. 2.2. Depending on the movement direction, this corrected distance is added proportionally to the computed position.

In the above example, all slack variables produced by the e stream will accumulate in the computed position streams, as the offset(by: -1, or: 0) operator refers to the last stream value (or 0 if that does not exist yet). As later shown in Sect. 5, multiple linear dependent slack variables can be combined without losing precision. Based on this, building a finite memory monitor for the above specification is possible. In fact, it is possible to translate the specification to one without slack variables:

```
input direction: Int
input raw_distance, position_x, position_y: Float
constant cos_45: Float := (1/2) * sqrt(2)

output d1 := if direction = 1
        then d1.offset(by: -1, or: 0.0) + 1.0
        else d1.offset(by: -1, or: 0.0)
output dn1 := if direction = -1
        then dn1.offset(by: -1, or: 0.0) + 1.0
        else dn1.offset(by: -1, or: 0.0)
output d3, dn3, d4, dn4 := ...

output delta_x := d1 - dn1 + d3*cos_45 - dn3*cos_45 - d4*cos_45 + dn4*cos_45
output epsilon_x := d1 + dn1 + d3 + dn3 + d4 + dn4
output raw_computed_pos_x := ...

output position_x_lower := raw_computed_pos_x - epsilon_x - delta_x
output position_x_upper := raw_computed_pos_x + epsilon_x + delta_x
trigger (position_x - position_x_lower) / (position_x_upper - position_x_lower) > 0.5
trigger (position_x_upper - position_x) / (position_x_upper - position_x_lower) > 0.5
```

Note that this specification is optimized by removing unreachable or equivalent cases. The raw_computed_pos_x is defined analogously to the computed_pos_x stream in Example 1 with the difference that it references the raw_distance input stream instead of the distance stream. Conceptually, this specification replaces the stream of slack variables e with eight individual slack variables, one for each direction. The streams d1 to d4 and their negative counterparts dynamically compute the coefficients of these slack variables, while the delta_x stream tracks the coefficient of the delta slack variable. The streams position_x_lower and position_x_upper reconstruct a precise lower and upper bound of the original computed_pos_x stream by applying interval arithmetic. In Sect. 5, we define a syntactical fragment of RLOLA for which such a transformation is always possible.

1.2 Related Work

In runtime verification, multiple logics have been studied to express valid system behavior, such as LTL [2], STL [19], or stream-based languages such as Lola [7], TeSSLa [6] or Striver [14]. In stream-based languages, the temporal history of measurements is represented as streams of values, and temporal properties are expressed through recursive stream equations involving time-offset accesses between these streams.

As established by Kauffman et al. [17], there are properties that cannot be monitored over unreliable channels that alter, delay, or lose data. While previous work was focused on missing or shifted events [18], this paper targets events that are present but mutated by measurement noise as specified by an error model.

While this could be encoded in first-order logic [8], the goal is to keep a strict memory bound on the resulting monitor. Kallwies et al. [16] handle missing events in the stream-based setting through symbolic input variables. The authors show that, in general, if streams are defined over real and boolean values, precise monitoring requires unbounded memory. Yet, this paper identifies a syntactic fragment in this domain that still allows for bounded memory monitors.

For temporal logics, there exist robust quantitative interpretations [9,10,13] that can handle inaccurate timestamps or measurement noise. Most such logics do not support measurement-related error models, leading to pessimistic verdicts. One exception is "truly robust" monitoring of Signal Temporal Logic [12], which also uses slack variables to express error models, but is significantly less expressive than stream-based specification languages.

2 Preliminaries

Runtime monitoring validates observed system behavior against a formal specification at runtime. The approach presented in this paper adapts the stream-based specification language Lola [7]. In the following, we provide an overview of its definition.

2.1 Lola

A Lola [7] specification consists of input streams, representing the observations made of the system, and output streams, which compute new values from input streams and other output streams. A Lola specification is a set of (recursive) equations over stream variables of the form:

$$o_1 = expr_1(i_1,...,i_m,\ o_1,...,o_n) \quad \cdots \quad o_n = expr_n(i_1,...,i_m,\ o_1,...,o_n)$$

where $o_1,...,o_n$ are output stream variables and $i_1,...,i_m$ are input stream variables and $expr_1,...,expr_n$ are stream expressions.

Stream expressions determine how the next value of an output stream is computed. They are defined as arithmetic and logic expressions over stream variables. They include *if ... then ... else ...* clauses, stream variable references, and a stream offset operator: .offset(by: *i*, or: *l*) for $i < 0 \in \mathbb{Z}$ and some literal l. Further, we use .last(or: *l*) as syntactic sugar for .offset(by: -1, or: *l*).

The semantics of Lola is defined by an evaluation model that relates input stream values to output stream values. For its full definition, we refer to the original Lola paper [7]. Notice that a specification can have multiple valid evaluation models. For example, the specification: output o = o has infinitely many evaluation models for any given vector of input streams $\tau_1,...,\tau_n$. Such specifications are called not well-defined due to their non-determinism. A specification is well-defined only if it assigns precisely one evaluation model to each vector of input streams $\tau_1, \ldots, \tau_n$. A syntactic criterion for well-definedness is given with the help of a dependency graph:

Definition 1 (Dependency Graph). *Let ϕ be a Lola specification. The dependency graph of ϕ is a directed weighted multi-graph $G = \langle V, E \rangle$ with $V = \{i_1, \ldots, i_m, o_1, \ldots, o_n\}$. An edge $e = \langle o_i, o_k, w \rangle$ is in E iff the expression of o_i contains o_k.offset(by: w, or: c) as a sub-expression (or $e = \langle o_i, i_k, w \rangle$ if i_k.offset(by: w, or: c) is a sub-expression). Analogously, edges with weight 0 are added for non-offset accesses.*

A specification is labeled *well-formed* iff its dependency graph does not contain any non-negative weight cycle, where the weight of a cycle is defined as the sum of all its edge weights.

2.2 Error Model

Following [12], we adapt the error model induced by the ISO norm 5725 [15] by decomposing the measurement error into a constant, but unknown per-sensor offset and a randomly varying per-measurement error. This decomposition directly correlates with the "trueness" and "precision" described in the ISO 5725 standard and is also reflected in Example 1 through the constant `delta` slack variable and the `e` stream of fresh slack variables. We adopt the definition of consistency from [12] and define when a series of sensor measurements is consistent with the unknown ground truth of a physical property.

Definition 2 (Consistency). *Let S be a sensor measuring a physical property at times $T \subseteq \mathbb{N}$ with a maximal sensor offset of $\delta \geq 0$ and a maximal random measurement error of $\epsilon \geq 0$. Let τ be the ground-truth time series. Then $m_S : T \to \mathbb{R}$ is a possible S time series over τ of sensor measurements iff*

$$\exists \Delta \in [-\delta, \delta] : \forall t \in T : \exists \varepsilon \in [-\epsilon, \epsilon] : \tau(t) + \varepsilon + \Delta = m_S(t).$$

We say the trajectory τ is consistent with m_S and denote this fact by $m_S \models \tau$.

Note that the consistency relation, as defined above, can be rewritten using affine arithmetic [11] as: $\tau(t) + \epsilon e_t + \delta d = m_S(t)$ if d is a slack constant and e_t is a per time-step fresh slack variable, ranging over the interval $[-1, 1]$.

3 Robust Lola

This section defines the syntax and semantics of RLOLA (*robust* Lola). RLOLA extends Lola with symbolic slack variables to represent error margins. To generate **slack variables** in RLOLA, we introduce the *Variable* value type.

An output stream of type *Variable* will produce a new slack variable in each time step or, in case of a constant stream, a single slack variable for the entire execution of the monitor.

```
input a_raw: Float
output e: Variable
constant d: Variable
output a := a_raw + 2 * e + 0.5 * d
```

Since slack variables are not explicitly bound to any values, streams of type *Variable* have no stream expressions. Instead, the variables symbolically represent a value in the range $[-1, 1]$. With streams of type *Variable* we can implement the measurement error model from Sect. 2.2 (like many other error models).

RLola Specifications. We define an RLOLA specification as a set of (recursive) equations over stream and slack variables as follows:

$$o_1 := expr_1(i_1, ..., i_I, \; o_1, ..., o_O, \; c_1, ..., c_C, \; c_1^V, ..., c_{V_c}^V, \; o_1^V, ..., o_{V_o}^V)$$
$$\vdots$$
$$o_O := expr_O(i_1, ..., i_I, \; o_1, ..., o_O, \; c_1, ..., c_C, \; c_1^V, ..., c_{V_c}^V, \; o_1^V, ..., o_{V_o}^V)$$

where $i_1, ..., i_I$ are input stream variables, $o_1, ..., o_O$ are output stream variables, $c_1, ..., c_C$ are constants, $c_1^V, ..., c_{V_c}^V$ are constant slack variables, $o_1^V, ..., o_{V_o}^V$ are slack variable streams, $expr_1, ..., expr_O$ are stream expressions, and $c_1 := C_1, ..., c_C := C_C$ are constant streams with $C_1, ..., C_C \in \mathbb{R} \cup \mathbb{B}$.

Omitted from the definition above are *trigger streams*. They are defined as boolean output streams specifying assertions that are communicated to a system operator upon violation. *Stream expressions*, the *dependency graph* and *well-formed* specifications are defined as for Lola in Sect. 2.1.

RLola Semantics. As for Lola, the semantics for RLOLA is defined by an evaluation model connecting input stream values to output stream values. Let ϕ be a robust Lola specification with: input stream variables $i_1, ..., i_I$, output stream variables $o_1, ..., o_O$, constants $c_1, ..., c_C$, constant slack variables $c_1^V, ..., c_{V_c}^V$, and slack variable streams $o_1^V, ..., o_{V_o}^V$.

Let $\tau_1, ..., \tau_I$ be streams of length N of input values. Let $\sigma_1, ..., \sigma_O$ be streams of length N of output values. Let $\zeta_1, ..., \zeta_{V_c}$ be streams of length N of constant values. Let $\sigma_1^V, ..., \sigma_{V_o}^V$ be streams of length N of slack values. A single evaluation of ϕ is then defined as: $\psi := \{\tau_1, ..., \tau_I, \sigma_1, ..., \sigma_O, \sigma_1^V, ..., \sigma_{V_o}^V, \zeta_1, ..., \zeta_{V_c}\}$.

An evaluation model of ϕ is then the possibly infinite set of evaluations such that for all evaluations, the following holds:

$$\forall 1 \leq t \leq N, 1 \leq i \leq I, 1 \leq o \leq O, 1 \leq o^V \leq V_o, 1 \leq c^V \leq V_c:$$
$$\sigma_o(t) := val(expr_o)(t)$$
$$\sigma_{o^V}^V(t) \in [-1, 1]$$
$$\zeta_{c^V}(t) \in [-1, 1]$$
$$\zeta_{c^V}(t) = \zeta_{c^V}(t-1), \text{ if } t > 0$$

where $val(expr_o)(t)$ is defined for

$$o_o := expr_o(i_1, ..., i_I, \ o_1, ..., o_O, \ c_1, ..., c_C, \ c_1^V, ..., c_{V_c}^V, \ o_1^V, ..., o_{V_o}^V)$$

with $c_j := C_j$ as follows:

$$val(i_j)(t) := \tau_j(t)$$
$$val(o_j)(t) := \sigma_j(t)$$
$$val(c_j)(t) := C_j$$
$$val(c_j^V)(t) := \zeta_j(t)$$
$$val(o_j^V)(t) := \sigma_j^V(t)$$
$$val(f(expr_1, ..., expr_k))(t) = f(val(expr_1)(t), ..., val(expr_k)(t))$$
$$val(expr.offset(by\!\!: i, \ or\!\!: l))(t) = \begin{cases} val(expr)(t+i) & for\ 1 \leq t+i \leq N \\ l & otherwise \end{cases}$$

An RLOLA monitor for a specification ϕ with the evaluation model φ and input streams $i_1, ..., i_I$ given the uncertain series of measurements $m_1, ..., m_I$ computes a (symbolic) representation of a set of evaluations

$$\varphi' := \{m_1, ..., m_I, \sigma_1, ..., \sigma_O, \sigma_1^V, ..., \sigma_{V_o}^V, \zeta_1, ..., \zeta_{V_c}\}$$

for any set of output streams $\sigma_1, ..., \sigma_O$, streams of slack values $\sigma_1^V, ..., \sigma_{V_o}^V$, and constant slack values $\zeta_1, ..., \zeta_{V_c}$ such that $\varphi' \subseteq \varphi$. Triggers are then evaluated existentially based on the set ψ'.

Boolean Conditions. With slack variables, stream equations may resolve to symbolically represented intervals instead of scalar values. We use the ternary predicates $>_p$ and $<_p$ to compare intervals to scalar thresholds in relation to an overlap percentage p. The overlap percentage sets a bound on the overlap of the interval with the threshold such that the predicate still evaluates to true:

The predicate $expr_i >_p c$ is satisfied for $p \in [0, 1]$ if the stream expression $expr_i$ resolves to range $[l, u]$ and $(u - c)/(u - l) > p$ holds. The definition for $<_p$ is analogous.

The explicit definition of an overlap percentage concretizes the *inconclusive* verdict found in other logics with robust semantics (cf. [9, 12]). There, comparing an interval of values to a scalar threshold produces an inconclusive verdict if the interval overlaps the threshold. The $>_p$ and $<_p$ predicates allow for a more precise assessment of the overlap.

4 Approximate Online Monitoring

We first present an online monitoring algorithm for RLOLA that over-approximates the semantics presented above. An evaluation algorithm for RLOLA has to manage two potentially unbounded quantities: the number of equations the monitor has to keep in memory and the length of these equations.

The number of equations in memory can be unbounded as, in general, the presented approach allows for refining or correcting earlier verdicts of the monitor at a later point in time, as slack variables can temporally relate measurement errors. Consider the scenario where the robot from Example 1 does not move, repeatedly measuring the same position. Such repeated measurements of the same physical value can increase the accuracy of the measured value, potentially leading to changes in past triggers. Yet, as shown in [12], to refine or correct previous monitor verdicts, the monitor would have to keep all previous stream equations in memory and solve a system of linear equations to evaluate trigger conditions across multiple time points. We argue that the monitor's constant memory footprint is more important than refining previous verdicts in an online monitoring setting, allowing the monitor to evict old stream equations.

The length of the equations can grow beyond any bound if more and more slack variables accumulate. Consider the following example. By definition, the equation for sum at time 3 includes the slack variables $e_1, e_2,$ and e_3. As time progresses, the equation for sum grows, accumulating more and more slackvariables. One approach to evaluate RLOLA specifications is to immediately interpret slack variables as the interval $[-1, 1]$.

```
input a_raw: Float
output e: Variable
constant d: Variable

output a := a_raw + 2 * e + 0.5 * d
output sum := sum.last(or: 0) + a
```

Interval Arithmetic. Interval arithmetic [20] lifts arithmetic operations such as addition and subtraction to intervals. An uncertain scalar value x can be represented as an interval $[a, b]$ of all possible values that x might have. An *interval* is defined as a set of real values $[a, b] = \{x \mid a \leq x \leq b\}$. Arithmetic operations and functions are then defined as follows: For two intervals $a = [a_l, a_u]$ and $b = [b_l, b_u]$ it holds that:

$$a + b = [a_l + b_l, a_u + b_u]$$
$$a - b = [a_l - b_u, a_u - b_l]$$
$$a * b = [\min(a_l b_l, a_l b_u, a_u b_l, a_u b_u), \max(a_l b_l, a_l b_u, a_u b_l, a_u b_u)]$$
$$a/b = a * \frac{1}{b} \text{ with } \frac{1}{b} = [b_u^{-1}, b_l^{-1}], \quad \text{if } 0 \notin b$$

In general, for any monotonic operation $\cdot$ it holds that:

$$a \cdot b = [\min(a_l \cdot b_l, a_l \cdot b_u, a_u \cdot b_l, a_u \cdot b_u), \max(a_l \cdot b_l, a_l \cdot b_u, a_u \cdot b_l, a_u \cdot b_u)]$$

Interval Approximation. In the following, we present a monitoring procedure that over-approximates the semantics of the RLOLA specification by translating it to a Lola specification defined over intervals using interval arithmetic. Note that Lola is generic regarding the value domains of streams and their supported operators, which enables this translation.

Interval Replacement. Let ϕ be an RLOLA specification with input stream variables $i_1, ..., i_I$, output stream variables $o_1, ..., o_O$, constants $c_1, ..., c_C$, constant slack variables $c_1^V, ..., c_{V_c}^V$, slack variable streams $o_1^V, ..., o_{V_o}^V$ and expressions $expr_1, ..., expr_O$. Let ϕ' be a Lola specification with expressions $expr'_1, ..., expr'_O$, where $expr'_i$ is equal to $expr_i$ with all references to $c_1^V, ..., c_{V_c}^V, o_1^V, ..., o_{V_o}^V$ replaced with the interval $[-1, 1]$. Boolean conditions, such as trigger conditions, are evaluated using the ternary operators defined in Sect. 3.

Proposition 1. *Let ϕ be an RLOLA specification and ϕ' be the Lola specification obtained from ϕ using interval replacement. Let ψ be the evaluation model of ϕ and ψ' be the evaluation model of ϕ'. If it holds for all sub-expressions of ϕ of the form*

$$\text{if } p \text{ then } expr_1 \text{ else } expr_2$$

that p does not (transitively) reference any slack variable, then it holds for fixed streams of input data $\tau_1, ..., \tau_I$ that if $\{\tau_1, ..., \tau_I, \sigma_1, ..., \sigma_O, \sigma_1^V, ..., \sigma_{V_o}^V, \zeta_1, ..., \zeta_{V_c}\} \in \psi$ then $\{\tau_1, ..., \tau_I, \sigma_1, ..., \sigma_O\} \in \psi'$.

The proposition states that *interval replacement* indeed produces a Lola specification that over-approximates an RLOLA specification. Intuitively, intervals reintroduce the aliasing problem, which, as described in Sect. 1, results in over-approximating measurement noise. The additional syntactic requirement on *if* conditions stems from conditionals being non-monotonic functions.

5 Precise Constant Memory Online Monitoring

We now present a syntactic fragment of RLOLA for which constant-memory monitors exist. We develop this result in multiple steps. First, we define two requirements that all specifications in the fragment must fulfill and show how slack variables can be pruned from the monitor if their coefficients are linearly dependent. Then, we give examples of increasing complexity, highlighting how these requirements ensure the collinearity of subsets of the slack variables.

Requirement 1. First, we syntactically limit stream expressions. They are required to be in one of the following two forms:

$$expr_i := c_s * o_i[o, d] + c_i^T \begin{pmatrix} i_1 \\ \vdots \\ i_I \end{pmatrix} + c_\epsilon^T \begin{pmatrix} o_1^V \\ \vdots \\ o_{V_o}^V \end{pmatrix} + c_\delta^T \begin{pmatrix} c_1^V \\ \vdots \\ c_{V_c}^V \end{pmatrix} \quad (1)$$

$$expr_i := \text{if } p \text{ then } expr_i^c \text{ else } expr_i^a \quad (2)$$

where $c_s \in \{0, 1\}$, p is a boolean stream expression and $c_i \in \mathbb{R}^I, c_\epsilon \in \mathbb{R}^{V_o}, c_\delta \in \mathbb{R}^{V_c}$. Intuitively, this requirement ensures that at every point in time, each equation entailed by a stream expression is an affine form [11].

Requirement 2. Second, we require that every output stream only occurs in dependency loops of equal weight. Concretely, let ϕ be a specification with output streams $o_1, ..., o_O$ and let $G = (V, E)$ be the dependency graph of ϕ, then:

$$\forall 1 \leq i \leq O. \exists c_o \in \mathbb{Z}. \forall \langle o_i \xrightarrow{o_1} ... \xrightarrow{o_n} o_i \rangle \in E. \sum_{1 \leq r \leq n} o_r = c_o$$

Intuitively, this requirement ensures that equations in the equation store are affine. For example, it prohibits calculating the Fibonacci sequence.

One exception from these requirements are trigger streams. As their value can, by definition, not be used by other streams and they are hence stateless, they can express arbitrary boolean assessments over output streams.

Consider Example 1; If the `distance` output stream is inlined, all stream expressions in the specification satisfy Requirement 1. Requirement 2 is also satisfied, as `computed_pos_x` and `computed_pos_y` are both only part of self-loops with weight -1.

We now develop the construction of constant-memory Lola monitors that monitor specifications of the fragment without loss of precision. We first define a method to reduce the number of slack variables in equations.

Definition 3 (Slack Variable Pruning). *Let $\epsilon \in [-1, 1]^j$ be a vector of slack variables and let $C \in \mathbb{R}^{k \times j}$ be a matrix of coefficients, then*

$$y = C(\epsilon_1, ..., \epsilon_j)^T$$

defines a zonotope over slack variables $\epsilon_1, ..., \epsilon_j$. To prune slack variables, we reduce the dimension of $\vec{\epsilon}$ by finding collinear column vectors of the matrix C to obtain an equivalent (pruned) representation of the zonotope:

$$y = C'(\epsilon_1, ..., \epsilon_l)^T$$

with $C' \in \mathbb{R}^{k \times l}$ for $l \leq j$. If two or more column vectors of C are collinear, it holds that $l < j$.

We use Definition 3 to prune variables from the equations the monitor maintains at runtime. For that, we define the state of a monitor as follows:

Monitoring State. Let ϕ be an RLOLA specification with output streams:

$$o_1 := expr_1 \quad ... \quad o_O := expr_O$$

A monitor manages two sets of equations called equation stores: R for resolved equations of the form: $\sigma_i(t) = c' + c_1\epsilon_1 + \cdots + c_s\epsilon_s$ and U for unresolved equations of the form $\sigma_i(t) = expr_i$. At time t for measurements $m_1, ..., m_I$ the following equations are added to R: $\tau_1(t) = m_1, ..., \tau_I(t) = m_I$ and $\sigma_1(t) = expr_1, ..., \sigma_O(t) = expr_O$ to U. If, through simplifications, equations from U become resolved, they are moved to R.

At any time point t, the sets U and R are called the monitoring state. We call the equations in R monitoring equations.

```
input a_raw: Float

output e: Variable
constant d: Variable

output a := a_raw + e + d
output sum2 := sum2.last(or: 0) + 2a
output sum3 := sum3.last(or: 0) + 3a
```

(a) The RLOLA specification with slack variables.

```
input a_raw: Float
constant e: Variable
constant d: Variable

output e_coeff :=
   e_coeff.last(or: 0) + 1
output sum2_raw :=
   sum2_raw.last(or: 0) + 2a_raw + 2d
output sum3_raw :=
   sum3_raw.last(or: 0) + 3a_raw + 3d
output sum_2 := sum2_raw + 2 * e_coeff * e
output sum_3 := sum3_raw + 3 * e_coeff * e
```

(b) The translated RLOLA specification without slack variables.

Fig. 2. An RLOLA specification where a slack variable occurs with different coefficients.

	1	2	3	4
sum2	$2e_1 + 2d$	$2e_1 + 2e_2 + 4d$	$2e_1 + 2e_2 + 2e_3 + 6d$	$2e_1 + 2e_2 + 2e_3 + 2e_4 + 8d$
sum3	$3e_1 + 3d$	$3e_1 + 3e_2 + 6d$	$3e_1 + 3e_2 + 3e_3 + 9d$	$3e_1 + 3e_2 + 3e_3 + 3e_4 + 12d$

Different Coefficients. As a first example, consider the specification in Fig. 2a and its partial monitoring state depicted below: The table depicts partial monitoring equations truncated to their slack variable part at time points one to four. As discussed in Sect. 4, one can see that the slack variables produced by e accumulate in the monitoring equations of sum2 and sum3. Yet, when rewriting the equations at time four as vectors, omitting the constant slack variable d:

$$\begin{pmatrix} 2,2,2,2 \\ 3,3,3,3 \end{pmatrix} (e_1, e_2, e_3, e_4)^T$$

it is easy to see that pruning, as defined in Definition 3, can reduce the number of slack variables to one, as all column vectors of the matrix are collinear. In fact, this holds for every time step due to Requirement 1 which ensures that slack variables only occur with a constant coefficient in stream equations. Based on this, Fig. 2b depicts an equivalent RLOLA specification using only constant slack variables.

Different Offsets. Next, consider the example where slack variables are used in streams that reference themselves with different offsets in Fig. 3a. Note that the constant slack variable d is omitted for simplicity. Again, consider the partial monitoring equations for this specification in the table below: Because

	1	2	3	4
sum	$2e_1$	$2e_1 + 2e_2$	$2e_1 + 2e_2 + 2e_3$	$2e_1 + 2e_2 + 2e_3 + 2e_4$
eo_sum	$3e_1$	$3e_2$	$3e_1 + 3e_3$	$3e_2 + 3e_4$

of the offset of -2, a slack variable e_i is added at either an even position *or*

```
input a_raw: Float
output e: Variable

output a := a_raw + e
output sum := sum.offset(by: -1, or: 0) + 2a
output eo_sum := eo_summ.offset(by: -2, or: 0) + 3a
```

(a) The RLOLA specification with slack variables.

```
input a_raw: Float
constant e_even: Variable
constant e_odd: Variable

output step := step.last(or: 0) + 1
output e_even_coeff := if step % 2 = 0 ∧ step % 1 = 0
                      then e_even_coeff.last(or: 0) + 1 else e_even_coeff.last(or: 0)
output e_odd_coeff := if step % 2 = 1 ∧ step % 1 = 0
                     then e_odd_coeff.last(or: 0) + 1 else e_odd_coeff.last(or: 0)
output sum_raw := sum_raw.last(or: 0) + a_raw
output eo_sum_raw := eo_sum_raw.offset(by: -2, or: 0) + a_raw
output sum := sum_raw + 2 * e_even_coeff * e_even + 2 * e_odd_coeff * e_odd
output eo_sum := if step % 2 = 0 ∧ step % 1 = 0
                 then eo_sum_raw + 3 * e_even_coeff * e_even
                 else eo_sum_raw + 3 * e_odd_coeff * e_odd
```

(b) The translated RLOLA specification without slack variables.

Fig. 3. A specification where slack variables accumulate under different offsets.

an odd position of eo_sum, never at both. This stems from the stream-based semantics of RLOLA. Because of this, we analyze these two cases separately. Consider the equations at time three and four in their vector representation:

$$\begin{pmatrix} 2,2,2 \\ 3,0,3 \end{pmatrix} (e_1, e_2, e_3)^T \qquad \begin{pmatrix} 2,2,2,2 \\ 0,3,0,3 \end{pmatrix} (e_1, e_2, e_3, e_4)^T \qquad \text{Both}$$

matrices can be pruned to reduce the number of slack variables to two. With the same argument as for different coefficients, this holds for all even and odd positions, respectively. We give an equivalent RLOLA specification that only uses constant slack variables in Fig. 3b. Note that the if conditions in the specification can be simplified. Yet, they are kept as is to demonstrate how the construction scales to arbitrary offsets in multiple streams as long as Requirement 2 is satisfied. In general, if a slack variable appears in multiple streams with different offsets $o_1, ..., o_k$, the above case distinction has to be extended to $s = o_1 * ... * o_k$ cases of offset combinations resulting in s constant slack variables.

Central Observation. When partitioning the monitoring equations of a specification in the fragment by case, the coefficients of the slack variables occurring in each case will always be equal. For example, in the above specification, the coefficients at even and at odd positions will always be equal. This is explained by the constant coefficients asserted by Requirement 1.

If **Clauses.** Lastly, we extend this case distinction to *if* clauses. Consider the following example:

```
input a_raw: Float
output e: Variable
output a := a_raw + e
output sum := if a_raw > 10
              then sum.offset(by: -1, or: 0) + 2a
              else sum.offset(by: -1, or: 0) + 5a
output eo_sum := eo_sum.offset(by: -2, or: 0) + 3a
```

To handle *if* clauses, we distinguish one case per if condition. Let a slack variable output stream be referenced in n output streams that contain *if* conditions. Let there be a total of k if conditions in their stream expressions. Then, a monitor has to handle $s * (n + k)$ slack variables where s is the previous bound on the number of slack variables.

In the above example, there are two different offsets (–1 and –2), and one stream contains a total of one if condition. Hence, to precisely monitor the above specification, the monitor has to distinguish $2*(1+1) = 4$ cases. In the following, we group the coefficients by their case: By Definition 3, the variables e_1 and e_5

	even	odd
a_raw $\leq$ 10	$\begin{pmatrix}5\\3\end{pmatrix} e_2$	$\begin{pmatrix}5\\3\end{pmatrix} e_1 + \begin{pmatrix}5\\3\end{pmatrix} e_5$
a_raw $>$ 10	$\begin{pmatrix}2\\3\end{pmatrix} e_4$	$\begin{pmatrix}2\\3\end{pmatrix} e_3$

of the above example can be pruned.

Following the central observation, it is easy to see that a monitor for the fragment only needs to keep a *single* constant slack variable for each case for each stream of slack variables. Figure 4 summarizes the construction.

The specifications generated by this construction can be evaluated, without any loss of precision, using the algorithm from Sect. 4. This is because all constant slack variables generated by the construction are only referenced once in streams that are *state-less*, meaning that they do not propagate through computations, preventing the aliasing problem.

Proposition 2. *The construction in Fig. 4 is correct and only requires a bounded number of slack variables.*

As the specification is finite, there can only be a bounded number of cases; hence, the number of slack variables is also bounded. The correctness of the construction follows from Definition 3 and from the fact that, by the requirements of the fragment, a slack variable can only occur in one case per output stream at each time step.

6 Evaluation

We evaluate our approach with respect to runtime and precision based on Example 1. We consider three variants of the specification: First, a Lola specification

---

Let $C_1, ..., C_k$ be the cases in which subsets of slack variables occur with equal coefficients in the monitoring equations.

1. For each case C_i introduce a constant slack variable d_i and construct a stream that counts how often this case occurs as follows:

   ```
   constant d_i: Variable
   output c_i := if C_i then c_i.offset(by:-1, or:0) + 1 else c_i.offset(by:-1, or:0)
   ```

2. For each output stream s and slack variable stream ϵ, where s references ϵ in cases $C_i, ..., C_j$ with coefficients $x_i, ..., x_j$ add a stream that reconstructs ϵ for s:

   ```
   output s_ε := c_i * x_i * d_i + ... + c_j * x_j * d_j
   ```

3. For each output stream s and constant slack variable δ, where s references δ in cases $C_i, ..., C_j$ with coefficients $x_i, ..., x_j$ add a stream that reconstructs δ for s:

   ```
   output s_δ := (c_i * x_i + ... + c_j * x_j) * δ
   ```

4. For each output stream s that references slack variable streams $\epsilon_1, ..., \epsilon_n$ and constant slack variables $\delta_1, ..., \delta_m$ construct a stream s_raw that is equal to s, apart that all references to slack-variables are removed. Construct a stream s' that reconstructs s from its partial sums.

   ```
   output s' := s_raw + s_ε_1 + ... + s_ε_n + s_δ_1 + ... + s_δ_m
   ```

Fig. 4. Construction of constant-memory monitors.

that does not take measurement errors into consideration. Second, a specification using the interval-based over-approximation presented in Sect. 4. Third, the RLOLA specification translated to regular Lola using the construction presented in Sect. 5. The experiments were conducted using the RTLola interpreter [5] on a MacBook Pro from 2020. A *ground truth* trace was randomly generated together with a mutated variant based on the error model presented in Sect. 2.2.

Figure 5a shows the error margins computed using interval arithmetic and slack variables around the ground truth x coordinates over time. While both error ranges grow over time, the graph visualizes the pessimistic over-approximation of interval arithmetic caused by the aliasing problem. It occurs due to the constant error `delta` in the example. In RLOLA this constant error is subtracted when the robot moves in opposite directions, while it is added in interval analysis.

Figure 5b compares the runtime of the three specifications in relation to the trace length. The running times were measured using the statistics-driven benchmarking library Criterion [1]. It shows that the plain Lola specification computes fastest, the interval-based specification is the second fastest, and the slack variable based specification has the highest computation time, taking 3.5 milliseconds for the whole trace of 1000 events. This is explained by the different number of auxiliary streams required to track the measurement errors in the different

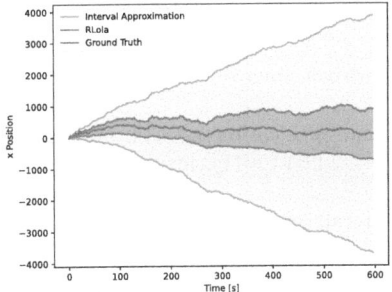 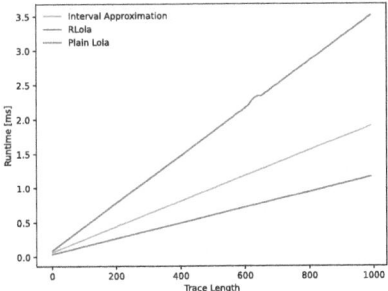

(a) Precision of the computed x-position for the interval approximation vs. the precise evaluation of the slack variables.

(b) Monitor run-time of the plain Lola specification, the interval approximation, and the RLOLA specification.

Fig. 5. Precision and running time of RLOLA.

approaches. The performance could be improved by adding native support for the underlying computational domains to the RTLola interpreter.

7 Conclusion

We have presented RLOLA, a robust extension of the monitoring framework Lola. In RLOLA, the addition of slack variables allows us to track measurement noise induced by inaccurate sensors throughout computations; boolean verdicts explicitly account for the resulting inaccuracies. We demonstrated that RLOLA monitors require, in general, an unbounded amount of memory. We addressed this issue with a complete, but approximate, online monitoring algorithm based on interval arithmetic and a construction of fully precise constant-memory monitors for a rich fragment of RLOLA. Lastly, we demonstrated effectiveness by evaluating the above methods with respect to running time and precision.

This paper has focused on *online* monitoring, where data is processed in real time, and where trigger conditions are evaluated based on the information available during runtime. An interesting question for future work is how to adapt this approach to *offline* monitoring. In offline monitoring, it is possible to evaluate trigger conditions with the benefit of hindsight: measurements that were obtained only *after* a certain condition was evaluated may still allow for a more precise re-analysis of the trigger value. At the same time, resource constraints are less of a concern for offline monitoring. In online monitoring, the bounded-memory guarantee is crucially important so that the monitor can run indefinitely on constrained hardware. In offline monitoring, it is generally affordable to re-evaluate trigger conditions using SMT-solving. A similar approach was recently proposed for the offline monitoring of robust Signal Temporal Logic [12].

References

1. Aparicio, J., Heisler, B.: Criterion - statistics-driven micro-benchmarking library (2023). https://crates.io/crates/criterion
2. Bauer, A., Leucker, M., Schallhart, C.: Runtime verification for LTL and TLTL. ACM Trans. Softw. Eng. Methodol. **20**(4), 14:1–14:64 (2011). https://doi.org/10.1145/2000799.2000800
3. Baumeister, J., et al.: Monitoring unmanned aircraft: specification, integration, and lessons-learned. In: Gurfinkel, A., Ganesh, V. (eds.) Computer Aided Verification. CAV 2024. LNCS, vol. 14682, pp. 207–218. Springer, Cham (2024). https://doi.org/10.1007/978-3-031-65630-9_10
4. Baumeister, J., Finkbeiner, B., Schirmer, S., Schwenger, M., Torens, C.: RTLola cleared for take-off: monitoring autonomous aircraft. In: Lahiri, S., Wang, C. (eds.) Computer Aided Verification. CAV 2020. LNCS, vol. 12225, pp. 28–39. Springer, Cham (2020). https://doi.org/10.1007/978-3-030-53291-8_3
5. Baumeister, J., et al.: RTLola interpreter - rust crate on crates.io (2023). https://crates.io/crates/rtlola-interpreter
6. Convent, L., Hungerecker, S., Leucker, M., Scheffel, T., Schmitz, M., Thoma, D.: TeSSLa: temporal stream-based specification language. In: Massoni, T., Mousavi, M.R. (eds.) SBMF 2018. LNCS, vol. 11254, pp. 144–162. Springer, Cham (2018). https://doi.org/10.1007/978-3-030-03044-5_10
7. D'Angelo, B., et al.: LOLA: runtime monitoring of synchronous systems. In: 12th International Symposium on Temporal Representation and Reasoning (TIME 2005), 23–25 June 2005, Burlington, Vermont, USA, pp. 166–174. IEEE Computer Society (2005). https://doi.org/10.1109/TIME.2005.26
8. Decker, N., Leucker, M., Thoma, D.: Monitoring modulo theories. In: Ábrahám, E., Havelund, K. (eds.) TACAS 2014. LNCS, vol. 8413, pp. 341–356. Springer, Heidelberg (2014). https://doi.org/10.1007/978-3-642-54862-8_23
9. Donzé, A., Ferrère, T., Maler, O.: Efficient robust monitoring for STL. In: Sharygina, N., Veith, H. (eds.) CAV 2013. LNCS, vol. 8044, pp. 264–279. Springer, Heidelberg (2013). https://doi.org/10.1007/978-3-642-39799-8_19
10. Donzé, A., Maler, O.: Robust satisfaction of temporal logic over real-valued signals. In: Chatterjee, K., Henzinger, T.A. (eds.) FORMATS 2010. LNCS, vol. 6246, pp. 92–106. Springer, Heidelberg (2010). https://doi.org/10.1007/978-3-642-15297-9_9
11. de Figueiredo, L.H., Stolfi, J.: Affine arithmetic: Concepts and applications. Numer. Algorithms **37**(1–4), 147–158 (2004). https://doi.org/10.1023/B:NUMA.0000049462.70970.B6
12. Finkbeiner, B., Fränzle, M., Kohn, F., Kröger, P.: A truly robust signal temporal logic: monitoring safety properties of interacting cyber-physical systems under uncertain observation. Algorithms **15**(4), 126 (2022). https://doi.org/10.3390/A15040126
13. Fränzle, M., Hansen, M.R.: A robust interpretation of duration calculus. In: Van Hung, D., Wirsing, M. (eds.) ICTAC 2005. LNCS, vol. 3722, pp. 257–271. Springer, Heidelberg (2005). https://doi.org/10.1007/11560647_17
14. Gorostiaga, F., Sánchez, C.: **Striver**: stream runtime verification for real-time event-streams. In: Colombo, C., Leucker, M. (eds.) RV 2018. LNCS, vol. 11237, pp. 282–298. Springer, Cham (2018). https://doi.org/10.1007/978-3-030-03769-7_16
15. ISO: ISO/IEC 5725:2023: Accuracy (trueness and precision) of measurement methods and results - Part 1: General principles and definitions. International Organization for Standardization, Geneva, Switzerland (July 2023)

16. Kallwies, H., Leucker, M., Sánchez, C.: Symbolic runtime verification for monitoring under uncertainties and assumptions. In: Bouajjani, A., Holík, L., Wu, Z. (eds.) Automated Technology for Verification and Analysis. ATVA 2022. LNCS, vol. 13505, pp. 117–134. Springer, Cham (2022). https://doi.org/10.1007/978-3-031-19992-9_8
17. Kauffman, S., Havelund, K., Fischmeister, S.: What can we monitor over unreliable channels? Int. J. Softw. Tools Technol. Transf. **23**(4), 579–600 (2021). https://doi.org/10.1007/S10009-021-00625-Z
18. Leucker, M., Sánchez, C., Scheffel, T., Schmitz, M., Thoma, D.: Runtime verification for timed event streams with partial information. In: Finkbeiner, B., Mariani, L. (eds.) RV 2019. LNCS, vol. 11757, pp. 273–291. Springer, Cham (2019). https://doi.org/10.1007/978-3-030-32079-9_16
19. Maler, O., Nickovic, D.: Monitoring temporal properties of continuous signals. In: Lakhnech, Y., Yovine, S. (eds.) FORMATS/FTRTFT -2004. LNCS, vol. 3253, pp. 152–166. Springer, Heidelberg (2004). https://doi.org/10.1007/978-3-540-30206-3_12
20. Moore, R.E., Kearfott, R.B., Cloud, M.J.: Introduction to Interval Analysis. SIAM, New Delhi (2009). https://doi.org/10.1137/1.9780898717716
21. Visconti, E., Bartocci, E., Loreti, M., Nenzi, L.: Online monitoring of spatio-temporal properties for imprecise signals. In: Arun-Kumar, S., Méry, D., Saha, I., Zhang, L. (eds.) 19th ACM-IEEE International Conference on Formal Methods and Models for System Design, Virtual Event, China, 20–22 November 2021, pp. 78–88. ACM (2021). https://doi.org/10.1145/3487212.3487344

Dynamic, Multi-objective Specification and Falsification of Autonomous CPS

Kevin Kai-Chun Chang[✉], Kaifei Xu, Edward Kim, Alberto Sangiovanni-Vincentelli, and Sanjit A. Seshia

University of California, Berkeley, Berkeley, CA 94709, USA
{kaichunchang,k.px,ek65,alberto,sseshia}@berkeley.edu

Abstract. Simulation-based falsification has proved to be an effective verification method for cyber-physical systems. Traditional approaches to falsification take as input a single or a set of temporal properties that must be satisfied by the system at all times. In this paper, we consider falsification of a more complex specification with two dimensions: multiple objectives with relative priorities and the evolution of these objectives characterized by time-varying priorities. We introduce the concept of *dynamic rulebooks* as a way to specify a prioritized multi-objective specification and its evolution over time. We develop a novel algorithm for falsifying a dynamic rulebook specification on a cyber-physical system. To evaluate our approach, we define scenarios and dynamic rulebook specifications for the domains of autonomous driving and human-robot interaction. Our experiments demonstrate that integrating dynamic rulebooks allows us to capture counterexamples more accurately and efficiently than when using static rulebooks. Moreover, our falsification framework identifies more numerous and more significant counterexamples as compared to previous approaches.

Keywords: Formal methods · Falsification · Specification · Dynamic Rulebooks · Cyber-physical systems · Autonomous driving · Human-robot interaction

1 Introduction

Simulation-based formal analysis, such as temporal logic falsification (e.g., [1,2,6,17]), has proved to be effective in finding safety violations in cyber-physical systems (CPS) and autonomous systems enabled by artificial intelligence (AI). Numerous approaches have been proposed over the past two decades (e.g., see [18]). However, traditional approaches to falsification take as input a single or a set of temporal properties (constraints) that must be satisfied by the system at all times. As described in [14], AI-enabled autonomous systems have two important features that necessitate advances in simulation-based verification: the specification of *multiple Boolean or quantitative constraints with relative priorities*, and the *dynamic nature of constraints* and their changing priority relations over time.

As a motivating example, consider a toy autonomous vehicle scenario shown in Fig. 1a, where the ego vehicle has no other moving vehicles or people around it but faces

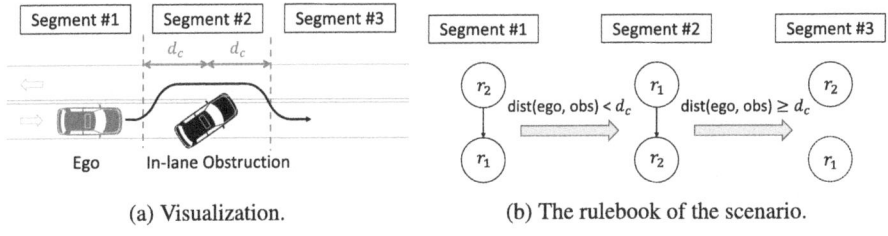

Fig. 1. Toy scenario with lane-keeping and obstruction avoidance.

an in-lane obstruction (such as a stalled car/road work barrier) that requires crossing the centerline of the road to avoid collision. However, this behavior violates traffic rules, presenting a scenario in which the autonomous vehicle must balance two constraints: "obeying traffic rules" and "avoiding the temporary obstruction." Different constraints may inherently conflict, as is evident in Fig. 1a, where the ego vehicle cannot simultaneously avoid the obstruction and adhere to traffic rules. In this case, *constraints become objectives as they cannot be satisfied simultaneously.* By doing so, we can handle constraints in a more flexible way, prioritizing and trading them off. In this example, it is reasonable to prioritize avoiding collision with the obstruction over strict adherence to traffic rules when the ego vehicle is close to the obstacle, acknowledging that temporarily crossing the centerline may be deemed safe if no oncoming traffic is present, while colliding with the obstacle poses potential harm to passengers in the ego vehicle.

In addition to managing multiple objectives, the dynamics of autonomous CPS must also be taken into account. In the aforementioned scenario, the priorities among objectives can evolve over time. While the ego vehicle should prioritize avoiding collision when close to the temporary obstruction, it should prioritize obeying traffic rules when the obstruction is still far away to avoid crossing the centerline prematurely. Additionally, once the vehicle successfully navigates around the obstruction, it can deactivate the "avoiding the obstruction" objective and refocus on "obeying traffic rules" until another obstruction is detected. This example illustrates how both the objectives and their priorities can change dynamically in an autonomous CPS.

Censi et al. [4] proposed a *rulebook* structure to specify a set of objectives and their priority relations. However, the set and the relations are static, making it inadequate for addressing the dynamic nature of CPS. Viswanadha et al. [16] gave a falsification framework for multi-objective CPS specified with rulebook structures. This framework also assumed static settings where the objectives and their priorities remain fixed throughout the scenario. To the best of our knowledge, no prior work has explored the falsification problem for dynamic, multi-objective specifications. In this paper, we address the gap by proposing a *dynamic, multi-objective specification* structure and give a *novel algorithm for falsification of such structures*. Our contributions are as follows.

- Formulation of *dynamic rulebooks* capable of specifying CPS where the set of objectives and priority relations can change over time.
- Development of an efficient *algorithm for falsifying* CPS whose requirements can be modeled with dynamic rulebooks.

- Introduction of a generic falsification framework that facilitates on-the-fly construction of rulebooks.
- Experimental demonstration of our specification formalism and falsification algorithm in the domains of autonomous driving and human-robot interaction.

The remainder of this paper is organized as follows: Sect. 2 formulates the concept of dynamic rulebook. Section 3 defines the dynamic and multi-objective CPS falsification problem. Section 4 details our falsification framework. Section 5 develops rules and scenarios in the domains of autonomous driving and human-robot interaction. Section 6 shows experimental results. Finally, Sect. 7 concludes this paper.

2 Formulation of Dynamic Rulebooks

To verify a dynamic, multi-objective CPS, it is essential to assess its behavior under various conditions or inputs. To formalize this, we introduce the concept of a *scenario*, represented as a closed transition system over a set of state variables $V = \{v_1, v_2, ..., v_n\}$ with domains $\{\mathcal{D}_{v_1}, \mathcal{D}_{v_2}, ..., \mathcal{D}_{v_n}\}$:

Definition 1 (Scenario). *A scenario M is a closed transition system $M = (V, V_0, \delta_P)$, where V is the set of state variables, V_0 is the set of initial value vectors of the state variables, and $\delta_P : (\mathcal{D}_{v_1} \times \mathcal{D}_{v_2} \times ... \times \mathcal{D}_{v_n}) \times (\mathcal{D}_{v_1} \times \mathcal{D}_{v_2} \times ... \times \mathcal{D}_{v_n}) \to \mathbb{B}$ is the transition relation. Here, $V := V_r \cup V_c$, where V_r is a set of random variables whose initial values are internally sampled by the scenario[1], while V_c is a set of random variables for which we need to sample their initial values. The transition relation $\delta_P(\vec{v}, \vec{v}')$ is true if and only if there is a transition from values $\vec{v}$ to $\vec{v}'$.*

The transition relation δ_P is determined by a set of parameters $P = \{p_1, p_2, ..., p_m\}$, which are not state variables, with domains $\{\mathcal{D}_{p_1}, \mathcal{D}_{p_2}, ..., \mathcal{D}_{p_m}\}$. We can then define the *input feature set* and the *input feature space* of a scenario:

Definition 2 (Input Feature Set and Input Feature Space). *The input feature set F encompasses all features used as inputs to a scenario M, determining the initial states and transitions of the scenario. Hence, $F = V_c \cup P$. The input feature space $\mathcal{F}$ is the domain that encompasses all the variables in F.*

Scenario 1 (Lane-Keeping and Obstruction Avoidance). *Here, we leverage the scenario depicted in Fig. 1 as a running example to elaborate on our formulation. In this scenario, V_c comprises the x and y positions of the ego vehicle, while the remaining state variables, such as the ego vehicle's orientation and model, are included in V_r. The transition relation updates the state variables based on the vehicle's dynamics in the simulation. The set of parameters P includes the target speed of the ego vehicle, the initial distance from the ego vehicle to the obstruction, and the distance to the obstruction at the start of lane change, which can affect the transition dynamics. For example, given the sampled target speed of the ego vehicle, the acceleration of the ego vehicle is*

---

[1] In probabilistic CPS modeling languages such as Scenic [8], internally-sampled variables can be implicitly sampled from prior distributions.

adjusted based on the difference between the current speed and the target speed, thus influencing the subsequent positions of the ego vehicle. Finally, the input feature set F consists of the parameters along with the positions of the ego vehicle, i.e., $F = V_c \cup P$.

Now, given a scenario M, our aim is to verify if, under an input feature vector $\vec{f} \in \mathcal{F}$, the trajectories of the scenario (i.e., the values of each state variable $v_i \in V$ at each timestamp) meet the desired constraints or objectives, referred to as *rules*. To evaluate if a rule is violated, we define the *violation score* of a rule as follows:

Definition 3 (Rule and Violation Score). *Given a scenario $M = (V, V_0, \delta_P)$, the violation score (VS) s of a rule r can be expressed as a function $s : \mathcal{F} \to \mathbb{R}$.[2] In this paper, we design the VS such that it is negative if and only if the corresponding rule is violated. Furthermore, the lower the VS, the more severely the rule is violated.*

Scenario 1 *(continued).* We define the two rules, r_1 and r_2, along with their VS. These rules are expressed using signal temporal logic (STL) formulas [11]:

– r_1 (avoiding the temporary obstruction):

$$\textbf{STL: } G_{[T_1,T_2]}(dist(x_0(t), x_{obs}(t)) \geq d_{safe});$$
$$\textbf{VS: } min_{[T_1,T_2]}(dist(x_0(t), x_{obs}(t)) - d_{safe}),$$

where $x_0(t)$ and $x_{obs}(t)$ are the positions of the ego vehicle and the in-lane obstruction, respectively; $G_{[T_1,T_2]}$ indicates the predicate inside the parentheses should always be true within the time interval $[T_1, T_2]$.

– r_2 (obeying the traffic rule of not crossing the centerline):

$$\textbf{STL: } G_{[T_1,T_2]}(dist(x_0(t), L) = 0); \textbf{VS: } - max_{[T_1,T_2]}(dist(x_0(t), L)),$$

where L denotes the polygon region of the lane, and $dist(x_0(t), L)$ indicates the minimum distance from the ego vehicle to the polygon. If the vehicle is within the polygon (i.e., it is on the lane), $dist(x_0(t), L) = 0$.

Indeed, VS is negative if and only if the ego vehicle violates the corresponding rule, and the lower the VS, the more severe the violation.

After defining the rules, we can introduce the *static rulebook* as proposed in [4], which specifies the rules and their priorities in a static multi-objective system.

Definition 4 (Static Rulebook). *A static rulebook B is a tuple $B = (R, \leq_R)$, where R is a set of rules and $\leq_R$ is a partial order on R indicating the relative priority of the rules. A static rulebook can be represented as a directed graph $G_B = (V_B, E_B)$, where each node in V_B represents a rule, and each edge in E_B indicates the priority relation between two rules. If there is an edge from node A to node B, then rule r_A has a higher priority than r_B.*

---

[2] We denote the function s in this way for simplicity. Actually, the function maps the trajectory generated under an input feature vector $\vec{f} \in \mathcal{F}$ to $\mathbb{R}$.

Finally, we propose the definition of *dynamic rulebook* for dynamic, multi-objective systems:

Definition 5 (Dynamic Rulebook). *The dynamic rulebook B_M for a scenario M is a tuple $B_M = (R_M, \leq_{R_M}, U_M)$. Similar to the static rulebook, R_M is a set of rules and $\leq_{R_M}$ is a partial order on R_M. However, the key difference lies in the dependency of R_M and $\leq_{R_M}$ on the state variables of the scenario M. As the state variables in M change, both R_M and $\leq_{R_M}$ can be updated, unlike in the static rulebook where R and $\leq_R$ remain fixed. Rules may be added or removed from R_M, and the priority among rules may also change. Formally, U_M is a transition function that defines these updates. Given the current R_M, $\leq_{R_M}$, and the values of the state variables in M, U_M outputs the updated R_M and $\leq_{R_M}$. A dynamic rulebook B_M can also be depicted as an evolving directed graph $G_{B_M} = (V_{B_M}, E_{B_M})$. With changes in state variables in M, nodes may be added or removed from the graph, and edges may be added, removed, or reversed.*

Property 1 (Segmentation of a Dynamic Rulebook). Each time the state variables in M change, R_M and $\leq_{R_M}$ of a dynamic rulebook may be updated. Thus, from another perspective, a dynamic rulebook can be viewed as a sequence of static rulebooks, denoted $B_M = \{B_1, B_2, B_3, ...\}$, where B_i is updated to B_{i+1} with some state changes. Similarly, the graphical representation of a dynamic rulebook can also be viewed as a sequence of directed graphs. We refer to the time segment corresponding to the static rulebook B_i as the i-th segment of scenario M.

For simplicity, unless otherwise specified, the "rulebook" refers to the "dynamic rulebook" throughout the remainder of this paper. The rulebook for Scenario 1 can be defined as follows:

Scenario 1 *(continued). As shown in Fig. 1b, the rulebook can evolve over time based on the position of the ego vehicle. Initially, when the ego vehicle is still far from the obstruction, r_2 has a higher priority than r_1 to prevent premature crossing of the centerline. As the ego vehicle approaches the obstruction (i.e., when the distance is less than a threshold d_c), r_1 gains priority to ensure the avoidance of the obstruction. Once the obstruction is successfully avoided (i.e., when the distance again exceeds d_c), r_1 is removed from the rulebook (indicated by the dashed circle in Fig. 1b).*

3 Problem Formulation

The *dynamic, multi-objective CPS falsification* problem can be formulated as follows:

Given a scenario $M = (V, V_0, \delta_P)$ along with the corresponding dynamic rulebook $B_M = (R_M, \leq_{R_M}, U_M)$, which can be viewed as a sequence of static rulebooks, our goal is to sample from the input feature space $\mathcal{F}$ to identify feature vectors that violate higher-priority rules and find more number of counterexamples, for all the static rulebooks in the sequence.

Formally, given two input feature vectors $\vec{f_1}$ and $\vec{f_2}$, $\vec{f_1}$ falsifies more than $\vec{f_2}$ for segment k if the following formula holds for the static rulebook B_k:

$$\forall i \cdot [s_i(\vec{f_2}) < s_i(\vec{f_1}) \\ \implies \exists j \cdot ((r_i <_{R_k} r_j) \land (s_j(\vec{f_1}) < s_j(\vec{f_2})))], \tag{1}$$

where r_i and r_j are rules with corresponding VS s_i and s_j, respectively. Recall that lower values output by s_i (or s_j) indicate more severe rule violations. Thus, the formula expresses that if $\vec{f_2}$ violates some rule i more severely than $\vec{f_1}$, then there must exist a higher-priority rule j such that $\vec{f_1}$ violates more severely than $\vec{f_2}$ on rule j. For simplicity, input feature vectors that lead to violations of some rules are called *counterexamples* in the remainder of the paper. Also, input feature vectors that falsify more severely are called "larger" counterexamples.

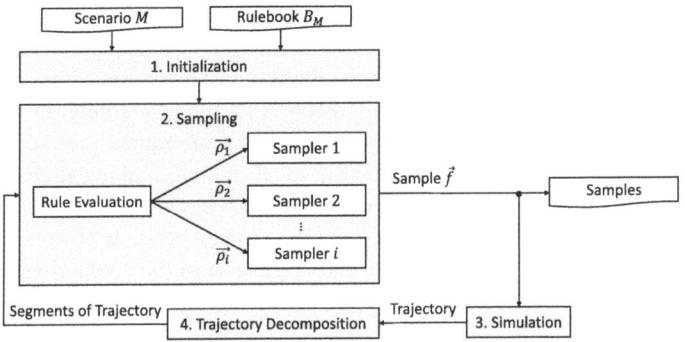

Fig. 2. Our falsification framework.

4 Our Framework

4.1 Overview of Our Framework

Figure 2 outlines our falsification framework. As explained in Property 1, a dynamic rulebook B_M can be understood as a sequence of static rulebooks $\{B_1, B_2, B_3, ...\}$. In our approach, we create a dedicated sampler for each static rulebook in the sequence (Step 1). During the sampling process (Step 2), in each iteration, one of these samplers is chosen to generate a sample. The selection of samplers follows a sequential style: first, Sampler 1 is chosen for N iterations, where N is a user-defined number; then Sampler 2 for another N iterations, then Sampler 3 for another N iterations, and so on. The generated sample is sent to the simulator for scenario simulation (Step 3), which produces a trajectory recording the state variable values in V at each timestamp $t \in [0, T]$, where T represents the simulation time interval. The trajectory is segmented into segments, each corresponding to a static rulebook (Step 4). Following trajectory decomposition, rules of each static rulebook $B_k = (R_k, \leq_{R_k})$ are evaluated on the corresponding segment.

The evaluation yields $\vec{\rho_k}$, encompassing the VS of all the rules in R_k, which is forwarded to the respective sampler as feedback. The sampler is then updated accordingly, and we proceed to sample for the next iteration (Step 2). This process iterates through Steps 2 to 4 until all samplers have been sampled N times.

4.2 Our Sampling Algorithm

In [16], the *multi-armed bandit (MAB)* sampling strategy is proposed, which is extended from [3] and the cross-entropy sampling algorithm [13]. This approach partitions each dimension of the sample space into multiple buckets and selects a bucket for sampling during each iteration. The fundamental principle of the sampler is to balance between exploitation and exploration: it seeks to identify samples that violate high-priority rules (exploitation), while also diversifying generated samples across the sample space (exploration). To achieve this balance, two matrices, $\mathcal{R}$ and $\mathcal{T}$, are employed. The exploitation matrix $\mathcal{R}$ records the source buckets of the current maximal counterexample, while the exploration matrix $\mathcal{T}$ is inversely proportional to the frequency of visits to each bucket. These matrices are then combined into a single matrix Q, from which the sampler selects the bucket with the highest corresponding value.

However, a limitation of the MAB approach is its reliance solely on information from the currently identified maximal counterexample. Consequently, in scenarios with complex rulebooks, it may become trapped in local optima, making it challenging to identify larger counterexamples. Moreover, the MAB sampler lacks a mechanism for distinguishing between different counterexamples. Specifically, it always increments the corresponding entry in $\mathcal{R}$ regardless of the magnitude of the counterexample.

To address these limitations, we introduce the concept of *error weight w*:

Definition 6 (Error Weight of a Rule). *For a rule r within a static rulebook $B = (R, \leq_R)$, suppose there are m number of rules which are lower in priority than r, the error weight w_r of r is defined as 2^m.*

Subsequently, whenever a counterexample is discovered, the error weights of the violated rules are aggregated to form the *error value e*, which indicates the magnitude of the counterexample.

Example 1 (Error Weight and Error Values). Consider a static rulebook $B = \{R, \leq_R\}$ consisting of four rules r_1, r_2, r_3, and r_4, where $r_4 >_R r_3 =_R r_2 >_R r_1$. The error weights for rules r_4, r_3, r_2, and r_1 are 8, 2, 2, and 1, respectively. If a counterexample violates r_4, r_2, and r_1, its error value will be $8 + 2 + 1 = 11$.

Proposition 1. *Given two counterexamples $\vec{f_1}$ and $\vec{f_2}$, $\vec{f_1}$ has a higher error value than $\vec{f_2}$ if it falsifies more than $\vec{f_2}$ based on the definition in Sect. 3.*

Algorithms 1, 2, and 3 detail our sampling approach. In the initialization phase (Algorithm 1), an error matrix $\mathcal{E}$ and a count matrix $\mathcal{C}$ are initialized. Both matrices are of size $d \times N$, where d is the dimension of the feature set and N represents the bucket size. Additionally, following Definition 6, the error weight of each rule is computed

---
Algorithm 1: Initialization of Sampler k

Input: The feature set F and the feature domain $\mathcal{F}$, the bucket size N, and the static rulebook $B_k = (R_k, \leq_{R_k})$

1   $d \leftarrow |F|$; // the dimension of the feature set
2   $\mathcal{E}_{d \times N} \leftarrow \mathcal{O}$; // initialize the error matrix as a zero matrix
3   $\mathcal{C}_{d \times N} \leftarrow \mathcal{J}$; // initialize the count matrix as an all-one matrix
4   $t \leftarrow 1$; // the iteration count
5   $i \leftarrow 0$;
6   $e_{max} \leftarrow 0$;
7   **foreach** *rule r in R_k* **do**
8 | $m \leftarrow$ number of rules have lower priorities than r;
9 | $\vec{w}[i] \leftarrow 2^m$; // the error weight
10 | $e_{max} \leftarrow e_{max} + 2^m$;
11 | $i \leftarrow i + 1$;
12   **end**
---

and stored in the error weight vector $\vec{w}$ (Lines 6 to 12). The sum of error weights, representing the maximum error value of a counterexample, is stored as e_{max}.

During the updating phase (Algorithm 2), a feedback vector $\vec{\rho_k}$ and a source bucket vector $\vec{b}$ are input. $\vec{\rho_k}$ consists of the output violation scores of all the rules in the rulebook. $\vec{b}$ contains the source buckets of the current sample. For example, if the i-th feature is sampled from the j-th bucket, then $\vec{b}[i] = j$. In Lines 1 to 6, the sampler computes the corresponding error value based on $\vec{\rho_k}$. In Lines 7 to 12, for each i-th dimension of the feature space, the source bucket $\vec{b}[i]$ is extracted. The error value is then added to the corresponding entry of $\mathcal{E}$, and e_{max} is added to the corresponding entry of $\mathcal{C}$. This ensures that if sampling from the j-th bucket for the i-th feature leads to a greater number of and larger counterexamples, $\mathcal{E}[i][j]$ will become larger. Similarly, the magnitude of entries in $\mathcal{C}$ reflects the sampling frequency from the corresponding bucket.

After sampler updating, in the sampling phase (Algorithm 3), we normalize the error matrix by performing element-wise division of $\mathcal{E}$ by $\mathcal{C}$ and set the result as the exploitation matrix $\mathcal{R}$. Since $\mathcal{R}$ is proportional to $\mathcal{E}$, it encourages the sampler to sample more from the buckets that have generated more and larger counterexamples. For the exploration aspect, we adopt the definition of from [16], setting the exploration matrix $\mathcal{T}$ as $\sqrt{\frac{\ln(t)}{\mathcal{C}}}$, where t is the current sampling iteration. Since the exploration matrix is inversely correlated to the sampling frequency $\mathcal{C}$, it encourages sampling from less frequently visited buckets. We then introduce a balance coefficient δ to control the balance between the two terms, combining them into matrix $\mathcal{Q}$. For each dimension of the feature space, the bucket corresponding to the highest entry value in $\mathcal{Q}$ is selected for sampling.

Example 2 demonstrates efficiency of our sampling approach over the MAB strategy:

Algorithm 2: Updating of Sampler k

Input: The feedback vector $\vec{\rho_k}$ and the source bucket vector $\vec{b}$

1 $e \leftarrow 0$;
2 **for** $i \leftarrow 0$ **to** $|R_k| - 1$ **do**
3   **if** $\vec{\rho_k}[i] < 0$ **then**
4          $e \leftarrow e + \vec{w}[i]$
5   **end**
6 **end**
7 **for** $i \leftarrow 0$ **to** d **do**
8      $j \leftarrow \vec{b}[i]$;
9      $\mathcal{E}[i][j] \leftarrow \mathcal{E}[i][j] + e$;
10     $\mathcal{C}[i][j] \leftarrow \mathcal{C}[i][j] + e_{max}$;
11     $t \leftarrow t + 1$;
12 **end**

Algorithm 3: Sampling from Sampler k

Input: The balance coefficient δ
Output: A feature vector (i.e., sample) $\vec{f} \in \mathcal{F}$ and a source bucket vector $\vec{b}$

1 $\mathcal{R} \leftarrow \mathcal{E}/\mathcal{C}$; // element-wise division
2 $\mathcal{T} \leftarrow \sqrt{\frac{ln(t)}{\mathcal{C}}}$; // element-wise division
3 $\mathcal{Q} \leftarrow \mathcal{R} + \sqrt{\delta} \cdot \mathcal{T}$;
4 **for** $i \leftarrow 0$ **to** d **do**
5      $j^* \leftarrow \mathrm{argmax}_j \mathcal{Q}[i][j]$;
6      $\vec{f}[i] \leftarrow$ uniformly randomly sample from the range of bucket j^*;
7      $\vec{b}[i] \leftarrow j^*$;
8 **end**

Example 2 (Comparison of Our Sampling Approach against the MAB approach). Consider a static rulebook $B = \{R, \leq_R\}$ consisting of five rules r_1, r_2, r_3, r_4, and r_5, where $r_5 >_R r_4 >_R r_3 >_R r_2 >_R r_1$. Suppose at some point during the falsification process, a counterexample is found that violates r_1, r_2, r_3, and r_4, making it the current maximal counterexample. Later, a larger counterexample is found that violates only r_5.

In the previous MAB approach, upon finding the new maximal counterexample, all information pertaining to previous counterexamples is discarded. Consequently, the sampler must "rediscover" the buckets associated with violations of r_1, r_2, r_3, and r_4. On the contrary, our sampling strategy leverages information from both types of counterexamples, facilitating the efficient discovery of even larger counterexamples (e.g. those violating all rules r_1, r_2, r_3, r_4, and r_5). Furthermore, employing our error weight scheme, the error values of the two counterexamples are 15 and 16, respectively. These values reflect the "importance" of the counterexamples and serves as weights during sampler updating.

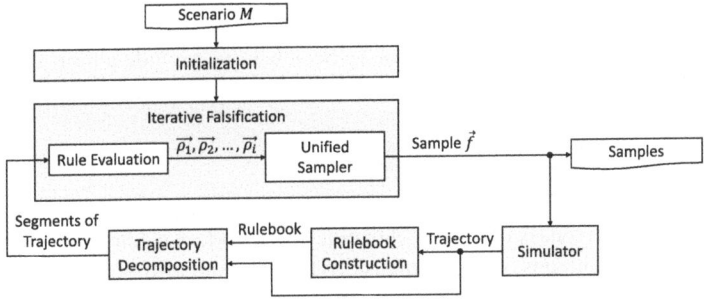

Fig. 3. Our generic falsification framework.

4.3 Extension to a Generic Framework

In our problem formulation, we assume the dynamic rulebook B_M is given. Specifically, the corresponding sequence of static rulebooks is predetermined before the falsification process starts. However, in some scenarios, updates to the rulebook may vary from one simulation iteration to another, depending on the trajectories of state variables. Under such circumstances, the falsification framework proposed in Sects. 4.1 and 4.2 becomes infeasible. An example of this type of scenario is provided in Scenario 4.

To accommodate this variability, we propose a more versatile framework employing a "unified" sampler, as shown in Fig. 3. Unlike dedicated samplers for individual static rulebooks, a single unified sampler generates samples throughout the entire falsification process. Moreover, the rulebook is not predefined; rather, it is constructed iteratively based on simulator-generated trajectories.

The initialization of the unified sampler mirrors Algorithm 1, with the key distinction that error weights are computed before each update. Sampling from the sampler also resembles Algorithm 3. For sampler updating, we have to consider the feedback vectors from all segments, $\vec{\rho_1}, \vec{\rho_2}, ..., \vec{\rho_i}$. To facilitate this, we introduce the concept of *normalized error value*:

Definition 7 (Normalized Error Value). *As defined in Sect. 4.2, the error value e of a counterexample is the sum of error weights of violated rules. The normalized error value e_{norm} is computed as the ratio of error value e to the maximum possible error value e_{max} (i.e., the error value when all rules are violated), expressed as $e_{norm} = \frac{e}{e_{max}}$.*

Taking the rulebook defined in Example 1 as an example, the maximum error value (e_{max}) is the sum of the error weights of all rules, which is 13. If a counterexample violates r_4, r_2, and r_1, its normalized error value (e_{norm}) will be $\frac{11}{13} \approx 0.846$.

Given rulebook B and feedback vectors $\vec{\rho_1}, \vec{\rho_2}, ..., \vec{\rho_i}$, the sampler computes error weights and normalized error values. Subsequently, segment-wise normalized error values are averaged to derive the *average error value e_{avg}*. Lastly, e_{avg} is added to the corresponding entry of $\mathcal{E}$, while the corresponding entry of $\mathcal{C}$ is incremented by 1, reflecting e_{avg}'s range between 0 and 1.

Although the generic falsification framework supports on-the-fly rulebook construction, it may not outperform the scenario-segmentation-based framework when the rulebook is available in advance. While the framework with a unified sampler can implicitly account for dependencies between segments, it also records less information compared to the framework with dedicated samplers. In Sect. 6.1, we provide a thorough comparison of the two frameworks.

5 Scenarios

To validate the effectiveness of our falsification framework, we construct multiple scenarios spanning the domains of autonomous driving and human-robot interaction. These scenarios are designed to simulate real-world situations while examining the variability of rulebooks. Before diving into specific scenarios, we first define four kinds of fundamental rules, along with their VS, that are essential in both domains [10,15]:

Rule A (Distance). *Two objects i and j, with positions $x_i(t)$ and $x_j(t)$, must maintain a safe distance from each other within a specified time interval, denoted as $r_{A,i,j}$.*

STL: $G_{[T_1,T_2]}(dist(x_i(t), x_j(t)) \geq d_{safe})$; **VS:** $min_{[T_1,T_2]}(dist(x_i(t), x_j(t))) - d_{safe}$

Rule B (Staying in Region). *An object i, with position $x_i(t)$, must stay within a specific region during a specified time interval, denoted as $r_{B,i,reg}$, where "reg" denotes the region.*

STL: $G_{[T_1,T_2]}(dist(x_i(t), reg) == 0)$; **VS:** $- max_{[T_1,T_2]}(dist(x_i(t), reg))$

Rule C (Reaching Goal). *An object i, with position $x_i(t)$, must reach its destination within a specified time interval, denoted as $r_{C,i,goal}$, where "goal" denotes the destination region.*

STL: $F_{[T_1,T_2]}(dist(x_i(t), goal) == 0)$; **VS:** $- min_{[T_1,T_2]}(dist(x_i(t), goal))$

Rule D (Lane Keeping). *An object i, with position $x_i(t)$, must not deviate too far from the center of a specified lane within a specified time interval, denoted as $r_{D,i,cent}$, where "cent" denotes the center of the lane.*

STL: $G_{[T_1,T_2]}(dist(x_i(t), cent) \leq d_{keep})$; **VS:** $d_{keep} - max_{[T_1,T_2]}(dist(x_i(t), cent))$

It's important to note that the above rules are abstract and can be refined into multiple instances in practical scenarios. For example, each pair of pedestrians, vehicles, or objects on the road may require a distinct instance of Rule A. Additionally, the safe distance d_{safe} and the lane-keeping distance d_{keep} may vary across different instances.

In addition to the obstruction avoidance scenario (Scenario 1), we have developed three additional scenarios within the autonomous driving domain. We use 0 to denote the ego vehicle, positive integers $(1, 2, ...)$ to represent other vehicles, and negative integers $(-1, -2, ...)$ to indicate pedestrians. For example, $r_{A,0,1}$ specifies the requirement to maintain a safe distance between the ego vehicle and vehicle 1.

Scenario 2 (Lane Change). *Fig. 4a illustrates a lane change scenario, and Fig. 4b illustrates the corresponding rulebook. In this scenario, the ego vehicle intends to transition from the right lane to the left lane. Prior to initiating the lane change, the vehicle*

Dynamic, Multi-objective Specification and Falsification 51

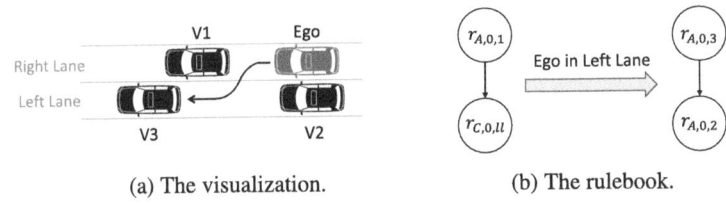

(a) The visualization. (b) The rulebook.

Fig. 4. The lane change scenario (Scenario 2).

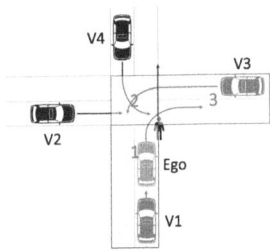 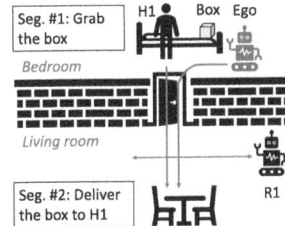

Fig. 5. The lane keeping and intersection crossing scenario (Scenario 3).

Fig. 6. The object fetching and delivery scenario (Scenario 5).

must maintain a safe distance from vehicle 1 ($r_{A,0,1}$) and attempt to overtake vehicle 2 to finish lane change ($r_{C,0,ll}$, where ll denotes the left lane). Upon successfully completing the lane change, the rules become maintaining a safe distance from vehicles 3 ($r_{A,0,3}$) and 2 ($r_{A,0,2}$).

A noteworthy aspect of the rulebook is the disjoint nature of nodes in the two segments. This feature enables the evaluation of our framework's performance under significant rule changes.

Scenario 3 (Lane Keeping and Intersection Crossing). *Figure 5 illustrates a lane keeping and intersection crossing scenario, segmented into three parts. In the first segment, the ego vehicle performs lane keeping on an incoming lane of an intersection. The goal is to reach the intersection (denoted as "inter"). Moving to the second segment, upon reaching the intersection, the ego vehicle aims to make a right turn amidst the presence of other vehicles and a pedestrian crossing and reach the outgoing lane (denoted as "ol"). Finally, in the third segment, the ego vehicle resumes lane keeping on the outgoing lane. Throughout this process, the ego vehicle must adhere to rules ensuring a safe distance from pedestrians and other vehicles, as well as remaining within the drivable area (denoted as "da"). Formally, the rulebook for this scenario is defined as follows:*

Segment 1: $r_{A,0,1} > r_{B,0,da} > r_{C,0,inter} > r_{D,0,cent}$
Segment 2: $r_{A,0,-1} > r_{A,0,1} = r_{A,0,2} = r_{A,0,3} = r_{A,0,4} > r_{B,0,da} > r_{C,0,ol}$
Segment 3: $r_{A,0,2} = r_{A,0,3} = r_{A,0,4} > r_{B,0,da} > r_{D,0,cent}$

Scenario 4 (Intersection Management). *In this scenario, we shift our perspective from the ego vehicle to a centralized intersection manager. This manager employs a* *first-come-first-serve principle to determine the passing order of vehicles at the intersection. Upon a vehicle's arrival, it informs the manager, who then adds it to the waiting queue. As the intersection becomes vacant, the manager allows the vehicle at the forefront of the queue to proceed while others must halt. The manager ensures the correct passing order while maintaining safe distances between vehicles.*

To model the rulebook for this scenario, rules are dynamically added or removed as vehicles arrive or depart. When a new vehicle joins the queue, distance rules between it and existing vehicles are appended to the rulebook, alongside a rule enforcing the sequential passing order. For example, assume the current waiting queue is $q = \{V_1, V_2, ..., V_i\}$ and a vehicle V_{i+1} arrives, rules $r_{A,1,i+1}, r_{A,2,i+1}, ..., r_{A,i,i+1}$ and a rule enforcing "V_i must exit the intersection before V_{i+1}" are added. Conversely, when a vehicle exits, the corresponding rules are removed. The distance rules hold higher priority than the passing order rule.

Given the varying order of vehicle arrivals and departures across simulations, the rulebook must be constructed on-the-fly during falsification.

For objects in the human-robot interaction (HRI) domain, we use 0 to denote the ego robot, positive integers to represent obstacles or other robots, and negative integers to indicate humans. For example, $r_{A,0,-1}$ specifies the requirement to maintain a safe distance between the ego robot and human 1.

Scenario 5 (Object Fetching and Delivery). *Figure 6 illustrates this scenario. In the first segment, the ego robot aims to grab a box of important documents from a bed while avoiding a human organizing clothes nearby. In the second segment, the human moves from the bedroom to the living room for work, and the ego robot must deliver the documents to the human while avoiding another robot vacuuming the area. Formally, the rulebook can be defined as follows:*

$$\text{Segment 1: } r_{A,0,-1} > r_{C,0,box}; \quad \text{Segment 2: } r_{A,0,1} > r_{C,0,-1}$$

A noteworthy aspect of this rulebook is that in Segment 1, the robot must maintain a safe distance from the human ($r_{A,0,-1}$), while in Segment 2, the robot aims to approach the human ($r_{C,0,-1}$). This reflects how interactions between objects in an autonomous CPS evolve over time.

6 Experiments

We conducted our experiments on a Ubuntu 20.04 Linux workstation equipped with a 3.7 GHz CPU and 64 GB of RAM. The scenarios are described using the Scenic programming language [7,8]. Scenic is a domain-specific probabilistic programming language tailored for formally describing scenarios in CPS, encompassing domains such as autonomous driving and robotics. The falsification framework is implemented in Python 3. In addition, our framework is seamlessly integrated with VerifAI [6], a formal verification environment offering a range of built-in sampling algorithms.

For the experiments in the autonomous driving domain, we utilized the Scenic built-in Newtonian simulator and the CARLA simulator [5]. For experiments in the robotics domain, we used the Meta Habitat 3.0 simulator [12] that offers modeling and simulation of both robots and humanoids. For each segment within every scenario in the autonomous driving domain, we selected three different random seeds and perform 300 iterations per seed, resulting in a total of 900 samples per segment. Similarly, for Scenario 3 in the HRI domain, we used three different random seeds with 200 iterations per seed, resulting in a total of 600 samples per segment. For each input feature, we divide its range into 5 buckets. The balance coefficient δ is set to 2 for the autonomous driving experiments and 1 for the HRI experiments.

To assess the capabilities of our falsification approach, we employ several metrics, including the maximum normalized error value among all samples (Max e_{norm}), the average normalized error value of all samples (Avg. e_{norm}), the percentage of the maximum counterexample out of all samples (Pct. Max CE), and the percentage of counterexamples out of all samples (Pct. CE). Note that due to its definition, e_{norm} may not be suitable for comparisons across different rulebooks.

6.1 Results

In this section, our aim is to address three research questions.

RQ1: Would using a dynamic rulebook result in finding more number of and larger counterexamples than a monolithic static rulebook? Table 1 compares the falsification results obtained using (1) dynamic rulebook with our sampling algorithm depicted in Fig. 2, (2) static rulebook with our sampling algorithm depicted in Fig. 2, and (3) static rulebook with the MAB algorithm, which has been shown to perform best among previous sampling approaches for static multi-objective systems in [16]. For experiments with static rulebooks, we combined the static rulebooks from each segment into a monolithic static rulebook, manually adjusting the priorities to encompass the requirements across all segments of a scenario. For Scenario 1, the monolithic static rulebook includes r_1 and r_2 with the same priority level. For Scenario 2, as the rules in the two static rulebooks are disjoint, they can be merged into a monolithic static rulebook directly. This results in a rulebook with 4 rules ($r_{A,0,1}, r_{C,0,ll}, r_{A,0,2}, r_{A,0,3}$) and 2 edges ($r_{A,0,1}$ pointing to $r_{C,0,ll}$ and $r_{A,0,3}$ pointing to $r_{A,0,2}$). For Scenario 3, the monolithic static rulebook includes all the rules, prioritizing $r_{A,0,-1}$ highest, followed by all r_A-type rules, then $r_{B,0,da}$, all r_C-type rules, and finally $r_{D,0,cent}$. Notably, for Scenario 3, however, the conflicting rules $r_{A,0,-1}$ (maintaining a safe distance from the human) in Segment 1 and $r_{C,0,-1}$ (approaching the human) in Segment 2 make it impossible to merge into a monolithic rulebook, highlighting the limitation of static rulebooks in addressing dynamic CPS requirements.

Table 1. Comparison of dynamic and static rulebooks.

Rulebook	Scen./Seg.	Max e_{norm}	Avg. e_{norm}	Pct. Max CE	Pct. CE	Scen./Seg.	Max e_{norm}	Avg. e_{norm}	Pct. Max CE	Pct. CE
Dynamic	1/1	1.000	**0.313**	31.3%	31.3%	3/1	0.733	**0.547**	7.7%	**99.0%**
Static		1.000	0.057	5.7%	5.7%		0.733	0.530	0.3%	98.3%
Static+MAB		1.000	0.057	5.7%	5.7%		0.733	0.521	2.0%	96.3%
Dynamic	1/2	1.000	**0.725**	58.8%	100.0%	3/2	0.976	**0.819**	20.7%	**98.0%**
Static		1.000	0.673	50.9%	100.0%		0.976	0.719	15.0%	96.3%
Static+MAB		1.000	0.623	43.4%	100.0%		0.976	0.734	11.3%	95.3%
Dynamic	1/3	1.000	**0.571**	57.1%	57.1%	3/3	0.867	**0.302**	4.0%	**62.0%**
Static		1.000	0.357	35.7%	35.7%		0.867	0.215	1.7%	**62.0%**
Static+MAB		1.000	0.341	34.1%	34.1%		0.867	0.229	1.3%	58.0%
Dynamic	2/1	1.000	**0.351**	15.4%	73.9%	5/1	1.000	0.743	53.2%	86.3%
Static		1.000	0.301	**16.1%**	57.8%		N.A.	N.A.	N.A.	N.A.
Static+MAB		1.000	0.262	9.6%	59.1%		N.A.	N.A.	N.A.	N.A.
Dynamic	2/2	1.000	**0.471**	45.0%	51.4%	5/2	1.000	0.836	75.3%	100.0%
Static		1.000	0.284	21.3%	42.6%		N.A.	N.A.	N.A.	N.A.
Static+MAB		1.000	0.279	21.6%	40.6%		N.A.	N.A.	N.A.	N.A.

Table 2. Comparison of sampling algorithms.

Algorithm	Scen./Seg.	Max e_{norm}	Avg. e_{norm}	Pct. Max CE	Pct. CE	Scen./Seg.	Max e_{norm}	Avg. e_{norm}	Pct. Max CE	Pct. CE
Ours	1/1	1.000	**0.313**	31.3%	31.3%	3/1	0.733	**0.547**	7.7%	**99.0%**
MAB		1.000	0.169	16.9%	16.9%		0.733	0.533	1.0%	98.7%
Halton		1.000	0.100	10.0%	10.0%		0.733	0.524	1.0%	97.7%
Ours	1/2	1.000	**0.725**	58.8%	100.0%	3/2	0.976	**0.819**	20.7%	**98.0%**
MAB		1.000	0.668	50.1%	100.0%		0.976	0.706	17.0%	95.3%
Halton		1.000	0.516	27.3%	100.0%		0.976	0.760	15.3%	93.0%
Ours	1/3	1.000	0.571	57.1%	57.1%	3/3	0.867	**0.302**	4.0%	**62.0%**
MAB		1.000	**0.753**	**75.3%**	**75.3%**		0.867	0.214	3.3%	61.7%
Halton		1.000	0.299	29.9%	29.9%		0.867	0.251	2.0%	57.0%
Ours	2/1	1.000	**0.351**	15.4%	73.9%	5/1	1.000	0.743	53.2%	86.3%
MAB		1.000	0.283	10.6%	63.4%		1.000	**0.776**	53.3%	**92.5%**
Halton		1.000	0.289	9.6%	67.1%		1.000	0.748	49.0%	**92.5%**
Ours	2/2	1.000	**0.471**	45.0%	51.4%	5/2	1.000	**0.836**	75.3%	100.0%
MAB		1.000	0.437	43.2%	44.8%		1.000	0.824	73.7%	100.0%
Halton		1.000	0.297	27.9%	33.3%		1.000	0.822	73.0%	100.0%

As shown in the table, across almost all segments, dynamic rulebooks yield higher Avg. e_{norm}, Pct. Max CE, and Pct. CE compared to static rulebooks. This improvement occurs because dynamic rulebooks decompose scenario requirements into a sequence of smaller static rulebooks, allowing the framework to precisely identify counterexamples relative to the rulebook of each segment, unlike static rulebooks which cannot differentiate between segments. Similarly, dynamic rulebooks yield higher Avg. e_{norm}, Pct. Max CE, and Pct. CE than the static rulebook with the MAB setting in all segments. Moreover, comparing the results of the static rulebook with the MAB setting to the dynamic rulebook with the MAB setting (row 2 in Table 2), the latter yields better results in the majority of segments, demonstrating that under different sampling algo-

Table 3. Analysis of the generic framework.

Scen./Seg.	Framework	Max e_{norm}	Avg. e_{norm}	Pct. Max CE	Pct. CE
4	Segmentation	N.A.	N.A.	N.A.	N.A.
	Unified	0.959	0.636	0.7%	100.0%
2/1	Segmentation	1.000	0.351	15.4%	73.9%
	Unified	1.000	0.303	13.1%	64.1%
2/2	Segmentation	1.000	0.471	45.0%	51.4%
	Unified	1.000	0.351	34.4%	36.6%

Table 4. Average violation scores of Scenario 2.

Algorithm/Rules	$r_{A,0,1}$	$r_{C,0,u}$	$r_{A,0,2}$	$r_{A,0,3}$
Ours	0.337	0.361	−2.439	−0.906
MAB	0.410	0.524	−2.683	−1.384
Halton	0.466	0.455	−1.364	−0.398

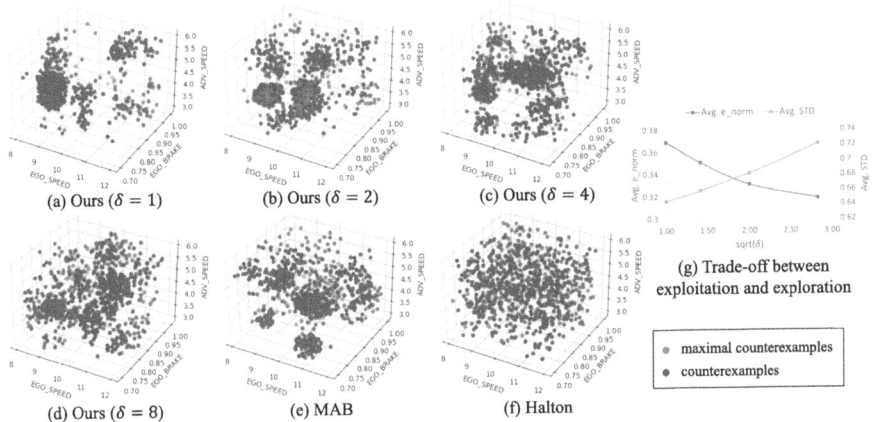

Fig. 7. The trade-off between exploitation and exploration in Scenario 2.

rithms, dynamic rulebooks still capture more and larger counterexamples than static rulebooks.

RQ2: Given a system specified with a dynamic rulebook, does our sampling algorithm identify a greater number of and larger counterexamples compared to previous sampling approaches? Table 2 compares the falsification results obtained using various sampling approaches. We compare our algorithm against multi-armed bandit (MAB) sampler, which is noted as the best previous sampling approach for multi-objective systems [16], and an efficient passive sampler, the Halton sampler [9]. Notably, the MAB sampler has been adapted for dynamic settings. The table shows that our framework yields a higher Avg. e_{norm}, Pct. Max CE, and Pct. CE than the MAB sampler in eight out of the ten segments, validating the effectiveness of our improvement to the MAB sampler. Similarly, our framework also outperforms the Halton sampler in almost all segments.

RQ3: Can our framework be adapted to diverse domains of applications? As illustrated in Tables 1 and 2, our framework demonstrates comparable or superior performance in scenarios from both the autonomous driving and human-robot interaction domains.

6.2 Discussion

In this section, we provide a thorough analysis of the generality, flexibility, and efficiency of our framework.

Analysis of Our Unified-Sampler-Based Approach. In Sect. 4.3, we propose a unified-sampler-based approach that supports on-the-fly rulebook construction. We validate its effectiveness with the intersection management scenario (Scenario 4). Since this scenario requires on-the-fly rulebook construction, the scenario-segmentation-based framework depicted in Sects. 4.1 and 4.2 become unavailable. As shown in Table 3, our unified sampler successfully identifies a large counterexample with a normalized error value of 0.959 (the maximum possible normalized error value is 1). Moreover, it identifies more than 100 types of counterexamples, demonstrating the effectiveness of our approach in scenarios with non-fixed rulebooks. However, for scenarios where the rulebooks are available in advance, the scenario-segmentation-based framework may still have an advantage. For instance, in Scenario 2, our scenario-segmentation-based framework achieves higher error values and a greater percentage of counterexamples than the unified-sampler-based approach. This is because the former creates a dedicated sampler for each time segment, allowing it to capture counterexamples more accurately.

Balance Between Exploitation and Exploration. There is a trade-off between exploitation and exploration during sampling. Our approach provides a flexible method to balance these two aspects. As shown in Algorithm 3, the balance coefficient δ is an input to the sampler, influencing the exploration term $\mathcal{T}$. A larger δ shifts the algorithm towards greater exploration. Figures 7(a) to (d) illustrate the sampled points for Segment 1 of Scenario 2 with varying δ values. As δ increases, the samples become more uniformly distributed across the sampling space. Furthermore, Fig. 7(g) plots the average normalized error (blue curve), representing exploitation, alongside the average standard deviations of the input features (orange curve), representing exploration. The trade-off between these two metrics is evident. Users can thus adjust the δ value according to their requirements, demonstrating the flexibility of our framework.

Additionally, Fig. 7(d) to (f) visually show that the diversity of our algorithm lies in between that of MAB and Halton while attaining highest average e_{norm}. This shows that our algorithm can better identify counterexamples while maintaining a higher diversity of samples than MAB.

Quantitative Falsification Results. In the computation of e_{norm}, we only consider whether each rule is violated or not. To further assess the degree of violation, we compute the average violation score (VS) for all samples. Recall from Definition 3 that a lower VS indicates a more severe violation. Using Scenario 2 as an example, Table 4 shows that our approach achieves a similar degree of violation as the MAB algorithm while consistently attaining a lower VS compared to the Halton sampler.

Runtime Analysis. For the largest scenario, Scenario 3, we compute the average runtime to generate a sample. The average sampling times for our algorithm, the MAB sampler, and the Halton sampler are 8.84s, 11.17s, and 14.15s, respectively. These results show the efficiency of our sampling algorithm.

7 Conclusion

Traditional approaches to multi-objective falsification of autonomous CPS fall short in capturing evolving priorities and objectives. To overcome this limitation, we introduced dynamic rulebooks to capture how objectives and their priorities change over time. In addition, we presented a falsification framework tailored for dynamic, multi-objective systems. Using experiments across various scenarios in the autonomous driving and human-robot interaction domains, we validated the effectiveness of our framework. Future work includes extending the application of dynamic rulebooks and our falsification algorithm to additional domains and real-world testing.

Acknowledgments. This work was supported in part by DARPA contract FA8750-23-C-0080 (ANSR), by Toyota and Nissan under the iCyPhy Center, by NSF grant 2303564, by C3DTI, and by Berkeley Deep Drive.

References

1. Abbas, H., Fainekos, G., Sankaranarayanan, S., Ivančić, F., Gupta, A.: Probabilistic temporal logic falsification of cyber-physical systems. ACM Trans. Embed. Comput. Syst. **12**(2s) (2013). https://doi.org/10.1145/2465787.2465797
2. Annpureddy, Y., Liu, C., Fainekos, G., Sankaranarayanan, S.: S-TALIRO: a tool for temporal logic falsification for hybrid systems. In: Abdulla, P.A., Leino, K.R.M. (eds.) TACAS 2011. LNCS, vol. 6605, pp. 254–257. Springer, Heidelberg (2011). https://doi.org/10.1007/978-3-642-19835-9_21
3. Carpentier, A., Lazaric, A., Ghavamzadeh, M., Munos, R., Auer, P.: Upper-confidence-bound algorithms for active learning in multi-armed bandits. In: Kivinen, J., Szepesvári, C., Ukkonen, E., Zeugmann, T. (eds.) ALT 2011. LNCS (LNAI), vol. 6925, pp. 189–203. Springer, Heidelberg (2011). https://doi.org/10.1007/978-3-642-24412-4_17
4. Censi, A., et al.: Liability, ethics, and culture-aware behavior specification using rulebooks. In: 2019 International Conference on Robotics and Automation (ICRA), pp. 8536–8542. IEEE (2019)
5. Dosovitskiy, A., Ros, G., Codevilla, F., Lopez, A., Koltun, V.: CARLA: an open urban driving simulator. In: Proceedings of the 1st Annual Conference on Robot Learning, pp. 1–16 (2017)
6. Dreossi, T., et al.: VERIFAI: a toolkit for the formal design and analysis of artificial intelligence-based systems. In: Dillig, I., Tasiran, S. (eds.) CAV 2019. LNCS, vol. 11561, pp. 432–442. Springer, Cham (2019). https://doi.org/10.1007/978-3-030-25540-4_25
7. Fremont, D.J., Dreossi, T., Ghosh, S., Yue, X., Sangiovanni-Vincentelli, A.L., Seshia, S.A.: Scenic: a language for scenario specification and scene generation. In: Proceedings of the 40th annual ACM SIGPLAN conference on Programming Language Design and Implementation (PLDI) (2019)
8. Fremont, D.J., et al.: Scenic: a language for scenario specification and data generation. Mach. Learn. **112**(10), 3805–3849 (2023)
9. Halton, J.H.: Algorithm 247: radical-inverse quasi-random point sequence. Commun. ACM **7**(12), 701–702 (1964)
10. Helou, B., et al.: The reasonable crowd: towards evidence-based and interpretable models of driving behavior. In: 2021 IEEE/RSJ International Conference on Intelligent Robots and Systems (IROS), pp. 6708–6715. IEEE (2021)

11. Maler, O., Nickovic, D.: Monitoring temporal properties of continuous signals. In: Lakhnech, Y., Yovine, S. (eds.) FORMATS/FTRTFT -2004. LNCS, vol. 3253, pp. 152–166. Springer, Heidelberg (2004). https://doi.org/10.1007/978-3-540-30206-3_12
12. Puig, X., et al.: Habitat 3.0: a co-habitat for humans, avatars and robots (2023)
13. Rubinstein, R.Y., Kroese, D.P.: The Cross-entropy Method: A Unified Approach to Combinatorial Optimization, Monte-Carlo Simulation, and Machine Learning, vol. 133. Springer, Heidelberg (2004). https://doi.org/10.1007/978-1-4757-4321-0
14. Seshia, S.A., Sadigh, D., Sastry, S.S.: Toward verified artificial intelligence. Commun. ACM **65**(7), 46–55 (2022)
15. Viswanadha, K., et al.: Addressing the IEEE AV test challenge with Scenic and VerifAI. In: 2021 IEEE International Conference on Artificial Intelligence Testing (AITest), pp. 136–142. IEEE (2021)
16. Viswanadha, K., Kim, E., Indaheng, F., Fremont, D.J., Seshia, S.A.: Parallel and multi-objective falsification with SCENIC and VERIFAI. In: Feng, L., Fisman, D. (eds.) RV 2021. LNCS, vol. 12974, pp. 265–276. Springer, Cham (2021). https://doi.org/10.1007/978-3-030-88494-9_15
17. Waga, M.: Falsification of cyber-physical systems with robustness-guided black-box checking. In: Proceedings of the 23rd International Conference on Hybrid Systems: Computation and Control, pp. 1–13 (2020)
18. Zhou, X., Gou, X., Huang, T., Yang, S.: Review on testing of cyber physical systems: methods and testbeds. IEEE Access **6**, 52179–52194 (2018). https://doi.org/10.1109/ACCESS.2018.2869834

Oblivious Monitoring for Discrete-Time STL via Fully Homomorphic Encryption

Masaki Waga[1](✉), Kotaro Matsuoka[1], Takashi Suwa[1],
Naoki Matsumoto[1], Ryotaro Banno[2], Song Bian[3], and Kohei Suenaga[1]

[1] Graduate School of Informatics, Kyoto University, Kyoto, Japan
mwaga@fos.kuis.kyoto-u.ac.jp
[2] Cybozu, Inc., Tokyo, Japan
[3] Beihang University, Beijing, China

Abstract. When monitoring a cyber-physical system (CPS) from a remote server, keeping the monitored data secret is crucial, particularly when they contain sensitive information, e. g., biological or location data. Recently, Banno et al. (CAV'22) proposed a protocol for online LTL monitoring that keeps data concealed from the server using *Fully Homomorphic Encryption (FHE)*. We build on this protocol to allow *arithmetic* operations over encrypted values, e. g., to compute a safety measurement combining distance, velocity, and so forth. Overall, our protocol enables oblivious online monitoring of *discrete-time real-valued signals* against signal temporal logic (STL) formulas. Our protocol combines two FHE schemes, CKKS and TFHE, leveraging their respective strengths. We employ CKKS to evaluate arithmetic predicates in STL formulas while utilizing TFHE to process them using a DFA derived from the STL formula. We conducted case studies on monitoring blood glucose levels and vehicles' behavior against the Responsibility-Sensitive Safety (RSS) rules. Our results suggest the practical relevance of our protocol.

Keywords: Monitoring · cyber-physical systems · signal temporal logic · fully homomorphic encryption · CKKS · TFHE

1 Background

Given the safety-critical nature of cyber-physical systems (CPSs), monitoring their behavior is crucial, e. g., to detect undesired behavior and prevent safety-critical situations beforehand. For instance, if a monitor detects a hardware issue in a car, the car should come to a safe stop immediately. Monitoring can also enhance the system's comfort. For example, it can enhance smooth traffic flow by advising drivers on appropriate velocity, which helps reduce traffic congestion.

Such specifications are often confidential since they may include proprietary or sensitive information. Although they can be kept unknown to the client by monitoring from a remote server, this exposes the monitored behavior to the server. Such exposure may cause additional security concerns when the monitored behavior contains confidential information, e. g., biological or location data.

Example 1 (remote vehicle monitoring). For smooth and safe driving, it is important to maintain proper velocity and distance from other vehicles. Since the desired velocity and distance are typically derived from the driver's visual observation or sensors on the car, a challenge arises when visibility is limited, e. g., on curving roads. Remote and centralized monitoring can enhance safety, e. g., a remote server receives driving data from each vehicle, conducts monitoring, and sends a precaution to a car if its preceding car is slow. However, this approach poses a potential privacy issue because tracking vehicle positions may reveal drivers' personal information (e. g., their home addresses); hence the monitored data should be kept unknown to the server. A more local monitoring approach may resolve this security issue but can introduce another issue: a potential leak of the concrete definition of the desired condition, which may be proprietary.

To address this issue, Banno et al. [1] introduced a protocol for LTL monitoring on a server without revealing monitored behavior. Their protocol uses *Fully Homomorphic Encryption (FHE)* [8], which enables computations on ciphertexts. The client sends a series of ciphertexts representing the monitored behavior to the server, and the server monitors it without decryption. Also, the monitoring occurs *online*, incrementally processing a stream of ciphertexts.

However, their protocol is limited to LTL formulas over *Boolean* propositions[1], i.e., the monitored behavior is limited to a series of Boolean values. Although their protocol can monitor various temporal behaviors, it cannot monitor a series of *numbers* against a specification containing *arithmetic* operations. Particularly, although it can compare numbers with constant thresholds by bit encoding of each value, it is not straightforward to extend their algorithms to efficiently handle specifications including arithmetic operations over multiple ciphertexts. Such limitation is due to their choice of the FHE scheme, specifically *FHE over the Torus (TFHE)* [5]. While TFHE excels at Boolean operations, it is known to be slow for arithmetic operations, e. g., multiplications.

Example 2. We continue with Example 1. Both of the above security concerns are resolved by oblivious monitoring, i. e., remotely monitoring driving data without revealing them to a server. However, the protocol in [1] cannot compare the vehicles' positions against a desired distance computed by arithmetic operations over multiple (encrypted) values, such as their velocities.

2 Oblivious Online Discrete-Time STL Monitoring

We enhance the protocol in [1] to accommodate specifications incorporating arithmetic operations. Specifically, our protocol enables oblivious online monitoring of discrete-time real-valued signals against the safety fragment of *signal temporal logic (STL)* [14] with polynomial constraints as predicates.

Our protocol uses the *Cheon-Kim-Kim-Song (CKKS) scheme* [4] in addition to TFHE to capitalize on their strengths. Specifically, we use CKKS for arithmetic evaluation and TFHE for logical evaluation. Figure 1 outlines our protocol. Before starting the protocol, the server constructs a DFA from the STL

---
[1] More precisely, their protocol supports regular languages over Booleans.

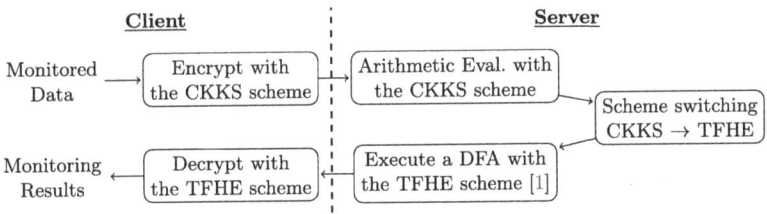

Fig. 1. Our oblivious online STL monitoring protocol with two FHE schemes: CKKS and TFHE. The DFA is constructed from the STL formula beforehand.

formula representing the monitored specification. The DFA receives a series of truth values of the arithmetic predicates in the STL formula. In our protocol, the client encrypts the monitored data using CKKS and sends the resulting ciphertexts to the server. The client can use either a public or a private key for encryption. We remark that multiple clients can participate in our protocol by sharing the public key. The server uses CKKS to evaluate the polynomial functions in the monitored STL formula. It then conducts scheme switching to obtain a ciphertext in TFHE representing the truth value of each predicate and executes the DFA using an algorithm from [1]. Finally, the resulting ciphertext is sent to the client and decrypted within TFHE. The server can only use a private key for decryption.

In summary, the following data are public in our protocol.

- The dimension of the monitored signal, i.e., the set $\mathcal{V}$ of variables.
- For each $x \in \mathcal{V}$, the range of x in the monitored signal[2].
- The security parameters of the FHE schemes.
- Public keys used for encryption.
- Special ciphertexts called *evaluation keys* used, e.g., in bootstrapping.

Notice that an upper bound of the depth of arithmetic operations (in particular, the multiplication) in CKKS can indirectly leak from the security parameters.

In contrast, we assume that the following data are private.

- The values of the monitored signal are concealed from the server.
- The private keys are concealed from the server.
- The monitored specification is concealed from the client.

Example 3. We continue with Example 2. We consider a specification: "If the (potentially obscured) vehicle ahead at a moderate distance has been driving slowly for more than two seconds, the ego vehicle should start decelerating". The desired velocity can be computed, for example, based on the *responsibility-sensitive safety (RSS)* model [17], which models the safe distance as a polynomial of both vehicles' velocities with some vehicle specific parameters as constants. Notice that such parameters can be kept secret. In our protocol, the vehicles encrypt their positions and velocities using a public key and send them

---

[2] More precisely, it is sufficient if for each $\mu(\sigma_i) \geq d$ in the specification, the server knows the range of $\mu(\sigma_i)$ for any valuation $\sigma_i \colon \mathcal{V} \to \mathbb{R}$ in the monitored signal.

to the server. Using CKKS, the server computes the desired distance $dist_{\text{good}}$ and compares it with the observed distance $x_{\text{front}} - x_{\text{ego}}$. Then, the truth value of $x_{\text{front}} - x_{\text{ego}} \geq dist_{\text{good}}$ is switched to TFHE and fed to the DFA constructed from the specification to detect the above undesired situation. Finally, an alert system (e. g., a digital road sign), which we assume has a private key, receives the monitoring result and sends a precaution to the driver.

Our use of the FHE schemes is based on the following observation about FHE-based stream processing:

> The CKKS scheme is suitable for element-wise pre-computation by polynomial arithmetic operations; The TFHE scheme is suitable for accumulation over a stream by (potentially) non-polynomial operations, including Boolean operations.

The reasoning behind this observation is summarized as follows.

- CKKS is dedicated to but efficient for polynomial arithmetic operations, whereas TFHE supports any operations, including Boolean operations.
- CKKS requires a bound of the depth of the operations to perform efficiently, while TFHE does not require it.

2.1 Scheme Switching Optimized with Value Range Information

To combine CKKS and TFHE, we propose a scheme-switching method based on [2] with the following improvements:

- Our method is based on a recent FHE operation called *homomorphic decomposition* [13], which is known to be more efficient than *homomorphic flooring* [12] used in [2] with minor improvements.
- We optimize scheme switching by ignoring the "lower bits" of the ciphertexts.
- We scale the ciphertexts assuming that the server knows the possible range of monitored signals as domain knowledge.

Conceptually, the scaling normalizes the encrypted values so that errors introduced by scheme switching do not cause overflow (as signed N-bit integers). Thanks to such normalization, our scheme switching can handle very small values even if we ignore the "lower bits" for optimization. We decide the scaling factor from the range of signals. See Sect. 3.2 of [19] for details.

3 Experimental Evaluation

We experimentally evaluated the practicality of our oblivious online STL monitoring protocol with our prototype toolkit ARITHHOMFA[3]. We implemented ARITHHOMFA in C++20. We use Microsoft SEAL [16] and TFHEpp [15] as the libraries for CKKS and TFHE, respectively. We used Spot 2.11.5 [7] to handle temporal logic formulas.

We aim to address the following research questions.

---

[3] ARITHHOMFA is publicly available at https://github.com/MasWag/arith_homfa.

Table 1. The STL formulas used in the experiments.

BGLvl$_1$	$\Box_{[100,700]}(glucose \geq 70)$	BGLvl$_7$	$\Box(glucose \geq 70 \wedge glucose < 180)$
BGLvl$_2$	$\Box_{[100,700]}(glucose < 350)$	BGLvl$_8$	$\Box(\Delta glucose \geq -5 \wedge \Delta glucose < 3)$
BGLvl$_4$	$\Box_{[600,700]}(glucose < 200)$	BGLvl$_{10}$	$\Box(glucose < 60 \Rightarrow \Diamond_{[0,25]} glucose \geq 60)$
BGLvl$_5$	$\neg\Diamond_{[200,600]}\Box_{[0,180]}(glucose \geq 240)$	BGLvl$_{11}$	$\Box(glucose > 200 \Rightarrow \Diamond_{[0,25]} glucose < 200)$
BGLvl$_6$	$\neg\Diamond_{[200,600]}\Box_{[0,180]}(glucose < 70)$	RSS	$\Box(S \wedge \mathcal{X}\neg S \Rightarrow \mathcal{X}(\varphi_{preBr} \wedge \varphi_{Br}))$

$$\varphi_{preBr} \equiv S\,\overline{\mathcal{R}}_{[0,\rho_{step}]}\,(A_{ego}^{maxAcc} \wedge A_{prec}^{maxBr}) \quad \varphi_{Br} \equiv S\,\overline{\mathcal{R}}_{[\rho_{step},+\infty)}\,(A_{ego}^{minBr} \wedge A_{prec}^{maxBr})$$

$$S \equiv (x_{ego} - x_{prec} < w \wedge x_{prec} - x_{ego} < w) \Rightarrow \dot{y}_{ego} < \dot{y}_{prec} \wedge \dot{y}_{ego} < \dot{y}_{prec} - d_{RSS}$$

$$A_{ego}^{maxAcc} \equiv \ddot{y}_{ego} < \ddot{y}_{maxAcc} \quad A_{ego}^{minBr} \equiv \ddot{y}_{ego} < -\ddot{y}_{minBr} \quad A_{prec}^{maxBr} \equiv \ddot{y}_{prec} \geq -\ddot{y}_{maxBr}$$

$$d_{RSS} = d_{ego}^{preBr} + d_{ego}^{Br} - d_{prec}^{Br} \quad d_{ego}^{preBr} = \dot{y}_{ego}\rho + 0.5\ddot{y}_{maxAcc}\rho^2$$

$$d_{ego}^{Br} = (\dot{y}_{ego} + \rho\ddot{y}_{maxAcc})^2/(2\ddot{y}_{minBr}) \quad d_{prec}^{Br} = \dot{y}_{prec}^2/(2\ddot{y}_{minBr})$$

Fig. 2. The auxiliary predicates and formulas in RSS. The constants are shown in Appendix B.2 of [19].

RQ1 How fast is the proposed workflow? Is it sufficient for practical usage?
RQ2 How does the optimization in Sect. 2.1 improve the efficiency?
RQ3 Does the use of CKKS improve the workflow's efficiency, for the benchmarks tractable by the approach in [1], which only uses TFHE scheme?
RQ4 Is the computational demand of the client low enough to be executed on a standard IoT device?

3.1 Benchmarks

For the experiments addressing RQ1–3, we used two benchmarks, BGLvl and RSS from practical applications. Table 1 shows the STL formulas we used, where the auxiliary predicates and formulas in RSS are shown in Fig. 2. Table 2 shows the size of the DFAs and the length of the monitored signals.

BGLvl is taken from [1]. It is a benchmark for monitoring of blood glucose levels of type 1 diabetes patients. The monitored signals are one-dimensional with $\mathcal{V} = \{glucose\}$. The term $\Delta glucose$ in BGLvl$_8$ represents the difference between two consecutive blood glucose levels, computed by CKKS in our algorithm. We used simglucose [20] to generate the monitored signals. STL formulas BGLvl$_1$–BGLvl$_6$ originate from [3]. STL formulas BGLvl$_7$–BGLvl$_{12}$ originate from [21].

RSS is a benchmark for monitoring driving behaviors of vehicles against the *Responsibility-Sensitive Safety (RSS)* model [17]. The monitored signal comprises eight dimensions: lateral position, longitudinal position, longitudinal velocity, and longitudinal acceleration of both the ego and the preceding vehicle, represented as $\mathcal{V} = \{x_i, y_i, \dot{y}_i, \ddot{y}_i \mid i \in \{ego, prec\}\}$. We generated the monitored signal using an unpublished 2D driving simulator. We used a variant of an STL formula taken from [10] encoding the RSS rule.

Table 2. Summary of the benchmarks. The columns $|L|$ and $|L^{\text{rev}}|$ show the number of states of $\mathcal{M}_\varphi$ and $\mathcal{M}_\varphi^{\text{rev}}$, respectively. The columns $|w|$ show the length of the monitored log. Cells labeled OOM indicate DFA construction was halted due to memory exhaustion.

	ARITHHOMFA		HOMFA		$|w|$
	$|L|$	$|L^{\text{rev}}|$	$|L|$	$|L^{\text{rev}}|$	
BGLvl$_1$	703	172,402	10,524	OOM	721
BGLvl$_2$	703	172,402	11,126	OOM	721
BGLvl$_4$	703	OOM	7026	OOM	721
BGLvl$_5$	72,603	OOM	OOM	OOM	721
BGLvl$_6$	72,603	OOM	OOM	OOM	721

	ARITHHOMFA		HOMFA		$|w|$
	$|L|$	$|L^{\text{rev}}|$	$|L|$	$|L^{\text{rev}}|$	
BGLvl$_7$	3	3	21	20	10,081
BGLvl$_8$	5	5	—	—	10,081
BGLvl$_{10}$	27	27	237	237	10,081
BGLvl$_{11}$	27	27	390	390	10,081
RSS	179	218	—	—	49

3.2 Experiments

To answer RQ1–3, we measured the time required for monitoring encrypted logs using BGLvl and RSS. For RQ2, we compared ARITHHOMFA with and without the optimization (ARITHHOMFA$_{\text{OPT}}$ and ARITHHOMFA$_{\text{NAIVE}}$) in Sect. 2.1. For RQ3, we compared ARITHHOMFA$_{\text{OPT}}$ with HOMFA [1], a tool for online oblivious *LTL* monitoring only with TFHE. To answer RQ4, we measured the time to *i)* encrypt random numbers to RLWE ciphertexts with either a public or private key within CKKS and *ii)* decrypt random LWE ciphertexts within TFHE. For the experiments addressing RQ4, we used randomly generated values because the values do not affect the time for encryption and decryption.

For the experiments addressing RQ1–3, we ran three approaches (ARITHHOMFA$_{\text{OPT}}$, ARITHHOMFA$_{\text{NAIVE}}$, and HOMFA) using two DFA execution algorithms (REVERSE and BLOCK) proposed in [1]. Thus, we have six configurations in total. We ran each configuration five times and took the mean runtime of these executions.

In ARITHHOMFA$_{\text{NAIVE}}$, we apply `HomDecomp` to 64bits, while in ARITHHOMFA$_{\text{OPT}}$, we apply `HomDecomp` to the first 24bits. For ARITHHOMFA, we used a block size (in BLOCK) of $B = 1$ and a bootstrapping interval (in REVERSE) of $I_{\text{boot}} = 200$, i.e., BLOCK returns the results for each input and bootstrapping is performed every time 200 ciphertexts are processed by REVERSE. For HOMFA, we used the same parameters as in [1][4]: $B = 1$ and $I_{\text{boot}} = 30000$. HOMFA is built with Spot 2.9.7 [7], which is also the same as [1]. ARITHHOMFA requires more frequent bootstrapping because the ciphertext obtained by scheme switching has larger noise. The choice of $B = 1$ is for the consistency with [1]. We used the default security parameters of SEAL and TFHEpp, which satisfy 128-bit security. See Appendix A of [19] for the concrete parameters.

We conducted the experiments for RQ1–3 on an AWS EC2 c6i.4xlarge instance (16 vCPU, 32 GB RAM) running Ubuntu 22.04. For the experiments for RQ4, we used two single-board computers (SBCs): one with and one without an Advanced Encryption Standard (AES) [6] hardware accelerator. Specifically, we used the Raspberry Pi 4 model B (ARM Cortex-A72 *without* a hardware AES accelerator) with 4 GiB RAM, running Ubuntu 23.04, and the NanoPi R6S with

---

[4] Our definition of block size B is slightly different from [1]. In their definition, the block size is 9 for HOMFA, which is the same as the experiments in [1].

Table 3. Summary of the runtime of ARITHHOMFA with and without the optimization in Sect. 2.1. The meaning of OOM is the same as Table 2. For each STL formula, the fastest configuration is highlighted.

	Runtime (sec.)				Runtime/valuation (sec.)			
	ARITHHOMFA$_{\text{OPT}}$		ARITHHOMFA$_{\text{NAIVE}}$		ARITHHOMFA$_{\text{OPT}}$		ARITHHOMFA$_{\text{NAIVE}}$	
	BLOCK	REVERSE	BLOCK	REVERSE	BLOCK	REVERSE	BLOCK	REVERSE
BGLvl$_1$	**2.33e+02**	4.75e+02	3.60e+02	6.13e+02	**3.23e-01**	6.59e-01	5.00e-01	8.50e-01
BGLvl$_2$	**2.29e+02**	4.76e+02	3.73e+02	6.18e+02	**3.18e-01**	6.60e-01	5.17e-01	8.58e-01
BGLvl$_4$	**1.83e+02**	OOM	3.28e+02	OOM	**2.54e-01**	OOM	4.55e-01	OOM
BGLvl$_5$	**3.30e+02**	OOM	4.59e+02	OOM	**4.58e-01**	OOM	6.36e-01	OOM
BGLvl$_6$	**3.74e+02**	OOM	4.68e+02	OOM	**5.19e-01**	OOM	6.50e-01	OOM
BGLvl$_7$	3.96e+03	**2.93e+03**	5.90e+03	5.06e+03	3.93e-01	**2.90e-01**	5.85e-01	5.01e-01
BGLvl$_8$	3.87e+03	**3.03e+03**	6.05e+03	5.09e+03	3.84e-01	**3.00e-01**	6.00e-01	5.05e-01
BGLvl$_{10}$	3.66e+03	**2.50e+03**	5.43e+03	4.26e+03	3.63e-01	**2.48e-01**	5.39e-01	4.23e-01
BGLvl$_{11}$	3.49e+03	**2.65e+03**	5.40e+03	4.23e+03	3.46e-01	**2.62e-01**	5.36e-01	4.19e-01
RSS	2.79e+01	**2.50e+01**	4.62e+01	3.87e+01	5.69e-01	**5.11e-01**	9.43e-01	7.89e-01

Table 4. Summary of the runtime of HOMFA. The meaning of OOM is the same as Table 2. The STL formulas HOMFA could not handle are omitted.

	Runtime (sec.)		Runtime/val. (sec.)			Runtime (sec.)		Runtime/val. (sec.)	
	BLOCK	REVERSE	BLOCK	REVERSE		BLOCK	REVERSE	BLOCK	REVERSE
BGLvl$_1$	7.33e+01	OOM	1.02e-01	OOM	BGLvl$_7$	9.58e+02	8.83e+00	9.50e-02	8.76e-04
BGLvl$_2$	7.36e+01	OOM	1.02e-01	OOM	BGLvl$_{10}$	1.12e+03	5.59e+01	1.11e-01	5.54e-03
BGLvl$_4$	2.05e+01	OOM	2.84e-02	OOM	BGLvl$_{11}$	1.15e+03	8.91e+01	1.14e-01	8.84e-03

a Rockchip RK3588S (ARM Cortex-A76 and Cortex-A55 *with* a hardware AES accelerator) and 8 GiB RAM, running Ubuntu 22.04.2 LTS.

In HOMFA, each blood glucose level was encoded using nine Boolean values via bit encoding, which is the same as [1]. For BGLvl$_8$ and RSS, we could not run HOMFA because the STL formulas include arithmetic operations.

Tables 3 and 4 show the mean runtime of ARITHHOMFA and HOMFA. Table 5 shows the mean runtime to encrypt and decrypt ciphertexts on SBCs.

3.3 RQ1: Performance on Practical Benchmarks

In the "ARITHHOMFA$_{\text{OPT}}$" block of "Runtime per valuation (sec.)" column of Table 3, we observe that for any formula in BGLvl, and for any algorithm, the mean runtime per signal valuation is at most 700 milliseconds when DFA construction was successful and the optimization is used. Furthermore, for any formula in BGLvl, the mean runtime per signal valuation is less than 500 milliseconds if an appropriate algorithm is chosen. This is much faster than the typical sampling intervals for blood glucose levels, e. g., 5 min for Dexcom G6 [11].

In the "ARITHHOMFA$_{\text{OPT}}$" block of "Runtime per valuation (sec.)" column of Table 3, we observe that for RSS, the mean runtime per signal valuation is less than 550 milliseconds for REVERSE and less than 650 milliseconds for BLOCK if the optimization is used. Since this closely aligns with the reaction time of human drivers [22], a delay of around 550 milliseconds is likely acceptable for driver alert systems by sending precautions. Overall, we answer RQ1 as follows.

> **Answer to RQ1**: ARITHHOMFA can monitor each signal valuation in less than 550 milliseconds if an appropriate method is used. This throughput is sufficient for monitoring blood glucose levels. Additionally, it is likely fast enough for monitoring driving behaviors as part of a driver alert system.

3.4 RQ2: Acceleration by the Optimized Scheme Switching

In the "Runtime per valuation (sec.)" column of Table 3, we observe that the performance improvement (per signal valuation) by our optimization in Sect. 2.1 was about 150 ms for BGLvl and about 250 ms for RSS. The runtime of ARITHHOMFA$_{\text{OPT}}$ was about 70% of that of ARITHHOMFA$_{\text{NAIVE}}$. This large reduction is because scheme switching is the dominant bottleneck among the overall process. Overall, we answer RQ2 as follows.

> **Answer to RQ2**: HOMFA is faster than ARITHHOMFA for the specifications that both can handle. For specifications with a huge DFA encoding, only ARITHHOMFA works due to the differences in DFA construction.

3.5 RQ3: Comparison with Purely TFHE-Based Approach

In the "Runtime (sec.)" columns of Tables 3 and 4, we observe that for benchmarks where both ARITHHOMFA and HOMFA work (e.g., BGLvl$_1$, BGLvl$_2$, BGLvl$_4$, BGLvl$_7$, BGLvl$_{10}$, and BGLvl$_{11}$ for BLOCK), HOMFA is more efficient due to the computational cost of scheme switching. In contrast, we observe that HOMFA cannot handle some STL formulas due to excessive memory consumption (e.g., BGLvl$_5$ and BGLvl$_6$ for BLOCK). This is due to the difference in the DFA size representing the same specification (Table 2). In HOMFA, each signal valuation is encoded by nine ciphertexts via bit encoding. In ARITHHOMFA, we have one ciphertext for each atomic proposition, which is at most two in BGLvl. This distinction results in the DFAs for ARITHHOMFA being much smaller than those for HOMFA. Overall, we answer RQ3 as follows.

> **Answer to RQ3**: HOMFA is faster than ARITHHOMFA for the specifications that both can handle. For specifications with a huge DFA encoding, only ARITHHOMFA works due to the differences in DFA construction.

3.6 RQ4: Computational Demand of the Client

Table 5 summarizes the mean runtime of encryption and decryption on SBCs. We observe that both the encryption and decryption processes consume considerably less time than the throughput of monitoring shown in the "Runtime per valuation (sec.)" column of Table 3. Therefore, we answer RQ4 as follows.

> **Answer to RQ4**: The client's computational demand in the proposed protocol is sufficiently low for standard IoT devices.

Table 5. Mean runtime to encrypt RLWE ciphertexts within CKKS and decrypt LWE ciphertexts within TFHE on SBCs.

	Enc. w/ public key [ms/value]	Enc. w/ private key [ms/value]	Decryption [ms/ciphertext]
NanoPi R6S (w/ AES accelerator)	6.82	2.21	1.17×10^{-3}
Raspberry Pi 4 (w/o AES accelerator)	12.7	4.44	1.72×10^{-3}

Table 6. Comparison of FHE-based monitoring methods.

	Used FHE Scheme	Arithmetic operations	Specification is secret
Ours	CKKS [4] and TFHE [5]	Yes	Yes
[1]	TFHE [5]	No	Yes
[18]	CKKS [4]	Yes	No

Furthermore, Table 5 shows that the encryption and decryption processes are faster on the NanoPi R6S than on the Raspberry Pi 4. This is likely due to the efficiency of the random number generation, which is enhanced by the hardware AES accelerator, as reported in [1] for TFHE.

4 Related Works

Table 6 summarizes FHE-based monitoring methods. As previously mentioned, our method is based on [1] and handles arithmetic operations by bridging the CKKS and TFHE schemes. Triakosia et al. [18] proposed a method for oblivious monitoring of manufacturing quality measures with CKKS. The approach in [18] is collaborative: the server conducts polynomial operations using CKKS, while the client conducts non-polynomial operations (e.g., branching) without using FHE techniques. This is done by *i)* decrypting the ciphertexts sent from the server, *ii)* conducting non-polynomial operations over plaintexts, *iii)* encrypting the result, and *iv)* sending it back to the server. This collaborative approach inherently allows the client to access the monitored specification. In contrast, our monitoring algorithm runs entirely on the server, thereby ensuring the specification remains confidential and not exposed to the client.

5 Conclusions and Future Work

Combining two FHE schemes, we proposed a protocol for online oblivious monitoring of safety STL formulas with arithmetic operations. We evaluated the proposed approach by monitoring blood glucose levels and vehicles' behavior. The experimental results suggest the practical relevance of our protocol.

Possible future directions include extending the protocol to handle more general signals, e. g., mixed signals [9].

Acknowledgments. This work is partially supported by JST PRESTO Grant No. JPMJPR22CA, JSPS KAKENHI Grant No. 22K17873 and 23KJ1319, and JST CREST Grant No. JPMJCR19K5, JPMJCR2012, and JPMJCR21M3.

References

1. Banno, R., Matsuoka, K., Matsumoto, N., Bian, S., Waga, M., Suenaga, K.: Oblivious online monitoring for safety LTL specification via fully homomorphic encryption. In: Shoham, S., Vizel, Y. (eds.) Computer Aided Verification. CAV 2022. LNCS, vol. 13371, pp. 447–468. Springer, Cham (2022). https://doi.org/10.1007/978-3-031-13185-1_22
2. Bian, S., et al.: HE3DB: an efficient and elastic encrypted database via arithmetic-and-logic fully homomorphic encryption. In: Meng, W., Jensen, C.D., Cremers, C., Kirda, E. (eds.) Proceedings of the 2023 ACM SIGSAC Conference on Computer and Communications Security, CCS 2023, Copenhagen, Denmark, 26–30 November 2023, pp. 2930–2944. ACM (2023)
3. Cameron, F., Fainekos, G., Maahs, D.M., Sankaranarayanan, S.: Towards a verified artificial pancreas: challenges and solutions for runtime verification. In: Bartocci, E., Majumdar, R. (eds.) RV 2015. LNCS, vol. 9333, pp. 3–17. Springer, Cham (2015). https://doi.org/10.1007/978-3-319-23820-3_1
4. Cheon, J.H., Kim, A., Kim, M., Song, Y.: Homomorphic encryption for arithmetic of approximate numbers. In: Takagi, T., Peyrin, T. (eds.) ASIACRYPT 2017. LNCS, vol. 10624, pp. 409–437. Springer, Cham (2017). https://doi.org/10.1007/978-3-319-70694-8_15
5. Chillotti, I., Gama, N., Georgieva, M., Izabachène, M.: TFHE: fast fully homomorphic encryption over the torus. J. Cryptol. **33**(1), 34–91 (2020)
6. Daemen, J., Rijmen, V.: Aes proposal: rijndael (1999)
7. Duret-Lutz, A., et al.: From spot 2.0 to spot 2.10: what's new? In: Shoham, S., Vizel, Y. (eds.) Computer Aided Verification. CAV 2022. LNCS, vol. 13372, pp. 174–187. Springer, Cham (2022). https://doi.org/10.1007/978-3-031-13188-2_9
8. Gentry, C.: Fully homomorphic encryption using ideal lattices. In: Mitzenmacher, M. (ed.) Proceedings of the 41st Annual ACM Symposium on Theory of Computing, STOC 2009, pp. 169–178. ACM (2009)
9. Havlicek, J., Little, S., Maler, O., Nickovic, D.: Property-based monitoring of analog and mixed-signal systems. In: Chatterjee, K., Henzinger, T.A. (eds.) FORMATS 2010. LNCS, vol. 6246, pp. 23–24. Springer, Heidelberg (2010). https://doi.org/10.1007/978-3-642-15297-9_3
10. Hekmatnejad, M., et al.: Encoding and monitoring responsibility sensitive safety rules for automated vehicles in signal temporal logic. In: Roop, P.S., Zhan, N., Gao, S., Nuzzo, P. (eds.) Proceedings of the 17th ACM-IEEE International Conference on Formal Methods and Models for System Design, MEMOCODE 2019, pp. 6:1–6:11. ACM (2019)
11. Klyve, D., Currie, K., Anderson Jr, J.H., Ward, C., Schwarz, D., Shelton, B.: Algorithm refinement in the non-invasive detection of blood glucose via bio-rfid^{TM} technology1. medRxiv, pp. 2023–05 (2023)

12. Liu, Z., Micciancio, D., Polyakov, Y.: Large-precision homomorphic sign evaluation using FHEW/TFHE bootstrapping. In: Agrawal, S., Lin, D. (eds.) Advances in Cryptology – ASIACRYPT 2022. ASIACRYPT 2022. LNCS, vol. 13792, pp. 130–160. Springer, Cham (2022). https://doi.org/10.1007/978-3-031-22966-4_5
13. Ma, S., Huang, T., Wang, A., Zhou, Q., Wang, X.: Fast and accurate: efficient full-domain functional bootstrap and digit decomposition for homomorphic computation. IACR Trans. Cryptogr. Hardw. Embed. Syst. **2024**(1), 592–616 (2024)
14. Maler, O., Nickovic, D.: Monitoring temporal properties of continuous signals. In: Lakhnech, Y., Yovine, S. (eds.) FORMATS/FTRTFT -2004. LNCS, vol. 3253, pp. 152–166. Springer, Heidelberg (2004). https://doi.org/10.1007/978-3-540-30206-3_12
15. Matsuoka, K., Banno, R., Matsumoto, N., Sato, T., Bian, S.: Virtual secure platform: a five-stage pipeline processor over TFHE. In: Bailey, M., Greenstadt, R. (eds.) 30th USENIX Security Symposium, USENIX Security 2021, pp. 4007–4024. USENIX Association (2021)
16. Microsoft SEAL (release 4.1), January 2023. https://github.com/Microsoft/SEAL, microsoft Research, Redmond, WA
17. Shalev-Shwartz, S., Shammah, S., Shashua, A.: On a formal model of safe and scalable self-driving cars. CoRR **abs/1708.06374** (2017)
18. Triakosia, A., Rizomiliotis, P., Tserpes, K., Tonelli, C., Senni, V., Federici, F.: Homomorphic encryption in manufacturing compliance checks. In: Katsikas, S., Furnell, S. (eds.) Trust, Privacy and Security in Digital Business. TrustBus 2022. LNCS, vol. 13582, pp. 81–95. Springer, Cham (2022). https://doi.org/10.1007/978-3-031-17926-6_6
19. Waga, M., et al.: Oblivious monitoring for discrete-time STL via fully homomorphic encryption. CoRR **abs/2405.16767** (2024). https://doi.org/10.48550/ARXIV.2405.16767
20. Xie, J.: Simglucose v0.2.1 (2018). https://github.com/jxx123/simglucose. Accessed 01 May 2023
21. Young, W., Corbett, J., Gerber, M.S., Patek, S., Feng, L.: DAMON: a data authenticity monitoring system for diabetes management. In: 2018 IEEE/ACM Third International Conference on Internet-of-Things Design and Implementation, IoTDI 2018, pp. 25–36. IEEE Computer Society (2018)
22. Zhang, X., Bham, G.H.: Estimation of driver reaction time from detailed vehicle trajectory data. In: Proceedings of the 18th Conference on Proceedings of the 18th IASTED International Conference: Modelling and Simulation, pp. 574–579. MOAS'07, ACTA Press, USA (2007)

Sampling-Based and Gradient-Based Efficient Scenario Generation

Vidisha Kudalkar[1](✉), Navid Hashemi[1], Shilpa Mukhopadhyay[2], Swapnil Mallick[1], Christof Budnik[3], Parinitha Nagaraja[3], and Jyotirmoy V. Deshmukh[1]

[1] University of Southern California, Los Angeles, USA
{kudalkar,navidhas,smallick,jdeshmuk}@usc.edu
[2] Texas A&M University, College Station, USA
shilpa2301@tamu.edu
[3] Siemens Corporation, Princeton, USA
{christof.budnik,parinitha.nagaraja}@siemens.com

Abstract. Safety-critical autonomous systems often operate in highly uncertain environments. These environments consist of many agents, some of which are being designed, and some represent the uncertain aspects of the environment. Testing autonomous systems requires generating diverse scenarios. However, the space of scenarios is very large, and many scenarios do not represent edge cases of the system. We want to develop a framework for automatically generating interesting scenarios. We propose to describe scenarios using a formal language. We show how we can extract interesting scenarios using scenario specifications from sampling-based approaches for scenario generation. We also introduce another technique for edge-case scenario generation using the gradient computation over STL. We demonstrate the capability of our framework in scenario generation in two case studies of autonomous systems involving the autonomous driving domain and the safety of human-robot systems in an industrial manufacturing context.

Keywords: Scenario Generation · Neurosymbolic Testing · Autonomous Systems · Temporal Logic

1 Introduction

Swift advancements in artificial intelligence have led to rapid growth of autonomous systems including self-driving vehicles, smart manufacturing systems, and unmanned aerial vehicles. These systems operate in open-world and real-time settings with pervasive uncertainty in their environment. For example, consider self-driving vehicles operating in urban environments; here, uncertainty includes extrinsic sources such as pedestrians, bicyclists, other cars, traffic lights, weather, and road conditions, and intrinsic sources such as uncertainties in correct object detection, trajectory prediction, localization, and scene understanding. As another example, consider a smart manufacturing system such as one described in [2], where humans and mobile robots cohabit on a factory floor with fixed manufacturing robotic manipulators. These systems often employ smart runtime monitoring to ensure safety by using sensors for real-time localization of various assets. The factory environment, though more well-structured than the open-world setting of cars, still has several sources of uncertainty; extrinsic sources such as human workers, lighting conditions, and electromagnetic interference, and intrinsic uncertainty related to the sensing errors in localization. Similar sources of uncertainty exist in other autonomous systems, such as unmanned aerial vehicles, smart warehouses, etc.

To assess the safety of such autonomous systems, a common mechanism is to construct a digital twin at an appropriate level of fidelity, and employ simulations to gauge the system behavior in many nominal and edge case *scenarios* [9,36]. Recently, modeling languages for specifying scenarios and tools for automatically generating scenarios have become a popular approach in testing autonomous cyber-physical systems [1,14,15,39]. The Scenic modeling language is one such formalism that has gained popularity. In Scenic, a scenario is defined as a collection of physical objects, with a probability distribution on their positions and other properties. A Scenic program is thus a probabilistic program that can generate many different concrete scenes by sampling from the distribution implied by the program. The overall approach of scenario generation in Scenic is based on rejection sampling. Scenic programs allow the user to specify *requirements* that constrain the set of scenes that will be generated (including temporal logic requirements specified in LTL). There are two main limitations to the current scenario generation approach in Scenic.

First, consider the situation where the high-level probabilistic program describes a very large collection of generic behaviors; for example, "up to ten workers walking through the smart factory," or "three cars traveling in three parallel lanes on a freeway." Scenic programs describing these scenarios would offer many degrees of freedom to each dynamic agent in the scene, leading to an astronomically large number of scenes in the implicit distribution. Furthermore, average scenarios (in a statistical sense) may only correspond to nominal system behaviors. For instance, "ten workers walking through the smart factory" may generate many scenarios where the workers walk in straight lines from their start to goal positions. In Scenic, requirements are used to constrain the generation of test scenarios to only interesting scenarios; for example, "at some time, two workers are within some δ distance of each other." However, the set of scenarios satisfying the requirement may have a very small measure in the overall distribution, making a rejection sampling-based approach inefficient as it is not requirement-driven.

The second challenge is that for broad scene descriptions, we may have several different sub-scenarios with differing requirements. For example, consider the Scenic program specifying "up to ten human workers walking through the factory floor", with the requirement "at least two workers enter the hazard region at the same time, and stay there for at least five seconds," and a different requirement: "at least three workers enter different hazard regions at the same time." If we adopt a requirements-driven sampling approach where we use optimization-guided tools for scenario sampling, and then with every new requirement, the scenario generation tool will have to repeat the process of rejection sampling to identify scenarios.

To address these challenges, we investigate two different strategies for scenario generation. The first strategy seeks to solve the second challenge problem. We propose the use of incremental sampling-based path planning methods to generate a very large set of scenarios consistent with a given scenario description. These could include methods based on the rapidly exploring random trees (RRT) algorithm [29] and its variants [23], or probabilistic roadmaps (PRMs) [24] and its variants. We assume that the given scenario requirement is in discrete-time Signal Temporal Logic (STL). We show that extracting scenarios satisfying a given discrete-time STL requirement can be done by an adaptation of the CTL model checking algorithm [11].

The second strategy seeks to solve the first challenge problem of requirement-driven scenario generation using a *neuro-symbolic* method. We use the observation from [20] that the quantitative semantics (robustness) of a discrete-time STL requirement can be underapproximated by a feedforward neural network with smooth activation functions (called LB4TL). With this encoding, if we have a black-box simulator, then we can use derivative-free nonlinear optimization methods for scenario generation using the LB4TL approximation of robustness to efficiently generate scenarios. If the simulation environment itself is differentiable (for example, Waymax [18]), then scenario generation can be efficiently solved by stochastic gradient descent.

To summarize, our main contributions to this paper are:

- We propose a coverage sampling-based approach to generate a scenario database (represented either as a tree or a forest) and extract interesting scenarios using a model checker for discrete-time STL. Our method allows extracting scenarios corresponding to multiple requirements after a single upfront generation of the scenario database.
- We propose a property-guided method that utilizes the gradient of discrete-time STL robustness to propose optimization-based and gradient-based techniques to efficiently generate scenarios corresponding to requirements that may be of tiny measure in the overall space of the implied scenarios.
- We demonstrate the scenario generation techniques using two case studies: smart manufacturing and autonomous driving.
- We present a case study where we interface our scenario generation tool with a physics-based Unity simulator to test the generated scenarios in a 3D environment.

2 Preliminaries

An environment is an abstract representation of the physical world containing mobile agents, sensors, and obstacles. We formalize an environment as follows:

Definition 1 (Environment). *An environment $\mathcal{E}$ is a tuple $\mathcal{L}, \mathcal{A}, \mathcal{Z}$, where: $\mathcal{L}$ is a finite or infinite set of locations in the environment, $\mathcal{A}$ is a set of dynamical, autonomous agents, and $\mathcal{Z}$ is a set of sensors that observe $\mathcal{E}$ and $\mathcal{A}$.*

For example, in a warehouse environment, we have multiple humans (agents) working in the factory around robot manipulators. The area around the robots is considered as hazard regions and these regions are not safe for humans to enter while the robots are operating. The environment can have a finite set of agents $\mathcal{A} = \{A_1, \ldots, A_n\}$. We define the agents as follows:

Definition 2 (Autonomous Agent). *An agent $\mathcal{A}_i$ is defined as a tuple $(S^i, U^i, \Delta^i, \pi^i, I^i)$ where S^i is a set of states of agent $\mathcal{A}_i$. At any time t, the agent is in state $s_t^i \in S^i$. U^i is the set of actions the agent can take, and we denote the action it takes at time t by u_t^i. Δ^i is a function mapping a state in S^i and an action in U^i to a next state (in S^i), π^i is a stochastic policy of the agents that represents a distribution over the set U^i conditioned by the current state, and I^i is a set of initial states s.t. $I^i \subset S^i$.*

Remark 1. We note that an agent can have several independent state variables, and the state space of the agent can be thought of as the Cartesian product of the domains of each of the state variables. We assume that the following state variables are always present: ℓ: the location of the agent in the environment, i.e., the value of this variable is in the set $\mathcal{L}$, and Θ: this variable defines the orientation of the agent in the environment; for 2-D environments, $\Theta = \{\theta\}$ or the angle between the agent's heading and the X-axis, and for 3-D environments, $\Theta = \{\phi, \theta, \psi\}$, the angle between the agent's heading with X, Y, Z axis respectively.

The environment can be equipped with sensors like cameras, RFID, lasers, etc. and we can observe the environment using these sensors. At every time t, the environment is updated as the agents transition into new states. We describe the environment at time t using the configuration. The configuration of the environment depends on the states of all agents $\mathcal{A}$.

Definition 3 (Configuration of an environment). *Formally, the configuration c_t at time t is defined as a vector $c_t = (s_t^1, s_t^2, \ldots, s_t^n)$.*

The environment is initialized using an initial configuration c_0 where each agent is in some initial state I^i. At every timestep t, the environment updates based on the actions of the agents $\mathcal{A}$. We denote this update as:

$$(s_t^1, s_t^2, \ldots, s_t^n) \xrightarrow{(u_t^1, u_t^2, \ldots, u_t^n)} (s_{t+1}^1, s_{t+1}^2, \ldots, s_{t+1}^n) \text{ s.t. } u_t^i \sim \pi^i(u \mid s = s_t^i)$$

We denote the states of all agents $(s_t^1, s_t^2, \ldots, s_t^n)$ by $\mathbf{s}_t$ and actions of all agents $(u_t^1, u_t^2, \ldots, u_t^n)$ by $\mathbf{u}_t$ at time t. Also, let $\mathcal{U} = U^1 \times \ldots \times U^n$.

Definition 4 (Scenario). *A scenario is defined as the finite sequence of configurations of length $L \in \mathbb{N}$ generated by the moves of the environment as $< c_0, c_1, c_2, \ldots, c_{L-1} >$. Formally, we can define a scenario of length $L \in \mathbb{N}$ as $\mathbf{s}_0 \xrightarrow{\mathbf{u}_0} \mathbf{s}_1 \xrightarrow{\mathbf{u}_1} \mathbf{s}_2 \xrightarrow{\mathbf{u}_2} \ldots \mathbf{s}_{L-1}$.*

We need a formal language to represent such scenario requirements. In this paper, we use Discrete-Time Signal Temporal Logic (DT-STL) to constrain the set of dynamic scenarios.

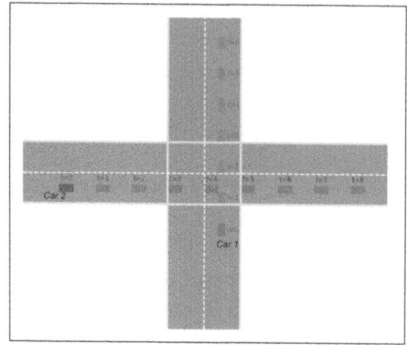
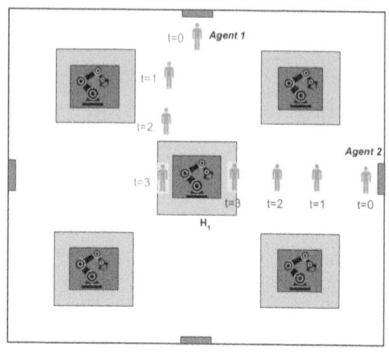

(a) car_1 and car_2 cross the intersection

(b) $human_1$ and $human_2$ enter the hazard region simultaneously

Fig. 1. Examples Scenarios: (a) Shows a scenario in the autonomous driving domain, and (b) shows a scenario in the industrial factory floor domain. (Color figure online)

Discrete-Time Signal Temporal Logic (STL). A DT-STL formula consists of atomic predicates connected using Boolean and temporal operators. An atomic predicate μ is written as $\mu = f(\mathbf{s}) \sim 0$, where f is a function over the states $\mathbf{s} = (s^1, s^2, \ldots, s^n)$, $\sim$ is a comparison operator such that $\sim \in \{<, \leq, >, \geq, =, \neq\}$. The temporal operators are always (**G**), eventually (**F**), until (**U**) and release (**R**). Each temporal operator is associated with a bounded integer time interval $\mathcal{I} = [a, b]$ where $a < b$ and $a, b \in \mathbb{Z}^{\geq 0}$. DT-STL syntax is formally defined as:

$$\varphi := \top \mid \mu \mid \neg\varphi \mid \varphi_1 \wedge \varphi_2 \mid \varphi_1 \mathbf{U}_\mathcal{I} \varphi_2 \mid \varphi_1 \mathbf{R}_\mathcal{I} \varphi_2$$

The remaining operators can be defined using these operators. The always operator is defined as $\mathbf{G}_\mathcal{I}\, \varphi \equiv \neg\, \mathbf{F}_\mathcal{I}\, \neg\varphi$ and eventually operator as $\mathbf{F}_\mathcal{I}\, \varphi \equiv \top\, \mathbf{U}_\mathcal{I}\, \varphi$.

Boolean Semantics of STL. Given a signal x and a time t, the Boolean semantics of any STL formula is inductively given by:

$$\begin{aligned}(x,t) &\models \mu &&\iff x \text{ satisfies } \mu \text{ at time } t \\ (x,t) &\models \neg\varphi &&\iff (x,t) \not\models \varphi \\ (x,t) &\models \varphi_1 \wedge \varphi_2 &&\iff (x,t) \models \varphi_1 \text{ and } (x,t) \models \varphi_2 \\ (x,t) &\models \varphi_1\, U_{[a,b]}\, \varphi_2 &&\iff \exists t' \in [t+a, t+b] \text{ s.t. } (x,t') \models \varphi_2 \\ & && \quad \text{and } \forall t'' \in [t, t'], (x, t'') \models \varphi_1\end{aligned}$$

An example of the scenario in the autonomous driving domain is "*Eventually car_1 and car_2 cross the intersection*", and we write this requirement using STL as ψ_1 (Eq. (1)). Figure 1a shows this scenario where car_1 is shown using red boxes and car_2 is shown using blue boxes, and both cars cross the intersection.

$$\psi_1 : \mathbf{F}_{[0,T]}\,[(car_1 \in intersection)] \bigwedge \mathbf{F}_{[0,T]}\,[(car_2 \in intersection)] \quad (1)$$

Another example in the industrial warehouse domain is $agent_1$ and $agent_2$ eventually enter hazard region H_1 simultaneously, and this is given by ψ_2 (Eq. (2)).

Figure 1b shows a scenario where $agent_1$ and $agent_2$ are highlighted in green and blue, resp., and both agents enter the hazard region H_1 at time $t = 3$.

$$\psi_2 : \mathbf{F}_{[0,T]}\left[(agent_1 \in H_1) \wedge (agent_2 \in H_1)\right] \tag{2}$$

Randomly Sampled Scenario: We can sample the scenarios randomly using Algorithm 1. First, we sample the initial configuration of the agents from the set of initial states (line 1). For each agent $\mathcal{A}_i$ where $i = 1 \ldots n$, we sample the states from time $t = 1 \ldots L - 1$ using the agent's policy and transition into a new state (lines 2–4).

Algorithm 1: Randomly sampled scenario

---
1 Sample initial configuration $(s_0^1, s_0^2, \ldots, s_0^n) \in \mathcal{I}^1 \times \mathcal{I}^2, \ldots, \mathcal{I}^n$;
2 **for** $i \leftarrow 1$ **to** n **do**
3 $\quad$ **for** $t \leftarrow 0$ **to** $L - 2$ **do**
4 $\quad\quad$ $u_t^i \sim \pi^i(u \mid s = s_t^i)$, $s_{t+1}^i \leftarrow \Delta^i(s_t^i, u_t^i)$;
5 $\quad$ **end**
6 **end**

2.1 Problem Definition

In this paper, we propose algorithms to generate a set of scenarios that capture the desired behavior of the agents in the system. In this paper, our goal is to find the set of scenarios where each scenario can be described using the trajectories $\pi = (\pi_0, \pi_1, \ldots, \pi_n)$ for the agents $A_0, A_1, \ldots, A_n$ that satisfy the requirement φ. To find the scenarios, we focus on two problems:

1. Given a dataset $\mathcal{D}$ of randomly sampled scenarios and a DT-STL scenario requirement φ, we aim to find the set of scenarios $\models \varphi$.
2. Given a DT-STL scenario requirement φ, we find the actions $\mathbf{u}_0, \mathbf{u}_1, \ldots, \mathbf{u}_{L-2}$ for all the agents $\mathcal{A}$ in the environment such that if we apply these actions we get a sequence of states, $\mathbf{s}_0 \xrightarrow{\mathbf{u}_0} \mathbf{s}_1 \xrightarrow{\mathbf{u}_1} \mathbf{s}_2 \xrightarrow{\mathbf{u}_2} \ldots \mathbf{s}_{L-1}$ and these sequence of states form a scenario s.t. $(\mathbf{s}_0, \mathbf{s}_1, \ldots, \mathbf{s}_{L-1}) \models \varphi$.

For the first problem, we use a sampling-based path-planning approach to obtain the variety of agent behaviors in the environment and extract desired behaviors by specifying a scenario specification φ using DT-STL as detailed in Sect. 3. We solve the second problem by learning a neural network control policy π_θ or the parameters θ such that, for any initial state $s_0 \in S_{init}$, the trajectory obtained using the control policy π_θ satisfies a given DTL-STL specification φ as outlined in Sect. 4.

3 Scenario Generation Using Path Planning and Model Checking

Incremental sampling-based path-planning algorithms are commonly used in the field of robotics. The Rapidly-exploring Random Trees algorithm (RRT) developed in [29], is widely used due to its speed to rapidly identify paths, even in

Algorithm 2: Coverage-based RRT algorithm

Input: Initial configurations I^i, Maximum iterations $steps_{max}$
1. $T_i = (V_i = \phi, E_i = \phi)$;
2. Goal points $G = \phi$;
3. Divide $\mathcal{E}$ into $p \times q$ blocks B_{ij};
4. **for** each block B_{ij} **do**
5.   Sample a set of goal points $G_{ij} \subset B_{ij}$;
6. $G = G \cup G_{ij}$;
7. $step \leftarrow 0$;
8. $s_0^i \leftarrow S_{init}^i.sample()$;
9. $V_i \leftarrow \{s_0^i\}$;
10. **while** $step < steps_{max}$ and $!(allGoalsReached)$ **do**
11. $x_{sample} \leftarrow S^i.sample()$;
12. $x_{near} \leftarrow \text{NearestNeighbour}(x_{sample})$;
13. $u \leftarrow \text{findaction}(x_{near})$;
14. $x_{new} \leftarrow f(x_{near}, u)$;
15.   **if** $collisionfree(x_{near}, x_{new})$ **then**
16. $V_i.add(x_{new})$;
17. $E_i.add(x_{near}, x_{new})$;
18. $step \leftarrow step + 1$;

high-dimensional environments. The RRT algorithm incrementally constructs a tree starting at a randomly sampled initial location (within the set of permitted initial locations). Nodes of the tree are agent locations, and edges indicate the action that moves the agent from the parent node to the child node. RRT has three main steps: (1) randomly sample a goal point in the state-space, (2) find the nearest node n on the tree to the goal point, (3) use a local optimizer to find an action to move the agent from n to a node that is the closest to the goal point within one time unit. These three steps are repeatedly invoked till some computation budget is reached. The vanilla RRT algorithm focuses on rapidly finding a feasible path to a target region, but may not provide sufficient coverage over the state space. We propose a variation of RRT to improve coverage over the state space.

Multi-agent RRTs for Building a Scenario Database. The Coverage-based RRT algorithm is outlined in Algorithm 2. We split the environment $\mathcal{E}$ into $p \times q$ blocks to systematically cover the working area of the agents. We define a block B_{ij} as the block located at row i and column j of $\mathcal{E}$ such that $0 \leq i \leq p-1$ and $0 \leq j \leq q-1$ and $B_{ij} \subset \mathcal{L}$. To ensure the coverage of the environment by the agents, we sample goal points from each block of the environment (lines 4–6). We defined the set of goal points $G = \cup_{i=0}^{p-1} \cup_{j=0}^{q-1} G_{ij}$ where G_{ij} is the set of goal points in B_{ij}. We incrementally construct a Coverage-based RRT $T_i = (V_i, E_i)$ for each agent $\mathcal{A}_i$ in the environment. We take a set of initial configurations I^i, and the maximum number of iterations $steps_{max}$ as input to the algorithm. The initial state s_0^i of an agent A_i is sampled from a set of initial configurations

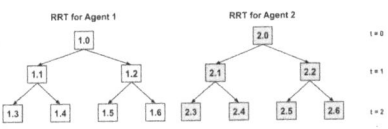
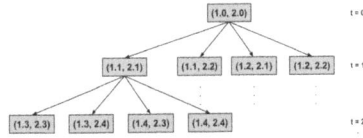

(a) Yellow nodes shows RRT for $Agent_1$ and purple nodes shows an RRT for $Agent_2$

(b) Multi-agent RRT is generated by combining nodes at each level

Fig. 2. Combining single agent RRTs into a multi-agent RRT

$I^i \in S^i$ (line 8). We initialize $V_i = \{s_0^i\}$ and $E_i = \phi$ (line 9). This initial state s_0^i is assigned as the root node of the RRT of the agent A_i. At each time t, a random configuration x_{sample} is sampled from the state space S^i (line 11). Next, the node $x_{near} \in V_i$ is searched in the tree T_i that is closest to x_{sample} using Euclidean distance (line 12). An input $u \in \mathcal{U}$ is determined to move the system from x_{near} to x_{sample} (line 13). For our agents, velocity v is one of the inputs that can be selected from $[v_{min}, v_{max}]$ and the steering angle $\theta \in [0, 2\pi]$. The input u is applied to identify the new node x_{new} using the dynamics of the system $f(x, u)$ (line 14). The dynamics of the system can be of the form $x_{t+1} = x_t + v_t \cos(\theta_t)\delta t$ and $y_{t+1} = y_t + v_t \sin(\theta_t)\delta t$. The path between x_{near} and x_{new} is checked for collisions before adding it to the tree T_i (line 15). If the path is collision-free, the x_{new} is added to the vertex set V_i, and the edge (x_{near}, x_{new}) is added to the edge set E_i (lines 16–17). The tree is iteratively built until there are $steps_{max}$ nodes in T_i or all the goals have been reached. At each node, we store the state s, inputs u, and time t to reach x_{new} from the root. Intuitively, the timestamp t at each node is the depth of node in the tree.

Combine RRTs to Generate a Multi-agent RRT. We combine the generated RRT for each agent into a multi-agent RRT. We consider the RRT of agent $\mathcal{A}_i$ as $\mathcal{T}_i = (V_i, E_i)$ where V_i is the set of nodes and E_i is the set of edges in tree $\mathcal{T}_i$. Each node in $\mathcal{T}_i$ is associated with the state s^i, action u^i, and a timestamp t. We combine the agent trees $\mathcal{T}_1, \mathcal{T}_2, \ldots, \mathcal{T}_n$ to generate a multi-agent RRT $\mathcal{T} = (\mathcal{V}, \mathcal{E})$, where $\mathcal{V} = \times_i V_i$,

$$\left((s_t^1, \ldots, s_t^n) \xrightarrow{u_t^1, \ldots, u_t^n} (s_{t+1}^1, \ldots, s_{t+1}^n)\right) \in \mathcal{E} \text{ if } \forall j \, \exists (s_t^j \xrightarrow{u_t^j} s_{t+1}^j) \in E^j,$$

Figure 2 shows the process of generating a multi-agent RRT. This approach ensures the integration of all nodes across all trees $\mathcal{T}_i$ and facilitates a temporal synchronized representation of all agents $\mathcal{A}$ in the environment.

Extracting Scenarios Using Model Checking. To extract scenarios satisfying a given DT-STL property φ, we use a standard backward model checking procedure [4,11]. Bounded-horizon DT-STL can be viewed as essentially a bounded-horizon LTL formula. To determine if there exist paths in the multi-agent RRT $\mathcal{T}$ satisfying such a formula is equivalent to model checking $\mathcal{T}$ with

φ	$\rho(\varphi, k)$	φ	$\rho(\varphi, k)$
$h(s_k) \geq 0$	$h(s_k)$	$\mathbf{F}_{[a,b]}\psi$	$\max_{k' \in [k+a, k+b]} \rho(\psi, k')$
$\varphi_1 \wedge \varphi_2$	$\min(\rho(\varphi_1, k), \rho(\varphi_2, k))$	$\varphi_1 \mathbf{U}_{[a,b]} \varphi_2$	$\max_{k' \in [k+a, k+b]} \left(\min \left(\rho(\varphi_2, k'), \min_{k'' \in [k, k']} \rho(\varphi_1, k'') \right) \right)$
$\varphi_1 \vee \varphi_2$	$\max(\rho(\varphi_1, k), \rho(\varphi_2, k))$	$\varphi_1 \mathbf{R}_{[a,b]} \varphi_2$	$\min_{k' \in [k+a, k+b]} \left(\max \left(\rho(\varphi_2, k'), \max_{k'' \in [k, k']} \rho(\varphi_1, k'') \right) \right)$
$\mathbf{G}_{[a,b]} \psi$	$\min_{k' \in [k+a, k+b]} \rho(\psi, k')$		

Fig. 3. Quantitative Semantics (Robustness value) of STL

respect to an equivalent CTL* formula $\mathbf{E}\varphi$. Recall that a standard backward model checking algorithm returns the set of states satisfying the given formula; if this set does not contain the initial states, then there is no scenario satisfying the requirement φ, and we require the RRT algorithm to be run for several more iterations. Otherwise, we can extract the set of paths in $\mathcal{T}$ that satisfy φ using a standard witness extraction algorithm for CTL* [4].

4 Neurosymbolic Scenario Generation

In what follows, we describe a neuro-symbolic procedure for scenario generation. The basic idea is to represent the scenario requirement φ as a cost function to be maximized; such a cost-based encoding is easily accomplished by the standard quantitative semantics of DT-STL. We note that we do not need to actually maximize the robust satisfaction of DT-STL, but *satisficing* scenarios are enough (i.e. scenarios that satisfy φ). However, we can still use an optimization-guided procedure and the optimizer's exploration process to identify such satisficing scenarios.

Quantitative Semantics of STL (or Robustness Value): The quantitative semantics of STL define a signed distance of a given trajectory from the set of trajectories satisfying or violating the given STL formula. There are many alternative semantics proposed in the literature [3,8,12,35]. We use the semantics from [8] which computes an approximation of the quantitative semantics. The main idea is to define a function $\rho(\varphi, s, k)$ that returns a numerical satisfaction degree of the formula. This is obtained by replacing the Boolean satisfaction of a predicate of the form $f(s) > 0$ with the numeric value $f(s)$, all disjunctions in the Boolean semantics of an STL formula with max, and conjunctions with min. We note that if $\rho(\varphi, s, k) > 0$ the STL formula φ is satisfied at time k, and we say that the formula φ is satisfied by a trajectory if $\rho(\varphi, s, 0) > 0$. The quantitative semantics of DT-STL is essentially the same, but with the caveat that time indices can only be integers.

The main idea that we pursue in this scenario generation technique is to represent the STL constraint as a smooth function of the scenario generation parameters, and utilize optimization techniques to find scenarios satisfying the constraint. There have been a number of methods for approximating STL semantics with smooth functions and neural networks [16,20,30]. There are two key differences in our approach: (1) we utilize the representation of a neural network-like computation graph representation of STL that guarantees that the value that it computes is a guaranteed lower bound for the actual STL robustness function first proposed in [20], (2) we leverage the most modern simulation environments are differentiable, and use stochastic gradient descent to find satisfying scenarios.

Given an STL formula φ, in [20], the authors represent the robustness computation in Eq. (3) as a tree, which can in turn be viewed as a neural network like computation graph. Special care is taken during the construction of this graph to reduce its depth through the use of associativity of min and max. Thus, $\max(a,b,c,d)$ is represented as $\max(\max(a,b),\max(c,d))$ rather than as $\max(a,\max(b,\max(c,d)))$. Furthermore, all instances of $\max(a,b)$ are replaced with $b + \text{swish}(a-b)$, and $\min(a,b)$ is replaced with $a - \text{softplus}(a-b)$.[1]

Given the set of agents $(A_1, \ldots, A_n)$ in the simulation environment, let $\mathbf{u}(\cdot) = \mathbf{u}_0, \ldots, \mathbf{u}_{L-1}$ be the sequence of joint actions executed by the agents. Recall that a joint action $\mathbf{u}_t = (u_t^1, \ldots, u_t^n)$. Let the resulting scenario be denoted $\mathbf{s}^{\mathbf{u}}$. We wish to sample scenarios from different action sequences and find a set of scenarios $\mathcal{S} = \{\mathbf{s} \mid \rho(\mathbf{s}, \varphi, 0) > 0\}$, i.e. a set of scenarios each satisfying φ. Ideally, we would like $|\mathcal{S}|$ to be at least the allocated test budget, i.e., a minimum number of scenarios. Furthermore, we would like the set $\mathcal{S}$ to be ϵ-separated[2] under a suitable distance metric[3] between scenarios. Formally ensuring such ϵ-separation is computationally expensive, but in the procedures described below, we provide mechanisms to ensure sufficient diversity in scenarios.

Scenario Generation with Black-box Optimization: We can perform scenario generation by considering the following optimization problem:

$$\mathbf{u}^* = \arg\max_{\mathbf{u} \in \mathcal{U}} \text{LB4TL}_\varphi(\mathbf{s}^{\mathbf{u}}) \tag{3}$$

For a general φ, LB4TL_φ is a non-convex function. Thus, we can use general blackbox optimization techniques such as CMAES [19], Particle Swarm Optimization [32], Nelder Mead [28] etc. to address problem (3). These optimizers typically have several random decision parameters, and iteratively approach the optimum. We record scenarios with positive robustness in a given optimizer run, and restart the optimizer with a different random seed to obtain a different scenario. While this does not guarantee that the scenarios identified will be sufficiently diverse, we empirically observe that it does give us diverse scenarios.

---

[1] The function $\text{swish}(x;\gamma_1) = \frac{x}{1+e^{-\gamma_1 x}}$, and the function $\text{softplus}(x;\gamma_2) = \frac{1}{\gamma_2}\log(1+e^{\gamma_2 x})$. Here, $\gamma_1, \gamma_2 > 0$ are user-defined parameters trading off smoothness and the accuracy of approximation.

[2] Let Y be a metric space with the metric d. Then, $X \subseteq Y$ is called ϵ-separated if for all $x_1, x_2 \in X$, $d(x_1, x_2) > \epsilon$.

[3] A scenario can be viewed as a vector of length T, and any vector norm can be thus be used to define distance between scenarios.

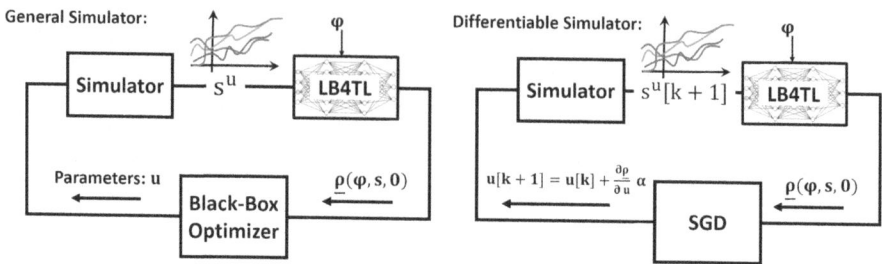

Fig. 4. Shows the computation graph utilized for neurosymbolic training process for satisficing parameters. In this paper, the learnable parameters **u**, are open-loop controllers $\mathbf{u} = \{a_0, a_1, \ldots, a_{T-1}\}$ and the symbolic part is LB4TL_φ that generates a guaranteed lower-bound for the robustness. The neurosymbolic training process aims to increase the output of the symbolic part to make it positive. The left computation graph is utilized if we don't have access to the simulator and the right figure is for when we have access to a differentiable simulator where k is the kth gradient step and α is the learning rate.

Scenario Generation for Differentiable Environments: Recently, there is a trend to design differentiable simulation environments. This means that the output of the simulator $\mathbf{s}^\mathbf{u}$ is a differentiable function of the actions/parameters of the simulator **u**. Examples of such environments include: Waymax [18], Brax [13], Tiny Differentiable Simulator [21], JAX [17]. With such environments, to generate the edge-case scenarios, we can utilize *stochastic gradient descent*. Let the initial guess for the sequence of actions (or the open-loop control policy) be denoted **u**[0]. We then use the following updates to the input actions:

$$\mathbf{u}[k+1] := \mathbf{u}[k] + \alpha \frac{\partial \rho(\varphi, \mathbf{s}^\mathbf{u}, 0)}{\partial \mathbf{u}} \approx \alpha \frac{\partial \text{LB4TL}_\varphi(\mathbf{s}^\mathbf{u})}{\partial \mathbf{s}^\mathbf{u}} \cdot \frac{\partial \mathbf{s}^\mathbf{u}}{\partial \mathbf{u}} \qquad (4)$$

Here, $\mathbf{u}[k]$ denotes the sequence of actions taken in the kth iteration, and α is a learning rate. For generating a diverse set of scenarios, we start with a different initial guess for the initial action sequence, which gives us a different scenario.

5 Case Studies

We evaluate our methods using two case studies: an industrial warehouse environment and an autonomous driving environment. In each case study, we demonstrate both of our techniques by generating the scenarios based on the requirements. The presented case studies would be challenging to existing test case generation techniques for several reasons: In the smart factory floor case study, the number of agents depends on the number of people allowed on the factory floor. This represents a unique challenge to test case generation tools that typically assume a fixed parameter space to explore. We argue that our RRT-based method allows composing scenarios of individual agents, thereby improving the scalability of scenario generation. In the autonomous driving case study, we require the construction of challenging test scenarios that are constrained to satisfy temporal logic specifications. While Scenic has some capabilities to accomplish such a setting, we show that the rejection sampling-based approach that Scenic utilizes underperforms our proposed approaches.

5.1 An Industrial Factory Floor Environment

In many industrial factory floors, mobile robots and fixed robotic manipulators are employed to perform various tasks like delivering packages to stations, assembling manufacturing parts, etc. Such robots are mostly operated in fenced areas because of the safety hazards they could cause to the humans around the factory. If the humans navigate close to the robots, the robots are turned off hampering the productivity. Monitoring the human activities near the working region of the robots could help avoid accidents and ensure the safety of humans working in factories. We derived our case study based on this use case.

In this case study, we have considered a $M \times M$ warehouse with n agents that maneuver in a squared area in the presence of k hazardous regions. Figure 1b shows a top-down view of the factory floor. The red regions represent the robots, and the gray regions surrounding the robots are the hazard regions. The agents can only enter through the doors of the warehouse (annotated in blue). Figure 5a shows our 3D warehouse simulation environment designed using Unity, which is used to test the generated scenarios. The agents in our environment follow the dynamics of the Dubins cars i.e. $x_{t+1}^i = x_t^i + v_t^i \cos(\theta_t^i)\delta t$ and $y_{t+1}^i = y_t^i + v_t^i \sin(\theta_t^i)\delta t$ for $i \in \{1, 2, \ldots, n\}$.

Example 1: RRT-MC Scenario Generation. In the first example, we have two agents in the warehouse environment with two manipulator robots, denoted in red regions in Fig. 5b and 5c. The robots are surrounded by hazard regions (marked with gray color). There are four doors to the warehouse, and the agents can enter only through these entrances into the warehouse. We want scenarios where all the agents walk only in safe regions and we represent this using $\varphi_1 = \bigwedge_{j=1}^{2} \mathbf{G}_{[0,T]} \left[\bigwedge_{i=1}^{2} p^i \notin H_j \right]$. Figure 5b shows the complete RRTs for both the agents, which are generated using Algorithm 2, and Fig. 5c shows all the scenarios that satisfy the requirement φ_1. The scenarios are extracted from the multi-agent RRT using the model-checking approach. In Fig. 6, we show the five scenarios that satisfy φ_1. We can see that the trajectories for both agents do not intersect with the hazard regions.

Example 2: Neurosymbolic Scenario Generation. In this case, we have five agents and four hazard regions. The agents are planned to satisfy the following specification formalized in Signal Temporal Logic, which represents the edge case. In other words, the agents meet in the vicinity of one of the hazard areas.

$$\varphi_2 = \bigvee_{j=1}^{4} \mathbf{F}_{[0,T]} \left[\bigwedge_{i,k \in [1,5]} (\mathbf{d}(p_i, p_k) < \epsilon \wedge \mathbf{d}(p_i, H_j) < \epsilon) \right] \wedge \bigwedge_{j=1}^{4} \mathbf{G}_{[0,T]} \left[\bigwedge_{i=1}^{5} p_i \notin H_j \right]$$

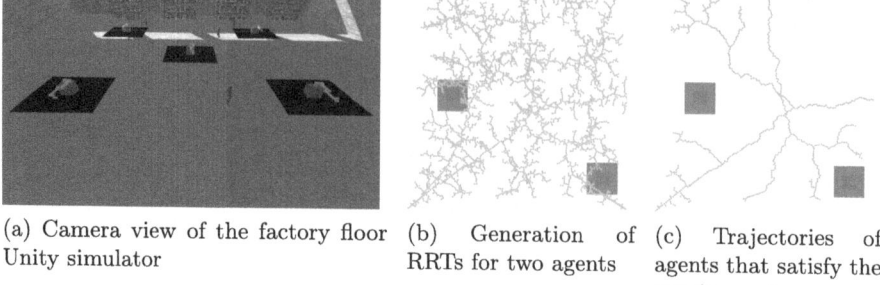

(a) Camera view of the factory floor Unity simulator
(b) Generation of RRTs for two agents
(c) Trajectories of agents that satisfy the requirement φ_1

Fig. 5. (a) shows Unity simulator for warehouse environment, (b) shows the generated RRT for two agents, and (c) shows the extracted trajectories from RRTs that satisfy the requirement φ_1.

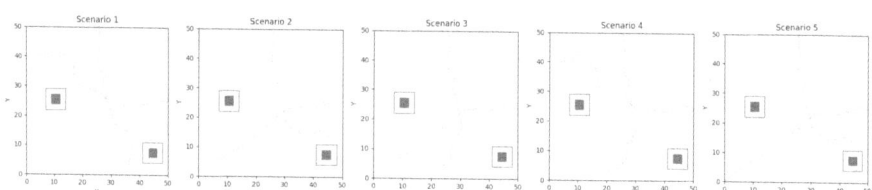

Fig. 6. The figure shows five scenarios that satisfy φ_1. In each scenario, we can see the trajectories of two agents that are always safe. These scenarios are generated using RRT and the model-checking approach.

p_i indicates the position of the agent $i \in \{1, 2, 3, 4, 5\}$ and H_j represents the jth hazardous area $j \in \{1, 2, 3, 4\}$. The specification implies the agents should meet together in the vicinity of one of the hazardous areas, while they are always avoiding all the hazardous regions. The agents will also start from one of the four doors provided for the room. Here the velocities are bounded within the interval $v^i \in [0, 3]$ and the horizon of the specification is $T = 50$ time-steps with sampling time $\delta t = 0.1$ s. Figure 7 shows five scenarios generated to satisfy φ_2. We have generated 25 scenarios. Assuming the sup-norm[4] as the distance between the scenarios, the scenarios are ϵ-separated with $\epsilon = 3.0683$. The maximum distance and the average distance are also 12.1254 and 8.2053 respectively.

5.2 Autonomous Driving

Autonomous driving is another popular area for scenario generation, as on-road testing of critical scenarios is not always possible. Our environment for this case study consists of a two-lane road, as shown in Fig. 8, where agents can drive from left to right. The car agents follow the dynamics of the Dubins cars. We consider that we have two car agents in the environemnt.

---

[4] For two vectors $V_1, V_2 \in \mathbb{R}^n$, we have: sup-norm$(V_1, V_2) = \max_i(\mid V_1(i) - V_2(i) \mid)$.

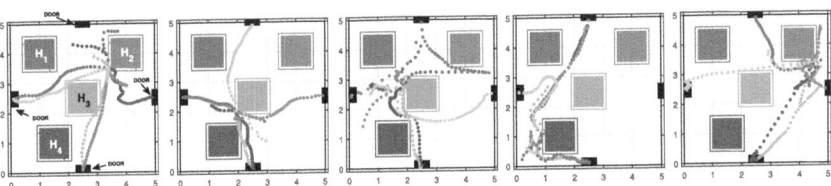

Fig. 7. This figure shows 5 different scenarios generated via Neurosymbolic technique. The scenario is the collection of 5 traces from the 5 agents, where the agents together satisfy the STL specification. The agents start from one of the doors and meet each other in the ϵ vicinity of one of the hazardous regions.

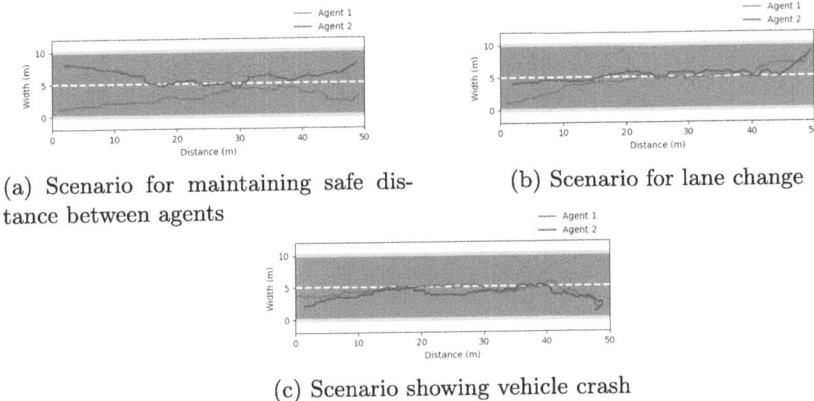

(a) Scenario for maintaining safe distance between agents

(b) Scenario for lane change

(c) Scenario showing vehicle crash

Fig. 8. Autonomous driving case study: A two-lane road where cars can navigate from left to right. A white dotted line separates the two lanes. The lane shown on the top is considered the left lane, and the bottom is the right lane.

In the first example, $\varphi_3 = \mathbf{G}_{[0,T]}\left[\bigwedge_{i,k\in\{1,\dots,n\}}(\mathbf{d}(c_i,c_j) > d_{safe})\right]$, we want the agents to always maintain at least d_{safe} distance from each other. We generated scenarios for this behavior using the requirement φ_3 and Fig. 8a shows an example scenario that satisfies φ_3. Next, we demonstrate the scenario where car agents change lanes. We assume that the agents start in the right lane, eventually merge into the left lane, and stay in the left lane. We represent this requirement by $\varphi_4 = \mathbf{F}_{[0,b]}\left[\mathbf{G}_{[b,L-b]}\left[\bigwedge_{i\in\{1,\dots,n\}}(lane(c_i) = left)\right]\right]$. We describe this scenario using φ_4, and Fig. 8b shows a scenario for this case. This figure shows the left lane on the top and the right lane on the bottom. Lastly, we show a crash scenario in Fig. 8c using $\varphi_5 = \mathbf{F}_{[0,T]}\left[\bigwedge_{i,k\in\{1,\dots,n\}}(\mathbf{d}(c_i,c_j) < \epsilon)\right]$. In this scenario, two car agents collide with each other at some time t.

84   V. Kudalkar et al.

Table 1. Shows the runtime and the distance between the scenarios. Note: For the RRT and model checking (RRT-MC) approach, the time for RRT generation is not included in the runtimes. Scenic could not generate any scenarios for φ_2 and φ_4 for 15 min.

Case Study	Requirement	Appraoch	Average Runtime (seconds)	Distance between scenarios	
				Mean	Std. Deviation
Industrial factory floor	φ_1	RRT-MC	0.02	0.50	0.31
		Neuro-symbolic	32.96	50.21	10.98
		Scenic	3.7	28.36	10.50
	φ_2	RRT-MC	14.87	2.63	2.17
		Neuro-symbolic	135.54	8.20	1.30
		Scenic	TIMEOUT	—	—
Autonomous Driving	φ_3	RRT-MC	0.11	0.11	0.07
		Neuro-symbolic	80.15	7.86	2.12
		Scenic	6.54	4.59	1.39
	φ_4	RRT-MC	0.27	3.18	0.70
		Neuro-symbolic	69.35	9.98	2.68
		Scenic	TIMEOUT	—	—
	φ_5	RRT-MC	0.07	0.09	0.07
		Neuro-symbolic	53.62	7.16	1.85
		Scenic	7.92	3.60	0.92

5.3 Results

We have performed our experiments for scenario generation using both of the proposed approaches. We also performed the same experiments with Scenic and to compare our results. We outlined our quantitative results in Table 1 by reporting runtimes and distance between scenarios for five requirements. In the RRT approach, there is an upfrount cost for generating the multi-agent RRT. Once the RRT is constructed, it can be reused for generating several scenarios based on various requirements and this scenario extraction is quite fast. To show this, we have used the same RRT for generating scenarios for for φ_3, φ_4 and φ_5 because the environment is exactly the same (Fig. 8). The time for generating RRT for autonomous driving case study is 1.49 seconds. The time to generate RRT for φ_1 is 26.14 seconds and φ_2 is 82.56 seconds. We do not reuse the multi-agent RRT here because the environments and number of agents are different. We observe from the Table 1 that the scenarios generated using path planning and model checking method are much faster than the Neurosymbolic technique but the Neurosymbolic methods generates much diverse scenarios.

The RRT approach is beneficial when there are several scenarios under independent constraints that need to be identified for testing, and reuse of generated trajectories is possible. The Neuro-symbolic approach is useful when there is a complex scenario constraint that needs to be satisfied and is more useful when we have a differentiable simulation environment. These are complementary approaches, and their application depends on the use case. While RRT-based method is better for reusing the generated trajectories for different scenario constraints, the Neuro-Symbolic approach is better for complex specifications with differentiable environments.

6 Related Work and Conclusions

Generating safety-critical scenarios is highly important for adaptive stress testing [41] and analyzing corner cases [34] in the research and development of autonomous cyber-physical systems [40].

Scenario Description Languages: Several scenario description languages have been proposed to define complex scenarios [1,31,37]. OpenScenario [1] offers a standardized approach and an XML format for modeling autonomous vehicle scenarios, where the motion of an agent is characterized through actions and triggers. These triggers are linked to the activities of other agents and their corresponding actions. GeoScenario [33], built on the foundation of OpenScenario, defines the behavior of a dynamic agent through its position and speed profiles, along with responsive triggers. Initially created to describe various scenes, Scenic [14], a probabilistic programming language, was later adapted to handle dynamic scenarios through actions specified by simulators, which may depend on the behavior of other traffic participants on the road. While Scenic relies on a rejection sampling approach to generate scenarios, we focus on a requirement-driven approach.

Scenario Based Testing: Originally developed for robot path and motion planning issues [22,23], Rapidly-exploring Random Trees (RRT) [29] have also shown promising results in the test generation domain [6,7,10,26] due to their capability to efficiently search high-dimensional spaces. Previous work the use of RRT for testing multi-robot controllers [25], autonomous racing maneuvers [5], vehicle control [27,38]. Since its introduction, numerous variants of RRT have been developed. One variant, known as Transition-based RRT (T-RRT) [22], merges the exploratory capabilities of the RRT algorithm, which swiftly expands random trees into unexplored areas, with the effectiveness of stochastic optimization methods, that employ transition tests to either accept or reject a new potential state. Another variant, RRT* [23], is demonstrably asymptotically optimal, meaning the cost of the solution it produces almost surely converges to the optimum.

Conclusion. In this paper, we consider the problem of scenario generation where the dynamic scenarios generated are required to satisfy given Discrete-Time STL requirements. We explore two different strategies for scenario generation. In the first, we use incremental sampling-based path-planning approaches to build a database of scenarios consistent with a given scenario description program (for example, in the probabilistic programming language Scenic). We then use model checking to extract scenarios matching the given requirement. In the second strategy, we explore a neuro-symbolic approach, where the given STL requirement is encoded with a smooth neural network and we use optimization-based methods to efficiently generate scenarios satisfying the requirement. We demonstrate our scenario generation technique on two different domains: industrial warehouse and autonomous driving.

References

1. Asam openscenario. https://www.asam.net/standards/detail/openscenario/. Accessed 19 May 2024
2. AG, S.: Siemens offers real-time locating system for a safe production environment and optimized production processes (2020). https://press.siemens.com/global/en/pressrelease/siemens-offers-real-time-locating-system-safe-production-environment-and-optimized
3. Akazaki, T., Hasuo, I.: Time robustness in MTL and expressivity in hybrid system falsification. In: Kroening, D., Păsăreanu, C.S. (eds.) CAV 2015. LNCS, vol. 9207, pp. 356–374. Springer, Cham (2015). https://doi.org/10.1007/978-3-319-21668-3_21
4. Baier, C., Katoen, J.P.: Principles of Model Checking. MIT Press, Cambridge (2008)
5. Bak, S., Betz, J., Chawla, A., Zheng, H., Mangharam, R.: Stress testing autonomous racing overtake maneuvers with RRT. In: 2022 IEEE Intelligent Vehicles Symposium (IV), pp. 806–812. IEEE (2022)
6. Branicky, M.S., Curtiss, M.M., Levine, J., Morgan, S.: Sampling-based planning, control and verification of hybrid systems. IEE Proc.-Control Theory Appl. **153**(5), 575–590 (2006)
7. Dang, T., Donzé, A., Maler, O., Shalev, N.: Sensitive state-space exploration. In: 2008 47th IEEE Conference on Decision and Control, pp. 4049–4054. IEEE (2008)
8. Donzé, A., Maler, O.: Robust satisfaction of temporal logic over real-valued signals. In: Chatterjee, K., Henzinger, T.A. (eds.) FORMATS 2010. LNCS, vol. 6246, pp. 92–106. Springer, Heidelberg (2010). https://doi.org/10.1007/978-3-642-15297-9_9
9. Dosovitskiy, A., Ros, G., Codevilla, F., Lopez, A., Koltun, V.: Carla: an open urban driving simulator. In: Conference on Robot Learning, pp. 1–16. PMLR (2017)
10. Dreossi, T., Dang, T., Donzé, A., Kapinski, J., Jin, X., Deshmukh, J.V.: Efficient guiding strategies for testing of temporal properties of hybrid systems. In: Havelund, K., Holzmann, G., Joshi, R. (eds.) NFM 2015. LNCS, vol. 9058, pp. 127–142. Springer, Cham (2015). https://doi.org/10.1007/978-3-319-17524-9_10
11. Emerson, E.A., Lei, C.L.: Modalities for model checking (extended abstract) branching time strikes back. In: Proceedings of the 12th ACM SIGACT-SIGPLAN Symposium on Principles of Programming Languages, pp. 84–96 (1985)
12. Fainekos, G.E., Pappas, G.J.: Robustness of temporal logic specifications. In: Havelund, K., Núñez, M., Roşu, G., Wolff, B. (eds.) FATES/RV -2006. LNCS, vol. 4262, pp. 178–192. Springer, Heidelberg (2006). https://doi.org/10.1007/11940197_12
13. Freeman, C.D., Frey, E., Raichuk, A., Girgin, S., Mordatch, I., Bachem, O.: Brax–a differentiable physics engine for large scale rigid body simulation. arXiv preprint arXiv:2106.13281 (2021)
14. Fremont, D.J., Dreossi, T., Ghosh, S., Yue, X., Sangiovanni-Vincentelli, A.L., Seshia, S.A.: Scenic: a language for scenario specification and scene generation. In: Proceedings of the 40th ACM SIGPLAN Conference on Programming Language Design and Implementation, pp. 63–78 (2019)

15. Fremont, D.J., et al.: Scenic: a language for scenario specification and data generation. Mach. Learn. **112**(10), 3805–3849 (2023)
16. Fronda, N., Abbas, H.: Differentiable inference of temporal logic formulas. IEEE Trans. Comput. Aided Des. Integr. Circuits Syst. **41**(11), 4193–4204 (2022)
17. Frostig, R., Johnson, M.J., Leary, C.: Compiling machine learning programs via high-level tracing. Syst. Mach. Learn. **4**(9) (2018)
18. Gulino, C., et al.: Waymax: an accelerated, data-driven simulator for large-scale autonomous driving research. Adv. Neural Inf. Process. Syst. **36** (2024)
19. Hansen, N., Müller, S.D., Koumoutsakos, P.: Reducing the time complexity of the derandomized evolution strategy with covariance matrix adaptation (CMA-ES). Evol. Comput. **11**(1), 1–18 (2003)
20. Hashemi, N., Hoxha, B., Prokhorov, D., Fainekos, G., Deshmukh, J.: Scaling learning based policy optimization for temporal tasks via dropout. arXiv preprint arXiv:2403.15826 (2024)
21. Heiden, E., Millard, D., Coumans, E., Sheng, Y., Sukhatme, G.S.: NeuralSim: augmenting differentiable simulators with neural networks. In: Proceedings of the IEEE International Conference on Robotics and Automation (ICRA) (2021). https://github.com/google-research/tiny-differentiable-simulator
22. Jaillet, L., Cortés, J., Siméon, T.: Transition-based RRT for path planning in continuous cost spaces. In: 2008 IEEE/RSJ International Conference on Intelligent Robots and Systems, pp. 2145–2150. IEEE (2008)
23. Karaman, S., Frazzoli, E.: Sampling-based algorithms for optimal motion planning. Int. J. Robot. Res. **30**(7), 846–894 (2011)
24. Kavraki, L.E., Kolountzakis, M.N., Latombe, J.C.: Analysis of probabilistic roadmaps for path planning. IEEE Trans. Robot. Autom. **14**(1), 166–171 (1998)
25. Kim, J., Esposito, J.M., Kumar, V.: An RRT-based algorithm for testing and validating multi-robot controllers. In: Robotics: Science and Systems, pp. 249–256. Boston, MA (2005)
26. Kim, J., Esposito, J.M., Kumar, V.: Sampling-based algorithm for testing and validating robot controllers. Int. J. Robot. Res. **25**(12), 1257–1272 (2006)
27. Koschi, M., Pek, C., Maierhofer, S., Althoff, M.: Computationally efficient safety falsification of adaptive cruise control systems. In: 2019 IEEE Intelligent Transportation Systems Conference (ITSC), pp. 2879–2886. IEEE (2019)
28. Lagarias, J.C., Reeds, J.A., Wright, M.H., Wright, P.E.: Convergence properties of the nelder-mead simplex method in low dimensions. SIAM J. Optim. **9**(1), 112–147 (1998)
29. LaValle, S.: Rapidly-exploring random trees: a new tool for path planning. Research Report, no. 9811 (1998)
30. Leung, K., Aréchiga, N., Pavone, M.: Backpropagation through signal temporal logic specifications: infusing logical structure into gradient-based methods. Int. J. Robot. Res. **42**(6), 356–370 (2023)
31. Majumdar, R., Mathur, A., Pirron, M., Stegner, L., Zufferey, D.: PARACOSM: a test framework for autonomous driving simulations. In: FASE 2021. LNCS, vol. 12649, pp. 172–195. Springer, Cham (2021). https://doi.org/10.1007/978-3-030-71500-7_9
32. Marini, F., Walczak, B.: Particle swarm optimization (PSO). A tutorial. Chemom. Intell. Lab. Syst. **149**, 153–165 (2015)
33. Queiroz, R., Berger, T., Czarnecki, K.: Geoscenario: an open dsl for autonomous driving scenario representation. In: 2019 IEEE Intelligent Vehicles Symposium (IV), pp. 287–294. IEEE (2019)

34. Riedmaier, S., Ponn, T., Ludwig, D., Schick, B., Diermeyer, F.: Survey on scenario-based safety assessment of automated vehicles. IEEE Access **8**, 87456–87477 (2020)
35. Rodionova, A., Lindemann, L., Morari, M., Pappas, G.J.: Combined left and right temporal robustness for control under STL specifications. IEEE Control Syst. Lett. (2022)
36. Rong, G., et al.: LGSVL simulator: a high fidelity simulator for autonomous driving. In: 2020 IEEE 23rd International Conference on Intelligent Transportation Systems (ITSC), pp. 1–6. IEEE (2020)
37. Schütt, B., Braun, T., Otten, S., Sax, E.: SceML: a graphical modeling framework for scenario-based testing of autonomous vehicles. In: Proceedings of the 23rd ACM/IEEE International Conference on Model Driven Engineering Languages and Systems, pp. 114–120 (2020)
38. Tuncali, C.E., Fainekos, G.: Rapidly-exploring random trees for testing automated vehicles. In: 2019 IEEE Intelligent Transportation Systems Conference (ITSC), pp. 661–666. IEEE (2019)
39. Vin, E., et al.: 3D environment modeling for falsification and beyond with scenic 3.0. In: Enea, C., Lal, A. (eds.) Computer Aided Verification. CAV 2023. LNCS, vol. 13964, pp. 253–265. Springer, Cham (2023). https://doi.org/10.1007/978-3-031-37706-8_13
40. Zhang, L., Peng, Z., Li, Q., Zhou, B.: Cat: closed-loop adversarial training for safe end-to-end driving. In: Conference on Robot Learning, pp. 2357–2372. PMLR (2023)
41. Zhong, Z., Tang, Y., Zhou, Y., Neves, V.D.O., Liu, Y., Ray, B.: A survey on scenario-based testing for automated driving systems in high-fidelity simulation. arXiv preprint arXiv:2112.00964 (2021)

HyperPart-X: Probabilistic Guarantees for Parameter Mining of Signal Temporal Logic Formulas in Cyber-Physical Systems

Tanmay Khandait[✉][iD] and Giulia Pedrielli[✉][iD]

School of Computing and Augmented Intelligence, Arizona State Univerisity, Tempe, USA
{tkhandai,gpedriel}@asu.edu

Abstract. Optimization-based falsification is an automatic test generation method for evaluating the safety of Cyber-Physical Systems (CPS) against formal requirements. In this work, we focus on temporal logic requirements and, more specifically on Parametric Signal Temporal Logic (pSTL). pSTL generalizes STL allowing to express the quantifiers of the logical operators as variables. This extends the falsification from searching for the inputs that violate the requirement to the inputs and the formula parametrizations that result into unsafe behaviors. The state-of-the-art Part-X, a recent algorithm for falsification, offers probabilistic falsification level sets and confidence-bounded results on inputs but is not tailored for pSTL. Our approach, HyperPart-X, builds on Part-X and solves the problem while also providing probabilistic guarantees on the estimated level set by adaptively branching the parameter space and intelligently sampling from both the parameter and input spaces in a coordinated and hierarchical approach. HyperPart-X is compared on synthetic functions and CPS benchmarks against uniform random and Part-X. Empirical results demonstrate that HyperPart-X returns level set estimates and guarantees, where Part-X fails to find a solution. Results also show that it can achieve the level set with the same associated confidence level as uniform random sampling using orders of magnitude less samples.

Keywords: pSTL · Test Generation · Probabilistic Guarantees · Falsification · Verification

1 Introduction

Signal Temporal Logic (STL) provides a formal framework for describing real-time properties of systems that exhibit both discrete and continuous dynamics, and it is used to express (un)desired behaviors of target systems that the user wishes to analyze [13]. Requirements can be formulated in STL using a combination of logical operators, temporal operators, timing intervals, and constraints on the magnitude of the signal. Logical operators such as AND, OR, NOT, along with temporal operators such as `Always`, `Eventually`, allow us to define the logical and temporal relationships within the formulas. Timing intervals can be specified to define when these conditions are true or false. Finally, the constraints on the magnitude of the signals are defined using real numbers.

Given a CPS-under-test, which we refer to as System-under-test (SUT), the robustness function is used to evaluate an input to the system and the generated trace with respect to a formal requirement. Formally, it is a distance metric that quantifies the distance of a system-generated trace from the set of states violating the requirement. It is, therefore, a real metric that takes positive values when the trace does not intersect the set and negative values otherwise (in which case the system is said to violate the requirement) [6], which transforms the problem of finding violations of a formal requirement into an optimization problem. Various methods have been proposed that utilize this for search-based test generation (SBTG) for falsification, where the goal is to identify CPS inputs, also called falsifying inputs, such that the corresponding output trajectories violate the requirement(s) [14,15,17]. While these techniques require the parameters of the magnitude and timing constraints to be precisely defined, there are instances where the parameters of the formal requirement being tested may not be known completely. For example, consider the F16 Ground Collision Avoidance System (GCAS) [16]. This autonomous system takes control of the aircraft when a pilot becomes incapacitated and relinquishes control when the pilot regains consciousness. A possible STL requirement is, $\varphi \equiv \Box_{[0,15]}$altitude ≥ 0, where given initial speed and height (fixed) and a specified input pose (pitch, roll, and yaw), the requirement states that the altitude of the aircraft should always be ≥ 0 from time $t = 0$ seconds to time $t = 15$ seconds [16]. We have three potential parameters: (i) the lower bound of the timing interval in the `Always` operator, (ii) the upper bound of the timing interval in the `Always` operator, and (iii) the threshold variable value for the $\geq$ operator. If the user wants to state this property leaving any of these parameters in their symbolic form, more expressiveness than the one from STL is needed. A solution is given by parametric Signal Temporal Logic (pSTL) that allows for the substitution of parameters in place of fixed threshold values in numerical comparisons and time delay constraints within temporal operators in an STL requirement. Considering the F16 case, one could inquire about the minimum duration for which a falsification can be found. A resulting pSTL requirement would be $\varphi_\lambda \equiv \Box_{[0,\lambda]}$altitude ≥ 0, where the upper bound of the *always* operator is parameterized.

When pSTL is used, the test generation goal is to determine parameter values that lead to falsifying inputs in addition to finding falsifying inputs for the corresponding parameter values. This extension of the falsification problem is called the *parameter-mining* problem [3]. Existing methods can be classified into passive and active parameter-mining approaches [3]. The passive parameter-mining approach finds the parameters (or regions) that are satisfying (or violating), assuming SUT inputs and associated traces are already given. This approach solves only for the parameter values that lead to falsification of the given traces. The *active parameter-mining* algorithms, on the other hand, search for parameter values while generating inputs. Algorithms from the earlier family assume the availability of input traces, while algorithms from the latter assume the robustness function to be monotonic with respect to the parameters of the pSTL. No algorithm has been proposed that actively mines for parameters without making any assumptions about the monotonicity of the robustness function associated with a pSTL. Moreover, neither of these approaches provides theoretical guarantees for the un-tested inputs, i.e., they do not analyze nor compute the probability of a certain parameter valuation falsifying the corresponding requirement or the volume of the parameter space that could possibly be falsified. A recently proposed algorithm, PART-X, performs test generation for CPS by estimating the 0-level set of the robustness landscape of a CPS induced by its safety requirements. The algorithm returns finite time probabilistic guarantees on the volume of the 0-level set (also called the *falsifying volume*) estimated by the algorithm at each iteration [17]. However, PART-X can only handle STLs.

In this work, we present the HYPERPART-X algorithm, which efficiently estimates the parameters of a pSTL formula. Specifically, it focuses on identifying parameters where the probability of a parameter having an associated falsification volume is below a user-defined threshold. The algorithm treats the level set of falsifying parameterizations as a probabilistic object and provides guarantees regarding its volume. HYPERPART-X achieves this by simultaneously searching the space of the formula parameters and the space of the SUT inputs by using an inner sampler. Thus, while the algorithm incrementally builds an estimate for the formula parameterization level set by intelligently sampling and adaptively partitioning the parameter space, it alternates with the *inner sampler* that builds an estimate of the falsification volume by reusing old inputs and sampling new inputs using PART-X. In effect, the overall algorithm is therefore an active parameter-mining approach that does not make any assumptions about the behavior of the pSTL formula.

To demonstrate its efficacy, the algorithm is tested on nonlinear non-convex optimization problems and CPS benchmarks, specifically the F16 GCAS and the Automatic Transmission (AT), which involve complex hybrid dynamics from both discrete and continuous components [7,16]. The empirical findings illustrate that HYPERPART-X successfully performs level set estimation and provides guarantees, even when the competitor PART-X fails to find a solution. Furthermore, HYPERPART-X can attain the level set with the same confidence level as a uniform random sampler while utilizing orders of magnitude lower number of samples.

The remainder of the paper is organized as follows, Sect. 2 reviews contributions from the parameter mining literature positioning this work in that context. Section 3 provides the background, while the problem formulation is provided in Sect. 4. The new HYPERPART-X algorithm is introduced in Sect. 5, while the numerical analysis and benchmark study are presented in Sect. 6. Finally, Sect. 7 draws the conclusions and the future research directions.

2 Related Work

The parameter-mining problem for STL has been widely studied, and several methods have been proposed [3]. In the context of this work, we distinguish two families of approaches that solve the parameter mining problem: (i) passive parameter-mining algorithms, and (ii) active parameter-mining algorithms.

Passive Parameter-Mining Algorithms. In this category of algorithms, a large number of contributions focus on computing the exact validity domain of a given specification, i.e., the set of parameters such that a given trajectory satisfies all the STLs within the set. The work in [1] searches the parameters in the validity domain of a given specification using a given set of inputs and associated traces. The proposed approach restricts the signals to finite sequences of (time-stamp, robustness value) pairs with linear interpolation between values, thereby allowing the validity domains to be expressed as Boolean combinations of linear constraints, and yields the exact validity domain at the cost of high computational complexity. As a result, an approach that focuses on computational efficiency approximates the validity domain to be ϵ-close to the exact validity domain in [4]. The goal of these approaches is to refine the bounds of the validity domain iteratively. While this problem is difficult to solve in general settings, restricting to a subset of pSTLs that have monotonic properties (also called monotonic pSTLs) yields a monotonic validity domain, and reduces the problem to a pareto-front identification problem [1]. Another method for the computation of approximate validity domains was proposed in [2], where the authors learn validity domains inductively by using validity signals, which is a signal that represents the set of parameter valuations for which a given formula is satisfied at each point in time.

Other approaches have also been proposed that focus on finding the optimal parameter value instead of the validity domain. One approach, TeLEx [9], mines parameters by solving a constrained optimization problem. The goal is to minimize the absolute value of the instantiated pSTL formula's robustness while ensuring that the instantiated formula is satisfied. They introduce a notion of tightness measure into the quantitative semantics for STL to make the temporal operators and predicates smooth and differentiable. This is solved using gradient-based methods. Several approaches were also proposed that embed machine learning to estimate optimal parameters [12,20,21]. In [12], the authors propose a computation graph to encode the pSTL formula, and apply backpropagation to learn the optimal parameters given a fixed set of traces. Given the encoding choice, the approach does not support mining of timing parameters.

Active Parameter-Mining Algorithms. This family of approaches aims to find the parameter value(s) for a pSTL formula such that all possible system traces satisfy the specification. Their approaches involve switching between mining parameters of a pSTL formula and sampling inputs that falsify an instantiated pSTL requirement. In [7], the authors actively mine a single-parameter monotonic pSTL formula. The goal is to exploit increasing/decreasing monotonicity to efficiently sample parameters that falsify the formula. The approach was generalized for mining multiple parameters in monotonic pSTL formulas in [8]. A similar approach is proposed in [10], where a candidate requirement is synthesized, and a falsification algorithm searches for inputs that falsify this requirement. If falsified, a new candidate requirement is synthesized and the process is repeated till no falsifying input is found. While applicable to non-monotonic cases, the authors recognize the inefficiency of the approach in such scenarios.

The approach proposed herein falls under the family of active mining algorithms as HYPERPART-X iteratively samples inputs and generates traces. Moreover, the assumption of monotonocity of a pSTL requirement is violated when the polarities of parameters are not fixed [1,10]. HYPERPART-X does not require assumptions on the nature of the robustness behavior of the parameters of the STL requirement and provides provable guarantees on the parameter set resulting from the approach.

3 Preliminaries

This section discusses the background techniques at the basis of the algorithmic design of HYPERPART-X. Section 3.1 introduces the semantics of STL and pSTL. Section 3.2 briefly introduces Gaussian processes (GP), used in HYPERPART-X as surrogates of different loss functions. Finally, we summarize the PART-X algorithm from [17].

3.1 Parametric Signal Temporal Logic (pSTL)

Let $\mathcal{M}$ represent the model of the black box SUT, composed of various software and hardware components. When simulating this model with initial conditions $\mathcal{X} \in \mathbb{R}^d$ and a set of time-varying inputs $\mathcal{U} \in \mathbb{R}^d$, the model generates a trace $\mathcal{Y}$, such that $\mathcal{Y} = \mathcal{M}(x)$, where $x \in \mathcal{X} \times \mathcal{U}$. Given a specification φ, the robustness of the trajectory $\mathcal{Y}$ generated by input x to the model $\mathcal{M}$ measures how close the output trace $\mathcal{Y}$ is to violating the specification. In this work, we employ Signal Temporal Logic (STL) to define a specification with the following syntax:

$$\varphi ::= y < a \mid \neg \varphi \mid \varphi \vee \varphi \mid \varphi \wedge \varphi \mid \varphi \, \mathrm{U}_I \, \varphi \mid \Box_I \, \varphi \mid \Diamond_I \, \varphi \tag{1}$$

where I represents a time interval over which the temporal and logical operators are evaluated. The robustness is calculated following the definition provided in [5]. If the robustness is positive, then the signal satisfies the specification. If the robustness is negative, the signal violates the specification. A zero robustness indicates undetermined Boolean satisfaction, implying the system may not be robust. In Eq. 1, for a given specification, the constants a and the interval I are fixed. By leaving these unspecified, we obtain pSTL:

$$\begin{aligned}\varphi_\lambda &::= y < \lambda_c \mid \neg \varphi \mid \varphi \vee \varphi \mid \varphi \wedge \varphi \mid \varphi \mathrm{U}_I \varphi \mid \Box_I \varphi \mid \Diamond_I \varphi \\ I &::= [\lambda_{T_1}, \lambda_{T_2}],\end{aligned} \tag{2}$$

where, $\lambda_c, \lambda_{T_1}, \lambda_{T_1} \in \mathbb{R}$, and $\lambda_{T_2} \geq \lambda_{T_1}$.

Evaluating the robustness of a model $\mathcal{M}$ against a specification φ_λ is a two-step process, where the model of the SUT is first evaluated under input x and then evaluated against φ_λ for specific values of λ. It is important to highlight that simulating the system is considerably more computationally expensive than monitoring a formula.

3.2 Gaussian Process Regression

The idea behind Gaussian process (GP) is to treat the original, possibly deterministic, function to model as a realization from a stochastic process, the GP. Under this interpretation, given a collection of n d-dimensional input points (locations) in $\mathbb{X} \subseteq \mathbb{R}^d$, and their corresponding function values denoted by $\mathcal{D} = \{\boldsymbol{x}_i, f(\boldsymbol{x}_i)\}_{i=1}^n$, where f is the unknown function, we estimate the Gaussian process $F(\boldsymbol{x}) = \mu + Z(\boldsymbol{x})$ with constant mean μ and $Z(\boldsymbol{x}) \sim \mathcal{GP}(0, \tau^2 \mathbf{R})$. Here, τ^2 represents the process variance and $\mathbf{R}$ represents the spatial correlation matrix with correlation function defined as $R_{ij} = \prod_{l=1}^{d} e^{(\theta_l |x_{il} - x_{jl}|)^2}$, for $i, j = 1, \cdots, n$ such that θ collects the correlation factor for smoothing the predictor with varying intensity.

The parameters μ and τ^2 can be estimated by maximum likelihood estimators as follows: $\hat{\mu} = \frac{\mathbf{1}_n^T \mathbf{R}^{-1} \mathbf{f}}{\mathbf{1}_n^T \mathbf{R}^{-1} \mathbf{1}_n}$, $\tau^2 = \frac{(\mathbf{f} - \mathbf{1}_n \hat{\mu})^T \mathbf{R}^{-1} (\mathbf{f} - \mathbf{1}_n \hat{\mu})}{n}$.

The best linear unbiased predictor $\hat{f}(\boldsymbol{x})$ and model variance $\hat{s}^2(\boldsymbol{x})$ for $\boldsymbol{x} \in \mathbb{X}$ are $\hat{f}(\boldsymbol{x}) = \hat{\mu} + \mathbf{r}(\boldsymbol{x})^T \mathbf{R}^{-1}(\mathbf{f} - \mathbf{1}_n \hat{\mu})$ and $\hat{s}^2(\boldsymbol{x}) = \tau^2 \left(1 - \mathbf{r}(\boldsymbol{x})^T \mathbf{R}^{-1} \mathbf{r}(\boldsymbol{x}) + \frac{(1 - \mathbf{1}_n^T \mathbf{R}^{-1} \mathbf{r}(\boldsymbol{x}))^2}{\mathbf{1}_n^T \mathbf{R}^{-1} \mathbf{1}_n}\right)$, where $\mathbf{r}(\boldsymbol{x})$ is defined as: $r_i(\boldsymbol{x}) = Corr(Z(\boldsymbol{x}), Z(\boldsymbol{x}_i)), \boldsymbol{x}_i \in \mathbb{X}$ [19].

In this work, we will use the model defined above as a surrogate for the an unknown function value. Specifically, given a training set of samples x and associated function values y, $\{\mathbf{x}_i, y_i\}_{i=1}^n$, we will predict the function value $\hat{Y}(\mathbf{x}_{n+1})$ at a new unsampled location $\mathbf{x}_{n+1}$. The robustness prediction will have the associated variance $s^2(\mathbf{x}_{n+1})$. Note that x, y here are just placeholder values, and will be defined appropriately when used.

3.3 PART-X Algorithm

Given an STL specification φ, identifying the set of counterexamples can be formulated as the problem of estimating the 0-level set, i.e., the set of inputs with non-positive robustness value. The algorithm PART-X, proposed in [17], approximates the robustness 0-level set with probabilistic guarantees to characterize its volume. The approach dynamically partitions the input space using local Gaussian processes for each subregion of the partition as a surrogate for the robustness function. In addition to identifying the 0-level set of the specification robustness, the partitioning approach also helps to circumvent issues that rise from the robustness function being discontinuous. In fact, the only assumption we need on the robustness function is that it is a locally smooth function

[17]. By leveraging the local surrogate models (Gaussian processes), the PART-X algorithm constructs a predictor for the robustness of non-evaluated inputs. This prediction is used to classify a region as positive (satisfying the requirement), negative (violating), or remaining. Independently from the classification, all subregions may undergo further classification into one of these two categories or stay remaining. If a region is classified as remaining or it is reclassified, it is partitioned in the subsequent iteration, provided that the volume after partitioning exceeds a user-specified minimum. Otherwise, the subregion is sampled but not branched. The algorithm concludes when the budget is exhausted or when all subregions reach the user-defined minimum volume. Upon completion, PART-X returns the estimates of the likelihood of encountering a falsifying input when none are found, and it determines the normalized volume of falsifying sets (0-level sets). The authors also prove that classification error is bounded at every iteration and that the classification error decreases as the algorithm progresses [17]. In effect, the 0-level set identified by the PART-X algorithm in fact contains the true 0-level set. In this work, we build upon the PART-X algorithm to solve the parameter mining problem with probabilistic guarantees

4 Problem Formulation

Let $\rho_\lambda(\mathcal{M}(x))$ denote the robustness function associated with a pSTL formula φ_λ instantiated with parameters $\lambda \in \Lambda \subseteq \mathbb{R}^{d_\Lambda}$ and the trace generated upon simulating inputs $x \in X \subseteq \mathbb{R}^{d_X}$. We denote the set of pSTL parameters $\lambda \in \Lambda \subseteq \mathbb{R}^{d_\Lambda}$, where d_Λ and d_X denote the dimensionality of the parameter and the input search space, respectively. Given a value of λ, X_0^λ is the 0-level set for the robustness function ρ_λ. We refer to $\widehat{Y}(\mathbf{x})$ as the surrogate for $\rho_\lambda(\mathcal{M}(x))$ in input locations that have not been evaluated. The following definition holds.

Definition 1 (Falsification Volume). *Given a set $S^\lambda \subset X$ with associated robustness surrogate q-th quantile predictor $\widehat{Y}_q(\mathbf{x})$, we refer to the falsification volume as the following stochastic quantity:*

$$V_f^q(S^\lambda) = \int_{S^\lambda} I_{\widehat{Y}_q(\mathbf{x}) \leq 0}(x)\, dx, \qquad (3)$$

where $I_{\widehat{Y}_q(\mathbf{x}) \leq 0}(x)$ is the indicator function.

Note that the falsification volume is stochastic because the predictor $\widehat{Y}_q(\mathbf{x})$ is built on sampled values of the robustness function $\rho_\lambda(\mathcal{M}(x))$.

Our HYPERPART-X algorithm builds an estimate for:

$$L_{\epsilon,\delta}^\Lambda \triangleq \{\lambda : P(V_f^q(X_0^\lambda) \leq \epsilon) \leq \delta\} \text{ s.t. } X_0^\lambda \triangleq \{x : \rho_\lambda(\mathcal{M}(x)) \leq 0\} \subseteq X, \quad (4)$$

where parameters δ, ϵ are user-defined and $L_{\epsilon,\delta}^\Lambda$ is the target level set. Given a value of λ, X_0^λ is the 0-level set for the robustness function ρ_λ. $V_f^q(\cdot)$ refers to the falsification volume, interpreted as a probabilistic object with an associated distribution (which our algorithm estimates). The constraint $P(V_f^q(X_0^\lambda) \leq \epsilon) \leq \delta$ ensures that the robustness associated with the selected parametrization λ has a corresponding 0-level set in the input space X_0 with non-0 measure. The outer objective in Eq. (4) is to determine the set (ϵ, δ)-level set $L_{\epsilon,\delta}^\Lambda$, i.e., the δ-level set defined in the parameter space Λ with respect to the function *probability of falsification*. This level set represents a region in the parameter space where the specified behavior, as defined by a user-defined pSTL formula φ_λ, is not satisfied with positive probability.

In essence, the inner objective function $P(V_f^q(X_0^\lambda) \leq \epsilon)$ finds regions of parameters that have an associated probability of falsification of at most ϵ. On the other hand, the outer constraint reports such a set or subset of parameters, defined by δ. HYPERPART-X utilizes PART-X in a nested manner, i.e., PART-X is used both in the input space to compute $V_f^q(X_0^\lambda)$ and in the parameter space to estimate the (ϵ, δ)-level set. It is important to note that the PART-X in the input space can be replaced with other 0-level set estimation algorithms (such as [18]). Since HYPERPART-X follows the PART-X algorithm to estimate $L_{\epsilon,\delta}^\Lambda$, the theoretical results that bound the classification error in the parameter space can be extended to HYPERPART-X. Existing methods in literature try to find parameters that have a falsification associated with them. HYPERPART-X allows the user decides the level of tightness they desire with respect to the parameters. It is important to highlight that our algorithm can estimate the same set as the existing methods by setting ϵ to a small value.

For ease of notation, we will hereafter refer to $P(V_f^q(X_0^\lambda) \leq \epsilon) - \delta$ as the (ϵ, δ)-*loss function*, denoted using $\mathbf{f}_{\epsilon,\delta}$. Our objective, therefore, is to estimate the level set of parameters λ such that $\mathbf{f}_{\epsilon,\delta}(\lambda) \leq 0$.

Explanatory Example. As an example to visually demonstrate the level sets elicited by the formulation, consider the parameterized version of the Himmelblau's function (Eq. (5)), where we add to the x variables, the λ variables to mimic a robustness function that results from a pSTL. The resulting function is non-linear and non-convex.

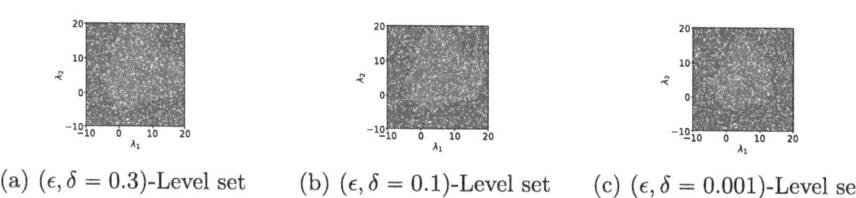

(a) $(\epsilon, \delta = 0.3)$-Level set (b) $(\epsilon, \delta = 0.1)$-Level set (c) $(\epsilon, \delta = 0.001)$-Level set

Fig. 1. Plots for non-linear, non-convex Himmelblau's function, whose target-level sets are known. For all the plots, $\epsilon = 0.1$.

$$\rho(x|\boldsymbol{\lambda} = (\lambda_1, \lambda_2)) = (x_1^2 + x_2 - \lambda_1)^2 + (x_2^2 + x_1 - \lambda_2)^2 - 40. \tag{5}$$

The input variables x define a 2-d space, i.e., $x \in X \subseteq \mathbb{R}^2$, while the parameters are defined in $\lambda \in \Lambda \subseteq \mathbb{R}^2$. Figure 1 displays parameterized Himmelblau's function (ϵ, δ)-level set of the parameter space. We sample 10,000 parameters $\lambda = (\lambda_1, \lambda_2) \in [-10, 20]^2$ and compute (ϵ, δ)-loss function using 1,000 inputs $\mathbf{x} = (x_1, x_2) \in [-5, 5]^2$ per parameter λ over a 100 repetitions. We depict (ϵ, δ)-level sets for a single ϵ value and multiple δ values. In Fig. 1, red points represent parameters within or on the level set ($\mathbf{f}_{\epsilon,\delta} \leq 0$), while green points lie outside ($\mathbf{f}_{\epsilon,\delta} > 0$), outlining the true (ϵ, δ)-level set in parameter space.

5 HYPERPART-X Algorithm

HYPERPART-X operates in both the parameter space and the input space, alternating between the two to effectively explore and optimize the system. At the parameter level, the algorithm sequentially samples and partitions the parameter space into subregions by using statistical quantities derived from the surrogate models for the (ϵ, δ)-loss function $\mathbf{f}_{\epsilon,\delta}$ learned within each subregion. HYPERPART-X keeps track of the subregions in the parameter space by maintaining a tree, that we refer to as Parameter Partitioning Tree (PPT). In the space of the inputs, locations are sampled to estimate the 0-level set of the robustness function given specific parameter values. This is referred to as the HYPERPART-X inner loop. An inner loop search is initiated only for specific values of the parameters that the algorithm adaptively selects. All the sampling distributions are continuously updated by maintaining the history of sampled inputs and their corresponding trajectories.

Each node in the PPT represents a subregion with an associated set of parameters and their corresponding (ϵ, δ)-loss function values. Gaussian processes are used as surrogates, allowing to define sampling distributions that aid in classifying a subregion. Specifically, every subregion can be classified with class γ based on the minimum and maximum q-quantile of the (ϵ, δ)-loss function. Let us denote the ith node of the PPT at the jth level at iteration k, with class γ, be denoted as $\Theta^\gamma_{i,j,k}$. The number of parameters mined in a subregion $\Theta^\gamma_{i,j,k}$ is denoted using $n^\Lambda_{i,j,k}$, while the total number of parameters mined so far is denoted using n^Λ. Similarly, the number of inputs sampled so far is denoted as n^X.

Algorithm 1 provides an overview of the proposed HYPERPART-X approach. At each iteration k, N^Λ_k parameters are sampled in the parameter space and N^X_k inputs are sampled in the input space (Line 4 in Algorithm 1). The (ϵ, δ)-loss function is then computed for the new parameters and updated for the previously sampled parameter by augmenting the associated filtration with the newly sampled inputs (Line 5 in Algorithm 1). The updated loss function is then used to classify the subregions of the parameter space(Line 6 in Algorithm 1). In this procedure, subregions are branched further in the next iteration based on their class γ. In case the available budget for sampling parameters is less than N^Λ_k, the algorithm distributes the available budget for sampling parameters across all the subregions based on their volume, updates the (ϵ, δ)-loss functions and classifies the subregions before the algorithm terminates (Line 9–12 in Algorithm 1). Upon termination, HYPERPART-X returns the estimates of the likelihood of a parameter λ satisfying $\mathbf{f}_{\epsilon,\delta} \leq 0$, and determines the normalized volume (ϵ, δ)-level set (line 13 in Algorithm 1).

Algorithm 1 Pseudocode for HYPERPART-X

1: **Input:** Parameter search space Λ, input search space X, parameter mining budget B_Λ, total input sampling budget B_X (we refer to this as *simulation budget*), inner loop local budget $B_X^l (\leq B_X)$, initialization budget for parameter space n_I^Λ, bayesian optimization budget for parameter space n_{BO}^Λ, continued sampling budget for parameter space n_{CS}^Λ, the initial sampling budget for input space n_i^X, define branching operator $\mathcal{P} : \Lambda \to (\Lambda_i)_i : \bigcup_i \Lambda_i = \Lambda, \bigcap_i \Lambda_i = \varnothing$, simulation function $\mathcal{M}$, pSTL formula φ_λ.

2: **Step 1:** Initialize the parameter-level tree with the root node representing the entire Λ space. This node will have a remaining class (r).

3: **while** $B_\Lambda - n^\Lambda \geq n_{CS}^\Lambda + \sum_{\Theta_{i,j,k}^\gamma : \gamma \in \{r, r+, r-\}} \left(\max(n_I^\Lambda - N_{i,j,k}^\Lambda, 0) + n_{BO}^\Lambda \right)$ **do**

4:     **Step 2:** Run Sampling the Parameter Space procedure.

5:     **Step 3:** Update (ϵ, δ)-loss function using Computing the (ϵ, δ)-loss function procedure.

6:     **Step 4:** Classify subregion using Classification of a Subregion in the Parameter Space procedure.

7: **end while**

8: **if** $B_\Lambda - n^\Lambda > 0$ **then**

9:     **Step 5:** Distribute the remaining budget $B_\Lambda - n^\Lambda$ between all subregions proportionally to volume.

10:     **Step 6:** Update (ϵ, δ)-loss function using Computing the (ϵ, δ)-loss function procedure.

11:     **Step 7:** Classify subregion using Classification of a Subregion in the Parameter Space procedure.

12: **end if**

13: Return the volume of (ϵ, δ)-level set.

It is important to emphasize that simulating the system is considerably more computationally expensive than monitoring a formula. The core benefit of our algorithm stems from the fact we have a user-defined upper bound on the number of inputs that can be simulated. HYPERPART-X intelligently samples inputs from the input space and reuses them throughout the algorithm by using the PART-X. On the other hand, the monitoring cost that the algorithm incurs is also bounded by a user-defined upper bound on the number of parameters that can be mined. HYPERPART-X adaptively samples and branches the parameter space to obtain the desired level set of parameters to the user. In the remainder of this section, we provide the key components of the HYPERPART-X algorithm.

Computing the (ϵ, δ)-***loss Function:*** Given a parameter $\lambda \in \Lambda$, the set of n^X sampled inputs $\{x_w\} \in X$ and their corresponding traces $\{\mathcal{M}(x_w)\}$, the user defined ϵ and δ threshold, and a pSTL formula φ_λ function instantiated with parameter λ, the (ϵ, δ)-loss function $\mathbf{f}_{\epsilon,\delta}(\lambda)$ is computed as follows. We first generate the dataset of $\mathcal{D}^X = \{x_w, \rho_\lambda(\mathcal{M}(x_w))\}$ of inputs and the robustness values of the resulting trajectories. We then estimate a Gaussian process and use the predictor $\hat{Y}(x)$ and associated variance $s^2(x)$ to estimate the falsification volume $V_f^q(X_0^\lambda)$ using a Monte-Carlo procedure. Consequently, we then compute the $\mathbf{f}_{\epsilon,\delta}(\lambda)$ using another Monte-Carlo procedure again.

Inner Loop Search: Given a set of parameters $\{\lambda_s\} \in \Theta_{i,j,k}^\gamma$, the budgets for local-search per parameter b_s, the set of n^X sampled inputs $\{x_w\} \in X$ and their corresponding traces $\{\mathcal{M}(x_w)\}$, the goal is to sample b_s inputs for a specific parameter location λ_s. We also require the user to define the necessary hyper-parameters for PART-X (Algorithm 4 in [17]) which include the initial sampling budget for input space n_I^X, the adaptive sampling budget for input space n_{BO}^X, the continued sampling budget for input space n_{CS}^X. Then, for a given parameter location λ_s, we first generate the dataset of $\mathcal{D}^X = \{x_w, \rho_{\lambda_s}(\mathcal{M}(x_w))\}_{w=1}^{n^X}$ of inputs and the robustness values of the resulting trajectories. All the n^X inputs resulting from previous inner searches are used to construct an Input Partitioning Tree (IPT) which is a collection of subregions in the inputs space. This is obtained by running PART-X without sampling and evaluating new input points. If $n^X = 0$, the IPT will only consist of the root node. Using the IPT, b_s inputs are sampled and the corresponding traces are stored by running the PART-X algorithm from [17]. Once this process is completed for all parameters in the set $\{\lambda_s\}$ the algorithm leaves the inner level search.

Classification of a Subregion in the Parameter Space: Consider a subregion $\Theta_{i,j,k}^\gamma$ in the parameter space having $n_{i,j,k}^\Lambda$ parameters denoted by the set $\{\lambda_s\}$. The dataset of parameters and their corresponding (ϵ, δ)-loss function values are first computed using the procedure detailed in Computing the (ϵ, δ)-loss function, which we denote as $\mathcal{D}_{i,j,k}^\Lambda = \{\lambda_s, \mathbf{f}_{\epsilon,\delta}(\lambda_s)\}$. We then estimate a Gaussian process and use the predictor $\hat{Y}_{i,j,k}(\lambda)$ and associated variance $s_{i,j,k}^2(\lambda)$ to estimate the falsification associated with the subregion. The estimation of the minimum and maximum q-quantile associated to the Gaussian process is

$$\min_{\lambda \in \Theta_{ijk}^\gamma} \left[\hat{Y}_{i,j,k}(\lambda) - Z_{1-q/2}\sqrt{s_{i,j,k}^2(\lambda)} \right], \max_{\lambda \in \Theta_{ijk}^\gamma} \left[\hat{Y}_{i,j,k}(\lambda) + Z_{1-q/2}\sqrt{s_{i,j,k}^2(\lambda)} \right].$$

A subregion is classified based on the values of the minimum and maximum q-quantile. At each iteration, a subregion can be classified as *positive* ($\gamma = +$) if the estimate of the minimum q-quantile is positive, *negative* ($\gamma = -$), if the estimate of the maximum q-quantile is negative, or *remaining* ($\gamma = \mathbf{r}$). A subregion with positive or negative could also be reclassified into another class. Thus, a subregion *reclassified from positive* has a class $\gamma = \mathbf{r}+$, and similarly, a subregion *reclassified from negative* has a class $\gamma = \mathbf{r}-$. If a region is classified as remaining ($\gamma \in \{\mathbf{r}\}$) or it is reclassified ($\gamma \in \{\mathbf{r}+, \mathbf{r}-\}$), it is partitioned in the subsequent iteration, provided that the volume after partitioning exceeds a user-specified minimum. If the volume after partitioning does not exceed a user-specified minimum, the subregion is classified as *unclassified*, denoted using $\gamma = \mathbf{u}$, and this subregion is neither sampled nor branched further.

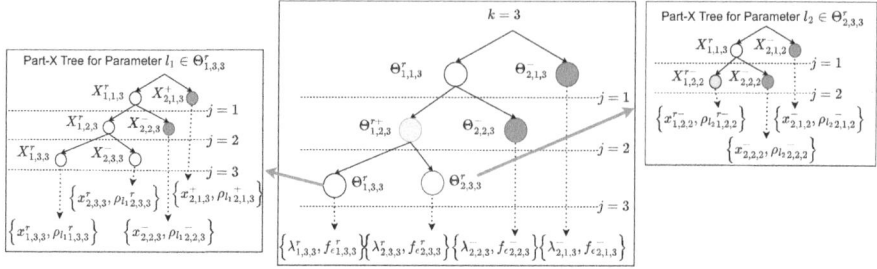

Fig. 2. The PPT generated using HYPERPART-X at start of iteration 3 in the outer loop along with the IPT generated by PART-X for some parameters constructed as part of the inner loop search.

Sampling the Parameter Space: Let B_Λ be the maximum number of parameters that can be mined, B_X be the maximum input sampling budget, B_X^l be the inner loop search budget. The algorithm samples parameters in each of the subregions represented by the leaf nodes of the parameter level tree depending on the class of the subregion. Consider a subregion $\Theta_{i,j,k}^\gamma$ in the parameter space having $n_{i,j,k}^\Lambda$ parameters. If the class $\gamma \in \{\mathbf{r}, \mathbf{r}+, \mathbf{r}-\}$, this subregion requires at least n_I^Λ parameters to be present to build its own Gaussian processes (and build the predictors $\hat{Y}_{i,j,k}(\lambda)$ and the associated variances $s_{i,j,k}^2(\lambda)$). Thus, $\max(n_I^\Lambda - n_{i,j,k}^\Lambda, 0)$ parameters are sampled randomly in the subregion. At this point, the algorithm checks if it has the capacity to enter the inner loop. If the inner loop search budget $B_X^l \geq B_X - n^X$, then the inner loop is triggered by supplying to it a set of parameters with respect to which inputs are to be sampled, along with the input sampling budget for each parameter. The budget allocations for every parameter is computed using a heuristic that assigns a higher budget to parameters whose $V_f^q(X_0^\lambda)$ is closer to but larger than the ϵ-threshold. The inner loop search budget b_s allocated to λ_s is defined as: $b_s \propto \frac{1}{\max(0, V_f^q(X_0^{\lambda_s})-\epsilon)}$ such that $\sum b_s = B_X^l$. Following this, additional n_{BO}^Λ parameters are sampled using a sequential Bayesian Optimization [11] approach with the objective of biasing the search for parameters towards the minimum of the (ϵ, δ)-loss function. On the other hand, subregions with class $\gamma \in \{+, -\}$ are allocated an overall budget of n_{CS}^Λ which are distributed proportional to the volumes of all subregions in this group, and the parameters are sampled randomly.

Figure 2 shows the HYPERPART-X PPT at the beginning of iteration $k = 3$ of the outer loop along with the IPT generated by PART-X for the parameters selected to trigger the inner loop search. At the start of iteration $k = 3$, there are four new subregions in the PPT: $\Theta_{1,3,3}^r$, $\Theta_{2,3,3}^r$, $\Theta_{2,2,3}^-$, and $\Theta_{2,1,3}^-$. Note that $\Theta_{1,2,3}^{r+}$ was a subregion that was classified as $\gamma = +$ at the start of the previous iteration and was reclassified at the end of the previous iteration, which resulted into its branching. Assuming that all budget constraints are met for iteration $k = 3$, the algorithm samples $N_{k=3}^\Lambda$ parameters in each of these subregions and $N_{k=3}^X$ inputs in the input space as part of the `Sampling the Parameter Space` procedure.

During this step, HYPERPART-X also invokes the `Inner Loop Search`. The IPT for a parameter location selected in $\Theta^r_{1,3,3}$ and $\Theta^r_{2,3,3}$ is shown. Once the parameters and inputs are sampled, the (ϵ, δ)-loss function is updated using `Computing the (ε,δ)-loss function` procedure and the class of the subregions are updated using `Classification of a Subregion in the Parameter Space` procedure. The nodes that still have class $\gamma \in \{\mathtt{r}, \mathtt{r+}, \mathtt{r-}\}$ will be branched further.

6 Results and Discussion

We demonstrate the performance of our method on three different classes of test benchmarks: (i) parameterized nonlinear non-convex reward functions that mimic the robustness from a pSTL, (ii) safety requirements from the F16-GCAS control system, and (iii) safety requirements from the Automatic Transmission (AT) benchmark presented in [8]. The first class of tests gives an opportunity to observe the capability of the proposed approach to identify geometrically complex shaped level sets much faster than competitors. The other two classes are CPS benchmarks, and allow us to prove our capabilities in more realistic settings showing how efficiently the approach, for the F16 case, can produce an estimate of requirement horizons that will be advisable to test the system safety. On the other hand, the AT benchmark shows the scalability of the proposed approach to increased input and parameter dimensions especially compared to approaches like PART-X that consider input and parameter space simultaneously.

These experiments illustrate that HYPERPART-X can successfully perform level set estimation and provide guarantees in the parameter space, while being sample-efficient in the input space. We compare the performance of HYPERPART-X to uniform random sampling (UR) and the PART-X algorithm. The UR sampler computes the true target level set by sampling 10^4 parameters, each with 10^4 input points, repeated 100 times, resulting in a total of 10^6 inputs and 10^{10} monitoring points. The closer the volume estimates to the UR, the better the performance. Given that simulation cost outweighs monitoring cost, we compare PART-X and HYPERPART-X by executing searches over the combined input and parameter spaces, ensuring both use the same number of simulations.

Non-linear Benchmarks: We consider mining the parameters of an over-parameterized version of Himmelblau's function (defined in Sect. 4, Eq. (5)) under two different *scenarios*. In the first scenario, the parameters $\lambda = (\lambda_1, \lambda_2) \in \Lambda = [-10, 20]^2$, and inputs $\mathbf{x} = (x_1, x_2) \in X = [-5, 5]^2$. HYPERPART-X was initialized with a total outer-loop budget $B_\Lambda = 1000$, and a total inner-loop budget $B_X = 2000$. The budget required to start an inner-loop search was set to $B^l_X = 500$ (SD1 in Table 1). A similar experiment was performed with $B_\Lambda = 2000$ (SD2 in Table 1). A total budget of 2000 simulations was assigned to PART-X. In the second scenario, the parameters are sampled from a larger domain for the parameter space, i.e., $\lambda = (\lambda_1, \lambda_2) \in \Lambda = [-10, 50]^2$. All the setup apart from the parameter-mining search space is same as in scenario 1 and are referred to as LD1 and LD2 in Table 1. For all the experiments detailed above, the ϵ was set to 0.1 and δ was set to 0.1.

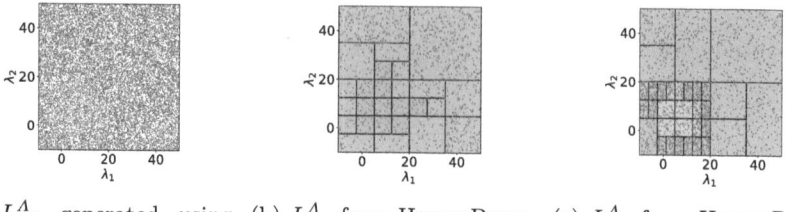

(a) $L^\Lambda_{\epsilon,\delta}$ generated using UR.

(b) $L^\Lambda_{\epsilon,\delta}$ from HYPERPART-X with $B_\Lambda = 1000$.

(c) $L^\Lambda_{\epsilon,\delta}$ from HYPERPART-X with $B_\Lambda = 2000$.

Fig. 3. Level set generated by the UR and the HYPERPART-X algorithm.

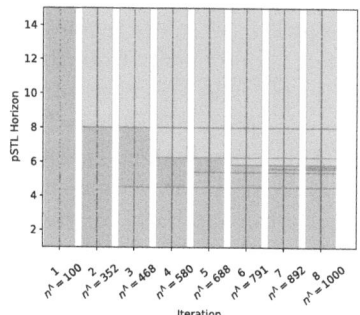

Fig. 4. Estimate of (ϵ, δ)-level intervals for the F16 GCAS case. Without generating new traces, the confidence on the interval estimation increases with the iterations. The middle region of undecided parameters consistently decreases.

F16 Ground Collision Avoidance System(F16): For this study, we use the F-16 benchmark in [16]. The GCAS system employs 16 continuous variables and piece-wise non-linear differential equations to simulate the autonomous maneuvering of the aircraft to prevent collisions with the ground. The benchmark, treats as inputs the initial roll, pitch, and yaw angles of the aircraft, namely ϕ, θ, ψ [16]. These angles have specific ranges: $[0.2\pi, 0.2833\pi]$, $[-0.5\pi, -0.54\pi]$, and $[0.25\pi, 0.378\pi]$, respectively. The initial altitude of the aircraft is set to $H_0 = 2335[\text{ft}]$, with a pose defined by the inputs. The trace generated from the simulation consists of the altitude at different time-stamps $H(t)$. In this scenario, the monitoring horizon is parametrized resulting in the following pSTL specification: "$\square_{[0,\lambda]}(\text{altitude} > 0)$", with $\lambda \in [1, 15][\text{s}]$.

HYPERPART-X was initialized with a total outer-loop budget $B_\Lambda = 1000$, and a total inner-loop budget $B_X = 2000$. The budget required to start an inner-loop search was set to $B_X^l = 500$. PART-X is assigned a total budget of 2000 simulations. The ϵ was set to 0.003 and δ was set to 0.1.

Table 1. Results obtained by HyperPart-X and benchmark algorithms.

Experiment	UR	q	PART-X Volume	Std Err	LCB	UCB	HYPERPART-X Volume	Std Err	LCB	UCB
SD 1	4.99E-01	50%	0.00E+00	0.00E+00	–	–	5.04E-01	1.53E-03	5.01E-01	5.07E-01
		95%	8.37E-01	1.51E-02	8.07E-01	8.67E-01	5.08E-01	1.49E-03	5.06E-01	5.11E-01
		99%	9.22E-01	4.98E-03	9.12E-01	9.32E-01	5.10E-01	1.46E-03	5.07E-01	5.13E-01
SD 2		50%	0.00E+00	0.00E+00	–	–	5.01E-01	9.43E-04	4.99E-01	5.03E-01
		95%	8.37E-01	1.51E-02	8.07E-01	8.67E-01	5.06E-01	8.96E-04	5.04E-01	5.08E-01
		99%	9.22E-01	4.98E-03	9.12E-01	9.32E-01	5.08E-01	8.96E-04	5.06E-01	5.09E-01
LD 1	1.27E-01	50%	7.91E-03	4.04E-03	0.00E+00	1.58E-02	1.75E-01	7.86E-02	1.26E-01	2.23E-01
		95%	3.70E-01	6.36E-02	2.46E-01	4.95E-01	1.76E-01	7.84E-02	1.28E-01	2.25E-01
		99%	5.80E-01	1.03E-01	3.79E-01	7.82E-01	1.77E-01	7.84E-02	1.28E-01	2.26E-01
LD 2		50%	7.91E-03	4.04E-03	0.00E+00	1.58E-02	1.44E-01	6.84E-02	1.02E-01	1.87E-01
		95%	3.70E-01	6.36E-02	2.46E-01	4.95E-01	1.46E-01	6.93E-02	1.03E-01	1.89E-01
		99%	5.80E-01	1.03E-01	3.79E-01	7.82E-01	1.48E-01	7.13E-02	1.03E-01	1.92E-01
F16	6.38E-01	50%	3.76E-04	4.50E-05	2.88E-04	4.64E-04	5.89E-01	6.55E-02	4.61E-01	7.17E-01
		95%	3.89E-03	1.08E-03	1.77E-03	6.00E-03	5.89E-01	6.55E-02	4.61E-01	7.17E-01
		99%	8.58E-03	2.51E-03	3.67E-03	1.35E-02	5.89E-01	6.55E-02	4.61E-01	7.17E-01
AT	9.27E-01	50%	9.78E-01	1.32E-02	9.52E-01	1.00E+00	9.31E-01	2.92E-03	9.25E-01	9.36E-01
		95%	1.00E+00	0.00E+00	–	–	9.33E-01	3.16E-03	9.26E-01	9.39E-01
		99%	1.00E+00	0.00E+00	–	–	9.33E-01	3.28E-03	9.27E-01	9.40E-01

Automatic Transmission (AT): We also show our results on the Simulink model of an automatic transmission controller characterized by hybrid dynamics, encompassing both continuous and discrete behaviors. The throttle and the brake signals over the specification horizon are considered as inputs, while the robustness depends on the continuous signals given by the engine speed ω (measured in RPM), and the vehicle speed v (measured in mph). The throttle input ranges from 0 to 100, and the input signals are parameterized using the `pchip` interpolation function, employing 7 control points for the throttle. As a result, the search in the input space is a 7-d problem.

For this benchmark, we consider the pSTL specifications from [8]. The pSTL of interest is $\varphi_{\lambda=(\lambda_1,\lambda_2)} = \Box_{[0,60]}((v \leq \lambda_1)$ and $(\omega \leq \lambda_2))$, requiring, globally, the vehicle speed (v) and engine speed (ω) to be below λ_1, λ_2, respectively. The search space for the parameter mining is as follows: $\lambda = (\lambda_1, \lambda_2) \in [0, 160] \times [3000, 8000]$.

HyperPart-X was initialized with a total outer-loop budget $B_\Lambda = 1000$, and a total inner-loop budget $B_X = 2000$. The budget required to start an inner-loop search was set to $B_X^l = 500$. Part-X is assigned a total budget of 2000 simulations. The ϵ was set to 0.1 and δ was set to 0.1.

Analysis of Results: The results for all algorithms are shown in Table 1. We report the mean ratio of the volume of the (ϵ, δ)-level set to the volume of the parameter search space, along with its standard error and confidence bounds computed over 10 replications at 95%. Finally, the q-column variants use the Gaussian processes at q-quantiles to estimate the volume of the (ϵ, δ) level set.

In the SD1, SD2, LD1 and LD2 benchmarks, we observe that HYPERPART-X approximates successfully the true level set volumes with significantly fewer samples. PART-X, on the other hand, fails to obtain a satisfactory performance in any example. Figure 3 shows the parameters and partitions mined by HYPERPART-X. The subregions classified $\gamma = \{-\}$ are shown in red (inside the (ϵ, δ)-level set), while those classified $\gamma = \{+\}$ are shown in green (outside the (ϵ, δ)-level set). The subregions classified as $\gamma = \{\texttt{r}, \texttt{r}^+, \texttt{r}^-\}$ are shown in blue. There are no subregions classified as $\gamma = \{\texttt{u}\}$. Visually, the parameters mined by HYPERPART-X tend to bias towards the regions that we actually intended on finding, as demonstrated in Fig. 3. Since we use Gaussian processes to estimate the volume at different confidence levels, higher confidence levels volume estimates will account for more uncertainty, leading to larger estimated volumes, which is also evident in Table 1.

For the "F16" benchmark, the regions and the obtained partitions are plotted for each iteration of the HYPERPART-X algorithm in Fig. 4, and follow the same color convention as Fig. 3. Intuitively, shorter pSTL horizons are considered to be "safer" (i.e., to not exhibit a failure), while longer simulations have a higher likelihood of resulting in a failure of the GCAS. Numerically, it can be observed from Table 1 that HYPERPART-X does well in comparision to PART-X and comes close to the ground truth with significantly fewer samples for all the benchmarks.

7 Conclusions

We present, for the first time, the HYPERPART-X algorithm that automatically generates test cases considering hierarchically both the modifiable parameters of a pSTL requirement (outer layer) and inputs to the CPS (inner layer). HYPERPART-X estimates the (ϵ, δ)-level set of the probability, for each parametrization of the STL, that a CPS has a falsification volume larger than some user-defined ϵ value. Here, we refer to falsification volume as the measure of the set containing falsifying inputs under a specific specification parametrization. Specifically, given an input space, a simulation tool (or test harness), a requirement, the range for the requirement parameters we wish to change, a target falsification volume level, and a significance level, HYPERPART-X attempts to classify the parameter space into violating, satisfying, and undecided subregions. The algorithm only performs monitoring of pre-simulated traces to evaluate parametrizations of the pSTL and may trigger, if the desired confidence is not reached, the inner-loop search, where falsification is run and both monitoring and simulation (harness execution) are performed.

The numerical results demonstrate that HYPERPART-X provides a sample-efficient and effective approach for estimating the δ-level set of the probability of a Cyber-Physical System (CPS) violating a given pSTL requirement. The next step in our research is to work on further increasing the efficiency of our algorithm by introducing heuristics to better distribute the input sampling budget, as well as to explore scalability to higher dimensions.

References

1. Asarin, E., Donzé, A., Maler, O., Nickovic, D.: Parametric identification of temporal properties. In: Khurshid, S., Sen, K. (eds.) RV 2011. LNCS, vol. 7186, pp. 147–160. Springer, Heidelberg (2012). https://doi.org/10.1007/978-3-642-29860-8_12
2. Bakhirkin, A., Ferrère, T., Maler, O.: Efficient parametric identification for STL. In: Proceedings of the 21st International Conference on Hybrid Systems: Computation and Control (Part of CPS Week), p. 177186. HSCC '18, Association for Computing Machinery, New York, NY, USA (2018). https://doi.org/10.1145/3178126.3178132
3. Bartocci, E., Mateis, C., Nesterini, E., Nickovic, D.: Survey on mining signal temporal logic specifications. Inf. Comput. **289**,104957 (2022). https://doi.org/10.1016/j.ic.2022.104957, https://www.sciencedirect.com/science/article/pii/S0890540122001122
4. Donzé, A.: Breach, a toolbox for verification and parameter synthesis of hybrid systems. In: Touili, T., Cook, B., Jackson, P. (eds.) CAV 2010. LNCS, vol. 6174, pp. 167–170. Springer, Heidelberg (2010). https://doi.org/10.1007/978-3-642-14295-6_17
5. Donzé, A., Maler, O.: Robust satisfaction of temporal logic over real-valued signals. In: Chatterjee, K., Henzinger, T.A. (eds.) FORMATS 2010. LNCS, vol. 6246, pp. 92–106. Springer, Heidelberg (2010). https://doi.org/10.1007/978-3-642-15297-9_9
6. Fainekos, G.E., Pappas, G.J.: Robustness of temporal logic specifications for continuous-time signals. Theor. Comput. Sci. **410**(42), 4262–4291 (2009)
7. Hoxha, B., Abbas, H., Fainekos, G.: Benchmarks for temporal logic requirements for automotive systems. In: Frehse, G., Althoff, M. (eds.) ARCH14-15. 1st and 2nd International Workshop on Applied veRification for Continuous and Hybrid Systems. EPiC Series in Computing, vol. 34, pp. 25–30. EasyChair (2015). https://doi.org/10.29007/xwrs, https://easychair.org/publications/paper/4bfq
8. Hoxha, B., Dokhanchi, A., Fainekos, G.: Mining parametric temporal logic properties in model-based design for cyber-physical systems. Int. J. Softw. Tools Technol. Transf. **20**, 79–93 (2018)
9. Jha, S., Tiwari, A., Seshia, S.A., Sahai, T., Shankar, N.: TeLEx: passive STL learning using only positive examples. In: Lahiri, S., Reger, G. (eds.) RV 2017. LNCS, vol. 10548, pp. 208–224. Springer, Cham (2017). https://doi.org/10.1007/978-3-319-67531-2_13
10. Jin, X., Donzé, A., Deshmukh, J.V., Seshia, S.A.: Mining requirements from closed-loop control models. IEEE Trans. Comput.-Aided Des. Integr. Circuits Syst. **34**(11), 1704–1717 (2015). https://doi.org/10.1109/TCAD.2015.2421907
11. Jones, D.R., Schonlau, M., Welch, W.J.: Efficient global optimization of expensive black-box functions. J. Glob. Optim. **13**, 455–492 (1998)
12. Leung, K., Aréchiga, N., Pavone, M.: Backpropagation through signal temporal logic specifications: infusing logical structure into gradient-based methods. Int. J. Robot. Res. **42**(6), 356–370 (2023). https://doi.org/10.1177/02783649221082115
13. Maler, O., Nickovic, D.: Monitoring temporal properties of continuous signals. In: Lakhnech, Y., Yovine, S. (eds.) FORMATS/FTRTFT -2004. LNCS, vol. 3253, pp. 152–166. Springer, Heidelberg (2004). https://doi.org/10.1007/978-3-540-30206-3_12
14. Mathesen, L., Pedrielli, G., Fainekos, G.: Efficient optimization-based falsification of cyber-physical systems with multiple conjunctive requirements. In: 2021 IEEE

17th International Conference on Automation Science and Engineering (CASE), pp. 732–737 (2021). https://doi.org/10.1109/CASE49439.2021.9551474
15. Mathesen, L., Pedrielli, G., Ng, S.H., Zabinsky, Z.B.: Stochastic optimization with adaptive restart: a framework for integrated local and global learning. J. Glob. Optim. **79**, 87–110 (2021)
16. Menghi, C., et al.: Arch-comp23 category report: falsification. In: Frehse, G., Althoff, M. (eds.) Proceedings of 10th International Workshop on Applied Verification of Continuous and Hybrid Systems (ARCH23). EPiC Series in Computing, vol. 96, pp. 151–169. EasyChair (2023). https://doi.org/10.29007/6nqs, https://easychair.org/publications/paper/wFh9
17. Pedrielli, G., et al.: Part-x: a family of stochastic algorithms for search-based test generation with probabilistic guarantees. IEEE Trans. Autom. Sci. Eng. (2023)
18. Qin, X., Xia, Y., Zutshi, A., Fan, C., Deshmukh, J.V.: Statistical verification of cyber-physical systems using surrogate models and conformal inference. In: 2022 ACM/IEEE 13th International Conference on Cyber-Physical Systems (ICCPS), pp. 116–126 (2022). https://doi.org/10.1109/ICCPS54341.2022.00017
19. Rasmussen, C.E., Williams, C.K., et al.: Gaussian Processes for Machine Learning, vol. 1. Springer, Berlin, Heidelberg (2006). https://doi.org/10.1007/978-3-540-28650-9_4
20. Vazquez-Chanlatte, M., Deshmukh, J.V., Jin, X., Seshia, S.A.: Logical clustering and learning for time-series data. In: Majumdar, R., Kunčak, V. (eds.) CAV 2017. LNCS, vol. 10426, pp. 305–325. Springer, Cham (2017). https://doi.org/10.1007/978-3-319-63387-9_15
21. Vazquez-Chanlatte, M., Ghosh, S., Deshmukh, J.V., Sangiovanni-Vincentelli, A., Seshia, S.A.: Time-series learning using monotonic logical properties. In: Colombo, C., Leucker, M. (eds.) RV 2018. LNCS, vol. 11237, pp. 389–405. Springer, Cham (2018). https://doi.org/10.1007/978-3-030-03769-7_22

Temporal Logics

faRM-LTL: A Domain-Specific Architecture for Flexible and Accelerated Runtime Monitoring of LTL Properties

Amrutha Benny[1], Sandeep Chandran[1(✉)], Rajshekar Kalayappan[2], Ramchandra Phawade[2], and Piyush P. Kurur[1]

[1] Indian Institute of Technology Palakkad, Palakkad 678623, Kerala, India
112004003@smail.iitpkd.ac.in, {sandeepchandran,ppk}@iitpkd.ac.in
[2] Indian Institute of Technology Dharwad, Dharwad 580007, Karnataka, India
{rajshekar.k,prb}@iitdh.ac.in

Abstract. State-of-the-art RV frameworks that implement runtime monitors in hardware synthesize monitoring circuits from formal specifications of properties. Such frameworks resynthesize or reconfigure monitoring circuits if the input properties change post-deployment. This is typically handled using reconfigurable fabrics such as FPGAs. Runtime monitors implemented on FPGAs have two disadvantages as compared to a fixed implementation (ASIC): (i) lower operating frequencies and (ii) inefficient use of area (on silicon). In this work, we propose an RV framework called *faRM-LTL*, that overcomes these two disadvantages by keeping the design of the runtime monitor unchanged even if the input properties change, thereby making it amenable for an ASIC implementation. We achieve this using a Linear Temporal Logic (LTL) Monitoring Instruction Set Architecture (LM-ISA), a compiler that translates properties specified in LTL into a sequence of LM-ISA instructions, and an associated programmable hardware runtime monitor that implements the LM-ISA. The flexibility of the faRM-LTL Monitor was evaluated on 53 LTL properties from several prior works. We also implemented the Monitor on an ASIC and found its area overhead to be under 0.5%.

Keywords: LTL monitor construction · Generic re-progr ammable monitors

1 Introduction

Runtime Verification (RV) is well-suited to verify the operation of large and complex systems. RV can also detect anomalous behaviors caused by factors other

---

This work is partially supported by IIT Palakkad Technology IHub Foundation (IPTIF) Technology Development Grant No. IPTIF/HRD/DF/011/SEP29.

Supplementary Information The online version contains supplementary material available at https://doi.org/10.1007/978-3-031-74234-7_7.

than design bugs because it monitors the functioning of the system in-field. As an example, state-of-the-art multi-core processors have been observed to yield incorrect results when specific computations are performed, in a particular order on specific cores [11,12,19,42]. Such errors have often led to corruption or loss of large volumes of data. Handling errors occurring in such complex and high-performance systems require runtime monitors to operate at-speed (verdicts given with minimal delay), and check properties of the system that may not be known at design-time.

Augmenting a base system (either software or hardware) with RV requires, a non-intrusive and light-weight instrumentation mechanism, and runtime monitors that identify incorrect behaviors. From the perspective of the underlying system, all software components (base system, instrumentation and runtime monitors) execute on processor cores. In systems where the instrumentation and monitoring is done in software, it typically takes several instructions (a few thousand processor clock cycles) to generate verdicts. This delay is dominated by the time taken to transfer instrumented information to the monitor through the memory hierarchy. Also, an additional processor core is reserved for executing the monitor itself. Such RV implementations are very flexible, and can quickly adapt to changes in the properties to be verified.

The high latency and the high resource overheads incurred is mitigated by implementing the instrumentation mechanisms and runtime monitors in hardware. A popular strategy for instrumentation in hardware is to use Design-for-Debug (DFD) structures that were embedded into the chip (processor die) during the design phase. DFD implementations such as ARM CoreSight [28] can typically generate execution traces that capture information such as the sequence of instruction execution, values written to registers by each instruction, and traps generated. Since the volume of information collected by on-chip instrumentation is large, they are used in conjunction with hardware runtime monitors.

Runtime monitors can either be implemented on the same chip as the system under observation (on-chip) or on a separate chip (off-chip). The latter requires the execution traces to be transferred across chips which is typically orders of magnitude slower than on-chip transfers. Runtime monitors in hardware can be implemented on reconfigurable fabrics such as FPGAs, or using dedicated circuitry (ASIC). FPGAs consist of programmable Lookup Tables (LUTs) where the output function of a logic gate to realize is written into these tables. Therefore, functionality realized by the FPGA can be changed by rewriting these tables. The operating frequency of FPGA is in the order of hundreds of MHz. An ASIC implementation uses dedicated circuitry (fixed) to achieve the desired functionality. Since the logic gates are implemented using transistors instead of LUTs, the area occupied is lower and the operating frequencies are in the order of a few GHz.

Several works have been proposed in the past that implement runtime monitors using off-chip FPGAs [32,44], on-chip ASICs [6] as well as on-chip FPGAs that are available in state-of-the-art hybrid SoCs [22,38] such as Xilinx Zynq. The time taken to generate verdicts in off-chip FPGAs are limited by both the off-chip communication as well as the lower operating frequencies of the FPGA. Implementations that use on-chip FPGAs reduce the time taken to generate verdicts by avoiding costly off-chip transfers. Finally, on-chip ASIC implementations are known to verify the system under observation at-speed, but lack flexibility to adapt to changes in properties to verify.

In this paper, we propose an RV framework that supports flexible and accelerated runtime monitoring of LTL properties, called *faRM-LTL*. The proposed framework uses on-chip runtime monitors that are amenable for ASIC implementation (circuit design does not change). However, we achieve the desired flexibility by adopting the same design principles as that of general-purpose processors. Specifically, we use a LTL Monitoring Instruction Set Architecture (LM-ISA) that forms the interface between on-chip hardware monitors, and input properties. Then, we use a compiler that translates LTL properties to a sequence of LM-ISA instructions. The sequence of LM-ISA instructions thus generated are passed on to the faRM-LTL monitor that is embedded adjacent to the on-chip DFD structures. Figure 1 shows the proposed Monitor within the context of the entire system.

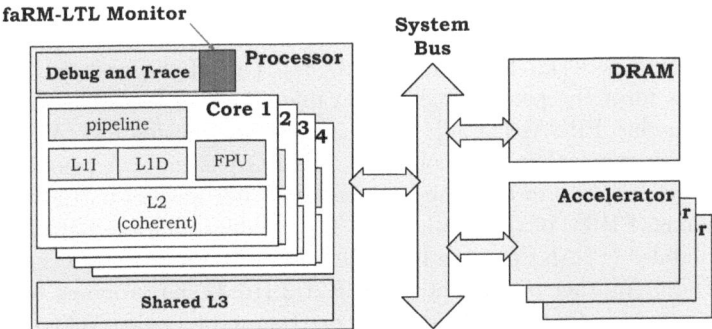

Fig. 1. A schematic of a system with a faRM-LTL monitor embedded in it. Each grey box is a die. Each die is manufactured independently and packaged into a chip before integrating them on a motherboard.

We evaluate faRM-LTL on 53 different LTL properties and observe that the number of LM-ISA instructions corresponding to the properties considered are few in number. We also synthesized[1] the proposed on-chip monitor using an ASIC flow and find that it occupies only 0.5% area of a typical processor, which is quite small and hence is feasible to be integrated into a general-purpose processor.

---

[1] In this work, we refer to the process of generating circuits from high-level specifications as synthesis, and generating a sequence of instructions from high-level specifications as compilation. Reconfiguration is used to refer to the process of changing the functionality realized by FPGAs.

The rest of the paper is organized as follows. Section 2 gives a brief survey of prior related works, Sect. 3 gives a quick background of the works that form the basis of the proposed work and motivates our proposed solution. Section 4 discusses the overview of our proposed solution first. It then discusses two approaches to generate LM-ISA instructions from input LTL specifications, and finally discusses the design of the faRM-LTL Monitor. The characterization of faRM-LTL on a wide variety of LTL properties, and the synthesis results of the proposed runtime monitors is discussed in Sect. 5. We summarize the overall work and identify directions for extending this work to build the entire framework and other opportunities for future research is discussed in Sect. 6.

2 Related Works

Traditionally, RV frameworks used software implementations [14,21] of instrumentation mechanisms and runtime monitors. The state-of-the-art frameworks are now well integrated into popular software tool-chains and source code analyzers such as the E-ACSL plugins [10,36] in Frama-C [25], AspectC++ compiler [39,40], and AspectJ [23]. These frameworks allow system developers to seamlessly apply RV to their applications. However, such monitors suffer from large delays in generating verdicts and incur high resource overheads.

Several proposals have used off-chip FPGAs extensively to improve the performance of monitors [4,7,9,16,31,32,35,37,44]. The off-chip transfer of the execution traces limit the performance achievable. This led researchers to explore the use of on-chip FPGAs [22,38]. There is a caveat in using FPGAs to achieve flexibility. The time taken to reconfigure an FPGA is high. A prior work that alleviates this proposes to load the bitstream files into several partially reconfigurable regions (PRRs) of the FPGA [44]. This enables multiple partial reconfiguration modules (PRMs) to time multiplex these PRRs to reduce the reconfiguration times. Another prominent work, R2U2 [16,32,35] proposes to generate hardware monitors for all the basic Metric Temporal Logic (MTL) operators and place them on the FPGAs. As the input properties change, only the interconnections between monitoring units corresponding to the basic operations are modified/reconfigured, thereby reducing the overall time taken to adapt to the changing property. Similarly, there are several techniques that have proposed to identify common sub-expressions among a list of candidate properties and implement them in hardware. Any subsequent processing of input trace can either be done in software or in FPGA, but the reconfiguration required would be lesser because the units implementing the common sub-expressions can be reused across several properties [22]. However, these works continue to be restricted by the relatively lower operating frequencies achieved on FPGAs.

An ASIC implementation of runtime monitors can operate at high frequencies. Therefore, such monitors are used to detect anomalous behaviors during post-silicon validation (a phase where initial silicon samples are tested for correctness before chips are cleared for mass production) [6]. However, such implementation of runtime monitors are rigid and cannot adapt to changes in input properties. The proposed faRM-LTL achieves the desired flexibility while being amenable to ASIC implementation by adopting an ISA driven approach.

2.1 Hardware Regex Matching Engines

The proposed LM-ISA is based on the "virtual machine approach" for regular expression matching [8]. CICERO [29] is a straight-forward hardware implementation of the virtual machine approach. CICERO engines are used to construct the proposed faRM-LTL Monitor that are embedded on-chip.

Regular expression matching has been extensively researched for the past several decades now. Over these years, several hardware accelerators have been proposed. The Micron Automata Processor (AP) is the most popular regular expression matching engine [13]. Since regular expression matching is inherently a memory-bound operation, all such hardware accelerators use spatial architectures (or other non-von Neumann architectures) where the comparison operation is performed close to the memory cells [20,24,27,33,34,43]. To the best of our knowledge, only off-chip implementations of these accelerators are available commercially. In this work, we have considered an implementation using CICERO instead of such accelerators because it is amenable to a range of low-level optimizations that are well known to ASIC designers. However, any of these accelerators could also serve our purpose if their on-chip implementations are feasible.

3 Background and Motivation

3.1 Syntax and Semantics of LTL

The syntax of LTL is as follows:

$$\varphi = true \mid p \mid \neg\varphi \mid \varphi_1 \wedge \varphi_2 \mid \mathcal{X}\varphi \mid \varphi_1 \, \mathcal{U} \, \varphi_2$$

where p is a proposition from a (finite) set of propositions P. $\mathcal{X}$ and $\mathcal{U}$ are *next-time* and *until* operators.

Semantics of LTL. Given an execution trace $\rho = \pi_0.\pi_1.\pi_2...$ of infinite length, where each $\pi_i \in 2^P$ for each $i \geq 0$, the semantics of the LTL operators are as shown below. Here (ρ, i) corresponds to $\pi_i.\pi_{i+1}.\pi_{i+2}...$, the suffix of ρ starting from i.

- $(\rho, i) \models true$.
- $(\rho, i) \models p$ iff $p \in \pi_i$.
- $(\rho, i) \models \neg\varphi$ iff $(\rho, i) \not\models \varphi$.
- $(\rho, i) \models \varphi_1 \wedge \varphi_2$ iff $(\rho, i) \models \varphi_1$ and $(\rho, i) \models \varphi_2$.
- $(\rho, i) \models \mathcal{X}\varphi$ iff $(\rho, i+1) \models \varphi$
- $(\rho, i) \models \varphi_1 \, \mathcal{U} \, \varphi_2$ iff $(\rho, j) \models \varphi_2$ for some $j \geq i$ and $(\rho, k) \models \varphi_1$ for all $i \leq k < j$

We say $\rho \models \varphi$ when $(\rho, 0) \models \varphi$. Other temporal operators such as *eventually* ($\diamond$) and *always* ($\square$) can be derived from these operators as shown below.

- $false \equiv \neg true$
- $\varphi_1 \vee \varphi_2 \equiv \neg(\neg\varphi_1 \wedge \neg\varphi_2)$
- $\varphi_1 \rightarrow \varphi_2 \equiv \neg\varphi_1 \vee \varphi_2$
- $\diamond\varphi \equiv true \, \mathcal{U} \, \varphi$
- $\square\varphi \equiv \neg\diamond\neg\varphi$

3.2 Runtime Verification of Properties Specified in LTL

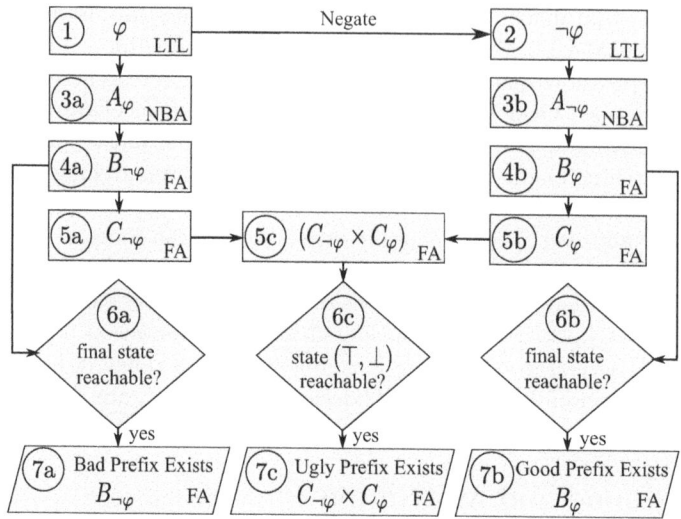

Fig. 2. Generation of Good, Bad and Ugly automata

The language accepted by an LTL expression is a set of strings of infinite length. In Verification, when a property is specified in LTL, the accepted language is a set of infinite-length streams of observations obtained from the system under observation. Clearly, in RV, observation streams of infinite length cannot be processed to determine satisfaction or refutation of the input property. So the idea of looking for finite length prefixes is employed [14,17,18,26,30].

Figure 2 describes the procedure. The LTL property φ is first converted to an equivalent Buchi Automaton A_φ (step 3a in Fig. 2). We consider the running example of the LTL property $\Box(a \to \neg(b\,\mathcal{U}\,c))$ to aid in the discussion. For this example, $P = \{a, b, c\}$, and the corresponding A_φ is given in Fig. 3. Here, $a\bar{b}c$ indicates that the propositions, a and c were $true$ but b was $false$. The letter I in the state label indicates that the state is an initial state.

We first derive the deterministic automaton $B_{\neg\varphi}$ from A_φ (step 4a in Fig. 2). Any infinite extension of a finite string that is accepted by $B_{\neg\varphi}$ will not satisfy A_φ. This is useful to give verdicts about an LTL property (interpreted over infinite strings) by just observing the system for a finite amount of time.

The subset construction procedure to derive $B_{\neg\varphi}$ is as follows. First, all those states in A_φ (and corresponding incoming and outgoing transitions) from where a cycle containing an accepting state is unreachable are removed. The set of initial states in A_φ are added to $B_{\neg\varphi}$ as the latter's initial states. Then for each state in this set, its outgoing transitions are considered. The transitions and the corresponding destination states (according to the subset construction

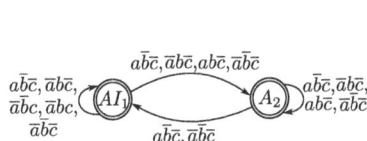

Fig. 3. $A_\varphi : \varphi = \Box(a \to \neg(b\,\mathcal{U}\,c))$ Letter I indicates initial states.

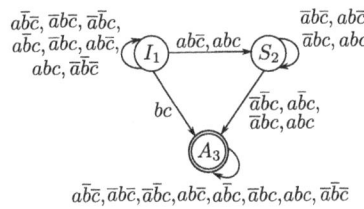

Fig. 4. $A_{\neg\varphi}$

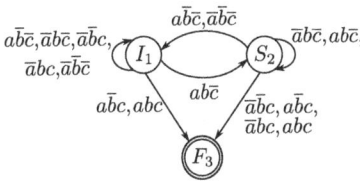

Fig. 5. $B_{\neg\varphi}$

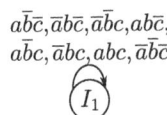

Fig. 6. B_φ

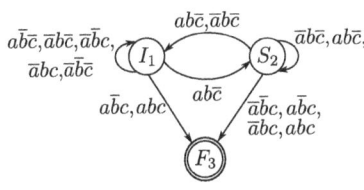

Fig. 7. $C_{\neg\varphi}$ (same as $B_{\neg\varphi}$)

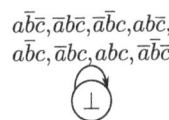

Fig. 8. C_φ

procedure) are added to $B_{\neg\varphi}$. The newly added states to $B_{\neg\varphi}$ are successively processed in a similar manner until all the reachable states in A_φ have been considered. The empty set is then marked as the accepting state of $B_{\neg\varphi}$. Intuitively, a run of the automaton $B_{\neg\varphi}$ that reaches the accepting state (empty set) would correspond to reaching a state in the NBA from where a cycle containing an accepting state is never reachable. In other words, the Buchi automaton will not accept any extension of the prefix string seen so far. If this accepting state is reachable, then we say the given LTL property has a *bad prefix*, which is captured by the finite automaton $B_{\neg\varphi}$ (step 7a in Fig. 2). A bad prefix is a stream of events s such that any infinite extension of s will not be accepted by A_φ, that is, the property φ is violated or refuted. Since such prefixes are finite, a refutation of property φ (if it has a bad prefix) can be detected by processing a finite trace of the current execution obtained from the system under observation. For the running example, $B_{\neg\varphi}$ is given in Fig. 5.

Similarly, we can start from the negation of the property $\neg\varphi$, construct $A_{\neg\varphi}$ and B_φ (for the running example, see Figs. 4 and 6), and see if a *good prefix* exists. If so, satisfactions of the property φ can be detected at runtime by processing a finite length execution trace.

C_φ is constructed from B_φ (step 5b in Fig. 2) by performing a full traversal (breadth first search) and replacing all states from where the accepting state is not reachable, by a single state with a self loop and the label $\bot$ (for the running example, see Fig. 8). If while processing an execution trace this state is reached, then there is no possibility of observing a good prefix. However, this does not mean that the property has been refuted – it only means that a statement regarding satisfaction cannot be made anymore. Similarly, $C_{\neg\varphi}$ can be constructed from $B_{\neg\varphi}$ (step 5a in Fig. 2) by replacing all states from where the accepting state is not reachable, by a single state with a self loop and the label $\top$. The cross-product $C_{\neg\varphi} \times C_\varphi$ is then constructed (step 5c in Fig. 2). If the state with the label $(\top, \bot)$ is reachable, then the property φ has an *ugly prefix*, which is captured by the finite automaton $C_{\neg\varphi} \times C_\varphi$ (step 7c in Fig. 2). An ugly prefix is a stream of events s such that any extension of s will neither lead to a good prefix nor a bad prefix. No verdict – satisfaction or refutation – can be made by observing the stream further.

3.3 Regular Expression Matching

Testing whether a candidate string belongs to the language described by a regular expression is a well-studied problem. The seminal algorithm by Ken Thompson [41] provides a linear time solution [29] that far outperforms classical backtracking based approaches. In this approach, at every point where the regular expression allows multiple forward paths towards acceptance, new virtual machines are spawned to explore the alternatives. At any time, the current symbol is processed by all active virtual machines. If the current symbol is not what a virtual machine was looking for, it dies. Else, it moves forward along its path to acceptance.

Table 1. CICERO's Instruction Set Architecture

Instruction	Description
MATCH OP	Compares OP with *cc. In case of match, PC+1 and cc+1. Else, thread dies.
MATCH_ANY	PC+1 and cc+1.
NO_MATCH OP	Compares OP with *cc. In case of no match, PC+1. Else, thread dies.
JUMP OP	Set PC to OP.
SPLIT OP	Spawn a new thread with PC = OP. The current thread's PC is incremented by 1.
ACCEPT_P	Accepts the sequence of characters seen so far.
END_WITHOUT_ACCEPTING	Thread dies.

PC: program counter (one per thread); cc: pointer to current character in the stream; *cc: character pointed to by cc

CICERO [29] is a hardware-based implementation of the Thompson's algorithm. Here, every path through the NFA that is live when checking for matches is a separate thread of execution. Under the Thompson's algorithm, each character in the input stream is visited only once. Therefore, when the current character pointer (cc) advances by one input character, all the threads that are alive needs to be executed. The instructions of these live threads have to be evaluated on the new input character available at (cc+1). Here This is done in a time-multiplexed fashion in the CICERO core. Table 1 lists instructions that can be executed by the threads when processing an input character.

The CICERO Compiler takes as input a regular expression and generates a sequence of CICERO instructions which is loaded into the instruction memory of a CICERO Engine. The CICERO Engine is then fed the stream of characters to be tested. The CICERO Engine signals a match when it finds that a substring in the input character stream matches (or satisfies) the regular expression.

3.4 Employing a Regular Expression Matcher as a Runtime Verification monitor

As discussed in Sect. 3.2, the refutation of an LTL property at runtime can be determined by detecting whether the execution trace of the current run obtained from the system under observation matches the *bad prefix*. Similarly, the satisfaction of an LTL property can be determined by detecting whether there is a match with the *good prefix*. A match with the *ugly prefix* can tell us whether further runtime verification is futile or not. Since the prefixes are automata, and every automaton has an equivalent regular expression that accepts the same language, we propose to employ the CICERO Engines to perform the prefix matching, and hence, to employ them as runtime monitors. The CICERO ISA, listed in Table 1, is therefore the LTL Monitoring ISA (LM-ISA) in this work.

4 faRM-LTL

4.1 Overview

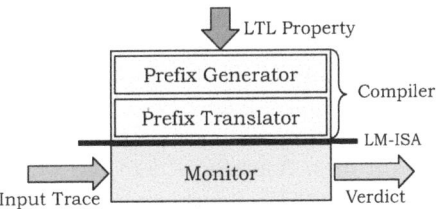

Fig. 9. Overview of faRM-LTL

Figure 9 shows the overview of the proposed framework and its components. We take as input, properties specified in LTL. The Prefix Generator generates the good, the bad, and the ugly prefix automata. The Prefix Translator then generates the LM-ISA programs for each of these prefix automata. We implemented the Prefix Generator and the Prefix Translator in Python (v3.10.12). The Monitor, that is composed of CICERO Engines, is then programmed with the generated LM-ISA programs. At runtime, execution traces from the system under observation are received at the Monitor, which looks for matches with the three different prefixes. If a match is found, the external world is notified for the initiation of suitable handling measures.

4.2 Prefix Generator

We used the LTL2BA tool [15] to generate the Buchi automaton from the input LTL property. The output of the LTL2BA tool was parsed and standardized (annotate each edge with the list of properties instead of short-hand notations) for further processing. Then our tool followed the procedure shown in Sect. 3.2 to generate the finite automata corresponding to the good, bad and ugly prefixes.

4.3 Prefix Translator

Once the prefixes have been determined, the Prefix Translator is used to generate LM-ISA machine code for each of them. In cases where a prefix does not exist, the generated LM-ISA program consists of a single END_WITHOUT_ACCEPTING instruction. We explore two approaches to do this compilation. We continue using the running example from Sect. 3.2 to explain the functioning of the two approaches.

Approach 1 Code Generation via Regular Expressions. The approach is described in Algorithm 1. We first convert the prefix, which is in the form of an automaton, to a regular expression. Considering the prefix described in Fig. 7, the regular expression obtained is $(((((a\bar{b}\bar{c}|\bar{a}b\bar{c})|\bar{a}\bar{b}c)|\bar{a}bc)|\bar{a}\bar{b}\bar{c})|((ab\bar{c}(\bar{a}b\bar{c}|ab\bar{c})*)(a\bar{b}\bar{c}|\bar{a}\bar{b}\bar{c}))) * ((a\bar{b}c|abc)|((ab\bar{c}(\bar{a}b\bar{c}|ab\bar{c})*)(((\bar{a}bc|a\bar{b}c)|\bar{a}bc)|abc)))$.

We employ the popular FAdo tool [3] to perform this conversion. We then employ the CICERO Compiler, which takes as input the regular expression, and generates LM-ISA machine code. The disassembled machine code for the running example is given in Table 2. Here, the execution starts with a single thread at $PC_1 = 0$. The first instruction SPLIT 41 spawns a second thread with $PC_2 = 41$ and increments PC_1 to 1. When a thread's $PC = 3$, the current input character (*cc) is compared with $ab\bar{c}$. In case of a match, the thread continues to the next PC ($PC = 4$), else it dies. A prefix is detected when at least one thread reaches $PC = 9$ which is the ACCEPT_P instruction.

When converting the automaton to the regular expression, the length of the regular expression can be exponential in the worst case in the size of the original automaton. The length of the LM-ISA program is linear in the length of the regular expression.

Approach 2 Direct Code Generation. In Approach 2, we seek to avoid the potentially expensive conversion of the prefix automaton to a regular expression. Instead, we opt to directly generate the LM-ISA machine code from the prefix automaton. The approach is detailed in Algorithm 2. The state traversal begins from the initial state, and all reachable states are visited exactly once. For each

Algorithm 1. Prefix Translator – Approach 1

1: **function** TRANSLATE(Finite Automaton F)
2:     $R = \text{generateRE}(F)$
3:     $I = \text{CICERO\_compiler}(R)$
4:     **return** I
5: **end function**

Table 2. Disassembled LM-ISA machine code corresponding to automaton 7 as generated by Approach 1

[0]	SPLIT 41	[11]	JUMP 9	[22]	JUMP 5	[33]	JUMP 0	[44]	JUMP 0
[1]	SPLIT 36	[12]	SPLIT 18	[23]	SPLIT 29	[34]	MATCH $\overline{a}\overline{b}\overline{c}$	[45]	MATCH $\overline{a}bc$
[2]	SPLIT 34	[13]	SPLIT 16	[24]	SPLIT 27	[35]	JUMP 0	[46]	JUMP 0
[3]	MATCH $ab\overline{c}$	[14]	MATCH $\overline{a}b\overline{c}$	[25]	MATCH $\overline{a}b\overline{c}$	[36]	SPLIT 39	[47]	SPLIT 50
[4]	SPLIT 23	[15]	JUMP 9	[26]	JUMP 23	[37]	MATCH $a\overline{b}\overline{c}$	[48]	MATCH $a\overline{b}c$
[5]	SPLIT 12	[16]	MATCH abc	[27]	MATCH $a\overline{b}c$	[38]	JUMP 0	[49]	JUMP 9
[6]	SPLIT 10	[17]	JUMP 9	[28]	JUMP 23	[39]	MATCH $\overline{a}\overline{b}c$	[50]	MATCH abc
[7]	MATCH $\overline{a}bc$	[18]	SPLIT 21	[29]	SPLIT 32	[40]	JUMP 0	[51]	JUMP 9
[8]	JUMP 9	[19]	MATCH $\overline{a}b\overline{c}$	[30]	MATCH $a\overline{b}c$	[41]	SPLIT 47		
[9]	ACCEPT_P	[20]	JUMP 5	[31]	JUMP 0	[42]	SPLIT 45		
[10]	MATCH $a\overline{b}c$	[21]	MATCH $a\overline{b}\overline{c}$	[32]	MATCH $\overline{a}\overline{b}c$	[43]	MATCH $\overline{a}\overline{b}c$		

Table 3. Disassembled LM-ISA machine code corresponding to automaton 7 as generated by Approach 2

I1_0:		[6]	SPLIT I1_3	S2_0:		[20]	SPLIT S2_3	[27]	NO_MATCH $\overline{a}\overline{b}\overline{c}$
[0]	SPLIT I1_1	[7]	MATCH abc	[14]	SPLIT S2_1	[21]	MATCH $a\overline{b}\overline{c}$	[28]	NO_MATCH $a\overline{b}c$
[1]	MATCH abc	[8]	JUMP F3_0	[15]	MATCH $\overline{a}b\overline{c}$	[22]	JUMP I1_0	[29]	NO_MATCH $\overline{a}\overline{b}c$
[2]	JUMP S2_0	I1_3:		[16]	JUMP S2_0	S2_3:		[30]	MATCH_ANY
I1_1:		[9]	NO_MATCH $a\overline{b}\overline{c}$	S2_1:		[23]	SPLIT S2_4	[31]	JUMP F3_0
[3]	SPLIT I1_2	[10]	NO_MATCH $a\overline{b}\overline{c}$	[17]	SPLIT S2_2	[24]	MATCH $\overline{a}b\overline{c}$	F3_0:	
[4]	MATCH $a\overline{b}\overline{c}$	[11]	NO_MATCH abc	[18]	MATCH $a\overline{b}c$	[25]	JUMP I1_0	[32]	ACCEPT_P
[5]	JUMP F3_0	[12]	MATCH_ANY	[19]	JUMP S2_0	S2_4:			
I1_2:		[13]	JUMP I1_0	S2_2:		[26]	NO_MATCH $a\overline{b}\overline{c}$		

state, the outgoing edges are considered and corresponding LM-ISA instructions are generated. The disassembled machine code for the running example is given in Table 3. Each transition in the prefix automaton is given a label stateID_symbolID (for example, I1_0). A thread is spawned for each outgoing transition of the automaton. The subsequent MATCH instruction in each thread compares the input character and only the matching thread survives, which then transitions to the next state using the JUMP instruction. A sequence of NO_MATCH instructions followed by a MATCH_ANY instruction is used to reduce the number of

Algorithm 2. Prefix Translator – Approach 2

1: insts ← [] ▷ list of LM-ISA instructions
2: q ← null
3: j ← 0
4: **function** TRANSLATE(Finite Automata F)
5:   toVisit ← []
6:   q ← Initial State
7:   **while** $q \neq$ null **do**
8:     visited[q] ← True
9:     **if** q is a Final State **then**
10:       emitAcceptIns()
11:     **else**
12:       outEdges ← prepare(F, q)
13:       j ← 0
14:       **for** i ← 0 to |outEdges| **do**
15:         e ← outEdges[i]
16:         **if** visited[e.dest] is False **then**
17:           **if** [e.dest] $\notin$ toVisit **then**
18:             toVisit.enqueue(e.dest)
19:           **end if**
20:         **end if**
21:         isLastEdge ← ($i ==$ (|outEdges| $- 1$)) ▷ last edge in outEdges
22:         emitEdge(e.dest, e.props_list, isLastEdge)
23:       **end for**
24:     **end if**
25:     q ← toVisit.dequeue()
26:   **end while**
27:   I ← assemble(insts)
28:   **return** I
29: **end function**

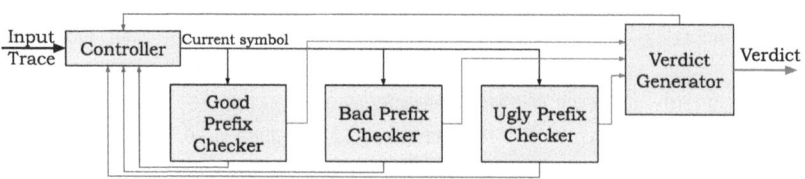

Fig. 10. Design of the faRM-LTL Monitor

threads spawned when the destination state for a majority of transitions is the same. The length of the LM-ISA program generated by Approach 2 is linear in the size of the prefix automaton.

Algorithm 3. Helper functions for Approach 2

```
 1: function PREPARE(F, q)
 2:     edges ← {}                                      ▷ <dest, props_list>
 3:     for all i ∈ Σ do
 4:         d ← F[q][i]
 5:         edges[d].dest = d
 6:         edges[d].props_list.append(i)
 7:     end for
 8:     return edges
 9: end function
10: function EMITACCEPTINS
11:     label ← "q_0"
12:     insts.append("{$label}: ")
13:     insts.append("    ACCEPT_P")
14: end function
15: function EMITEDGE(dest, props, isLastEdge)
16:     if props.len() × 3 > |Σ| − props.len() + 2 then
17:         label ← "q_j"
18:         insts.append("{label}: ")
19:         if not isLastEdge then
20:             j ← j + 1
21:             insts.append("    SPLIT {$q_$j}")
22:         end if
23:         for all p ∈ Σ do
24:             if p ∉ props then
25:                 insts.append("    NO_MATCH {$p}")
26:             end if
27:         end for
28:         insts.append("    MATCH_ANY")
29:         insts.append("    JUMP {$dest}_0")
30:     else
31:         for all p ∈ props do
32:             label ← "q_j"
33:             insts.append("{$label}: ")
34:             if not isLastEdge || p is the not last prop in props then
35:                 j ← j + 1
36:                 insts.append("    SPLIT {$q_$j}")
37:             end if
38:             insts.append("    MATCH {$prop}")
39:             insts.append("    JUMP {$dest}_0")
40:             return
41:         end for
42:     end if
43:     return
44: end function
```

4.4 Monitor

Figure 10 shows the proposed design of the faRM-LTL Monitor. It consists of three CICERO Engines – the Good Prefix Checker, the Bad Prefix Checker, and the Ugly Prefix Checker – each with its own instruction memory. The implementation of the Monitor is largely based around the CICERO Regex coprocessor engine available in the open source [2]. We made minor modifications to the CICERO regex engine such as making the engine accept only one symbol at a time instead of buffering a few symbols. The Monitor instantiates three of these modified CICERO engines. The trace produced by the system under observation is received at the Controller. The Controller forwards each trace symbol to all three Checkers (one symbol at a time). When any one of the Checkers detects a prefix match, it informs the Controller and the Verdict Generator, and the monitoring stops. If it was the Good Prefix Checker (or Bad Prefix Generator) that detected the match, the Verdict Generator issues a `satisfied` (or `refuted`) verdict. If it was the Ugly Prefix Checker that detected the match, the Verdict Generator issues an `inconclusive` verdict. Since the prefixes encountered in practice are not too large, we do not have to support multiple topologies of CICERO engines, and hence we have simplified the controller. We implemented the Monitor in SystemVerilog.

5 Experiments

We evaluate the proposed framework on 53 properties from an earlier work [5]. The details of the properties such as the formula size and its maximum nesting depth, the corresponding sizes of the bad, good and ugly prefix automata and the sizes of the corresponding regular expressions is given in [1]. These properties were compiled on a laptop with an Intel Core i5-10210u (10th generation, mobile CPU) processor and 8 GB RAM. Each property was compiled five times and the average time taken is reported (the variations in the time taken across the five runs was negligible).

Figure 11 shows the sizes of the prefix automata (B_ϕ and $B_{\neg\phi}$ in Sect. 3.2) for each property, as well as the number of instructions in the corresponding LM-ISA programs produced by the two approaches. For the size of the automata, we report the sum of the number of states and the number of transitions as done in [5]. If a property does not have a good (bad) prefix, then the bars corresponding to the good (bad) prefix monitor automaton and good (bad) prefix monitor programs are not shown in the figure. We observe that as expected, with increasing size of the prefix automaton, the sizes of the LM-ISA programs increase. We also observe that Approach 2 generates fewer or equal number of instructions as compared to Approach 1 in 48 (out of 53) cases. Moreover, even in cases where the number of instructions generated by Approach 2 is higher, it is higher only by a maximum of 2 instructions (as seen in the case of P41). This indicates there are some inefficiencies introduced by the heuristics used for eliminating states when generating the regular expression from the finite automaton (under Approach 1), which is avoided by Approach 2. Finally, the

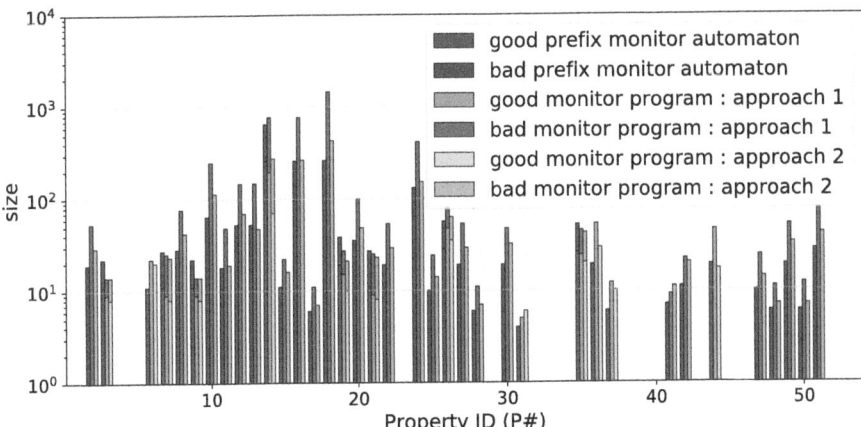

Fig. 11. Sizes of prefix monitor automata and corresponding LM-ISA programs produced using the two approaches

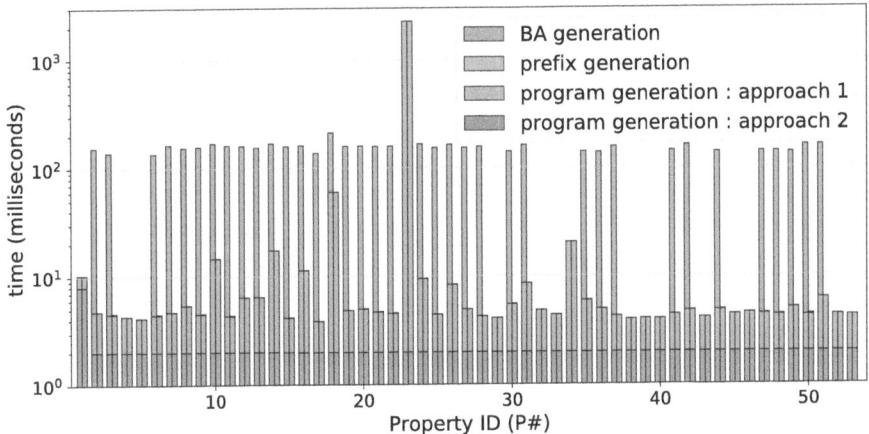

Fig. 12. Breakup of the time taken for compilation

total number of LM-ISA instructions generated per monitorable LTL property by Approach 2 is only 55.03 instructions on average and a maximum of 428 instructions (as seen in the case of P18).

Figure 12 shows the breakup of the time taken by the different stages of the faRM-LTL Compiler. For non-monitorable properties, the program generation bars are not shown. The time taken for program generation using Approach 2 is so small (< 1 ms) in terms of the scale of the graph that the corresponding bars are not clearly visible. We observe that Approach 2 is faster than Approach 1 by 96.1% on average (geomean; considering only monitorable properties). This saving is because we avoid generating regular expression from the finite automaton. We also observe that Approach 2 is faster than Approach 1 in all the cases evaluated. Approach 2 takes 7.46 ms on average to compile an LTL property, and a maximum of 60.02 ms (as seen in the case of P18).

5.1 Weakly Monitorable Properties

Weakly monitorable properties are those properties that have an ugly prefix but not all of its prefixes are ugly [30]. Therefore, it is still possible to get a verdict for such properties by observing a finite-length trace.

Table 4. Instruction counts for weakly monitorable properties (using Approach 2)

Property	ugly	bad	good	Compile time (ms)
$((a\|\|\square \diamond b)$ && $\mathcal{X}b)$	7	5	7	8.51
$((a\|\|\square \diamond a)$ && $\mathcal{X}b)$	7	5	7	7.98
$\square \diamond a$ && $\mathcal{X}b$	5	5	1	5.54
$\square \diamond a \|\| \mathcal{X}b$	5	1	5	5.63

Table 4 shows the number of LM-ISA instructions generated using Approach 2 for ugly, bad and good prefixes corresponding to the weakly monitorable properties mentioned in [30]. We note that the number of instructions corresponding to the ugly prefixes and the time taken to compile them are small. The corresponding numbers using Approach 1 follow similar trends as discussed above.

5.2 Area Overhead

We used the Cadence Genus tool with the freepdk 45nm standard cell library to synthesize the faRM-LTL Monitor. Each of the Prefix Checkers have an internal instruction memory that can store 1024 instructions (each instruction is 32 bits). This is well-provisioned to handle complex LTL properties.

We observed that the Monitor occupies an area of 2.04 mm^2 (0.5% of a typical 400 mm^2 processor die), and hence is small enough to embed into the same die. We also observe that the critical path of the Monitor remains unchanged (1300 ns) as compared to the original CICERO engine.

6 Conclusions

We proposed an RV framework for runtime monitoring of LTL properties of complex and high-performance systems. The proposed framework automatically compiles the input properties into a corresponding sequence of LM-ISA instructions. These LM-ISA instructions are then executed on a hardware monitor to verify properties. Since the hardware design of the runtime monitor does not change with changes in the input properties, the runtime monitor is amenable to be implemented alongside processor cores. Our experiments on 53 different LTL properties show that the time taken to compile these LTL properties is only 7.46 ms on average, and the hardware monitor occupies only around 2 mm^2 when synthesized using the ASIC flow.

References

1. An Appendix to faRM-LTL: A Domain-Specific Architecture for Flexible and Accelerated Runtime Monitoring of LTL Properties. https://unarthal.gitlab.io/assets/pdfs/characterization.pdf
2. Cicero regex coprocessor. https://github.com/DanieleParravicini/regex_coprocessor
3. Almeida, A., Almeida, M., Alves, J., Moreira, N., Reis, R.: FAdo and GUItar: tools for automata manipulation and visualization. In: Maneth, S. (ed.) CIAA 2009. LNCS, vol. 5642, pp. 65–74. Springer, Heidelberg (2009). https://doi.org/10.1007/978-3-642-02979-0_10
4. Backasch, R., Hochberger, C., Weiss, A., Leucker, M., Lasslop, R.: Runtime verification for multicore SOC with high-quality trace data. ACM Trans. Des. Autom. Electron. Syst. **18**(2) (2013). https://doi.org/10.1145/2442087.2442089
5. Bauer, A., Leucker, M., Schallhart, C.: Runtime verification for LTL and TLTL. ACM Trans. Softw. Eng. Methodol. (TOSEM) **20**(4), 1–64 (2011)
6. Boulé, M., Zilic, Z.: Automata-based assertion-checker synthesis of PSL properties. ACM Trans. Des. Autom. Electron. Syst. **13**(1) (2008). https://doi.org/10.1145/1297666.1297670
7. Convent, L., Hungerecker, S., Scheffel, T., Schmitz, M., Thoma, D., Weiss, A.: Hardware-based runtime verification with embedded tracing units and stream processing. In: Colombo, C., Leucker, M. (eds.) RV 2018. LNCS, vol. 11237, pp. 43–63. Springer, Cham (2018). https://doi.org/10.1007/978-3-030-03769-7_5
8. Cox, R.: Regular expression matching: the virtual machine approach (2009). http://swtch.com/rsc/regexp/regexp2.html
9. Decker, N., et al.: Rapidly adjustable non-intrusive online monitoring for multi-core systems. In: Cavalheiro, S., Fiadeiro, J. (eds.) SBMF 2017. LNCS, vol. 10623, pp. 179–196. Springer, Cham (2017). https://doi.org/10.1007/978-3-319-70848-5_12
10. Delahaye, M., Kosmatov, N., Signoles, J.: Common specification language for static and dynamic analysis of c programs. In: Proceedings of the 28th Annual ACM Symposium on Applied Computing, pp. 1230–1235 (2013)
11. Dixit, H.D., Boyle, L., Vunnam, G., Pendharkar, S., Beadon, M., Sankar, S.: Detecting silent data corruptions in the wild. arXiv preprint arXiv:2203.08989 (2022)
12. Dixit, H.D., et al.: Silent data corruptions at scale. arXiv preprint arXiv:2102.11245 (2021)
13. Dlugosch, P., Brown, D., Glendenning, P., Leventhal, M., Noyes, H.: An efficient and scalable semiconductor architecture for parallel automata processing. IEEE Trans. Parallel Distrib. Syst. **25**(12), 3088–3098 (2014). https://doi.org/10.1109/TPDS.2014.8
14. Drusinsky, D.: The temporal rover and the ATG rover. In: Havelund, K., Penix, J., Visser, W. (eds.) SPIN 2000. LNCS, vol. 1885, pp. 323–330. Springer, Heidelberg (2000). https://doi.org/10.1007/10722468_19
15. Gastin, P., Oddoux, D.: Fast LTL to Büchi automata translation. In: Berry, G., Comon, H., Finkel, A. (eds.) CAV 2001. LNCS, vol. 2102, pp. 53–65. Springer, Heidelberg (2001). https://doi.org/10.1007/3-540-44585-4_6

16. Geist, J., Rozier, K.Y., Schumann, J.: Runtime observer pairs and Bayesian network reasoners on-board FPGAs: flight-certifiable system health management for embedded systems. In: Bonakdarpour, B., Smolka, S.A. (eds.) RV 2014. LNCS, vol. 8734, pp. 215–230. Springer, Cham (2014). https://doi.org/10.1007/978-3-319-11164-3_18
17. Havelund, K., Roşu, G.: Monitoring java programs with java PathExplorer. Electr. Notes Theor. Comput. Sci. **55**(2), 200–217 (2001)
18. Havelund, K., Rosu, G., Clancy, D.: Java PathExplorer: a runtime verification tool. In: International Space Conference (2001)
19. Hochschild, P.H., et al.: Cores that don't count. In: Proceedings of the Workshop on Hot Topics in Operating Systems, pp. 9–16 (2021)
20. Huang, Y., Chen, Z., Li, D., Yang, K.: CAMA: energy and memory efficient automata processing in content-addressable memories. In: 2022 IEEE International Symposium on High-Performance Computer Architecture (HPCA), pp. 25–37 (2022). https://doi.org/10.1109/HPCA53966.2022.00011
21. Jin, D., Meredith, P.O., Lee, C., Roşu, G.: JavaMOP: efficient parametric runtime monitoring framework. In: 2012 34th International Conference on Software Engineering (ICSE), pp. 1427–1430. IEEE (2012)
22. Jindal, N., et al.: Dhoom: reusing design-for-debug hardware for online monitoring. In: Proceedings of the 56th Annual Design Automation Conference 2019, pp. 1–6 (2019)
23. Kiczales, G., Hilsdale, E., Hugunin, J., Kersten, M., Palm, J., Griswold, W.G.: An overview of AspectJ. In: Knudsen, J.L. (ed.) ECOOP 2001. LNCS, vol. 2072, pp. 327–354. Springer, Heidelberg (2001). https://doi.org/10.1007/3-540-45337-7_18
24. Kong, L., et al.: Software-hardware codesign for efficient in-memory regular pattern matching. In: Proceedings of the 43rd ACM SIGPLAN International Conference on Programming Language Design and Implementation, pp. 733–748. PLDI 2022, Association for Computing Machinery, New York, NY, USA (2022). https://doi.org/10.1145/3519939.3523456
25. Kosmatov, N., Signoles, J.: A lesson on runtime assertion checking with Frama-C. In: Legay, A., Bensalem, S. (eds.) RV 2013. LNCS, vol. 8174, pp. 386–399. Springer, Heidelberg (2013). https://doi.org/10.1007/978-3-642-40787-1_29
26. Kupferman, O., Vardi, M.Y.: Model checking of safety properties. Formal Meth. Syst. Des. **19**, 291–314 (2001)
27. Liu, H., Ibrahim, M., Kayiran, O., Pai, S., Jog, A.: Architectural support for efficient large-scale automata processing. In: 2018 51st Annual IEEE/ACM International Symposium on Microarchitecture (MICRO), pp. 908–920 (2018). https://doi.org/10.1109/MICRO.2018.00078
28. Mijat, R.: Better trace for better software: introducing the new arm coresight system trace macrocell and trace memory controller. ARM, White Paper (2010)
29. Parravicini, D., Conficconi, D., Sozzo, E.D., Pilato, C., Santambrogio, M.D.: Cicero: a domain-specific architecture for efficient regular expression matching. ACM Trans. Embedd. Comput. Syst. (TECS) **20**(5s), 1–24 (2021)
30. Peled, D., Havelund, K.: Refining the safety–liveness classification of temporal properties according to monitorability. In: Margaria, T., Graf, S., Larsen, K.G. (eds.) Models, Mindsets, Meta: The What, the How, and the Why Not? LNCS, vol. 11200, pp. 218–234. Springer, Cham (2019). https://doi.org/10.1007/978-3-030-22348-9_14
31. Reinbacher, T., Függer, M., Brauer, J.: Runtime verification of embedded real-time systems. Formal Meth. Syst. Des. **44**, 203–239 (2014)

32. Reinbacher, T., Rozier, K.Y., Schumann, J.: Temporal-logic based runtime observer pairs for system health management of real-time systems. In: Ábrahám, E., Havelund, K. (eds.) TACAS 2014. LNCS, vol. 8413, pp. 357–372. Springer, Heidelberg (2014). https://doi.org/10.1007/978-3-642-54862-8_24
33. Sadredini, E., Rahimi, R., Lenjani, M., Stan, M., Skadron, K.: Impala: algorithm/architecture co-design for in-memory multi-stride pattern matching. In: 2020 IEEE International Symposium on High Performance Computer Architecture (HPCA), pp. 86–98 (2020). https://doi.org/10.1109/HPCA47549.2020.00017
34. Sadredini, E., Rahimi, R., Verma, V., Stan, M., Skadron, K.: eAP: a scalable and efficient in-memory accelerator for automata processing. In: Proceedings of the 52nd Annual IEEE/ACM International Symposium on Microarchitecture, pp. 87–99. MICRO '52, Association for Computing Machinery, New York, NY, USA (2019). https://doi.org/10.1145/3352460.3358324
35. Schumann, J., Moosbrugger, P., Rozier, K.Y.: R2U2: monitoring and diagnosis of security threats for unmanned aerial systems. In: Bartocci, E., Majumdar, R. (eds.) RV 2015. LNCS, vol. 9333, pp. 233–249. Springer, Cham (2015). https://doi.org/10.1007/978-3-319-23820-3_15
36. Signoles, J., Kosmatov, N., Vorobyov, K.: E-ACSL, a runtime verification tool for safety and security of C programs (tool paper). In: RV-CuBES, pp. 164–173 (2017)
37. Solet, D., Béchennec, J.L., Briday, M., Faucou, S., Pillement, S.: Hardware runtime verification of embedded software in SoPC. In: 2016 11th IEEE Symposium on Industrial Embedded Systems (SIES), pp. 1–6. IEEE (2016)
38. Solet, D., Béchennec, J.L., Briday, M., Faucou, S., Pillement, S.: Hardware runtime verification of embedded software in SoPC. In: 2016 11th IEEE Symposium on Industrial Embedded Systems (SIES), pp. 1–6 (2016). https://doi.org/10.1109/SIES.2016.7509425
39. Spinczyk, O., Lohmann, D.: The design and implementation of AspectC++. Knowl.-Based Syst. **20**(7), 636–651 (2007)
40. Spinczyk, O., Lohmann, D., Urban, M.: AspectC++: an AOP extension for C++. Softw. Dev. J. **5**(68–76) (2005)
41. Thompson, K.: Programming techniques: regular expression search algorithm. Commun. ACM **11**(6), 419–422 (1968)
42. Wang, S., Zhang, G., Wei, J., Wang, Y., Wu, J., Luo, Q.: Understanding silent data corruptions in a large production CPU population. In: Proceedings of the 29th Symposium on Operating Systems Principles, pp. 216–230 (2023)
43. Wen, Z., Kong, L., Le Glaunec, A., Mamouras, K., Yang, K.: BVAP: energy and memory efficient automata processing for regular expressions with bounded repetitions. In: Proceedings of the 29th ACM International Conference on Architectural Support for Programming Languages and Operating Systems, Volume 2, pp. 151–166. ASPLOS 2024, Association for Computing Machinery, New York, NY, USA (2024). https://doi.org/10.1145/3620665.3640412
44. Zhou, W., Hu, F., Ma, J.: Improving flexibility in embedded system runtime verification with python. In: 2022 IEEE International Symposium on Software Reliability Engineering Workshops (ISSREW), pp. 281–282. IEEE (2022)

Efficient Offline Monitoring for Dynamic Metric Temporal Logic

Konstantinos Mamouras(✉)

Rice University, Houston, TX 77005, USA
mamouras@rice.edu

Abstract. We propose an efficient offline monitoring algorithm for properties written in DMTL (Dynamic Metric Temporal Logic), a temporal formalism that combines MTL (Metric Temporal Logic) with regular expressions. Our algorithm has worst-case running time that is polynomial in the size of the temporal specification and linear in the length of the input trace. In particular, our monitoring algorithm needs time $O(m^3 \cdot n)$, where m is the size of the DMTL formula and n in the length of the input trace.

Keywords: offline monitoring · metric temporal logic · regular expressions · dynamic logic · nondeterministic automata

1 Introduction

Monitoring is a lightweight verification technique for checking at runtime that a program or system behaves as desired. It has proved to be effective for evaluating the correctness of the behavior of complex systems, where static verification is computationally intractable. This includes cyber-physical systems (CPSs) that consist of both computational and physical processes. A *monitor* is a program that observes the execution trace of the system and emits values that indicate events of interest or other actionable information.

It is common to specify monitors using special-purpose formalisms such as variants of temporal logic [65], regular expressions [45], and other domain-specific programming languages [13]. In the context of cyber-physical systems, logics that are interpreted over signals are frequently used. This includes Metric Temporal Logic (MTL) [47] and Signal Temporal Logic (STL) [51].

Linear Temporal Logic (LTL) [65] cannot express all regular properties and is therefore expressively weaker than regular expressions. MTL inherits this lack of expressiveness. Several extensions of LTL have been considered in order to make it expressively complete for the class of regular properties [21,77].

We focus here on properties that are interpreted over discrete-time signals and are specified using an extension of MTL with regular expressions. We call this formalism **Dynamic Metric Temporal Logic** or DMTL. Its syntax is based on the dynamic modalities of Dynamic Logic [67] and it is similar to LDL (Linear Dynamic Logic) [21]. DMTL provides the dynamic temporal connectives $\langle r_I$ (past diamond) and $|r\rangle_I$ (future diamond), where r is a regular expression and I is an interval that specifies the domain of temporal quantification.

Main Contribution. We propose a novel algorithm for the efficient offline monitoring of DMTL (Theorem 5) with unrestricted past-time and future-time dynamic temporal connectives. Our algorithm goes beyond existing algorithms by considering a more expressive specification language that fuses metric temporal logic and regular expressions. Efficient monitoring algorithms for MTL have been considered before [41,71] (as well as in the setting of quantitative semantics [56]), but the fusion of MTL with regular expressions poses challenges that cannot be addressed by prior approaches. Monitoring for MDL (Metric Dynamic Logic, which is essentially the same formalism as what we call DMTL here) has been considered in [14,68]. These works propose algorithms whose time complexity is at least exponential in the size of the temporal specification.

In order to obtain our monitoring algorithm, we devise specialized data structures and algorithms for dealing with the dynamic temporal connectives $\langle r_I$ and $|r\rangle_I$. These algorithms are expressed using the NFA for an appropriate abstraction of the regular expression r. The main challenge is dealing with the intervals I, which are succinctly represented in binary notation. The key feature of our algorithm is that it needs time-per-item that is polynomial in the size of the specification φ (in fact, $O(|\varphi|^3)$) and constant in the size of the input signal. Each past-time (resp., future-time) dynamic temporal connective is handled with a left-to-right (resp., right-to-left) pass over the trace.

2 Dynamic Metric Temporal Logic

We start this section by presenting the syntax of DMTL (Dynamic Metric Temporal Logic), a logical formalism that fuses metric temporal logic and regular expressions. The syntax that we use is based on LDL (Linear Dynamic Logic) [21] with the time interval annotations of MTL (Metric Temporal Logic) [47]. We interpret DMTL over discrete signals that can be either finite or infinite. In the case of finite signals we use a truncated semantics, in the spirit of [30]. We consider a qualitative (Boolean) semantics (Definition 4), which is given in terms of the satisfaction relation $\models$.

For integers $i, j \in \mathbb{Z}$ we define the intervals $[i, j] = \{n \in \mathbb{Z} \mid i \leq n \leq j\}$ and $[i, \infty) = \{n \in \mathbb{Z} \mid i \leq n\}$. For a set I of integers and $n \in \mathbb{Z}$, define $n + I = \{n + i \mid i \in I\}$ and $n - I = \{n - i \mid i \in I\}$.

For an alphabet D, we write D^* for the set of all finite strings over D. We denote by ε the empty string. For subsets of strings $A, B \subseteq D^*$, we define $A \cdot B = \{uv \mid u \in A \text{ and } v \in B\}$. We also define the *n-fold concatenation* A^n as follows: $A^0 = \{\varepsilon\}$ and $A^{n+1} = A^n \cdot A$.

The two-element set of Boolean values is $\mathbb{B} = \{0, 1\}$. Given a set A, a function $p : A \to \mathbb{B}$ represents a subset of A.

Definition 1 (Regular Expressions). Regular expressions $\mathsf{RExp}(D)$ are given by the following grammar:

$$r, r_1, r_2 ::= \varepsilon \mid p \mid r_1 + r_2 \mid r_1 \cdot r_2 \mid r^*,$$

where $p: D \to \mathbb{B}$ is an atomic predicate. Every regular expression r is interpreted as a subset $\mathcal{L}(r) \subseteq D^*$ as follows:

$$\mathcal{L}(\varepsilon) = \{\varepsilon\} \qquad \mathcal{L}(r_1 + r_2) = \mathcal{L}(r_1) \cup \mathcal{L}(r_2) \qquad \mathcal{L}(r^*) = \bigcup_{n \geq 0} \mathcal{L}(r)^n$$
$$\mathcal{L}(p) = \{u \in D \mid p(u) = 1\} \qquad \mathcal{L}(r_1 \cdot r_2) = \mathcal{L}(r_1) \cdot \mathcal{L}(r_2)$$

We say that r *denotes* the language $\mathcal{L}(r)$.

The set $\mathsf{Mat}(m, n, A)$ consists of all matrices with m rows and n columns whose entries are elements of the set A. So, $\mathsf{Mat}(1, n)$ consists of row vectors of size n. Similarly, $\mathsf{Mat}(m, 1)$ consists of column vectors of size m. When no confusion arises, we sometimes identify $\mathsf{Mat}(1, 1, A)$ with A. For a matrix $M : \mathsf{Mat}(m, n, A)$ and integer indexes i and j with $0 \leq i < m$ and $0 \leq j < n$, we write $M(i, j) : A$ for the entry of M at the i-th row and j-th column. We write $\mathsf{Mat}(m, n)$ as abbreviation for $\mathsf{Mat}(m, n, \mathbb{B})$. That is, $\mathsf{Mat}(m, n)$ is the set of Boolean matrices with m rows and n columns.

Definition 2. A *nondeterministic finite automaton* (NFA) over D is a tuple $\mathcal{A} = (Q, \mathsf{init}, \Delta, \mathsf{fin})$, where Q is a finite set of n states, $\mathsf{init} : \mathsf{Mat}(1, n)$ is the initialization (row) vector, $\Delta : \mathsf{Mat}(n, n, D \to \mathbb{B})$ is the *transition matrix*, and $\mathsf{fin} : \mathsf{Mat}(n, 1)$ is the finalization (column) vector. The automaton $\mathcal{A}$ denotes a function $[\![\mathcal{A}]\!] : D^* \to \mathbb{B}$, given as follows:

$$[\![\mathcal{A}]\!](a_1 a_2 \ldots a_n) = \mathsf{init} \cdot \Delta[a_1] \cdot \Delta[a_2] \cdots \Delta[a_n] \cdot \mathsf{fin},$$

where $\Delta[a] : \mathsf{Mat}(n, n)$ and $\Delta[a](i, j) = \Delta(i, j)(a)$ for all indexes i, j.

Every regular expression r can be converted into an equivalent nondeterministic automaton $\mathcal{A}_r$ with $|r|$ states, which means that $[\![\mathcal{A}_r]\!]$ is the characteristic function of the language $\mathcal{L}(r) \subseteq D^*$. That is, for every $u \in D^*$, we have that: $[\![\mathcal{A}_r]\!] = 1$ iff $u \in \mathcal{L}(r)$. We will be using this fact freely in Sect. 3 to describe the monitoring algorithm for DMTL.

We will consider a temporal formalism interpreted over *traces* that are finite or infinite sequences of *data items* from a set D. We write D^* (resp., D^+) for the set of all finite (resp., non-empty finite) sequences over D, and $D^\omega = \omega \to D$ for the set of all infinite sequences over D, where ω is the first infinite ordinal (i.e., the set of natural numbers). We also define $D^\infty = D^* \cup D^\omega$. We write ε for the empty sequence and $|u|$ for the length of a trace, where $|u| = \omega$ if u is infinite. A finite sequence $u \in D^*$ can be viewed as a function from $[0, |u| - 1]$ to D, that is, $u = u(0)u(1) \ldots u(|u| - 1)$.

Definition 3 (Syntax). Let D be a set of data items. The set $\mathsf{DMTL}(D)$ of *temporal formulas* is built from atomic predicates $p : D \to \mathbb{B}$ using the Boolean connectives $\neg$ and $\vee$, and the unary dynamic temporal connectives $\langle r \rangle_I$ and $|r\rangle_I$, where r is a regular expression and I is an interval of the form $[a, b]$ or $[a, \infty)$ with $0 \leq a \leq b < \omega$. More precisely, the formulas and regular expressions of DMTL are defined by mutual induction according to the following grammar:

$$u, [i,j] \models \varepsilon \iff i = j$$
$$u, [i,j] \models \varphi? \iff j = i+1 \text{ and } u, i \models \varphi$$
$$u, [i,j] \models r_1 + r_2 \iff u, [i,j] \models r_1 \text{ or } u, [i,j] \models r_2$$
$$u, [i,j] \models r_1 \cdot r_2 \iff u, [i,k] \models r_1 \text{ and } u, [k,j] \models r_2 \text{ for some } k \text{ with } i \leq k \leq j$$
$$u, [i,j] \models r^* \iff i = j \text{ or there is a decomposition } \mathcal{S} \text{ of } [i,j] \text{ such that}$$
$$\qquad u, [k,\ell] \models r \text{ for every interval } [k,\ell] \text{ in } \mathcal{S}$$

$$u, i \models p \iff p(u(i)) = 1$$
$$u, i \models \neg \varphi \iff u, i \not\models \varphi$$
$$u, i \models \varphi_1 \vee \varphi_2 \iff u, i \models \varphi_1 \text{ or } u, i \models \varphi_2$$
$$u, i \models |r\rangle_I \varphi \iff \text{there is } j < |u| \text{ with } j \in i + I \text{ s.t. } u, [i,j] \models r \text{ and } u, j \models \varphi$$
$$u, i \models \varphi \langle r|_I \iff \text{there is } j \geq 0 \text{ with } j \in i - I \text{ such that}$$
$$\qquad u, j \models \varphi \text{ and } u, [j+1, i+1] \models r$$

Fig. 1. Boolean semantics for DMTL.

$$\varphi, \varphi_1, \varphi_2 ::= p \mid \neg \varphi \mid \varphi_1 \vee \varphi_2 \mid \varphi\langle r_I \mid |r\rangle_I \varphi \qquad \text{[formulas]}$$
$$r, r_1, r_2 ::= \varepsilon \mid \varphi? \mid r_1 + r_2 \mid r_1 \cdot r_2 \mid r^* \qquad \text{[regular expressions]}$$

We write DMTL(D) and DRExp(D) for the set of formulas and regular expressions respectively that the grammar above defines.

For a temporal connective $X \in \{\langle r|, |r\rangle\}$, we write X_a as an abbreviation for $X_{[a,a]}$ and X as an abbreviation for $X_{[0,\infty)}$. The usual temporal connectives P (sometime in the past), S (since), F (sometime in the future) and U (until) can be considered as the following abbreviations:

$$\mathsf{P}_I \varphi = \varphi \langle \top^*|_I \qquad \mathsf{F}_I \varphi = |\top^*\rangle_I \varphi \qquad \varphi \mathsf{S}_I \psi = \psi \langle (\varphi?)^*|_I \qquad \varphi \mathsf{U}_I \psi = |(\varphi?)^*\rangle_I \psi$$

where $\top : D \to \mathbb{B}$ is the predicate that always returns 1, i.e., $\top(u) = 1$ for every $u \in D$. Conjunction $\wedge$ can be defined in terms of $\neg$ and $\vee$. The duals $|r]_I$ and $[r|_I$ of $|r\rangle_I$ and $\langle r|_I$ respectively can also be seen as abbreviations: $|r]_I \varphi = \neg |r\rangle_I \neg \varphi$ and $\varphi[r|_I = \neg((\neg \varphi)\langle r|_I)$.

A *decomposition* of an interval $[i,j]$ (where $i \leq j$) is a nonempty finite sequence of intervals $[i_1, j_1], [i_2, j_2], \ldots, [i_n, j_n]$ with $i_1 = i$, $j_n = j$, and $j_k = i_{k+1}$ for every $k = 1, 2, \ldots, n - 1$.

For a trace u and an interval $[i,j]$ with $0 \leq i \leq j \leq |u|$, we write $u[i..j] = u(i)u(i+1)\ldots u(j-1)$ for the substring of u at location $[i,j]$. In particular, we have that $u[i..i] = \varepsilon$ and $u[i..i+1] = u(i)$.

Definition 4 (Boolean Semantics). We interpret the formulas in DMTL(D) over traces from D^∞ and at specific time points. The regular expressions of DMTL are interpreted over time intervals. The Boolean semantics involves two *satisfaction relations*, which are defined in Fig. 1.

– For a regular expression r, a trace $u \in D^\infty$ and two positions $0 \leq i \leq j \leq |u|$, we write $u, [i,j] \models r$ when r is true in u at the interval $[i,j]$.

$$\rho(\varepsilon, u, [i,j]) = \begin{cases} 1, & \text{if } i = j \\ 0, & \text{otherwise} \end{cases}$$

$$\rho(\varphi?, u, [i,j]) = \begin{cases} \rho(\varphi, u, i), & \text{if } j = i+1 \\ 0, & \text{otherwise} \end{cases}$$

$$\rho(r_1 + r_2, u, [i,j]) = \rho(r_1, u, [i,j]) \sqcup \rho(r_2, u, [i,j])$$

$$\rho(r_1 \cdot r_2, u, [i,j]) = \bigsqcup_{i \le k \le j} \Big(\rho(r_1, u, [i,k]) \sqcap \rho(r_2, u, [k,j]) \Big)$$

$$\rho(r^*, u, [i,j]) = \bigsqcup_{i \le k_1 \le \cdots \le k_n \le j} \Big(\rho(r, u, [i,k_1]) \sqcap \rho(r, u, [k_1,k_2]) \sqcap \cdots \sqcap \rho(r, u, [k_n,j]) \Big)$$

$$\rho(p, u, i) = p(u(i))$$
$$\rho(\neg \varphi, u, i) = \neg \rho(\varphi, u, i)$$
$$\rho(\varphi \lor \psi, u, i) = \rho(\varphi, u, i) \sqcup \rho(\psi, u, i)$$
$$\rho(\langle r \rangle_I \varphi, u, i) = \bigsqcup_{j \in i+I, \, j < |u|} \Big(\rho(r, u, [i,j]) \sqcap \rho(\varphi, u, j) \Big)$$
$$\rho(\varphi \langle r|_I, u, i) = \bigsqcup_{j \in i-I, \, j \ge 0} \Big(\rho(\varphi, u, j) \sqcap \rho(r, u, [j+1, i+1]) \Big)$$

Fig. 2. Some properties of the interpretation function for DMTL.

- For a formula $\varphi \in \mathsf{DMTL}(D)$, a trace $u \in D^\infty$ and a position $0 \le i < |u|$, we write $u, i \models \varphi$ when φ is true in u at position i.

We define the *(formula) interpretation function* $\rho : \mathsf{DMTL}(D) \times D^\infty \times \omega \to \mathbb{B}$, where $\rho(\varphi, u, i)$ is defined when $0 \le i < |u|$, as follows:

$$\rho(\varphi, u, i) = 1, \text{ if } u, i \models \varphi \qquad \rho(\varphi, u, i) = 0, \text{ if } u, i \not\models \varphi$$

For a formula φ and a trace $u \in D^\infty$, then we write $\rho(\varphi, u)$ to denote the trace v with $|v| = |u|$ given by $v(i) = \rho(\varphi, u, i)$ for every $0 \le i < |u|$. Similarly, we define the *(regular expression) interpretation function* $\rho : \mathsf{DRExp}(D) \times D^\infty \times (\mathbb{N} \times \mathbb{N}) \to \mathbb{B}$, where $\rho(r, u, [i,j])$ is defined when $0 \le i \le j \le |u|$, as follows:

$$\rho(\varphi, u, [i,j]) = 1, \text{ if } u, [i,j] \models r \qquad \rho(\varphi, u, [i,j]) = 0, \text{ if } u, [i,j] \not\models r$$

Notice that $u, i \models \varphi$ iff $u, [i, i+1] \models \varphi?$. Another way to describe this property is as follows: $\rho(\varphi, u, i) = \rho(\varphi?, u, [i, i+1])$.

The set $\mathbb{B} = \{0, 1\}$ of Boolean values is a lattice. We write $\sqcap$ for the meet operation (i.e., conjunction) and $\sqcup$ for the join operation (i.e., disjunction).

Figure 2 shows some properties that the interpretation function of Definition 4 satisfies. These properties are an immediate consequence of the definition of the satisfaction relation $\models$ from Fig. 1.

From DMTL to Regular Expression Matching. Let $r \in \mathsf{DRExp}(D)$ be a regular expression of DMTL. The expression r may contain subexpressions of the form $\varphi?$, where φ is a temporal formula. Let $\varphi_0, \varphi_1, \ldots, \varphi_{K-1}$ be an enumeration of the maximal subexpressions of the form $\varphi?$ that r contains. We will see now how to reduce the interpretation of $\varphi_K \langle r$ to the interpretation of a pure regular expression.

Define $\varphi_K \langle r$ and $r' = \pi_K \cdot r[\pi_i/\varphi_i?]$, where $r[\pi_i/\varphi_i?]$ results from r by replacing each $\varphi_i?$ by π_i. Each $\pi_i : \mathbb{B}^{K+1} \to \mathbb{B}$ is the i-th projection function. We call r' the *abstraction* of the formula $\varphi_K \langle r$.

This abstraction operation is similar to the "oracle-projection" operation used in [55] to deal with regular expressions that contain lookaround assertions.

Let $u \in D^*$ be a finite trace and i be a time instance with $0 \leq i < |u|$. The main observation is that $u, i \models \varphi_K \langle r$ iff $\tau[0..i+1] \in \mathcal{L}(r')$, where $\tau = \rho(\varphi_0, u) \times \cdots \times \rho(\varphi_{K-1}, u) \times \rho(\varphi_K, u)$.

3 Efficient Monitoring

Given a temporal property φ and a trace u, the *monitoring problem* asks to compute $\rho(\varphi, u)$ (see Definition 4). In other words, the output of monitoring is a tape $v : \mathbb{B}^*$ with length $|v| = |u|$ so that $v(i) = \rho(\varphi, u, i)$ for every $0 \leq i < |u|$.

DMTL monitoring can be reduced to a small set of computational primitives. In order to efficiently monitor formulas that involve the temporal connectives $\langle r_I$ and $|r \rangle_I$, we provide specialized algorithms that are presented later in Fig. 3, Fig. 4, Fig. 5, and Fig. 6. The base expressions in each r are of the form $\varphi?$, where φ is a temporal formula.

The temporal connective $\langle r_I$ is handled with a left-to-right pass over the input trace. For the formula $\varphi_K \langle r_I$, let $\varphi_0?, \varphi_1? \ldots, \varphi_{K-1}?$ be an enumeration of the maximal temporal subexpressions $\varphi_i?$ that appear in r. Evaluating the formula $\varphi_K \langle r_I$ over a trace $u \in D^\infty$ is the same as evaluating the formula $(\varphi_K \langle r_I)[\pi_i/\varphi_i]$ that results from $\varphi_K \langle r_I$ by replacing each φ_i by π_i, over

$$\tau = \rho(\varphi_0, u) \times \rho(\varphi_1, u) \times \cdots \times \rho(\varphi_{K-1}, u) \times \rho(\varphi_K, u) : (\mathbb{B}^{K+1})^*.$$

We write $\pi_i : A_0 \times A_1 \times \cdots \times A_K \to A_i$ for the i-th projection. So, the monitoring of $\varphi_K \langle r_I$ can be performed in two stages: (1) monitoring each of the $\varphi_0, \varphi_1, \ldots, \varphi_{K-1}, \varphi_K$ formulas, and (2) propagating the output signals from the first stage into a monitor for the formula $\pi_K \langle r[\pi_i/\varphi_i]_I$. Notice that $r[\pi_i/\varphi_i]$ is a pure regular expression, that is, there is no nesting of regular and temporal operators.

The key observation from the previous paragraph is that the original formula $\varphi_K \langle r_I$ is true in u (original trace) at time instant i iff the rewritten formula $\pi_K \langle r[\pi_i/\varphi_i]_I$ is true in the trace τ (output tapes from maximal temporal subformulas) at time instant i. In turn, this is equivalent to the pure regular expression $r' = \pi_K \cdot r[\pi_i/\varphi_i?]$ matching over the appropriate interval (determined by I).

The temporal connective $|r \rangle_I$ is handled with a right-to-left pass over the input trace. The computation is completely symmetric to the past-time case, so we omit the discussion.

```
// D = B^{K+1} is the type of input data items
// n = # states of the automaton A = (Q, init, Δ, fin) : NFA(D) for p·r
```
$\mathrm{Mat}(1,n)$ $vec \leftarrow \mathbb{0}_{\mathsf{Mat}(1,n)}$ // row vector for automaton configuration
```
// Invariant for the configuration row vector vec:
// Suppose that the input history is [x_0, x_1, ..., x_{N-1}] ∈ D*.
// Then,  vec = ⊔_{i=0}^{N-1}(init · Δ[x_i] · Δ[x_{i+1}] ··· Δ[x_{N-1}]).
```
Function $\mathrm{Next}(D\ x)$:
$\quad vec \leftarrow vec \sqcup \mathrm{init}$ // re-initialize: a new automaton execution is spawned
$\quad$ // the automaton takes a transition:
$\quad vec \leftarrow vec \cdot \Delta[x]$ // vector-matrix multiplication
$\quad$ **return** $vec \cdot \mathrm{fin}$ // emit output value

Fig. 3. Monitor for the formula $\varphi \langle r_{[0,\infty)}$.

3.1 Monitor for the Formula $p\langle r_{[0,\infty)}$

Based on the previous discussion, we will assume from now on that a formula of the form $\varphi \langle r_I$ contains only atomic predicates in r that are projections (i.e., π_i for some index i). We also assume that φ is a projection atomic predicate.

Since r is a pure regular expression (that is, every occurrence of the ? operator is applied to atomic propositions), the monitoring of the formula $p\langle r_{[0,\infty)}$ amounts to matching the regular expression $p? \cdot r$. As shown in Fig. 3, the monitoring algorithm constructs the automaton $\mathcal{A} = (Q, \mathrm{init}, \Delta, \mathrm{fin})$: $\mathrm{NFA}(D)$ for $p? \cdot r$ and simulates its execution. Let u be a finite trace and $\ell = |u| \geq 1$ be its length. We have that:

$$\rho(p\langle r_{[0,\infty)}, u, \ell - 1) = \bigsqcup_{i=0}^{\ell-1} \Big(\rho(p, u, i) \sqcap \rho(r, u, [i+1, \ell])\Big)$$
$$= \bigsqcup_{i=0}^{\ell-1} \Big(\rho(p? \cdot r, u, [i, \ell])\Big)$$
$$= \bigsqcup_{i=0}^{\ell-1} \Big(\mathrm{init} \cdot \Delta[u(i)] \cdots \Delta[u(i_1)] \cdots \Delta[u(\ell-1)] \cdot \mathrm{fin}\Big)$$
$$= X_\ell \cdot \mathrm{fin}, \text{ where}$$
$$X_0 = \mathbb{0}_{\mathsf{Mat}(1,n)} \quad \text{and} \quad X_{i+1} = (X_i + \mathrm{init}) \cdot \Delta[u(i)]$$

For example, for the trace $u = u_0 u_1 u_2$, we would have

$$X_3 = (((\mathbb{0} + \mathrm{init}) \cdot \Delta[u_0] + \mathrm{init}) \cdot \Delta[u_1] + \mathrm{init}) \cdot \Delta[u_2]$$
$$= \mathrm{init} \cdot \Delta[u_0] \cdot \Delta[u_1] \cdot \Delta[u_2] + \mathrm{init} \cdot \Delta[u_1] \cdot \Delta[u_2] + \mathrm{init} \cdot \Delta[u_2].$$

The algorithm maintains a row vector vec that represents the configuration of the automaton. At every step, the initialization row vector is added to vec (which essentially means that a new thread of execution is spawned at that moment) and then vec is multiplied with the transition matrix $\Delta[x]$, where x is the current data item. The output is $vec \cdot \mathrm{fin} \in \mathbb{B}$, where fin is the finalization column vector of the automaton. This algorithm uses space $O(n)$ to store vec and time-per-item $O(n^2)$ to perform a vector-matrix multiplication, where n is the number of states of $\mathcal{A}$.

```
// D = B^{K+1} is the type of input data items
// n = # states of the automaton A = (Q, init, Δ, fin) : NFA(D) for p · r
// State for UpdateWnd_a:   buf, wnd, m, z, agg.
[D; a] buf ← [nil; a] // input buffer: fill array of size a with nil items
// window -- fill array of size a with identity matrices:
[Mat(n, n); a] wnd ← [1_{Mat(n,n)}; a]
Nat m ← 0 // size of new block
Mat(n, n) z ← 1_{Mat(n,n)} // aggregate of new block: identity matrix
Mat(n, n) agg ← 1_{Mat(n,n)} // initial overall aggregate: identity matrix
Function UpdateWnd_a(D x):
    buf[m] ← x // new item is placed on the buffer
    wnd[m] ← Δ[x] // evict oldest matrix, replace with Δ[x]
    m ← m + 1 // new block enlarged
    z ← z · Δ[x] // update aggregate for new block: matrix multiplication
    if m = a then // the new block is full
        for i ← a − 2 to 0 do // convert new block to old block
        |   wnd[i] ← wnd[i] · wnd[i + 1] // matrix multiplication
        m ← 0 // empty new block
        z ← 1_{Mat(n,n)} // identity matrix
    agg ← wnd[m] · z // update overall aggregate: matrix multiplication

// State for Next:
Nat ℓ ← 0 // counter for number of items consumed so far (up to a items)
Mat(1, n) vec ← 0_{Mat(1,n)} // row vector for automaton configuration
Function Next(D x):
    D old ← buf[m] // oldest item gets evicted from the input buffer
    UpdateWnd_a(x) // update the window data structure with current item
    if ℓ < a then // no item evicted from the input buffer
    |   ℓ ← ℓ + 1 // increment ℓ
        return 0 // the formula is false
    else // ℓ = a: item evicted from the input buffer
        vec ← vec ⊔ init // re-initialize: a new automaton execution is spawned
        vec ← vec · Δ[old] // automaton transition: vector-matrix multiplication
        return vec · agg · fin // emit output value
```

Fig. 4. Monitor for the formula $p \langle r_{[a,\infty)}$, where $a \geq 1$.

3.2 Monitor for the Formula $p \langle r_{[a,\infty)}$ Where $a \geq 1$

As shown in Fig. 4, the monitoring algorithm constructs the automaton $\mathcal{A} = (Q, \text{init}, \Delta, \text{fin}) : \text{NFA}(D)$ for $p?\cdot r$ and simulates its execution. Let u be a finite trace and $\ell = |u|$ be its length. If $\ell \leq a$, then $\rho(p\langle r_{[a,\infty)}, u, \ell - 1) = 0$. If $\ell \geq a+1$, then we have:

$$\rho(p\langle r_{[a,\infty)}, u, \ell - 1) =$$
$$\bigsqcup_{i=0}^{\ell-1-a} \Big(\rho(p, u, i) \sqcap \rho(r, u, [i+1, \ell]) \Big) =$$
$$\bigsqcup_{i=0}^{\ell-1-a} \Big(\rho(p? \cdot r, u, [i, \ell]) \Big) =$$

$$\bigsqcup_{i=0}^{\ell-1-a}\left(\text{init} \cdot \Delta[u(i)] \cdots \Delta[u(\ell-1-a)] \cdot \Delta[u(\ell-a)] \cdots \Delta[u(\ell-1)] \cdot \text{fin}\right) =$$
$$\left(\sum_{i=0}^{\ell-1-a}\text{init} \cdot \Delta[u(i)] \cdots \Delta[u(\ell-1-a)]\right) \cdot \left(\Delta[u(\ell-a)] \cdots \Delta[u(\ell-1)]\right) \cdot \text{fin}.$$

We see above that the value can be expressed as the product of a row vector $vec : \mathsf{Mat}(1, n)$, a matrix $agg : \mathsf{Mat}(n, n)$, and the finalization column vector $\text{fin} : \mathsf{Mat}(n, 1)$. Intuitively, the row vector vec is the configuration of the automaton $\mathcal{A}$ after consuming all the input except for the last a data items. So, vec can be computed by executing the automaton $\mathcal{A}$ using input that is delayed by a steps. This delay of the input can be realized efficiently using a ring buffer. The matrix agg is the product of the transition matrices for the last a data items. This corresponds to a sliding-window computation, which means that at every step the window over which the product is computed shifts one step to the right.

The algorithm of Fig. 4 gives an efficient implementation of the ring buffer for computing vec and the algorithm for computing agg. The key data structures of the algorithm are buf, wnd, agg, m, and z. The arrays buf and wnd are split into a "new block" containing entries that correspond to the last m items and an "old block". Suppose that the last a input items are the following:

$$[x_0, x_1, \ldots, x_{a-m-1}, \underbrace{x_{a-m}, \ldots, x_{a-2}, x_{a-1}}_{\text{last } m \text{ input items}}], \text{ where } x_{a-1} \text{ is the last item.}$$

Then, the ring buffer buf (array of size a with elements of type D) has the following contents:

$$buf = [\ \underbrace{x_{a-m}, \ldots, x_{a-2}, x_{a-1}}_{\text{new block: last } m \text{ input items}}, \underbrace{x_0, x_1, \ldots, x_{a-m-1}}_{\text{old block}}].$$

The window wnd (array of size a with elements of type $\mathsf{Mat}(n, n)$) has the following contents:

$$wnd = [\underbrace{\Delta[x_{a-m}], \ldots, \Delta[x_{a-2}], \Delta[x_{a-1}]}_{\text{new block: } m \text{ matrices}}, \underbrace{y_0, y_1, \ldots, y_{a-m-1}}_{\text{old block: } a-m \text{ matrices}}], \text{ where}$$
$$y_i = \Delta[x_i] \cdot \Delta[x_{i+1}] \cdots \Delta[x_{a-m-1}] \text{ for every } i = 0, \ldots, a-m-1$$

The key invariant for the matrix $z : \mathsf{Mat}(n, n)$ is that it is always the product

$$z = \Delta[x_{a-m}] \cdots \Delta[x_{a-2}] \cdot \Delta[x_{a-1}]$$

of the transition matrices for the last m items. Finally, the matrix $agg : \mathsf{Mat}(n, n)$ is the product (aggregate) of the transition matrices for the entire window:

$$agg = y_0 \cdot z = \Delta[x_0] \cdots \Delta[x_{a-m-1}] \cdot \Delta[x_{a-m}] \cdots \Delta[x_{a-1}].$$

When a new item x arrives, we evict the aggregate y_0 corresponding to the oldest item x_0 and replace it by $\Delta[x]$. Thus, the new block is expanded with the additional matrix $\Delta[x]$ and therefore we also update the aggregates z and agg.

```
// D = 𝔹^{K+1} is the type of input data items
// n = # states of the automaton 𝒜 = (Q, init, Δ, fin) : NFA(D) for p · r
// s = b + 1 ≥ 1 is the size of the window
// State for PUpdateWndVM_s:  wndm, wndv, k, zm, zv, aggm, aggv.
[Mat(n,n); s] wndm ← [𝟙_{Mat(n,n)}; s]  // fill array of size s with identity matrices
[Mat(1,n); s] wndv ← [𝟘_{Mat(1,n)}; s]  // fill array of size s with zero row vectors
Nat k ← 0  // size of new block
Mat(n,n) zm ← 𝟙_{Mat(n,n)}  // matrix aggregate of new block: identity matrix
Mat(1,n) zv ← 𝟘_{Mat(1,n)}  // vector aggregate of new block: zero row vector
Mat(n,n) aggm ← 𝟙_{Mat(n,n)}  // initial matrix aggregate: identity matrix
Mat(1,n) aggv ← 𝟘_{Mat(1,n)}  // initial vector aggregate: zero row vector
```

Function PUpdateWndVM$_s$(D x):
    $wndm[k] \leftarrow \Delta[x]$ // evict oldest matrix, replace with $\Delta[x]$
    $wndv[k] \leftarrow$ init $\cdot \Delta[x]$ // evict oldest vector, replace with init $\cdot \Delta[x]$
    $k \leftarrow k + 1$ // new block enlarged
    // update matrix aggregate for new block (matrix multiplication):
    $zm \leftarrow zm \cdot \Delta[x]$
    // update vector aggregate for new block (vector-matrix multiplication):
    $zv \leftarrow zv \cdot \Delta[x] +$ init $\cdot \Delta[x]$
    if $k = s$ **then** // the new block is full
        for $i \leftarrow s - 2$ **to** 0 **do** // convert new block to old block
            $wndm[i] \leftarrow wndm[i] \cdot wndm[i+1]$ // matrix multiplication
            // vector-matrix multiplication:
            $wndv[i] \leftarrow wndv[i] \cdot wndm[i+1] + wndv[i+1]$
        $k \leftarrow 0$ // empty new block
        $zm \leftarrow \mathbb{1}_{Mat(n,n)}$ // identity matrix
        $zv \leftarrow \mathbb{0}_{Mat(1,n)}$ // zero row vector
    // update overall matrix aggregate (matrix multiplication):
    $aggm \leftarrow wndm[k] \cdot zm$
    // update overall vector aggregate (vector-matrix multiplication):
    $aggv \leftarrow wndv[k] \cdot zm + zv$

Function Next(T x):
    PUpdateWndVM$_{b+1}(x)$ // update the data structure
    return $aggv \cdot$ fin // emit output value

Fig. 5. Monitor for the formula $p\langle r_{[0,b]}$.

When the new block becomes full (i.e., $m = a$) then we convert it to an old block by performing all partial products from right to left. This conversion requires $a - 1$ applications of matrix multiplication, but it is performed once every a items. So, the algorithm needs $O(n^3)$ amortized time-per-item and $O(a \cdot n^2)$ space to store the window of matrices.

Finally, notice that the updating of *vec* is very similar to the monitor of Fig. 3. The main difference is that the input items are delayed by a steps using the ring buffer *buf*.

3.3 Monitor for the Formula $p \langle r_{[0,b]}$

As shown in Fig. 5, the monitoring algorithm constructs the automaton $\mathcal{A} = (Q, \text{init}, \Delta, \text{fin}) : \mathsf{NFA}(D)$ for the regular expression $p? \cdot r$. Let u be a finite trace and $\ell = |u|$ be its length. We have:

$$\rho(p\langle r_{[0,b]}, u, \ell - 1) = \bigsqcup_{i=\max(0,\ell-1-b)}^{\ell-1} \left(\rho(p, u, i) \sqcap \rho(r, u, [i+1, \ell-1]) \right)$$
$$= \left(\sum_{i=\max(0,\ell-1-b)}^{\ell-1} \text{init} \cdot \Delta[u(i)] \cdots \Delta[u(\ell-1)] \right) \cdot \text{fin}.$$

We see above that the value can be expressed as the product of a row vector $aggv : \mathsf{Mat}(1, n)$ and the finalization column vector $\text{fin} : \mathsf{Mat}(n, 1)$. Intuitively, the row vector $aggv$ is the configuration of the automaton $\mathcal{A}$ (with re-initialization at every step) after consuming the last $s = b + 1$ data items. It corresponds to a sliding-window aggregation, which means that at every step the window over which the aggregate is computed shifts one step to the right[1].

The algorithm of Fig. 5 gives an efficient implementation of the algorithm for computing $aggv$. The key data structures of the algorithm are $wndm$ (window of matrices), $wndv$ (window of row vectors), k, zm, zv, $aggm$ (overall matrix aggregate), and $aggv$ (overall vector aggregate). The arrays $wndm$ and $wndv$ are split between a "new block" containing entries that correspond to the last k items and an "old block". Suppose that the last s input items are the following:

$$[x_0, x_1, \ldots, x_{s-k-1}, \underbrace{x_{s-k}, \ldots, x_{s-2}, x_{s-1}}_{\text{last } k \text{ input items}}], \text{ where } x_{s-1} \text{ is the last item.}$$

The window $wndm$ (array of size s with elements of type $\mathsf{Mat}(n,n)$) has the following contents:

$$wndm = [\underbrace{\Delta[x_{s-k}], \ldots, \Delta[x_{s-2}], \Delta[x_{s-1}]}_{\text{new block: } k \text{ matrices}}, \underbrace{ym_0, ym_1, \ldots, ym_{s-k-1}}_{\text{old block: } s-k \text{ matrices}}], \text{ where}$$

$$ym_i = \Delta[x_i] \cdot \Delta[x_{i+1}] \cdots \Delta[x_{s-k-1}] \text{ for every } i = 0, \ldots, s - k - 1$$

The window $wndv$ (array of size s with elements of type $\mathsf{Mat}(1,n)$) has the following contents:

$$wndv = [\underbrace{\text{init} \cdot \Delta[x_{s-k}], \ldots, \text{init} \cdot \Delta[x_{s-1}]}_{\text{new block: } k \text{ row vectors}}, \underbrace{yv_0, yv_1, \ldots, yv_{s-k-1}}_{\text{old block: } s-k \text{ row vectors}}], \text{ where}$$

$$yv_t = \sum_{i=t}^{s-k-1} \left(\text{init} \cdot \prod_{j=i}^{s-k-1} \Delta[x_j] \right) \text{ for every } t = 0, \ldots, s - k - 1$$

The key invariants for the matrix $zm : \mathsf{Mat}(n, n)$ (new block matrix aggregate) and the row vector $zv : \mathsf{Mat}(1, n)$ (new block vector aggregate) are the following:

$$zm = \Delta[x_{s-k}] \cdots \Delta[x_{s-2}] \cdot \Delta[x_{s-1}] \qquad zv = \sum_{i=s-k}^{s-1} \left(\text{init} \cdot \prod_{j=i}^{s-1} \Delta[x_j] \right)$$

---

[1] Notice that this aggregation is not the same as the aggregation of Fig. 4, which is simply a product of transition matrices.

// $D = \mathbb{B}^{K+1}$ is the type of input data items
// $n = $ # states of the automaton $\mathcal{A} = (Q, \text{init}, \Delta, \text{fin}) : \text{NFA}(D)$ for $p \cdot r$
// State for UpdateWnd_a: buf, wnd, m, z, agg.
// State for PUpdateWndVM_s with $s = b - a + 1 \geq 1$:
// $wndm$, $wndv$, k, zm, zv, $aggm$, $aggv$.

Nat $\ell \leftarrow 0$ // counter for number of items consumed so far (up to a items)

Function Next(T x):
> D $old \leftarrow buf[m]$ // oldest item gets evicted from the input buffer
> // update the window data structure for the interval $[0, a-1]$:
> $\text{UpdateWnd}_a(x)$
> **if** $\ell < a$ **then** // no item evicted from input buffer
>> $\ell \leftarrow \ell + 1$ // increment ℓ
>> **return** 0 // the formula is false
>
> **else** // $\ell = a$: item evicted from the input buffer
>> // update the data structure for the interval $[a, b]$:
>> $\text{PUpdateWndVM}_{b-a+1}(old)$
>> **return** $aggv \cdot agg \cdot \text{fin}$ // emit output value

Fig. 6. Monitor for the formula $p\langle r_{[a,b]}$, where $a \geq 1$.

Notice that zm is the product of transition matrices for last k items. Finally, the overall matrix aggregate $aggm : \text{Mat}(n, n)$ and the overall vector aggregate $aggv : \text{Mat}(1, n)$ satisfy the following invariants:

$$aggm = ym_0 \cdot zm$$
$$= \Delta[x_0] \cdots \Delta[x_{s-k-1}] \cdot \Delta[x_{s-k}] \cdots \Delta[x_{s-1}]$$
$$aggv = yv_0 \cdot zm + zv$$
$$= \left(\sum_{i=0}^{s-k-1} \text{init} \cdot \prod_{j=i}^{s-k-1} \Delta[x_j]\right) \cdot \prod_{j=s-k}^{s-1} \Delta[x_j] + \left(\sum_{i=s-k}^{s-1} \text{init} \cdot \prod_{j=i}^{s-1} \Delta[x_j]\right)$$
$$= \left(\sum_{i=0}^{s-k-1} \text{init} \cdot \prod_{j=i}^{s-1} \Delta[x_j]\right) + \left(\sum_{i=s-k}^{s-1} \text{init} \cdot \prod_{j=i}^{s-1} \Delta[x_j]\right)$$
$$= \sum_{i=0}^{s-1} \left(\text{init} \cdot \prod_{j=i}^{s-1} \Delta[x_j]\right)$$

When a new item x arrives, we evict the aggregates ym_0, yv_0 corresponding to the oldest item x_0 and replace them by $\Delta[x]$ and $\text{init} \cdot \Delta[x]$ respectively. Thus, the new block is expanded and therefore we also update the aggregates zm, zv, $aggm$, and $aggv$. When the new block becomes full (i.e., $m = s$) then we convert it to an old block. This conversion requires $s - 1$ applications of matrix multiplication and vector-matrix multiplication, but it is performed once every s items. So, the algorithm needs $O(n^3)$ amortized time-per-item and $O(s \cdot n^2)$ space to store the windows of matrices and vectors.

3.4 Monitor for the Formula $p\langle r_{[a,b]}$

As shown in Fig. 6, the monitoring algorithm constructs the automaton $\mathcal{A} = (Q, \text{init}, \Delta, \text{fin}) : \mathsf{NFA}(D)$ for the regular expression $p? \cdot r$. Let u be a finite trace and $\ell = |u|$ be its length. We have:

$\rho(p\langle r_{[a,b]}, u, \ell - 1) =$
$\bigsqcup_{i=\max(0,\ell-1-b)}^{\ell-1-a} \big(\rho(p, u, i) \sqcap \rho(r, u, [i, \ell - 1])\big) =$
$\bigsqcup_{i=\max(0,\ell-1-b)}^{\ell-1-a} \big(\text{init} \cdot \Delta[u(i)] \cdots \Delta[u(\ell - 1 - a)] \cdot \Delta[u(\ell - a)] \cdots \Delta[u(\ell - 1)] \cdot \text{fin}\big) =$
$\Big(\sum_{i=\max(0,\ell-1-b)}^{\ell-1-a} \text{init} \cdot \Delta[u(i)] \cdots \Delta[u(\ell - 1 - a)]\Big) \cdot \Big(\Delta[u(\ell - a)] \cdots \Delta[u(\ell - 1)]\Big) \cdot \text{fin}.$

We see above that the value can be expressed as the product of a row vector $aggv : \mathsf{Mat}(1, n)$, a matrix $agg : \mathsf{Mat}(n, n)$, and the finalization column vector $\text{fin} : \mathsf{Mat}(n, 1)$. Intuitively, the row vector $aggv$ is the vector aggregate computed with the algorithm of Fig. 5 (procedure PUpdateWndVM$_s$ with size $s = b-a+1$). The difference here is that $aggv$ is delayed by a steps, which can be accomplished using a buffer of size a. The matrix agg is the product of the transition matrices for the last a data items. This corresponds to the sliding-window computation described in Fig. 4 (procedure UpdateWnd$_a$).

The online monitor of Fig. 6 includes the state needed for UpdateWnd$_a$ (buf, wnd, m, z, agg) and the state needed for PUpdateWndVM$_s$ with size $s = b-a+1$ ($wndm$, $wndv$, k, zm, zv, $aggm$, $aggv$). Suppose that the last $b+1$ input items are the following:

$[\; \underbrace{x_0, x_1, \ldots, x_{b-a}}_{b - a + 1 \text{ input items}}, \underbrace{x_{b-a+1}, \ldots, x_{b-1}, x_b}_{\text{last } a \text{ input items}}]$, where x_b is the last item.

From the invariants for the procedures UpdateWnd$_a$ and PUpdateWndVM$_{b-a+1}$ we already know that the following hold:

$$aggv = \sum_{i=0}^{b-a} \big(\text{init} \cdot \prod_{j=i}^{b-a} \Delta[x_j]\big) \qquad agg = \Delta[x_{b-a+1}] \cdots \Delta[x_{b-1}] \cdot \Delta[x_b]$$

We conclude that $aggv \cdot agg \cdot \text{fin} = \sum_{i=0}^{b-a} \big(\text{init} \cdot \prod_{j=i}^{b} \Delta[x_j] \cdot \text{fin}\big)$, which is the desired output value.

The algorithm needs $O(n^3)$ amortized time-per-item and $O(b \cdot n^2)$ space to store the windows of matrices and vectors.

3.5 Overall Monitoring Algorithm

The algorithm proceeds in a bottom-up manner, computing the output $\rho(\psi, u)$ for every subformula ψ of φ. The base case of an atomic formula $p : D \to \mathbb{B}$ is trivial. The Boolean connectives negation $\neg$ and disjunction $\vee$ are easy to handle. The "box" connectives $|r]_I$ and $[r|_I$ are encoded using negation the "diamond" connectives. We discussed earlier in Sects. 3.1, 3.2, 3.3 and 3.4 how to handle the past diamond connective $\langle r_I$ with 4 different algorithms for each form of the time interval I: $[0, \infty)$, $[a, \infty)$ with $a \geq 1$, $[0, b]$, and $[a, b]$ with $a \geq 1$. All these algorithms proceed with a single left-to-right pass over the input trace (and the output tapes of the maximal strict subformulas).

The case of the *future* diamond connective $|r\rangle_I$ is completely symmetric to the case $\langle r_I$. The difference is that the future connective requires a *right-to-left* pass over the input.

Theorem 5. *For a DMTL formula φ and a finite input trace u, the monitoring problem can be solved in time $O(|\varphi|^3 \cdot \ell)$, where ℓ is the length of the trace u.*

Proof. The main arguments for the correctness of the overall monitoring algorithm (i.e., the invariants for the data structures) have already been provided in Sects. 3.1, 3.2, 3.3 and 3.4. We have also seen for every case of the formulas of the form $\varphi = \psi \langle r_I$ that the amortized complexity is $O(|\varphi|^3)$ per data item. Since the amortized per-item running time is an average over the entire input stream, the overall running time is $O(|\varphi|^3 \cdot \ell)$ *in the worst case*. The complexity analysis for formulas of the form $\varphi = |r\rangle_I \psi$ is analogous. The remaining cases of Boolean connectives are straightforward. □

The space requirements of the algorithm are exponential in the size of the specification φ because of the succinct representation of the time intervals I.

The polynomial complexity bound of Theorem 5 is interesting because the DMTL formalism combines regular expressions with metric temporal connectives that express a kind of "counting". The operator $\{m,n\}$ of *counting* (or *bounded repetition*) in regular expressions is similar. The pattern $r\{m,n\}$ describes the repetition of r from m to n times. Bounded repetition makes regular expressions exponentially more succinct and thus raises algorithmic challenges. See, for example, [36] for relevant results and pointers to relevant literature. Recent works [46,48,72,75] use automata with counters or bit vectors for efficient matching. For some special cases of intervals I, more efficient algorithms may apply [35].

The bottom-up monitoring algorithm described in this section performs left-to-right (resp., right-to-left) passes over the input trace for past-time (resp., future-time) temporal connectives. For the special case where there are only past-time or only future-time connectives, it would be possible to perform a single pass (similarly to [55] for lookaround assertions). In this case, it seems that the algorithm could be conveniently described using streaming dataflow constructs (see, e.g., [15,44,49,54,70]), as is done in [60] for MTL.

As a final remark, it may be possible to use the algorithms of this section in the context of quantitative formalisms and query languages for streaming data [19,32]. For example, Quantitative Regular Expressions (QREs) [6,9,59] and associated automata-theoretic models with registers [5,7,8] could be extended with "counting" features similar to DMTL's connectives. QREs have been used to express complex online detection algorithms for medical monitoring [3,4]. Extending their syntax with "counting" features may provide convenience of expression, thus making them suitable for more applications.

4 Related Work

The syntax of our temporal formalism DMTL is based on Dynamic Logic [37,67], and also on the more recent work on ForSpec [10], PSL [1,28], SystemVerilog [2,17,74], and LDL [21]. Pnueli and Zaks [64,66] consider runtime verification for PSL using a class of transducers that they call temporal testers. Morin-Allory and Borrione [62] use PVS to prove the correctness of monitors that are synthesized from PSL specifications. Das et al. [20] present an approach for synthesizing SystemVerilog assertions in hardware. Armoni et al. [11] use deterministic automata to monitor temporal specifications. Eisner [27] discusses the use of PSL in dynamic and runtime verification. Boulé and Zilic [16] use an automata-based approach for the synthesis of assertion checkers from PSL properties. Morin-Allory et al. [63] validate several rewrite rules for PSL properties using PVS. Javaheri et al. [43] studies the synthesis in hardware of PSL regular expressions. Eisner and Fisman [29] discuss extensions to temporal logic that are included in SVA and/or PSL and the semantic issues that they raise. Witharana et al. [76] present both pre-silicon and post-silicon assertion-based approaches for hardware validation. MDL (Metric Dynamic Logic) is considered in [14,68].

The monitoring of LTL properties with only future-time temporal connectives is considered in [38]. The monitoring of LTL with only past-time temporal connectives ("past-time LTL") is studied in [39,40]. The main observation is that the semantics of past-time LTL can be defined recursively so that the monitoring algorithm only needs to look one step backwards. Markey and Schnoebelen [61] discuss the complexity of offline monitoring for LTL (with both future-time and past-time temporal connectives) specifications. Finkbeiner and Sipma [34] propose monitoring algorithms that make use of alternating automata. The online monitoring of LTL with both past-time and future-time temporal connectives is discussed in [71] (Sect. 4.2 on "Linear Temporal Logics").

Thati and Roşu [71] study online monitoring for MTL with past-time ("since") and future-time ("until") temporal connectives. For the special case of past-time MTL, the online monitoring algorithm has better time and space complexity. Reinbacher et al. [69] consider an online monitoring algorithm for past-time MTL specifications and its FPGA realization. The FPGA implementation of STL monitors is considered in [41].

Basin et al. [14] propose an online MDL monitoring algorithm over traces with timestamped data items. In order to deal with the unavoidable unbounded lookahead needed for temporal connectives such as $U_{[0,\infty)}$, the proposed algorithm produces non-standard output, which does not only consist of Boolean values. Raszyk et al. [68] consider multi-head monitoring of MDL. A multi-head monitor has multiple pointers, which are called reading heads, in the system trace. The proposed MDL monitoring algorithm requires space that is exponential in the formula size, but it is independent of the constants in the time intervals I that annotate the temporal connectives.

There are various approaches for interpreting future-time connectives in the context of online monitoring. For example, [23] assumes the availability of a predictor to interpret future connectives, and [26] considers robustness intervals: the tightest intervals which cover the robustness for all possible extensions of the available trace. Reelay [73] uses only past-time connectives. The transducer-based framework of [60] can be used to monitor temporal properties which depend on bounded future input by allowing some bounded delay in the output.

While this paper focuses on qualitative (Boolean) semantics, it may be possible to generalize the techniques to quantitative interpretations of the specification language. There is a large body of work on monitoring for quantitative interpretations of temporal formalisms. We discuss some related works below.

Fainekos and Pappas [31] define the robustness degree of satisfaction in terms of the distance of the signal from the set of desirable ones (or its complement). They also suggest an under-approximation of the robustness degree which can be effectively monitored. This is called the *robustness estimate* and is defined by induction on MTL/STL formulas, by interpreting conjunction (resp., disjunction) as inf (resp., sup) over the set $\mathbb{R}^{\pm\infty}$ of the extended real numbers.

In [42], the authors study a generalization of the robustness degree by considering idempotent semirings of real numbers. They also propose an online monitoring algorithm that uses symbolic weighted automata. While this approach computes the precise robustness degree in the sense of [31], the construction of the relevant automata incurs a doubly exponential blowup if one considers STL specifications. In [18], it is observed that an extension of the robustness estimate to bounded distributive lattices can be effectively monitored, but this is explored for the more limited formalism of past-time MTL. The paper [56] considers an algebraic semantics based on semirings, which is too abstract to define a metric notion of signed distance and robustness degree. Semirings are also used in [12], where the authors consider a spatio-temporal logic. Complete lattices are used in [57,58], where the focus is on online monitoring over continuous-time signals.

A key ingredient for the efficient monitoring of STL is a streaming algorithm for sliding-window maximum [22,25]. The tool Breach [24], which is used for the falsification of temporal specifications over hybrid systems, uses the sliding-maximum algorithm of [50].

The compositional construction of automata-based monitors from temporal specifications has also been considered in [33,52,53].

5 Conclusion

We have studied the problem of offline monitoring for DMTL, a formalism that combines MTL with regular expressions. We propose the first polynomial-time algorithm for offline monitoring. More specifically, our algorithm has time complexity $O(m^3 \cdot n)$, where m is the size of the DMTL formula and n is the length of the input trace. Other approaches for monitoring that translate the specification into a single automaton cannot achieve our polynomial time complexity bound, since the resulting automaton can be of at least exponential size.

Acknowledgments. This research was supported in part by the US National Science Foundation award CCF 2319572.

References

1. IEEE standard for Property Specification Language (PSL). IEEE STD 1850–2010 (Revision of IEEE STD 1850–2005), pp. 1–182 (2010). https://doi.org/10.1109/IEEESTD.2010.5446004
2. IEEE standard for SystemVerilog–unified hardware design, specification, and verification language. IEEE STD 1800–2023 (Revision of IEEE STD 1800–2017), pp. 1–1354 (2024). https://doi.org/10.1109/IEEESTD.2024.10458102
3. Abbas, H., Alur, R., Mamouras, K., Mangharam, R., Rodionova, A.: Real-time decision policies with predictable performance. Proc. IEEE Spec. Issue Des. Autom. Cyber-Phys. Syst. **106**(9), 1593–1615 (2018). https://doi.org/10.1109/JPROC.2018.2853608
4. Abbas, H., Rodionova, A., Mamouras, K., Bartocci, E., Smolka, S.A., Grosu, R.: Quantitative regular expressions for arrhythmia detection. IEEE/ACM Trans. Comput. Biol. Bioinf. **16**(5), 1586–1597 (2019). https://doi.org/10.1109/TCBB.2018.2885274
5. Alur, R., Fisman, D., Mamouras, K., Raghothaman, M., Stanford, C.: Streamable regular transductions. Theor. Comput. Sci. **807**, 15–41 (2020). https://doi.org/10.1016/j.tcs.2019.11.018
6. Alur, R., Mamouras, K.: An introduction to the StreamQRE language. Dependable Softw. Syst. Eng. **50**, 1–24 (2017). https://doi.org/10.3233/978-1-61499-810-5-1
7. Alur, R., Mamouras, K., Stanford, C.: Automata-based stream processing. In: Chatzigiannakis, I., Indyk, P., Kuhn, F., Muscholl, A. (eds.) Proceedings of the 44th International Colloquium on Automata, Languages, and Programming (ICALP 2017). Leibniz International Proceedings in Informatics (LIPIcs), vol. 80, pp. 112:1–112:15. Schloss Dagstuhl–Leibniz-Zentrum fuer Informatik, Dagstuhl, Germany (2017). https://doi.org/10.4230/LIPIcs.ICALP.2017.112
8. Alur, R., Mamouras, K., Stanford, C.: Modular quantitative monitoring. Proc. ACM Programm. Lang. **3**(POPL), 50:1–50:31 (2019). https://doi.org/10.1145/3290363
9. Alur, R., Mamouras, K., Ulus, D.: Derivatives of quantitative regular expressions. In: Aceto, L., Bacci, G., Bacci, G., Ingólfsdóttir, A., Legay, A., Mardare, R. (eds.) Models, Algorithms, Logics and Tools. LNCS, vol. 10460, pp. 75–95. Springer, Cham (2017). https://doi.org/10.1007/978-3-319-63121-9_4
10. Armoni, R., et al.: The ForSpec temporal logic: a new temporal property-specification language. In: Katoen, J.-P., Stevens, P. (eds.) TACAS 2002. LNCS, vol. 2280, pp. 296–311. Springer, Heidelberg (2002). https://doi.org/10.1007/3-540-46002-0_21
11. Armoni, R., Korchemny, D., Tiemeyer, A., Vardi, M.Y., Zbar, Y.: Deterministic dynamic monitors for linear-time assertions. In: Havelund, K., Núñez, M., Roşu, G., Wolff, B. (eds.) FATES/RV -2006. LNCS, vol. 4262, pp. 163–177. Springer, Heidelberg (2006). https://doi.org/10.1007/11940197_11
12. Bartocci, E., Bortolussi, L., Loreti, M., Nenzi, L.: Monitoring mobile and spatially distributed cyber-physical systems. In: Proceedings of the 15th ACM-IEEE International Conference on Formal Methods and Models for System Design, pp. 146–155. MEMOCODE 2017, ACM, New York, NY, USA (2017). https://doi.org/10.1145/3127041.3127050
13. Bartocci, E., et al.: Specification-based monitoring of cyber-physical systems: a survey on theory, tools and applications. In: Bartocci, E., Falcone, Y. (eds.) Lectures on Runtime Verification. LNCS, vol. 10457, pp. 135–175. Springer, Cham (2018). https://doi.org/10.1007/978-3-319-75632-5_5

14. Basin, D., Krstić, S., Traytel, D.: Almost event-rate independent monitoring of metric dynamic logic. In: Lahiri, S., Reger, G. (eds.) RV 2017. LNCS, vol. 10548, pp. 85–102. Springer, Cham (2017). https://doi.org/10.1007/978-3-319-67531-2_6
15. Benveniste, A., Caspi, P., Edwards, S.A., Halbwachs, N., Le Guernic, P., de Simone, R.: The synchronous languages 12 years later. Proc. IEEE **91**(1), 64–83 (2003). https://doi.org/10.1109/JPROC.2002.805826
16. Boulé, M., Zilic, Z.: Automata-based assertion-checker synthesis of PSL properties. ACM Trans. Des. Autom. Electr. Syst. **13**(1), 4:1–4:21 (2008). https://doi.org/10.1145/1297666.1297670
17. Bustan, D., Korchemny, D., Seligman, E., Yang, J.: SystemVerilog assertions: past, present, and future SVA standardization experience. IEEE Des. Test Comput. **29**(2), 23–31 (2012). https://doi.org/10.1109/MDT.2012.2183336
18. Chattopadhyay, A., Mamouras, K.: A verified online monitor for metric temporal logic with quantitative semantics. In: Deshmukh, J., Ničković, D. (eds.) RV 2020. LNCS, vol. 12399, pp. 383–403. Springer, Cham (2020). https://doi.org/10.1007/978-3-030-60508-7_21
19. D'Angelo, B., et al.: LOLA: runtime monitoring of synchronous systems. In: Proceedings of the 12th International Symposium on Temporal Representation and Reasoning (TIME 2005), pp. 166–174. IEEE, USA (2005). https://doi.org/10.1109/TIME.2005.26
20. Das, S., Mohanty, R., Dasgupta, P., Chakrabarti, P.: Synthesis of system Verilog assertions. In: Proceedings of the Design Automation & Test in Europe Conference (DATE 2006), vol. 2, pp. 1–6. IEEE, USA (2006). https://doi.org/10.1109/DATE.2006.243776
21. De Giacomo, G., Vardi, M.Y.: Linear temporal logic and linear dynamic logic on finite traces. In: Twenty-Third International Joint Conference on Artificial Intelligence, pp. 854–860 (2013). https://www.ijcai.org/Proceedings/13/Papers/132.pdf
22. Deshmukh, J.V., Donzé, A., Ghosh, S., Jin, X., Juniwal, G., Seshia, S.A.: Robust online monitoring of signal temporal logic. Formal Meth. Syst. Des. **51**(1), 5–30 (2017). https://doi.org/10.1007/s10703-017-0286-7
23. Dokhanchi, A., Hoxha, B., Fainekos, G.: On-line monitoring for temporal logic robustness. In: Bonakdarpour, B., Smolka, S.A. (eds.) RV 2014. LNCS, vol. 8734, pp. 231–246. Springer, Cham (2014). https://doi.org/10.1007/978-3-319-11164-3_19
24. Donzé, A.: Breach, a toolbox for verification and parameter synthesis of hybrid systems. In: Touili, T., Cook, B., Jackson, P. (eds.) CAV 2010. LNCS, vol. 6174, pp. 167–170. Springer, Heidelberg (2010). https://doi.org/10.1007/978-3-642-14295-6_17
25. Donzé, A., Ferrère, T., Maler, O.: Efficient robust monitoring for STL. In: Sharygina, N., Veith, H. (eds.) CAV 2013. LNCS, vol. 8044, pp. 264–279. Springer, Heidelberg (2013). https://doi.org/10.1007/978-3-642-39799-8_19
26. Dreossi, T., Dang, T., Donzé, A., Kapinski, J., Jin, X., Deshmukh, J.V.: Efficient guiding strategies for testing of temporal properties of hybrid systems. In: Havelund, K., Holzmann, G., Joshi, R. (eds.) NFM 2015. LNCS, vol. 9058, pp. 127–142. Springer, Cham (2015). https://doi.org/10.1007/978-3-319-17524-9_10
27. Eisner, C.: PSL for runtime verification: theory and practice. In: Sokolsky, O., Taşıran, S. (eds.) RV 2007. LNCS, vol. 4839, pp. 1–8. Springer, Heidelberg (2007). https://doi.org/10.1007/978-3-540-77395-5_1
28. Eisner, C., Fisman, D.: A Practical Introduction to PSL. Springer, Boston, MA (2007). https://doi.org/10.1007/978-0-387-36123-9

29. Eisner, C., Fisman, D.: Functional specification of hardware via temporal logic. In: Handbook of Model Checking, pp. 795–829. Springer, Cham (2018). https://doi.org/10.1007/978-3-319-10575-8_24
30. Eisner, C., Fisman, D., Havlicek, J., Lustig, Y., McIsaac, A., Van Campenhout, D.: Reasoning with temporal logic on truncated paths. In: Hunt, W.A., Somenzi, F. (eds.) CAV 2003. LNCS, vol. 2725, pp. 27–39. Springer, Heidelberg (2003). https://doi.org/10.1007/978-3-540-45069-6_3
31. Fainekos, G.E., Pappas, G.J.: Robustness of temporal logic specifications for continuous-time signals. Theoret. Comput. Sci. **410**(42), 4262–4291 (2009). https://doi.org/10.1016/j.tcs.2009.06.021
32. Faymonville, P., et al.: StreamLAB: stream-based monitoring of cyber-physical systems. In: Dillig, I., Tasiran, S. (eds.) CAV 2019. LNCS, vol. 11561, pp. 421–431. Springer, Cham (2019). https://doi.org/10.1007/978-3-030-25540-4_24
33. Ferrère, T., Maler, O., Ničković, D., Pnueli, A.: From real-time logic to timed automata. J. ACM **66**(3), 19:1–19:31 (2019). https://doi.org/10.1145/3286976
34. Finkbeiner, B., Sipma, H.: Checking finite traces using alternating automata. Formal Meth. Syst. Des. **24**(2), 101–127 (2004). https://doi.org/10.1023/B:FORM.0000017718.28096.48
35. Ganardi, M., Hucke, D., König, D., Lohrey, M., Mamouras, K.: Automata theory on sliding windows. In: Niedermeier, R., Vallée, B. (eds.) Proceedings of the 35th Symposium on Theoretical Aspects of Computer Science (STACS 2018). Leibniz International Proceedings in Informatics (LIPIcs), vol. 96, pp. 31:1–31:14. Schloss Dagstuhl–Leibniz-Zentrum fuer Informatik, Dagstuhl, Germany (2018). https://doi.org/10.4230/LIPIcs.STACS.2018.31
36. Gelade, W.: Succinctness of regular expressions with interleaving, intersection and counting. Theoret. Comput. Sci. **411**(31), 2987–2998 (2010). https://doi.org/10.1016/j.tcs.2010.04.036
37. Harel, D., Kozen, D., Tiuryn, J.: Dynamic Logic. MIT Press, Cambridge (2000)
38. Havelund, K., Roşu, G.: Monitoring programs using rewriting. In: Proceedings 16th Annual International Conference on Automated Software Engineering (ASE 2001), pp. 135–143. IEEE, USA (2001). https://doi.org/10.1109/ASE.2001.989799
39. Havelund, K., Roşu, G.: Synthesizing monitors for safety properties. In: Katoen, J.-P., Stevens, P. (eds.) TACAS 2002. LNCS, vol. 2280, pp. 342–356. Springer, Heidelberg (2002). https://doi.org/10.1007/3-540-46002-0_24
40. Havelund, K., Roşu, G.: Efficient monitoring of safety properties. Int. J. Softw. Tools Technol. Transfer **6**(2), 158–173 (2004). https://doi.org/10.1007/s10009-003-0117-6
41. Jakšić, S., Bartocci, E., Grosu, R., Kloibhofer, R., Nguyen, T., Ničković, D.: From signal temporal logic to FPGA monitors. In: 2015 ACM/IEEE International Conference on Formal Methods and Models for Codesign (MEMOCODE 2015), pp. 218–227. IEEE, USA (2015). https://doi.org/10.1109/MEMCOD.2015.7340489
42. Jakšić, S., Bartocci, E., Grosu, R., Ničković, D.: An algebraic framework for runtime verification. IEEE Trans. Comput. Aided Des. Integr. Circuits Syst. **37**(11), 2233–2243 (2018). https://doi.org/10.1109/TCAD.2018.2858460
43. Javaheri, F.N., Morin-Allory, K., Borrione, D.: Synthesis of regular expressions revisited: from PSL SEREs to hardware. IEEE Trans. Comput. Aided Des. Integr. Circuits Syst. **36**(5), 869–882 (2017). https://doi.org/10.1109/TCAD.2016.2600241
44. Kahn, G.: The semantics of a simple language for parallel programming. Inf. Process. **74**, 471–475 (1974)

45. Kleene, S.C.: Representation of events in nerve nets and finite automata. In: Shannon, C.E., McCarthy, J. (eds.) Automata Studies, pp. 3–41. No. 34 in Annals of Mathematics Studies, Princeton University Press (1956)
46. Kong, L., et al.: Software-hardware codesign for efficient in-memory regular pattern matching. In: Proceedings of the 43rd ACM SIGPLAN International Conference on Programming Language Design and Implementation, pp. 733–748. PLDI 2022, ACM, New York, NY, USA (2022). https://doi.org/10.1145/3519939.3523456
47. Koymans, R.: Specifying real-time properties with metric temporal logic. Real-Time Syst. **2**(4), 255–299 (1990). https://doi.org/10.1007/BF01995674
48. Le Glaunec, A., Kong, L., Mamouras, K.: Regular expression matching using bit vector automata. Proc. ACM Programm. Lang. **7**(OOPSLA1), 92:1–92:30 (2023). https://doi.org/10.1145/3586044
49. Lee, E.A., Messerschmitt, D.G.: Static scheduling of synchronous data flow programs for digital signal processing. IEEE Trans. Comput. **C-36**(1), 24–35 (1987). https://doi.org/10.1109/TC.1987.5009446
50. Lemire, D.: Streaming maximum-minimum filter using no more than three comparisons per element. CoRR abs/cs/0610046 (2006). http://arxiv.org/abs/cs/0610046
51. Maler, O., Nickovic, D.: Monitoring temporal properties of continuous signals. In: Lakhnech, Y., Yovine, S. (eds.) FORMATS/FTRTFT -2004. LNCS, vol. 3253, pp. 152–166. Springer, Heidelberg (2004). https://doi.org/10.1007/978-3-540-30206-3_12
52. Maler, O., Nickovic, D., Pnueli, A.: Real time temporal logic: past, present, future. In: Pettersson, P., Yi, W. (eds.) FORMATS 2005. LNCS, vol. 3829, pp. 2–16. Springer, Heidelberg (2005). https://doi.org/10.1007/11603009_2
53. Maler, O., Nickovic, D., Pnueli, A.: From MITL to timed automata. In: Asarin, E., Bouyer, P. (eds.) FORMATS 2006. LNCS, vol. 4202, pp. 274–289. Springer, Heidelberg (2006). https://doi.org/10.1007/11867340_20
54. Mamouras, K.: Semantic foundations for deterministic dataflow and stream processing. In: ESOP 2020. LNCS, vol. 12075, pp. 394–427. Springer, Cham (2020). https://doi.org/10.1007/978-3-030-44914-8_15
55. Mamouras, K., Chattopadhyay, A.: Efficient matching of regular expressions with lookaround assertions. Proc. ACM Programm. Lang. **8**(POPL), 92:1–92:31 (2024). https://doi.org/10.1145/3632934
56. Mamouras, K., Chattopadhyay, A., Wang, Z.: Algebraic quantitative semantics for efficient online temporal monitoring. In: TACAS 2021. LNCS, vol. 12651, pp. 330–348. Springer, Cham (2021). https://doi.org/10.1007/978-3-030-72016-2_18
57. Mamouras, K., Chattopadhyay, A., Wang, Z.: A compositional framework for quantitative online monitoring over continuous-time signals. In: Feng, L., Fisman, D. (eds.) RV 2021. LNCS, vol. 12974, pp. 142–163. Springer, Cham (2021). https://doi.org/10.1007/978-3-030-88494-9_8
58. Mamouras, K., Chattopadhyay, A., Wang, Z.: A compositional framework for algebraic quantitative online monitoring over continuous-time signals. Int. J. Softw. Tools Technol. Transfer **25**(4), 557–573 (2023). https://doi.org/10.1007/s10009-023-00719-w
59. Mamouras, K., Raghothaman, M., Alur, R., Ives, Z.G., Khanna, S.: StreamQRE: modular specification and efficient evaluation of quantitative queries over streaming data. In: Proceedings of the 38th ACM SIGPLAN Conference on Programming Language Design and Implementation, pp. 693–708. PLDI 2017, ACM, New York, NY, USA (2017). https://doi.org/10.1145/3062341.3062369

60. Mamouras, K., Wang, Z.: Online signal monitoring with bounded lag. IEEE Trans. Comput. Aided Des. Integr. Circuits Syst. **39**(11), 3868–3880 (2020). https://doi.org/10.1109/TCAD.2020.3013053
61. Markey, N., Schnoebelen, P.: Model checking a path. In: Amadio, R., Lugiez, D. (eds.) CONCUR 2003. LNCS, vol. 2761, pp. 251–265. Springer, Heidelberg (2003). https://doi.org/10.1007/978-3-540-45187-7_17
62. Morin-Allory, K., Borrione, D.: Proven correct monitors from PSL specifications. In: Proceedings of the Design Automation & Test in Europe Conference (DATE 2006), vol. 1, pp. 1–6. IEEE, USA (2006). https://doi.org/10.1109/DATE.2006.244079
63. Morin-Allory, K., Boulé, M., Borrione, D., Zilic, Z.: Validating assertion language rewrite rules and semantics with automated theorem provers. IEEE Trans. Comput. Aided Des. Integr. Circuits Syst. **29**(9), 1436–1448 (2010). https://doi.org/10.1109/TCAD.2010.2049150
64. Pnueli, A., Zaks, A.: PSL model checking and run-time verification via testers. In: Misra, J., Nipkow, T., Sekerinski, E. (eds.) FM 2006. LNCS, vol. 4085, pp. 573–586. Springer, Heidelberg (2006). https://doi.org/10.1007/11813040_38
65. Pnueli, A.: The temporal logic of programs. In: Proceedings of the 18th Annual Symposium on Foundations of Computer Science (SFCS 1977), pp. 46–57. IEEE, USA (1977). https://doi.org/10.1109/SFCS.1977.32
66. Pnueli, A., Zaks, A.: On the merits of temporal testers. In: Grumberg, O., Veith, H. (eds.) 25 Years of Model Checking. LNCS, vol. 5000, pp. 172–195. Springer, Heidelberg (2008). https://doi.org/10.1007/978-3-540-69850-0_11
67. Pratt, V.R.: Semantical considerations on Floyd-Hoare logic. In: Proceedings of the 17th IEEE Annual Symposium on Foundations of Computer Science (SFCS 1976), pp. 109–121. IEEE, USA (1976). https://doi.org/10.1109/SFCS.1976.27
68. Raszyk, M., Basin, D., Traytel, D.: Multi-head monitoring of metric dynamic logic. In: Hung, D.V., Sokolsky, O. (eds.) ATVA 2020. LNCS, vol. 12302, pp. 233–250. Springer, Cham (2020). https://doi.org/10.1007/978-3-030-59152-6_13
69. Reinbacher, T., Függer, M., Brauer, J.: Real-time runtime verification on chip. In: Qadeer, S., Tasiran, S. (eds.) RV 2012. LNCS, vol. 7687, pp. 110–125. Springer, Heidelberg (2013). https://doi.org/10.1007/978-3-642-35632-2_13
70. Stephens, R.: A survey of stream processing. Acta Inform. **34**(7), 491–541 (1997). https://doi.org/10.1007/s002360050095
71. Thati, P., Roşu, G.: Monitoring algorithms for metric temporal logic specifications. Electr. Notes Theor. Comput. Sci. **113**, 145–162 (2005). https://doi.org/10.1016/j.entcs.2004.01.029, proceedings of the Fourth Workshop on Runtime Verification (RV 2004)
72. Turoňová, L., Holík, L., Lengál, O., Saarikivi, O., Veanes, M., Vojnar, T.: Regex matching with counting-set automata. Proc. ACM Programm. Lang. **4**(OOPSLA), 218:1–218:30 (2020). https://doi.org/10.1145/3428286
73. Ulus, D.: The Reelay monitoring tool (2020). https://doganulus.github.io/reelay/. Accessed 20 Aug 2020
74. Vijayaraghavan, S., Ramanathan, M.: A Practical Guide for SystemVerilog Assertions. Springer, Boston, MA (2006). https://doi.org/10.1007/b137011
75. Wen, Z., Kong, L., Le Glaunec, A., Mamouras, K., Yang, K.: BVAP: energy and memory efficient automata processing for regular expressions. In: Proceedings of the 29th ACM International Conference on Architectural Support for Programming Languages and Operating Systems, Volume 2, pp. 151–166. ASPLOS 2024, ACM, New York, NY, USA (2024). https://doi.org/10.1145/3620665.3640412

76. Witharana, H., Lyu, Y., Charles, S., Mishra, P.: A survey on assertion-based hardware verification. ACM Comput. Surv. **54**(11s), 225:1–225:33 (2022). https://doi.org/10.1145/3510578
77. Wolper, P.: Temporal logic can be more expressive. Inf. Control **56**(1–2), 72–99 (1983). https://doi.org/10.1016/S0019-9958(83)80051-5

TIMELYMON: A Streaming Parallel First-Order Monitor

Lennard Reese[✉][iD], Rafael Castro G. Silva[✉][iD], and Dmitriy Traytel[✉][iD]

Department of Computer Science, University of Copenhagen, Copenhagen, Denmark
{lere,rasi,traytel}@di.ku.dk

Abstract. First-order monitors analyze data-carrying event streams. When event streams are generated by distributed systems, it may be difficult to ensure that events arrive at the monitor in the right order. We develop a new monitoring tool for metric first-order temporal logic, called TIMELYMON, that can process out-of-order events. Using the stream processing framework Timely Dataflow, TIMELYMON also supports parallelized monitoring. We demonstrate TIMELYMON's good performance and scalability on synthetic and real-world benchmarks.

Keywords: Monitoring · Temporal logic · Stream processing

1 Introduction

First-order monitors detect complex temporal patterns in data-carrying event streams. Metric first-order temporal logic (MFOTL) [5] (Sect. 2) is a powerful language for expressing the temporal patterns. Monitors like DejaVu [15], MonPoly [6], and VeriMon [2] use (variants of) MFOTL as their input language.

Patterns expressed by MFOTL formulas are interpreted over event streams that are subdivided into time-points. A time-point consists of a time-stamp and a database, i.e., a finite set of events. From the point of view of the monitor, events coming from a single database happen concurrently. Existing monitors either restrict the databases to be singleton sets [7,15] or process entire databases at once and in-order [2,6]. Both these modes of operation limit the existing tools' suitability for monitoring distributed systems in which individual concurrent events may arrive at the monitor out-of-order [3,4]. The plausible workaround based on reordering of the events in a component wrapping the monitor has been proposed [3]. However, the monitor is idle while it waits for delayed events in this approach.

In this work, we develop a monitoring tool for MFOTL that supports the *streaming* mode of operation (Sect. 3), i.e., the processing of individual events that may arrive out-of-order. Our monitor's output is also presented to the user event-wise and possibly out-of-order. This has the advantage that whenever future temporal operators are involved users may get to see verdicts much earlier than in traditional monitors, which output verdicts for entire time-points at once.

A somewhat surprising advantage of the streaming setting is that we can reuse mostly the same data structures for both past and future operators and can even support unbounded future operators without completely stalling the monitor.

An additional challenge for MFOTL monitoring, which we also tackle, is scalability. Typically, MFOTL monitors are sequential algorithms that are quickly overwhelmed by high volume and high velocity event streams. Parallelization is the main approach for tackling such scalability issues. The approaches for parallelizing MFOTL monitors can be grouped in two categories. The *black box* parallelization approach uses the sequential monitors without modifications (as a black box) to process independent slices of the input [1,11,27]. The alternative is *white box* parallelization, in which the monitoring algorithm is itself parallelized [14,17,25].

Generic data stream processing frameworks like Apache Flink [10] and Timely Dataflow [24] are useful tools for implementing black and white box parallel monitors as they enforce a program structure that is susceptible to a high degree of parallelism while hiding the pitfalls of parallel programming from their users.

We use Timely Dataflow [23,24] to implement our streaming MFOTL monitor, called TIMELYMON, as a white box parallel monitor. Timely Dataflow organizes its programs as a graph of stream transformers, called operators. Given a monitorable [5] MFOTL formula, we map every MFOTL operator occurring in it to a Timely Dataflow operator that inputs the verdicts from the subformulas and outputs the verdicts according to the MFOTL operator's semantics. Parallelized evaluation of Timely Dataflow operators naturally results in out-of-order verdicts for subformulas, which meshes well with our streaming mode of operation.

We demonstrate TIMELYMON's reasonable performance and good scalability on a standard first-order benchmark [20] (Sect. 4) and a real-world example. We also extend the benchmark by incorporating different degrees of the input being out-of-order. TIMELYMON is publicly available [26], along with build and usage instructions and our experiments.

Related Work. TIMELYMON processes out-of-order event streams. In the area of stream runtime verification, pioneered by Lola [12], in-order processing is the norm. An exception is TeSSLa [22], which can process multiple non-synchronized streams, but requires each of them to be in-order. We do not impose any order requirements, but require that the events are labeled with their "true" position so that one has the information to reconstruct the sorted input in principle.

Decentralized runtime monitoring [13] uses multiple monitors to check a centralized specification via multiple decentralized specifications. Each operator in TIMELYMON can be viewed as one decentralized monitor with a partial view of the monitored system. Bonakdarpour et al. [9,18] discussed decentralized run-time verification with a focus on fault-tolerance and crash-resiliency and focuses on LTL, whereas TIMELYMON supports MFOTL. Timely Dataflow has no built-in fault-tolerance mechanisms, although different approaches have been proposed [21,28].

The traditional MFOTL monitors MONPOLY [6], DEJAVU [15], and VERIMON [2] all assume in-order inputs. This restriction also extends to the black box parallel monitors using these tools [1,27]. Basin et al. [3] note this limitation and incorporate watermark-based reordering in the black box monitor, with the aforementioned downside of the monitor having to wait for complete input prefixes.

A exception to in-order MFOTL monitors is Basin et al.'s [7] (closed-source) monitor POLÍMON [19], which supports out-of-order processing for metric temporal logic extended with freeze quantifiers. Their streams store precisely one value per register (which the freeze quantifiers refer to) at a time-point, whereas for us one time-point consists of a set of events. Their logic, also called half-order temporal logic [16], is much less expressive than MFOTL. Nonetheless, we use a variant of their observations data structure to optimize our Once and Eventually operators.

2 Preliminaries

We briefly recall metric first-order temporal logic (MFOTL).

Metric First-Order Temporal Logic. Let $\mathbb{I}$ be the set of nonempty intervals over $\mathbb{N}$. An interval $[b, b') \in \mathbb{I}$ denotes $\{a \in \mathbb{N} \mid b \leq a \land a < b'\}$, where $b \in \mathbb{N}$, $b' \in \mathbb{N} \cup \{\infty\}$, and $b < b'$. We fix a domain $\mathbb{D}$, a set of event names $\mathbb{E}$, and the function $\iota : \mathbb{E} \to \mathbb{N}$ that assigns each $e \in \mathbb{E}$ the arity $\iota(e)$. Additionally, we consider a set of variables $\mathbb{V}$ such that $\mathbb{V} \cap (\mathbb{D} \cup \mathbb{E}) = \varnothing$. MFOTL formulas $\alpha, \beta, \ldots$ are defined as follows:

$$\alpha, \beta := e(\bar{t}) \mid t_1 \approx t_2 \mid \neg \alpha \mid \alpha \land \beta \mid \alpha \lor \beta \mid \exists x.\, \alpha \mid \alpha \,\mathsf{S}_I\, \beta \mid \alpha \,\mathsf{U}_I\, \beta$$

The predicate $e(\bar{t})$ consists of an event name $e \in \mathbb{E}$ and a finite sequence of arguments $\bar{t} = t_1, \ldots, t_{\iota(e)}$, where each $t_i \in \mathbb{V} \cup \mathbb{D}$. Similarly, equality $\approx$ is applied to arguments from $\mathbb{V} \cup \mathbb{D}$. Boolean operators and the existential quantifier are standard. The temporal operators S ("since") and U ("until") are annotated with an interval $I \in \mathbb{I}$. From this minimal MFOTL syntax, we derive additional operators in a standard fashion: $\top := \exists x.\, x \approx x$ ("truth"), $\alpha \to \beta := \neg \alpha \lor \beta$ ("implication"), $\forall x.\, \alpha := \neg \exists x.\, \neg \alpha$ ("universal quantification"), $\Diamondblack_I \alpha := \top \,\mathsf{S}_I\, \alpha$ ("once"), $\Diamond_I \alpha := \top \,\mathsf{U}_I\, \alpha$ ("eventually"), and $\Box_I \alpha := \neg \Diamond_I \alpha$ ("always").

A *database* D is a finite set of events and each event has the form $e(d_1, \ldots d_{\iota(r)})$ for $e \in \mathbb{E}$ and $d_i \in \mathbb{D}$. A *time-stamped database* is a pair of a time-stamp $\tau \in \mathbb{N}$ and a database D. An event stream is an infinite sequence $\rho = \langle \tau_i, D_i \rangle_{i \in \mathbb{N}}$ of time-stamped databases. Each time-stamped database in ρ is called a time-point and is identified by its index i. Time-stamps in the event stream must (1) monotonically increase: $\forall i \in \mathbb{N}.\, \tau_i \leq \tau_{i+1}$ and (2) always eventually make progress: $\forall \tau.\, \exists i.\, \tau < \tau_i$.

MFOTL formulas are evaluated over event streams and valuations for the formula's free variables. The valuation $v : \mathbb{V} \to \mathbb{D}$ maps variables to domain values. The standard semantics of an MFOTL formula α is given by a satisfaction relation of the form $v, i \models \alpha$. We refer to Basin et al. [5,8] for a formal definition.

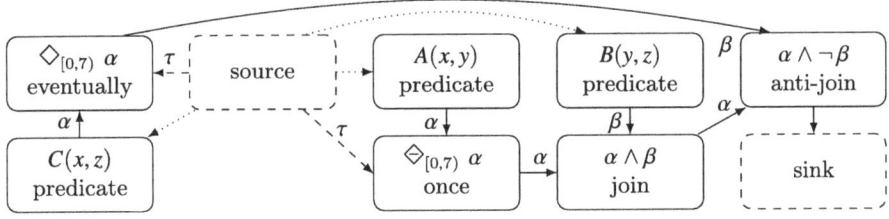

Fig. 1. Dataflow graph for the formula $(\Diamond_{[0,7)} A(x,y)) \wedge B(y,z) \wedge \neg (\Diamond_{[0,7)} C(x,z))$.

The objective for our monitor is to (eventually) compute correct verdicts, also called *satisfactions*, for each time-point i, i.e., satisfying valuations v applied to the formula's free variables. To ensure that the set of satisfactions for any time-point is finite, we syntactically restrict the formulas we consider as is done in some but not all MFOTL monitors [2,6]. Such restriction allow monitors to use finite relations (or tables) instead of binary decision diagrams [15] or automata [5] to represent sets of satisfactions, which benefits performance. Specifically, we make the following restrictions, which are also present in the MonPoly and VeriMon monitors:

1. negated formulas may occur only on the right-hand side of a conjunction $\alpha \wedge \neg \beta$ and moreover β's free variables must be contained in α's in such cases or on the left-hand side of a $(\neg \alpha) \mathsf{S}_I \beta$ or $(\neg \alpha) \mathsf{U}_I \beta$;
2. (negated) equalities between variables may only appear on the right-hand side of a conjunction $\alpha \wedge x \approx y$ (and $\alpha \wedge \neg x \approx y$) and moreover x or y (x and y when negated) must be contained in α's free variables in such cases;
3. in formulas of the form $\alpha \vee \beta$, α and β must have the same free variables;
4. in formulas of the form $\alpha \mathsf{U}_I \beta$ and $\alpha \mathsf{S}_I \beta$, the free variables of α must be contained in β's. (This also applies when α is a negated formula as in 1.)

3 Monitoring Algorithm Overview

TIMELYMON creates a dataflow graph from the MFOTL formula's abstract syntax tree. Usually, the mapping from MFOTL operators to Timely Dataflow operators is one-to-one, but not always. For example, formulas of the form $\alpha \wedge \neg \beta$ are translated into a single, binary anti-join operator. Also, we optimize the derived operators $\Diamondblack$ and $\Diamond$ by using dedicated operators.

Figure 1 shows the dataflow graph constructed for the example formula $(\Diamond_{[0,7)} A(x,y)) \wedge B(y,z) \wedge \neg (\Diamond_{[0,7)} C(x,z))$. The inputs of each binary operator are labeled with the role of the incoming input stream from the operator's point of view. Even though $\Diamondblack$ and $\Diamond$ are derived from S and U, we use dedicated, optimized operators for them in the dataflow graph. All temporal operators receive an additional input (denoted by τ) over which time-stamps are communicated.

Our operators exchange three kinds of events. We use MFOTL's time-points as the notion of time in Timely Dataflow. Thus, all exchanged events are labeled with a time-point. The source operator emits individual data events of the form $e(d_1,\ldots,d_{\iota(e)})$ to the predicates operators (dotted connections). Furthermore, the source operator emits time-stamp events of the form (τ_i) mapping a time-point i to its time-stamp τ_i (dashed connections) to temporal operators. The other operators exchange subformula satisfaction events (solid connections). A satisfaction v is represented by a vector of domain values $(d_1,\ldots,d_{\iota(e)})$ that are interpreted as the values assigned by v to the subformula's free variables (listed in some canonical order).

TIMELYMON operators make no assumption on the order in which it receives the events. Also, as soon as a satisfaction according to the operator's semantics is found, it is immediately output. Each parallel worker in Timely Dataflow executes the entire dataflow on different portions of the data. We specify for each operator how to distribute the data across workers. For example, the incoming events to be processed by the predicate operators are simply hashed onto the worker's identity: one worker may receive the event $A(1,2)$, another one may receive $B(2,3)$. Later operators may require the redistribution of the data across the workers. For example, the join operator must ensure that the same worker receives the matching satisfaction $(1,2)$ for variables (x,y) and $(2,3)$ for variables (y,z) to correctly compute the resulting satisfaction $(1,2,3)$ for variables (x,y,z). Therefore, our algorithm (re)distributes the events before the join operator by hashing the values from the join key, i.e., the common variables of α and β. Similarly, for the temporal operators we use the variables of α for hashing (unless α has no free variables, in which case we broadcast the trivial α tuples to all workers and hash on β's variables).

We sketch how our algorithm processes each MFOTL operator.

Predicate. Upon receiving an event $e(d_1,\ldots,d_{\iota(e)})$, the operator for the predicate $e(x_1,\ldots,x_{\iota(e)})$ creates the corresponding satisfaction $(d_1,\ldots,d_{\iota(e)})$. The operator performs matching due to constants and repeated variables that may occur, which may filter out certain events. For example, the predicate $A(x,5,x)$ matches the event $A(1,5,1)$ yielding the satisfaction (1) for the variable list (x). The same predicate does not match events $A(1,4,1)$ or $A(1,5,2)$—no satisfaction is output.

Existential Quantifier. The operator for the existential quantifier $\exists x.\ \alpha$ projects away (i.e., removes) the variable x from the satisfactions it receives for α.

Disjunction. The binary operator for $\alpha \vee \beta$ outputs the satisfactions it receives on either input. Recall that α and β are assumed to have the same free variables.

Conjunction. We use four operators to handle conjunctions. Whenever equalities are involved we consider two cases: (1) The operator for formulas of the form $\alpha \wedge x \approx y$ or $\alpha \wedge \neg x \approx y$ where both x and y are free in α filters α's satisfactions using the (negated) equality constraint. (2) The operator for formulas of the form $\alpha \wedge x \approx y$ where only one of x and y is free in α extends α's satisfactions with the new variable (copying the old variable's value). The regular conjunction

time-point	0	1	2	3	4
time-stamp	1		3	3	7
α with variable list (x)			(1)	(1),(2)	(1),(2)
β with variable list (x,y)	(1,2),(3,1)		(2,1)	(4,3)	(2,1),(4,5)
$\alpha \, S_{[1,5)} \, \beta$ with variable list (x,y)					(2,1)

Fig. 2. Example partial inputs and outputs for $\alpha \, S_{[1,5)} \, \beta$

$\alpha \wedge \beta$ proceeds symmetrically whenever it receives a new input for α or β. For both inputs, the operator stores all previously received satisfactions grouped by time-point. Upon receiving a new satisfaction for α at time-point i, the operator joins it with all matching previously received satisfactions for β at i and outputs the result. The conjunction with a negated subformula $\alpha \wedge \neg \beta$ is evaluated using a binary anti-join operator. This operator is non-streaming, in the sense that it must wait until it receives all β satisfactions for a time-point i before producing an output at i.

Temporal Operators. We exemplify the inner workings of our streaming temporal operators $\alpha \, S_I \, \beta$ and $\alpha \, U_I \, \beta$. The operators have three inputs: one for time-stamps and two for the subformulas α and β. Recall that we assume that α's free variables are contained in those of β. We focus on the S case.

Consider the partial trace in Fig. 2. It shows the received satisfactions for α and β and the computed output $(2,1)$ for $\alpha \, S_{[1,5)} \, \beta$ at time-point 4. The operator works under the assumption that none of the time-points is complete. That is, it may receive new inputs for any of the time-points 0–4. The operator has not yet received any input at time-point 1; even this time-point's time-stamp is unknown. Nonetheless and unlike traditional monitors, the operator was able to already output a satisfaction at time-point 4. To do so, it was sufficient to note the $(2,1)$ input for β at time-point 2 and the two (1) inputs for α at time-points 3 and 4 together with the quantitative interval check: $7-3 \in [1,5)$. We call such patterns of inputs resulting in S satisfactions β-α-sequences. Because α may have fewer variables than β, a single input for α may be relevant for different β-α-sequences.

Continuing our example, we note that both receiving new inputs for α and β may trigger new output for S. For example, upon receiving the satisfaction (1) at time-point 1 for α the operator can output satisfactions $(1,2)$ at time-points 2 and 3 and possibly also at 1 if it learns that the time-stamp at time-point 1 is different from 1 (but not at 0 and 4, which fail the interval constraint). Alternatively, upon receiving the satisfaction $(1,2)$ for β at time-point 1 with time-point 2, we can output the satisfaction $(1,2)$ at time-points 2 and 3 (but not at 0, 1, and 4).

4 Empirical Evaluation

We evaluate TIMELYMON to provide answers to the following research questions:

RQ1: Does our monitor produce the same verdicts as the verified tool VeriMon?
RQ2: How does TIMELYMON perform in comparison to MonPoly and VeriMon?
RQ3: How does TIMELYMON scale with respect to the number of events?
RQ4: How does TIMELYMON scale with respect to the number of workers?
RQ5: How does the order of the events impact TIMELYMON's performance?
RQ6: Does TIMELYMON output verdicts earlier than MonPoly?

4.1 Experimental Setup

We used the synthetic benchmark generation tool by Krstić and Schneider [20] to conduct our experiments. Our traces were generated for the built-in *temporal three-way conjunctions* family of query patterns $\mathcal{F}_3$. A three-way conjunction is a specific temporal pattern that involves three distinct event types A, B, and C, with integer data values. The family is parameterized by lists of variables v_A, v_B, v_C (called variable patterns) and is given by the following parametric MFOTL formula:

$$(\Diamond_{[0,b]} A(v_A)) \wedge B(v_B) \wedge (\Diamond_{[0,b]} C(v_C))$$

We used the three supported variable patterns: Star $v_A = (w,x)$, $v_B = (w,y)$, $v_C = (w,z)$, Linear $v_A = (w,x)$, $v_B = (x,y)$, $v_C = (y,z)$, and Triangle $v_A = (x,y)$, $v_B = (y,z)$, $v_C = (z,x)$. We also consider the Negated Triangle formula, which includes an anti-join: $(\Diamond_{[0,b]} A(x,y)) \wedge B(y,z) \wedge \neg (\Diamond_{[0,b]} C(z,x))$. The interval's upper bound b is denoted by the superscript ^{b} on a pattern's name, e.g., Star^7. To benchmark Since and Until we use two additional parametric formulas, which are referred to by combining the variable pattern and the operator, e.g., Star Until or Triangle Since.

$$B(v_A) \, \mathsf{S}_{[0,45]} \, ((\Diamond_{[0,45]} A(v_B)) \wedge C(v_C)) \qquad B(v_A) \, \mathsf{U}_{[0,45]} \, ((\Diamond_{[0,45]} A(v_B)) \wedge C(v_C))$$

The benchmark supports adjusting the relative frequency of each event's type. We use 10% for A, 50% for B, and 40% for C. For each variable pattern, we used the benchmark to randomly generated finite prefixes of event streams of different lengths ranging from 50 to 500 time-points with 1 000 events per time-point.

The benchmark has the capability to delay a given fraction of events, which mimics real-world scenarios where there is no guarantee of order. We use this feature but also consider other cases that exhibit a higher degree of disorder. We examine five different orders in which events are given to TIMELYMON:

In-order: Events are sent in the correct order, with ascending time-points.
Delayed: Events are sent mainly in order. For each time-point, a subset of the data is delayed and moved to a later point in the input. The maximum delay (move distance md) and the fraction of delayed events can be specified (standard deviation sd) by the user. We use $md = 5$ and $sd = 25\%$.
Reversed: Events are sent in the reverse order, with descending time-points.
Out-of-order (time-points): Entire time-points are shuffled. The monitor receives time-points (consisting of a set of events) in an arbitrary order.

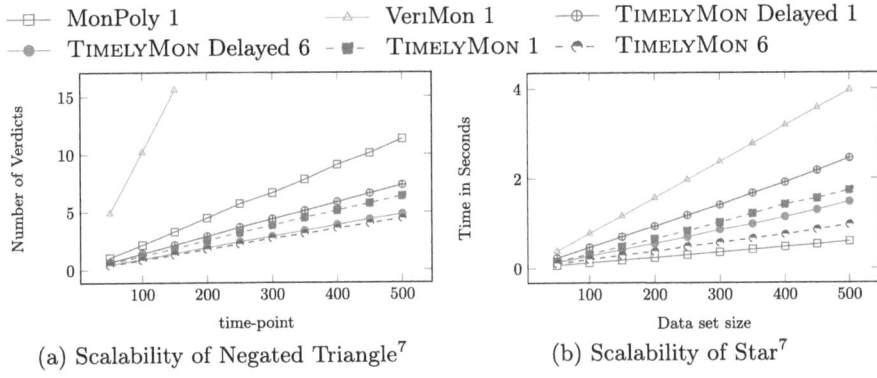

Fig. 3. Load scalability results

Out-of-order (events): Individual events are shuffled. The monitor receives events (labeled with their time-point and time-stamp) in an arbitrary order.

To test TIMELYMON with real-world data, we used the Wikipedia API [29] that streams all changes in real-time. The produced stream is mildly out-of-order. Moreover, it does not contain watermarks so that it is not clear by how much individual events may be delayed. We reduce each JSON objects in this stream to a time-stamped event containing the event-type, username, and the bot label. We used a simple python script to interact with the API, and to sanitize and transform the data into the format suitable for TIMELYMON. Our objective was to identify users that are not labeled as bots but exhibit bot-like behavior. Our policy outputs users u not labeled as bots (i.e., have label 0) that perform five edits (event ed) within (too) close proximity (1–2 s) to each other:

$$ed(u,0) \wedge \diamondsuit_{[1,2]} (ed(u,0) \wedge \diamondsuit_{[1,2]} (ed(u,0) \wedge \diamondsuit_{[1,2]} (ed(u,0) \wedge \diamondsuit_{[1,2]} ed(u,0))))$$

4.2 Data and Analysis

All experiments were run on an Apple M2 Pro 10 Core CPU at 3.30 GHz, and 16 GB of RAM. For each synthetic experiment we ran 5 executions and recorded the average execution time. For **RQ1**, we observed that there was no difference in the verdicts produced by all monitors (even though TIMELYMON's verdicts were ordered differently than VeriMon's and MonPoly's as expected).

A direct comparison between TIMELYMON, MonPoly, and VeriMon is only fair when considering one worker and an *in-order* event sequence, as the latter tools are restricted to this setting. TIMELYMON scales worse than MonPoly but better than VeriMon in terms of trace length 3b. Therefore, for **RQ2**, we cannot claim any performance gain in equal testing scenarios (i.e., without parallelism).

For **RQ3**, as shown in Figs. 3a and 3b, processing time expectedly increases proportionally with increased numbers of the events. In the one worker scenario,

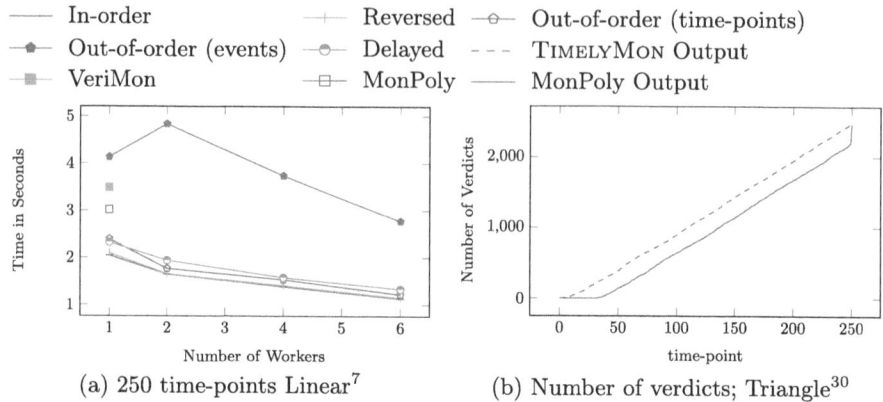

Fig. 4. Anticipation and parallel scalability results

our monitor spends (approximately) five times more time to process 250 time-points than it does for 50 time-points. On the other hand, with six workers, our monitor still has competitive execution times for 500 time-points compared to the other monitors. In response to **RQ4**, in general, increasing the number of workers resulted in a significant reduction of execution time for all benchmarks. For example, the execution time was reduced by almost 40% for the Delayed input order when increasing from 1 to 2 workers in Fig. 4a.

Out of the considered tools, only TIMELYMON can process events out-of-order. Regarding **RQ5**, out-of-order (events) setting presents the most challenging cases for TIMELYMON, as shown in Fig. 4a. In this scenario, the execution time increases significantly with a large number of time-points. The larger the set of out-of-order time-points in the partial sequence data structure, the higher the likelihood of gaps and the number of optimised updates. Apart from this corner case, TimelyMon's performance is robust with respect to delaying a fraction of events.

To answer question **RQ6**, we record the numbers of output tuples for TIMELYMON and MonPoly after each time-point in the in-order experiment. Figure 4b show the result: TIMELYMON is always equal or ahead of MonPoly. We computed the average, minimal and maximal difference by how much TIMELYMON leads:

Formula	Average	Minimum	Maximum
Triangle[30]	247	1	302
Star[30]	240	0	292

Due to the event-wise processing and the ability to output as soon as possible, TIMELYMON produces output ahead of MonPoly. We also note the advantage of our approach in the real-world scenario, where TIMELYMON continuously produces output, whereas MonPoly would need to buffer, sort, and only produce output when receiving watermarks. The API has an enforced timeout; we ran TimelyMon for 13.34 min on 6 cores with a peak memory consumption of 54 MB.

Acknowledgments. This research is supported by a Novo Nordisk Fonden start package grant (NNF20OC0063462). We thank Galina Peycheva for her past-only dynamic-programming-based monitor implementation in Timely Dataflow [25], which served as the starting point for the development of TimelyMon. We thank David Basin, Srđan Krstić, and Joshua Schneider for insightful discussions about different approaches to parallel, out-of-order monitoring.

References

1. Basin, D.A., Caronni, G., Ereth, S., Harvan, M., Klaedtke, F., Mantel, H.: Scalable offline monitoring of temporal specifications. Formal Meth. Syst. Des. **49**(1–2), 75–108 (2016). https://doi.org/10.1007/s10703-016-0242-y
2. Basin, D.A., et al.: VeriMon: a formally verified monitoring tool. In: Seidl, H., Liu, Z., Pasareanu, C.S. (eds.) ICTAC 2022. LNCS, vol. 13572, pp. 1–6. Springer, Cham (2022). https://doi.org/10.1007/978-3-031-17715-6_1
3. Basin, D.A., Gras, M., Krstić, S., Schneider, J.: Scalable online monitoring of distributed systems. In: Deshmukh, J., Ničković, D. (eds.) RV 2020. LNCS, vol. 12399, pp. 197–220. Springer, Cham (2020). https://doi.org/10.1007/978-3-030-60508-7_11
4. Basin, D.A., Harvan, M., Klaedtke, F., Zalinescu, E.: Monitoring data usage in distributed systems. IEEE Trans. Softw. Eng. **39**(10), 1403–1426 (2013). https://doi.org/10.1109/TSE.2013.18
5. Basin, D.A., Klaedtke, F., Müller, S., Zalinescu, E.: Monitoring metric first-order temporal properties. J. ACM **62**(2), 15:1–15:45 (2015). https://doi.org/10.1145/2699444
6. Basin, D.A., Klaedtke, F., Zalinescu, E.: The MonPoly monitoring tool. In: Reger, G., Havelund, K. (eds.) RV-CuBES 2017. Kalpa Publications in Computing, vol. 3, pp. 19–28. EasyChair (2017). https://doi.org/10.29007/89hs
7. Basin, D.A., Klaedtke, F., Zalinescu, E.: Runtime verification over out-of-order streams. ACM Trans. Comput. Log. **21**(1), 5:1–5:43 (2020). https://doi.org/10.1145/3355609
8. Basin, D.A., Krstic, S., Schneider, J., Traytel, D.: Correct and efficient policy monitoring, a retrospective. In: André, É., Sun, J. (eds.) ATVA 2023. LNCS, vol. 14215, pp. 3–30. Springer, Cham (2023). https://doi.org/10.1007/978-3-031-45329-8_1
9. Bonakdarpour, B., Fraigniaud, P., Rajsbaum, S., Rosenblueth, D.A., Travers, C.: Decentralized asynchronous crash-resilient runtime verification. J. ACM **69**(5), 34:1–34:31 (2022). https://doi.org/10.1145/3550483
10. Carbone, P., Katsifodimos, A., Ewen, S., Markl, V., Haridi, S., Tzoumas, K.: Apache Flink^{TM}: stream and batch processing in a single engine. IEEE Data Eng. Bull. **38**(4), 28–38 (2015). http://sites.computer.org/debull/A15dec/p28.pdf
11. Chen, F., Roşu, G.: Parametric trace slicing and monitoring. In: Kowalewski, S., Philippou, A. (eds.) TACAS 2009. LNCS, vol. 5505, pp. 246–261. Springer, Heidelberg (2009). https://doi.org/10.1007/978-3-642-00768-2_23

12. D'Angelo, B., et al.: LOLA: runtime monitoring of synchronous systems. In: 12th International Symposium on Temporal Representation and Reasoning (TIME 2005), 23–25 June 2005, Burlington, Vermont, USA, pp. 166–174. IEEE Computer Society (2005). https://doi.org/10.1109/TIME.2005.26
13. Falcone, Y.: On decentralized monitoring. In: Nouri, A., Wu, W., Barkaoui, K., Li, Z.W. (eds.) VECoS 2021. LNCS, vol. 13187, pp. 1–16. Springer, Cham (2022). https://doi.org/10.1007/978-3-030-98850-0_1
14. Hansen, E.H.P.: Streaming Algorithms for Metric First-Order Temporal Operators. Bachelor's thesis, University of Copenhagen (2022)
15. Havelund, K., Peled, D., Ulus, D.: First-order temporal logic monitoring with BDDs. Formal Meth. Syst. Des. **56**(1), 1–21 (2020). https://doi.org/10.1007/s10703-018-00327-4
16. Henzinger, T.A.: Half-order modal logic: how to prove real-time properties. In: Dwork, C. (ed.) PODC 1990, pp. 281–296. ACM (1990). https://doi.org/10.1145/93385.93429
17. Jannelli, V.: A White-Box Parallel Monitor for Metric First-Order Temporal Logic. Bachelor's thesis, ETH Zürich (2021)
18. Kazemlou, S., Bonakdarpour, B.: Crash-resilient decentralized synchronous runtime verification. In: 37th IEEE Symposium on Reliable Distributed Systems, SRDS 2018, Salvador, Brazil, 2–5 October 2018, pp. 207–212. IEEE Computer Society (2018). https://doi.org/10.1109/SRDS.2018.00032
19. Klaedtke, F.: POLIMON: checking temporal properties over out-of-order streams at runtime (2024)
20. Krstić, S., Schneider, J.: A benchmark generator for online first-order monitoring. In: Deshmukh, J., Ničković, D. (eds.) RV 2020. LNCS, vol. 12399, pp. 482–494. Springer, Cham (2020). https://doi.org/10.1007/978-3-030-60508-7_27
21. Lattuada, A.: You may not need synchronization (in streaming systems). Ph.D. thesis, ETH Zurich (2022)
22. Leucker, M., Sánchez, C., Scheffel, T., Schmitz, M., Schramm, A.: TeSSLa: runtime verification of non-synchronized real-time streams. In: Haddad, H.M., Wainwright, R.L., Chbeir, R. (eds.) SAC 2018, pp. 1925–1933. ACM (2018). https://doi.org/10.1145/3167132.3167338
23. McSherry, F.: Github: Timely dataflow. https://github.com/TimelyDataflow/timely-dataflow/
24. Murray, D.G., McSherry, F., Isard, M., Isaacs, R., Barham, P., Abadi, M.: Incremental, iterative data processing with timely dataflow. Commun. ACM **59**(10), 75–83 (2016). https://doi.org/10.1145/2983551
25. Peycheva, G.: Real-time verification of datacenter security policies via online log analysis. Master's thesis, ETH Zürich (2018)
26. Reese, L., Silva, R.C.G., Traytel, D.: Development repository of TIMELYMON (2024). https://git.ku.dk/kfx532/timelymon/-/releases/RV24_Tool_Paper
27. Schneider, J., Basin, D.A., Brix, F., Krstić, S., Traytel, D.: Scalable online first-order monitoring. Int. J. Softw. Tools Technol. Transf. **23**(2), 185–208 (2021). https://doi.org/10.1007/s10009-021-00607-1
28. Selvatici, L.: A Streaming System with Coordination-Free Fault-Tolerance. Master's thesis, ETH Zurich (2020)
29. Wikimedia Foundation, I.: Event platform/eventstreams. https://stream.wikimedia.org/v2/ui/#/?streams=mediawiki.recentchange

Specification and Visualization

Adding State to Stream Runtime Verification

Manuel Caldeira, Hannes Kallwies[✉][ID], Martin Leucker[✉][ID], and Daniel Thoma[✉]

Institute for Software Engineering and Programming Languages,
University of Lübeck, Lübeck, Germany
{kallwies,leucker,thoma}@isp.uni-luebeck.de

Abstract. Stream Runtime Verification (SRV) is gaining traction for monitoring systems with data streams, but it struggles with specifying state-based systems and control flow. While automata models like state charts excel at representing states, functional languages offer solutions like monads (e.g., in Haskell) to elegantly handle state and data streams together. Other approaches exist in Lustre/Esterel or Rust. However, for SRV frameworks like TeSSLa, no such approach exists so far. This paper extends TeSSLa's syntax by building on a monadic type to simplify for improved control flow specifications.

Keywords: Stream runtime verification · Automata · Monads

1 Introduction

Runtime Verification [15] deals with checking individual runs of systems whether they meet a given correctness property. Stream Runtime Verification (SRV) [20] is gaining significant attention, particularly in monitoring systems that generate continuous data streams. Prominent tools for SRV are the pioneer LOLA [8], its real-time extension RTLola [4], Striver [12], and the Temporal Stream-based Specification Language (TeSSLa) [14], on which we build in this paper. In SRV, equational specifications are used which offer a powerful tool due to their conciseness, ease of understanding, and clear semantics. This approach perfectly aligns with modelling data flow, allowing for straightforward analysis of data streams.

However, a key limitation of equational specifications lies in their treatment of state-based systems. Specifying control flow, a core element of state-based systems, becomes cumbersome. At the same time, automata models, like state charts, hybrid systems, and timed automata directly model state-based systems and their transitions and are a popular in RV as well. Automata have been successfully applied in RV to monitor temporal logics like LTL [9,15], used as specification formalisms in tools [6] and developed into expressive formalisms for quantified properties [1,19].

Therefore, it seems beneficial to bridge the gap between the strengths of both state-based and stream-based approaches. Functional languages have dealt with similar issues, and concepts like monads [22] have emerged as a solution. Notably, Haskell provides excellent support for monads [18]. With its do-notation it has also established the idea of mapping an imperative-style syntax to monads by chaining continuations using the monad's bind-operator. An alternative approach is the async-await-syntax for futures that has been developed in the context of C# and F# [21] and has been adopted by many innovative, emerging languages like Rust [16]. The declarative Lustre and imperative Esterel [13] have shown the advantages of both paradigms for synchronous programming. A similar technique of chaining continuations has also be used to give a semantics to Esterel in terms of streams [3] and to translate a deterministic fragment of the Discrete Duration Calculus to Lustre [10].

This paper presents a novel syntactic extension to TeSSLa, building on the addition of a monadic type. This addition simplifies the process of specifying control flow within TeSSLa. Therefore, several challenges had to be addressed. Firstly, TeSSLa treats time as a first-class citizen, introducing complexities. Secondly, ensuring finite stream graphs is crucial for practical applications, especially when targeting FPGA backend implementations. Finally, type inference within TeSSLa presents its own set of difficulties.

This paper presents the first approach to runtime verification that leverages a monadic type within a temporal stream-based language. By extending TeSSLa with suitable syntax extension and a monadic type, we aim to simplify the specification of control flow.

The work was mainly developed in the thesis of the first author which also serves as an extended reference [5]. The implementation is open source[1] and an executable[2] is available. Further documentation on TeSSLa can also be found on its website[3].

2 States in TeSSLa Yesterday

TeSSLa. TeSSLa (short for Temporal Stream Based Specification Language) is a stream runtime verification (SRV) formalism and toolchain [7,14] which is especially suited for the description of real-time properties. Similar to other SRV languages, like LOLA [15] or Striver [11], TeSSLa describes the property to be monitored as a stream transformation. Therefore a TeSSLa specification consists of input and intermediate stream definitions. Input streams are those that originate from the observed system and whose values are incrementally passed to the TeSSLa monitor, which is generated from the specification. The intermediate streams are defined in the specification by application of stream operators on input and intermediate streams. TeSSLa is built upon six basic

---

[1] https://git.tessla.io/tessla/tessla/-/tree/feature-imperative-tessla.
[2] https://git.tessla.io/tessla/tessla/-/jobs/artifacts/feature-imperative-tessla/file/target/imperative-tessla.zip?job=deploy.
[3] https://tessla.io/.

core-operators, e.g. for executing (called lifting) functions on the current stream values, or retrieving the last event from a specific stream. Finally, some of the intermediate streams in the specification can also be marked as output streams. The events from these streams are then emitted by the monitor during its execution and reflect the result of the runtime verification process. Beyond this basic concept the standard TeSSLa implementation [14] offers several additional features, e.g. capabilities for defining macros and functions (for lifting) in a functional style or access to several predefined operations and functions in a standard library.

A special focus of TeSSLa lies on the specification of real-time properties. Compared to early SRV languages like LOLA, it operates on timed streams, i.e. such where every event has a timestamp from a global clock attached. With corresponding operators it is possible to retrieve these timestamps in the specification and compute with them (e.g. to determine latencies) and to emit output events at arbitrary timestamps, not necessarily synchronous to input events. Due to this asynchronicity every future-independent, monotonic and continuous stream transformation can be described by a TeSSLa specification [7]. However, specific scenarios require complex constructions which are often unintuitive and cause hard-to-read code, which is unfavorable, especially for a specification language, which should allow for a high-level description of properties. Representative for such a scenario is the description of control flows. To illustrate this, we introduce a small running example.

Coffee Machine. Figure 1 shows a simple state machine modelling a coffee maker. Initially, the coffee machine is in an idle state. When a user presses the button it starts the brewing process. After 20 s a cup then has been released and filled with coffee. The machine detects when the cup is taken by the user and returns to the idle state. In addition, the machine keeps track of the number of cups n pro-

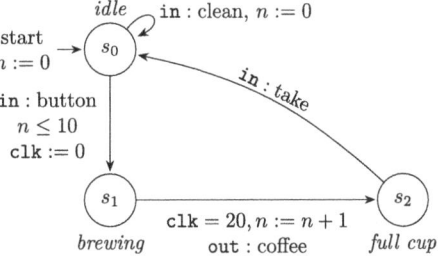

Fig. 1. Coffee machine as timed automaton

duced. When n exceeds 10 the machine has to be cleaned. All theses aspects, control flow, timing and some additional data constraints can be represented concisely using state machines.

When it comes to description of this scenario in a TeSSLa specification, e.g. to monitor the correct behavior of the coffee machine, the main obstacle is the nature of TeSSLa as a dataflow language. The only possibility to express the current state of the coffee machine (i.e. the automaton) is to define a dedicated intermediate stream to hold this information. In the particular example the state consists of the discrete automaton state (s_i) and the current value of n. Whenever an input occurs (e.g. the pressing of a button of the machine) the last value from this state stream and the inputs are used to determine the new state stream value. The outputs (e.g. coffee in the running example) can

```
1   in button: Events[Unit]; in take: Events[Unit]; in clean: Events[Unit]
2
3   def automatonLogic(lastS: Option[(Int, Int)], button: Option[Unit],
4         take: Option[Unit], clean: Option[Unit], timeout: Option[Unit]) = {
5     def state = getSome(lastS)._1
6     def n = getSome(lastS)._2
7
8     def t0 = state == 0 && isSome(button) && n <= 10
9     def t1 = state == 1 && isSome(timeout)
10    def t2 = state == 2 && isSome(take)
11    def t3 = state == 0 && isSome(clean)
12
13    def newState = if t0 then 1 else if t1 then 2 else if t2
14        then 0 else state
15    def newN = if t1 then n + 1 else if t3 then 0 else n
16    def coffee = t1
17    Some(((newState, newN), coffee))
18  }
19
20  def timerReset: Events[Unit] = lift(button, last(automatonState, button),
21    (b, s) => if isSome(b) && getSome(s)._1 == 0 && getSome(s)._2 <= 10 then
22              Some(()) else None)
23  def timeout = delay(const(20, timerReset), timerReset)
24  def trigger = mergeUnit4(button, take, clean, timeout)
25  def transitionResult = lift5(last(automatonState, trigger), button, take,
26                                clean, timeout, automatonLogic)
27  def automatonState: Events[(Int, Int)] =
28    default(transitionResult._1, (0,0))
29  [...]
```

Listing 1. Coffee machine example in TeSSLa

then be determined on basis of this state or within the transition computation. When time is involved, as in the example above, an additional stream has to be introduced which has to bear an event whenever the time runs out which again triggers the computation described above.

Listing 1 shows an excerpt of such an implementation in conventional TeSSLa. The state is maintained in the stream `automatonState` which is a tuple of two integers representing the automaton state and the current value of n. Whenever one of the external actions like button presses (input streams) or the stream `timeout` (which implements the timing behavior of the transition between s_1 and s_2 in the automaton with help of operator **delay**) carries an event, the last value of `automatonState` is recovered (line 24 of Listing 1) and the function `automatonLogic` which is defined in lines 3–17 is called on this last state and the current values of the input streams and the timeout. In this function the successor state (including the new value of n) is then computed according to the transition rules of the automaton and the value of the `coffee` output is determined. Based on the resulting value, the new event of `automatonState` is set in line 26.

Overall, the implementation contains a lot of boilerplate code to handle the triggering of the new state computation and storing the transition result to stream `automatonState`, while the actual automaton description finds itself in lines 8–14. Especially the handling of the timed transition (lines 19–22) requires complex, partially redundant code to avoid a self-recursion of stream `timerReset`.

```
1   in button: Events[Unit]
2   in clean:  Events[Unit]
3   in take:   Events[Unit]
4
5   defer def idle(n: Int) = waitFor {
6     clean => call idle(0)
7     button => {
8       call brewing
9       call idle(n + 1)
10    }
11  }
12
13  def brewing = proc {
14    call sleep(20)
15    yield ()
16    call waitUntil(take)
17  }
18
19  def coffee = run(idle(0))
20
21  out coffee
```

Listing 2. New TeSSLa

3 States in TeSSLa Today

The challenges when trying to express state-based specifications like the coffee machine from Fig. 1 in TeSSLa are twofold: firstly, TeSSLa is a purely functional language. While this is very well suited to express and reason about compositions of stream-transforming operations, it makes it difficult to express the idea of modification of state and control flow in a natural way. Secondly, the asynchronous nature of TeSSLa (streams do not have to carry events at the same points in time) makes it more difficult to express synchronous transition conditions between states triggered by events on streams and delays.

In order to handle both challenges we have introduced a new, procedural syntax to TeSSLa. The main idea is to introduce procedures with imperative-style control-flow. Semantically, these procedures maintain a *current timestamp* starting at 0 and are executed continually. Time inside a procedure moves forward by calling waitFor and thereby waiting for one ore more conditions. A condition can refer to the arrival of events on other streams as well as a point in time. In-between waitFor-calls a procedure can output a value to a single output stream using yield. Procedures can handover control flow to another procedure until it returns using the call keyword. In order to obtain the stream of outputs produced by a procedure it has to be executed using run. A procedure can be called, via call or run, arbitrarily in parallel without multiple instances affecting each other.

Procedures are represented by standard TeSSLa definitions of type Proc[V, Y] where V is the type of value returned to a caller and Y is the type of values yielded to the output stream. However, to distinguish the procedural syntax it has to be wrapped in a proc-block unless it is only a single, procedural action.

Listing 2 shows a specification for the coffee machine example using the new syntax. The output stream coffee is defined as the output of executing the procedure idle with argument 0 (line 19). Procedure idle is defined as a single

```
1   def extra = waitFor {
2     button2 => {
3       def start = now
4       waitFor {
5         button1 .or await start + 1s => call idle
6         button2 => if (getSomeOrElse(temp?, 0) < 50) then {
7           call program(call count)
8         } else {
9           call idle
10         }
11       }
12     }
13   }
14   def count = waitFor {
15     button1 => 1 + (call count)
16     button2 => 0
17   }
```

Listing 3. Advanced features

waitFor-block (line 5) with two cases: arrival of an event on clean in which idle is called recursively with n reset to 0, and button in which brewing is called first and once control is returned idle is called recursively with n increased by 1. idle never returns. Such infinite recursions are possible as long as time keeps being moved forward by waitFor actions and the calls occur in tail position. If, like in this case, the recursion is unguarded and only depends on arguments, available at compile time, the procedure has to be marked as defer to avoid compile-time expansion.

Procedure brewing is defined by single proc block. It first calls the procedure sleep to wait for 20 s, then yields a Unit-value and finally calls waitUntil to wait for an event on stream take before returning. sleep and waitUntil are procedures from the standard library that can be implemented easily using the general waitFor syntax.

Listing 3 demonstrates several advanced features not used in the running example. Suppose we want to add a programming mode that is entered by "double clicking" a second button but only may be entered, when the brewing unit has cooled down enough. Once entered, the coffee size can be changed by pressing the first button repeatedly and confirming with the second button.

Procedure extra first waits for button2 to be pressed, after which in line 3 the current time stamp is saved as start. Then, the procedure waits for one of two cases in line 4: (1) button1 is pressed, or the time point start + 1s has been reached. (2) button2 is pressed a second time within the 1 s limit. In the latter case the procedure reads the current value of the stream temp using the ?-operator. The result of reading a value from a stream can be none as a current value might not be available. The standard library function getSomeOrElse inserts a default value where necessary. If the value read is less than 50, the procedure moves to line 7. Here, call is used as a sub-expressions. This allows to call procedures inside of nested expressions. In this example, the procedure count is called, which counts the number of times button1 is pressed, returning the total number once button2 is pressed. This number is then passed as an argument to procedure program.

```
1   in a: Events[Unit]
2   in b: Events[Unit]
3   in c: Events[Unit]
4
5   defer def q0(stack: List[Bool]): Proc[Unit, Bool] = waitFor {
6       a => call q0(List.prepend(true, stack))
7       b => call q0(List.prepend(false, stack))
8       c => call q1(stack)
9   }
10
11  defer def q1(stack: List[Bool]): Proc[Unit, Bool] = waitFor {
12      a => if(!List.isEmpty(stack) && List.head(stack))
13          then call q0(List.tail(stack)) else call qf
14      b => if(!List.isEmpty(stack) && !List.head(stack))
15          then call q0(List.tail(stack)) else call qf
16      c => call q0(stack)
17  }
18
19  def qf: Proc[Unit, Bool] = waitFor {
20      a .or b => {
21          yield false
22          call qf
23      }
24  }
25
26  out run(q0(List.empty))
```

Listing 4. Deterministic push-down automaton

Our aim was to integrate the procedural syntax seamlessly with the purely functional basis of the language. An established way to handle control flow and side-effects like state-modifications, events and timeouts in purely functional languages are monadic types, i.e. types that can encode the effects available to the programmer and define two additional operations `Pure[V](v: V): M[V]` and `FlatMap[V1, V2](m: M[V1], f: V1 => M[V2]): M[V2]`. `Pure` just allows to convert regular values into the monadic type, whereas `FlatMap` allows to chain functions expressed over said type together.

Consider the procedure **brewing** from Listing 2. Using a monadic interface for the type `Proc` and a constructor for the action `yield` it could be represented by the following purely functional program.

```
1   def brewing: Proc[Unit, Unit] = FlatMap(sleep(20), (x) =>
2       FlatMap(Yield(()), (y) => WaitUntil(take)))
```

To support the complete syntax, we can follow the same approach of using `FlatMap` to chain a continuation function to an action it depends on. We just need to extend the type `Proc` by further constructors mirroring the syntactic constructs:

```
1   type Proc[V, Y]
2   def Pure[V](value: V): Proc[V, Nothing]
3   def FlatMap[V1, V2, Y](proc: Proc[Y, V1], f: V1 => Proc[Y, V2])
4   def Yield[Y](value: Y): Proc[Y, Unit]
5   def Read[V](stream: Events[V]): Proc[Nothing, Option[A]]
6   def Now: Proc[Nothing, Time]
7   def WaitUntil[V, Y](cases: List[(Case, Proc[V, Y])]): Proc[V, Y]
```

Internally, `Proc` is implemented as an enum type representing the possible control flow of the program. Correspondingly, `run` is then implemented by a generic TeSSLa specification executing instances of `Proc`.

Generally, the procedural extension can express common deterministic models of control flow like automata very well. To exemplify this, Listing 4 shows a representation of a push-down automaton accepting the language

$$S := aSa \mid bSb \mid c \mid aSaS \mid bSbS \mid cS.$$

Control states are represented by the procedures q0, q1 and qf and the stack is represented by a list that is passed along from state to state. Stack symbols a prepended and removed accordingly. Examples for further automata models, finite automata, counter automata, timed automata and register automata, as well as a reformulation of a specification for a robotics application originally published in [2] can be found on the tool website[4].

4 Implementation

Figure 2 shows the architecture of the TeSSLa compiler with modified phases in blue (1st, 2nd) and new phases in red (3rd, 5th). The compiler exhibits a phase based architecture, starting with parsing implemented using the parser generator Antlr [17]. The next phase, desugaring, takes the abstract syntax tree (AST) generated by Antlr and translates it into a simplified AST removing any syntactic sugar, e.g. operators and special syntax like if-expressions are translated into function calls. The type-checker infers types for all declarations, checks explicitly given types and resolves imports. The macro expansion phase identifies all function calls that can be evaluated at compile time and expands them. Then, the AST is passed to one of the backends for interpretation or code generation.

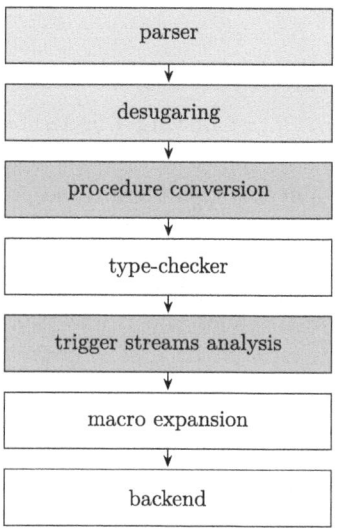

Fig. 2. Compiler architecture

To implement the new procedural syntax, we have extended the grammar for Antlr correspondingly. The transformation from the procedural syntax into functional expressions over the Proc-type is already implemented in the desugaring phase. This facilitates to implement the new features without adding explicit support to all further phases and type-checking in particular. This approach is possible, as all transformation points where calls to flatMap have to be inserted are marked by call on the syntactic level.

The procedure conversion phase handles converting procedures that do not yield any output. Such a procedure can be freely combined with procedures

---

[4] https://git.tessla.io/tessla/tessla/-/blob/feature-imperative-tessla/imperative/README.md.

yielding outputs of any type. TeSSLa's type system does however currently not allow to express this kind of convertibility. Therefore, this phase detects typical cases before type checking and inserts appropriate conversion calls. We plan to extend TeSSLa in the future by a more general mechanism for type-class resolution and replace this phase by appropriate type declarations.

The run keyword is implemented as a standard TeSSLa function in the standard library by a generic specification executing the Proc type triggered by all streams the executed procedures depend on. As TeSSLa stream transformation graphs are generated at compile time and then just executed at runtime, these triggering streams have to be determined at compile time. The trigger streams analysis phase computes an over-approximation of the streams a procedure might read or wait for and inserts this information as an extra argument to run.

5 Conclusions and Future Work

We presented an approach of representing control-flow in TeSSLa that is transferable to similar steam-based formalism. The provided examples demonstrate how state-based formalisms involving complex aspects like time and data can be expressed concisely using the new syntax. While the inherent control flow of the formalism was lost using only stream equations it could be represented easily using the procedural syntax. We believe such procedural extensions have the potential to greatly improve the readability and maintainability of stream-based specifications and can provide some of the benefits of automaton based RV to stream-based RV. While many kinds of automata can be expressed directly, TeSSLa is limited to determinism and non-deterministic modells cannot be represented directly.

During development and experimentation we identified several limitations that we plan to tackle in future work. Currently, procedures can only output values to a single stream. A syntax for addressing multiple output streams would be useful especially when outputs to multiple destinations occur asynchronously.

When reading values from streams a current value might not be available. It is however a common pattern that a procedure waits for an event on some stream and then reads its value immediately. In this case, the value is guaranteed to be available which should be reflected by the type system.

The procedure conversion phase of the current implementation could be eliminated, if TeSSLa would support a general type-class mechanism. This would also help to avoid manual type annotations in certain edge cases.

The TeSSLa compiler tries to expand functions at compile-time where possible. This helps to reduce the complexity of a specification before being passed to low-level backends like micro-controllers or FPGAs. When using infinite recursions like for idle in Listing 2 this has to be disabled using the defer keyword. While such recursions did not serve a use-case in TeSSLa before, they do with procedures. The compiler should heuristically detect these cases.

References

1. Barringer, H., Falcone, Y., Havelund, K., Reger, G., Rydeheard, D.: Quantified event automata: towards expressive and efficient runtime monitors. In: Giannakopoulou, D., Méry, D. (eds.) FM 2012. LNCS, vol. 7436, pp. 68–84. Springer, Heidelberg (2012). https://doi.org/10.1007/978-3-642-32759-9_9
2. Begemann, M.J., Kallwies, H., Leucker, M., Schmitz, M.: TeSSLa-ROS-Bridge - runtime verification of robotic systems. In: Ábrahám, E., Dubslaff, C., Tarifa, S.L.T. (eds.) ICTAC 2023. LNCS, vol. 14446, pp. 388–398. Springer, Cham (2023). https://doi.org/10.1007/978-3-031-47963-2_23
3. Berry, G., Cosserat, L.: The ESTEREL synchronous programming language and its mathematical semantics. In: Brookes, S.D., Roscoe, A.W., Winskel, G. (eds.) CONCURRENCY 1984. LNCS, vol. 197, pp. 389–448. Springer, Heidelberg (1985). https://doi.org/10.1007/3-540-15670-4_19
4. Biewer, S., Finkbeiner, B., Hermanns, H., Köhl, M.A., Schnitzer, Y., Schwenger, M.: RTLola on board: testing real driving emissions on your phone. In: TACAS 2021, Part II. LNCS, vol. 12652, pp. 365–372. Springer, Cham (2021). https://doi.org/10.1007/978-3-030-72013-1_20
5. Caldeira Cabral, M.: An imperative syntax extension for stream runtime verification. Bachelor's thesis, Universität zu Lübeck (2024)
6. Colombo, C., Pace, G.J., Schneider, G.: LARVA—safer monitoring of real-time java programs (tool paper). In: Hung, D.V., Krishnan, P. (eds.) Seventh IEEE International Conference on Software Engineering and Formal Methods, SEFM 2009, Hanoi, Vietnam, 23–27 November 2009, pp. 33–37. IEEE Computer Society (2009). https://doi.org/10.1109/SEFM.2009.13
7. Convent, L., Hungerecker, S., Leucker, M., Scheffel, T., Schmitz, M., Thoma, D.: TeSSLa: temporal stream-based specification language. In: Massoni, T., Mousavi, M.R. (eds.) SBMF 2018. LNCS, vol. 11254, pp. 144–162. Springer, Cham (2018). https://doi.org/10.1007/978-3-030-03044-5_10
8. D'Angelo, B., et al.: LOLA: runtime monitoring of synchronous systems. In: TIME, pp. 166–174. IEEE Computer Society (2005)
9. Giannakopoulou, D., Havelund, K.: Automata-based verification of temporal properties on running programs. In: 16th IEEE International Conference on Automated Software Engineering (ASE 2001), Coronado Island, San Diego, CA, USA, 26–29 November 2001, pp. 412–416. IEEE Computer Society (2001). https://doi.org/10.1109/ASE.2001.989841
10. Gonnord, L., Halbwachs, N., Raymond, P.: From discrete duration calculus to symbolic automata. In: Maraninchi, F., Girault, A., Pouzet, M. (eds.) Proceedings of the Third International Workshop on Synchronous Languages, Applications, and Programs, SLAP 2004, Satellite Event of ETAPS 2004. Electronic Notes in Theoretical Computer Science, Barcelona, Spain, 28 March 2004, vol. 153, pp. 3–18. Elsevier (2004). https://doi.org/10.1016/J.ENTCS.2006.02.022
11. Gorostiaga, F., Sánchez, C.: Striver: stream runtime verification for real-time eventstreams. In: Colombo, C., Leucker, M. (eds.) RV 2018. LNCS, vol. 11237, pp. 282–298. Springer, Cham (2018). https://doi.org/10.1007/978-3-030-03769-7_16
12. Gorostiaga, F., Sánchez, C.: Stream runtime verification of real-time event streams with the Striver language. Int. J. Softw. Tools Technol. Transf. **23**(2), 157–183 (2021)
13. Halbwachs, N.: Synchronous Programming of Reactive Systems. Springer, New York (1993). https://doi.org/10.1007/978-1-4757-2231-4

14. Kallwies, H., Leucker, M., Schmitz, M., Schulz, A., Thoma, D., Weiss, A.: TeSSLa - an ecosystem for runtime verification. In: Dang, T., Stolz, V. (eds.) RV 2022. LNCS, vol. 13498, pp. 314–324. Springer, Cham (2022). https://doi.org/10.1007/978-3-031-17196-3_20
15. Leucker, M., Schallhart, C.: A brief account of runtime verification. J. Log. Algebraic Methods Program. **78**(5), 293–303 (2009)
16. Nystrom, B.: What color is your function? (2015). https://journal.stuffwithstuff.com/2015/02/01/what-color-is-your-function/
17. Parr, T.: The Definitive ANTLR 4 Reference, 2 edn. Pragmatic Bookshelf (2013)
18. Peyton Jones, S.L., Wadler, P.: Imperative functional programming. In: Proceedings of the 20th ACM SIGPLAN-SIGACT Symposium on Principles of Programming Languages, POPL 1993, pp. 71–84. Association for Computing Machinery (1993)
19. Reger, G.: Automata based monitoring and mining of execution traces. Ph.D. thesis, University of Manchester, UK (2014). http://www.manchester.ac.uk/escholar/uk-ac-man-scw:225931
20. Sánchez, C.: Online and offline stream runtime verification of synchronous systems. In: Colombo, C., Leucker, M. (eds.) RV 2018. LNCS, vol. 11237, pp. 138–163. Springer, Cham (2018). https://doi.org/10.1007/978-3-030-03769-7_9
21. Syme, D.: The early history of F#. Proc. ACM Program. Lang. **4**(HOPL), 75:1–75:58 (2020)
22. Wadler, P.: The essence of functional programming. In: Proceedings of the 19th ACM SIGPLAN-SIGACT Symposium on Principles of Programming Languages, POPL 1992, pp. 1–14. Association for Computing Machinery (1992)

The Complexity of Data-Free Nfer

Sean Kauffman[1]($\boxtimes$)[iD], Kim Guldstrand Larsen[2][iD], and Martin Zimmermann[2][iD]

[1] Queen's University, Kingston, Canada
sean.k@queensu.ca
[2] Aalborg University, Aalborg, Denmark
{kgl,mzi}@cs.aau.dk

Abstract. Nfer is a Runtime Verification language for the analysis of event traces that applies rules to create hierarchies of time intervals. This work examines the complexity of the evaluation and satisfiability problems for the data-free fragment of nfer. The evaluation problem asks whether a given interval is generated by applying rules to a known input, while the satisfiability problem asks if an input exists that will generate a given interval.

By excluding data from the language, we obtain polynomial-time algorithms for the evaluation problem and for satisfiability when only considering inclusive rules. Furthermore, we show decidability for the satisfiability problem for cycle-free specifications and undecidability for satisfiability of full data-free nfer.

Keywords: Interval Logic · Complexity · Runtime Verification

1 Introduction

Nfer is an interval logic for analyzing and comprehending event traces that has been used in a wide range of applications, from anomaly detection in autonomous vehicles [14] to spacecraft telemetry analysis [17]. However, its high complexity demands that users restrict the features they incorporate into their applications to ensure tractability. Despite this, no work exists that examines the runtime complexity of nfer without data; an obvious restraint on the power of the language that more closely resembles propositional interval logics like Halpern and Shoham's logic of intervals (HS) and Duration Calculus [26]. These languages still tend to be undecidable in the general case, however, so it is unclear if this restriction on nfer helps with tractability. In this paper, we show that evaluation of the data-free variant of nfer is tractable and, furthermore, satisfiability for this variant is tractable with additional restrictions.

Supported by Digital Research Centre Denmark (DIREC) and the Natural Sciences and Engineering Research Council of Canada (NSERC) [ref. RGPIN-2024-04280].

Supplementary Information The online version contains supplementary material available at https://doi.org/10.1007/978-3-031-74234-7_11.

© The Author(s), under exclusive license to Springer Nature Switzerland AG 2025
E. Ábrahám and H. Abbas (Eds.): RV 2024, LNCS 15191, pp. 174–191, 2025.
https://doi.org/10.1007/978-3-031-74234-7_11

Nfer was developed by scientists from NASA's et Propulsion Laboratory (JPL) in collaboration with other researchers to analyze event traces from remote systems like spacecraft [16–18]. In nfer, specifications consist of rules that describe and label relationships between time periods called intervals. Applying nfer rules to an event trace yields a hierarchy of these intervals that is easier for humans and machines to comprehend than the raw events.

Nfer typically operates on intervals with data, but here we define a data-free fragment of the language. Data-free nfer is expressive enough for many use cases, having appeared, for example, to analyze the Sequential Sense-Process-Send (SSPS) dataset [17]. Data-free nfer is also the target for an algorithm to mine rules from real-time embedded systems [15].

Recent work analyzing the evaluation complexity of nfer has shown that it is undecidable for the full language, but with various decidable fragments [20, 21]. These fragments mostly remain intractable, however, with PTIME complexity only possible by employing a meta-constraint on the size of the results that may not be practical in many cases. Those works did not examine data-free nfer as a fragment, however, despite it being an obvious restriction with precedent in the literature. A major advantage of restricting nfer to the data-free fragment is that the satisfiability problem becomes interesting. With data, it is trivial to show that satisfiability for nfer is undecidable. This follows from the results in [21] where nfer is shown to have undecidable evaluation. One can encode a Turing machine using nfer rules and satisfiability asks if there is an initial tape such that the machine terminates.

Without data, however, it is much less obvious if satisfiability is undecidable. In fact, we show that satisfiability for the full data-free nfer language is still undecidable, but we achieve decidability by restricting to a cycle-free or inclusive-only fragment, the latter of which we demonstrate is decidable in PTIME. That the satisfiability of inclusive, data-free nfer is decidable in PTIME has exciting implications for practitioners, since these checks can be implemented in event-trace analysis tools [13]. We also show that the evaluation problem for data-free nfer is in PTIME without any artificial restrictions on the size of the result from meta-constraints.

All proofs omitted due to space restrictions can be found in [19].

Related Work. Other works have examined the complexity of interval-based logics. Halpern et al. introduced an interval temporal logic and examined its decidability in [11]. Chaochen et al. found decidable and undecidable fragments of an extension of that work, Duration Calculus [7], over both discrete and dense time [6]. Bolander et al. later introduced Hybrid Duration Calculus (HDC) that added the ability to name an interval and refer to it in a formula [4]. They showed that HDC can express Allen's relations and is decidable over discrete and dense time domains with non-elementary complexity.

Other works have investigated the complexity of HS [12], a modal logic based on Allen's Temporal Logic (ATL). Montanari et al. examined the satisfiability problem for the subset of HS over the natural numbers with only *begins/begun by* and *meets* operators and proved it to be EXPSPACE-complete [23]. The same authors later proved that adding the *met by* operator increases the complexity of the language to be decidable only over finite total orders [22]. Aceto et al. later examined the expressive power of all fragments of HS over total orders [1].

2 Data-Free Nfer

We denote the set of nonnegative integers as $\mathbb{N}$. The set of Booleans is given as $\mathbb{B} = \{true, false\}$. We fix a finite alphabet Σ of event identifiers and a finite alphabet $\mathcal{I}$ of interval identifiers such that $\Sigma \subseteq \mathcal{I}$. A word is a sequence of identifiers $\sigma = \sigma_0 \sigma_1 \cdots \sigma_{|\sigma|-1}$ where $\sigma_i \in \Sigma$. Given a word σ, we define the non-empty subsequence $\sigma_{[s,e]} = \sigma_s \cdots \sigma_e$, where $0 \leq s \leq e \leq |\sigma| - 1$.

An event represents a named state change in an observed system. An event is a pair (η, t) where $\eta \in \Sigma$ is its identifier and $t \in \mathbb{N}$ is the timestamp when it occurred. The set of all events is $\mathbb{E} = \Sigma \times \mathbb{N}$. A trace is a sequence of events $\tau = (\eta_0, t_0)(\eta_1, t_1) \cdots (\eta_{n-1}, t_{n-1})$ where $n = |\tau|$ and $t_i \leq t_j$ for all $i < j$.

Intervals represent a named period of state in an observed system. An interval is a triple (η, s, e) where $\eta \in \mathcal{I}$ is its identifier, and $s, e \in \mathbb{N}$ are the starting and ending timestamps where $s \leq e$. We denote the set of all intervals by $\mathbb{I}$. A set of intervals is called a *pool* and the set of all pools is $\mathbb{P} = 2^{\mathbb{I}}$. We say that an interval $i = (\eta, s, e)$ is labeled by η and define the accessor functions $id(i) = \eta$, $start(i) = s$, and $end(i) = e$. An interval of duration zero is an *atomic* interval.

Syntax. The data-free `nfer` syntax consists of *rules*. There are two forms of rules: inclusive and exclusive. Inclusive rules test for the existence of two intervals matching a temporal constraint. Exclusive rules test for the existence of one interval and the absence of another interval matching a temporal constraint. When such a pair is found, a new interval is produced with an identifier specified by the rule and timestamps taken from the matched intervals. We define the syntax of these rules as follows:

– Inclusive rules have the form $\eta \leftarrow \eta_1 \oplus \eta_2$ and
– exclusive rules have the form $\eta \leftarrow \eta_1 \text{ unless } \ominus \eta_2$

where $\eta, \eta_1, \eta_2 \in \mathcal{I}$ are identifiers, $\oplus \in \{\textbf{before}, \textbf{meet}, \textbf{during}, \textbf{coincide}, \textbf{start}, \textbf{finish}, \textbf{overlap}, \textbf{slice}\}$ is a *clock predicate* on three intervals (one for each of η, η_1, and η_2), and $\ominus \in \{\textbf{after}, \textbf{follow}, \textbf{contain}\}$ is a clock predicate on two intervals (one for each of η_1 and η_2). For a rule $\eta \leftarrow \eta_1 \oplus \eta_2$ or $\eta \leftarrow \eta_1 \text{ unless} \ominus \eta_2$ we say that η appears on the left-hand and the η_i appear on the right-hand side.

Semantics. The semantics of the `nfer` language is defined in three steps: the semantics R of individual rules on pools, the semantics S of a specification (a list of rules) on pools, and the semantics T of a specification on traces of events.

We first define the semantics of inclusive rules with the interpretation function R. Let Δ be the set of all rules. Semantic functions are defined using the brackets $[\![\_]\!]$ around syntax being given semantics.

$$R [\![\_]\!] : \Delta \to \mathbb{P} \to \mathbb{P}$$
$$R [\![\eta \leftarrow \eta_1 \oplus \eta_2]\!] \pi =$$
$$\{ i \in \mathbb{I} : i_1, i_2 \in \pi \ . \ id(i) = \eta \wedge id(i_1) = \eta_1 \wedge id(i_2) = \eta_2 \wedge \oplus(i, i_1, i_2) \}$$

In the definition, an interval i is a member of the produced pool when two existing intervals in π match the identifiers η_1 and η_2 and the temporal constraint $\oplus$. The identifier of i is given in the rule and $\oplus$ defines its start and end timestamps.

The clock predicates referenced by $\oplus$ are shown in Table 1. These relate two intervals using the familiar ATL temporal operators [2] and also specify the start and end timestamps of the produced intervals. For the example **before**(i, i_1, i_2), i_1 and i_2 are matched when i_1 ends **before** i_2 begins. The generated interval i has start and end timestamps inherited from the intervals i_1 and i_2, i.e., no new timestamps are generated by applying **before**(i, i_1, i_2). This is true for all other rules as well.

Table 1. Formal definition of nfer clock predicates for inclusive rules

$\oplus$	Constraints on $i, i_1,$ and i_2
before	$end(i_1) < start(i_2) \wedge start(i) = start(i_1) \wedge end(i) = end(i_2)$
meet	$end(i_1) = start(i_2) \wedge start(i) = start(i_1) \wedge end(i) = end(i_2)$
during	$start(i_2) = start(i) \leq start(i_1) \wedge end(i_1) \leq end(i_2) = end(i)$
coincide	$start(i_1) = start(i_2) = start(i) \wedge end(i_1) = end(i_2) = end(i)$
start	$start(i_1) = start(i_2) = start(i) \wedge end(i) = \max(end(i_1), end(i_2))$
finish	$end(i) = end(i_1) = end(i_2) \wedge start(i) = \min(start(i_1), start(i_2))$
overlap	$start(i_1) < end(i_2) \wedge start(i_2) < end(i_1) \wedge$ $start(i) = \min(start(i_1), start(i_2)) \wedge end(i) = \max(end(i_1), end(i_2))$
slice	$start(i_1) < end(i_2) \wedge start(i_2) < end(i_1) \wedge$ $start(i) = \max(start(i_1), start(i_2)) \wedge end(i) = \min(end(i_1), end(i_2))$

We now define the semantics of exclusive rules with the function R.

$$R [\![\eta \leftarrow \eta_1 \textbf{ unless } \ominus \eta_2]\!] \pi =$$
$$\{ i \in \mathbb{I} : i_1 \in \pi \ . \ id(i) = \eta \wedge id(i_1) = \eta_1 \wedge$$
$$start(i) = start(i_1) \wedge end(i) = end(i_1) \wedge$$
$$\neg \ (\exists \ i_2 \in \pi \ . \ i_2 \neq i_1 \wedge id(i_2) = \eta_2 \wedge \ominus(i_1, i_2) \ ) \ \}$$

Like with inclusive rules, exclusive rules match intervals in the input pool π to produce a pool of new intervals. The difference is that exclusive rules produce new intervals where one existing interval in π matches the identifier η_1 and no intervals exist in π that match the identifier η_2 such that the clock predicate $\ominus$ holds for the η_1-labeled and the η_2-labeled interval.

The three possibilities referenced by ⊖ are shown in Table 2. These clock predicates relate two intervals using familiar ATL temporal operators while the timestamps of the produced interval are copied from the included interval rather than being defined by the clock predicate. For the example **after**(i_1, i_2), i_1 and i_2 would be matched (if i_2 existed) if i_1 begins after i_2 ends, and this match would result in *no* interval being produced. If such an interval i_2 is absent, an interval is produced with timestamps matching i_1.

Table 2. Formal definition of nfer clock predicates for exclusive rules

⊖	Constraints on i_1 and i_2
after	$start(i_1) > end(i_2)$
follow	$start(i_1) = end(i_2)$
contain	$start(i_2) \geq start(i_1) \land end(i_2) \leq end(i_1)$

The interpretation function S defines the semantics of a finite list of rules, called a specification. Given a specification $\delta_1 \cdots \delta_n \in \Delta^*$ and a pool $\pi \in \mathbb{P}$, $S[\![\_]\!]$ recursively applies $R[\![\_]\!]$ to the rules in order, passing each instance the union of π with the intervals returned by already completed calls.

$$S[\![\_]\!] : \Delta^* \to \mathbb{P} \to \mathbb{P}$$

$$S[\![\delta_1 \cdots \delta_n]\!]\,\pi = \begin{cases} S[\![\delta_2 \cdots \delta_n]\!]\,(\pi \cup R[\![\delta_1]\!]\,\pi) & \textbf{if } n > 0 \\ \pi & \textbf{otherwise} \end{cases}$$

An nfer specification $D \in \Delta^*$ forms a directed graph $G(D)$ with vertices for the rules in D connected by edges representing identifier dependencies. An edge exists in $G(D)$ from δ to δ' iff there is an identifier η that appears on the left-hand side of δ and the right-hand side of δ'. We say that D contains a cycle if $G(D)$ contains one; otherwise D is cycle-free.

The rules in a cycle in an nfer specification must be iteratively evaluated until a fixed point is reached. As intervals may never be destroyed by rule evaluation, inclusive rules may be repeatedly evaluated, safely. However, exclusive rules may not be evaluated until the intervals on which they depend are known to be present or absent.

For example, suppose a specification with the two rules $\delta_1 = c \leftarrow a$ **meet** b and $\delta_2 = a \leftarrow c$ **meet** b. Given $\pi = \{(a, 0, 1), (b, 1, 2), (b, 2, 3), (b, 3, 4), (d, 4, 5)\}$, we have $R[\![\delta_1]\!]\pi = \{(c, 0, 2)\}$ and $R[\![\delta_2]\!](\pi \cup R[\![\delta_1]\!]\pi) = \{(a, 0, 3)\}$. The rules must be applied a second time to reach a fixed point that includes the interval $(c, 0, 4)$. Now consider the consequences if the specification also contained the exclusive rule $\delta_3 = b \leftarrow d$ **unless follow** c. After the first evaluation, $(c, 0, 4)$ is not yet produced, so evaluating δ_3 would generate $(b, 4, 5)$, an incorrect result. As such, *exclusive rules may not appear in cycles* but may appear in a specification that contains cycles among inclusive rules.

To find the cycles in a specification, we compute the strongly-connected components of the directed graph $G(D)$ formed by the rules in D. Each strongly connected component represents either a cycle or an individual rule outside of a cycle. We then sort the components in topological order and iterate over each component until a fixed point is reached.

The interpretation function $T[\![\_]\!]$ defines the semantics of a specification applied to a trace of events. To ensure consistency with prior work and to simplify our presentation, we overload $T[\![\_]\!]$ to operate on an event trace $\tau \in \mathbb{E}^*$ by first converting τ to the pool $\{init(e) : e \text{ is an element of } \tau\}$ where $init(\eta, t) = (\eta, t, t)$.

$$T[\![\_]\!] : \Delta^* \to \mathbb{P} \to \mathbb{P}$$
$$T[\![\,\delta_1 \cdots \delta_n\,]\!]\, \pi = \pi_{\ell+1,1}.\ \pi_{1,1} = \pi \wedge$$
$$\mathcal{D} = \mathrm{SCC}(\delta_1 \cdots \delta_n) \wedge (D_1 \cdots D_\ell) = topsort(\mathcal{D})\ .$$
$$\pi_{i+1,1} = \bigcup\nolimits_{j>0} \pi_{i,j}.\ \pi_{i,j+1} = S[\![\,D_i\,]\!]\,(\pi_{i,j})$$

where $\mathrm{SCC}(\delta_1 \cdots \delta_n)$ is the set $\mathcal{D}$ of strongly connected components of the graph $G(\delta_1 \cdots \delta_n)$ and $topsort(\mathcal{D})$ is a topological sort of these components.

3 Satisfiability

We are interested in the existential nfer satisfiability problem: Given a specification D, a set of identifiers Σ, and a target identifier η_T, is there an input trace of events $\tau \in \mathbb{E}^+$ with identifiers in Σ such that an η_T-labeled interval is in $T[\![D]\!]\,\tau$? The nfer satisfiability problem is interesting in part because of the restriction of input identifiers to $\Sigma \subseteq \mathcal{I}$. If $\eta_T \in \Sigma$, then any specification is trivially satisfiable. When $\eta_T \notin \Sigma$, however, then a η_T-labeled interval must be derived. This problem is non-trivial and, as we shall see, undecidable in general.

To see how data-free nfer specifications may be satisfiable or not, consider the following two example specifications for the target identifier η_T and input identifiers $\Sigma = \{a, b\}$:

$$D_{\mathrm{sat}} = \begin{cases} A \leftarrow a \textbf{ before } b \\ B \leftarrow A \textbf{ meet } b \\ \eta_T \leftarrow A \textbf{ overlap } B \end{cases} \qquad D_{\mathrm{unsat}} = \begin{cases} A \leftarrow b \textbf{ before } X \\ B \leftarrow a \textbf{ meet } b \\ \eta_T \leftarrow a \textbf{ overlap } B \end{cases}$$

A satisfying event trace for D_{sat} is $\tau_1 = (a, 1), (b, 2)$, since $T[\![D_{\mathrm{sat}}]\!]\,\tau_1 = \{(a, 1, 1), (b, 2, 2), (A, 1, 2), (B, 1, 2), (\eta_T, 1, 2)\}$. For D_{unsat}, no η_T-labeled interval can be produced because **overlap** requires one of the two matched intervals to have positive duration: for an interval i, $end(i) - start(i) > 0$. Since a-labeled intervals must be initial, they are atomic (zero duration). That leaves B-labeled intervals produced by another rule. The rule that produces B-labeled intervals, however, only matches initial intervals with the same timestamps. As such, any B-labeled interval will also have zero duration, and the **overlap** rule will never be matched. Finally, the **before** rule can never be applied, as no X-labeled interval can be generated.

3.1 Data-Free nfer Satisfiability is Undecidable

In this section, we show the undecidability of the data-free nfer satisfiability problem by a reduction from the emptiness problem for the intersection of two Context-Free Grammars (CFGs). The undecidability result relies on the recursive nature of nfer, i.e., an η-labeled interval can be produced from another η-labeled interval, and on its negation capabilities, i.e., via exclusive rules.

Theorem 1. *The data-free nfer satisfiability problem is undecidable.*

We now show how to simulate a CFG G with data-free nfer rules with a designated identifier η_G so that a word w is accepted by the CFG iff applying the rules to events that correspond to w generates an interval over the same period with identifier η_G. Then the intersection of two CFGs G_1 and G_2 is nonempty if and only if applying the corresponding rules generates, for some sequence of events corresponding to a word, two intervals with the same starting and ending timestamps, one with identifier η_{G_1} and one with η_{G_2}. The existence of two such intervals can again be captured by a data-free nfer rule producing an interval with a target identifier.

Formally, a CFG is a four-tuple (V, Σ, P, S), where V is a finite set of non-terminals (or variables), Σ is the finite set of terminals that are disjoint from V, P is a finite set of productions of the form $v \to w$ where $v \in V$ and $w \in (V \cup \Sigma)^*$, and S is the initial non-terminal. We assume, without loss of generality, that a CFG is in Chomsky-normal form [8].[1] This means that all productions are in one of two forms: $A \to BC$ or $A \to a$ where $A, B, C \in V$, $a \in \Sigma$, and $S \notin \{B, C\}$.

Given a grammar (V, Σ, P, S), where $A \in V$, $w, x, y \in (V \cup \Sigma)^*$, and $(A \to x) \in P$, then we say that wAy yields wxy, written $wAy \Rightarrow wxy$. We write $w \overset{*}{\Rightarrow} y$ if $w = y$ or there exists a sequence of strings $x_1, x_2, \ldots, x_n$ for $n \geq 0$ such that $w \Rightarrow x_1 \Rightarrow x_2 \Rightarrow \cdots \Rightarrow x_n \Rightarrow y$. The language of the grammar is $\{w \in \Sigma^* : S \overset{*}{\Rightarrow} w\}$. If a word is in the language of the grammar we say it has a derivation in the grammar. Deciding if the intersection of the languages of two CFGs is empty is undecidable [3].

We use grammar $G_x = (V_x, \Sigma_x, P_x, S_x)$ accepting $\{a(a^n)(b^n) : n > 0\}$ as a running example, where $V_x = \{A, B, M, M', S_x\}$, $\Sigma_x = \{a, b\}$, and $P_x = \{A \to a, B \to b, S_x \to AM, M \to AB, M \to AM', M' \to MB\}$. The string aab has the derivation $S_x \Rightarrow AM \Rightarrow AAB \Rightarrow AAb \Rightarrow Aab \Rightarrow aab$.

We present six types of data-free nfer rules to simulate the intersection of two CFGs $G = (V, \Sigma, P, S)$ and $G' = (V', \Sigma, P', S')$, where $V \cap V' = \varnothing$ and $P \cap P' = \varnothing$. The first four steps are necessary to account for events with coincident timestamps and because simulating a CFG requires the sequential composition of non-terminals, while nfer rules cannot perform sequential composition directly on atomic intervals. Then the final two steps map the productions of a CFG and their intersection directly to data-free nfer rules. The six types of rules are:

1. Rules to label non-unique timestamps in an event trace so that they can be filtered out. We do so, because event traces in nfer are allowed to have events

---
[1] Note that we, w.l.o.g., disregard the empty word.

with the same timestamps while there is only one letter at each position of a word. So, to simplify our translation between event traces and words, we just filter out events with non-unique timestamps.
2. Rules that then perform the actual event filtering to only include events with unique timestamps.
3. Rules that label every interval in a trace by its starting event, i.e. where some event occurs at the start and some other event occurs at the end, we label the interval by the starting event.
4. Rules that select the minimal starting-event-labeled intervals, i.e. the intervals where no other interval is subsumed by that interval. The result of this step is a set of contiguous intervals labeled by their starting event. These minimal intervals are totally ordered and in one-to-one correspondence with the original events with unique timestamps. Thus, we have transformed the event trace into an *equivalent* pool of intervals.
5. Rules that simulate the productions of the CFGs on the pool of minimal starting-event-labeled intervals. The generated intervals encode a derivation tree. The word corresponding to the event trace is accepted by a CFG if an interval is generated that is labeled by that grammar's initial non-terminal.
6. A rule that labels an interval by a given target label if the simulation of the two CFGs labeled the same interval by their initial non-terminals. The interval is generated if the word corresponding to the same event trace is accepted by both CFGS.

We begin by relating event traces to words. Event traces form a total preorder as some timestamps may be equal, while the symbols in a word are totally ordered by their index (no two symbols have the same index). To convert a word to an event trace, we add a timestamp equal to the index of the event. Given a word $\sigma \in \Sigma^*$, $TRACE(\sigma) = (\sigma_0, 0), (\sigma_1, 1), \ldots, (\sigma_{n-1}, n-1)$ where $n = |\sigma|$. For example, $TRACE(aab) = (a, 0), (a, 1), (b, 2)$.

When converting an event trace to a word, however, we must only consider events with unique timestamps. The following example trace illustrates the reasoning at this step: consider $\tau_x = (a, 0), (a, 1), (a, 2), (b, 2), (b, 3), (b, 4)$ where both an a-labeled and a b-labeled event occur at timestamp 2. To convert τ_x to a word, we want to order its identifiers using only their timestamps, and, consequently, the two events with timestamp 2 cannot be ordered. As such, we ensure that only events with unique timestamps affect the generation of intervals involved in simulating a CFG. Before we show how to generate those intervals we define formally what we mean by unique timestamps.

Given a trace $\tau = (\eta_0, t_0), (\eta_1, t_1), \ldots, (\eta_{n-1}, t_{n-1})$, t_i is unique in τ if for all $j \neq i$ we have $t_j \neq t_i$. Let $UNIQ(\tau) = \{t_{i_0}, t_{i_1}, \ldots, t_{i_{k-1}}\}$ be the set of unique timestamps in τ such that $t_{i_j} < t_{i_{j'}}$ for all $j < j'$, i.e., we enumerate the unique timestamps of τ in increasing order. Then, $WORD(\tau) = \eta_{i_0}, \eta_{i_1}, \ldots, \eta_{i_{k-1}}$.

We now define data-free `nfer` rules that capture the definition of $WORD$. The rules first generate atomic `SPOIL` intervals where multiple events share timestamps and then filter the events to only those that do not share timestamps with those `SPOIL` intervals.

Given the alphabet Σ, we define rules to generate SPOIL intervals for non-unique timestamps. We let SPOIL be a new identifier (SPOIL $\notin \Sigma$).

$$D_1 = \{\text{SPOIL} \leftarrow a \text{ coincide } b : (a,b) \in \Sigma \times \Sigma \wedge a \neq b\} \quad (1)$$

For example, applying D_1 to the example trace τ_x defined above results in the following intervals: $T[\![D_1]\!](\tau_x) = \{(a, 0, 0), (a, 1, 1), (a, 2, 2), (b, 2, 2), (\text{SPOIL}, 2, 2), (b, 3, 3), (b, 4, 4)\}$. Figure 1 shows this example on a timeline. In the top of the figure, the solid line shows time progressing from left to right, with the identifiers appearing in the trace given below their associated timestamps. The new SPOIL-labeled interval is shown below the timeline, having been generated by the rules in D_1 shown on the right. The remainder of the figure relates to steps 2, 3, and 4.

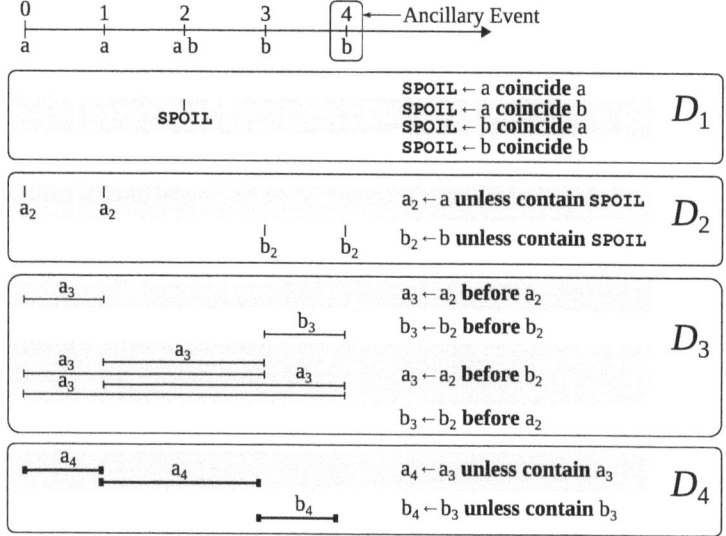

Fig. 1. Example of applying steps 1–4 from the proof of Theorem 1

Proposition 1. *Given a trace τ, $T[\![D_1]\!](\tau)$ characterizes $WORD(\tau)$ in the following sense: $\{t : (\text{SPOIL}, t, t) \in T[\![D_1]\!](\tau)\}$ is the difference between the set of timestamps in τ and $UNIQ(\tau)$.*

Now, we can define rules that filter the events to only those with unique timestamps by excluding any that coincide with SPOIL-labeled intervals. These rules ensure that the nfer simulation of a CFG uses exactly the same events that are used in $WORD$: those with unique timestamps. Note that the intervals generated by the rules in D_i for steps $i \in \{2, 3, 4\}$ are labeled by identifiers annotated by the step number (a_i) where $a \in \Sigma$ and $a_i \notin V \cup V' \cup \Sigma$.

$$D_2 = \{a_2 \leftarrow a \text{ unless contain SPOIL} : a \in \Sigma\} \quad (2)$$

Figure 1 shows the result of applying D_2 to the result of $T[\![D_1]\!](\tau_x)$. The intervals $(a_2, 0, 0)$ and $(a_2, 1, 1)$ annotate a-labeled intervals that do not coincide with a SPOIL-labeled interval, while $(b_2, 3, 3)$ and $(b_2, 4, 4)$ annotate the b-labeled intervals that do not coincide with a SPOIL-labeled interval. No such annotated intervals are produced at timestamp 2, where the rules in D_1 generated a SPOIL-labeled interval.

Recall that the intervals that result from the rules in D_2 are still atomic, i.e. they are effectively events and have a duration of zero. The next step is to use those atomic intervals to generate every interval in the trace with a positive duration (restricted to those with unique starting and ending timestamps in the original trace τ). We label every such interval with a label derived from its start.

$$D_3 = \{a_3 \leftarrow a_2 \textbf{ before } b_2 : (a, b) \in \Sigma \times \Sigma\} \tag{3}$$

As shown in Fig. 1, the intervals generated by applying D_3 in our example are $(a_3, 0, 1)$ from the rule $a_3 \leftarrow a_2 \textbf{ before } a_2$, $(b_3, 3, 4)$ from $b_3 \leftarrow b_2 \textbf{ before } b_2$, and $(a_3, 1, 3)$, $(a_3, 0, 3)$, $(a_3, 1, 4)$, $(a_3, 0, 4)$ from $a_3 \leftarrow a_2 \textbf{ before } b_2$.

Now, we introduce rules that filter the intervals produced by the rules in D_3 so that only the *minimal* intervals remain. A minimal interval is one where no other interval (with the same label) is subsumed by it. The resulting intervals form a contiguous sequence covering all unique timestamps in τ where their meeting points are the atomic intervals produced by D_2.

$$D_4 = \{a_4 \leftarrow a_3 \textbf{ unless contain } a_3 : a \in \Sigma\} \tag{4}$$

The reason for generating this contiguous sequence of intervals is that we need to transform the input into elements that are *sequentially composable* using data-free nfer rules. To understand why, recall our example event trace: $\tau_x = (a, 0), (a, 1), (a, 2), (b, 2), (b, 3), (b, 4)$. As seen in Fig. 1, the atomic intervals that result from applying D_1 and D_2 to this trace are $\{(a_2, 0, 0), (a_2, 1, 1), (b_2, 3, 3), (b_2, 4, 4)\}$. Because these intervals do not overlap (they are atomic and have unique timestamps) we can see from Table 1 that the only clock predicate that can match two subsequent intervals (i.e., no labeled interval exists between the end of the first and beginning of the second) is **before**. The rules in D_3, then, do that (match intervals using **before** rules) but these match both subsequent and non-subsequent intervals. Applying the rule $a_3 \leftarrow a_2 \textbf{ before } b_2$, for example, produces $(a_3, 1, 3)$, $(a_3, 0, 3)$, $(a_3, 1, 4)$, and $(a_3, 0, 4)$. To match only subsequent intervals requires the rules from step four (in D_4). Applying $a_4 \leftarrow a_3 \textbf{ unless contain } a_3$ only generates $(a_4, 0, 1), (a_4, 1, 3)$ because they do not *contain* another a_3-labeled interval, while $(a_3, 0, 3)$, $(a_3, 1, 4)$, and $(a_3, 0, 4)$ do contain $(a_3, 0, 1)$ and $(a_3, 1, 2)$.

At this point, we must discuss what we call the *Ancillary Event Phenomenon*. Because we must generate sequentially composable intervals to simulate a CFG, and because these intervals must label the time *between* events, inevitably one event per trace must be unrepresented by such intervals. Since we choose to label the intervals by their starting event, the final event in the trace with a unique timestamp does not label an interval. We call this the *ancillary event* in a trace. In τ_x, the ancillary event is $(b, 4)$.

After applying $D_1 \cup D_2 \cup D_3 \cup D_4$, we have the intervals $(a_4, 0, 1), (a_4, 1, 3)$, and $(b_4, 3, 4)$. These intervals are now *sequentially composable* because they (uniquely) **meet** at timestamps 1 and 3, meaning we can use the **meet** clock predicate to match only the contiguous intervals and no others.

With the sequentially composable intervals produced by the rules in D_4, we now can simulate the productions of the two CFGs. Recall that P and P' are the disjoint sets of these productions.

$$D_5 = \{ A \leftarrow a_4 \text{ \textbf{coincide} } a_4 : (A \to a) \in P \cup P' \} \cup \\ \{ A \leftarrow B \text{ \textbf{meet} } C : (A \to BC) \in P \cup P' \} \tag{5}$$

Unlike the rules from $D_1 \cup D_2 \cup D_3 \cup D_4$, the rules in D_5 may contain cycles and must be iterated over until a fixed point is reached.

Figure 2 shows the result of applying D_5 to the running example. Each rule in D_5, shown on the right side of the figure, maps to a production in P_x and the intervals they produce simulate a derivation for τ_x in G_x. Applying $A \leftarrow a_4$ **before** a_4 produces $(A, 0, 1)$ and $(A, 1, 3)$, while $B \leftarrow b_4$ **before** b_4 produces $(B, 3, 4)$. Then, applying $M \leftarrow A$ **meet** B produces $(M, 1, 4)$ and applying $S_x \leftarrow A$ **meet** M produces $(S_x, 0, 4)$. As S_x is the initial non-terminal for G_x, an S_x-labeled interval in the fixed point indicates that the trace τ_x during that interval is in the language of G_x.

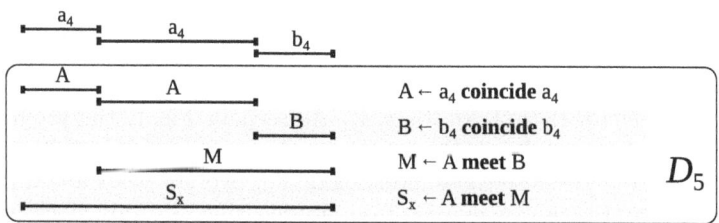

Fig. 2. Example of applying step 5 from the proof of Theorem 1

Next, we show that the data-free nfer simulation has the desired properties. We begin by showing correctness for a single grammar, starting with soundness.

Lemma 1. *Given a CFG $G = (V, \Sigma, P, S)$ and a word $\sigma \in \Sigma^*$, fix an identifier $a \in \Sigma$ for the ancillary event. Then, $\sigma \in \mathcal{L}(G) \Leftrightarrow (S, 0, |\sigma| - 1) \in T[\![\bigcup_{i=1}^{5} D_i]\!] (TRACE(\sigma \cdot a))$.*

Proof. The proof is by induction over $j - i$, showing that for a non-terminal $A \in V$, $A \stackrel{*}{\Rightarrow} \sigma_{[i,j]} \Leftrightarrow (A, i, j) \in T[\![\bigcup_{i=1}^{5} D_i]\!] (TRACE(\sigma \cdot a))$. □

We now show completeness for a single grammar.

Lemma 2. *Given a CFG $G = (V, \Sigma, P, S)$ and a trace $\tau \in \mathbb{E}^*$ such that $|\tau| \geq 2$, let t be the second largest timestamp in $UNIQ(\tau)$ and let $\sigma = WORD(\tau)$. Then, $(S, 0, t) \in T[\![\bigcup_{i=1}^{5} D_i]\!](\tau) \Leftrightarrow \sigma_{[0,|\sigma|-2]} \in \mathcal{L}(G)$.*

Proof. By induction over $j - i$, showing that for a non-terminal $A \in V$ and $\tau = (\eta_0, t_0) \cdots (\eta_{n-1}, t_{n-1})$, $A \stackrel{*}{\Rightarrow} WORD(\tau_{[i,j]}) \Leftrightarrow (A, t_i, t_j) \in T[\![\bigcup_{i=1}^{5} D_i]\!](\tau)$. □

Finally, we check that a word is accepted by both grammars by labeling as η_T where the timestamps of any S-and-S'-labeled intervals are the same. If any word has a derivation in both G and G', then applying $\bigcup_{i=1}^{6} D_i$ to the corresponding trace will result in a η_T-labeled interval in the fixed point.

$$D_6 = \{\eta_T \leftarrow S \textbf{ coincide } S'\} \qquad (6)$$

For example, suppose a second grammar G'_x was introduced accepting the language a^+b^+, where its initial non-terminal was S'_x. The word aab is in the language of G'_x and so applying $\bigcup_{i=1}^{5} D_i$ for G'_x to the trace τ_x would yield a fixed point containing the interval $(S'_x, 0, 4)$. Since $(S_x, 0, 4)$ coincides with this interval, applying the rule in D_6 will yield $(\eta_T, 0, 4)$.

Lemma 3. *Given CFGs G and G' and a word $\sigma \in \Sigma^*$, fix an identifier $a \in \Sigma$ for the ancillary event. Then, $\sigma \in \mathcal{L}(G) \cap \mathcal{L}(G') \Leftrightarrow (\eta_T, 0, |\sigma| - 1) \in T[\![\bigcup_{i=1}^{6} D_i]\!](TRACE(\sigma \cdot a))$.*

Proof. Lemma 1 implies that the CFGs G and G' are simulated by $\bigcup_{i=1}^{5} D_i$ for a word σ and applying D_6 finds words in the language of both grammars. □

Lemma 4. *Given CFGs G and G' and a trace $\tau \in \mathbb{E}^*$ such that $|\tau| \geq 2$, let t be the second largest timestamp in $UNIQ(\tau)$ and let $\sigma = WORD(\tau)$. Then, $(\eta_T, 0, t) \in T[\![\bigcup_{i=1}^{6} D_i]\!](\tau) \Leftrightarrow \sigma_{[0,|\sigma|-2]} \in \mathcal{L}(G) \cap \mathcal{L}(G')$.*

Proof. Lemma 2 implies that the CFGs G and G' are simulated by $\bigcup_{i=1}^{5} D_i$ for a trace τ and applying D_6 finds words in the language of both grammars. □

Now, we can prove Theorem 1.

Proof. Applying Lemmas 3 and 4 we obtain that $\mathcal{L}(G) \cap \mathcal{L}(G')$ is non-empty if and only if there is a $\tau \in \mathbb{E}^+$ such that $(\eta_T, \_, \_) \in T[\![\bigcup_{i=1}^{6} D_i]\!](\tau)$. This shows that the undecidable non-emptiness problem for the intersection of two CFGs can be reduced to the data-free nfer satisfiability problem. □

As satisfiability of data-free nfer is undecidable, we now turn our attention to examining fragments with decidable satisfiability. We identify two such fragments: Inclusive nfer, where only inclusive rules are permitted, and Cycle-free nfer, where specifications can be evaluated without a fixed-point computation.

3.2 Inclusive Data-Free nfer Satisfiability is in PTIME

We begin our study with the case where an nfer specification may contain cycles but only contains inclusive rules.

Theorem 2. *The data-free, inclusive* nfer *satisfiability problem is in* PTIME.

We show that there is a polynomial-time algorithm that determines if an input trace τ exists such that an η_T-labeled interval is in $T[\![D]\!]\tau$ for a given specification D. To do this, we show how the satisfiability of a data-free Inclusive-nfer specification can be proven through an analysis of the rules without guessing a witnessing trace. This is due to the monotone nature of inclusive nfer rules: new events added to an input trace only add intervals and cannot invalidate existing ones. We leverage this fact to show how only two factors influence the satisfiability of cycle-free, inclusive nfer specifications: producibility from events in Σ and the requirement of positive duration for some intervals.

To begin, observe that inclusive nfer rules are monotone in nature. The interpretation functions R, S, and T only add intervals; they never remove them. Furthermore, if the rule is inclusive, R only tests for the existence of intervals; it only tests for non-existence in the case of exclusive rules. This means that we may always introduce new events into an input trace without needing to keep track of prior results. The consequence is that ensuring that a η_T-labeled interval appears in a fixed-point of $T[\![D]\!]\tau$ only requires showing that a rule δ_T exists in D with η_T on its left-hand side and that δ_T may be matched by intervals resulting from Σ-labeled events. This concept is very similar to graph reachability and we define it here inductively.

Definition 1. *Let Σ be a set of input identifiers and D an inclusive* nfer *specification. An identifier η is producible by D iff $\eta \in \Sigma$ or if there exists a rule $(\eta \leftarrow \eta_1 \oplus \eta_2) \in D$ and both η_1 and η_2 are producible by D.*

We now prove that satisfiability for an nfer specification using only rules with the **before** operator is equivalent to producibility. We discuss specifications with only **before**-rules here because they allow us to ignore the interaction between events, which have zero duration, and nfer operators which require positive duration. We address this complication after proving Proposition 2.

Proposition 2. *Given a set of input identifiers Σ and a target identifier η_T, an* nfer *specification D_b containing only* **before** *rules is satisfiable iff η_T is producible by D_b.*

Proof. If $\eta_T \in \Sigma$, then D_b is satisfied by the trace $(\eta_T, 0)$. If $\eta_T \notin \Sigma$, then for D_b to be satisfiable there must be a rule δ_T in D_b with η_T on its left-hand side. Next, observe from the definition of **before** in Table 1 that the only requirement of δ_T to produce a η_T-labeled interval is that there exist intervals i_1 and i_2 such that $end(i_1) < start(i_2)$. Clearly, if $id(i_1) \in \Sigma$ and $id(i_2) \in \Sigma$ we can create an input trace that satisfies this. If either identifier on the right-hand side of δ_T is not in Σ, then apply the same logic inductively for that identifier.

The reverse follows by a similarly straightforward induction: if a η_T-labeled interval is producible then D_b is satisfiable. □

To permit inclusive operators beyond **before**, we must address the requirement of *positive duration*. To see why we need to address positive duration, take, for example, the **overlap** operator. Again from Table 1, we see that **overlap** requires that $start(i_1) < end(i_2)$ and $start(i_2) < end(i_1)$. If we assume a zero duration for i_2, we still must have positive duration for i_1: $start(i_1) < start(i_2) = end(i_2) < end(i_1)$, and the same holds for i_2 if we assume zero duration for i_1. This means that, for an **overlap**-rule to match, at least one interval it matches must have positive duration. As such, **overlap**-rules cannot match two initial intervals (events), as they have zero duration.

Thus, producibility is insufficient to show satisfiability for inclusive-**nfer** specifications. We must augment our definition of what is producible to account for what intervals may be produced with positive duration.

Table 3 defines two functions from rules to sets of subsets of identifiers, $\text{match}_+ : \Delta \to 2^{2^{\mathcal{I}}}$ and $\text{add}_+ : \Delta \to 2^{2^{\mathcal{I}}}$. The match_+ function returns the identifiers that must appear in intervals with positive duration for a given rule to match (produce an interval). The add_+ function returns the identifiers that must appear in intervals with positive duration for a given rule to produce an interval with a positive duration. Both functions return values in Conjunctive-Normal Form (CNF), meaning that at least one element of each set must have positive duration. For example, $\text{match}_+(\eta \leftarrow \eta_1 \text{ meet } \eta_2) = \varnothing$ because **meet** can match two intervals with zero duration, but $\text{add}_+(\eta \leftarrow \eta_1 \text{ meet } \eta_2) = \{\eta_1, \eta_2\}$ because at least one of the two intervals it matches must have positive duration for the result to have positive duration.

Table 3. Positive duration requirements on $\delta = (\eta \leftarrow \eta_1 \oplus \eta_2)$ in CNF (for the sake of readability, we identify a set of sets by a list of sets)

$\oplus$	before	meet	during	coincide	start	finish	overlap	slice
$\text{match}_+(\delta)$	$\varnothing$	$\varnothing$	$\varnothing$	$\varnothing$	$\varnothing$	$\varnothing$	$\{\eta_1,\eta_2\}$	$\{\eta_1,\eta_2\}$
$\text{add}_+(\delta)$	$\varnothing$	$\{\eta_1,\eta_2\}$	$\{\eta_2\}$	$\{\eta_1\},\{\eta_2\}$	$\{\eta_1,\eta_2\}$	$\{\eta_1,\eta_2\}$	$\{\eta_1,\eta_2\}$	$\{\eta_1,\eta_2\}$

Definition 2. *Let Σ be a set of input identifiers and D an inclusive* **nfer** *specification. An identifier η is* positive-duration capable *in D iff there exists a rule $(\eta \leftarrow \eta_1 \oplus \eta_2) = \delta \in D$ such that for all $A \in \text{add}_+(\delta)$, there exists an identifier in A that is positive-duration capable in D.*

Note that **before**-rules δ are always positive-duration capable, as we have $\text{add}_+(\delta) = \emptyset$ for such δ. We now define duration-sensitive producibility for identifiers in an inclusive **nfer** specification using match_+ and the definition of positive-duration capable identifiers.

Definition 3. *Let Σ be a set of input identifiers and D an inclusive* **nfer** *specification. An identifier η is* duration-sensitive producible *by D iff $\eta \in \Sigma$ or if* there exists a rule $(\eta \leftarrow \eta_1 \oplus \eta_2) = \delta \in D$ such that η_1 and η_2 are both duration-sensitive producible by D and for all $M \in \text{match}_+(\delta)$, there exists an identifier in M that is positive-duration capable in D.

It should be clear that the consequence of Definition 3 is the following lemma.

Lemma 5. *Given a target identifier η_T, an inclusive* nfer *specification D is satisfiable iff η_T is duration-sensitive producible by D.*

Now, we can prove Theorem 2.

Proof. By Lemma 5, satisfiability for data-free inclusive nfer is equivalent to duration-sensitive producibility. As duration-sensitive producibility is defined inductively, there is a straightforward polynomial-time satisfiability algorithm implementing Definition 3. □

3.3 Cycle-Free Data-Free nfer Satisfiability is Decidable

Next, we consider data-free nfer with inclusive and exclusive rules, but without cycles. Here, our decidability result is obtained by a transformation to *monadic first order logic* (MFO) (see, e.g., [10] for details) over strings.

Theorem 3. *The cycle-free data-free* nfer *satisfiability problem is decidable.*

Proof. Given a cycle-free specification D, we will, for each identifier η, construct an MFO formula $\varphi_{D,\eta}(t_0, t_1)$ with free variables t_0, t_1, such that η is satisfiable with respect to D iff $\varphi_{D,\eta}(t_0, t_1)$ is satisfiable, i.e. there exists a string (word) w over 2^Σ and an assignment $v : \{t_0, t_1\} \to \{0, \ldots, |w| - 1\}$ such that $w, v \models \varphi_{D,\eta}(t_0, t_1)$. Note, that for an event identifier $\eta \in \Sigma$, $\eta(\cdot)$ is a monadic predicate, where $\eta(t)$ evaluates to true in a string w over 2^Σ at position t if and only if the set of w at position t contains η. That is $w, v \models \eta(t)$ if and only if $\eta \in w_{v(t)}$.

Now from w, v, where $w, v \models \varphi_{D,\eta}(t_0, t_1)$, a satisfying input trace for η may be obtained as the concatenation $\tau_{w,v} = (w_{t_0}, t_0)(w_{t_0+1}, t_0+1) \ldots (w_{t_1}, t_1)$, where for a set $\sigma = \{\eta_1, \ldots, \eta_k\} \subseteq \Sigma$ and $t \in \mathbb{N}$, we denote by (σ, t) the (any) string $(\eta_1, t)(\eta_2, t) \cdots (\eta_k, t)$.

Since D is cycle-free, we may order the identifiers by a topological sort of the directed graph formed by the rules. The construction of $\varphi_{D,\eta}(t_0, t_1)$ now proceeds by induction on this order. In the base case, η is an event identifier. Here $\varphi_{D,\eta}(t_0, t_1) = (t_0 = t_1 \wedge \eta(t_0))$. For the inductive case, $\varphi_{D,\eta}(t_0, t_1)$ is obtained by a disjunction of all the rules for η in D, i.e.:

$$\varphi_{D,\eta}(t_0, t_1) = \bigvee\nolimits_{\eta \leftarrow \eta_1 \text{ op } \eta_2 \in D} \psi_{D, \eta_1 \text{ op } \eta_2}(t_0, t_1)$$

where **op** $\in \{\oplus, \textbf{unless } \ominus\}$. Here the definition $\psi_{D, \eta_1 \text{ op } \eta_2}(t_0, t_1)$ is obtained using the MFO formulas for η_1 and η_2 from the induction hypothesis. Here we just give the definition for two rules, one inclusive and one exclusive rule, leaving the remaining rules for the reader to provide.

$\psi_{D,\eta_1 \text{ before } \eta_2}(t_0, t_1) = \exists t'_0, t'_1.\ t_0 \leq t'_1 < t'_0 \leq t_1 \wedge \varphi_{D,\eta_1}(t_0, t'_1) \wedge \varphi_{D,\eta_2}(t'_0, t_1)$

$\psi_{D,\eta_1 \text{ unless after } \eta_2}(t_0, t_1) = \varphi_{D,\eta_1}(t_0, t_1) \wedge \forall t'_0, t'_1.\ (t'_0 \leq t'_1 < t_0 \leq t_1) \Rightarrow$
$\neg \varphi_{D,\eta_2}(t'_0, t'_1)$

Thus, decidability of MFO satisfiability over finite strings [5,9,25] yields decidability of cycle-free data-free nfer satisfiability. □

Though the reduction to MFO in Theorem 3 yields the desired decidability result, it comes with a non-elementary complexity [24]. We leave it open whether the problem has elementary complexity.

4 Evaluation of Data-Free nfer

The evaluation problem for nfer asks, given a specification D, a trace τ of events, and a target identifier η_T, is there an η_T-labeled interval in $T[\![D]\!]\tau$? The problem has been extensively studied in the presence of data, with complexities ranging from undecidable (for arbitrary data and cycles in the rules) to PTIME (for finite data under the minimality constraint). We refer to [21] for an overview of the results. One case that has not been considered thus far is the complexity of the evaluation problem for data-free nfer.

Obviously, the result from [21] for finite-data covers the case of data-free specifications, but without the "minimality" meta-constraint that artificially limits the size of the result, evaluation with only inclusive rules is PSPACE-complete (without cycles) and respectively EXPTIME-complete (with cycles). Here, we show that these results depend on the availability of (finite) data: data-free nfer can be evaluated in polynomial time (even without minimality).

Theorem 4. *The evaluation problem for data-free* nfer *is in* PTIME.

Proof. Consider an input consisting of a specification D, a trace τ of events, and a target identifier η_T, and let k be the number of unique timestamps in τ.

Recall that an interval is completely specified by its identifier in $\mathcal{I}$ and its starting and ending timestamp. Hence, as the application of rules does not create new timestamps (cf. Table 1 and Table 2), the number of intervals in $T[\![D]\!]\tau$ is bounded by $k^2|\mathcal{I}|$. Furthermore, whether a rule is applicable to two intervals can be checked in constant time. Thus, one can compute $T[\![D]\!]\tau$ in polynomial time and then check whether it contains an η_T-labeled interval. □

5 Conclusion and Future Work

We have studied the complexity of the satisfiability and evaluation problems for Data-free nfer. We proved that the evaluation problem is in PTIME and the satisfiability problem is undecidable in the general case, but decidable for cycle-free specifications and in PTIME for specifications with only inclusive rules.

There are still open questions around the complexity of nfer that may be interesting. We showed that satisfiability for data-free nfer is decidable for cycle-free specifications, but we do not prove a tight bound and we suspect it may be possible to achieve improvements on the non-elementary upper-bound we give. Another open question is if satisfiability is decidable for restricted cases of nfer *with data*, for example if specifications are cycle-free and data is finite. We are also interested in the complexity of *monitoring* nfer. Here and in other works, nfer is presented with an offline semantics. A naïve monitoring algorithm might simply recompute produced intervals each time a new event arrives, but we suspect that better monitoring complexity can be achieved without requiring assumptions beyond temporal ordering. We hope that this work inspires others to examine the complexity of other modern Runtime Verification (RV) languages.

References

1. Aceto, L., Della Monica, D., Goranko, V., Ingólfsdóttir, A., Montanari, A., Sciavicco, G.: A complete classification of the expressiveness of interval logics of Allen's relations: the general and the dense cases. Acta Informatica **53**(3), 207–246 (2016). https://doi.org/10.1007/s00236-015-0231-4
2. Allen, J.F.: Maintaining knowledge about temporal intervals. Commun. ACM **26**(11), 832–843 (1983)
3. Bar-Hillel, Y., Perles, M., Shamir, E.: On formal properties of simple phrase structure grammars. STUF - Lang. Typology Universals **14**(1–4), 143–172 (1961). https://doi.org/10.1524/stuf.1961.14.14.143
4. Bolander, T., Hansen, J.U., Hansen, M.R.: Decidability of a hybrid duration calculus. Electron. Notes Theor. Comput. Sci. **174**(6), 113–133 (2007). https://doi.org/10.1016/j.entcs.2006.11.029. Proceedings of the International Workshop on Hybrid Logic (HyLo 2006)
5. Büchi, J.R.: Weak second-order arithmetic and finite automata. Math. Log. Q. **6**(1–6), 66–92 (1960). https://doi.org/10.1002/malq.19600060105. https://onlinelibrary.wiley.com/doi/abs/10.1002/malq.19600060105
6. Chaochen, Z., Hansen, M.R., Sestoft, P.: Decidability and undecidability results for duration calculus. In: Enjalbert, P., Finkel, A., Wagner, K.W. (eds.) STACS 1993. LNCS, vol. 665, pp. 58–68. Springer, Heidelberg (1993). https://doi.org/10.1007/3-540-56503-5_8
7. Chaochen, Z., Hoare, C., Ravn, A.P.: A calculus of durations. Inf. Process. Lett. **40**(5), 269–276 (1991). https://doi.org/10.1016/0020-0190(91)90122-X
8. Chomsky, N.: On certain formal properties of grammars. Inf. Control **2**(2), 137–167 (1959). https://doi.org/10.1016/S0019-9958(59)90362-6
9. Elgot, C.C.: Decision problems of finite automata design and related arithmetics. Trans. Am. Math. Soc. **98**(1), 21–51 (1961). http://www.jstor.org/stable/1993511
10. Grädel, E., Thomas, W., Wilke, T. (eds.): Automata, Logics, and Infinite Games: A Guide to Current Research. LNCS, vol. 2500. Springer, Heidelberg (2002). https://doi.org/10.1007/3-540-36387-4
11. Halpern, J., Manna, Z., Moszkowski, B.: A hardware semantics based on temporal intervals. In: Diaz, J. (ed.) ICALP 1983. LNCS, vol. 154, pp. 278–291. Springer, Heidelberg (1983). https://doi.org/10.1007/BFb0036915

12. Halpern, J.Y., Shoham, Y.: A propositional modal logic of time intervals. J. ACM **38**(4), 935–962 (1991). https://doi.org/10.1145/115234.115351
13. Kauffman, S.: Log analysis and system monitoring with nfer. Sci. Comput. Program. **225**, 102909 (2023). https://doi.org/10.1016/j.scico.2022.102909
14. Kauffman, S., Dunne, M., Gracioli, G., Khan, W., Benann, N., Fischmeister, S.: Palisade: a framework for anomaly detection in embedded systems. J. Syst. Architect. **113**, 101876 (2021). https://doi.org/10.1016/j.sysarc.2020.101876
15. Kauffman, S., Fischmeister, S.: Mining temporal intervals from real-time system traces. In: International Workshop on Software Mining (SoftwareMining 2017), pp. 1–8. IEEE (2017). https://doi.org/10.1109/SOFTWAREMINING.2017.8100847
16. Kauffman, S., Havelund, K., Joshi, R.: `nfer` – a notation and system for inferring event stream abstractions. In: Falcone, Y., Sánchez, C. (eds.) RV 2016. LNCS, vol. 10012, pp. 235–250. Springer, Cham (2016). https://doi.org/10.1007/978-3-319-46982-9_15
17. Kauffman, S., Havelund, K., Joshi, R., Fischmeister, S.: Inferring event stream abstractions. Formal Methods Syst. Des. **53**, 54–82 (2018). https://doi.org/10.1007/s10703-018-0317-z
18. Kauffman, S., Joshi, R., Havelund, K.: Towards a logic for inferring properties of event streams. In: Margaria, T., Steffen, B. (eds.) ISoLA 2016. LNCS, vol. 9953, pp. 394–399. Springer, Cham (2016). https://doi.org/10.1007/978-3-319-47169-3_31
19. Kauffman, S., Larsen, K.G., Zimmermann, M.: The complexity of data-free Nfer (2024). https://arxiv.org/abs/2407.03155
20. Kauffman, S., Zimmermann, M.: The complexity of evaluating Nfer. In: Aït-Ameur, Y., Crăciun, F. (eds.) TASE 2022. LNCS, vol. 13299, pp. 388–405. Springer, Cham (2022). https://doi.org/10.1007/978-3-031-10363-6_26
21. Kauffman, S., Zimmermann, M.: The complexity of evaluating nfer. Sci. Comput. Program. **231**, 103012 (2024). https://doi.org/10.1016/j.scico.2023.103012
22. Montanari, A., Puppis, G., Sala, P.: Maximal decidable fragments of Halpern and Shoham's modal logic of intervals. In: Abramsky, S., Gavoille, C., Kirchner, C., Meyer auf der Heide, F., Spirakis, P.G. (eds.) ICALP 2010. LNCS, vol. 6199, pp. 345–356. Springer, Heidelberg (2010). https://doi.org/10.1007/978-3-642-14162-1_29
23. Montanari, A., Puppis, G., Sala, P., Sciavicco, G.: Decidability of the interval temporal logic ABB over the natural numbers. In: Theoretical Aspects of Computer Science, STACS 2010, pp. 597–608. Schloss Dagstuhl - Leibniz-Zentrum für Informatik (2010). https://hal.archives-ouvertes.fr/hal-00717798
24. Stockmeyer, L.J.: The complexity of decision problems in automata theory and logic. Ph.D. thesis, MIT (1974)
25. Trakhtenbrot, B.A.: Finite automata and the logic of one-place predicates. Siberskii Matematicheskii Zhurnal **3**(1), 103–131 (1962)
26. Valentin Goranko, A.M., Sciavicco, G.: A road map of interval temporal logics and duration calculi. J. Appl. Non-Classical Logics **14**(1–2), 9–54 (2004). https://doi.org/10.3166/jancl.14.9-54

RTLolaMo³Vis - A Mobile and Modular Visualization Framework for Online Monitoring

Jan Baumeister[✉][iD], Bernd Finkbeiner[iD], Jan Kautenburger, and Clara Rubeck

CISPA Helmholtz Center for Information Security, 66123 Saarbrücken, Germany
{jan.baumeister,finkbeiner,jan.kautenburger,clara.rubeck}@cispa.de

Abstract. Runtime monitoring facilitates human oversight of safety-critical systems by collecting and aggregating data from sensors and other system components and by issuing alerts whenever the safety specification is violated. It is critical that the collected data is presented in a way that helps the user to quickly assess the situation. Most monitoring tools have only limited support for data visualization. We present RTLolaMo³Vis, an online runtime monitoring framework that is mobile, modular, and supports the graphical visualization of the monitoring data in real time. RTLolaMo³Vis is highly configurable, from data collection to the final visualization, which makes it applicable to a wide spectrum of applications. The design of RTLolaMo³Vis follows the monitoring-based visualization approach, which minimizes the additional code for visualization by preprocessing the data in the monitor. We demonstrate the modularity and efficiency of RTLolaMo³Vis on simulated drone flights and real-world communication data. On standard mobile phones and tablet computers, RTLolaMo³Vis processes the monitoring output at a frequency of 100 Hz without any data loss.

Keywords: Runtime Verification · Stream-based Monitoring · Data Visualization

1 Introduction

Embedded software and cyber-physical systems (CPS) are at the heart of modern applications like autonomous cars and planes, medical devices, and civic infrastructures. In such systems, computer programs make decisions and take actions that affect the safety and well-being of humans. Runtime verification technology like real-time monitoring can play a crucial role in increasing the

---

This work was partially supported by the Aviation Research Program LuFo of the German Federal Ministry for Economic Affairs and Energy as part of "Volocopter Sicherheitstechnologie zur robusten eVTOL Flugzustandsabsicherung durch formales Monitoring" (No. 20Q1963C), by the German Research Foundation (DGF) as part of TRR 248 (389792660), and by the European Research Council (ERC) Grant HYPER (101055412).

© The Author(s), under exclusive license to Springer Nature Switzerland AG 2025
E. Ábrahám and H. Abbas (Eds.): RV 2024, LNCS 15191, pp. 192–202, 2025.
https://doi.org/10.1007/978-3-031-74234-7_12

trust in such systems by collecting and aggregating data from sensors and other system components. The aggregated data helps the human user to assess the safety of the running system and to intervene in critical situations.

It is far from trivial, however, to present the information available in the monitor in a way that helps the user to quickly understand the situation. Most monitoring tools have some support for displaying the collected data, but the visualization is often surprisingly limited. Many tools still rely on a textual interface with "alert" messages. Textual output is prone to mix-ups and often hard to read, especially in hectic situations where many alerts arrive simultaneously. Additionally, the textual output makes it difficult to connect emitted triggers to the input data that causes them, thus making it harder to find faults. The TeSSLa visualizer [18] and the RTLola Playground [13] provide graphical visualizations of output streams, but in both tools the data can only be visualized in retrospect, once all data has been collected. An effective visualization for CPS should both be *online*, i.e., available in real time so that the user can understand bad situations as quickly as possible, and *mobile*, i.e., available on small devices such as mobile phones, so that it can be deployed without extensive computing infrastructure. An example where such a visualization has been realized in a limited application context is the *RTLola on Board* app [8]. RTLola on Board is a mobile application for Android phones that connects to the On-Board-Diagnostics (OBD) port of a car and displays data on automotive exhaust emissions in real time while the car is being driven. The app has been useful in finding violations of the regulatory framework currently valid in the European Union.

In this paper, we present RTLolaMo^{3}Vis, a visualization framework that is, similar to the RTLola on Board app, capable of displaying the information in real time and in a mobile setting, but is universally applicable in a wide spectrum of application domains. RTLolaMo^{3}Vis is a mobile application for Android and iOS devices built on top of the RTLola monitoring language and framework [5]. Users of the visualization framework have a range of options to customize the specification used in the monitor, the type of input data, as well as the visualization output.

The design principle behind RTLolaMo^{3}Vis is *monitoring-based visualization* [3], which keeps the additional code for the visualization to a minimum and relies on the monitor itself to carry out the many data processing steps that are needed to prepare the visualization. This includes various types of data filtering and aggregation, the synchronization of asynchronous inputs, the identification of graph points and trigger values, and the management of the user's attention. All these computations are carried out by a monitor specified in RTLola. Around this RTLola-based core we then build a mobile application that accepts data as configured by the user, passes the data to the monitor, and then visualizes the monitoring results as graphs or in textual form as configured by the user. We demonstrate the effectiveness and functionality of our approach by monitoring and visualizing data gathered during various simulations. This includes a drone flight in AirSim [2], flight data from the Microsoft Flight Simulator[1], and real-

---

[1] https://www.flightsimulator.com/.

world communication data. These experiments highlight the modular nature of our approach, its easy usability, and the insights a user can gain from a customized visualization. The remainder of the paper is structured as follows. In Sect. 2, we give a brief overview of RTLola. We detail the tasks needed to implement a modular mobile framework for online monitoring in Sect. 3. In Sect. 4, we describe the implementation and our experience with the practical application of RTLolaMo³Vis.

1.1 Related Work

The importance of visualizing data streams for effective data analysis and decision-making in real-time environments was highlighted by Krstajić and Keim [19] and is being applied in various areas [12,15,24,25]. However, the field of runtime monitoring mainly relies on the textual representation of the monitor output [10,11,14,16,18,20]. In general, each tool could be combined with an external visualization but does not support a native solution for stream visualization. Some monitoring frameworks support data visualization for offline monitoring, in the form of browser-based playgrounds [13,18] or support visualization for a concrete online monitoring setup [8]. In comparison, this paper presents an approach for visualizing data generated from a monitor running in real-time, which is due to different configurations not tailored to a concrete setup. Besides visualizing the output of the monitor, we follow the approach of combining visualization and monitoring as presented by Baumeister et al. [3]. Here, the monitor performs some of the visualization tasks, such as data filtering or synchronization.

2 RTLola

RTLola is a stream-based specification language that uses stream equations to describe the transformation of incoming data streams to output streams and a set of trigger conditions. A satisfying trigger condition represents a safety violation. The runtime monitor is generated from the formal description given by the specification. The following specification exemplifies RTLola and we refer the reader to [4,13] for more details [6].

```
1  input vel: Float64, timestamp: Float64
2  output diff_too_high := abs(vel - vel.last(or:vel)) > 10.0
3  trigger diff_too_high "Difference is greater than 10.0"
4
5  output filtered_vel eval when !diff_too_high with vel
6  output avg_vel @1Hz := filtered_vel.aggregate(over: 2s, using: average).defaults(to: 0.0)
7  output vel_point := (timestamp.hold(or:0.0), avg_vel, diff_too_high.aggregate(over: 1s,
       using: exists))
```

The specification detects big velocity changes and prepares the data for the visualization. First, it declares two input streams: The first stream `vel` represents the velocity given by the inertial measurement unit (IMU), and the second stream `time` contains the current time. The output stream `diff_too_high` computes the difference between the currently measured velocity and the last seen velocity. If the velocity difference exceeds the threshold of 10.0 units, the output stream evaluates to true, and subsequently, a trigger will be thrown.

Next, the specification prepares the monitor output for the visualization following the monitoring-based visualization approach [3]. More concretely, the specification in this example first filters the velocity to exclude noisy sensor readings with the output stream `filtered_vel`. Next, the `avg_vel` stream computes the average velocity using a sliding window. This operation accumulates all values over a 2-s duration, as the visualization cannot plot every data point. Additionally, the stream is annotated by an explicit frequency of `1Hz` to ensure that too frequent data points do not overload the visualization. Lastly, we define `vel_point` representing a concrete point in a plot. The `time` and `avg_vel` streams represent the x- and y-coordinates of the plot. In our setup, a single point can appear in two colors, depending on the value of the last element in the tuple, specifying whether the point causes a trigger. Here, the plot visualizes whether `diff_too_high` was true in the last second. This demonstrates how we can leverage RTLola to perform visualization tasks like data synchronization, or filtering while monitoring a system.

3 Framework

This section gives a general overview of the tool to build a visualization for the monitor output. In summary, it receives data from a system, passes them to the monitoring framework, and visualizes the monitor output using graphs and textual triggers. Figure 1 illustrates our structure, introducing a configurable 5-step approach. With the start of the application, each step receives a separate configuration that is not tied to one specific setup. Then, the framework validates the compatibility between the configurations to guarantee a safe execution.

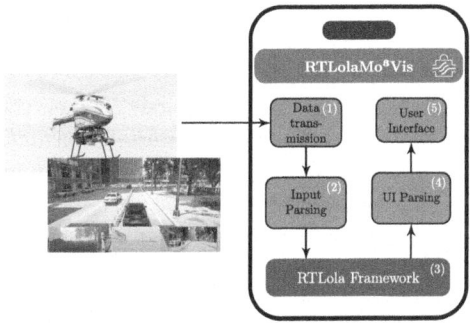

Fig. 1. RTLolaMo^{3}Vis setup

(1) **Data Transmission**: First, the framework receives data from the monitored system, supporting multiple communication protocols, and passes the data to the input parser.
(2) **Input Parsing**: This step translates incoming data to the format expected by the monitoring framework. Via a configuration it is compatible with a range of system setups, thus making it modular and adaptable. RTLola, the underlying specification language, can handle asynchronous data, making it necessary for our configuration to process various input types.
(3) **Monitoring Framework**: The core of our framework is the RTLola monitor, but our approach is applicable to all stream-based monitoring frameworks. Our setup passes the processed input to the monitor to identify violations of the specified properties. Additionally, the specification prepares the

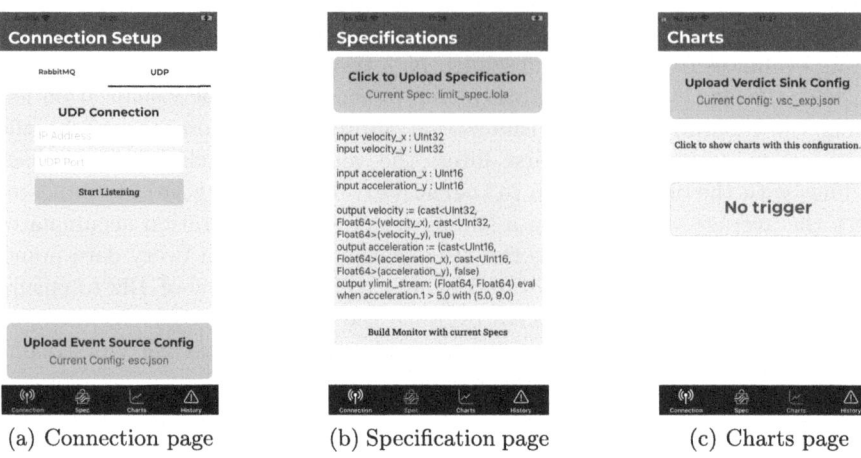

Fig. 2. Layout of RTLolaMo³Vis

data for visualization as shown in Sect. 2, e.g., by filtering the input data and data synchronization. Therefore, after all configurations are provided, the framework checks if the specification is compatible with the visualization. Furthermore, the framework validates if the expected inputs align with the specification.
(4) **UI Parsing**: The UI Parsing takes the monitor output and translates it into the expected user interface format. Consequently, the modularization of this step is tailored to the concrete visualization.
(5) **User Interface**: Given the output from the previous step, the visualization displays plots of stream values, along with triggers and their associated messages. As configuration, the framework expects a description of the plots and checks for compatibility with the specification, i.e., it is only possible to plot what the specification computes.

4 Implementation and Experiments

This section discusses the concrete implementation of the application. After providing the technical setup, we describe concrete configurations for each step in Sect. 3 to achieve a modular setup.

4.1 Technical Setup

RTLolaMo³Vis[2] is implemented in Xamarin Forms [17], a cross-platform mobile application development toolkit. This toolkit uses shared code written in C# and produces an Android and an iOS application. The RTLola Interpreter [7] serves as the underlying monitoring framework. To embed the Rust-based [23] RTLola

---

[2] The app is publicly available at GitHub.

```
1  {
2    "timestamp": "Float64",
3    "msg_id": "UInt8",
4    "payload": {
5      "payload_id": "msg_id",
6      "1": {
7        "data": {
8          "velocity_x": "Float64",
9          "velocity_y": "Float64"
10       }
11     }
12     "2" : {
13       "data" : { "alt": "Float64" }
14  }}}
```

(a) Event source configuration

```
1  {
2    "Plots": [
3      {
4        "Id": "0",
5        "X": "Time",
6        "Y": "Average velocity",
7        "Series": [
8          {
9            "Stream": "vel_point",
10           "Connected": "True",
11           "Color": "Blue"
12         }
13       ],
14       "Limits": { "x": "limit" }
15  }]}
```

(b) Verdict sink configuration

Fig. 3. Example of an event source and verdict sink configuration

monitor into external build systems, we built a C-compatible API and compiled the API with *cargo lipo* [9]. This compiler creates a universal library used in the iOS version of the app and a dynamic-link library (DLL) for Android. Besides data transmission and the concrete user interface, all steps of the pipeline presented in Sect. 3 are implemented in the pre-compiled library. Note that RTLola can be replaced by other runtime monitoring frameworks easily if they provide an implementation that uses roughöy the same input-output interface and be compiled into a DLL and fat library.

4.2 Visualization Pipeline

(1) **Data Transmission**: The implementation of the data transmission uses existing Xamarin libraries and supports two setups: The first setup utilizes UDP [26] for fast and easy transmission of byte streams while the second setup uses RabbitMQ [22] for a more reliable transmission. Figure 2a displays the start page of our tool in which the user provides the configuration for this stage.

(2) **Input Parsing**: Our implementation achieves modularity using an *event source configuration*. This configuration is an ordered JSON file that defines a modular parser for a given byte stream. This parser defines different messages to achieve a partial input assignment, e.g., the payload of a message differs depending on the sensor that sends the data resulting in different updates of the input streams.

Figure 3a exemplifies a configuration defining a parser with two messages, one for the velocity and one for the altitude. First, the example defines the header of each message containing a timestamp and a message ID. The next entry splits the parser into different cases determined by the msg_id. The following numbers define the parsing for each message: The first message, identified with the message ID 1, assigns velocity_x and velocity_y to the equally named input streams in the specification. The second message defines the parsing for the altitude sensor following the same structure. Note that an event source configuration must be compatible with the given specification, i.e., the configuration must contain a fitting definition for each input stream of the specification in at least one message ID.

(3) **Monitoring Framework**: The implementation uses the RTLola interpreter as monitoring framework. As configuration, it gets a specification written in the RTLola specification language.

(4) **UI Parsing**: The configuration in this step defines the overall structure of the visualization and is shared with the user interface. This so-called *verdict sink configuration* is given as a JSON file and defines a list of graphs. Each graph also called plot consists of the following entries exemplified in Fig. 3b:

Id: A unique identifier for each plot.

X, Y: An x- and y-axis description.

Series: A description of the series in the plot, i.e., a line in the graph. Each entry assigns the series to a stream in the specification via the "Stream" entry. As described in Sect. 2, a stream contains the x- and y-coordinates in the plot as well as an indication of the color. The additional attributes "Connected" and "Color" are explained in the user interface step as they only define the appearance of the final visualization.

Limits: A limit entry sets the lower and upper bounds for an axis on a plot. Each limit entry is directly linked to a specific data stream in the specification. When this stream is updated, the new stream values are interpreted as the updated boundaries, and the visualization automatically removes any values that fall outside these limits.

A common use case is visualizing velocity over time, where it's often more useful for the user to restrict the view to a specific timeframe rather than the entire execution duration. As time progresses and older data becomes less relevant, updating the associated limit stream automatically removes any values with timestamps outside the newly defined boundaries.

If an entry is empty, the implementation uses a default value or notifies the user. Additionally, the implementation prepares the visualization of the trigger messages. In our setup, triggers include one of the keywords ALERT, ADVISORY, CAUTION, WARNING, or ERROR at the beginning of the trigger message. These so-called *importances* classify different severities of triggers in the visualization. Besides trigger messages, the implementation prepares errors and messages from the monitoring framework, e.g., parsing or communication errors, which we refer to as *logs*.

(5) **Visualization**: Our implementation splits the visualization into two independent views: the trigger visualization and graphs of stream values. Triggers and logs are entered into the trigger data store and displayed on the trigger history page, as shown in Fig. 4b. This page sorts trigger messages into their specific categories or to ADVISORY if no importance is defined in the specification. Logs are in the ERROR category. The appearance of plots is defined in the verdict sink configuration presented in the previous step. Our user interface supports the visualization of a set of plots collecting a series

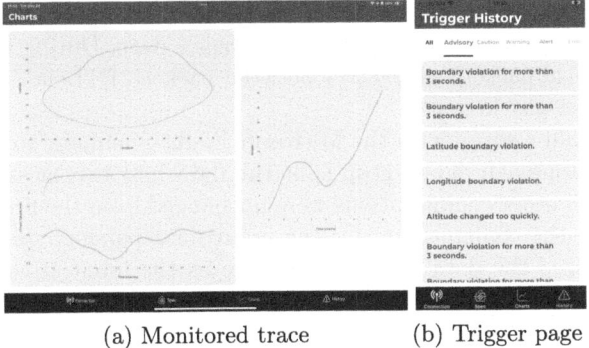

(a) Monitored trace (b) Trigger page

Fig. 4. Mobile monitoring in connection with AirSim.

of data points, as illustrated in Fig. 4a. All points are entered into the chart data store according to the plot- and series ID they were paired with during UI Parsing. The implementation uses Livecharts [21] as a plotting library and an `Observablecollection` in the charts data store. This data store ensures that each point added or removed to the store is propagated to the user interface. Since each series corresponds to a stream in the specification, a data point contains the x- and y-coordinates and a boolean value. The `"Color"` attribute assigns each series a color. This color is taken if the boolean value of the data point is false. The second color defines an alternative color of a data point. In our case study, this alternative color indicates a violation of a trigger related to the data point for which we define the second color as the trigger color. The default color and trigger color are blue and red respectively. The attribute `"Connected"` of series defines whether the points of a series are connected, i.e., whether the series is a line or a scatter plot. However, this connection does not smooth the connecting line. If the application receives a new limit, all points in any series of the corresponding plot are checked for out-of-bound values.

5 Evaluation

We evaluated our approach in three setups to demonstrate modularity, efficiency, and usability. Each experiment ran RTLolaMo[3]Vis on an iPhone SE (2020) and an iPad Pro 5th generation. The first setup is based on the AirSim [2] drone simulator and sends the data via UDP. As configurations, we use extended versions from Sect. 2 and Sect. 4, included in the appendix. The experiment defines three plots: one with the latitude and longitude, one with two velocity series, and one for the altitude. Each series was annotated with a trigger, e.g., if the position violated a geofence. Figure 4 shows two screenshots taken during the run, one of the plotted charts and one of the visualized textual triggers. As defined in our configuration, triggered points are marked red, and non-triggered points are marked green. The iPad and iPhone were able to visualize all three plots. Figure 4b presents the corresponding trigger page. During this flight, the simulator sent 640 packets with 0.75 s between packets. RTLolaMo^{3}Vis handled the data without any losses.

Next, we build a setup with the Microsoft Flight Simulator to test the modularity of our approach. This setup split the data into two messages: position and velocity. All other configurations were unchanged from the first experiment. After replacing the configuration for the input data parsing, step 2 in Sect. 3, the tool visualized the data as expected, even as the input streams were split into two messages. Here, we transmitted the first message every 0.5 s and the second message every second without data loss.

Lastly, we evaluate our tool on a dataset of IP addresses that try to log into a web application. We designed a new specification and configuration for this setup and reached a frequency of 100Hz without any data loss. Compared to the previous setup, this experiment required minor plotting.

6 Conclusion

This paper introduces a new mobile application called RTLolaMo^{3}Vis for online runtime verification. RTLolaMo^{3}Vis follows the approach of combining monitoring and visualization and emphasizes modularity. We realize this design principle using a 5-step approach. After receiving the data, the Input Parsing specifies the mapping between the input data and the monitor input defined in the specification. The monitor evaluates the input based on the specification, the UI Parsing prepares the data for the visualization, and the user interface visualizes streams and trigger messages. Each step takes a separate configuration with the start of the application resulting in a highly modular application. We demonstrate the effectiveness and practical usability of our approach by monitoring simulated drone flights and network communication. This real-world application of RTLolaMo^{3}Vis showcases how easy it is to deploy and highlights the usefulness of graph-oriented visualization compared to previous text-only monitor outputs.

In the future, mobile applications like RTLolaMo^{3}Vis can be expanded and enhanced to include more visualization options and greater modularity. One aspect is to increase the modularity of input parsing. Specifically, we plan to allow users to include their pre-compiled library for Input Parsing instead of including it in the monitor. We aim to inspire other developers of runtime verification frameworks to focus more on the practical applicability of their frameworks to enable the development of more real-world applications and easy access to runtime verification tools.

References

1. Adolf, F.-M., Faymonville, P., Finkbeiner, B., Schirmer, S., Torens, C.: Stream runtime monitoring on UAS. In: Lahiri, S., Reger, G. (eds.) RV 2017. LNCS, vol. 10548, pp. 33–49. Springer, Cham (2017). https://doi.org/10.1007/978-3-319-67531-2_3

2. Airsim. https://microsoft.github.io/AirSim. Accessed 26 May 2024
3. Baumeister, J., Finkbeiner, B., Gumhold, S., Schledjewski, M.: Real-time visualization of stream-based monitoring data. In: Dang, T., Stolz, V. (eds.) RV 2022. LNCS, vol. 13498, pp. 325–335. Springer, Cham (2022). https://doi.org/10.1007/978-3-031-17196-3_21
4. Baumeister, J., et al.: Monitoring unmanned aircraft: specification, integration, and lessons-learned. In: Gurfinkel, A., Ganesh, V. (eds.) CAV 2024. LNCS, vol. 14682, pp. 207–218. Springer, Cham (2024). https://doi.org/10.1007/978-3-031-65630-9_10
5. Baumeister, J., Finkbeiner, B., Schirmer, S., Schwenger, M., Torens, C.: RTLola cleared for take-off: monitoring autonomous aircraft. In: Lahiri, S.K., Wang, C. (eds.) CAV 2020, Part II. LNCS, vol. 12225, pp. 28–39. Springer, Cham (2020). https://doi.org/10.1007/978-3-030-53291-8_3
6. Baumeister, J., Finkbeiner, B., Schwenger, M., Torfah, H.: FPGA stream-monitoring of real-time properties. ACM Trans. Embed. Comput. Syst. **18**(5s) (2019). https://doi.org/10.1145/3358220
7. Baumeister, J., Kohn, F., Oswald, S., Schwenger, M.: RTLola interpreter. https://docs.rs/rtlola-interpreter/latest/rtlola_interpreter/
8. Biewer, S., Finkbeiner, B., Hermanns, H., Köhl, M.A., Schnitzer, Y., Schwenger, M.: RTLola on board: testing real driving emissions on your phone. In: Groote, J.F., Larsen, K.G. (eds.) TACAS 2021. LNCS, vol. 12652, pp. 365–372. Springer, Cham (2021). https://doi.org/10.1007/978-3-030-72013-1_20
9. Cargo lipo. https://github.com/TimNN/cargo-lipo. Accessed 15 May 2024
10. D'Angelo, B., et al.: LOLA: runtime monitoring of synchronous systems. In: 12th International Symposium on Temporal Representation and Reasoning (TIME 2005), pp. 166–174 (2005). https://doi.org/10.1109/TIME.2005.26
11. Donzé, A., Ferrère, T., Maler, O.: Efficient robust monitoring for STL. In: Sharygina, N., Veith, H. (eds.) CAV 2013. LNCS, vol. 8044, pp. 264–279. Springer, Heidelberg (2013). https://doi.org/10.1007/978-3-642-39799-8_19
12. Elsisi, M., Tran, M.Q., Mahmoud, K., Mansour, D.E.A., Lehtonen, M., Darwish, M.M.F.: Towards secured online monitoring for digitalized GIS against cyber-attacks based on IoT and machine learning. IEEE Access **9**, 78415–78427 (2021). https://doi.org/10.1109/ACCESS.2021.3083499
13. Finkbeiner, B., Kohn, F., Schledjewski, M.: Leveraging static analysis: an IDE for RTLola. In: André, É., Sun, J. (eds.) ATVA 2023, Part II. LNCS, vol. 14216, pp. 251–262. Springer, Cham (2023). https://doi.org/10.1007/978-3-031-45332-8_13
14. Gorostiaga, F., Sánchez, C.: **Striver**: stream runtime verification for real-time event-streams. In: Colombo, C., Leucker, M. (eds.) RV 2018. LNCS, vol. 11237, pp. 282–298. Springer, Cham (2018). https://doi.org/10.1007/978-3-030-03769-7_16
15. Hautte, S., et al.: A dynamic dashboarding application for fleet monitoring using semantic web of things technologies. Sensors **20**, 1152 (2020). https://doi.org/10.3390/s20041152
16. Havelund, K., Roşu, G.: Synthesizing monitors for safety properties. In: Katoen, J.-P., Stevens, P. (eds.) TACAS 2002. LNCS, vol. 2280, pp. 342–356. Springer, Heidelberg (2002). https://doi.org/10.1007/3-540-46002-0_24
17. Hermes, D., Mazloumi, N.: Building Xamarin. Forms Mobile Apps Using XAML: Mobile Cross-Platform XAML and Xamarin. Forms Fundamentals. Apress (2019)
18. Kallwies, H., Leucker, M., Schmitz, M., Schulz, A., Thoma, D., Weiss, A.: TeSSLa-an ecosystem for runtime verification. In: Dang, T., Stolz, V. (eds.) RV 2022. LNCS, vol. 13498, pp. 314–324. Springer, Cham (2022). https://doi.org/10.1007/978-3-031-17196-3_20

19. Krstajić, M., Keim, D.A.: Visualization of streaming data: observing change and context in information visualization techniques. In: 2013 IEEE International Conference on Big Data, pp. 41–47 (2013).https://doi.org/10.1109/BigData.2013.6691713
20. Omer, M., Peled, D.: Runtime verification prediction for traces with data. In: Katsaros, P., Nenzi, L. (eds.) RV 2023. LNCS, vol. 14245, pp. 148–167. Springer, Cham (2023). https://doi.org/10.1007/978-3-031-44267-4_8
21. Orozco, A.R.: LiveCharts2 (2021). https://github.com/beto-rodriguez/LiveCharts2
22. Rabbitmq: One broker to queue them all. https://www.rabbitmq.com. Accessed 15 May 2024
23. Rust. https://www.rust-lang.org. Accessed 15 May 2024
24. Stylianides, N., Dikaiakos, M., Gjermundrød, H., Panayi, G., Kyprianou, T.: Intensive care window: real-time monitoring and analysis in the intensive care environment. IEEE Trans. Inf Technol. Biomed. **15**(1), 26–32 (2011). https://doi.org/10.1109/TITB.2010.2091141
25. Tran, M.Q., et al.: Reliable deep learning and IoT-based monitoring system for secure computer numerical control machines against cyber-attacks with experimental verification. IEEE Access **10**, 23186–23197 (2022). https://doi.org/10.1109/ACCESS.2022.3153471
26. User Datagram Protocol. RFC 768 (1980). https://doi.org/10.17487/RFC0768. https://www.rfc-editor.org/info/rfc768

Deep Neural Networks

Case Study: Runtime Safety Verification of Neural Network Controlled System

Frank Yang[1], Sinong Simon Zhan[1], Yixuan Wang[1], Chao Huang[2], and Qi Zhu[1(✉)]

[1] Electrical and Computer Engineering, Northwestern University, Evanston, USA
{frankyang2024,SinongZhan2028,yixuanwang2024,qzhu}@u.northwestern.edu
[2] School of Electronics and Computer Science, University of Southampton, Southampton, UK
Chao.Huang@soton.ac.uk

Abstract. Neural networks are increasingly used in safety-critical applications such as robotics and autonomous vehicles. However, the deployment of neural-network-controlled systems (NNCSs) raises significant safety concerns. Many recent advances overlook critical aspects of verifying control and ensuring safety in real-time scenarios. This paper presents a case study on using POLAR-Express, a state-of-the-art NNCS reachability analysis tool, for runtime safety verification in a Turtlebot navigation system using LiDAR. The Turtlebot, equipped with a neural network controller for steering, operates in a complex environment with obstacles. We developed a safe online controller switching strategy that switches between the original NNCS controller and an obstacle avoidance controller based on the verification results. Our experiments, conducted in a ROS2 Flatland simulation environment, explore the capabilities and limitations of using POLAR-Express for runtime verification and demonstrate the effectiveness of our switching strategy.

Keywords: Safety verification · Neural Network Controlled System

1 Introduction

The increasing complexity of control strategies used in cyber-physical systems (CPSs) [34], specifically those based on neural networks, has revolutionized decision-making and control in several critical domains, including healthcare [58, 59], robotics [48,49,61], transportation [14,39,55], building control [53,56,57], and industrial automation [9,54]. These advanced control approaches excel at handling complex and dynamic environments due to their ability to learn and adapt from data. However, assuring the safety and stability of these systems for the nonlinearity of control systems and their closed-loop formation with dynamic systems remains a significant challenge [4,42,64,66].

Frank Yang, Simon Sinong Zhan, Yixuan Wang, and Qi Zhu's work is partially supported by US National Science Foundation grants 2324936 and 2328973. Chao Huang's work is supported by the grant EP/Y002644/1 under the EPSRC ECR International Collaboration Grants program, funded by the International Science Partnerships Fund (ISPF) and the UK Research and Innovation.

Literature in this domain primarily focuses on developing methodologies to assess and guarantee the reliability and robustness of neural network decisions. Early approaches often relied on static analysis techniques that scrutinized network structures and weights to predict behavior under various inputs [1,26,46]. Recent advancements have introduced more dynamic methods, such as formal verification and reachability analysis [2,18,40,50], which offer more nuanced insights into network behaviors across potential operational scenarios. The Simplex-based Reachability Analysis [7,16] guarantees system overall safety by integrating a verified safety controller and decision logic that switches between complex and safety controllers. While making significant contributions on real-time reachability, the use of these verification tools in realistic environments with machine-learning components remains largely unexplored. Our work uses POLAR-Express [50], a state-of-the-art verification tool to perform online reachability analysis for realistic robotic systems with neural network control and LiDAR sensing. We demonstrate the effectiveness of POLAR-Express for online reachability analysis by safely navigating robots in complex environments with obstacle constraints. The main contributions of this paper are as follows:

- We present a comprehensive study demonstrating the feasibility of performing runtime verification by POLAR-Express on Turtlebot for safe navigation.
- We provide a safe online controller switching strategy to avoid unknown obstacles based on the runtime verification result.

2 Related Work

Runtime Verification for Control. Runtime Verification (RV) plays a crucial role in the real-time operation of autonomous systems, such as autonomous vehicles [25], transportation networks [41] and medical devices [35]. In control theory, techniques such as adaptive control and robust control are employed to manage uncertainties and ensure stability in real-time scenarios [5,63]. From the formal methods perspective, model checking, which utilizes temporal logic specifications like linear temporal logic (LTL) and signal temporal logic (STL), forms the backbone of verification processes on the system's trajectories [8,15,22,30,44,60,62]. Moreover, the integration of stochastic quantification tools with temporal logic through conformal prediction frameworks offers a formal statistical guarantee of system reliability under dynamic conditions [10,37]. These developments have fostered innovative hybrid approaches that combine the strengths of control theory and formal methods to tackle complex verification challenges in real-time systems [3,45].

NNCS Verification. The verification of neural networks has emerged as a critical research area [65]. Tools like Reluplex [31], Marabou [32], and Sherlock [17] employ techniques derived from formal methods to ensure that neural networks adhere to specified safety and performance criteria. Others methods includes optimization-based over-approximation [17,46], and hybrid system approximation [29]. Alongside these, with the existing techniques for verifying dynamic systems [11,13], a series of works have attained considerable maturity, providing formal analysis for neural network controlled systems (NNCSs) [2,18–20,24,33,38,47,50–52]. However, most of these approaches have not demonstrated the capability to verify NNCSs in a runtime environment. [28] presented the feasibility of Verisig [27,29] using high-dimensional LiDAR measurements as the NNCS input, albeit in a simplistic setting for runtime requirements.

3 POLAR-Express Case Study

3.1 Preliminary

NNCS. We consider the explicit dynamics of an NNCS as $\dot{s} = f(s,a)$ where the state variable is $s \in \mathcal{S} \subseteq \mathbb{R}^n$, control input is $a \in \mathcal{A} \subseteq \mathbb{R}^m$, and the dynamic $f : \mathbb{R}^n \times \mathbb{R}^m \to \mathbb{R}^n$ is a Lipschitz continuous function, ensuring a unique solution of the ODE. Such a system can be controlled by a feedback NN controller κ_{nn}, at i-th ($i = 0, 1, \cdots$) sampling period $i\delta$, κ_{nn} reads the system state $s_{i\delta}$, generates a control input $a = \kappa_{nn}(s_{i\delta})$, and the system evolves according to $\dot{s} = f(s,a)$ within the period of $[i\delta, (i+1)\delta]$. The *flowmap* function $\varphi(s_0, t) : \mathbb{R}^n \times \mathbb{R}_{\geq 0} \to \mathbb{R}^n$ is to describe the solution of the NNCS, which maps the initial state s_0 to the system state $\varphi(s_0, t)$ at time t starting from s_0. We call a state s' *reachable* if there exist $s_0 \in S$ and $t \in \mathbb{R}_{\geq 0}$ with $s' = \varphi(s_0, t)$. A reachable set $\mathcal{S}_r^T$ is a collection of all reachable states within a time range $T = \mathbb{R}_{\geq 0}$ given an initial space $\mathcal{S}_0 = \{s_0\}$, i.e., $\mathcal{S}_r^T = \{\varphi(s_0, t), \mid s_0 \in \mathcal{S} \land t \in T\}$. Intuitively, once the reachable set $\mathcal{S}_r^T$ is non-overlapping with the unsafe sets $\mathcal{S}_u$, safety is guaranteed for such an NNCS throughout the time horizon T.

POLAR-Express. POLAR-Express [50] is a reachability analysis tool for NNCS based on polynomial arithmetic, developed upon POLAR [23]. It uses Bernstein polynomial interpolation to over-approximate the non-differentiable activation functions to enable layer-by-layer Taylor-Models (TMs) propagation for general feed-forward neural networks. The output over-approximation from the neural network is combined with Flow* [12] for next-step reachable set computation. This process repeats with the previous reachable set result as the input set for the next step and thus rolls out the overall reachable set step by step within the entire time horizon. Moreover, to tighten the over-approximation, POLAR-Express stores the TM intervals symbolically with their linear transformation matrix and only evaluates the remainder interval at the end. This approach is called symbolic remainder, which reduces the accumulation of over-approximation error in TM by avoiding the wrapping effect in linear mappings.

3.2 Task Specification

We control the Turtlebot 3 Burger (Details in Appendix A) in the ROS2 Flatland simulation to execute a left turn via an NN controller in a structured environment bounded by 5-m walls (Fig. 1). The Turtlebot is equipped with LiDAR sensing capabilities, enabling it to localize and detect obstacles within its surroundings. While the NN controller computes the desired speed and steering angle for the left turn, POLAR-Express runs in real-time to verify the controller's safety. To create dynamic

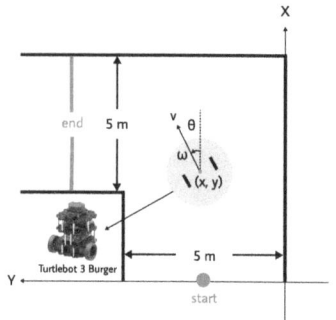

Fig. 1. Turtlebot Task Overview

and uncertain environments, we introduced random obstacles during navigation, which do not exist in the training phase of the NN controller. This scenario ensured that some of the NN control signals would be unsafe, thereby requiring POLAR-Express to capture unsafe maneuvers in real time and demanding a safe control adaptation strategy.

3.3 Runtime Verification (POLAR-Express) Based Safe Control

Figure 2a outlines this case study's safe closed-loop control framework. We use POLAR-Express to compute reachable sets of NN controller κ_{nn} for Turtlebot at runtime. In case of a potential collision, the Turtlebot is switched to a backup obstacle avoidance controller κ_b for safety. We switch back to the NN controller if it is verified to be safe after the obstacle avoidance controller takes over. We introduce the details of each component in the following.

Turtlebot Dynamics and Localization. We model the Turtlebot's dynamics as $\dot{x} = \cos(\theta)v$, $\dot{y} = \sin(\theta)v$, $\dot{\theta} = \omega$ [43]. where θ is the orientation angle around x-axis and (x, y) is the localized position, $s = [x, y, \theta] \in \mathcal{S}$. $a = [v, \omega] \in \mathcal{A}$ is the control input signal, representing linear velocity and angular velocity, generated by the controller. Given a global map of the environment and the laser scan data from the LDS-01, the Turtlebot can localize its position by the Adaptive Monte-Carlo Localization (AMCL) approach implemented in the Nav2 package [6].

NN Controller κ_{nn}. We construct an NN controller $\kappa_{nn} : \mathbb{R}^3 \to \mathbb{R}^2$ with two hidden layers with a size of 64 neurons and ReLU activation functions. The controller takes the localized (x, y, θ) as input and outputs the linear velocity and angular velocity (v, ω) for the Turtlebot, i.e., $a_{nn} = (v, \omega) = \kappa_{nn}(x, y, \theta)$. To train the network, we collected 100 trajectories from expert demonstration data at 20 Hz in a simulation environment using the Nav2 goal package, moving the robot from a desired starting position to an end zone, and thus obtaining a dataset of $\{(x, y, \theta, v, \omega)\}$. We then train the NN controller via supervised learning to reduce an MSE loss as $\|\kappa_{nn}(x, y, \theta) - (v, \omega)\|^2$. It is worth noting that there are no obstacles in the environment during offline training.

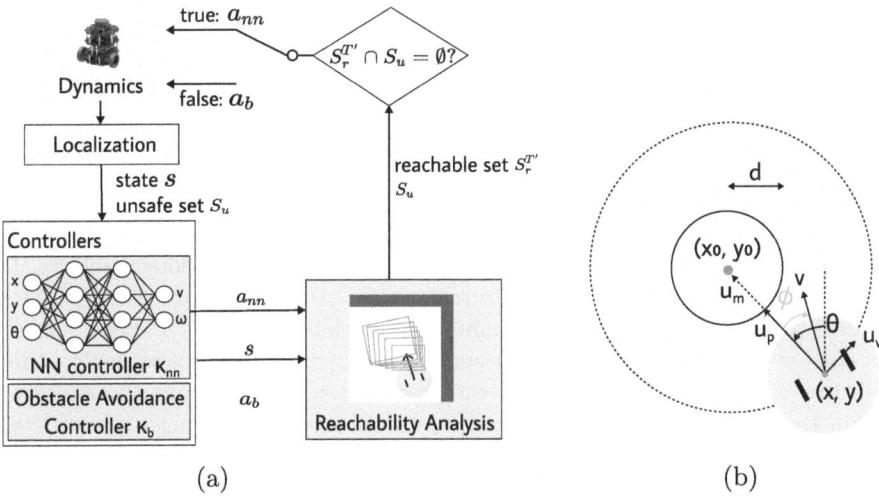

Fig. 2. a. The case study framework. We use POLAR-Express to determine the switch between an NN controller and an obstacle avoidance controller. **b.** The obstacle avoidance controller design moves the Turtlebot counterclockwise while keeping a safe distance.

Obstacle Avoidance Controller κ_b. If the runtime verification result of κ_{nn} is unsafe, we switch to the obstacle avoidance controller κ_b. Given the obstacle position, κ_b move the Turtlebot around the obstacle counterclockwise while keeping a constant distance d by adapting the algorithm in [36], as shown in Fig. 2b. Let (x, y) be the robot's localized position and (x_0, y_0) be the obstacle's center. The distance vector from the robot is $u_m = \begin{bmatrix} x_0 - x \\ y_0 - y \end{bmatrix}$. To maintain a safe distance d, we compute $u_p = u_m - \frac{u_m}{\|u_m\|} * d$, which points toward the obstacle if $\|u_m\| \geq d$, and vice versa. To move in parallel with the obstacle, we rotate u_p by 90°: where R=$\begin{bmatrix} 0, -1 \\ 1, 0 \end{bmatrix}$. Combining both components, the desired motion and angle for safe obstacle avoidance is $u = u_p + u_v$ and $\phi = \arctan(u_x, u_y)$, where u_x and u_y are the projections of u onto x- and y-axes, respectively. Considering Turtlebot's physical limits (0.22 m/s linear and 2.84 rad/s angular), we cap the desired steering velocity v while setting it to $\|u\|$. Similarly, we cap the desired steering angle ω while setting it to the difference between ϕ and current orientation θ. The control input of κ_b becomes

$$a_b = (v, \omega) = (\min(0.22, \|u\|), \min(2.84, \phi - \theta))$$

It is important to note that κ_b is a fallback mechanism to steer the robot to safety when κ_{nn} is deemed unsafe by runtime verification. For the scope of this work, we assume that κ_b is guaranteed to safely navigate the robot around the obstacle to a stable point where κ_{nn} can resume control.

Obstacle Detection as Unsafe Regions $\mathcal{S}_u$. We introduce obstacles of random size and location on the NNCS trajectory for online navigation. Note that the neural network does not have any knowledge of the random obstacle on the map. Rather, these obstacles can be detected and localized by the sensing ability of the Turtlebot at runtime. The location of these obstacles is treated as the unsafe region $\mathcal{S}_u$ for the safety verification of the neural network controlled Turtlebot by POLAR-Express.

Controller Switching Logic. As mentioned, Turtlebot can detect and localize the obstacles' locations as unsafe regions $\mathcal{S}_u$. At runtime, we use POLAR-Express to compute an over-approximation of reachable set for κ_{nn} starting from the current state s within a time horizon T' as $\mathcal{S}_r^{T'}$. If $\mathcal{S}_u$ overlaps with $\mathcal{S}_r^{T'}$, this indicates a potential collision between Turtlebot under κ_{nn} and the obstacle within time horizon T', and therefore we switch to κ_b producing a_b for safety. While operating under κ_b, the robot continues to perform online reachability analysis for κ_{nn}. If $\mathcal{S}_u$ is no longer overlapping with $\mathcal{S}_r^{T'}$, i.e., $S_r^{T'} \cap S_u = \emptyset$, the robot switches back to κ_{nn}, as its control input is verified to be safe. This synergistic approach leverages κ_{nn} for efficient task execution and relies on κ_b and reachability analysis to guarantee safety in complex and cluttered environments; the switching logic can be carried entirely online.

4 Experiments

The simulation was performed on a Dell XPS 15 with an i7 processor, performing reachability analysis every 0.2 s in the callback function of the ROS2 Flatland simulation. POLAR-Express can be customized by adjusting key hyperparameters such as the degree of the Taylor Model (TM), the order of the Bernstein Polynomial approximation (BP), and the number of verification steps (please see [11,50] for more details of these hyper-parameters). By default, we assign the order of TM as 2 and the order of BP as 2 with 10 verification steps. With the default parameters, our framework operates effectively in both single (Fig. 3b) and multiple obstacle avoidance scenarios (Fig. 3c). Our well-trained κ_{nn} driving agent responds to obstacles detected with the reachable set computation by POLAR-Express timely and correctly activating the guarding condition, which then switches to the κ_b controller, also shown in Fig. 4. The κ_{nn} resumes control once the agent steers around the obstacle and the reachable set no longer overlaps with unsafe areas (Fig. 3b, Fig. 4). In the multiple-obstacles scenario, our runtime framework consistently manages several controller switches, ensuring safety throughout the operation (Fig. 3c). To comprehensively evaluate the case study, we then explore different parameter settings for POLAR-Express in different runtime scenarios, which may affect the tightness and computation efficiency of the reachable set.

Verification Time Steps. The verification time step determines the temporal horizon over which POLAR-Express computes the reachable set of the robot's

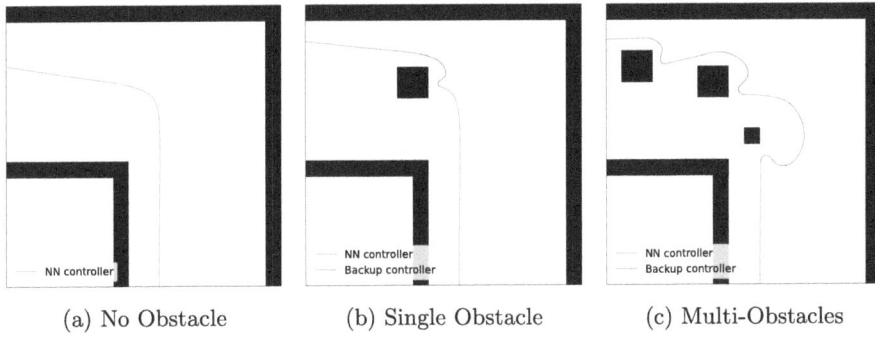

Fig. 3. The navigation trajectory of Turtlebot with our runtime verification based control by κ_{nn} (green) and κ_b (red) for **a)**. No obstacles, **b)**. navigating around a single obstacle, and **c)**. navigating through multiple obstacles. The connection points of green and red are the controller switching points. (Color figure online)

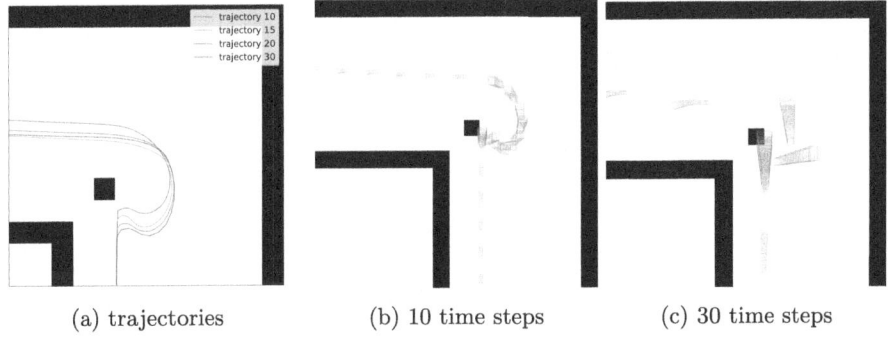

Fig. 4. Trajectories and runtime reachable set visualization by POLAR-Express with varying verification time steps: green boxes and red boxes show runtime reachable sets using the NN and the obstacle avoidance controller, respectively. (Color figure online)

future states. As observed in Fig. 4a, longer verification time steps predict further and react to obstacles further ahead, while shorter steps react closer to obstacles. Although this predictive capability is desirable, increasing the verification time step introduces several drawbacks, as shown below.

Longer verification time steps increase the computational cost and may not satisfy the real-time verification requirement, as evidenced by the runtimes for different time steps in Table 1. Figure 4 demonstrates that we continue using κ_{nn} if its runtime reachable set (green bounding boxes) does not overlap with the obstacle, and switch to κ_b otherwise, indicated by the red runtime reachable set. The visualization shows that controllers with longer verification time steps, such as 30 (Fig. 4c), compute less frequently than those with shorter time steps, like 10 (Fig. 4b). Secondly, longer verification time steps can cause the controller to become more conservative and less task-critical, spending more time on obsta-

Table 1. The verification time step vs. runtime (s)

Verification Steps	10	15	20	30
Runtime (s)	0.18	0.26	0.35	0.53
Task Total Time Usage(s)	77.73	80.05	82.32	89.31
Obstacle Avoidance Controller Time Usage(s)	20.97	22.37	25.19	28.99
Obstacle Avoidance Controller Utilization (%)	26.97	27.94	30.6	32.46

cle avoidance and delaying task completion (Table 1). Lastly, longer verification steps may lead to an excessive accumulation of over-approximation error in the reachable set. This can result in an overly conservative evaluation of κ_{nn}'s safety, causing a premature switch to κ_b and consequent performance degradation.

Overall, trajectory planning systems face a trade-off between computational complexity and safety considerations. Longer verification time steps ensure safer navigation by exploring more potential paths and identifying obstacles earlier, but this comes at the cost of increased computational time and data sparsity, potentially causing delayed verification decisions and reduced task criticality. Conversely, shorter verification time steps may be computationally more efficient but risk overlooking potential obstacles or failing to plan adequately. Striking the right balance between these factors is crucial for performance and safety.

Timing of Runtime Verification with POLAR-Express. In this section, we evaluate the runtime performance of POLAR-Express by conducting experiments with different combinations of Taylor Model (TM) degrees and Bernstein Polynomial (BP) approximation orders, which determines the accuracy of NN approximation and dynamic systems propagation. Intuitively, higher order degrees of the polynomials within POLAR-Express provide more powerful and accurate approximations but come with more computation burden.

The bar graph in Fig. 5 represents the runtime for various TM degrees and BP orders. Each runtime data is collected from the callback function and averaged for 10 trajectories. The POLAR-Express setup is fixed at 10 verification steps. In our evaluation, high TM degrees directly result in longer runtimes. We found that an increase in BP order does not drastically increase the time cost of the verification. Since the simulation is set to run the callback function every 0.2 s, only combinations with an average runtime of less than 0.2 s are considered valid for real-time performance. Based on this criterion, the valid combinations include TM degrees up to 3.

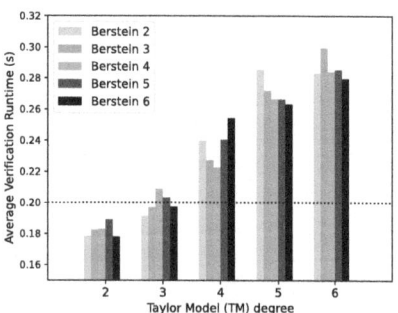

Fig. 5. The 10-step verification runtime of POLAR-Express with different TM and BP orders.

5 Conclusion and Future Work

This paper presents a runtime verification case study where an autonomous Turtlebot, equipped with a neural network (NN) controller, navigates a structured environment using only LiDAR measurements and POLAR-Express for runtime reachability analysis. Our research can expand in several directions: 1) Adapting our framework to accommodate system uncertainties and stochastic policies is a potential area for further development. 2) Incorporating scheduling techniques from the real-time systems for runtime verification could enhance system-level efficiency, where we can opportunistically call the verification engine only when it is necessary. 3) The switching logic of this case study is static and relatively simple, overlooking the fact that the obstacle avoidance controller could enter states that are not recoverable by the NN controllers. This could also be a future direction for improving this work.

A Turtlebot Specification

To emulate real robot operations, we designed a robot testbed using the Flatland simulation environment. This setup replicates the dynamics of the Turtlebot 3 Burger, a differential wheeled robot equipped with two independently driven wheels and a LiDAR sensor [21]. Its maximum translational and angular velocities are 0.22 m/s and 2.84 rad/s, respectively. It has a 360-degree Laser Distance Sensor (LDS-01) capable of scanning the environment at 300 rpm, with a distance range of 120 mm to 3600 mm and a sample rate of 1.8k Hz. Given the Turtlebot's LiDAR scanning distance range, we set up a simulation with 5-meter bounded walls (Fig. 1) to ensure the robot receives appropriate laser scan values for localization.

References

1. Albarghouthi, A., et al.: Introduction to neural network verification. Found. Trends® Program. Lang. **7**(1–2), 1–157 (2021)
2. Althoff, M.: An introduction to CORA 2015. In: Proceedings of the Workshop on Applied Verification for Continuous and Hybrid Systems, pp. 120–151 (2015)
3. Alur, R.: Principles of Cyber-Physical Systems. MIT Press, Cambridge (2015)
4. Alur, R., et al.: The algorithmic analysis of hybrid systems. Theoret. Comput. Sci. **138**(1), 3–34 (1995)
5. Astrom, K.J., Murray, R.M.: Feedback Systems: An Introduction for Scientists and Engineers. Princeton University Press, Princeton (2010)
6. Author(s): Development of an automated benchmark for the analysis of nav2 controllers (unpublished)
7. Bak, S., Johnson, T., Caccamo, M., Sha, L.: Real-time reachability for verified simplex design. ACM Trans. Embed. Comput. Syst. **15**(26), 1–27 (2016)
8. Bauer, A., Leucker, M., Schallhart, C.: Runtime verification for LTL and TLTL. ACM Trans. Softw. Eng. Methodol. (TOSEM) **20**(4), 1–64 (2011)

9. Breivold, H.P., Sandström, K.: Internet of things for industrial automation-challenges and technical solutions. In: 2015 IEEE International Conference on Data Science and Data Intensive Systems, pp. 532–539. IEEE (2015)
10. Cairoli, F., Bortolussi, L., Paoletti, N.: Learning-based approaches to predictive monitoring with conformal statistical guarantees. In: Katsaros, P., Nenzi, L. (eds.) RV 2023. LNCS, vol. 14245, pp. 461–487. Springer, Cham (2023). https://doi.org/10.1007/978-3-031-44267-4_26
11. Chen, X., Ábrahám, E., Sankaranarayanan, S.: Flow*: an analyzer for non-linear hybrid systems. In: Sharygina, N., Veith, H. (eds.) CAV 2013. LNCS, vol. 8044, pp. 258–263. Springer, Heidelberg (2013). https://doi.org/10.1007/978-3-642-39799-8_18
12. Chen, X., Sankaranarayanan, S., Abrahám, E.: Flow* 1.2: more effective to play with hybrid systems. In: Applied Verification for Continuous and Hybrid Systems, pp. 152–159 (2015)
13. Chutinan, A., Krogh, B.H.: Computational techniques for hybrid system verification. IEEE Trans. Autom. Control **48**(1), 64–75 (2003)
14. Deka, L., Khan, S.M., Chowdhury, M., Ayres, N.: Transportation cyber-physical system and its importance for future mobility. In: Transportation Cyber-Physical Systems, pp. 1–20. Elsevier (2018)
15. Desai, A., Dreossi, T., Seshia, S.A.: Combining model checking and runtime verification for safe robotics. In: Lahiri, S., Reger, G. (eds.) RV 2017. LNCS, vol. 10548, pp. 172–189. Springer, Cham (2017). https://doi.org/10.1007/978-3-319-67531-2_11
16. Desai, A., Ghosh, S., Seshia, S.A., Shankar, N., Tiwari, A.: SOTER: a runtime assurance framework for programming safe robotics systems. In: 2019 49th Annual IEEE/IFIP International Conference on Dependable Systems and Networks (DSN), pp. 138–150 (2019). https://doi.org/10.1109/DSN.2019.00027
17. Dutta, S., Chen, X., Jha, S., Sankaranarayanan, S., Tiwari, A.: Sherlock-a tool for verification of neural network feedback systems: demo abstract. In: Proceedings of the 22nd ACM International Conference on Hybrid Systems: Computation and Control, pp. 262–263 (2019)
18. Dutta, S., Chen, X., Sankaranarayanan, S.: Reachability analysis for neural feedback systems using regressive polynomial rule inference. In: Proceedings of the 22nd ACM International Conference on Hybrid Systems: Computation and Control, pp. 157–168 (2019)
19. Fan, J., Huang, C., Chen, X., Li, W., Zhu, Q.: ReachNN*: a tool for reachability analysis of neural-network controlled systems. In: Hung, D.V., Sokolsky, O. (eds.) ATVA 2020. LNCS, vol. 12302, pp. 537–542. Springer, Cham (2020). https://doi.org/10.1007/978-3-030-59152-6_30
20. Fan, J., Huang, C., Li, W., Chen, X., Zhu, Q.: Towards verification-aware knowledge distillation for neural-network controlled systems: Invited paper. In: 2019 IEEE/ACM International Conference on Computer-Aided Design (ICCAD), pp. 1–8 (2019). https://doi.org/10.1109/ICCAD45719.2019.8942059
21. Gross, D.: An implementation approach of the gap navigation tree using the TurtleBot 3 burger and ROS kinetic. Master's thesis, University of Applied Sciences Vorarlberg (2020). https://opus.fhv.at/frontdoor/deliver/index/docId/3888/file/Gross_Daniel_Robot_Navigation_using_ROS.pdf
22. Havelund, K., Peled, D.: An extension of LTL with rules and its application to runtime verification. In: Finkbeiner, B., Mariani, L. (eds.) RV 2019. LNCS, vol. 11757, pp. 239–255. Springer, Cham (2019). https://doi.org/10.1007/978-3-030-32079-9_14

23. Huang, C., Fan, J., Chen, X., Li, W., Zhu, Q.: POLAR: a polynomial arithmetic framework for verifying neural-network controlled systems. In: Bouajjani, A., Holík, L., Wu, Z. (eds.) ATVA 2022. LNCS, vol. 13505, pp. 414–430. Springer, Cham (2022). https://doi.org/10.1007/978-3-031-19992-9_27
24. Huang, C., Fan, J., Li, W., Chen, X., Zhu, Q.: ReachNN: reachability analysis of neural-network controlled systems. ACM Trans. Embed. Comput. Syst. (TECS) **18**(5s), 1–22 (2019)
25. Huang, J., et al.: ROSRV: runtime verification for robots. In: Bonakdarpour, B., Smolka, S.A. (eds.) RV 2014. LNCS, vol. 8734, pp. 247–254. Springer, Cham (2014). https://doi.org/10.1007/978-3-319-11164-3_20
26. Huang, X., Kwiatkowska, M., Wang, S., Wu, M.: Safety verification of deep neural networks. In: Majumdar, R., Kunčak, V. (eds.) CAV 2017. LNCS, vol. 10426, pp. 3–29. Springer, Cham (2017). https://doi.org/10.1007/978-3-319-63387-9_1
27. Ivanov, R., Carpenter, T., Weimer, J., Alur, R., Pappas, G., Lee, I.: Verisig 2.0: verification of neural network controllers using taylor model preconditioning. In: Silva, A., Leino, K.R.M. (eds.) CAV 2021. LNCS, vol. 12759, pp. 249–262. Springer, Cham (2021). https://doi.org/10.1007/978-3-030-81685-8_11
28. Ivanov, R., Carpenter, T.J., Weimer, J., Alur, R., Pappas, G.J., Lee, I.: Case study: verifying the safety of an autonomous racing car with a neural network controller. In: Proceedings of the 23rd International Conference on Hybrid Systems: Computation and Control, pp. 1–7 (2020)
29. Ivanov, R., Weimer, J., Alur, R., Pappas, G.J., Lee, I.: Verisig: verifying safety properties of hybrid systems with neural network controllers. In: Proceedings of the 22nd ACM International Conference on Hybrid Systems: Computation and Control, pp. 169–178 (2019)
30. Jakšić, S., Bartocci, E., Grosu, R., Ničković, D.: An algebraic framework for runtime verification. IEEE Trans. Comput. Aided Des. Integr. Circuits Syst. **37**(11), 2233–2243 (2018)
31. Katz, G., Barrett, C., Dill, D.L., Julian, K., Kochenderfer, M.J.: Reluplex: an efficient SMT solver for verifying deep neural networks. In: Majumdar, R., Kunčak, V. (eds.) CAV 2017. LNCS, vol. 10426, pp. 97–117. Springer, Cham (2017). https://doi.org/10.1007/978-3-319-63387-9_5
32. Katz, G., et al.: The marabou framework for verification and analysis of deep neural networks. In: Dillig, I., Tasiran, S. (eds.) CAV 2019. LNCS, vol. 11561, pp. 443–452. Springer, Cham (2019). https://doi.org/10.1007/978-3-030-25540-4_26
33. Kochdumper, N., Althoff, M.: Constrained polynomial zonotopes. Acta Inform. **60**(3), 279–316 (2023)
34. Lee, E.A., Seshia, S.A.: Introduction to Embedded Systems: A Cyber-Physical Systems Approach. MIT Press, Cambridge (2016)
35. Leucker, M., Schmitz, M., à Tellinghusen, D.: Runtime verification for interconnected medical devices. In: Margaria, T., Steffen, B. (eds.) ISoLA 2016. LNCS, vol. 9953, pp. 380–387. Springer, Cham (2016). https://doi.org/10.1007/978-3-319-47169-3_29
36. Li, J., Sun, J., Chen, G.: A multi-switching tracking control scheme for autonomous mobile robot in unknown obstacle environments. Electronics **9**(1) (2020). https://doi.org/10.3390/electronics9010042, https://www.mdpi.com/2079-9292/9/1/42
37. Lindemann, L., Qin, X., Deshmukh, J.V., Pappas, G.J.: Conformal prediction for STL runtime verification. In: Proceedings of the ACM/IEEE 14th International Conference on Cyber-Physical Systems (with CPS-IoT Week 2023), pp. 142–153 (2023)

38. Liu, E.I., Althoff, M.: Computing specification-compliant reachable sets for motion planning of automated vehicles. In: 2021 IEEE Intelligent Vehicles Symposium (IV), pp. 1037–1044 (2021). https://doi.org/10.1109/IV48863.2021.9575739
39. Liu, X., Huang, C., Wang, Y., Zheng, B., Zhu, Q.: Physics-aware safety-assured design of hierarchical neural network based planner. In: 2022 ACM/IEEE International Conference on Cyber-Physical Systems (ICCPS) (2022)
40. Lopez, D.M., Choi, S.W., Tran, H.D., Johnson, T.T.: NNV 2.0: the neural network verification tool. In: Enea, C., Lal, A. (eds.) CAV 2023. LNCS, vol. 13965, pp. 397–412. Springer, Cham (2023). https://doi.org/10.1007/978-3-031-37703-7_19
41. Qian, Z., Zhong, S., Sun, G., Xing, X., Jin, Y.: A formal approach to design and security verification of operating systems for intelligent transportation systems based on object model. IEEE Trans. Intell. Transp. Syst. (2022)
42. Sastry, S.: Nonlinear Systems: Analysis, Stability, and Control, vol. 10. Springer, Heidelberg (2013)
43. Siwek, M., Panasiuk, J., Baranowski, L., Kaczmarek, W., Prusaczyk, P., Borys, S.: Identification of differential drive robot dynamic model parameters. Materials (Basel) **16**(2), 683 (2023). https://doi.org/10.3390/ma16020683
44. Su, H., Feng, S., Zhan, S., Zhan, N.: Switching controller synthesis for hybrid systems against STL formulas. arXiv preprint arXiv:2406.16588 (2024)
45. Tabuada, P.: Verification and Control of Hybrid Systems: A Symbolic Approach. Springer, Heidelberg (2009). https://doi.org/10.1007/978-1-4419-0224-5
46. Wang, S., et al.: Beta-CROWN: efficient bound propagation with per-neuron split constraints for neural network robustness verification. Adv. Neural. Inf. Process. Syst. **34**, 29909–29921 (2021)
47. Wang, Y., Huang, C., Wang, Z., Wang, Z., Zhu, Q.: Design-while-verify: correct-by-construction control learning with verification in the loop. In: Proceedings of the 59th ACM/IEEE Design Automation Conference, DAC 2022, pp. 925–930. Association for Computing Machinery, New York (2022). https://doi.org/10.1145/3489517.3530556
48. Wang, Y., et al.: Joint differentiable optimization and verification for certified reinforcement learning. In: Proceedings of the ACM/IEEE 14th International Conference on Cyber-Physical Systems (with CPS-IoT Week 2023), pp. 132–141 (2023)
49. Wang, Y., et al.: Enforcing hard constraints with soft barriers: safe reinforcement learning in unknown stochastic environments. In: International Conference on Machine Learning, pp. 36593–36604. PMLR (2023)
50. Wang, Y., et al.: Polar-express: efficient and precise formal reachability analysis of neural-network controlled systems. IEEE Trans. Comput.-Aided Design Integr. Circuits Syst. (2023)
51. Wang, Z., Huang, C., Wang, Y., Hobbs, C., Chakraborty, S., Zhu, Q.: Bounding perception neural network uncertainty for safe control of autonomous systems. In: DATE 2021: Proceedings of the Conference on Design, Automation and Test in Europe (2021)
52. Wang, Z., Huang, C., Zhu, Q.: Efficient global robustness certification of neural networks via interleaving twin-network encoding. In: DATE 2022: Proceedings of the Conference on Design, Automation and Test in Europe (2022)
53. Wei, T., Wang, Y., Zhu, Q.: Deep reinforcement learning for building HVAC control. In: 2017 54th ACM/EDAC/IEEE Design Automation Conference (DAC), pp. 1–6 (2017). https://doi.org/10.1145/3061639.3062224
54. Wollschlaeger, M., Sauter, T., Jasperneite, J.: The future of industrial communication: automation networks in the era of the internet of things and industry 4.0. IEEE Industr. Electron. Mag. **11**(1), 17–27 (2017)

55. Xiong, G., Zhu, F., Liu, X., Dong, X., Huang, W., Chen, S., Zhao, K.: Cyber-physical-social system in intelligent transportation. IEEE/CAA J. Autom. Sinica **2**(3), 320–333 (2015)
56. Xu, S., et al.: Accelerate online reinforcement learning for building HVAC control with heterogeneous expert guidances. In: Proceedings of the 9th ACM International Conference on Systems for Energy-Efficient Buildings, Cities, and Transportation, BuildSys 2022, pp. 89–98. Association for Computing Machinery, New York (2022). https://doi.org/10.1145/3563357.3564064
57. Xu, S., Wang, Y., Wang, Y., O'Neill, Z., Zhu, Q.: One for many: transfer learning for building HVAC control. In: Proceedings of the 7th ACM International Conference on Systems for Energy-Efficient Buildings, Cities, and Transportation, BuildSys 2020, pp. 230–239. Association for Computing Machinery, New York (2020). https://doi.org/10.1145/3408308.3427617
58. Xue, B., Alba, C., Abraham, J., Kannampallil, T., Lu, C.: Prescribing large language models for perioperative care: what's the right dose for pre-trained models? arXiv preprint arXiv:2402.17493 (2024)
59. Xue, B., et al.: Assisting clinical decisions for scarcely available treatment via disentangled latent representation. In: Proceedings of the 29th ACM SIGKDD Conference on Knowledge Discovery and Data Mining, pp. 5360–5371 (2023)
60. Zapridou, E., Bartocci, E., Katsaros, P.: Runtime verification of autonomous driving systems in CARLA. In: Deshmukh, J., Ničković, D. (eds.) RV 2020. LNCS, vol. 12399, pp. 172–183. Springer, Cham (2020). https://doi.org/10.1007/978-3-030-60508-7_9
61. Zhan, S.S., Wang, Y., Wu, Q., Jiao, R., Huang, C., Zhu, Q.: State-wise safe reinforcement learning with pixel observations. In: 6th Annual Learning for Dynamics and Control Conference (2024)
62. Zhang, Z., An, J., Arcaini, P., Hasuo, I.: Online causation monitoring of signal temporal logic. In: Enea, C., Lal, A. (eds.) CAV 2023. LNCS, vol. 13964, pp. 62–84. Springer, Cham (2023). https://doi.org/10.1007/978-3-031-37706-8_4
63. Zhou, K., Doyle, J.C.: Robust and Optimal Control. Prentice Hall (1996)
64. Zhu, Q., et al.: Safety-assured design and adaptation of learning-enabled autonomous systems. In: Proceedings of the 26th Asia and South Pacific Design Automation Conference, ASPDAC 2021, pp. 753–760. Association for Computing Machinery, New York (2021). https://doi.org/10.1145/3394885.3431623
65. Zhu, Q., et al.: Verification and design of robust and safe neural network-enabled autonomous systems. In: 2023 59th Annual Allerton Conference on Communication, Control, and Computing (Allerton), pp. 1–8. IEEE (2023)
66. Zhu, Q., et al.: Know the unknowns: addressing disturbances and uncertainties in autonomous systems. In: Proceedings of the 39th International Conference on Computer-Aided Design, ICCAD 2020. Association for Computing Machinery, New York (2020). https://doi.org/10.1145/3400302.3415768

Gaussian-Based and Outside-the-Box Runtime Monitoring Join Forces

Vahid Hashemi[1], Jan Křetínský[2,3], Sabine Rieder[1,2,3(✉)], Torsten Schön[4], and Jan Vorhoff[1,4]

[1] Audi AG, Ingolstadt, Germany
sabine.rieder@tum.de
[2] Masaryk University, Brno, Czechia
[3] Technical University of Munich, Munich, Germany
[4] AImotion Bavaria, Technische Hochschule Ingolstadt, Ingolstadt, Germany

Abstract. Since neural networks can make wrong predictions even with high confidence, monitoring their behavior at runtime is important, especially in safety-critical domains like autonomous driving. In this paper, we combine ideas from previous monitoring approaches based on observing the activation values of hidden neurons. In particular, we combine the Gaussian-based approach, which observes whether the current value of each monitored neuron is similar to typical values observed during training, and the Outside-the-Box monitor, which creates clusters of the acceptable activation values, and, thus, considers the correlations of the neurons' values. Our experiments evaluate the achieved improvement.

Keywords: Runtime Monitoring · Neural Networks · Out-of-Model-Scope Detection

1 Introduction

Neural Networks (NNs) show impressive results on a variety of computer vision tasks [2,12,20,23]. However, studies demonstrate that even state-of-the-art NNs experience reduced accuracy when processing so-called *Out-Of-Distribution (OOD) data*, which follows a different distribution than the *In-Distribution (ID) data* used during training [15,17,18]. Furthermore, even very well-trained NNs fail to reach perfect accuracy on the testing data, although it is ID. Such unavoidable inaccuracy poses a significant challenge in safety-critical domains

---

The authors would like to thank all partners within the Hi-Drive project for their cooperation and valuable contribution. This project has received funding from the European Union's Horizon 2020 research and innovation program under grant agreement No 101006664 and the MUNI Award in Science and Humanities (MUNI/I/1757/2021) of the Grant Agency of Masaryk University. The sole responsibility of this publication lies with the authors. Neither the European Commission nor CINEA - in its capacity of Granting Authority - can be made responsible for any use that may be made of the information this document contains.

like autonomous driving and highlights the need for runtime monitors that hint at uncertain, and, thus, possibly erroneous, predictions.

Out-Of-Model-Scope (OMS) detection [5] is the task of identifying inputs leading to incorrect predictions. Monitors targeting the OMS setting aim to identify OOD and ID data for which the NN produces incorrect results, but, in contrast to OOD detection, should not notify of correctly processed OOD data. Since the primary objective of runtime monitoring is identifying erroneous outcomes, OMS detection is more adequate in a safety-critical context than OOD detection. Nevertheless, OOD detection may serve as a valuable proxy to attain the ultimate goal of OMS detection.

In this work, we combine ideas of two existing lightweight OOD detection approaches, namely the Gaussian monitor [6] and the Outside-the-Box monitor [8] (short: Box monitor) and evaluate the combination for OMS detection. Both approaches base their OOD decision on the activation values of an inner, typically the penultimate, layer. The Box monitor records the activation values of known data and creates areas of previously seen activation value vectors in the form of unions of hyperrectangles. Inputs producing values inside the box are assumed to be safe. The Gaussian monitor [6] instead models the activation values of a neuron as a Gaussian distribution and computes intervals that contain *likely* values of this distribution. Consequently, it ignores outliers in training and warns against rare values. However, the Gaussian monitor does not use the information of correlations between neurons used in the Box monitor as it, technically, only considers one hyperrectangle. Our combination of the two approaches enriches the Gaussian monitor with information about these correlations among the individual neurons. As the amount of computations increases with the number of monitored neurons, we decrease the number of monitored neurons by using partial gradient descent.

Our basic experiments in the OMS setting show that considering the correlations of neurons improves the detection capabilities of the vanilla Gaussian monitor for the complex CIFAR-10 [10] dataset. In contrast, on the simpler GTSRB [9] dataset, the combination of the Box monitor and the Gaussian monitor achieves similar results as the latter. Interestingly, reducing the number of monitored neurons does not drastically decrease performance for the combined monitor, which altogether allows for more efficient runtime monitoring.

Our contribution can be summarized as follows:

- We extend the monitor presented in [6] to benefit from clustering of activation values from the Box monitor [8].
- As the computation requirements increase with the size of the NN, we investigate monitoring only the most relevant neurons of the NN.
- We evaluate the presented monitoring approaches for OMS detection on the CIFAR-10 and GTSRB datasets.

2 Related Work

As our work focuses on detecting OMS data based on the activation values of hidden layers in the NN, we mention related work following the sane approach. The survey by Yang et al. [22] presents a more comprehensive overview of OOD detection approaches.

Cheng et al. [3] focus on the status (equal to zero or above zero) of ReLU neurons on known safe data and store it as a "pattern". Patterns observed at runtime are accepted if they are close to already stored patterns. Henzinger et al. [8] consider the activation values and build safe areas in the form of hyperrectangles based on the observed values. Lukina et al. [13] extend the approach to incrementally adapt at runtime and create a quantitative measure of how unknown a new sample is. Hashemi et al. [6] model the activation values of a neuron with a Gaussian distribution and build an interval containing common activation values centered around the mean of the distribution. Sun et al. [19] use the distance of an activation value to its k-nearest neighbor in a set of previously recorded activation values as OOD score. Morteza and Li [14] assume that the activation values of ID data follow a multivariate Gaussian distribution and measure the sum of values proportional to each class log-likelihood of the in-distribution data. Lee et al. [11] fit a class-dependent multivariate Gaussian distribution to the observed activation values of a softmax classifier and compute a score based on the Mahalanobis-distance. Corbière et al. [4] suggest using an NN trained on the neuron activation values of the penultimate layer as a monitor. This NN is supposed to predict the probability of the monitored NN making a correct prediction for the input.

3 Preliminaries

3.1 Neural Networks

An NN consists of m layers L_1 to L_m and each layer l contains s_l neurons. Each neuron of layer $l > 1$ first computes its pre-activation value $\mathbf{z}$ as weighted sum of activation values from neurons of the precious layer. The neuron's activation value $\mathbf{a}$ is obtained by applying an activation function $f_l : \mathbb{R} \to \mathbb{R}$ to the pre-activation value. With a slight abuse of notation, we write $f_l(\mathbf{z})$ when we refer to component-wise application of f_l on $\mathbf{z}$. We formalize the computations for a layer l with weight matrix $W_l \in \mathbb{R}^{s_{l-1} \times s_l}$, bias $\mathbf{b_l}$ and input $\mathbf{x} \in D \subseteq \mathbb{R}^n$ as:

$$\mathbf{a}_0 = \mathbf{x} \qquad \mathbf{z}_l = W_l^T \mathbf{a}_{l-1} + \mathbf{b_l} \qquad \mathbf{a}_l = f_l(\mathbf{z}_l)$$

The last layer provides the classification result, meaning the mapping of datapoint $\mathbf{x}$ to a set of r different labels $Y = \{y_1, \ldots, y_r\}$.

3.2 Monitors

Gaussian Monitor [6]. The approach consists of three steps: Training of the monitor, threshold setting and runtime evaluation. In the training process, for each neuron and class, a Gaussian distribution is fitted to the neuron's activation values observed for several ID inputs. We then compute an interval for each neuron containing approximately 95% of recorded activation values based on the empirical rule [21]. Due to the use of the empirical rule, it is barely ever the case that all neurons produce values contained in their respective intervals. This is rectified by setting a threshold on the number of neurons that need to produce such values. A higher threshold will lead to the monitor classifying more images as OOD and vice versa. We consider a set of known safe images not used for training the monitor for setting this threshold. Lastly, when the NN receives a new sample as input, the neurons' activation values and the predicted class are observed. Each neuron votes if its value lies inside the bounds for the predicted class, and the outcome of the vote is compared to the threshold.

Box Monitor [8]. Henzinger et al. suggest using multidimensional boxes for monitoring, one set of boxes for each class. The boxes are computed based on activation values observed on ID inputs. These values are clustered with the K-Means algorithm and each cluster results in one box. As there exists a trade-off between the number of correctly identified OOD points and wrongly identified ID data, it is possible to modify the coarseness of the boxes by enlarging them by a factor of γ. During runtime, the authors expect ID data to produce activation vectors contained in the boxes and OOD data to produce values outside of it.

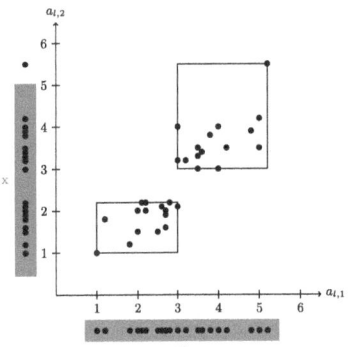
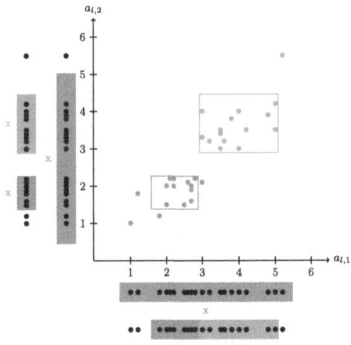

(a) Comparison of the Gaussian monitor and the Box monitor. The figure is based on [6].

(b) Comparison of Gaussian monitor and the clustered Gaussian monitor. The colors denote the assigned point cluster.

Fig. 1. Comparison of different monitors. The axes represent the neurons and their activation values, and the points are the vectors of activation values observed for a particular input. Boxes depict safe areas of the Box and the combined monitor. The points below each axis show the activation values mapped to the specific axis with x highlighting the mean. The boxes below the axes depict the activation values the Gaussian monitor accepts. (Color figure online)

Difference Between Gaussian and Box Monitor. Figure 1a depicts the differences between the two described monitors. While the Box Monitor considers the relationship between neurons, the Gaussian monitor models the behavior of each single neuron more precisely and is less affected by outliers.

3.3 Neuron Selection via Gradient Analysis

Due to the additional complexity each new neuron brings to monitoring, Cheng et al. [3] propose, among other things, only observing the most relevant neurons in the monitored layer L_l. They identify these neurons through the absolute value of the partial gradient $|\frac{\partial a_{m,j}}{\partial a_{l,t}}|$ for activation value $a_{m,j}$ of neuron $N_{m,j}$ in the output layer L_m, and the activation $a_{l,t}$ of a neuron $N_{l,t} \in L_l$. The partial derivatives depend on the activation function's derivatives and vary for each input. A special case is monitoring last hidden layer without any non-linear computation. In this particular case, as pointed out by Cheng et al. [3], the partial derivatives are the weights between the two layers. The paper is unclear on handling the case with different partial derivatives for various inputs.

4 Methodology

4.1 Combining Gaussian Monitor and Box Monitor

We combine the Box monitor and the Gaussian monitor to obtain a monitor robust to outliers (like the Gaussian monitor) and aware of neuron correlations (like the Box monitor). The monitor is trained based on an observation of k activation vectors for each class c. These k activation vectors are obtained from correctly classified ID data and are clustered using K-Means similar to the creation of the Box monitor. Overall, we obtain several clusters per class. The Gaussian Monitor is called on each cluster separately and computes a Gaussian distribution for each neuron and its activation values belonging to the clusters. Based on the distribution, intervals containing 95% of the data are computed as before and boxes are build based on these intervals. Figure 1b shows the boxes for different clusters (depicted by different colors). For an input to be accepted, its activation value needs to be contained in one of the boxes. While the Gaussian monitor from Fig. 1a would have accepted an activation value of $(2,4)$, the new monitor will mark it correctly as previously unseen. Furthermore, the combined monitor is more sensitive to cluster outliers than the Box monitor. The sensitivity can be fine tuned by setting a threshold on how many neurons need to produce values contained inside the intervals of a specific cluster. Due to the new structure of the monitor, we use a procedure similar to Henzinger et al. [8] for detecting outliers at runtime. When a new input is observed, we compute the Euclidean distance of its activation value vector to the centroids of each cluster and compare to the closest ones. For each cluster, each neuron still votes on whether its activation is in the interval and thus valid and an alarm will be triggered if the number is lower than the threshold.

One can also use a multivariate Gaussian distribution for each cluster and compute the Mahalanobis distance similar to the suggestion by Lee et al. [11].

4.2 Neuron Selection for Monitoring

To improve the runtime performance of our proposed monitors, we adhere to the suggestion made by Cheng et al. [3] to only observe the neurons with the most significant impact on the expected class score determined by partial gradient analysis. We compute a score $abs\_score_{j,t}^l$ for a particular class y_j and a neuron $N_{l,t}$ of layer l based on the partial derivative of several known safe inputs. We define $S_j \subset D$ as a set of known safe inputs of class j. To calculate the $abs\_score_{j,t}^l$ for the $N_{l,t}$, we sum up the absolute value of the partial gradient $\frac{\partial a_{m,j}(x_i)}{\partial a_{l,t}(x_i)}$ for each input vector $\mathbf{x}_i \in S_j$, where $a_{m,j}(x_i)$ represents the activation value of neuron $N_{m,j}$ when the NN is applied to x_i:

$$abs\_score_{j,t}^l = \sum_{i=1}^{|S_j|} \left| \frac{\partial a_{m,j}(x_i)}{\partial a_{l,t}(x_i)} \right|.$$

While we can apply this technique of selection relevant neurons to the NN we want to monitor, there is also the possibility to use a *monitoring NN* [4]. In this case, we first train an NN on the (pre-)activation values of the original NN for each class to detect potentially misclassified images. Given the set of safe activation values A_j^l for class j and layer l and the set of activation $\bar{A}_j^l$ for images of the training data that do not lead to the class prediction, an NN, defined as NET_j^l, is created to output a score between 0 and 1 that encodes the confidence the monitoring NN has that the prediction made by the monitored NN is correct. Basing our neuron selection on the partial gradient of such a monitoring NN uses the fact that this NN has obtained a deeper understanding of the original NN.

5 Evaluation

In our experiments, we evaluate (RQ1) the influence of neuron selection, (RQ2) the combination of the multivariate Gaussian monitor with clustering and (RQ3) the overall performance of our suggested combination of methods.

5.1 Experimental Setup and Implementation

Datasets. For our experiments, we use two datasets, GTSRB [9], a dataset consisting of German traffic signs, and CIFAR-10 [10], which contains objects from different classes like plane, car, or bird. We evaluate our proposed monitors with the Monitizer framework [1], which allows us to implement a monitor and evaluate it on various types of OOD data. As we are interested in OMS detection, we generalize this framework by excluding OOD images from evaluation if the monitored NN still made a correct prediction and adding a new category of misclassified ID images. The OMS data classes contain images from an entirely new dataset, different noises and perturbations like light and contrast changes applied to known data, and objects not contained in the training data, but placed in a similar environment as the one known to the NN. The technical report [7] contains a visualization of the datasets and OMS data.

Network Architectures. For CIFAR-10 images, we use an NN consisting of 6 convolutional layers with ReLU activation function and max-pooling operation followed by 4 linear layers with ReLU activation function [16]. The NN for GTSRB consists of 2 convolutional layers with ReLU activation and max-pooling operation followed by 3 linear layers with ReLU activation function. Both architectures are illustrated in the technical report [7].

Preparation of Monitors. For training the monitors, meaning generating the intervals and boxes, and threshold setting, we use the pre-activations of the NN for correctly classified input images, following the suggestion of previous works [3,8]. We focus on pre-activation values as we have obtained better results on them compared to the activation values. The images for threshold setting have not been used for clustering and computing intervals. We adjust our monitors' thresholds to receive no alarm on 90% of the correctly classified ID dataset.

Quality Measure and Plots. The plots show the True Positive Rate (TPR) (sometimes also called *recall*) of our experiments, meaning the number of correct alarms divided by the number of OMS images for each of our OMS datasets. This is the most relevant metric as our datasets only consist of OMS examples. The monitors' performance on data within the model-scope is fixed by the threshold.

5.2 Results

RQ1: Neuron Selection. Table 1 displays the TPR for the clustered Gaussian monitor when monitoring the pre-activation values of all neurons in the last hidden layer versus monitoring only 75%, 50% or 25% of the neurons for CIFAR-10. The results indicate that monitoring less neurons tends to decrease the TPR. However, when comparing the selection of 100% with the selection of only 25%, the decrease is mostly not significant, while reducing the number of monitored neurons by 75% drastically reduces computation efforts. Table 1 also displays the TPR when selecting 75% of the neurons for monitoring based on partial gradient descent of the monitoring NN. Our monitoring NN consists of 3 linear layers with ReLU activation function followed by one layer with Sigmoid activation function. It shows that the results obtained when using the gradients computed on the monitoring NN perform slightly better in some settings than the ones for the original NN but are mostly similar.

RQ2: Clustering the Multivariate Gaussian [11]. Table 2 displays the TPR of the monitor when using a different number of clusters for the pre-activation values or the last hidden layer of the CIFAR-10 NN. Using clusters or increasing their number reduces performance on all test settings.

RQ3: Overall Results. Table 3 shows the TPR for the different monitors using the best configurations for the CIFAR-10 and the GTSRB dataset. We compare

Table 1. Comparison of the TPR for the clustered Gaussian monitor with 3 Clusters when only using the $x\%$ most relevant neurons (partial gradient descent on the original or the monitoring NN) for the pre-activation values of the last hidden layer of the CIFAR-10 NN.

Monitors	Wrong ID	GTSRB	DTD	Gaussian	SaltAnd Pepper	Contrast	Gaussian Blur	Invert	Rotate	Light	Cifar100
Original NN											
100%	21.71	39.00	15.00	19.49	26.20	32.42	17.02	21.76	20.74	24.58	20.00
75%	17.74	44.00	13.00	13.62	12.44	28.82	9.21	14.14	13.32	22.05	17.00
50%	20.05	41.00	21.00	16.43	17.35	31.32	11.25	16.86	17.11	24.36	18.00
25%	19.59	36.00	21.00	18.34	22.89	29.58	12.05	18.73	20.27	21.99	12.00
Monitoring NN											
75%	17.67	39.00	17.00	14.75	18.51	28.42	12.62	15.81	15.07	20.77	14.00

Table 2. TPR of the multivariate Gaussian monitor applied to the pre-activation values of the last hidden layer (CIFAR-10) with different numbers of clusters.

Monitors	Wrong ID	GTSRB	DTD	Gaussian	SaltAnd Pepper	Contrast	Gaussian Blur	Invert	Rotate	Light	Cifar100
No Clusters	24.21	57.00	12.00	18.93	15.64	42.48	12.47	21.99	20.57	34.47	25.00
2 Clusters	20.05	51.00	10.00	15.84	13.03	37.54	9.62	17.96	17.21	29.93	24.00
3 Clusters	16.20	43.00	8.00	12.90	10.63	33.48	7.34	15.03	14.29	25.19	21.00

Table 3. Comparison of the different monitors on the CIFAR-10 (top table) and the GTSRB dataset (lower table). In the first 3 rows, we consider the pre-activation values of the last hidden layer. The last row considers the activation value of the second-to-last hidden layer without clustering (similar to [6]).

Monitors	Wrong ID	GTSRB	DTD	Gaussian	SaltAnd Pepper	Contrast	Gaussian Blur	Invert	Rotate	Light	Cifar100
Univariate Gaussian, 3 Clusters	21.71	39.00	15.00	19.49	26.20	32.42	17.02	21.76	20.74	24.58	20.00
Univariate Gaussian, No Clusters	5.20	19.00	4.00	3.37	1.56	11.99	2.53	3.99	3.18	9.13	3.00
Univariate Gaussian, [6]	10.82	19.00	4.00	7.75	5.58	19.95	4.97	8.13	6.94	15.76	8.00

Monitors	Wrong ID	CIFAR10	DTD	Gaussian	SaltAnd Pepper	Contrast	Gaussian Blur	Rotate	Invert	Light	CTS
Univariate Gaussian, 3 Clusters	49.93	75.00	76.56	44.45	80.42	97.26	38.68	48.28	87.06	65.47	62.83
Univariate Gaussian, No Clusters	21.65	53.91	64.84	27.90	46.12	87.87	20.82	26.42	74.62	46.28	36.44
Univariate Gaussian, [6]	41.13	70.31	73.44	42.07	80.20	97.26	28.72	46.50	75.02	50.69	49.14

our monitors to the Gaussian monitor as Hashemi et al. [6] already demonstrated that it performs at least as well as the Box monitor. Our proposed runtime monitors demonstrate better results than the Gaussian monitor in all our test settings by at least 10% on the CIFAR-10 dataset. Also on the GTSRB dataset, the clustered Gaussian monitor performs at least as well as the Gaussian monitor [6], but the improvement is not as noticeable anymore. All monitors attain notably higher TPRs when assessed on the GTSRB dataset than on the CIFAR-10 dataset.

5.3 Discussion

Combining the research findings of Hashemi et al. [6] and Henzinger et al. [8] has demonstrated that pre-clustering the NN's activations before constructing the Gaussian monitor is superior to a Gaussian monitor without clusters. This is particularly evident when using slightly more complex datasets, such as CIFAR-10. On the less complex GTSRB dataset the new monitor achieves at least similar results to the baseline method making our approach applicable to simpler datasets and beneficial for more complex datasets. Clustering activation values for the multivariate Gaussian monitor [11] did not improve performance.

By selecting and monitoring only the most relevant neurons, identified through partial gradient descent on several inputs, the monitor's performance is not drastically decreased. This enables more efficient monitoring of activation values.

6 Conclusion and Future Work

In this work, we applied the Gaussian monitor [6] for OOD detection for NNs to the setting of OMS detection and extended it. Our new monitors consider the correlations of neurons by pre-clustering the activation values similar to [8]. We found that clustering the activation values before applying the Gaussian monitor outperforms the approach without clustering. We also saw that the number of monitored neurons can be reduced while maintaining comparable detection capabilities. This reduces the amount of computation required in each monitoring step, which is essential for executing the monitors fast. In future work, we want to evaluate on more datasets and investigate the possibility of combining monitoring of several layers.

References

1. Azeem, M., Grobelna, M., Kanav, S., Kretinsky, J., Mohr, S., Rieder, S.: Monitizer: automating design and evaluation of neural network monitors. arXiv preprint arXiv:2405.10350 (2024). https://doi.org/10.48550/arXiv.2405.10350
2. Chen, L.C., Papandreou, G., Kokkinos, I., Murphy, K., Yuille, A.L.: DeepLab: semantic image segmentation with deep convolutional nets, atrous convolution, and fully connected CRFS. IEEE Trans. Pattern Anal. Mach. Intell. **40**(4), 834–848 (2018). https://doi.org/10.1109/TPAMI.2017.2699184
3. Cheng, C.H., Nührenberg, G., Yasuoka, H.: Runtime monitoring neuron activation patterns. In: 2019 Design, Automation & Test in Europe Conference & Exhibition (DATE), pp. 300–303 (2019). https://doi.org/10.23919/DATE.2019.8714971
4. Corbière, C., Thome, N., Bar-Hen, A., Cord, M., Pérez, P.: Addressing failure prediction by learning model confidence. In: Proceedings of the 33rd International Conference on Neural Information Processing Systems, pp. 2902–2913 (2019). https://dl.acm.org/doi/10.5555/3454287.3454548

5. Guérin, J., Delmas, K., Ferreira, R., Guiochet, J.: Out-of-distribution detection is not all you need. In: Proceedings of the Thirty-Seventh AAAI Conference on Artificial Intelligence and Thirty-Fifth Conference on Innovative Applications of Artificial Intelligence and Thirteenth Symposium on Educational Advances in Artificial Intelligence. AAAI 2023/IAAI 2023/EAAI 2023. AAAI Press (2023). https://doi.org/10.1609/aaai.v37i12.26732
6. Hashemi, V., Křetínský, J., Mohr, S., Seferis, E.: Gaussian-based runtime detection of out-of-distribution inputs for neural networks. In: Feng, L., Fisman, D. (eds.) RV 2021. LNCS, vol. 12974, pp. 254–264. Springer, Cham (2021). https://doi.org/10.1007/978-3-030-88494-9_14
7. Hashemi, V., Křetínský, J., Rieder, S., Schön, T., Vorhoff, J.: Gaussian-based and outside-the-box runtime monitoring join forces. arXiv preprint (2024)
8. Henzinger, T.A., Lukina, A., Schilling, C.: Outside the box: abstraction-based monitoring of neural networks. In: De Giacomo, G., Catala, A., Dilkina, B. (eds.) ECAI 2020 : 24th European Conference on Artificial Intelligence. Frontiers in Artificial Intelligence and Applications, vol. 325, pp. 2433–2440. IOS Press, Amsterdam (2020). https://doi.org/10.3233/FAIA200375
9. Houben, S., Stallkamp, J., Salmen, J., Schlipsing, M., Igel, C.: Detection of traffic signs in real-world images: the German traffic sign detection benchmark. In: International Joint Conference on Neural Networks, no. 1288 (2013)
10. Krizhevsky, A.: Learning multiple layers of features from tiny images. University of Toronto, Toronto, Canada, Technical report (2009)
11. Lee, K., Lee, K., Lee, H., Shin, J.: A simple unified framework for detecting out-of-distribution samples and adversarial attacks. In: Advances in Neural Information Processing Systems, vol. 31 (2018)
12. Liu, L., et al.: Deep learning for generic object detection: a survey. Int. J. Comput. Vis. **128**(2), 261–318 (2020). https://doi.org/10.1007/s11263-019-01247-4
13. Lukina, A., Schilling, C., Henzinger, T.A.: Into the unknown: active monitoring of neural networks. In: Feng, L., Fisman, D. (eds.) RV 2021. LNCS, vol. 12974, pp. 42–61. Springer, Cham (2021). https://doi.org/10.1007/978-3-030-88494-9_3
14. Morteza, P., Li, Y.: Provable guarantees for understanding out-of-distribution detection. In: Proceedings of the AAAI Conference on Artificial Intelligence, vol. 36, pp. 7831–7840 (2022)
15. Ovadia, Y., et al.: Can you trust your model's uncertainty? Evaluating predictive uncertainty under dataset shift. In: Proceedings of the 33rd International Conference on Neural Information Processing Systems, pp. 14003–14014 (2019). https://dl.acm.org/doi/abs/10.5555/3454287.3455541
16. Ramesh, V.: CIFAR-10 PyTorch implementation (2021). https://github.com/iVishalr/cifar10-pytorch. Accessed 04 Dec 2023
17. Shafaei, A., Schmidt, M.W., Little, J.: A less biased evaluation of out-of-distribution sample detectors. In: British Machine Vision Conference (2019). https://doi.org/10.48550/arXiv.1809.04729
18. Shankar, V., Dave, A., Roelofs, R., Ramanan, D., Recht, B., Schmidt, L.: Do image classifiers generalize across time? In: 2021 IEEE/CVF International Conference on Computer Vision (ICCV), pp. 9641–9649 (2021). https://doi.org/10.1109/ICCV48922.2021.00952
19. Sun, Y., Ming, Y., Zhu, X., Li, Y.: Out-of-distribution detection with deep nearest neighbors. In: International Conference on Machine Learning, pp. 20827–20840. PMLR (2022)
20. Tan, M., Le, Q.V.: EfficientNet: rethinking model scaling for convolutional neural networks. ArXiv (2019). https://doi.org/10.48550/arXiv.1905.11946

21. Wackerly, D., Mendenhall, W., Scheaffer, R.L.: Mathematical Statistics with Applications. Cengage Learning (2014). ISBN 9781111798789
22. Yang, J., Zhou, K., Li, Y., Liu, Z.: Generalized out-of-distribution detection: a survey. arXiv preprint arXiv:2110.11334 (2021)
23. Zhao, C., Sun, Q., Zhang, C., Tang, Y., Qian, F.: Monocular depth estimation based on deep learning: an overview. Sci. China Technol. Sci. **63**(9), 1612–1627 (2020). https://doi.org/10.1007/s11431-020-1582-8

Box-Based Monitor Approach for Out-of-Distribution Detection in YOLO: An Exploratory Study

Weicheng He, Changshun Wu[(✉)][iD], and Saddek Bensalem[iD]

University Grenoble Alpes, VERIMAG, Grenoble, France
{weicheng.he,changshun.wu,saddek.bensalem}@univ-grenoble-alpes.fr

Abstract. Deep neural networks (DNNs), despite their impressive performance in various tasks, often produce overconfident predictions on out-of-distribution (OoD) data, which can lead to severe consequences, especially in safety-critical applications. Monitoring OoD samples for DNNs at runtime is thus essential. Although this problem has been extensively studied in image classification and recently in object detection with the Faster R-CNN architecture, the state-of-the-art series of You Only Look Once (YOLO) remains underexplored. This short paper presents an initial exploration into OoD detection for YOLO models, proposing a box-based monitor approach. The core idea is to use a data structure with a geometric shape of boxes to enclose regions in the logit space where the neural network makes decisions on in-distribution (ID) data. This structure serves as a reference to monitor the behavior of the network during deployment. Our preliminary results demonstrate that this box-based monitor outperforms several existing logits-based scoring methods, achieving a significant 20% reduction in false positive rates for OoD samples while maintaining a high true positive rate for ID samples. We hope that our work will spark meaningful discussion and inspire future research efforts, highlighting both the potential and the challenges of integrating OoD detection with the YOLO architecture for effective runtime monitoring.

Keywords: Out-of-distribution detection · Object detection neural networks · YOLO

1 Introduction

Due to the inherent complexity of programming-specific application functionalities and the necessity for models to perform well on existing and new data, deep neural networks (DNNs) are crucial in many applications. However, they face safety challenges, such as robustness problem [24] (imperceptible perturbations can deceive network decision making) and out-of-distribution (OoD) problems [12] (networks tend to generalize to inputs that do not belong to the training classes). Despite various verification techniques, ensuring their safety remains incomplete [9,15,18,23,30]. Systems must be observed during operation, for example, using online monitoring techniques [4,6,7,13,20]. DNN monitoring can be divided into two main types: control task-oriented and visual perception-oriented. Control task-oriented monitoring deals with tasks where data-driven control systems operate under formal specifications, making it relatively straightforward to define and verify expected behaviors. In contrast, visual perception-oriented monitoring addresses the complex nature of data-driven visual perception systems, where intricate and often opaque characterizations make it challenging to formally verify and validate the behavior of the system using mathematics and logic. Our work falls into the latter category, concentrating on monitoring DNN-implemented object detection components. Specifically, we aim to discard the network's predictions when presented with OoD samples.

The OoD detection problem has received extensive attention in tasks like image and natural language processing classification [1–3,11,12,14,16,19]. However, this problem has only recently been addressed in object detection, a more prevalent application in real-world scenarios. Yet, the object detection models considered have typically been Faster R-CNN [22], which, while effective, may not match the accuracy and speed of the YOLO series model. YOLO series is regarded as the state-of-the-art (SOTA) implementation of object detection DNNs and is widely acclaimed for real-time applications [8,25,26]. In this exploratory study, we begin by highlighting the persistence of the OoD problem in YOLO despite its SOTA performance in object detection. Given the complexity of YOLO's structure and the difficulty in identifying specific learned features for each prediction, we propose focusing on the logits (output) space within the detection head for OoD detection. Specifically, we extend the *box abstraction-based monitor*, a technique effective in image classification tasks [13,28,29]. The core idea of this monitor is to enclose regions in the logit space where the neural network makes decisions using a data structure of geometric shape of boxes. When the DNN makes predictions, the monitor evaluates whether the corresponding logit falls within these enclosed regions. If they do, the decision is considered ID; otherwise, it's classified as OoD. Our experimental results demonstrate that our boxed monitor approach significantly reduces the number of erroneous detections compared to existing methods based on the logit space. This underscores the effectiveness of our method in addressing the inherent OoD problem in YOLO.

This paper is structured as follows. Section 2 defines the OoD detection problem. Section 3 details the proposed Boxed Monitor for the YOLO model. In Sect. 4, we conduct experiments to validate our monitor across various OoD datasets. Section 5 covers related and future works. The final section concludes the paper.

2 Problem Statement

Given a Deep Neural Network (DNN) implemented system, it is essential to define and OoD samples. A DNN classifier or object detector selects the class with the highest probability as the result. OoD samples are those whose true class does not belong to the training set Y_{train}. This represents a semantic shift from a distributional perspective, implying the input falls outside the model's generalization capabilities. In traditional system design terms, OoD samples are analogous to illegal inputs (e.g., a string input in a numerical processing program). Due to the inherent nature of DNNs making overconfident predictions on OoD samples, it is crucial to have a detector (or monitor) to oversee the decision-making process.

An OoD detector can be considered as a classifier $g : X \to \{0,1\}$, where 0 indicates ID and 1 indicates OoD. One common method involves designing a scoring function $S : X \to \mathbb{R}$, such as [10,19]. For a given sample $\mathbf{x}$, compute the score $S(\mathbf{x})$ and establish a threshold τ such that:

$$g(\mathbf{x}) = \begin{cases} 0 & \text{if } S(\mathbf{x}) \geq \tau \\ 1 & \text{if } S(\mathbf{x}) < \tau \end{cases}$$

Another approach involves feature space abstraction, which is employed to represent an infinite state space using a more computationally efficient data structure. This allows for a simplified yet effective representation of the feature space, making it feasible to manage and analyze without the need to exhaustively explore every possible state. It usually first observes historical data $\{\mathbf{x}_i\}_{i=1}^n$ and their feature representations $F = \{f(\mathbf{x}_i)\}_{i=1}^n$ (the outputs from a layer close to the DNN's output layer), and then defines equivalence classes in F such that neighboring features belong to the same distribution. One classical method is to use a finite set of geometric shapes, e.g., n-dimentional box [7,13,28,29], to abstract each equivalence class. Subsequently, an ID is approximated by a finite set of geometric shapes in the corresponding feature space. In this case, a sample $\mathbf{x}$ is considered in-distribution (ID) if its feature representation $f(\mathbf{x})$ falls within the abstracted feature space of ID data; otherwise, it is considered OoD.

3 Approach

3.1 Basic Notions

YOLO. This work focuses on the YOLO (You Only Look Once) model, a prominent object detection framework composed of three main components: the backbone, the neck, and the detection head, as shown in Fig. 1. The YOLO model's workflow begins with the input image being fed into the backbone, where multi-level features are extracted. These feature maps are then processed through the neck, which aggregates and refines the features before passing them to the detection head. The detection head performs further computations and post-processing to produce the final output: a list of detected objects with their corresponding bounding boxes, class labels, and confidence scores. YOLO's single-stage, end-to-end design offers significant computational efficiency over multi-stage detectors like Faster R-CNN. However, this design also brings complexity, particularly in the feature extraction process, which makes it challenging to

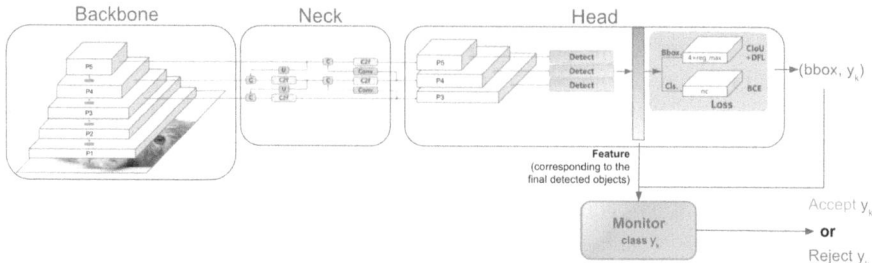

Fig. 1. YOLOv8 architecture and the integration of Boxed Monitor. For monitor construction, features are extracted from the output of YOLOv8 Detection Head.

isolate object-specific features critical for OoD detection methods. Given these challenges, we propose focusing on the logits space within the detection head for OoD detection. The logits space offers a more suitable choice due to its lower dimensionality and its ability to provide a high-level, discriminative representation of the input data. Our investigation takes an exploratory approach, initially concentrating on the logits space to lay the groundwork for future exploration of other feature spaces. This approach will enable subsequent work to extend or propose new OoD detection methods within the YOLO model.

Tight Box Abstraction for a Dataset [5,13,28]. In n-dimensional geometric space, a box is a continuous set, often used to abstract some point sets. It consists of n intervals, each corresponding to the upper and lower bounds that each dimension can take. For a dataset $X = \{\mathbf{x}^1, \ldots, \mathbf{x}^m\}$, we define its *tight box abstraction* as $B(X) \stackrel{\text{def}}{=} \{(x_1, \ldots, x_n) \in \mathbb{R}^n \mid a_i \leq x_i \leq b_i, i \in [1 \cdots n]\}$ where $a_i = \min(\{\mathbf{x}_i^j\})$ and $b_i = \max(\{\mathbf{x}_i^j\})$ for $i \in [1 \cdots n]$ and $j \in [1 \cdots m]$. For simplicity, we encode a box abstraction as a list of intervals as follows: $[[a_1, b_1], \ldots, [a_n, b_n]]$.

3.2 Monitor Construction

Box-Based Monitor Construction for YOLO. Considering an object detector with fixed parameters, we represent its training dataset as $D_{train} = \{(\mathbf{x}^i, gt_j^i = (bbox_j^i, label_j^i)), i \in [1, \ldots, m], j \in [1, \ldots, o_i]\}$ where there are m images and $\sum_{i=1}^{m} o_i$ labeled objects. Each image $\mathbf{x}^i$ in the dataset contains ground truth information gt^i regarding the bounding box coordinates $bbox_j^i$ and the label $label_j^i$ for each object instance. During the inference phase, the YOLO object detector f produces detection instances $p = f(\mathbf{x}) = \{p_j = (bbox_j^*, label_j^*, conf_j), j \in [1, \ldots, o^*]\}$ for an image $\mathbf{x}$, with $conf_j$ indicating the confidence score for the classification of a detection instance. Based on the definitions above, a boxed-abstraction-based monitor $\mathcal{B}_y = \{B^1, \ldots, B^{k_y}\}$ is constructed for each output class y of the YOLOv8 model following four main steps:

- Step 1: Feature extraction. For each semantic label $y \in \mathcal{Y}$, z_y denotes a logits vector corresponding to a prediction instance p_j with label y, where $conf_j > \gamma$, with γ being the confidence threshold for predictions that maximizes the YOLO model's micro F1 score. The logits vector z_y is extracted from the output of the Detect head of the YOLOv8 model. F_y represents a tensor that concatenates all logits vectors z_y corresponding to label y extracted from the training set.
- Step 2: Partition of features. The features within F_y are partitioned into a set of k_y subsets, denoted as $\pi(F_y) = \{F_y^1, \ldots, F_y^{k_y}\}$.
- Step 3: Abstraction building. $\mathcal{B}_y = \{B^1, \ldots, B^{k_y}\}$, where B^j is a tight box abstraction for subset F_y^j for $j \in [1 \cdots k_y]$.
- Step 4: Box enlargement. We enlarge boxes of the monitor to address cases where ID True Positive Rate (TPR) falls below the threshold of 95%. This refinement begins by sorting detection instances p in ascending order by the minimum distance of their logits vectors z_y to any box in the monitor $\mathcal{B}_y$ using Eq. (1).

$$\mathsf{dist}(z_y, \mathcal{B}_y) \stackrel{\text{def}}{:=} \min_{j \in [1 \cdots k_y]} \{d(z_y, B_y^j)\} \quad (1)$$

Boxes are then enlarged to encompass sorted object instances until an ID TPR of 95% is achieved.

3.3 Monitor Deployment

During the inference phase, the **monitor will reject a prediction** $p_i = (bbox_i^*, label_i^*, conf_i)$ **corresponding to an input x** if $\nexists j \in [1 \cdots k_y]$ such that the logits vector **z**, which corresponds the prediction p_i in the logit space, lies within B_j. The containment verification $\mathbf{z} \in B_j$, which compares **z** against the lower and upper bounds of the box on each dimension, can be executed with a linear complexity related to the number of neurons monitored.

4 Experiments

We conducted experiments across various real-world object detection datasets to assess the effectiveness of our proposed Boxed Monitor within the YOLO architecture. We have implemented Boxed Monitor by developing utility modules for *feature extraction* within YOLOv8 model based on its official implementation by Ultralytics library and *monitor construction* using Scikit-learn library.

4.1 Experiment Setup

The evaluation protocol outlined in VOS [10] is followed in this study, using two ID datasets: BDD100k and PASCAL-VOC, along with two OoD datasets

Table 1. OoD counts comparison between YOLO and Faster R-CNN

ID	Method	mean Average Precision ↑	OoD Counts ↓ (OoD: MS-COCO/OpenImage)	Difference (%)
BDD100k	Faster R-CNN	31.5	2671/1577	
	YOLOv8s	**37.7**	**968/621**	**↓ 64%/61%**
PASCAL-VOC	Faster R-CNN	72.2	1224/2091	
	YOLOv8s	**83.7**	**714/1579**	**↓ 42%/24%**

derived from MS-COCO and Open-Images. Each OoD dataset excludes images containing ID objects. Regarding the model architecture, our primary focus in this study is on the YOLOv8 and YOLOv10. We train the YOLOv8 model on each ID dataset by fine-tuning pre-trained weights for 100 epochs. For YOLOv10 training, we fine-tuned the YOLOv10-small (YOLOv10s) model, which was pre-trained on the COCO dataset. This fine-tuning process was conducted separately for each ID dataset, with training continuing for 150 epochs per dataset. For the evaluation metric of monitor performance, we consider *FPR95*, representing the rate of false positives among OoD samples while maintaining a 95% true positive rate for ID samples. It is worth noting that a "false positive" denotes an object erroneously identified as an ID object despite belonging to the OoD categories. A lower FPR95 value indicates a more effective monitor in accurately detecting OoD objects.

The experiments were conducted using the following processes: Initially, preliminary experiments were undertaken to evaluate the OoD problem in the YOLO model compared to the Faster R-CNN model. Afterward, feature extraction was performed on the training sets using the pre-trained YOLO model. Subsequently, the monitor was constructed leveraging the extracted features. We then utilized the YOLO model to generate predictions and extract features from the ID validation sets and the OoD datasets. During the evaluation phase, Boxed Monitor made a verdict on each predicted instance based on the corresponding feature. After analyzing the evaluation results, a confusion matrix was computed to determine the FPR95 for each dataset. Finally, the performance of the Boxed Monitor was benchmarked against existing OoD detection methods in terms of FPR95.

4.2 Results

The OoD Problem for YOLO. We evaluated two YOLO models, one trained on BDD100K and the other on PASCAL-VOC, against two OoD datasets: COCO and OpenImages, and quantified their predictions. Theoretically, these two models should not produce any detections on these datasets because they do not contain any ID objects, similar to illegal inputs in software systems. Our experimental results reveal that YOLO does exhibit the OoD problem, though it performs slightly better than Faster R-CNN. Detailed comparisons are provided in Table 1.

Table 2. OoD detection performance comparison between Boxed Monitor and other OoD detection methods for YOLOv8 and YOLOv10; For each OoD dataset, the categories are disjoint with the ID dataset. Numbers in **bold** texts imply the method's superiority.

ID	Method	FPR95 ↓ (OoD: MS-COCO/OpenImage)	
		YOLOv8	YOLOv10
BDD100k	MSP	72.75/72.11	60.23/62.47
	EBO	69.60/75.46	68.59/71.17
	MLS	69.65/75.50	68.24/70.99
	MDS	72.42/69.82	62.93/65.21
	Boxed Monitor (ours)	**52.80/49.76**	**56.49/48.07**
PASCAL-VOC	MSP	60.69/65.22	52.36/71.13
	EBO	77.97/81.42	69.11/81.64
	MLS	77.94/81.43	69.10/81.63
	MDS	61.24/82.42	50.45/86.24
	Boxed Monitor (ours)	**56.98/58.36**	**40.41/48.71**

Effectiveness. Our Boxed Monitor achieves superior performance in terms of FPR95 across various datasets. We compared the proposed Boxed Monitor with recent competitive OoD detection baselines, including *Maximum Softmax Probability* [12], *Energy score* [19], *Maximum logit scores* [11], *Mahalanobis distance* [16]. All the selected baseline methods are also logits-based (like the Boxed Monitor), assigning an OoD score to each input to indicate the likelihood of a sample being within the ID.

The experimental results in Table 2 demonstrates that Boxed Monitor outperforms the competitive baseline methods by a margin for both ID datasets. In particular, when the ID dataset is BDD100k, Boxed Monitor reduces the FPR95 from 69.6% to 52.8% for MS-COCO, from 69.82% to 49.76% for OpenImage. This represents an improvement of 16.8% and 20.06%, respectively.

Figure 2 showcases a qualitative analysis of predictions on several OoD images using the YOLOv8 model (top) compared against OoD detections by Boxed Monitor (bottom). We utilize PASCAL-VOC as the ID dataset. As demonstrated, Boxed Monitor effectively identifies most object instances predicted by the YOLO model as OoD objects in these images. However, it is noteworthy that Boxed Monitor is susceptible to some failures, particularly in cases where an object shares similar characteristics with an ID class. An instance is provided in the right-most column of Fig. 2, where the model mis-detects a zebra as a horse, which Boxed Monitor does not flag as an OoD object.

5 Related and Future Work

Related Work. In traditional software programs, inputs are typically subjected to type checking; if a type inconsistency is detected, the program will not process

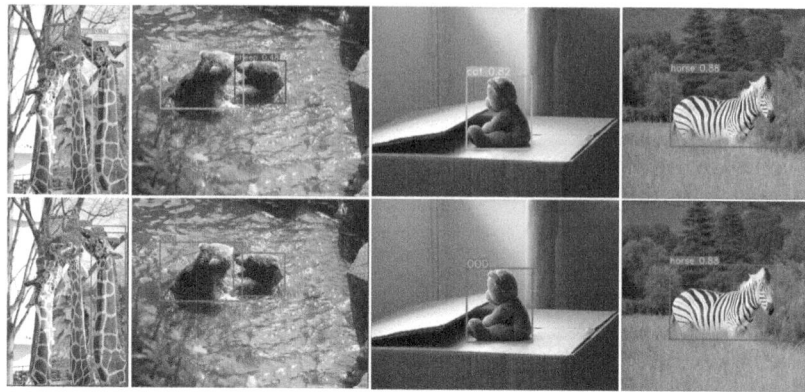

Fig. 2. Visualization of detected objects on the OoD images (from MS-COCO). The ID dataset is PASCAL-VOC. **Top:** predictions from YOLO object detector. **Bottom:** OoD detections by Boxed Monitor

the input. However, DNNs do not have this built-in mechanism and often face the OoD problem, where the model cannot discern whether an input is OoD and may still assign high confidence to such data. The challenge of identifying OoD inputs for DNNs has been widely explored in the context of image classification [11,12,16,17,21]. The exploration of OoD detection methods in the context of object detection is still in its infancy, focusing primarily on Faster R-CNN and transformer-based models, as demonstrated in studies like VOS [10] and SAFE [27]. The VOS method generates synthetic outliers during model training to shape an uncertainty decision boundary at the border of learned features from ID data, assuming that these features follow a Gaussian distribution. An alternative approach, SAFE [27], involves extracting features and training a multi-layer perceptron on a surrogate task of discerning perturbed from clean ID data. However, both methods rely on identifying a layer where one can interpret the learned features for a model's prediction, which becomes challenging when dealing with the YOLO architecture. This is compounded by the fact that the learning process of YOLO has not been fully elucidated. That is, it remains unclear what the semantic meaning of the learned features is for a specific prediction, which encompasses both object localization and classification within an image. To the best of our knowledge, Boxed Monitor is the first method to specifically address OoD object detection for the YOLO architecture.

Future Work. As indicated in Table 2, although the Boxed Monitor achieved the best performance among all methods, the FPR95 metric still exceeds 50%. This suggests that over half of the OoD instances remain undetected by Boxed Monitor and highlights the need for further improvement in future research. We are currently exploring the potential to enhance Boxed Monitor through the use of explainable artificial intelligence techniques, enabling us to decipher and leverage the learned discriminative features from other layers. This could pave the way for extending other OoD detection methods based on learned features. Another future work direction involves investigating whether our proposed Boxed Monitor affects the real-time efficiency of the underlying YOLO model, given YOLO's renowned speed.

6 Conclusion

This exploratory study introduces a box abstraction-based OoD monitoring method to YOLO architecture. Notably, this method is easy to implement and does not require any structural modifications to the underlying model or retraining procedures. Our experimental results demonstrate superior performance compared to existing OoD detection techniques, with a notable 20% reduction in false positive rates for OoD samples while maintaining a true positive rate of 95% for ID samples. We hope that this study will spark greater interest in investigating OoD challenges specific to the YOLO model, while also fostering continuous enhancements in OoD detection capabilities tailored for YOLO.

Acknowledgments. This study was funded by the European Union's Horizon 2020 research and innovation programme under grant agreement No. 956123 - FOCETA.

Disclosure of Interests. The authors have no competing interests.

References

1. Arora, U., Huang, W., He, H.: Types of out-of-distribution texts and how to detect them. In: Proceedings of the EMNLP 2021 - 2021 Conference on Empirical Methods in Natural Language Processing, pp. 10687–10701. Association for Computational Linguistics (ACL) (2021)
2. Chen, S., Bi, X., Gao, R., Sun, X.: Holistic sentence embeddings for better out-of-distribution detection. In: Findings of the Association for Computational Linguistics: EMNLP 2022, pp. 6676–6686. Association for Computational Linguistics, Abu Dhabi (2022)
3. Chen, S., Yang, W., Bi, X., Sun, X.: Fine-tuning deteriorates general textual out-of-distribution detection by distorting task-agnostic features. In: Findings of the Association for Computational Linguistics: EACL 2023, pp. 552–567 (2023)
4. Cheng, C.H.: Provably-robust runtime monitoring of neuron activation patterns. In: 2021 Design, Automation & Test in Europe Conference & Exhibition (DATE), pp. 1310–1313. IEEE (2021)
5. Cheng, C.H., Huang, C.H., Brunner, T., Hashemi, V.: Towards safety verification of direct perception neural networks. In: DATE, pp. 1640–1643. IEEE (2020)
6. Cheng, C.H., Nührenberg, G., Yasuoka, H.: Runtime monitoring neuron activation patterns. In: 2019 Design, Automation & Test in Europe Conference & Exhibition (DATE), pp. 300–303. IEEE (2019)
7. Cheng, C.H., Wu, C., Seferis, E., Bensalem, S.: Prioritizing corners in OoD detectors via symbolic string manipulation. In: Bouajjani, A., Holík, L., Wu, Z. (eds.) ATVA 2022. LNCS, vol. 13505, pp. 397–413. Springer, Cham (2022). https://doi.org/10.1007/978-3-031-19992-9_26

8. Cheng, T., Song, L., Ge, Y., Liu, W., Wang, X., Shan, Y.: YOLO-world: real-time open-vocabulary object detection. In: Proceedings of the IEEE Conference Computer Vision and Pattern Recognition (CVPR) (2024)
9. Dreossi, T., Fremont, D.J., Ghosh, S., Kim, E., Ravanbakhsh, H., Vazquez-Chanlatte, M., Seshia, S.A.: VERIFAI: a toolkit for the formal design and analysis of artificial intelligence-based systems. In: Dillig, I., Tasiran, S. (eds.) CAV 2019. LNCS, vol. 11561, pp. 432–442. Springer, Cham (2019). https://doi.org/10.1007/978-3-030-25540-4_25
10. Du, X., Wang, Z., Cai, M., Li, Y.: VOS: learning what you don't know by virtual outlier synthesis. In: ICLR (2022)
11. Hendrycks, D., et al.: Scaling out-of-distribution detection for real-world settings. In: ICML (2022)
12. Hendrycks, D., Gimpel, K.: A baseline for detecting misclassified and out-of-distribution examples in neural networks. In: ICLR (2016)
13. Henzinger, T.A., Lukina, A., Schilling, C.: Outside the box: abstraction-based monitoring of neural networks. In: ECAI 2020, pp. 2433–2440. IOS Press (2020)
14. Huang, H., Li, Z., Wang, L., Chen, S., Dong, B., Zhou, X.: Feature space singularity for out-of-distribution detection. In: Proceedings of the Workshop on Artificial Intelligence Safety 2021 (SafeAI 2021) (2021)
15. Huang, X., Kwiatkowska, M., Wang, S., Wu, M.: Safety verification of deep neural networks. In: Majumdar, R., Kunčak, V. (eds.) CAV 2017, Part I. LNCS, vol. 10426, pp. 3–29. Springer, Cham (2017). https://doi.org/10.1007/978-3-319-63387-9_1
16. Lee, K., Lee, K., Lee, H., Shin, J.: A simple unified framework for detecting out-of-distribution samples and adversarial attacks. In: NeurIPS (2018)
17. Liang, S., Li, Y., Srikant, R.: Enhancing the reliability of out-of-distribution image detection in neural networks. In: ICLR (2018)
18. Liu, C., et al.: Algorithms for verifying deep neural networks. Found. Trends® Optim. **4**(3-4), 244–404 (2021)
19. Liu, W., Wang, X., Owens, J., Li, Y.: Energy-based out-of-distribution detection. In: Advances in Neural Information Processing Systems (2020)
20. Lukina, A., Schilling, C., Henzinger, T.A.: Into the unknown: active monitoring of neural networks. In: Feng, L., Fisman, D. (eds.) RV 2021. LNCS, vol. 12974, pp. 42–61. Springer, Cham (2021). https://doi.org/10.1007/978-3-030-88494-9_3
21. Papernot, N., McDaniel, P.: Deep k-nearest neighbors: towards confident, interpretable and robust deep learning. arXiv preprint arXiv:1803.04765 (2018)
22. Ren, S., He, K., Girshick, R., Sun, J.: Faster R-CNN: towards real-time object detection with region proposal networks. In: NeurIPS (2015)
23. Seshia, S.A., Sadigh, D., Sastry, S.S.: Toward verified artificial intelligence. Commun. ACM **7**, 46–55 (2022)
24. Szegedy, C., et al.: Intriguing properties of neural networks. In: ICLR. Citeseer (2014)
25. Wang, A., et al.: YOLOv10: real-time end-to-end object detection (2024)
26. Wang, C., et al.: Gold-YOLO: efficient object detector via gather-and-distribute mechanism. In: Oh, A., Naumann, T., Globerson, A., Saenko, K., Hardt, M., Levine, S. (eds.) Advances in Neural Information Processing Systems, vol. 36, pp. 51094–51112. Curran Associates, Inc. (2023)
27. Wilson, S., Fischer, T., Dayoub, F., Miller, D., Sünderhauf, N.: SAFE: sensitivity-aware features for out-of-distribution object detection. In: Proceedings of the IEEE/CVF International Conference on Computer Vision (ICCV), pp. 23565–23576 (2023)

28. Wu, C., Falcone, Y., Bensalem, S.: Customizable reference runtime monitoring of neural networks using resolution boxes. In: Katsaros, P., Nenzi, L. (eds.) RV 2023. LNCS, vol. 14245, pp. 23–41. Springer, Cham (2023). https://doi.org/10.1007/978-3-031-44267-4_2
29. Wu, C., He, W., Cheng, C.H., Huang, X., Bensalem, S.: BAM: box abstraction monitors for real-time OoD detection in object detection. arXiv preprint arXiv:2403.18373 (2024)
30. Wu, M., Wicker, M., Ruan, W., Huang, X., Kwiatkowska, M.: A game-based approximate verification of deep neural networks with provable guarantees. Theor. Comput. Sci. **807**, 298–329 (2020)

Distributed Systems

Distributed Monitoring of Timed Properties

Léo Henry[1], Thierry Jéron[2], Nicolas Markey[2(✉)], and Victor Roussanaly[3]

[1] University College London, London, UK
[2] IRISA, CNRS and Inria and Univ. Rennes, Rennes, France
Thierry.Jeron@inria.fr, nicolas.markey@irisa.fr
[3] Université de Lorraine, Nancy, France

Abstract. In formal verification, runtime monitoring consists of observing the execution of a system in order to decide as quickly as possible whether or not it satisfies a given property. We consider monitoring in a distributed setting, for properties given as reachability timed automata. In such a setting, the system is made of several components, each equipped with its own local clock and monitor. The monitors observe events occurring on their associated component, and receive timestamped events from other monitors through FIFO channels. Since clocks are local, they cannot be perfectly synchronized, resulting in imprecise timestamps. Consequently, they must be seen as intervals, leading monitors to consider possible reorderings of events. In this context, each monitor aims to provide, as early as possible, a verdict on the property it is monitoring, based on its potentially incomplete and imprecise knowledge of the current execution. In this paper, we propose an on-line monitoring algorithm for timed properties, robust to time imprecision and partial information from distant components. We first identify the date at which a monitor can safely compute a verdict based on received events. We then propose a monitoring algorithm that updates this date when new information arrives, maintains the current set of states in which the property can reside, and updates its verdict accordingly.

Keywords: Distributed systems · timed automata · observation · approximation

1 Introduction

Formal verification is a branch of computer science that aims to check whether computer systems satisfy their requirements. This includes model checking [3,10] and deductive verification [15,20], which work offline and check properties of all behaviours of the system under study. In contrast, runtime verification [4,23] is a set of efficient techniques to monitor the behaviour of a *running* system, and to detect, as early as possible during execution, whether some properties are violated. This domain of formal verification has been extensively studied over the last 25 years, and is now mature enough to be applied in various application domains.

As real-life systems typically comprise several connected components, runtime verification has to handle situations where the behaviours of the components are only partially known and may be imprecise: each component is equipped with a monitor, and monitors exchange information asynchronously with each other.

Because the system is distributed, we assume that each monitor only has access to a local clock, which may slightly drift w.r.t a reference clock. Hence the dates of the events are only known with a limited precision, and the exact order of the events occurring on different subsystems may be unknown. We assume that communications between local monitors are FIFO; this way, when a monitor receives the information that some event took place on some subsystem, it also knows all the events that have occurred earlier on that subsystem.

Thanks to these hypotheses, each monitor can determine a time in the past for which it currently has enough information to decide whether the property it is checking already held, or failed to hold, at that time. We consider real-time properties modelled as *timed automata* (TA) [1]; the expressiveness of these models allows to account for the precise timing of events, which magnifies the impact of the lack of an observable global clock.

Example 1. Consider a private (*e.g.*, enterprise, university) network with a set of terminals and servers containing user account data logged in and a router connected to them. Properties of interest can be that (1) all machines should remain connected to the network and (2) no account should be logged in more than one terminal at a time. Even if two terminals signal that they are connected to a given account, a monitor has to wait to ensure that no "log out" message is pending from one of the two terminals. Plus, once such signals are received, the approximate timings may lead to situations where two terminals may or may not have been connected to the same user session at the same time, with no ability to conclude.

Our contributions. We present a monitoring algorithm for properties expressed as (deterministic) TAs in a distributed setting without a global clock. Each monitor keeps track of the most recent date at which it has collected the full history (relying on the assumption that communications with other monitors are FIFO). The prefix of the collected trace at this time already contains uncertainty, due to the absence of a global clock, which entails that reordering events from distinct components must be considered. The computation of a verdict is based on the incremental update of a structure that encodes the set of states compatible with the prefix of the collected trace up to the time of interest. We show that the monitoring algorithm is sound and complete.

Related Works. This paper studies distributed runtime verification for timed properties described as timed automata [1]. Several related approaches have been developed in the literature. Extensions of Linear-time Temporal Logic (LTL) integrating dense time have been explored for runtime verification and monitor synthesis [6]. Among them, Metric Temporal Logic (MTL) is of particular interest as it is directly related to TAs [25] and is equipped with a progression function allowing to evaluate formulas at runtime [28]. Similarly, Timed Regular Expressions are as expressive as TAs and can be translated to TAs [2]. The tool Montre [29] monitors them using timed pattern matching. Monitoring TA models has been realized in the case of one-clock non-deterministic TAs [19]. Pinisetty *et al.* [26] introduce a predictive setting for runtime verification of timed properties, leveraging reachability analysis to anticipate the detection of verdicts.

The aforementioned approaches consider that the monitored system is *centralized* and the decision procedure is fed with a unique trace containing complete observations. *Decentralized* runtime verification [7] (see also a recent overview in [13]) handles separate traces corresponding to each monitor. Decentralized (also called synchronous) methods however assume the existence of a global clock shared by all components and monitors. We relax this assumption here, and consider *asynchronous distributed monitoring* (or *distributed monitoring* for short). For a discussion on the links and differences between synchronous and asynchronous methods, see [16].

Most approaches in decentralized runtime verification take as input Linear-time Temporal Logic formulas [7,11,17] or finite-state automata [12,14]. These approaches monitor specifications of discrete time, which does not account for the physical time that impacts the evaluation of the specifications nor the moment at which monitors perform their evaluation and deliver their verdicts. An approach close to ours is [5], in which properties are specified in an extension of Metric Temporal Logic to tackle both timing and data values. Similar to us, the authors also deal with out-of-order messages, but also failures and lost messages. However, they consider that local clocks are accurate.

Distributed runtime verification exhibits similarities with diagnosis [30,31] ([9] for TAs), which aims to identify the occurrence of a fault and the component(s) responsible for it after a finite number of discrete steps, and has to cope with partial observation. Our approach differs from diagnosis, as we assume that monitors'(combined) local information suffices to detect violations; diagnosis does not aim to check membership to an arbitrary timed regular expression. The approach of [21] for robust diagnosis shares several common aspects with ours. While centralized, it considers diagnosis where communication between the system and the diagnoser is subject to varying latency, clock drift and out-of-order observation. The problem is different but is similar in spirit: incrementally building a verdict based on approximate and partial timed observations. Moreover some constructions have clear similarities, which is not surprising: in both cases the language of runs compatible with the current partial and approximate observation has to be considered. Other approaches comparable to ours perform monitoring on timed properties in a decentralized [27] or distributed [18] fashion. Our own approach discusses distributed monitoring directly on timed automata models.

2 Preliminaries

We present the basic hypotheses about our formalization of the distributed monitoring problem in Sect. 2.1, the notions of words and languages at play in Sect. 2.2 and 2.3, and timed automata in Sect. 2.4.

2.1 Distributed Timed Systems

We consider systems made of n independent components $(C_i)_{1 \leq i \leq n}$. Each C_i is observed by a local monitor M_i. The components being independent, we assume that each C_i has its own finite alphabet of actions Act_i, disjoint from the alphabets of the other components. We write $\mathsf{Act} = \bigsqcup_{1 \leq i \leq n} \mathsf{Act}_i$ for the alphabet of all actions. For an action $a \in \mathsf{Act}_i$, we write $\mathsf{Comp}(a) = i$. An action a fired by component C_i is observed and timestamped by its monitor M_i, giving rise to an *event* (a, t) in $\mathsf{Act}_i \times \mathbb{R}_{\geq 0}$. We assume the following about the system:

Respective knowledge: monitors know each others' alphabets of actions;
Communication: monitors send messages to their peers, carrying the timestamped events they observed (and events they learnt about from other monitors) in the order in which they observed them. We assume that local events can be strictly ordered.
Communication channels: communications between monitors obey a FIFO policy with no message loss: messages are received in the order they were sent, and any sent message is eventually received, although no upper bound on communication delays is assumed.
Communication topology: the connectivity is such that a monitor M_i can receive messages (either directly or indirectly) from any monitor M_j managing some action appearing in M_i's property.
Local liveness: at any given time, each monitor will eventually have a local observation in the future, and will eventually send it to the other monitors.
Time approximation: monitors do not share a global clock, but one can assume that each local clock has a maximal skew ε with respect to a global *reference clock*[1]. We suppose that clocks are non-decreasing.

Most of these assumptions are easy to satisfy. A FIFO policy can be achieved by numbering the events exchanged between one monitor and another, ensuring that a monitor can handle events in the order they were sent. Local liveness can be ensured by adding empty events that are sent when no events have been observed for a long duration. The main practical constraints are the absence of message losses, and the bound on clock skews. However, even these assumptions can be mitigated. Message losses can be detected using the message numbering, while a mechanism such as Network Time Protocol (NTP) can be used to limit the skew to ε.

---

[1] Our approach can be easily generalized to different ε for each monitor, with our theorems depending on the greatest one.

We consider that each monitor is in charge of verifying some property (given as a timed automaton, see Sect. 2.4). As the monitoring algorithms and properties are symmetric for each such monitor, we restrict our dissertation to a fixed monitor M_i and assume that the entire set Act of actions is necessary for its property (some of these actions are still observed by other monitors).

2.2 Timed Words and Languages

We consider intervals in $\mathbb{R}$, denoted $\mathcal{I}(\mathbb{R})$. For an interval $I = \langle l, u \rangle$, with $\langle \in \{(, [\}$ and $\rangle \in \{),]\}$, we write $\mathsf{lb}(I) = l$, $\mathsf{ub}(I) = u$ for its lower and upper bounds. For two intervals I_1, I_2 of $\mathbb{R}$, we write $I_1 \prec I_2$ if $\mathsf{ub}(I_1) \leq \mathsf{lb}(I_2)$; when this condition is met, the intervals intersect in at most one point. We also consider intervals of natural numbers and write $[\![1; m]\!]$ for $\{k \in \mathbb{N} \mid 1 \leq k \leq m\}$.

Timed Words and Languages. We consider *timed words* built on the alphabet of actions Act as (finite or infinite) sequences $\sigma = (a_k, t_k)_{k \in [\![1;m]\!]}$[2] of *events* in Act $\times$ $\mathbb{R}_{\geq 0}$ whose sequence of *dates* $(t_k)_{k \in [\![1;m]\!]}$ is non-decreasing. We write $\sigma[k] = (a_k, t_k)$ for its k-th event. For any interval I of $\mathbb{R}_{\geq 0}$, we write $\sigma_{|I}$ for the subword of σ restricted to dates in I, and $\sigma_{|t}$ as a shorthand for $\sigma_{|[0,t]}$ with $t \in \mathbb{R}_{\geq 0}$. For a finite timed word $\sigma = (a_k, t_k)_{k \in [\![1;m]\!]}$, we write $|\sigma| = m$ for its length, $\mathsf{firstt}(\sigma) = t_1$ and $\mathsf{lastt}(\sigma) = t_m$ respectively for the dates of its first and last events; for the empty word γ, we let $\mathsf{firstt}(\gamma) = \mathsf{lastt}(\gamma) = 0$. Two timed words σ_1 and σ_2 can be concatenated into $\sigma_1 \cdot \sigma_2$ if, and only if, $\mathsf{lastt}(\sigma_1) \leq \mathsf{firstt}(\sigma_2)$. For any interval $I \subseteq \mathbb{R}_{\geq 0}$, we write $\mathsf{TT}_I(\mathsf{Act})$ for the set of timed words in $(\mathsf{Act} \times I)^*$, and $\mathsf{TT}(\mathsf{Act}) = \mathsf{TT}_{\mathbb{R}_{\geq 0}}(\mathsf{Act})$. A language of timed words is any subset of $\mathsf{TT}(\mathsf{Act})$.

For two languages of timed words L_1 and L_2, their concatenation $L_1 \cdot L_2$ is defined and equal to $\{\sigma_1 \cdot \sigma_2 \mid \sigma_1 \in L_1, \sigma_2 \in L_2\}$ if, and only if, $\sup\{\mathsf{lastt}(\sigma_1) \mid \sigma_1 \in L_1\} \leq \inf\{\mathsf{firstt}(\sigma_2) \mid \sigma_2 \in L_2\}$. The restriction to an interval naturally generalizes to languages: for a language $L \subseteq \mathsf{TT}(\mathsf{Act})$ and an interval I of $\mathbb{R}$, $L_{|I} = \{\sigma_{|I} \mid \sigma \in L\}$.

Projections on Monitors. In our setting, Act is the disjoint union of alphabets Act_i. For a timed word σ, we write $\mathsf{p}_i(\sigma)$ for the projection on the actions monitored by M_i, defined by induction as $\mathsf{p}_i(\gamma) = \gamma$ for the empty word, and $\mathsf{p}_i(\sigma \cdot (a, t)) = \mathsf{p}_i(\sigma) \cdot (a, t)$ if $a \in \mathsf{Act}_i$ and $\mathsf{p}_i(\sigma \cdot (a, t)) = \mathsf{p}_i(\sigma)$ otherwise.

Conversely, we define a tensor operation on timed words $\sigma_1 \otimes \sigma_2$ that merges the events while re-ordering them by ascending timestamps. This operation is such that $\sigma = \otimes_{i \in [\![1;n]\!]} \mathsf{p}_i(\sigma)$.

2.3 Approximate Timed Words

If we had perfect clocks, timed words as defined above would be the model of choice for representing the knowledge of the monitors; restriction to intervals

---

[2] We abusively use such a notation for both finite and infinite sequences.

would be used to identify the part of the knowledge that each monitor knows is complete (as opposed to the part of the knowledge where informations from some of the components did not arrive yet).

In the context of distributed monitoring, we consider that the clocks of the monitors may be imprecise, resulting in a potential drift of up to a uniform bound ε w.r.t. a reference clock. Because of this, we have to rely on a notion of *approximate timed words*, and to define restriction to intervals for this new model.

Because of timing imprecisions, an event (a, t), made of action a timestamped with t by the monitor that observed it, may have happened anywhere in the interval $[t-\varepsilon, t+\varepsilon] \cap \mathbb{R}_{\geq 0}$ with respect to the reference clock[3]. Thus, while the information collected by a monitor has the form of a timed word $\sigma = (a_k, t_k)_{k \in [\![1;m]\!]}$, the real date of each event (a_k, t_k) lies in the interval $I_k = [t_k - \varepsilon, t_k + \varepsilon] \cap \mathbb{R}_{\geq 0}$. We call *approximate timed word of* σ, the sequence $\nu(\sigma) = (a_k, I_k)_{k \in [\![1;m]\!]}$.

Approximate Timed Words. An *approximate timed word* (ATW for short) is a sequence of pairs $\nu = (a_k, I_k)_{k \in [\![1;m]\!]}$ such that, for all $k \in [\![1;m]\!]$, $a_k \in \mathsf{Act}$ and $I_k \in \mathcal{I}(\mathbb{R})$ is an interval (open or closed for generality). We denote by $\mathsf{ATW}(\mathsf{Act})$ the set of approximate timed words on Act.

With any approximate timed word, we associate two languages: its *ordered* language and its *non-ordered* language. Intuitively, the *ordered language* of ν is the language of timed words that respect the order of the events and the intervals given by ν, while the *non-ordered language* will be the union of the ordered languages for all possible reorderings of the events.

The ordered semantics defines a "tube" of timed words with the same untimed projection. It is defined as follows:

$$[\![(a_k, I_k)_{k \in [\![1;m]\!]}]\!]_{\mathsf{ord}} = \{(a_k, t_k)_{k \in [\![1;m]\!]} \in \mathsf{TT}(\mathsf{Act}) \mid \forall k \in [\![1;m]\!].t_k \in I_k\}$$

By definition of $\mathsf{TT}(Act)$, the sequence $(t_k)_{k \in [\![1;m]\!]}$ is non-decreasing, which induces constraints on subsequent t_k's. Notice that $[\![\nu]\!]_{\mathsf{ord}} = \emptyset$ when $I_k = \emptyset$ for some k, or if no increasing sequences of dates can be found in the sequence $(I_k)_{k \in [\![1;m]\!]}$.

In order to define the *non-ordered language* of ν, we introduce the subset $\mathcal{F}(\nu)$ of permutations of events in ν that respect the strict order of events sharing the same component (each monitor knows the order of events occurring in the component it supervises). We define it as follows, with $\mathsf{Perms}([\![1;m]\!])$ being the set of permutations of $[\![1;m]\!]$:

$$\mathcal{F}((a_k, I_k)_{k \in [\![1;m]\!]}) = \{f \in \mathsf{Perms}([\![1;m]\!]) \mid \forall k, l \in [\![1;m]\!].$$
$$(\mathsf{Comp}(a_k) = \mathsf{Comp}(a_l) \wedge k < l) \Rightarrow f(k) < f(l)\}.$$

Then for $f \in \mathcal{F}(\nu)$, we abuse the notation and write $f(\nu)$ for the ATW $(a_{f(k)}, I_{f(k)})_{k \in [\![1;m]\!]}$. Finally, we define the *(non-ordered) language* of ν as the

---

[3] Intersection with $\mathbb{R}_{\geq 0}$ is used to rule out events with negative dates.

set of timed words that respect both the intervals given by ν, and the strict local order on each component:

$$[\![\nu]\!] = \bigcup_{f \in \mathcal{F}(\nu)} [\![f(\nu)]\!]_{\mathsf{ord}}.$$

Intuitively, this language includes commutations of events that occurred at sufficiently close dates on different components: indeed, if $\nu = \nu_1 \cdot (b_k, t) \cdot (b_l, t') \cdot \nu_2$ with $\mathsf{Comp}(b_k) \neq \mathsf{Comp}(b_l)$ and $|t - t'| \leq 2\varepsilon$, then $[\![\nu]\!]$ contains timed words with form $\sigma_1 \cdot (b_k, t) \cdot (b_l, t') \cdot \sigma_2$ and $\sigma_1 \cdot (b_l, t' - \varepsilon) \cdot (b_k, t + \varepsilon) \cdot \sigma_2$.

Back to the monitoring problem, given some monitor and an observation prefix σ that is sufficient (in some sense clarified later), considering the imprecision due to the skew ε in the approximate timed word $\nu(\sigma)$, the non-ordered language $[\![\nu(\sigma)]\!]$ is the set of executions that could produce this observation prefix, hence that has to be considered for monitoring.

Operations on Approximate Timed Words. We now focus on defining a restriction of approximate timed words to an interval of dates. This will be useful for the incremental update of the monitor's knowledge (see Sect. 3.3). Semantically, the restriction of an ATW ν to an interval I is the set of restrictions to I of all the timed words contained in $[\![\nu]\!]$. In this section, we present a syntactic definition, which will be the basis of an effective computation.

To this aim, we first define *intersection*: for $\nu = (a_k, I_k)_{k \in [\![1;m]\!]}$ and an interval I, the intersection of ν with I is the ATW $\nu_{\cap I} = (a_k, I_k \cap I)_{k \in [\![1;m]\!]}$. Notice that $[\![\nu_{\cap I}]\!]_{\mathsf{ord}} = [\![\nu_{\cap I}]\!] = \emptyset$ if $I_k \cap I = \emptyset$ for some $k \in [\![1;m]\!]$.

Our syntactic definition of restriction adapts the notion of subword. For any interval I of $\mathbb{R}_{\geq 0}$, and two ATW ν' and ν'', we say that $\nu' = \nu'_1 \cdots \nu'_n$ is a *subword* of $\nu'' = \nu''_1 \cdot \nu'_1 \cdots \nu''_n \cdot \nu'_n \cdot \nu''_{n+1}$ *conditioned by* I, written $\nu' \preceq_I \nu''$, if, and only if,

- for all $l \in [\![1; n+1]\!]$, for any (a_k, I_k) in ν''_l, $\neg(I_k \subseteq I)$: all events in ν''_l (which are dropped) *may occur outside of* I;
- for all $l \in [\![1; n]\!]$, for any $(a'_{k'}, I'_{k'})$ in ν'_l, $I'_{k'} \cap I \neq \emptyset$: all events in ν'_l (which are not dropped) *may occur in* I;
- there is $f \in \mathcal{F}(\nu'')$ s.t. $f(\nu'') = \nu_1 \cdot \nu' \cdot \nu_3$ for some ν_1 and ν_3: this encodes the fact that two events in the same component can not be permuted.

We can now define the (syntactic) *restriction* of an approximate timed word ν to an interval I as $\nu_{|I} = \{\nu'_{\cap I} \mid \nu' \preceq_I \nu\}$. As a shorthand, for a timestamp T, we write $\nu_{|[0,T]} = \nu_{|T}$. We overload the term *restriction* of ν to I because of the characterization of Lemma 1 below: the syntactic restriction corresponds to the semantic approach of taking the language of timed words associated with ν, and restricting each of its words. This provides us with a way of representing, manipulating and computing restriction of ATW to intervals:

Lemma 1. *For any approximate timed word ν and any timestamp T, it holds $\cup_{\nu' \in \nu_{|T}} [\![\nu']\!] = [\![\nu]\!]_{|T}$.*

Following this, we write $[\![\nu_{|T}]\!]$ for $\bigcup_{\nu' \in \nu_{|T}} [\![\nu']\!]$.

Example 2. Consider the approximate timed word $\nu = (a, [1,3])(b, [2,4])(c, [3,5])$, and $I = [0,3]$ with the components of the actions being pair-wise different. Then:

- $\nu_{\cap I}$ is the approximate timed word $(a, [1,3])(b, [2,3])(c, \{3\})$.
- assuming that all three events occur on different components (and can then be freely swapped), the set $\{\nu' \mid \nu' \preceq_I \nu\}$ is

$$\{\epsilon, (a, [1,3]), (a, [1,3])(b, [2,4]), (a, [1,3])(c, [3,5]),$$
$$(a, [1,3])(b, [2,4])(c, [3,5]), (b, [2,4]), (b, [2,4])(c, [3,5]), (c, [3,5])\}$$

(in other terms, all subwords are allowed, since all intervals intersect I and none of them are included in I). It follows that $\nu_{|I}$ is the union of ϵ, $(a, [1,3])$, $(a, [1,3])(b, [2,3])$, $(a, [1,3])(c, [3,3])$, $(a, [1,3])(b, [2,3])(c, [3,3])$, $(b, [2,3])$, $(b, [2,3])(c, [3,3])$ and $(c, [3,3])$.

Now, assume that b and c relate to the same component, so that they cannot be swapped. In this case, $(a, [1,3])(c, [3,5])$ is no longer a subword of ν for I, because the third condition is no longer fulfilled.

2.4 Formalism for Timed Systems

We monitor properties given as TAs, which are standard formalism for expressing properties of time-constrained systems: the aim of our monitoring procedure is to decide if the execution we are (partially and imprecisely) observing is (or will be) accepted by a given timed automaton. We introduce the formalism of timed automata in thie section.

Let X be a finite set of clocks. A clock valuation is a function $v \colon X \to \mathbb{R}_{>0}$. We write $\mathcal{V}(X)$ for the set of valuations. The initial valuation is $\mathbf{0} \colon x \in X \mapsto 0$; a time elapse for a delay $t \in \mathbb{R}_{\geq 0}$ maps valuation v to $v + t \colon x \mapsto v(x) + t$, and a clock reset for a subset $X' \subseteq X$ maps v to $v_{[X']}$ such that $v_{[X']}(x) = v(x)$ if $x \notin X'$, and $v_{[X']}(x) = 0$ otherwise.

A *zone* is a finite conjunction of clock constraints of the forms $x_1 \bowtie n$ and $x_1 - x_2 \bowtie n$, with $x_1, x_2 \in X$, $\bowtie \in \{<, \leq, =, \geq, >\}$ and $n \in \mathbb{N}$. We write $\mathcal{Z}(X)$ for the set of zones of X. We write $v \models z$ and say that v *satisfies* z when the values of the clocks in v satisfy the constraints in z.

Definition 2. *A timed automaton (TA) is a tuple $\mathcal{A} = (\mathcal{L}, \ell_{init}, \mathsf{Act}, X, E)$ where $\mathcal{L}$ is a finite set of locations containing the initial location ℓ_{init}, Act and X are finite sets of actions and clocks respectively, and $\mathrm{E} \subseteq \mathcal{L} \times \mathcal{Z}(X) \times \mathsf{Act} \times 2^X \times \mathcal{L}$ is the set of transitions. For a transition $(\ell, g, a, z, \ell') \in \mathrm{E}$, we call ℓ its source, ℓ' its target, g and a its guard and action and z its reset set. We call configurations of $\mathcal{A}$ the triples $(\ell, \mathrm{v}, t) \in \mathcal{L} \times \mathcal{V} \times \mathbb{R}_{\geq 0}$, and initial configuration the configuration $(\ell_{init}, \mathbf{0}, 0)$.*

Remark 1. We add to the usual notion of configuration a date representing the instant at which the system is in this configuration (after a given behaviour). We do this because our reasoning is based on timestamps, not delays, following the definition of timed words based on observations. This can be readily implemented by giving an additional clock (which is never reset) to the TA.

A timed word $\sigma = (a_i, t_i)_{1 \leq i}$ is *a trace* of a timed automaton if, starting from the initial configuration $(\ell_{init}, \mathbf{0}, 0)$, one can find a sequence $\rho = ((\ell_{i-1}, v_{i-1}, t_{i-1}) \xrightarrow{\delta_i} (\ell_{i-1}, v_{i-1} + \delta_i, t_{i-1} + \delta_i) \xrightarrow{e_i} (\ell_i, v_i, t_{i-1} + \delta_i))_{1 \leq i}$ with $e_i = (\ell_{i-1}, g_i, a_i, z_i, \ell_i) \in E$, $\delta_i = t_i - t_{i-1}$ (with $t_0 = 0$), and at each step $v_{i-1} + \delta_i \models g_i$ and $v_i = (v_{i-1} + \delta_i)_{[z_i]}$. Such a sequence ρ is called a (finite or infinite) *run*, and we write $\mathrm{trace}(\rho) = \sigma$. A timed word σ is a *partial* trace if there exists a timed word σ' such that $\sigma' \cdot \sigma$ is a trace. A partial trace thus corresponds to a *partial run* that does not (necessarily) start from $(\ell_{init}, \mathbf{0}, 0)$. For a (partial) trace σ with $\mathrm{firstt}(\sigma) \geq t$, we write $(\ell, v, t) \xrightarrow{\sigma}_t (\ell', v', t')$ when σ leads from configuration (ℓ, v, t) to configuration (ℓ', v', t').

A timed automaton is said *deterministic* if for any two transitions (ℓ, g, a, z, ℓ') and (ℓ, g', a, z', ℓ') such that $g \cap g' \neq \emptyset$, it holds $g = g'$ and $z = z'$. It is said *complete* when for any configuration (ℓ, v, t) and action $a \in \mathsf{Act}$, there is at least a transition (ℓ, g, a, z, ℓ') such that $v \models g$. When considering complete deterministic automata, the *trace*function defined above is a bijection, and we identify traces with their associated runs. In this context, we add the possibility of having a final delay after a trace: for a configuration (ℓ, v, t), a date t'' and a (partial) trace σ such that $\mathrm{firstt}(\sigma) \geq t$ and $\mathrm{lastt}(\sigma) = t' \leq t''$ we write $(\ell, v, t) \; \mathsf{after}_t^{t''} \; \sigma$ for the unique configuration (ℓ', v'', t'') such that $(\ell, v, t) \xrightarrow{\sigma}_t (\ell', v', t') \xrightarrow{t'' - t'} (\ell', v'', t'')$, i.e., reached from (ℓ, v, t) after the trace σ followed by the delay $t'' - t'$. This can be generalized to sets of configurations and languages: for a set of configurations S and a language of timed words L, such that $\inf\{\mathrm{firstt}(\sigma) \mid \sigma \in L\} \geq t$ and $\sup\{\mathrm{lastt}(\sigma) \mid \sigma \in L\} \leq t''$, $S \; \mathsf{after}_t^{t''} \; L = \{(\ell', v', t'') \mid \exists (\ell, v, t) \in S, \exists \sigma \in L, (\ell', v', t'') = (\ell, v, t) \; \mathsf{after}_t^{t''} \; \sigma\}$. Finally, we define the corresponding notion when no date is given: $S \; \mathsf{after} \; L = \{(\ell', v', t') \mid \exists (\ell, v, t) \in S, \exists \sigma \in L, \exists t', (\ell', v', t') = (\ell, v, t) \; \mathsf{after}_t^{t'} \; \sigma\}$. Notice that in this last definition, t and t' are not bound and can range on all values such that $\mathsf{after}_t^{t'}$ is defined.

Modelling Properties. The property associated with monitor M_i is defined by a deterministic and complete TA $\mathcal{A}_i$ and a subset $\mathcal{F}_i$ of locations specifying a reachability property[4]: we write $[\![\mathcal{A}_i, \mathcal{F}_i]\!]$ for the set of (runs of) finite traces σ that end in some location of $\mathcal{F}_i$ when applied to $\mathcal{A}_i$ from its initial configuration $(\ell_{init}, \mathbf{0}, 0)$; we extend $[\![\mathcal{A}_i, \mathcal{F}_i]\!]$ (abusively keeping the same notation) to include runs of infinite traces σ for which there is a length k such that all prefixes of σ of length larger than k are in $[\![\mathcal{A}_i, \mathcal{F}_i]\!]$.

---

[4] We here restrict to deterministic and complete TAs for simplicity, but generalization to non-deterministic and incomplete TAs is easy.

Given a property specified by $\mathcal{A}_i$ and $\mathcal{F}_i$, a finite trace σ is a *good prefix* (resp. *bad prefix*) if for all *infinite* continuations $\sigma \cdot \sigma' \in (\mathsf{Act} \times \mathbb{R}_{\geq 0})^\omega$ of σ, $\sigma \cdot \sigma' \in [\![\mathcal{A}_i, \mathcal{F}_i]\!]$ (resp. $\sigma \cdot \sigma' \notin [\![\mathcal{A}_i, \mathcal{F}_i]\!]$). In terms of automata, this means that the prefix reached some configuration in $\mathcal{L}_i \times \mathcal{V} \times \mathbb{R}_{\geq 0}$ from which it will always eventually stay in $\mathcal{F}_i \times \mathcal{V} \times \mathbb{R}_{\geq 0}$ (resp. it never visited and will never visit $\mathcal{F}_i$). We note this set of configurations $\mathit{Inev}(\mathcal{F}_i)$ (resp. $\mathit{Never}(\mathcal{F}_i)$). Good prefixes (resp. bad prefixes) are then traces of runs in $[\![\mathcal{A}_i, \mathit{Inev}(\mathcal{F}_i)]\!]$ (resp. $[\![\mathcal{A}_i, \mathit{Never}(\mathcal{F}_i)]\!]$). Starting from $\mathcal{F}_i$, the state sets $\mathit{Inev}(\mathcal{F}_i)$ and $\mathit{Never}(\mathcal{F}_i)$ can be computed offline by a zone-based co-reachability analysis [8]. Thanks to this, we restrict our focus to the reachability of pairs of locations and zones without loss of generality. These notions can be extended to languages, thus to approximate timed words. A language $L \in \mathsf{TT}_{\mathsf{Act}}$ is a *good* (resp. *bad*) *language prefix* if $L \subseteq [\![\mathcal{A}_i, \mathit{Inev}(\mathcal{F}_i)]\!]$ (resp. $L \subseteq [\![\mathcal{A}_i, \mathit{Never}(\mathcal{F}_i)]\!]$). These can also be computed using $\mathit{Inev}(\mathcal{F}_i)$ and $\mathit{Never}(\mathcal{F}_i)$.

3 Monitoring with Complete Information

The role of monitoring algorithms is to provide us with verdicts when analyzing executions of the system. Since we want this to be performed online, verdicts should be given as soon as possible, based on the observation of a finite execution prefix. However, in the context of distributed systems, the observation collected by a monitor at a given date may be imperfect, with missing events and approximate dates. We first identify the points in time where we have enough information to decide a verdict in Sect. 3.1, and then define our verdicts of interest in Sect. 3.2. Using this, we explain the data structure we use and its related operations in Sect. 3.3, and explain how to compute a verdict in Sect. 3.4.

3.1 Point of Certainty

When the components of the system perform actions, their corresponding monitors $(M_j)_{j \in [\![1;n]\!]}$ instantly *observe* these actions and timestamp them with the value of their (local) clock. However, they need to wait for the communication of other monitors in order to *collect* the information about the other components' events.

Communication Policy. We consider the simple policy in which each monitor M_j instantly sends its observations (action performed and timestamp) to every other monitor M_i that needs it for checking its property, grouping in the same message all the events that occurred at the same instant[5]. As there are no bounds in communication delays, monitors still have to deal with partial and out-of-order information. Moreover, local time approximation induces imprecision in event

---

[5] This technical detail is useful for Proposition 3 to ensure that all events of same date issued from the same component are collected simultaneously. It can be implemented by waiting any non null delay before sending a message aggregating the observations.

dates. To make monitoring sound, we first determine the time point at which we can safely monitor with no missing event.

Formally, consider the *global observation* σ^o such that at a given global time t^g, the observation collected by all monitors is hence $\sigma^o_{|t^g}$. We know that the *global trace* σ^g of the run of the system is such that $\sigma^g \in [\![\nu(\sigma^o)]\!]$. This trace can not be observed, yet it is the one we want to monitor, hence we will start our reasoning from (prefixes of) the language $[\![\nu(\sigma^o)]\!]$.

Moreover, no single monitor has access to $\sigma^o_{|t^g}$ at time t^g due to the need for synchronization. Let the *collected trace* at t by M_i, written $\sigma_i(t)$, be the monitoring information gathered by a monitor M_i at the M_i-local time t. It is composed of a subset of the global observation $\sigma^o_{|t+\varepsilon}$, containing at least its own local observation $\mathsf{p}_i(\sigma^o)_{|t}$ and events received from other monitors, forming for each monitor M_j a timed word $\mathsf{p}_j(\sigma^o)_{|t_j}$ with $t_j \leq t+2\varepsilon$. Indeed, communication being FIFO, M_i receives the information from each individual M_j in order, but potentially with M_j-local timestamps up to $t + 2\varepsilon$, as both the M_i-local time t and the M_j-local time can skew by a maximum of ε from the global time.

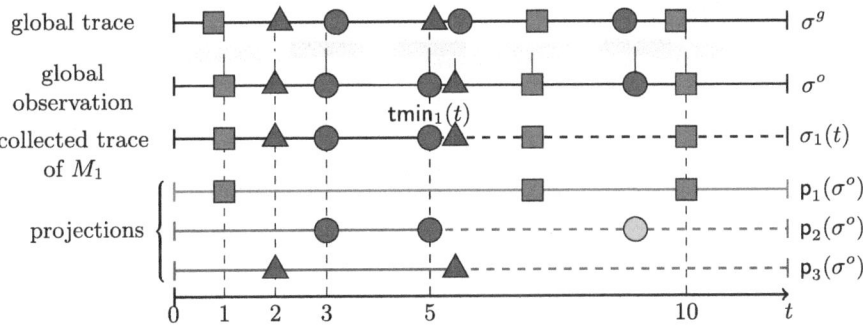

Fig. 1. A global finite trace σ^g (top), its corresponding global observation σ^o at local M_i-time t (below) with rectangles figuring global time approximation ($\varepsilon = 0.7$), the collected trace $\sigma_1(t) = (a,1)(c,2)(b,3)(b,5)(c,5.5)(a,7)(a,10)$ (middle), *i.e.*, observation of M_1 completed with some events received from M_2 and M_3, the projections observed locally by three monitors M_1, M_2, M_3 at t (bottom). Dashed lines represent information uncertainty, *e.g.*, M_1 ignores what happened after the last event received from each of the other monitors.

For M_i at M_i-local date t, consider the set

$$\{(j,t_j) \in [\![1;n]\!] \times \mathbb{R}_{\geq 0} \mid j \neq i \wedge \big(\mathsf{lastt}(\mathsf{p}_j(\sigma_i(t))) = t_j\big)\} \cup \{(i,t)\}$$

of pairs made of the index j of each monitor coupled with the timestamp of the last observation received from M_j by M_i. Let $(\mathsf{jtmin}_k)_{k\in[\![1;n]\!]} = (\mathsf{jmin}_k, \mathsf{tmin}_k)_{k\in[\![1;n]\!]}$ be the sequence obtained by ordering this set of pairs by ascending timestamp[6]. Initially, those timestamps are all 0, and any order may

---

[6] We should write $(\mathsf{jtmin}_k(t))_{k\in[\![1;n]\!]} = (\mathsf{jmin}_k(t), \mathsf{tmin}_k(t))_{k\in[\![1;n]\!]}$, *i.e.*, parametrize by t, but we will often forget t when clear from the context.

be chosen. Then, this sequence with its ordering can be easily maintained on-the-fly when new events are observed or received by M_i. Clearly, $(\mathsf{jmin}_1, \mathsf{tmin}_1)$ identifies the monitor M_j for which M_i is aware of the earliest timestamp (in its local time). In the absence of a skew, M_i would be sure to have complete information from all other monitors at time tmin_1, with jmin_1 being the monitor for which the last event known by M_i (if any) is the oldest. However, as time is approximated, and since verdicts should be given on global traces, knowing all events at local times up to tmin_1 only certifies that all events have been recorded for global time up to $\mathsf{tmin}_1 - \varepsilon$, as seen in Example 3. Notice that this also entails that the verdict can be given at t only if $t \geq \varepsilon$.

Example 3. In Fig. 1, for monitor M_1, $\mathsf{jmin}_1 = 2$ at time t. Yet, if the verdict was given with respect to observations after the last event from M_2, the last event from M_3, which happened before it but was marked with a later timestamp, would be missed. The verdict should thus restrict to the earliest possible global date for the last event of M_2, namely $\mathsf{tmin}_1 - \varepsilon$.

Conversely, we are sure that for all monitors, we collected some event with timestamp at least tmin_1. As local times are non-decreasing and communications are FIFO, no monitor can send a new observation with global time below $\mathsf{tmin}_1 - \varepsilon$. Thus, we know that all events of global time below $\mathsf{tmin}_1 - \varepsilon$ have already been collected by M_i. The set of possible traces of the system corresponding to that observation is $\nu(\sigma_i(t))_{|\mathsf{tmin}_1 - \varepsilon}$. This is the purpose of the first part of the following proposition. The second part claims that, indeed, the observation at $\mathsf{tmin}_1(t) - \varepsilon$ is in the set of "tubes" of possible observations of σ^g restricted to $\mathsf{tmin}_1(t) - \varepsilon$.

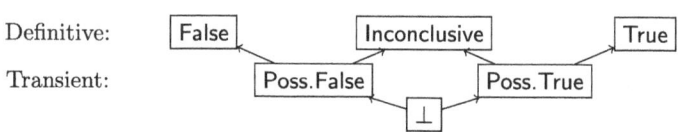

Fig. 2. Hasse diagram of the verdict preorder

Proposition 3. *For any monitor M_i, at any local time $t \geq \varepsilon$, $\sigma^g_{|\mathsf{tmin}_1(t)-\varepsilon}$ belongs to $[\![\nu(\sigma_i(t))_{|\mathsf{tmin}_1(t)-\varepsilon}]\!]$. Similarly, $\sigma_i(t)_{|\mathsf{tmin}_1(t)-\varepsilon}$ belongs to $[\![\nu(\sigma^g)_{|\mathsf{tmin}_1(t)-\varepsilon}]\!]$.*

3.2 Verdicts at $\mathsf{tmin}_1 - \varepsilon$

As demonstrated by Proposition 3, at global time $\mathsf{tmin}_1 - \varepsilon$ the global trace $\sigma^g_{|\mathsf{tmin}_1-\varepsilon}$ necessarily belongs to the language of traces compatible with the collected trace for M_i at local time t, restricted to $\mathsf{tmin}_1 - \varepsilon$. Consequently, this is a sufficient language to ensure safe monitoring, in the sense that a *definitive* verdict (True, False or Inconclusive) for this language built from a current observed trace cannot be changed by future observations.

To go a step further, we add *transient* verdicts to the definitive verdicts: Poss.True(resp. Poss.False) means that the property can not be falsified (resp. verified), although it is still possible to reach an Inconclusive verdict instead of a True (resp. False) one. The induced pre-order of verdicts $\lesssim$ is displayed in Fig. 2. The *verdict function* $V(t)$ then links at each date t the compatible traces $[\![\nu(\sigma_i(t))_{|\mathsf{tmin}_1(t)-\varepsilon}]\!]$ with the property specified by $\mathcal{A}_i$. Formally $V(t)$ is

- True when $[\![\nu(\sigma_i(t))_{|\mathsf{tmin}_1(t)-\varepsilon}]\!]$ is a good language prefix;
- False when $[\![\nu(\sigma_i(t))_{|\mathsf{tmin}_1(t)-\varepsilon}]\!]$ is a bad language prefix;
- Inconclusive when $[\![\nu(\sigma_i(t))_{|\mathsf{tmin}_1(t)-\varepsilon}]\!]$ intersects both languages $[\![\mathcal{A}_i, Inev(\mathcal{F}_i)]\!]$ and $[\![\mathcal{A}_i, Never(\mathcal{F}_i)]\!]$;
- Poss.True when $[\![\nu(\sigma_i(t))_{|\mathsf{tmin}_1(t)-\varepsilon}]\!]$ intersects $[\![\mathcal{A}_i, Inev(\mathcal{F}_i)]\!]$ but no higher verdict (True or Inconclusive) applies;
- Poss.False when $[\![\nu(\sigma_i(t))_{|\mathsf{tmin}_1(t)-\varepsilon}]\!]$ intersects $[\![\mathcal{A}_i, Never(\mathcal{F}_i)]\!]$ but no higher verdict (False or Inconclusive) applies;
- $\bot$ by default, if none of these conditions holds.

Because properties are specified by complete TAs, all traces and their continuations are traces of the TA, and since good/bad prefixes are closed under continuation, verdicts can only progress to higher verdicts in the above pre-order:

Lemma 4. *For a fixed monitor M_i with a property $(\mathcal{A}_i, \mathcal{F}_i)$, for any $t' > t$, we have $V(t) \lesssim V(t')$.*

In particular, *definitive* verdicts remain true eternally as soon as they hold. We say that σ is ε -*conclusive* when $\nu(\sigma)$ yields a definitive non-Inconclusive verdict (recall that $\nu(\sigma)$ depends on ε for the size of its intervals). Equivalently:

Definition 5. *For a fixed monitor M_i with a property $(\mathcal{A}_i, \mathcal{F}_i)$ and a skew ε, we say that a timed word σ is ε-conclusive when $[\![\nu(\sigma)]\!]$ is either a good or a bad language prefix.*

3.3 Data Structure

So far, we have defined verdicts with respect to the language $[\![\nu(\sigma_i(t))_{|\mathsf{tmin}_1(t)-\varepsilon}]\!]$. However, in order to incrementally compute verdicts when new observations arrive, it will be more adequate to manipulate sets of configurations reached after this language. The next proposition justifies the adequacy of this approach.

Proposition 6. *The verdict $V(t)$ at M_i-local date t can be computed by checking whether the set of configurations $(\ell_{init}, \mathbf{0}, 0)$ $\mathbf{after}_0^{\mathsf{tmin}_1(t)-\varepsilon}$ $[\![\nu(\sigma_i(t))_{|\mathsf{tmin}_1(t)-\varepsilon}]\!]$ intersects or is included in* $\mathrm{Inev}(\mathcal{F}_i)$ *or* $\mathrm{Never}(\mathcal{F}_i)$.

In the following, we proceed in steps to define the computation of the above set of configurations: first, we decompose the computation on *unordered* languages into computations on *ordered ones*, where permutations of events are fixed (Proposition 8). We encode them in a data structure R(t) that represents both the set of configurations reached after some trace in $[\![\nu(\sigma_i(t))_{|\text{tmin}_1(t)-\varepsilon}]\!]$, and the remaining events necessary for incremental computation. Then, we intersect the sets of configurations with the precise time of interest ($\text{tmin}_1 - \varepsilon$) to obtain the equality with the above set (Proposition 10). Finally, we show how to incrementally update the proposed data structure when new observations are collected.

Decomposition of $\{(\ell_{init}, \mathbf{0}, 0)\}$ *after* $[\![\nu(\sigma_i(t))_{|\text{tmin}_1(t)-\varepsilon}]\!]$. The separation of an unordered language into a union of ordered ones requires considering permutations of the restriction $\nu(\sigma_i(t))_{|\text{tmin}_1(t)-\varepsilon}$. For this, we define the *decomposition* of an ATW ν at some date T, as the set of all possible prefixes of $\nu_{|T}$ paired with the set of events that are yet to be accounted for, as this set will be necessary to incrementally update the data structure.

Definition 7. *The decomposition of $\nu \in$ ATW(Act) at global time T is*

$$\mathcal{D}(\nu, T) = \{(f(\nu_1); \nu_2) \mid \nu = \nu_1 \otimes \nu_2 \wedge \nu_1 \preceq_{[0,T]} \nu \wedge f \in \mathcal{F}(\nu_1)\}.$$

For a pair $(\nu_1; \nu_2)$ in $\mathcal{D}(\nu, T)$, ν_1 corresponds to a permutation of an element in $\nu_{|T}$, while ν_2 lists the remaining events that are not taken into account in ν_1. We can then use the decomposition to express the unordered language of a restriction as a union of ordered ones as follows.

Proposition 8. $[\![\nu_{|T}]\!] = \bigcup_{(\nu_1;\nu_2)\in\mathcal{D}(\nu,T)} [\![\nu_1 \cap [0,T]]\!]_{ord}$.

We are now ready to define our data structure R(t) (we should write $R_i(t)$ but the monitor is clear from the context), which encodes the configurations reached through each ν_1 in the decomposition, associated with its remainder ν_2:

Definition 9. *For a monitor M_i and a local time t, we define R(t), as*

$$R(t) = \{(\{(\ell_{init}, \mathbf{0}, 0)\} \text{ after } [\![\nu_1]\!]_{ord}; \nu_2) \mid (\nu_1; \nu_2) \in \mathcal{D}(\nu(\sigma_i(t)), \text{tmin}_1(t) - \varepsilon)\}.$$

The set R(t) represents a set of configurations in which the system can be after some sequence of events in $\nu(\sigma_i(t))_{|\text{tmin}_1(t)-\varepsilon}$. A restriction to dates before $\text{tmin}_1(t) - \varepsilon$ is still necessary (see the intersection with $[0, T]$ in Proposition 8). In order to add this constraint, we call *state of* R(t) the set of configurations $\text{state}(R(t)) = \bigcup_{(S,\nu_2)\in R(t)}\{(\ell, v, t) \in S \mid t = \text{tmin}_1(t) - \varepsilon\}$ and get the desired equality:

Proposition 10. $\text{state}(R(t)) = \{(\ell_{init}, \mathbf{0}, 0)\} \text{ after}_0^{\text{tmin}_1(t)-\varepsilon} [\![\nu(\sigma_i(t))_{|\text{tmin}_1(t)-\varepsilon}]\!]$.

Example 4. Let us consider the example from Fig. 1 with the collected trace at time $t = 10$ being $\sigma_i(t) = (a, 1)(c, 2)(b, 3)(b, 5)(c, 5.5)(a, 7)(a, 10)$ and the skew $\varepsilon = 0.7$. We have $\text{tmin}_1 - \varepsilon = 4.8$. We first have to consider the set C of all possible configurations reached by an interleaving of the first three observations $(a, 1)(c, 2)(b, 3)$. Then, we have to consider every case for the events $(b, 5)(c, 5.5)$ that can occur before or after $\text{tmin}_1 - \varepsilon$. R(10) is then composed of the following elements, for each $c \in C$:

- $(c; \nu((b,5)(c,5.5)(a,7)(a,10)))$, meaning that all events occur after time 4.8;
- $(c \text{ after } [\![(b, [4.3, 5.7])]\!]_{\text{ord}}; \nu((c, 5.5)(a, 7)(a, 10)))$, considering that the event b happened before time 4.8;
- $(c \text{ after } [\![(c, [4.8, 6.2])]\!]_{\text{ord}}; \nu((b, 5)(a, 7)(a, 10)))$, considering that c occured before time 4.8.
- the two elements $(c \text{ after } [\![(b, [4.3, 5.7])(c, [4.8, 6.2])]\!]_{\text{ord}}; \nu((a, 7)(a, 10)))$ and $(c \text{ after } [\![(c, [4.8, 6.2])(b, [4.3, 5.7])]\!]_{\text{ord}}; \nu((a, 7)(a, 10)))$ considering that both b and c occurred before time 4.8, thus both orderings should be considered.

Note that R(10) contains configurations that can only be reached if the collected events occur after $\text{tmin}_1 - \varepsilon$, but they do not appear in $\text{state}(\text{R}(10))$, since we only consider configurations that are reached at time $\text{tmin}_1 - \varepsilon$, meaning that the events leading to these configurations must have occurred before this time.

Updates of R. When time passes, new events may be collected. If they do not change tmin_1, the only updates to R is their addition to ν_2. If tmin_1 changes at $t' > t$ because of newly collected events ν', then the combination of $\text{R}(t)$ and ν' contains all the necessary information to update R, as each element of $\text{R}(t)$ encodes all of $\nu(\sigma_i(t))_{|\text{tmin}_1(t) - \varepsilon}$. Thus, updating the structure is only a matter of selecting, for each $(S, \nu_2) \in \text{R}(t)$, the possible sub-words of $\nu_2 \cdot \nu'$ to apply after S.

Proposition 11. *Let $t' \geq t$ and ν' be the sequence of events received in the interval $(t, t']$ (i.e., such that $\sigma_i(t') = \sigma_i(t) \otimes \nu'$), then*

$$\text{R}(t') = \{(S \text{ after } [\![\nu'_1]\!]_{\text{ord}}; \nu'_2) \mid (S; \nu_2) \in \text{R}(t), (\nu'_1, \nu'_2) \in \mathcal{D}(\nu_2 \otimes \nu', \text{tmin}_1(t') - \varepsilon)\}.$$

Intuitively, for each pair (S, ν_2) in $\text{R}(t)$, the extension of ν_2 with the newly collected events ν' is decomposed at $\text{tmin}_1(t') - \varepsilon$. For each possible element (ν'_1, ν'_2) in this decomposition, $\text{R}(t')$ builds the pair made of the set S after $[\![\nu'_1]\!]_{\text{ord}}$ associated with the remainder ν'_2. We call $next(\text{R}(t), t')$ the function that computes $\text{R}(t')$ at the time t' when $\text{tmin}_1(.)$ changes according to Proposition 11. We now have a data structure that can be used to compute the set of configurations needed to infer verdicts (Proposition 10) and can be updated incrementally based on the new collected observations and $\text{tmin}_1(\cdot) - \varepsilon$ (Proposition 11).

3.4 Monitoring at $\text{tmin}_1(.) - \varepsilon$

The previous discussions lead to the monitoring algorithm presented in Algorithm 1. It uses a triple of boolean values (I, N, C) encoding the intersection of $\text{state}(\text{R})$ respectively with $Inev(\mathcal{F}_i)$, $Never(\mathcal{F}_i)$ and the complement of their union. The algorithm starts with R being the initial state with no remaining events, the minimal time for monitoring $\text{tmin} = \varepsilon$, jtmin initially set to $(k, 0)_{k \in [\![1; n]\!]}$. Each new collected sequence of observations from a monitor M_j (recall that monitors group all events with same date in a unique message) is added to all continuations ν in R, and jtmin is updated. If tmin_1 has changed, tmin and R are updated (as discussed above). The update of (I, N, C) determines the verdict which is returned if definitive (a lazy evaluation of (I, N, C) optimizes the update, I and N being non-decreasing, while C is non-increasing). We do not detail here the communication of verdicts between monitors which could help anticipate their termination.

Algorithm 1: The monitor M_i's algorithm to monitor at $\text{tmin}_1(.) - \varepsilon$.

Init: $R = \{((\ell_{init}, \mathbf{0}, \mathbf{0}); [\,])\}$; $\text{tmin} = \varepsilon$; $\text{jtmin} = (k, 0)_{k \in [\![1;n]\!]}$; $\text{verdict}(i) := \bot$;
$(I, N, C) := ((\ell_{init}, \mathbf{0}, \mathbf{0}) \in Inev(\mathcal{F}_i), (\ell_{init}, \mathbf{0}, \mathbf{0}) \in Never(\mathcal{F}_i), \neg(I \vee N))$;

1 **while** $True$ **do**
2   **Receive** sequence $(a_1, t_a) \ldots (a_n, t_a)$ from monitor $M_j, j \in [\![1;n]\!]$;
3     $R := \{(S, \nu \otimes \nu((a_1, t_a) \ldots (a_n, t_a))) \mid (S, \nu) \in R\}$;
4   update jtmin ;
5   **if** $\text{tmin}_1 > \text{tmin}$ **then**
6         $\text{tmin} := \text{tmin}_1$;
7         $R := next(R, \text{tmin}_1 - \varepsilon)$;
8         $I := I \vee (\text{state}(R) \cap Inev(\mathcal{F}_i) \neq \emptyset)$;
9         $N := N \vee (\text{state}(R) \cap Never(\mathcal{F}_i) \neq \emptyset)$;
10        $C := C \wedge (\text{state}(R) \cap \overline{Inev(\mathcal{F}_i) \cup Never(\mathcal{F}_i)}) \neq \emptyset$;
11   **switch** (I, N, C) **do**
12   **case** $(1, 1, *)$ **do** return (verdict (i):=Inconclusive);
13   **case** $(1, 0, 0)$ **do** return (verdict (i):=True) ;
14   **case** $(0, 1, 0)$ **do** return (verdict (i):=False);
15   **case** $(1, 0, 1)$ **do** verdict (i):=Poss.True;
16   **case** $(0, 1, 1)$ **do** verdict (i):=Poss.False;

Proposition 12. *Algorithm 1 sets the verdict to $V(t)$.*

We can prove the following soundness and completeness of the monitoring algorithm. Notice that completeness is limited to 2ε-conclusive executions.

Theorem 13. *Monitoring at $\text{tmin}_1(.) - \varepsilon$ is sound and complete where, for any local monitor M_i and its property $(\mathcal{A}_i, \mathcal{F}_i)$:*

soundness *means that for any global trace $\sigma^g \in TT(\text{Act})$ produced at date $T \in \mathbb{R}_{\geq 0}$, if $\text{verdict}(i) = \text{True}$ at time T, then σ^g is a good prefix of $(\mathcal{A}_i, \mathcal{F}_i)$ (respectively, if $\text{verdict}(i) = \text{False}$ at time T, then σ^g is a bad prefix of $(\mathcal{A}_i, \mathcal{F}_i)$). Furthermore, if $\text{verdict}(i) = \text{Inconclusive}$, then neither σ^g nor its possible continuations are 2ε-conclusive on $(\mathcal{A}_i, \mathcal{F}_i)$.*
completeness *means that for any global trace $\sigma^g \in TT(\text{Act})$, if a prefix of σ^g is 2ε-conclusive and good (respectively, bad) on $(\mathcal{A}_i, \mathcal{F}_i)$ then there exists some date $T \in \mathbb{R}_{\geq 0}$ such that $\text{verdict}(i) = \text{True}$ (respectively, $\text{verdict}(i) = \text{False}$).*

4 Conclusion

This paper presents a distributed approach to monitor properties specified as deterministic timed automata when faced with approximation on events dates. The approach relies on the identification of the point in time at which sufficient information has been gathered by the local monitor to compute a verdict and the incremental computation of the set of states of the property compatible with the collected observation at this point in time This requires the careful account of potential permutations of events emanating from distant components.

This method allows to apply monitoring on complex systems that are *distributed* in space and whose behaviours *depend strongly on time*, further increasing the reach of this popular runtime verification method. It is interesting to notice the timely nature of this contribution, as the interest for distributed systems is developing not only in verification (see related works) but also in model learning ([22,24] discrete time), which could soon allow to automatically generate models of systems and specifications, allowing—at longer term—for fully black-box distributed tools requiring no expert knowledge.

While we ensured the soundness and completeness of our algorithm, its efficiency still needs to be experimented. Future works should include the implementation and test of this algorithm against realistic models and properties. This implementation could be then compared to the one presented in [27] that allows decentralized monitoring of regular timed expressions (but without clock skew), which can be generated from a timed automaton. Additionally, our algorithm could be extended in several ways. First, with additional hypotheses (*e.g.*, maximal throughput of components), we could issue verdicts earlier by anticipating the occurrence of events. This would require an extension of the structure R, adding a level of uncertainty. The balance between the gain of anticipation and the cost of updating this structure would certainly be an issue and requires experimental tuning. Using similar techniques, we believe we can handle properties defined by non-deterministic timed automata, at least for one-clock automata [19]. Finally, we can also try to reduce the communication overhead. Indeed, we assumed that all the local observations are forwarded to every other monitor, which can be improved in several ways, depending on the system topology.

Acknowledgements. This work was partially supported by the EPSRC Standard Grant CLeVer (EP/S028641/1).

References

1. Alur, R., Dill, D.L.: A theory of timed automata. Theor. Comput. Sci. **126**(2), 183–235 (1994)
2. Asarin, E., Caspi, P., Maler, O.: Timed regular expressions. J. ACM **49**(2), 172–206 (2002)
3. Baier, C., Katoen, J.P.: Principles of Model-Checking. MIT Press, Cambridge, May 2008

4. Bartocci, E., Falcone, Y. (eds.): Lectures on Runtime Verification. LNCS, vol. 10457. Springer, Cham (2018). https://doi.org/10.1007/978-3-319-75632-5
5. Basin, D., Klaedtke, F., Zălinescu, E.: Runtime verification over out-of-order streams. ACM Trans. Comput. Log. **21**(1), 1–43 (2019)
6. Bauer, A., Leucker, M., Schallhart, C.: Runtime verification for LTL and TLTL. ACM Trans. Softw. Eng. Methodol. **20**(4), 14:1–14:64 (2011)
7. Bauer, A., Falcone, Y.: Decentralised LTL monitoring. In: Giannakopoulou, D., Méry, D. (eds.) FM 2012. LNCS, vol. 7436, pp. 85–100. Springer, Heidelberg (2012). https://doi.org/10.1007/978-3-642-32759-9_10
8. Bengtsson, J., Yi, W.: Timed automata: semantics, algorithms and tools. In: Desel, J., Reisig, W., Rozenberg, G. (eds.) ACPN 2003. LNCS, vol. 3098, pp. 87–124. Springer, Heidelberg (2004). https://doi.org/10.1007/978-3-540-27755-2_3
9. Bouyer, P., Henry, L., Jaziri, S., Jéron, T., Markey, N.: Diagnosing timed automata using timed markings. Int. J. Softw. Tools Technol. Transf. **23**(2), 229–253 (2021)
10. Clarke, E.M., Henzinger, T.A., Veith, H., Bloem, R. (eds.): Handbook of Model Checking. Springer-Verlag, Cham (2018). https://doi.org/10.1007/978-3-319-10575-8
11. Colombo, C., Falcone, Y.: Organising LTL monitors over distributed systems with a global clock. Form. Methods Syst. Des. **49**(1–2), 109–158 (2016)
12. El-Hokayem, A., Falcone, Y.: On the monitoring of decentralized specifications: semantics, properties, analysis, and simulation. ACM Trans. Softw. Eng. Methodol. **29**(1), 1:1–1:57 (2020)
13. Falcone, Y.: On decentralized monitoring. In: Nouri, A., Wu, W., Barkaoui, K., Li, Z.W. (eds.) VECoS 2021. LNCS, vol. 13187, pp. 1–16. Springer, Cham (2022). https://doi.org/10.1007/978-3-030-98850-0_1
14. Falcone, Y., Cornebize, T., Fernandez, J.-C.: Efficient and generalized decentralized monitoring of regular languages. In: Ábrahám, E., Palamidessi, C. (eds.) FORTE 2014. LNCS, vol. 8461, pp. 66–83. Springer, Heidelberg (2014). https://doi.org/10.1007/978-3-662-43613-4_5
15. Filliâtre, J.-C.: Deductive software verification. Int. J. Softw. Tools Technol. Transf. **13**(5), 397–403 (2011)
16. Francalanza, A., Pérez, J.A., Sánchez, C.: Runtime verification for decentralised and distributed systems. In: Bartocci, E., Falcone, Y. (eds.) Lectures on Runtime Verification. LNCS, vol. 10457, pp. 176–210. Springer, Cham (2018). https://doi.org/10.1007/978-3-319-75632-5_6
17. Gallay, F., Falcone, Y.: Decentralized LTL enforcement. In: Ganty, P., Bresolin, D. (eds.), Proceedings 12th International Symposium on Games, Automata, Logics, and Formal Verification, GandALF 2021, Padua, Italy, 20–22 September 2021, volume 346 of EPTCS, pp. 135–151 (2021)
18. Ganguly, R., et al.: Distributed runtime verification of metric temporal properties. J. Parallel Distrib. Comput. **185**, 104801 (2024)
19. Grez, A., Mazowiecki, F., Pilipczuk, M., Puppis, G., Riveros, C.: The monitoring problem for timed automata. *CoRR*, abs/2002.07049, 2020
20. Hoare, C.A.R.: An axiomatic basis for computer programming. Commun. ACM **12**(10), 576–580 (1969)
21. Kohl, M.A., Hermanns, H.: Model-based diagnosis of real-time systems: robustness against varying latency, clock drift, and out-of-order observations. ACM Trans. Embed. Comput. Syst. **22**(4), 68:1–68:48 (2023)
22. Labbaf, F., Groote, J.F., Hojjat, H., Mousavi, M.R.: Compositional learning for interleaving parallel automata. In: Kupferman, O., Sobocinski, P. (eds.) Foundations of Software Science and Computation Structures. FoSSaCS 2023. LNCS, vol.

13992, pp. 413–435. Springer, Cham (2023). https://doi.org/10.1007/978-3-031-30829-1_20
23. Leucker, M., Schallart, C.: A brief account of runtime verification. J. Log. Algebr. Program. **78**(5), 293–303 (2009)
24. Neele, T., Sammartino, M.: Compositional automata learning of synchronous systems. In: Lambers, L., Uchitel, S. (eds.) Fundamental Approaches to Software Engineering. FASE 2023. LNCS, vol. 13991, pp. 47–66. Springer, Cham (2023). https://doi.org/10.1007/978-3-031-30826-0_3
25. Nickovic, D., Maler, O.: AMT: a property-based monitoring tool for analog systems. In: Raskin, J.-F., Thiagarajan, P.S. (eds.) FORMATS 2007. LNCS, vol. 4763, pp. 304–319. Springer, Heidelberg (2007). https://doi.org/10.1007/978-3-540-75454-1_22
26. Pinisetty, S., Jéron, T., Tripakis, S., Falcone, Y., Marchand, H., Preoteasa, V.: Predictive runtime verification of timed properties. J. Syst. Softw. **132**, 353–365 (2017)
27. Roussanaly, V., Falcone, Y.: Decentralised runtime verification of timed regular expressions. In: Artikis, A., Posenato, R., Tonetta, S. (eds.), 29th International Symposium on Temporal Representation and Reasoning, TIME 2022, 7–9 November 2022, Virtual Conference, volume 247 of *LIPIcs*, pp. 6:1–6:18. Schloss Dagstuhl - Leibniz-Zentrum für Informatik, 2022
28. Thati, P., Rosu, G.: Monitoring algorithms for metric temporal logic specifications. Electron. Notes Theor. Comput. Sci. **113**, 145–162 (2005)
29. Ulus, D.: MONTRE: a tool for monitoring timed regular expressions. In: Majumdar, R., Kunčak, V. (eds.) CAV 2017. LNCS, vol. 10426, pp. 329–335. Springer, Cham (2017). https://doi.org/10.1007/978-3-319-63387-9_16
30. Wang, Y., Yoo, T.-S., Lafortune, S.: Diagnosis of discrete event systems using decentralized architectures. Discret. Event Dyn. Syst. **17**(2), 233–263 (2007)
31. Yin, X., Lafortune, S.: Codiagnosability and coobservability under dynamic observations: transformation and verification. Autom. **61**, 241–252 (2015)

Towards Efficient Runtime Verified Linearizable Algorithms

Gilde Valeria Rodríguez[1]([✉]) [iD] and Armando Castañeda[2] [iD]

[1] Posgrado en Ciencia e Ingeniería de la Computación, Universidad Nacional Autónoma de México, Mexico City, Mexico
`gildevroji@gmail.com`
[2] Instituto de Matemáticas, Universidad Nacional Autónoma de México, Mexico City, Mexico
`armando.castaneda@im.unam.mx`

Abstract. An asynchronous, fault-tolerant, sound and complete algorithm for runtime verification of linearizability of concurrent algorithms was proposed in [7]. This solution relies on the snapshot abstraction in distributed computing. The fastest known snapshot algorithms use complex constructions, hard to implement, and the simplest ones provide large step complexity bounds or only weak termination guarantees. Thus, the snapshot-based verification algorithm is not completely satisfactory. In this paper, we propose an alternative solution, based on the collect abstraction, which can be optimally implemented in a simple manner. As a final result, we offer a simple and generic methodology that takes any presumably linearizable algorithm and produces a lightweight runtime verified linearizable version of it.

Keywords: Asynchronous concurrent algorithms · Distributed runtime verification · Fault-tolerance · Linearizability

1 Introduction

Context. Runtime verification techniques for *concurrent shared-memory algorithms* have been mostly focused on low-level properties such as data races or deadlocks (see [2,13,17,25]). Techniques for high-level properties, e.g., *linearizability* [21] and *sequential consistency* [24], are still underdeveloped. Except for [7], the proposed solutions for high-level properties [5,10,11,14,15] are incomplete, fault-free or partially-synchronous (see the related work section below).

A model has recently been proposed [7], for the theoretical study of runtime verification of high-level properties of concurrent algorithms, where a *verifier* $\mathcal{V}$ interacts with an algorithm $\mathcal{A}$ under inspection, with the aim of detecting if the responses of $\mathcal{A}$ are correct. The model assumes processes are *asynchronous* and *crash-prone*, and $\mathcal{A}$ is a *black-box*. These conditions impose a challenging setting [6] where the *communication interface* (which captures the current execution of $\mathcal{A}$) and the *monitoring system* (which tests if the captured execution is correct) need to be *asynchronous*, *fault-tolerant* and *decoupled* from $\mathcal{A}$.

© The Author(s), under exclusive license to Springer Nature Switzerland AG 2025
E. Ábrahám and H. Abbas (Eds.): RV 2024, LNCS 15191, pp. 262–281, 2025.
https://doi.org/10.1007/978-3-031-74234-7_17

Runtime Verification of Linearizability. Unsurprisingly, to some extent, a simple indistinguishability argument shows that linearizability, the gold standard for correctness of concurrent implementations, is impossible to runtime verify [7]. Namely, for common objects such as pool, queue, stack and even consensus, there is no verifier that is *sound* and *complete*.

The main result in [7], however, is that any *presumably* linearizable algorithm $\mathcal{A}$ can be transformed into an algorithm $\mathcal{A}^*$ "wrapping" $\mathcal{A}$ such that $\mathcal{A}^*$ is linearizable if and only if $\mathcal{A}$ is linearizable. In $\mathcal{A}^*$, outputs to operations are obtained through $\mathcal{A}$, and additional code produces information that "sketches" the current execution (of $\mathcal{A}^*$). The execution's sketches allows the existence of a sound and complete verifier $\mathcal{V}^*$ that runtime verifies linearizability of $\mathcal{A}^*$ (hence indirectly verifying $\mathcal{A}$) such that if a process reports ERROR, it is able to provide a *witness* supporting its claim, namely, a non-linearizable execution of $\mathcal{A}^*$.

It turns out that from $\mathcal{A}^*$ and $\mathcal{V}^*$, and from known algorithms [3,34], a lightweight *runtime verified* implementation $\mathcal{B}^*$ can be obtained, where processes are split into two groups, *producers* and *verifiers*. Producers are in charge of producing responses to operations' invocations, using $\mathcal{A}$ (the implementation wrapped by $\mathcal{A}^*$) and executing a constant number of additional instructions to record the sketch of the current execution. The verifiers are in charge of verifying if the recorded execution is correct, reporting ERROR if necessary. In this way, discarding the verification tasks, the step complexity of $\mathcal{B}^*$ is the same as $\mathcal{A}$ plus a constant additive factor.

Limitations of $\mathcal{A}^*$, $\mathcal{V}^*$ and $\mathcal{B}^*$. The key building block in the solution proposed in [7] is the *snapshot* abstraction [1], which allows a process to *atomically* read all entries of a shared array. This seemingly simple operation has been extensively studied in the distributed computing literature, and has proven to be extremely useful in the design of concurrent algorithms (being [7] yet one more example of this fact). Although there are snapshot algorithms with good theoretical step complexity bounds, it is not clear that these algorithms perform well in practical settings. Furthermore, the fastest known algorithms (e.g. [22]) are based on clever but complex constructions, and the simplest algorithms have large step complexity or only provide weak termination guarantees [1]. Critical for deriving $\mathcal{B}^*$ are the *decoupled* snapshot algorithms [3,34], which provide good theoretical step complexity bounds, but are based on complex constructions too. Thus, despite the strong properties of $\mathcal{A}^*$, $\mathcal{V}^*$ and $\mathcal{B}^*$, they are not completely satisfactory in the context of runtime verification, as one of the main targets in this context is to have commutation interfaces and monitoring systems as simple and efficient as possible, ideally not interfering with the system under inspection (e.g. [2,4,8,32]). This is the issue we study in this paper.

Contributions. We search for more efficient and simpler solutions than those proposed in [7], with the hope that they turn into runtime verified solutions with good performance in practical settings.

In a nutshell, we propose a new wrapper $\mathcal{A}^+$ and verifier $\mathcal{V}^+$ for linearizability, based on the *collect* abstraction, which allows a process to *non-atomically* read all entries of a shared array. Being non-atomic, collect provides strictly weaker guarantees than snapshot. A benefit of collect, however, is that optimal implementations are extremely simple. Simplicity of $\mathcal{A}^+$ and $\mathcal{V}^+$ comes with a price: the analysis of them is considerably more difficult than that of $\mathcal{A}^*$ and $\mathcal{V}^*$. The main challenge is capturing the current execution of $\mathcal{A}^+$ and verifying it in $\mathcal{V}^+$, relying only in the weak properties of collect. That this is possible it is not obvious at all, and the related analysis is the main technical contribution of the paper. Furthermore, using a novel, simple and efficient *decoupled* collect implementation that we propose here, we are able to obtain from $\mathcal{A}^+$ and $\mathcal{V}^+$ a lightweight runtime verified algorithm $\mathcal{B}^+$, simpler than $\mathcal{B}^*$, whose additive factor is very low, equal to *five*.

Due to space constraints, all proofs and complementary discussions will appear in the journal version of the paper.

Related Work. Distributed runtime verification of fault-tolerant distributed systems is considered and emergent and important topic, that poses several challenges that are yet to be solved (see [6,9,12,16,26,31]). As far as we know, besides [7], there is no distributed runtime verification algorithm (for any high-level property) that is fully asynchronous and fault-tolerant.

The definition of the runtime verification problem in [7] is based on Pnueli's approach [29]. The interactive model in that work provides a clean framework where the discrepancies between the actual execution of the algorithm under inspection and the detected execution in the verifier can be analyzed. It is a common topic in the runtime verification literature that, for several reasons, the detected execution may be imprecise or even incomplete (see survey [33]). The results in [7] hold for a generalization of linearizability. Here, for clarity, we focus on linearizability, but our results can be extended to that generalization as well.

Runtime verification of linearizability has been studied in [10,11], in asynchronous failure-free shared memory models with centralized monitoring systems. Specific code is added to a *white-box* algorithm in order to record the execution in a *log* (a sequence of events) that later is verified by a single process. Hence the runtime verification algorithm is neither fully distributed nor fault-tolerant. Events must be *atomically* recorded in the log, which necessarily requires consensus or the use of locks [20,28,30]. High-level operations are divided in *mutators* and *observers*. For mutators, the user has to add code that records its linearization point, and for observers, invocations and responses are recorded separately. It is known that there are linearizable implementations whose linearization points are *not fixed* [27], thus the approach in [10,11] is not complete. Also, it is not explained in [10,11] the relation between the actual execution of the algorithm under inspection and the execution recorded in the log.

A series of works [5,14,15] propose runtime verification solutions for *task solvability* [19]. These works consider a shared memory system that solves a series of tasks, and the aim is to runtime verify that the outputs for each task are correct, i.e. they satisfy the inputs/outputs relation specifying the task. To do so, an asynchronous fault-tolerant shared memory algorithm runs every time a task in the series is solved, and it is assumed that the verification algorithm terminates before the processes solve the next task. Thus, the proposed solution is distributed and fault-tolerant but it is *not* fully asynchronous. Another main difference with [5,14,15] is that the solutions proposed here, and in [7], can detect validity violations in a finer way, as real-time relations of the actual execution are taken into account, whereas in [5,14,15] only input-output pairs are used in the verification algorithm. For example, by observing only input-output pairs, for consensus it is impossible to detect when a process ran solo and decided a value distinct from its input, which violates validity. That scenario, in contrast, can be detected by our verifier through the views mechanism.

2 Preliminaries

Implementations and Executions. We consider a standard concurrent shared memory system (e.g. [21]) with $n \geq 2$ *asynchronous* processes, $p_1, \ldots, p_n$, which may *crash* at any time in any execution, except for at least one. The *index* of process p_i is i. Processes communicate by invoking *atomic* operations on the locations of the shared memory, such a simple *read/write*, or more powerful operations such as *Compare&Set* or *Fetch&Add*. Shared base objects are denoted with uppercase letters ($\mathcal{O}$); local variables used by a process for performing local computations are denoted with lowercase letter subscripted with the index of the process (local variables op_i and $resp_i$ by process p_i).

An *implementation* of a sequential object $\mathcal{O}$ (e.g. a queue) is a *distributed algorithm* $\mathcal{A}$ consisting of n local state machines, $A_1, \ldots, A_n$. Each A_i specifies the shared memory operations and local computations p_i executes to respond its invocations to a high-level operations of $\mathcal{O}$ (from now on simply called operations). Each of these base objects operations and local computations is a *step*. Below we use the terms implementation and algorithm interchangeably.

An *execution* of an implementation $\mathcal{A}$ is a possibly infinite sequence of steps as specified by $\mathcal{A}$, plus invocations and responses to operations, satisfying the usual *well-formedness* properties [21] (i.e., each process starts a new operation only if its previous operation has a matching response). *Correct* processes and *complete* and *pending* operations in an execution are defined in the usual way, as well as the *step complexity* of an implementation.

Linearizability. For an execution E of $\mathcal{A}$, $E|p_i$ denotes the sequence of invocations and responses of p_i in E. Executions E and F are *equivalent* if $\forall p_i$, $E|p_i = F|p_i$. For operations op and op' of E, op *precedes* op', denoted $op \prec_E op'$, if and only if the response of op appears before the invocation of op'. The operations are *concurrent*, denoted $op \,||_E\, op'$, if neither $op \prec_E op'$ nor $op' \prec_E op$.

A finite execution E of $\mathcal{A}$ is *linearizable* [21] if it is possible to obtain an execution F by appending responses to some pending operations of E, and by removing the remaining pending operations, such that there exists a sequential execution S of $\mathcal{O}$ with F and S being equivalent and $\prec_F \,\subseteq\, \prec_S$. We say that $\mathcal{A}$ is *linearizable* if each of its finite executions are linearizable. We let the predicate $\mathsf{LIN}(E)$ to be true if and only if E is linearizable.

An execution F is *quasi-equivalent* to an execution E if for each p_i, $E|p_i = F|p_i \cdot x$, where x is the empty string or a single response. Thus, if E and F are equivalent, one is quasi-equivalent to the other, but not necessarily vice versa.

Lemma 1 (Quasi-equivalence and linearizability). *Let E be any linearizable execution and F be any execution that is quasi-equivalent to E such that $\prec_F \subseteq \prec_E$. Then, F is linearizable.*

Progress Conditions. $\mathcal{A}$ is *wait-free* if in every infinite execution, every correct process completes infinitely many operations [18], and it is *lock-free* if in every infinite execution, infinitely many operations are complete [21]. The notions of wait-freedom and lock-freedom naturally extend to specific operations or fragments of pseudocode.

The Collect Object. The *collect* object [23] is a useful abstraction frequently used in shared memory algorithms. It can be seen as a shared array with n entries. Each process p_i can write v in the i-th entry using the $write(i, v)$ operation; the processes can read the whole memory using the $collect()$ operation, which is *not atomic* (hence the object cannot be specified by a sequential object) and hence for each entry it returns either the last written value in it or one of the values of the writes in that entry that are concurrent with the collect. Thus, an invocation to $collect()$ spans an *interval of time*, representing the time it needs to collect the values in the entries of the shared array.

The collect object can be easily and optimally wait-free implemented using a shared array M. When p_i invokes $write(i, v)$, it writes v in $M[i]$, and when it invokes $collect()$ it reads one by one, in some arbitrary order, the entries of M and returns the vector of values it obtains. We consider a collect implementation in Algorithms 2 and 5.

3 An Interactive Model for Runtime Verification

In this section, we introduce the model and settings used throughout the rest of the paper, which also recalls some of the main contributions of [7]. We proposed an interactive model for asynchronous wait-free runtime verification of correctness properties of implementations. In it, an algorithm $\mathcal{A}$ that is *presumably* linearizable with respect to $\mathcal{O}$ *interacts* with a *verifier* $\mathcal{V}$, which is nothing else than a wait-free algorithm as guarantees that every call finishes its execution in a finite number of steps.

Algorithm 1 contains the generic structure of a wait-free verifier, tailored for linearizability (with respect to $\mathcal{O}$) in Line 8. The verifier *conceptually* receives as input the algorithm $\mathcal{A}$ it seeks to verify. Wlog, it assumes that $\mathcal{A}$ provides a single operation, $Apply(op)$, whose input op is a description of the actual operation is invoked and its inputs. For simplicity, it is assumed data-independence between each operation description op.[1] The processes in $\mathcal{V}$ interact with $\mathcal{A}$ by invoking, infinitely often and *at asynchronous times*, non-deterministically chosen operations of $\mathcal{A}$ (Lines 1, 4 and 5). The processes exchange information using the shared memory M (Lines 3, 6 and 7) in order for them to decide whether the current execution so far is linearizable with respect to $\mathcal{O}$ (Line 8) and, if not

---

[1] We can eliminate this assumption; we assume it to simplify the algorithm.

report ERROR together with the execution that *witnesses* their claim (Line 9), and the interaction continues.

Algorithm 1. Generic structure of a verifier $\mathcal{V}$. Generic code for process p_i.

Shared Variables:
    Shared memory M
Operation Verify($\mathcal{A}$) **is**
1: **while** true **do**
2:     $op_i \leftarrow$ non-deterministically chosen high-level operation
3:     Code to announce in M the invocation to Apply(op_i) of $\mathcal{A}$
4:     Invoke operation Apply(op_i) of $\mathcal{A}$
5:     $resp_i \leftarrow$ response from operation Apply(op_i) of $\mathcal{A}$
6:     Code to announce in M the response $resp_i$
7:     $exec_i \leftarrow$ Code that obtains from M the execution so far of $\mathcal{A}$
8:     **if** $\neg \mathsf{LIN}(exec_i)$ **then**
9:         report (ERROR, $exec_i$)
end Verify

The model makes the following assumptions:

1) Lines 3, 6 and 7 are wait-free, which discards the use of locks. The aim of this assumption for the verifier is to "preserve" the progress properties of $\mathcal{A}$ (if locks were allowed, the resulting system that integrates $\mathcal{A}$ and $\mathcal{V}$ loses the progress properties of $\mathcal{A}$, i.e., lock-freedom or wait-freedom).
2) Being designed for studying the distributed issues related to the task of distributed runtime verification (i.e., the discrepancies between the actual execution, and the execution each process detects in $\mathcal{V}$), it assumes every process is able to locally test if a finite execution is linearizable (Line 8), and the cost of these local computations is neglected.
3) $\mathcal{A}$ is a black-box, namely, its specification is unaccessible. Thus, in any execution (interaction) with $\mathcal{A}$, the execution of $\mathcal{A}$ only contains invocation and responses, and no the internal computations of it. Furthermore, $\mathcal{A}$ being a black-box implies that no verifier can be specifically designed for $\mathcal{A}$, it should properly work for any possible linearizable implementation $\mathcal{A}' \neq \mathcal{A}$.
4) No crash failures occur and hence all executions (interactions) of a verifier can be infinite. This assumption does not prevent $\mathcal{V}$ for being crash-tolerant as the system is asynchronous and linearizability is tested at finite times.

Thus, the challenge is to design wait-free code for Lines 4, 6 and 7 such that the processes are able detect the current execution of $\mathcal{A}$, which then each process can locally test for linearizability.

For common sequential objects such as queue, stack and consensus, there is no wait-free verifier that is sound and complete [7], namely, it is not true that processes report ERROR if and only if the current execution of $\mathcal{A}$ is not linearizable.

However, it is possible to "wrap" *any* $\mathcal{A}$ in an algorithm $\mathcal{A}^*$ that outputs responses to operations, together with information of its current execution, a "sketch" of it, such that the following stronger problem is solvable. In this version, if the current execution of $\mathcal{A}^*$ is linearizable, the processes in $\mathcal{V}$ are allowed to report ERROR if they "discover" a non-linearizable execution of $\mathcal{A}^*$. Below, for every execution E of a verifier with input $\mathcal{A}^*$, $E|\mathcal{A}^*$ denotes the sequence of invocation and responses of $\mathcal{A}^*$. This is the execution of $\mathcal{A}^*$ in E. The algorithm $\mathcal{A}^*$ [7] is equivalent to the Algorithm 2, only differs in Line 5; a snapshot operation is executed in $\mathcal{A}^*$[2].

Definition 1 (Strong Distributed Runtime Verification). *A wait-free verifier $\mathcal{V}_{\mathcal{O}}$ distributed runtime verifies linearizability of an object $\mathcal{O}$ if, in every infinite execution E of $\mathcal{V}_{\mathcal{O}}$ with an arbitrary input algorithm $\mathcal{A}^*$, the following conditions are satisfied:*

⋄ *Strong soundness: If for every finite prefix E' of E, then $\mathsf{LIN}(E'|\mathcal{A}^*)$, either no process reports ERROR or a process reports ERROR together with a witness.*

⋄ *Completeness. If E has a finite prefix E' such that $\neg\mathsf{LIN}(E'|\mathcal{A}^*)$, at least one process reports ERROR together with a witness.*

Linearizability of $\mathcal{O}$ is distributed runtime verifiable if there is a wait-free verifier that distributed runtime verifies linearizability of $\mathcal{O}$.

In the sequel we show a new wrapper $\mathcal{A}^+$, simpler and more efficient than $\mathcal{A}^*$, such that the problem of strong distributed runtime verification is solvable for any sequential object $\mathcal{O}$. Simplicity and efficiency of $\mathcal{A}^+$, however, comes with a more complex analysis.

4 The Wrapper $\mathcal{A}^+$

Let $\mathcal{A}$ be any implementation of object an $\mathcal{O}$ that is presumably linearizable. Our aim is to produce (in a systematic manner) a new implementation $\mathcal{A}^+$ from $\mathcal{A}$. The produced implementation outputs information about its current execution, additionally to response operations that are obtained through $\mathcal{A}$. As we will see, this additional information is not accurate, it only "sketches" the current execution, however, such sketches are good enough to runtime verify $\mathcal{A}^+$.

Algorithm 2. The wrapper $\mathcal{A}^+$. Pseudocode of process p_i.

Shared Variables:
  N = Wait-free collect object with each entry initialized to $\emptyset$
Local Persistent Variable:
  $uset_i$ = an unbounded set initialized to $\emptyset$
Operation Apply(op_i) **is**
1: $uset_i \leftarrow uset_i \cup \{(p_i, op_i)\}$
2: N.write($i, uset_i$)
3: Invoke operation Apply(op_i) of $\mathcal{A}$
4: $y_i \leftarrow$ response from operation Apply(op_i) of $\mathcal{A}$
5: $c_i \leftarrow N$.collect()
6: $\lambda_i \leftarrow \bigcup_{k \in \{1,2,\ldots,n\}} c_i[k]$
7: **return** (y_i, λ_i)
   end Apply

---

[2] $\mathcal{A}^*$ can invoke any high-level operation of $\mathcal{A}$, denoted as Apply(op_i) [7].

The implementation $\mathcal{A}^+$ is presented in Algorithm 2. As anticipated, the processes use $\mathcal{A}$ to obtain responses to operations (Lines 3 and 4). In order to produce a sketch of the current execution (of $\mathcal{A}^+$), each process p_i first announces its next operation in its corresponding entry of N (Lines 1 and 2), then collects the sets in N (Line 5) and finally returns the response y_i and the union λ_i of all collected sets (Lines 6 and 7). The set λ_i, with pairs (p_j, op_j), is the *view* of operation (p_i, op_i). Intuitively, the view of (p_i, op_i) is the (unordered) set of operations, complete and pending, that p_i is aware of while executing op_i.

In any execution of $\mathcal{A}^+$, every operation has an "inner" operation that corresponds to the invocation and to the response from $\mathcal{A}$. In the sequel, for any execution E of $\mathcal{A}^+$, we let $E|\mathcal{A}$ denote the subsequence with the invocation and responses of $\mathcal{A}$. This is the execution of $\mathcal{A}$ in E.

$\mathcal{A}^+$ assumes entries of N can store sets of unbounded size. This unrealistic assumption can be eliminated with linked lists: each p_i stores in the shared memory a double linked list that only p_i can modify but anyone can read. In this way, in Line 2, p_i writes in N a pointer to its most recent cell in its list.

Analyzing $\mathcal{A}^+$. Due to the optimal collect implementation in Sect. 2:

Lemma 2 (Step complexity of $\mathcal{A}^+$). *In $\mathcal{A}^+$, every operation op takes the number of steps $\mathcal{A}$ takes for the same operation plus n reads and 1 write.*

$\mathcal{A}^+$ preserves the progress and correctness properties of $\mathcal{A}$. While progress is due to the fact that N is wait-free, linearizability follows from Lemma 1 and the fact that any execution E of $\mathcal{A}^+$ is quasi-equivalent to $E|\mathcal{A}$ and $\prec_E \subseteq \prec_{E|\mathcal{A}}$.

Lemma 3 (Progress and correctness of $\mathcal{A}^+$). *$\mathcal{A}^+$ is wait-free (resp. lock-free) if and only if $\mathcal{A}$ is wait-free (resp. lock-free). Moreover, $\mathcal{A}^+$ is linearizable (disregarding views) if and only if $\mathcal{A}$ is linearizable.*

We now identify a subset of the executions of $\mathcal{A}^+$ such that if it were possible to detect at runtime such executions, one can runtime verify linearizability.

Tight Executions. Consider an operation op_i of p_i in an execution E of $\mathcal{A}^+$. Its collect in Line 5 Algorithm 2 is made of a sequence of at most n reads (it could be $< n$ if op_i is pending). Let e be any of these reads, and $N[j]$ be the entry it reads. We say that e is *fresh* if either e reads a set $\neq \emptyset$ and op_i is the first operation of p_i, or the set e reads from $N[j]$ is distinct from the set the previous operation of p_i reads from $N[j]$ (in the operation's collect). The *latest* fresh read (of op_i) is the fresh read that appears latest in E, and the *tail* of the collect are the reads that follow the latest fresh read. Intuitively, the latest fresh read is the latest step where op_i "discovers" fresh information of the ongoing execution. The latest fresh read of an operation is well-defined as p_i inserts (p_i, op_i) in $N[i]$ before collecting.

An execution T of $\mathcal{A}^+$ is *tight* if for every operation: 1) if pending, it has its write in Line 2 but no read step of its collect in Line 5 and the pair written in Line 2 appears in the collect of a complete operation; 2) its invocation and steps in Line 1 appear all right before its write; 3) if complete, the tail of its collect (if any) and its response *appear all right*[3] after its latest fresh read.

In other words, in a tight execution, the beginning and end of a complete operation correspond to its write and its latest fresh read.

It turns out that any execution E of $\mathcal{A}^+$ can be modified to obtain its *associated* tight execution $T(E)$: 1) remove every pending operation with no write in Line 2 or whose pair written in Line 2 does not appear in the collect of a complete operation; 2) for every operation with a pending collect (i.e. with $< n$ reads), remove all these reads; then, for every remaining operation: 3) move forward, right before its write step, its invocation and its local steps in Line 1; 4) move backward, right before its latest fresh read, the tail of its collect (if any); and if the operation is complete, move backward the local steps in Line 6 and its response, otherwise insert at that place the corresponding local steps in Line 6 and response. Intuitively, $T(E)$ represents the execution the processes perceive through their views in E.

Figure 1 depicts a 3-process execution E of $\mathcal{A}^+$ and its associated tight execution $T(E)$. The latest fresh read of op_a is r_2, as it reads from $N[2]$ the set containing the pair written by p_2 in op_b and r_3 reads $\emptyset$ from $N[3]$. Thus, in $T(E)$, op_a spans the interval that goes from its write to r_2. Note that op_{a+1} is not in $T(E)$ as its pair written in Line 2 does not appear in the collect of a complete operation. Also note that op_b and op_c are concurrent in E, but op_b precedes op_c in $T(E)$.

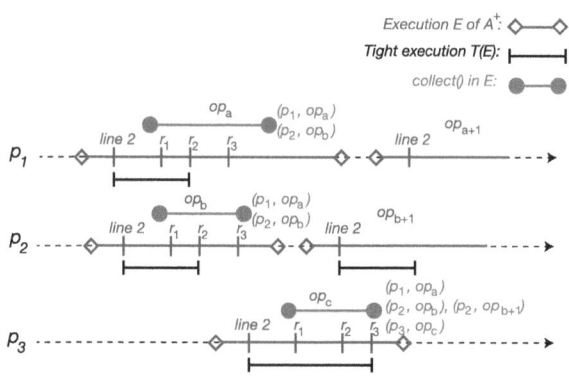

Fig. 1. A tight execution of $\mathcal{A}^+$

Lemma 4 ($T(E)$ is an execution of $\mathcal{A}^+$). *For every execution E of $\mathcal{A}^+$, $T(E)$ is an execution of $\mathcal{A}^+$.*

Lemma 5 (E and $T(E)$). *Let E be an execution of $\mathcal{A}^+$. For any two operations op_a and op_b of E, complete or pending, such that op_a and op_b appear in $T(E)$:*

---

[3] The response event happens immediately, e.g., the tight execution in Fig. 1.

$$op_a \prec_E op_b \implies op_a \prec_{T(E)} op_b$$

$$op_a \parallel_E op_b \land op_a \prec_{T(E)} op_b \implies op_a \prec_{E|\mathcal{A}} op_b$$

Corollary 1. *Let E be an execution of $\mathcal{A}^+$. Then,*

$$\neg\mathsf{LIN}(E) \implies \neg\mathsf{LIN}(T(E)).$$

The results above show that, if somehow the tight execution $T(E)$ of the current execution E can be detected in a verifier, linearizability can be runtime verified. For completeness, $\neg\mathsf{LIN}(E) \implies \neg\mathsf{LIN}(T(E))$, by Corollary 1, and hence the processes can report ERROR. For the case of strong soundness, we have two cases: 1) if $\mathsf{LIN}(T(E))$ then the processes do not report ERROR; 2) but if $\neg\mathsf{LIN}(T(E))$, then it must be the case that there is a pair of concurrent operations of E that one of them precedes the other in $T(E)$ (as in the second case of Lemma 5), i.e., $T(E)$ does not accurately capture E, it is only a "sketch" of E. However, $T(E)$ is an execution of $\mathcal{A}^+$, by Lemma 4, hence the processes have "discovered" that, although the current execution is linearizable, $\mathcal{A}^+$ is not linearizable (and thus $\mathcal{A}$ is not linearizable either, by Lemma 3).

5 From Views to Tight Executions

Now we show that views encode tight executions. This is our most relevant contribution on the technical side. The difficulty of it is due the weak guarantees provided by the collect operation. This is different from [7], where snapshots facilitates obtaining an execution from views (taken with snapshots).

For the rest of the section, fix an arbitrary finite tight execution E of $\mathcal{A}^+$.

Lemma 6 (Properties of Views). *Consider the views $\lambda_{i,e}$ and $\lambda_{j,f}$ in the responses of complete operations op_e and op_f of E by processes p_i and p_j (possibly with $p_i = p_j$). Then:*

1) Self-inclusion: $(p_i, op_e) \in \lambda_{i,e}$.
2) Containment in precedence: if $op_e \prec_E op_f$, $\lambda_{i,e} \subset \lambda_{j,f}$.
3) Non-empty intersection: if $op_e \parallel_E op_f$, $\lambda_{i,e} \cap \lambda_{j,f} \neq \emptyset$.

Lemma 6 suggests that it should be possible to obtain E by analyzing the contention and intersection between views in E. This is essentially what the local Algorithm 3 achieves using those operations, as we show next.

Let λ_E be the set containing every 4-tuple $(p_i, op_e, y_{i,e}, \lambda_{i,e})$, where op_e is a complete operation of p_i in E, with response $y_{i,e}$ and view $\lambda_{i,e}$. Algorithm 3, which is local to each process, takes λ_E, analyzes the views in it, and produces an execution X_E in two phases. We use $X_E[a:b]$ to denote a substring of X_E from index a to b, such that $0 \leq a < b \leq |X_E| - 1$.

In the first phase, Lines 1–10, the algorithm processes, in an arbitrary order, the tuples in λ_E. Each iteration of the do-while loop takes a tuple $(p_i, op_e, y_{i,e}, \lambda_{i,e})$ and inserts the invocation and response of operation op_e of

p_i somewhere in X_E. The invocation and response are denoted with the pairs (p_i, op_e) and $(y_{i,e}, \lambda_{i,e})$, respectively. The position where the *invocation pair* (p_i, op_e) is inserted (Line 7) is obtained from function pos_{inv}, Algorithm 4. Roughly speaking, pos_{inv} returns the "earliest" time in the execution constructed so far that precedes all operations whose views contain (p_i, op_e) (hence justifying those views). Similarly, the position where the *response pair* $(y_{i,e}, \lambda_{i,e})$ is inserted (Line 9) is obtained from function pos_{res}, Algorithm 4. This position, intuitively, corresponds to the "earliest" point in time where no invocation pair that is *not* in $\lambda_{i,e}$ has occurred (hence justifying the view $\lambda_{i,e}$).

Algorithm 3. From λ_E to X_E

Operation $X(\lambda_E)$ is:
1:    $\varphi \leftarrow \emptyset$ ▷ the subset of 4-tuples already processed
2:    $X_E \leftarrow \epsilon$
3:    **do**   ▷ adding the complete operations
4:        $\gamma \leftarrow$ any 4-tuple in $\lambda_E \setminus \varphi$
5:        $\varphi \leftarrow \varphi \cup \{\gamma\}$
6:        $inv \leftarrow pos_{inv}(\gamma, X_E)$
7:        $X_E \leftarrow X_E[0 : inv - 1] \cdot (\gamma.p, \gamma.op) \cdot X_E[inv : |X_E| - 1]$
8:        $last \leftarrow pos_{res}(\gamma, X_E)$
9:        $X_E \leftarrow X_E[0 : last - 1] \cdot (\gamma.y, \gamma.\lambda) \cdot X_E[last : |X_E| - 1]$
10: **while** $\varphi \neq \lambda_E$
11: **for** $i \leftarrow 0$ to $|X_E| - 1$ ▷ adding the pending invocations
12:      **if** $[i]$ is a *response pair* **then** $(y_j, \lambda_j) \leftarrow X_E[i]$
13:      $\beta \leftarrow$ set with every $(p, op) \in \lambda_j$ s.t. $\nexists\, k \in X_E$ s.t. $X_E[k] = (p, op)$
14:      **while** $\beta \neq \emptyset$
15:         $\psi \leftarrow$ any *invocation pair* in β
16:         $X_E \leftarrow X_E[0 : i - 1] \cdot \psi \cdot X_E[i : |X_E| - 1]$
17:         $\beta \leftarrow \beta \setminus \{\psi\}$
18: **return** X_E
      end $X(\lambda_E)$

After the first phase, X_E might have (complete) operations whose views have invocation pairs that do not appear in X_E (as invocations), in which case X_E is not well-formed. This can happen if an operation that is pending in E appears in a view of a tuple (operation) of λ_E. The second phase, Lines 11–17, fixes this issue. It checks, in index-ascending order, if there is a response pair whose view has invocation pairs that do not appear in X_E, and if so, it inserts all of them, in an arbitrary order, right before the response pair (hence justifying its view).

For example, Fig. 1 shows a tight execution E of $\mathcal{A}^+$, in which the set of all 4-tuples is:

$$\lambda_E = \{(p_1, op_a, y_{1,a}, \lambda_{1,a}), (p_2, op_b, y_{2,b}, \lambda_{2,b}), (p_3, op_c, y_{3,c}, \lambda_{3,c})\}$$
$$\lambda_{1,a} = \{(p_1, op_a), (p_2, op_b)\}$$
$$\lambda_{2,b} = \{(p_1, op_a), (p_2, op_b)\}$$
$$\lambda_{3,c} = \{(p_1, op_a), (p_2, op_b), (p_2, op_{b+1}), (p_3, op_c)\}$$

Algorithm 3 produces the following execution:

$$X_E = \{(p_1, op_a), (p_2, op_b), (y_{2,b}, \lambda_{2,b}), (y_{1,a}, \lambda_{1,a}), (p_3, op_c), (p_2, op_{b+1}), (y_{3,c}, \lambda_{3,c})\}.$$

Observe that the execution $T(E)$ in Fig. 1 is exactly described by X_E. The invocation pair (p_1, op_{a+1}) is not in X_E as it is not in the views of the 4-tuples in λ_E.

The order of some invocation pairs and response pairs is not relevant, as their order does not affect the precedence or concurrence of any operation. For example, the execution X'_E below, which can be produced by Algorithm 3 too, is equivalent to X_E with $\prec_{X_E} = \prec_{X'_E}$:

$$X'_E = \{(p_2, op_b), (p_1, op_a), (y_{1,a}, \lambda_{1,a}), (y_{2,b}, \lambda_{2,b}), (p_3, op_c), (p_2, op_{b+1}), (y_{3,c}, \lambda_{3,c})\}.$$

The following lemma is the key to prove that X_E indeed captures E (Theorem 1). It describes the order of precedence and concurrency of operations based on containment and inclusion between views in λ_E. The lemma uses the following notation: 1) for any operation op_i of X_E, $cmplt(op_i)$ is true if and only if op_i is complete in X_E; 2) for each complete operation op_a in X_E of process p_i, $y_{i,a}$ and $\lambda_{i,a}$ denote the response and view of op_a such that $(p_i, op_a, y_{i,a}, \lambda_{i,a}) \in \lambda_E$; and 3) for views $\lambda_{i,a}$ and $\lambda_{j,b}$, $incomp(\lambda_{i,a}, \lambda_{j,b})$ is true if and only if $\lambda_{i,a} \not\subseteq \lambda_{j,b} \wedge \lambda_{j,b} \not\subseteq \lambda_{i,a}$.

Algorithm 4. Functions pos_{inv}, pos_{res} and hb

Operation $pos_{inv}(\gamma, X_E)$ **is:**
1:   $p_i, op_e, \lambda_{i,e} \leftarrow \gamma.p, \gamma.op, \gamma.\lambda$
2:   $index \leftarrow 0$
3:   **while** $index \leq |X_E| - 1$ **do**
4:       **if** $X_E[index]$ is an *invocation pair* **then**
5:           $(p_j, op_f) \leftarrow X_E[index]$
6:           **if** $(p_i, op_e) \in \lambda_{j,f} \wedge [\,((p_j, op_f) \notin \lambda_{i,e}) \vee \exists (p_k, op_g) \in \lambda_{j,f}$ s.t. $hb(p_k, op_g, \lambda_{k,g}, p_j, op_f, \lambda_{j,f}) \wedge \neg hb(p_k, op_g, \lambda_{k,g}, p_i, op_e, \lambda_{i,e})\,]$ **then**
7:               **return** $index$
8:       **if** $X_E[index]$ is a *response pair* **then**
9:           $(y_{j,f}, \lambda_{j,f}) \leftarrow X_E[index]$
10:          **if** $(p_i, op_e) \in \lambda_{j,f} \vee [(\lambda_{i,e} \not\subseteq \lambda_{j,f}) \wedge (\lambda_{j,f} \not\subseteq \lambda_{i,e})]$ **then**
11:              **return** $index$
12:      $index \rightarrow index + 1$
13: **return** $index$
     end pos_{inv}

Operation $pos_{res}(\gamma, X_E)$ **is:**
14: $p_i, op_e, \lambda_{i,e} \leftarrow \gamma.p, \gamma.op, \gamma.\lambda$
15: $index \leftarrow 0$
16: **while** $index \leq |X_E| - 1$ **do**
17:      **if** $X_E[index]$ is an *invocation pair* **then**
18:          $(p_j, op_f) \leftarrow X_E[index]$
19:          **if** $hb(p_i, op_e, \lambda_{i,e}, p_j, op_f, \lambda_{j,f})$ **then**
20:              **return** $index$
21:      **if** $X_E[index]$ is a *response pair* **then**
22:          $(y_{j,f}, \lambda_{j,f}) \leftarrow X_E[index]$
23:          **if** $[\lambda_{i,e} \subseteq \lambda_{j,f}] \vee [(\lambda_{j,f} \not\subseteq \lambda_{i,e}) \wedge (\lambda_{i,e} \not\subseteq \lambda_{j,f}) \wedge \exists (p_k, op_g) \in \lambda_{j,f} \oplus \lambda_{i,e}$ s.t. $hb(p_i, op_e, \lambda_{i,e}, p_k, op_g, \lambda_{k,g})]$ ▷ $\oplus$ denotes the symmetric difference **then**
24:              **return** $index$
25:      $index \rightarrow index + 1$
26: **return** $index$
     end pos_{res}

Operation $hb(p_i, op_i, \lambda_{i,i}, p_j, op_j, \lambda_{j,j})$ **is:**
27: **if** $(p_j, op_j) \notin \lambda_{i,i} \wedge (p_i, op_i) \in \lambda_{j,j} \wedge [\lambda_{i,i} \subset \lambda_{j,j}]$ **then return** *true*
     end hb

Lemma 7 (Relating X_E and λ_E). *Let op_a be a complete operation in X_E by process p_i, and op_b be a complete or pending operation in X_E by process p_j.*

1. $op_a \prec_{X_E} op_b \iff$
   $\bigl(cmplt(op_b) \land \lambda_{i,a} \subset \lambda_{j,b} \land (p_i, op_a) \in \lambda_{j,b} \land (p_j, op_b) \notin \lambda_{i,a} \bigr) \lor$
   $\bigl(\neg cmplt(op_b) \land (p_j, op_b) \notin \lambda_{i,a} \bigr)$
2. $op_a \parallel_{X_E} op_b \iff$
   $\bigl(cmplt(op_b) \land (p_i, op_a) \in \lambda_{j,b} \land (p_j, op_b) \notin \lambda_{i,a} \land incomp(\lambda_{i,a}, \lambda_{j,b}) \bigr) \lor$
   $\bigl(cmplt(op_b) \land (p_i, op_a) \in \lambda_{j,b} \land (p_j, op_b) \in \lambda_{i,a} \land (incomp(\lambda_{i,a}, \lambda_{j,b}) \lor \lambda_{i,a} \subset \lambda_{j,b}) \bigr) \lor$
   $\bigl(\neg cmplt(op_b) \land (p_j, op_b) \in \lambda_{i,a} \bigr)$

We can prove Theorem 1, the main result of this section. The proof consists in showing that, in E, if one operation precedes the other, their views satisfy one of the two clauses in the first item of Lemma 7, and, similarly, if two operations are concurrent, their views satisfy one of the clauses in the second item.

Theorem 1 (Relating X_E and E). *For every tigh execution E of $\mathcal{A}^+$, E and X_E are equivalent with $\prec_E = \prec_{X_E}$. Consequently,*

$$\text{LIN}(E) \iff \text{LIN}(X_E).$$

6 The Verifier $\mathcal{V}^+$

In this section we present a verifier $\mathcal{V}^+$ that runtime verifies linearizability of any algorithm $\mathcal{A}^+$ obtained using the generic transformation in Sect. 4. The verifier appears in Algorithm 5. In every iteration of the while loop, process p_i invokes a non-deterministically chosen operation op_i of $\mathcal{A}^+$ (Lines 3 to 5), and inserts in $M[i]$ the 4-tuple with the response y_i and the view λ_i it obtains from $\mathcal{A}^+$ (Line 7). Then, p_i collects all tuples in M (Line 8), and defines the set τ_i with all the tuples in the collect (Line 9). A tricky part of the verifier is that, due to asynchrony (details below), applying Algorithm 3 to τ_i, might give an execution $X(\tau_i)$ with no relation with the actual execution of $\mathcal{A}^+$. Thus, p_i uses first the local function $refine()$ that returns a subset τ_i' of τ_i (Line 10), which is the input to Algorithm 3. As we will see, $X(\tau_i')$ is indeed related to the actual execution of $\mathcal{A}^+$, and hence is the execution p_i tests against linearizability (Lines 11 and 12).

Algorithm 5. Verifier $\mathcal{V}^+$ for linearizability of any algorithm $\mathcal{A}^+$. Pseudocode of process p_i.

Shared Variables:
  M = Wait-free collect object with each entry initialized to $\emptyset$
Local Persistent Variable:
  res_i = an unbounded set initialized to $\emptyset$
Operation Verify($\mathcal{A}^+$) **is**
 1:   $res_i \leftarrow \emptyset$
 2:   **while** true **do**
 3:     $op_i \leftarrow$ non-deterministically chosen operation
 4:     Invoke operation Apply(op_i) of $\mathcal{A}^+$
 5:     $(y_i, \lambda_i) \leftarrow$ response from operation Apply(op_i) of $\mathcal{A}^+$
 6:     $res_i \leftarrow res_i \cup \{(p_i, op_i, y_i, \lambda_i)\}$
 7:     M.write(i, res_i)
 8:     $c_i \leftarrow M$.collect()
 9:     $\tau_i \leftarrow \bigcup_{k \in \{1,2,\ldots,n\}} c_i[k]$
10:     $\tau'_i \leftarrow refine(\tau_i)$
11:     **if** $\neg\mathsf{LIN}(X(\tau'_i))$ **then**
12:       report(ERROR, $X(\tau'_i)$)
     end Verify

Before defining function $refine()$[4], we explain the necessity of it through an example. Basically, the reason is that $X(\tau_i)$ might not be a well-formed execution, making useless testing linearizability of it. For example, Fig. 2(a) shows an 3-process execution E of $\mathcal{V}^+$, due to asynchrony, the collect of operation op_a of p_1, "misses" the two operations of p_2, op_b and op_{b+1}, but it reads the 4-tuple corresponding to operation op_c of p_3. Thus, τ_1 contains only two tuples. The problem is that the view $\lambda_{3,c}$ of op_c has the invocation pairs of the four operations, and hence τ_1 encodes two pending operations of p_2, which is impossible. In fact, the result of applying Algorithm 3 to τ_1, $X(\tau_1)$, is a non-well-formed execution, as shown in Fig. 2(b).

After all, the problem of obtaining non-well-formed executions is inherent to asynchrony, i.e. that τ_i might be a proper subset of $\lambda_{T(E|\mathcal{A}^+)}$ (recall that $\lambda_{T(E|\mathcal{A}^+)}$ is the set with all 4-tuples of complete operations of $T(E|\mathcal{A}^+)$). However, there exists a subset τ'_i of τ_i such that $X(\tau'_i)$ is an execution of $\mathcal{A}^+$. Roughly speaking, this set corresponds to the maximal subset of τ_i such that every process has at most one pending operation. In the example in Fig. 2(a), that subset contains only the 4-tuple corresponding to the operation of op_a of p_1.

---

[4] Theorem 1 appears to be a straightforward way to verify $\mathcal{A}^+$, but due to asynchrony we do not obtain an X_E thought $\mathcal{V}^+$; however, we can transform any $X(\tau_i)$ into a well-formed execution $X(\tau'_i)$ which is also an sketch of an execution $\mathcal{A}^+$ as X_E.

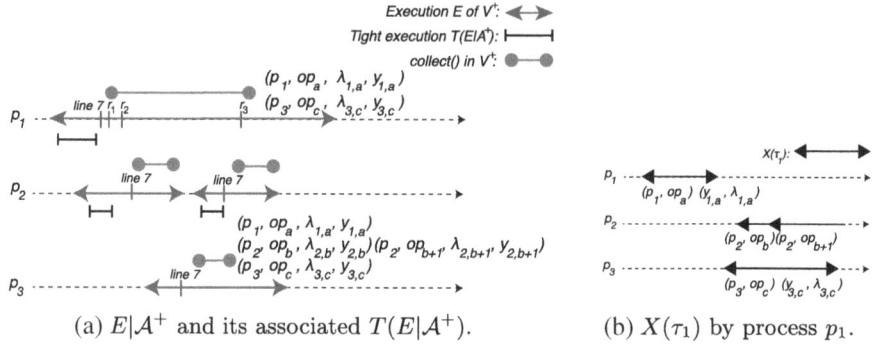

Fig. 2. Discrepancies between $X(\tau_1)$ and $T(E|\mathcal{A}^+)$.

Let E be any finite execution of $\mathcal{V}^+$, and let τ_i be the set obtained by process p_i in Line 9 in its last iteration of the while loop. Consider the set $\lambda_{T(E|\mathcal{A}^+)}$ with the 4-tuples of the complete operations in the tight execution $T(E|\mathcal{A}^+)$ associated to $E|\mathcal{A}^+$. Note that $\tau_i \subseteq \lambda_{T(E|\mathcal{A}^+)}$. An invocation pair (p, op) is τ_i-*pending* if: (1) (p, op) appears in the view of a 4-tuple of τ_i, and (2) there are no y and λ such that $(p, op, y, \lambda) \in \tau_i$. We define $refine(\tau_i)$ as the maximal subset of τ_i such that for each of its tuples (p, op, y, λ), there are no pair of τ_i-pending invocation pairs $(p', op'), (p'', op'') \in \lambda$ such that $p' = p''$ and $op' \neq op''$.

Lemma 8 (Non-emptiness of τ_i'). *Let E be any finite execution of $\mathcal{V}^+$, and let τ_i' be the set obtained by process p_i in Line 10 in its last iteration of the while loop. Then, τ_i' contains every 4-tuple that appears in M right before the first read of p_i's collect in its last iteration of the while loop.*

We now argue that, despite asynchrony, $X(\tau_i')$ indeed captures an execution of $\mathcal{A}^+$, possibly different from the current one. The proof consists in showing that there exists an execution F where some operations of the current execution are missing such that its tight execution $T(F|\mathcal{A}^+)$ is exactly $X(\tau_i')$.

Lemma 9 ($X(\tau_i')$ is an execution of $\mathcal{A}^+$). *Let E be any finite execution of $\mathcal{V}^+$, and let τ_i' be the set obtained by process p_i in Line 10 in its last iteration of the while loop.*
There exist a finite execution F of $\mathcal{V}^+$ such that:
1) $T(F|\mathcal{A}^+)$ and $X(\tau_i')$ are equivalent with $\prec_{X(\tau_i')} = \prec_{T(F|\mathcal{A}^+)}$, and
2) $F|\mathcal{A}^+$ is an execution of $\mathcal{A}^+$.

The previous lemma together with Lemmas 1 and 4 imply:

Corollary 2 ($X(\tau_i')$ and the current execution). *Let E be any finite execution of $\mathcal{V}^+$, and let τ_i' be the set obtained by process p_i in Line 10 in its last iteration of the while loop. There exists a finite execution F of $\mathcal{V}^+$ such that:*

$$\mathsf{LIN}(X(\tau_i')) \iff \mathsf{LIN}(T(F|\mathcal{A}^+))$$

Finally, we prove our main result, correctness of $\mathcal{V}^+$ in Theorem 2. For strong soundness, the proof shows that if $X(\tau'_i)$ is not linearizable, it is fine that processes report ERROR, since $X(\tau'_i)$ is an execution of $\mathcal{A}^+$. For completeness, it shows that if the current execution of $\mathcal{A}^+$ is not linearizable and, due to asynchrony, p_i locally computes an execution $X(\tau'_i)$ that is linearizable, then eventually, after a finite number of iterations of the do-while loop, p_i collects from M the non-linearizable behavior of $\mathcal{A}^+$ and hence at that moment $X(\tau'_i)$ is not linearizable.

Theorem 2 (Correctness of $\mathcal{V}^+$). *The verifier $\mathcal{V}^+$ runtime verifies linearizability of any object $\mathcal{O}$ with any input algorithm $\mathcal{A}^+$. Furthermore, $\mathcal{V}^+$ satisfies the following stability property: if a process reports* ERROR *in an infinite execution E of $\mathcal{V}^+$ and $\neg$LIN$(E'|\mathcal{A}^+)$ for some finite prefix E', then eventually every process reports* ERROR *forever.*

7 The Lightweight Runtime Verified $\mathcal{B}^+$

We now show that $\mathcal{A}^+$ and $\mathcal{V}^+$ can be combined to obtain a lightweight crash-tolerant *runtime verified* algorithm $\mathcal{B}^+$, where processes are split into two groups, *producers*, $p_1, p_2, \ldots, p_x$, and *verifiers*, $v_1, v_2, \ldots, v_y$. Intuitively, in $\mathcal{B}^+$, producers and verifiers execute in parallel $\mathcal{A}^+$ and $\mathcal{V}^+$, with the difference that producers *do not* return views of operations. Algorithm 6 describes $\mathcal{B}^+$. Producers produce responses to operations using $\mathcal{A}$ (Lines 2 and 3), the algorithm wrapped in $\mathcal{A}^+$, and record the sketch of the current execution of $\mathcal{B}^+$ (Lines 1, 4 and 5). Verifiers are in charge of verifying, from time to time, the execution that producers have recorded so far (Lines 7 to 16).

Producers and verifiers communicate through two wait-free *decoupled* collect objects. In the spirit of known decoupled snapshot algorithms [3,34], a decoupled collect object separates collects in two actions: obtaining a *reference* and obtaining the *actual* values. An x-dimensional decoupled collect object stores a set in each of its entries[5], and provides three operations: $Insert(i, v)$ that allows producer p_i to insert v in the i-th set, $TakeCollect()$ that allows any process to take a *reference* (an integer) of a collect of the sets, and $GetCollect(ref)$ that retrieves the actual values in the collect with reference ref. In the full version of the paper, we present a simple and wait-free decoupled collect algorithm in which $Insert(i, v)$ executes two shared memory operations and $TakeCollect()$ executes a single shared memory operation.

---

[5] We focus on the case that each entry stores an evergrowing set, but the definition can be generalized.

Algorithm 6. The lightweight runtime verified linearizable algorithm $\mathcal{B}^+$.

Shared Variables:
    S, V : x-dimensional wait-free decoupled collect objects with each entry initialized to $\emptyset$
Operation Apply(op_i) **is**   ▷ Code for producer p_i
 1:    $S.Insert(i, (p_i, op_i))$
 2:    Invoke operation Apply(op_i) of $\mathcal{A}$
 3:    $y_i \leftarrow$ response from operation Apply(op_i) of $\mathcal{A}$
 4:    $ref_i \leftarrow S.TakeCollect()$ ▷ Obtains a reference to the view of operation (p_i, op_i)
 5:    $V.Insert(i, (p_i, op_i, y_i, ref_i))$
 6:    **return** y_i
    end Apply

Operation Verify() **is**   ▷ Code for verifier v_j
 7:    **while** $true$ **do**
 8:        $c_j \leftarrow V.GetCollect(V.TakeCollect())$ ▷ Obtains a collect of V in two steps
 9:        $\tau_j \leftarrow \emptyset$
10:        **for** $r_j \leftarrow 1$ up to x **do**
11:            **for** each $(p_j, op_j, y_j, ref_j) \in c_j[r_j]$ **do**
12:                $\tau_j \leftarrow \tau_j \cup \{(p_i, op_i, y_i, C.GetCollect(ref_j))\}$ ▷ Actual view of operation (p_i, op_i)
13:        $\tau_j' \leftarrow refine(\tau_j)$
14:        **if** $\neg LIN(X(\tau_j'))$ **then**
15:            **report**(ERROR, $X(\tau_j')$)
16:        **Sleep** for T units of time   ▷ T is an application dependent constant
    end Verify

The following theorem assumes that there is at least one correct producer and at least one correct verifier in any execution of $\mathcal{B}^+$.

Theorem 3 (Correctness of $\mathcal{B}^+$). *Let $\mathcal{A}$ be any algorithm that is presumably linearizable, and consider its related runtime verified algorithm $\mathcal{B}^+$ as defined above. Then,*

1) $\mathcal{B}^+$ is linearizable if and only if $\mathcal{A}$ is linearizable;
2) $\mathcal{B}^+$ is wait-free (resp. lock-free) if and only if $\mathcal{A}$ is wait-free (resp. lock-free);
3) $\mathcal{B}^+$'s operation step complexity is $\mathcal{A}$'s step complexity plus five;
4) in $\mathcal{B}^+$'s executions, if a verifier reports ERROR, it provides a non-linearizable execution of $\mathcal{B}^+$, and if the current execution is not linearizable, eventually all correct verifiers report ERROR forever.

8 Conclusions

We provided a fault-tolerant asynchronous wrapper $\mathcal{A}^+$ and its corresponding verifier $\mathcal{V}^+$ based on simple collects, which considerably improve the previous solution proposed in [7]. Based on the wrapper $\mathcal{A}^+$ and on a novel decoupled collect algorithm, we also proposed a lightweight asynchronous crash-tolerant runtime verified linearizable algorithm $\mathcal{B}^+$, in which the communication interface and the monitoring system are decoupled, a property that allows independent optimization on any of these components.

Acknowledgments. Gilde Valeria Rodríguez is the recipient of a PhD fellowship of CONAHCYT. Armando Castañeda is supported by the research project DGAPA-PAPIIT IN108723.

References

1. Afek, Y., Attiya, H., Dolev, D., Gafni, E., Merritt, M., Shavit, N.: Atomic snapshots of shared memory. J. ACM **40**(4), 873–890 (1993). https://doi.org/10.1145/153724.153741
2. Bartocci, E., Falcone, Y. (eds.): Lectures on Runtime Verification - Introductory and Advanced Topics. Lecture Notes in Computer Science, vol. 10457. Springer, Cham (2018)https://doi.org/10.1007/978-3-319-75632-5
3. Bashari, B., Woelfel, P.: An efficient adaptive partial snapshot implementation. In: Miller, A., Censor-Hillel, K., Korhonen, J.H. (eds.) PODC 2021: ACM Symposium on Principles of Distributed Computing, Virtual Event, Italy, 26–30 July 2021, pp. 545–555. ACM (2021). https://doi.org/10.1145/3465084.3467939
4. Berkovich, S., Bonakdarpour, B., Fischmeister, S.: Runtime verification with minimal intrusion through parallelism. Formal Methods Syst. Des. **46**(3), 317–348 (2015). https://doi.org/10.1007/s10703-015-0226-3
5. Bonakdarpour, B., Fraigniaud, P., Rajsbaum, S., Rosenblueth, D.A., Travers, C.: Decentralized asynchronous crash-resilient runtime verification. J. ACM **69**(5), 34:1–34:31 (2022). https://doi.org/10.1145/3550483
6. Bonakdarpour, B., Fraigniaud, P., Rajsbaum, S., Travers, C.: Challenges in fault-tolerant distributed runtime verification. In: Margaria, T., Steffen, B. (eds.) ISoLA 2016, Part II. LNCS, vol. 9953, pp. 363–370. Springer, Cham (2016). https://doi.org/10.1007/978-3-319-47169-3_27
7. Castañeda, A., Rodríguez, G.V.: Asynchronous wait-free runtime verification and enforcement of linearizability. In: Oshman, R., Nolin, A., Halldórsson, M.M., Balliu, A. (eds.) Proceedings of the 2023 ACM Symposium on Principles of Distributed Computing, PODC 2023, Orlando, FL, USA, 19–23 June 2023, pp. 90–101. ACM (2023). https://doi.org/10.1145/3583668.3594563
8. Decker, N., Gottschling, P., Hochberger, C., Leucker, M., Scheffel, T., Schmitz, M., Weiss, A.: Rapidly adjustable non-intrusive online monitoring for multi-core systems. In: Cavalheiro, S., Fiadeiro, J. (eds.) SBMF 2017. LNCS, vol. 10623, pp. 179–196. Springer, Cham (2017). https://doi.org/10.1007/978-3-319-70848-5_12
9. El-Hokayem, A., Falcone, Y.: Can we monitor all multithreaded programs? In: Colombo, C., Leucker, M. (eds.) RV 2018. LNCS, vol. 11237, pp. 64–89. Springer, Cham (2018). https://doi.org/10.1007/978-3-030-03769-7_6
10. Elmas, T., Tasiran, S.: Vyrdmc: Driving runtime refinement checking with model checkers. In: Barringer, H., Finkbeiner, B., Gurevich, Y., Sipma, H. (eds.) Proceedings of the Fifth Workshop on Runtime Verification, RV@CAV 2005, Edinburgh, UK, 12 July 2005. Electronic Notes in Theoretical Computer Science, vol. 144, pp. 41–56. Elsevier (2005). https://doi.org/10.1016/j.entcs.2006.02.003
11. Elmas, T., Tasiran, S., Qadeer, S.: VYRD: verifying concurrent programs by runtime refinement-violation detection. In: Sarkar, V., Hall, M.W. (eds.) Proceedings of the ACM SIGPLAN 2005 Conference on Programming Language Design and Implementation, Chicago, IL, USA, 12–15 June 2005, pp. 27–37. ACM (2005). https://doi.org/10.1145/1065010.1065015
12. Falcone, Y.: On decentralized monitoring. In: Nouri, A., Wu, W., Barkaoui, K., Li, Z.W. (eds.) VECoS 2021. LNCS, vol. 13187, pp. 1–16. Springer, Cham (2022). https://doi.org/10.1007/978-3-030-98850-0_1
13. Falcone, Y., Havelund, K., Reger, G.: A tutorial on runtime verification. In: Broy, M., Peled, D.A., Kalus, G. (eds.) Engineering Dependable Software Systems, NATO Science for Peace and Security Series, D: Information and Communication

Security, vol. 34, pp. 141–175. IOS Press (2013). https://doi.org/10.3233/978-1-61499-207-3-141
14. Fraigniaud, P., Rajsbaum, S., Travers, C.: Locality and checkability in wait-free computing. Distrib. Comput. **26**(4), 223–242 (2013). https://doi.org/10.1007/s00446-013-0188-x
15. Fraigniaud, P., Rajsbaum, S., Travers, C.: A lower bound on the number of opinions needed for fault-tolerant decentralized run-time monitoring. J. Appl. Comput. Topol. **4**(1), 141–179 (2020). https://doi.org/10.1007/s41468-019-00047-6
16. Francalanza, A., Pérez, J.A., Sánchez, C.: Runtime verification for decentralised and distributed systems. In: Bartocci, E., Falcone, Y. (eds.) Lectures on Runtime Verification. LNCS, vol. 10457, pp. 176–210. Springer, Cham (2018). https://doi.org/10.1007/978-3-319-75632-5_6
17. Havelund, K., Goldberg, A.: Verify your runs. In: Meyer, B., Woodcock, J. (eds.) VSTTE 2005. LNCS, vol. 4171, pp. 374–383. Springer, Heidelberg (2008). https://doi.org/10.1007/978-3-540-69149-5_40
18. Herlihy, M.: Wait-free synchronization. ACM Trans. Program. Lang. Syst. **13**(1), 124–149 (1991). https://doi.org/10.1145/114005.102808
19. Herlihy, M., Kozlov, D.N., Rajsbaum, S.: Distributed Computing Through Combinatorial Topology. Morgan Kaufmann (2013). https://store.elsevier.com/product.jsp?isbn=9780124045781
20. Herlihy, M., Shavit, N.: The Art of Multiprocessor Programming. Morgan Kaufmann (2008)
21. Herlihy, M., Wing, J.M.: Linearizability: a correctness condition for concurrent objects. ACM Trans. Program. Lang. Syst. **12**(3), 463–492 (1990). https://doi.org/10.1145/78969.78972
22. Inoue, M., Masuzawa, T., Chen, W., Tokura, N.: Linear-time snapshot using multi-writer multi-reader registers. In: Tel, G., Vitányi, P. (eds.) WDAG 1994. LNCS, vol. 857, pp. 130–140. Springer, Heidelberg (1994). https://doi.org/10.1007/BFb0020429
23. Kuznetsov, P., Guerraoui, R.: Algorithms for Concurrent Systems. EPFL Press (2018)
24. Lamport, L.: How to make a multiprocessor computer that correctly executes multiprocess programs. IEEE Trans. Comput. **28**(9), 690–691 (1979). https://doi.org/10.1109/TC.1979.1675439
25. Leucker, M., Schallhart, C.: A brief account of runtime verification. J. Log. Algebraic Methods Program. **78**, 293–303 (2009). https://doi.org/10.1016/j.jlap.2008.08.004
26. Lourenço, J.M., Fiedor, J., Křena, B., Vojnar, T.: Discovering concurrency errors. In: Bartocci, E., Falcone, Y. (eds.) Lectures on Runtime Verification. LNCS, vol. 10457, pp. 34–60. Springer, Cham (2018). https://doi.org/10.1007/978-3-319-75632-5_2
27. Lynch, N.A., Vaandrager, F.W.: Forward and backward simulations: I. Untimed systems. Inf. Comput. **121**(2), 214–233 (1995). https://doi.org/10.1006/inco.1995.1134
28. Moir, M., Shavit, N.: Concurrent data structures. In: Mehta, D.P., Sahni, S. (eds.) Handbook of Data Structures and Applications. Chapman and Hall/CRC (2004). https://doi.org/10.1201/9781420035179.ch47
29. Pnueli, A., Zaks, A.: PSL model checking and run-time verification via testers. In: Misra, J., Nipkow, T., Sekerinski, E. (eds.) FM 2006. LNCS, vol. 4085, pp. 573–586. Springer, Heidelberg (2006). https://doi.org/10.1007/11813040_38

30. Raynal, M.: Concurrent Programming - Algorithms, Principles, and Foundations. Springer, Cham (2012). https://doi.org/10.1007/978-3-642-32027-9
31. Sánchez, C., et al.: A survey of challenges for runtime verification from advanced application domains (beyond software). Formal Methods Syst. Des. **54**(3), 279–335 (2019). https://doi.org/10.1007/s10703-019-00337-w
32. Soueidi, C., El-Hokayem, A., Falcone, Y.: Opportunistic monitoring of multi-threaded programs. In: Lambers, L., Uchitel, S. (eds.) FASE 2023. LNCS, vol. 13991, pp. 173–194. Springer, Cham (2023). https://doi.org/10.1007/978-3-031-30826-0_10
33. Taleb, R., Hallé, S., Khoury, R.: Uncertainty in runtime verification: A survey. Comput. Sci. Rev. **50**, 100594 (2023). https://doi.org/10.1016/J.COSREV.2023.100594
34. Wei, Y., Ben-David, N., Blelloch, G.E., Fatourou, P., Ruppert, E., Sun, Y.: Constant-time snapshots with applications to concurrent data structures. In: Lee, J., Petrank, E. (eds.) PPoPP 2021: 26th ACM SIGPLAN Symposium on Principles and Practice of Parallel Programming, Virtual Event, Republic of Korea, 27 February–3 March 2021, pp. 31–46. ACM (2021). https://doi.org/10.1145/3437801.3441602

Approximate Distributed Monitoring Under Partial Synchrony: Balancing Speed & Accuracy

Borzoo Bonakdarpour[1], Anik Momtaz[1], Dejan Ničković[2], and N. Ege Saraç[3(✉)]

[1] Michigan State University, East Lansing, USA
{borzoo,momtazan}@msu.edu
[2] AIT Austrian Institute of Technology, Wien, Austria
dejan.nickovic@ait.ac.at
[3] Institute of Science and Technology Austria (ISTA), Klosterneuburg, Austria
esarac@ista.ac.at

Abstract. In distributed systems with processes that do not share a global clock, *partial synchrony* is achieved by clock synchronization that guarantees bounded clock skew among all applications. Existing solutions for distributed runtime verification under partial synchrony against temporal logic specifications are exact but suffer from significant computational overhead. In this paper, we propose an *approximate* distributed monitoring algorithm for Signal Temporal Logic (STL) that mitigates this issue by abstracting away potential interleaving behaviors. This conservative abstraction enables a significant speedup of the distributed monitors, albeit with a tradeoff in accuracy. We address this tradeoff with a methodology that combines our approximate monitor with its exact counterpart, resulting in enhanced efficiency without sacrificing precision. We evaluate our approach with multiple experiments, showcasing its efficacy in both real-world applications and synthetic examples.

Keywords: distributed systems · approximate monitoring · partial synchrony

1 Introduction

Distributed systems are networks of independent agents that work together to achieve a common objective. They come in many different forms. For example, cloud computing uses distribution of resources and services over the internet to offer to their users a scalable infrastructure with transparent on-demand access to computing power and storage. Swarms of drones is another family of distributed systems where individual drones collaborate to accomplish tasks like search and rescue or package delivery. While each drone operates independently, it also communicates and coordinates with others to successfully achieve their

---

This work was supported in part by the ERC-2020-AdG 101020093. This work is ponsored in part by the United States NSF CCF-2118356 award. This research was partially funded by A-IQ Ready (Chips JU, grant agreement No. 101096658).

© The Author(s) 2025
E. Ábrahám and H. Abbas (Eds.): RV 2024, LNCS 15191, pp. 282–301, 2025.
https://doi.org/10.1007/978-3-031-74234-7_18

common objectives. The individual agents in a distributed system typically do not share a global clock. To coordinate actions across multiple agents, clock synchronization is often needed. While perfect clock synchronization is impractical due to network latency and node failures, algorithms such as the Network Time Protocol (NTP) allow agents to maintain a *bounded skew* between the synchronized clocks. We then say that a distributed system has *partial synchrony*.

Formal verification of distributed system is a notoriously hard problem, due to the combinatorial explosion of all possible interleavings in the behaviors collected from individual agents. *Runtime verification (RV)* provides a more pragmatic approach in which a behavior of a distributed system is observed and its correctness is checked against a formal specification. We consider the *distributed RV* setting where this task is performed by a single central monitor observing the independent agents (as opposed to *decentralized RV* where the monitoring task itself is distributed). Remotely related to the problem of distributed RV under partial synchrony are distributed RV in the fully *synchronous* [5,8,9] and *asynchronous* [6,7,12,17,19,21] settings as well as benchmarking tools [2] for assessing monitoring overhead. The problem of distributed RV under partial synchrony assumption has been studied for Linear Temporal Logic (LTL) [11] and Signal Temporal Logic (STL) [18] specification languages. The proposed solutions use Satisfiability-Modulo-Theory (SMT) solving to provide sound and complete distributed monitoring procedures. Although distributed RV monitors consume only a single distributed behavior at a time, this behavior can have an excessive number of possible interleavings. Put another way, although RV deals only with the verification of a single execution at run time, it is still prone to evaluating an explosion of combinations. Hence, the exact distributed monitors from the literature can still suffer from significant computational overhead. This phenomenon has been observed even under partial synchrony [10,11], and becomes problematic even for offline monitoring of a large set of log files.

To mitigate this issue, we propose a new approach for *approximate* RV of STL under partial synchrony. In essence, we conservatively abstract away potential interleavings in distributed behaviors, resulting in their overapproximation. This abstraction simplifies the representation of distributed behaviors into a set of Boolean expressions, taking into account regions of uncertainty created by clock skews. We define monitoring operations that evaluate temporal specifications over such expressions, which result in monitoring verdicts on overapproximated behaviors. This approximate solution yields an inevitable tradeoff between *accuracy* and *speedup*. For applications where reduced accuracy is not acceptable, we devise a methodology that combines approximate and exact monitors, with the aim to benefit from the enhanced efficiency without sacrificing precision. Approximate monitoring is also valuable in the sequential setting, with applications including monitoring with state estimation [4,23], quantitative monitoring and its resource-precision tradeoffs [13–15], and various other uses [1,3].

We implemented our approach in a prototype tool and performed thorough evaluations on both synthetic and real-world case studies (mutual separation in swarm of drones and a water distribution system). We first demonstrated that in many experiments, our approximate monitors achieve speedups of up to 5 orders of magnitude compared to the exact SMT-based solution. We empirically characterized the classes of specifications and behaviors for which our approximate monitors achieve good precision. We finally showed that combining exact and approximate distributed RV yields significant efficiency gains on average without sacrificing precision, even with low-accuracy approximate monitors.

2 Preliminaries

We denote by $\mathbb{B} = \{\top, \bot\}$ the set of Booleans, $\mathbb{R}$ the set of reals, $\mathbb{R}_{\geq 0}$ the set of nonnegative reals, and $\mathbb{R}_{>0}$ the set of positive reals. An interval $I \subseteq \mathbb{R}$ of reals with the end points $a < b$ has length $|b - a|$.

Let Σ be a finite *alphabet*. We denote by Σ^* the set of finite words over Σ and by ϵ the empty word. For $u \in \Sigma^*$, we respectively write prefix(u) and suffix(u) for the sets of prefixes and suffixes of u. We also let infix$(u) = \{v \in \Sigma^* \mid \exists x, y \in \Sigma^* : u = xvy\}$. For a nonempty word $u \in \Sigma^*$ and $1 \leq i \leq |u|$, we denote by $u[i]$ the ith letter of u. Given $u \in \Sigma^*$ and $\ell \geq 1$, we denote by u^ℓ the word obtained by concatenating u by itself $\ell - 1$ times. Moreover, given $L \subseteq \Sigma^*$, we define first$(L) = \{u[0] \mid u \in L\}$. For sets $L_1, L_2 \subseteq \Sigma^*$ of words, we let $L_1 \cdot L_2 = \{u \cdot v \mid u \in L_1, v \in L_2\}$. For tuples $(u_1, \ldots, u_m)$ and $(v_1, \ldots, v_m)$ of words, we let $(u_1, \ldots, u_m) \cdot (v_1, \ldots, v_m) = (u_1 v_1, \ldots, u_m v_m)$.

We define the function destutter : $\Sigma^* \to \Sigma^*$ inductively. For all $\sigma \in \Sigma \cup \{\epsilon\}$, let destutter$(\sigma) = \sigma$. For all $u \in \Sigma^*$ such that $u = \sigma_1 \sigma_2 v$ for some $\sigma_1, \sigma_2 \in \Sigma$ and $v \in \Sigma^*$, we define it as follows:

$$\text{destutter}(u) = \begin{cases} \text{destutter}(\sigma_2 v) & \text{if } \sigma_1 = \sigma_2 \\ \sigma_1 \cdot \text{destutter}(\sigma_2 v) & \text{otherwise} \end{cases}$$

For a set $L \subseteq \Sigma^*$ of finite words, we define destutter$(L) = \{\text{destutter}(u) \mid u \in L\}$. We extend destutter to tuples of words in a synchronized manner: for all $\sigma \in \Sigma \cup \{\epsilon\}$ let destutter$(\sigma, \ldots, \sigma) = (\sigma, \ldots, \sigma)$. Given a tuple $(u_1, \ldots, u_m) = (\sigma_{1,1}\sigma_{1,2}v_1, \ldots, \sigma_{m,1}\sigma_{m,2}v_m)$ of words of the same length, destutter$(u_1, \ldots, u_m)$ is defined as expected:

$$\text{destutter}(u_1, \ldots, u_m) = \begin{cases} \text{destutter}(\sigma_{1,2}v_1, \ldots, \sigma_{m,2}v_m) & \text{if } \sigma_{i,1} = \sigma_{i,2} \text{ for all } 1 \leq i \leq m \\ (\sigma_{1,1}, \ldots, \sigma_{m,1}) \cdot \text{destutter}(\sigma_{1,2}v_1, \ldots, \sigma_{m,2}v_m) & \text{otherwise} \end{cases}$$

Moreover, given an integer $k \geq 0$, we define stutter$_k$: $\Sigma^* \to \Sigma^*$ such that stutter$_k(u) = \{v \in \Sigma^* \mid |v| = k \land \text{destutter}(v) = \text{destutter}(u)\}$ if $k \geq |\text{destutter}(u)|$, and stutter$_k(u) = \emptyset$ otherwise.

Signal Temporal Logic (STL) [16]. Let $A, B \subset \mathbb{R}$. A function $f : A \to B$ is *right-continuous* iff $\lim_{a \to c^+} f(a) = f(c)$ for all $c \in A$, and *non-Zeno* iff for every bounded interval $I \subseteq A$ there are finitely many $a \in I$ such that f is not continuous at a. A *signal* is a right-continuous, non-Zeno, piecewise-constant function $x : [0, d) \to \mathbb{R}$ where $d \in \mathbb{R}_{>0}$ is the duration of x and $[0, d)$ is its temporal domain. Let $x : [0, d) \to \mathbb{R}$ be a signal. An *event* of x is a pair $(t, x(t))$

where $t \in [0,d)$. An *edge* of x is an event $(t, x(t))$ such that $\lim_{s \to t^-} x(s) \neq \lim_{s \to t^+} x(s)$. In particular, an edge is *rising* if $\lim_{s \to t^-} x(s) < \lim_{s \to t^+} x(s)$, and it is *falling* otherwise. A signal $x : [0, d) \to \mathbb{R}$ can be represented finitely by its initial value and edges: if x has m edges, then $x = (t_0, v_0)(t_1, v_1) \ldots (t_m, v_m)$ such that $t_0 = 0$, $t_{i-1} < t_i$, and (t_i, v_i) is an edge of x for all $1 \leq i \leq m$.

Let AP be a set of *atomic propositions*. The syntax of STL is given by the grammar $\varphi := p \mid \neg \varphi \mid \varphi \wedge \varphi \mid \varphi \mathcal{U}_I \varphi$ where $p \in \mathsf{AP}$ and $I \subseteq \mathbb{R}_{\geq 0}$ is an interval.

A *trace* $w = (x_1, \ldots, x_n)$ is a finite vector of signals. We express atomic propositions as functions of trace values at a time point t, i.e., a proposition $p \in \mathsf{AP}$ over a trace $w = (x_1, \ldots, x_n)$ is defined as $f_p(x_1(t), \ldots, x_n(t)) > 0$ where $f_p : \mathbb{R}^n \to \mathbb{R}$ is a function. Given intervals $I, J \subseteq \mathbb{R}_{\geq 0}$, we define $I \oplus J = \{i + j \mid i \in I, j \in J\}$, and we simply write t for the singleton set $\{t\}$.

We recall the finite-trace qualitative semantics of STL defined over $\mathbb{B}$. Let $d \in \mathbb{R}_{>0}$ and $w = (x_1, \ldots, x_n)$ with $x_i : [0, d) \to \mathbb{R}$ for all $1 \leq i \leq n$. Let φ_1, φ_2 be STL formulas and let $t \in [0, d)$.

$$(w, t) \models p \iff f_p(x_1(t), \ldots, x_n(t)) > 0$$
$$(w, t) \models \neg \varphi_1 \iff \overline{(w, t) \models \varphi_1}$$
$$(w, t) \models \varphi_1 \wedge \varphi_2 \iff (w, t) \models \varphi_1 \wedge (w, t) \models \varphi_2$$
$$(w, t) \models \varphi_1 \mathcal{U}_I \varphi_2 \iff \exists t' \in (t \oplus I) \cap [0, d) :$$
$$(w, t') \models \varphi_2 \wedge \forall t'' \in (t, t') : (w, t'') \models \varphi_1$$

We simply write $w \models \varphi$ for $(w, 0) \models \varphi$. We additionally use the following standard abbreviations: $\texttt{false} = p \wedge \neg p$, $\texttt{true} = \neg \texttt{false}$, $\varphi_1 \vee \varphi_2 = \neg(\neg \varphi_1 \wedge \neg \varphi_2)$, $\Diamond_I \varphi = \texttt{true} \mathcal{U}_I \varphi$, and $\Box_I \varphi = \neg \Diamond_I \neg \varphi$. Moreover, the untimed temporal operators are defined through their timed counterparts on the interval $[0, \infty)$.

Distributed Semantics of STL [18]. We consider an asynchronous and loosely-coupled message-passing system of $n \geq 2$ reliable agents producing a set of signals $x_1, \ldots, x_n$, where for some $d \in \mathbb{R}_{>0}$ we have $x_i : [0, d) \to \mathbb{R}$ for all $1 \leq i \leq n$. The agents do not share memory or a global clock. Only to formalize statements, we speak of a *hypothetical* global clock and denote its value by T. For local time values, we use the lowercase letters t and s. For a signal x_i, we denote by V_i the set of its events, and by E_i the set of its edges. We represent the local clock of the ith agent as an increasing and divergent function $c_i : \mathbb{R}_{\geq 0} \to \mathbb{R}_{\geq 0}$ that maps a global time T to a local time $c_i(T)$.

We assume that the system is *partially synchronous*: the agents use a clock synchronization algorithm that guarantees a bounded clock skew with respect to the global clock, i.e., $|c_i(T) - c_j(T)| < \varepsilon$ for all $1 \leq i, j \leq N$ and $T \in \mathbb{R}_{\geq 0}$, where $\varepsilon \in \mathbb{R}_{>0}$ is the maximum clock skew.

Definition 1. *A distributed signal is a pair $(S, \rightsquigarrow)$, where $S = (x_1, \ldots, x_n)$ is a vector of signals and $\rightsquigarrow$ is the happened-before relation between events defined as follows: (1) For every agent, the events of its signals are totally ordered, i.e., for all $1 \leq i \leq n$ and all $(t, x_i(t)), (t', x_i(t')) \in V_i$, if $t < t'$ then $(t, x_i(t)) \rightsquigarrow$*

$(t', x_i(t'))$. (2) *Every pair of events whose timestamps are at least ε apart is totally ordered, i.e., for all $1 \leq i, j \leq n$ and all $(t, x_i(t)) \in V_i$ and $(t', x_j(t')) \in V_j$, if $t + \varepsilon \leq t'$ then $(t, x_i(t)) \rightsquigarrow (t', x_j(t'))$.*

The notion of *consistent cut* captures possible global states.

Definition 2. *Let $(S, \rightsquigarrow)$ be a distributed signal of n signals, and $V = \bigcup_{i=1}^{n} V_i$ be the set of its events. A set $C \subseteq V$ is a* consistent cut *iff for every event in C, all events that happened before it also belong to C, i.e., for all $e, e' \in V$, if $e \in C$ and $e' \rightsquigarrow e$, then $e' \in C$.*

We denote by $\mathbb{C}(T)$ the set of consistent cuts at global time T. Given a consistent cut C, its *frontier* $\mathsf{fr}(C) \subseteq C$ is the set consisting of the last events in C of each signal, i.e., $\mathsf{fr}(C) = \bigcup_{i=1}^{n} \{(t, x_i(t)) \in V_i \cap C \mid \forall t' > t : (t', x_i(t')) \notin V_i \cap C\}$.

Definition 3. *A* consistent cut flow *is a function* $\mathsf{ccf} : \mathbb{R}_{\geq 0} \to 2^V$ *that maps a global clock value T to the frontier of a consistent cut at time T, i.e., $\mathsf{ccf}(T) \in \{\mathsf{fr}(C) \mid C \in \mathbb{C}(T)\}$.*

For all $T, T' \in \mathbb{R}_{\geq 0}$ and $1 \leq i \leq n$, if $T < T'$, then for every pair of events $(c_i(T), x_i(c_i(T))) \in \mathsf{ccf}(T)$ and $(c_i(T'), x_i(c_i(T'))) \in \mathsf{ccf}(T')$ we have $(c_i(T), x_i(c_i(T))) \rightsquigarrow (c_i(T'), x_i(c_i(T')))$. We denote by $\mathsf{CCF}(S, \rightsquigarrow)$ the set of all consistent cut flows of the distributed signal $(S, \rightsquigarrow)$.

Observe that a consistent cut flow of a distributed signal induces a vector of synchronous signals which can be evaluated using the standard STL semantics described above. Let $(S, \rightsquigarrow)$ be a distributed signal of n signals $x_1, \ldots, x_n$. A consistent cut flow $\mathsf{ccf} \in \mathsf{CCF}(S, \rightsquigarrow)$ yields a trace $w_{\mathsf{ccf}} = (x'_1, \ldots x'_n)$ on the temporal domain $[0, d)$ such that $(c_i(T), x_i(c_i(T))) \in \mathsf{ccf}(T)$ implies $x'_i(T) = x_i(c_i(T))$ for all $1 \leq i \leq n$ and $T \in [0, d)$. The set of traces of $(S, \rightsquigarrow)$ is given by $\mathsf{Tr}(S, \rightsquigarrow) = \{w_{\mathsf{ccf}} \mid \mathsf{ccf} \in \mathsf{CCF}(S, \rightsquigarrow)\}$ (Fig. 1).

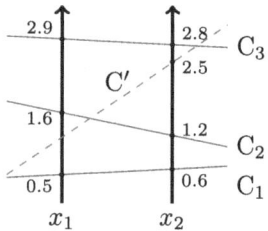

Fig. 1. A distributed signal in with consistent cuts C_1, C_2, C_3 constituting a consistent cut flow. Note that C' is a non-example since $(2.5, x_2(2.5)) \in \mathsf{fr}(C')$ and $(1.6, x_1(1.6)) \notin \mathsf{fr}(C')$, but $(1.6, x_1(1.6))$ happened before $(2.5, x_2(2.5))$.

We define the satisfaction of an STL formula φ by a distributed signal $(S, \rightsquigarrow)$ over a three-valued domain $\{\top, \bot, ?\}$ Notice that we quantify universally over traces for both satisfaction and violation.

$$[(S, \rightsquigarrow) \models \varphi] = \begin{cases} \top & \text{if } \forall w \in \mathsf{Tr}(S, \rightsquigarrow) : w \models \varphi \\ \bot & \text{if } \forall w \in \mathsf{Tr}(S, \rightsquigarrow) : w \models \neg\varphi \\ ? & \text{otherwise} \end{cases}$$

3 Overapproximation of the STL Distributed Semantics

To address the computational overhead in exact distributed monitoring, we define STL$^+$, a variant of STL whose syntax is the same as STL but semantics provide a sound approximation of the STL distributed semantics. In particular, given a distributed signal $(S, \rightsquigarrow)$, STL$^+$ considers an approximation $\mathsf{Tr}^+(S, \rightsquigarrow)$ of the set $\mathsf{Tr}(S, \rightsquigarrow)$ of synchronous traces where $\mathsf{Tr}(S, \rightsquigarrow) \subseteq \mathsf{Tr}^+(S, \rightsquigarrow)$. A signal $(S, \rightsquigarrow)$ satisfies (resp. violates) an STL$^+$ formula φ iff all the traces in $\mathsf{Tr}^+(S, \rightsquigarrow)$ belong to the language of φ (resp. $\neg \varphi$).

$$[(S, \rightsquigarrow) \models \varphi]_+ = \begin{cases} \top & \text{if } \forall w \in \mathsf{Tr}^+(S, \rightsquigarrow) : w \models \varphi \\ \bot & \text{if } \forall w \in \mathsf{Tr}^+(S, \rightsquigarrow) : w \models \neg \varphi \\ ? & \text{otherwise} \end{cases}$$

Throughout the paper, we assume φ is *copyless*, i.e., each signal $x \in S$ occurs in φ at most once. Moreover, the signals are Boolean, non-Zeno, piecewise-constant, and have no edge at time 0. We assume Boolean signals only for convenience; all the concepts and results generalize to non-Boolean signals because finite-length piecewise-constant signals use only a finite number of values. We note that our approach is a sound overapproximation also for non-copyless formulas, although potentially less precise. In Sects. 4 and 5, we respectively define Tr^+ and present an algorithm to compute the semantics of STL$^+$.

Theorem 1. *For every STL formula φ and every distributed signal $(S, \rightsquigarrow)$, if $[(S, \rightsquigarrow) \models \varphi]_+ = \top$ (resp. $\bot$) then $[(S, \rightsquigarrow) \models \varphi] = \top$ (resp. $\bot$).*

Notice that both the distributed semantics of STL and the semantics of STL$^+$ quantify universally over the set of traces for the verdicts $\top$ and $\bot$. Therefore, Theorem 1 holds for the verdicts $\top$ and $\bot$, but not for $?$.

4 Overapproximation of Synchronous Traces

In this section, given a distributed signal $(S, \rightsquigarrow)$, we describe an overapproximation $\mathsf{Tr}^+(S, \rightsquigarrow)$ of its set $\mathsf{Tr}(S, \rightsquigarrow)$ of synchronous traces. First, we present the notion of *canonical segmentation*, a systematic way of partitioning the temporal domain of a distributed signal to track partial synchrony. Second, we introduce *value expressions*, sets of finite words representing signal behavior in a time interval. Finally, we define Tr^+ and show that it soundly approximates Tr.

Canonical Segmentation. Consider a Boolean signal x with a rising edge at time $t > \varepsilon$. Due to clock skew, this edge occurs in the range $(t - \varepsilon, t + \varepsilon)$ from the monitor's perspective. This range is an *uncertainty region* because within it, the monitor can only tell that x changes from 0 to 1. Formally, given an edge $(t, x(t))$, we define $\theta_{\text{lo}}(x, t) = \max(0, t - \varepsilon)$ and $\theta_{\text{hi}}(x, t) = \min(d, t + \varepsilon)$ as the endpoints of the edge's uncertainty region.

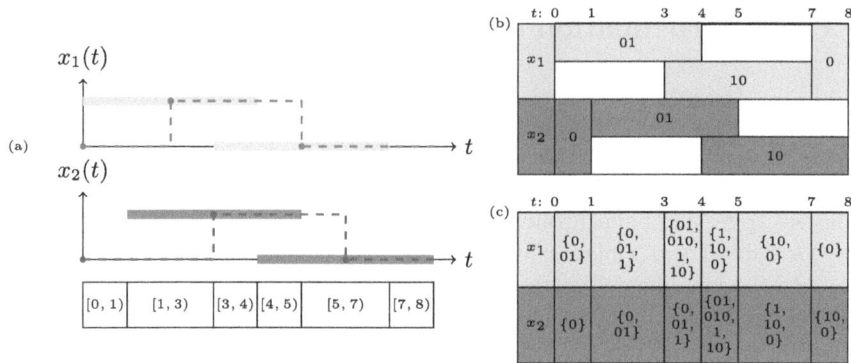

Fig. 2. (a) A distributed signal $(S, \leadsto)$ with x_1 (top, red) and x_2 (bottom, blue) whose edges are marked with solid balls and their uncertainty regions are given as semi-transparent boxes around the edges. The resulting canonical segmentation G_S is shown below the graphical representation of the signals. (b) The uncertainty regions of $(S, \leadsto)$ and the corresponding value expressions. (c) The tabular representation of the function γ for $(S, \leadsto)$, e.g., $\gamma(x_1, [3,4)) = (\mathsf{suffix}(01) \cdot \mathsf{prefix}(10)) \setminus \{\epsilon\} = \{01, 010, 1, 10\}$. (Color figure online)

Given a temporal domain $I = [0, d) \subset \mathbb{R}_{\geq 0}$, a *segmentation* of I is a partition of I into finitely many intervals $I_1, \ldots, I_k$, called *segments*, of the form $I_j = [t_j, t_{j+1})$ such that $t_j < t_{j+1}$ for all $1 \leq j \leq k$. By extension, a segmentation of a collection of signals with the same temporal domain I is a segmentation of I.

Let $(S, \leadsto)$ be a distributed signal of n signals. The *canonical segmentation* G_S of $(S, \leadsto)$ the segmentation of S where the segment endpoints match the temporal domain and uncertainty region endpoints. Formally, we define G_S as follows. For each signal x_i, where $1 \leq i \leq n$, let F_i be the set of uncertainty region endpoints. Let $F = \{0, d\} \cup \bigcup_{i=1}^{n} F_i$ and let $(s_j)_{1 \leq j \leq |F|}$ be a nondecreasing sequence of clock values corresponding to the elements of F. Then, the canonical segmentation of $(S, \leadsto)$ is $G_S = \{I_1, \ldots, I_{|F|-1}\}$ where $I_j = [s_j, s_{j+1})$ for all $1 \leq j < |F|$. We show an example in Fig. 2a.

Value Expressions. Consider a Boolean signal x with a rising edge within an uncertainty region of (t_1, t_2). As mentioned, the monitor only knows that x changes from 0 to 1 in this interval. This knowledge is represented as a finite word $v = 01$ over the alphabet $\Sigma = \{0, 1\}$. This representation, called a *value expression*, encodes the uncertain behavior of an observed signal relative to the monitor. Formally, a value expression is an element of Σ^*, where Σ is the finite alphabet of signal values. Given a signal x and an edge $(t, x(t))$, the value expression corresponding to the uncertainty region $(\theta_{\mathrm{lo}}(x, t), \theta_{\mathrm{hi}}(x, t))$ is $v_{x,t} = v_- \cdot v_+$, where $v_- = \lim_{s \to t^-} x(s)$ and $v_+ = \lim_{s \to t^+} x(s)$. We omit the concatenation symbol $\cdot$ when the letters are clear from context. This definition is general because finite-length piecewise-constant real-valued signals will only have a finite number of values, making Σ finite.

Notice that (i) uncertainty regions may overlap, and (ii) the canonical segmentation may split an uncertainty region into multiple segments. Consider a signal x with a rising edge in $(1, 5)$ and a falling edge in $(4, 8)$. The corresponding value expressions are respectively $v_1 = 01$ and $v_2 = 10$. Notice that the behavior of x in the interval $[1, 4)$ can be expressed as $\mathsf{prefix}(v_1)$, encoding whether the rising edge has happened yet. Similarly, the behavior in $[4, 5)$ is given by $\mathsf{suffix}(v_1) \cdot \mathsf{prefix}(v_2)$, which captures whether the edges occur in this interval (thanks to prefixing and suffixing) and the fact that the rising edge happens before the falling edge (thanks to concatenation).

Formally, given a distributed signal $(S, \rightsquigarrow)$, we define a function $\gamma : S \times G_S \to 2^{\Sigma^*}$ that maps each signal and segment of the canonical segmentation to a set of value expressions, capturing the signal's potential behaviors in the given segment. Let x be a signal in S, and let $R_1, \ldots, R_m$ be its uncertainty regions where $R_i = (t_i, t'_i)$ and the corresponding value expression is v_i for all $1 \leq i \leq m$. Now, let $I \in G_S$ be a segment with $I = [s, s')$ and for each $1 \leq i \leq m$ define the set V_i of value expressions capturing how I relates with R_i in Eq. (1).

The last case happens only when $I \cap R_i$ is empty. We define γ as follows:

$$\gamma(x, I) = \mathsf{destutter}(V_1 \cdot V_2 \cdot \ldots \cdot V_m) \setminus \{\epsilon\}$$

$$V_i = \begin{cases} \{v_i\} & \text{if } t_i = s \wedge s' = t'_i \\ \mathsf{prefix}(v_i) & \text{if } t_i = s \wedge s' < t'_i \\ \mathsf{suffix}(v_i) & \text{if } t_i > s \wedge s' = t'_i \\ \mathsf{infix}(v_i) & \text{if } t_i > s \wedge s' < t'_i \\ \{\epsilon\} & \text{otherwise} \end{cases} \quad (1)$$

Observe that $\gamma(x, I)$ contains all the potential behaviors of x in segment I by construction. However, it is potentially overapproximate because the sets $V_1, \ldots, V_m$ contain redundancy by definition, and the concatenation does not ensure that an edge is considered exactly once – see Fig. 2b and Fig. 2c.

Overapproximation of Tr. Consider a distributed signal $(S, \rightsquigarrow)$ of n signals, and let G_S be its canonical segmentation. We describe how the function γ defines a set $\mathsf{Tr}^+(S, \rightsquigarrow)$ of synchronous traces that overapproximates the set $\mathsf{Tr}(S, \rightsquigarrow)$. Consider $x \in S$, and let x' be a signal with the same temporal domain, and let $I = [s, s')$ be a segment in G_S. Let $(t_1, x'(t_1)), \ldots, (t_\ell, x'(t_\ell))$ be the edges of x' in segment I with $t_i < t_{i+1}$ for all $1 \leq i < \ell$. The signal x' is I-consistent with x iff the value expression $x'(s) \cdot x'(t_1) \cdot \ldots \cdot x'(t_\ell)$ belongs to $\gamma(x, I)$. Moreover, x' is consistent with x iff it is I-consistent with x for all $I \in G_S$. Now, let $S = (x_1, \ldots, x_n)$ and define $\mathsf{Tr}^+(S, \rightsquigarrow)$ as follows:

$$\mathsf{Tr}^+(S, \rightsquigarrow) = \{(x'_1, \ldots, x'_n) \mid x'_i \text{ is consistent with } x_i \text{ for all } 1 \leq i \leq n\}$$

Example 1. Recall $(S, \rightsquigarrow)$ and its γ function from Fig. 2. Consider the synchronous trace $w \in \mathsf{Tr}(S, \rightsquigarrow)$ where the rising edges of both signals occur at time 3 and the falling edges at time 5. Such a signal w would be included in $\mathsf{Tr}^+(S, \rightsquigarrow)$ since for each $i \in \{1, 2\}$, the value expression 1 is contained in $\gamma(x_i, [3, 4))$ and $\gamma(x_i, [4, 5))$, while 0 is contained in the remaining sets γ maps x_i to. Now, consider a synchronous trace (x'_1, x'_2) where both signals are initially 0, have rising edges at time 2 and 3.5, and falling edges at time 3 and 5. This trace does not belong to $\mathsf{Tr}(S, \leadsto)$ since x_1' and x_2' have more edges than x_1 and x_2. However, it belongs to $\mathsf{Tr}^+(S, \leadsto)$ since x_1' and x_2' are consistent with x_1 and x_2. Specifically, for each $i \in \{1, 2\}$, the value expression 01 is contained in $\gamma(x_i, [1, 3))$ and $\gamma(x_i, [3, 4))$, the expression 1 is contained in $\gamma(x_i, [4, 5))$, and 0 is contained in the remaining sets γ maps x_i to.

Finally, we prove that Tr^+ overapproximates Tr.

Lemma 1. *For every distributed signal* $(S, \leadsto)$, *we have* $\mathsf{Tr}(S, \leadsto) \subseteq \mathsf{Tr}^+(S, \leadsto)$.

5 Monitoring Algorithm

In this section, for a distributed signal $(S, \leadsto)$, we describe an algorithm to compute $[(S, \leadsto) \models \varphi]_+$ using the function γ from Sect. 4 without explicitly computing $\mathsf{Tr}^+(S, \leadsto)$. We introduce the *asynchronous product* of value expressions to capture interleavings within segments, then evaluate *untimed* and *timed operators*. Finally, we combine these steps to compute the *semantics* of STL$^+$. We also discuss an efficient implementation of the monitoring algorithm using *bit vectors*, heuristics to enhance *generalization* for real-valued signals, and a method to *combine* our approach with exact monitoring.

Asynchronous Products. Consider the value expressions $u_1 = 0 \cdot 1$ and $u_2 = 1 \cdot 0$ encoding the behaviors of two signals within a segment. Since behaviors within a segment are asynchronous, to capture their potential interleavings, we consider how the values in u_1 and u_2 can align. In particular, there are three potential alignments: (i) the rising edge of u_1 happens before the falling edge of u_2, (ii) the falling edge of u_2 happens before the rising edge of u_1, and (iii) they happen simultaneously. We respectively represent these with the tuples $(011, 110)$, $(001, 100)$, and $(01, 10)$ where the first component encodes u_1 and the second u_2. Formally, given two value expressions u_1 and u_2 (resp. sets L_1 and L_2 of value expressions), we define their *asynchronous product* as follows:

$$u_1 \otimes u_2 = \{\mathsf{destutter}(v_1, v_2) \mid v_i \in \mathsf{stutter}_k(u_i), k = |u_1| + |u_2| - 1, i \in \{1, 2\}\}$$
$$L_1 \otimes L_2 = \{u_1 \otimes u_2 \mid u_1 \in L_1, u_2 \in L_2\}$$

Asynchronous products of value expressions allow us to lift value expressions to satisfaction signals of formulas.

Example 2. Recall $(S, \leadsto)$ and its γ function given in Fig. 2. To compute the value expressions encoding the satisfaction of $x_1 \wedge x_2$ in the segment $[1, 3)$, we first compute the asynchronous product $\gamma(x_1, [3, 4)) \otimes \gamma(x_2, [3, 4))$, and then the bitwise conjunction of each pair in the set. For example, taking the expression 010 for x_1 and 01 for x_2, the product contains the pair $(010, 011)$. Its bitwise conjunction is 010, encoding a potential behavior for the satisfaction of $x_1 \wedge x_2$.

Untimed Operations. As hinted in Example 2, to compute the semantics, we apply bitwise operations on value expressions and their asynchronous products to transform them into encodings of satisfaction signals of formulas. For example, to determine $[(S, \leadsto) \models \Diamond(x_1 \wedge x_2)]_+$, we first compute for each segment in G_S the set of value expressions for the satisfaction of $x_1 \wedge x_2$, and then from these compute those of $\Diamond(x_1 \wedge x_2)$. This compositional approach allows us to evaluate arbitrary STL$^+$ formulas.

First, we define bitwise operations on Boolean value expressions encoding atomic propositions. Then, we use these to evaluate untimed STL formulas over sets of value expressions. Let u and v be Boolean value expressions of length ℓ. We denote by $u \,\&\, v$ the bitwise-and operation, by $u \mid v$ the bitwise-or, and by $\sim\! u$ the bitwise-negation. We also define the *bitwise strong until* operator:

$$u\mathsf{U}^0 v = \left(\max_{i \leq j \leq \ell} \left(\min \left(v[j], \min_{i \leq k \leq j} u[k] \right) \right) \right)_{1 \leq i \leq \ell}$$

As usual, we derive *bitwise eventually* as $\mathsf{E}u = 1^\ell \mathsf{U}^0 u$, *bitwise always* as $\mathsf{A}u = \sim\!(\mathsf{E}\sim\! u)$, and *bitwise weak until* as $u\mathsf{U}^1 v = (u\mathsf{U}^0\, v) \mid (\mathsf{A}u)$. The distinction between U^0 and U^1 will be useful when we incrementally evaluate a formula. Finally, note that the output of these operations is a value expression of length ℓ. For example, if $u = 010$, we have $\mathsf{E}u = 110$ and $\mathsf{A}u = 000$.

Let $(S, \leadsto)$ be a distributed signal. Consider an atomic proposition $p \in \mathsf{AP}$ encoded as $x_p \in S$ and let φ_1, φ_2 be two STL formulas. We define the evaluation of untimed formulas with respect to $(S, \leadsto)$ and a segment $I \in G_S$ inductively:

$[(S, \leadsto), I \models p] = \gamma(x_p, I)$
$[(S, \leadsto), I \models \neg\varphi_1] = \{\sim\! u \mid u \in [(S, \leadsto), I \models \varphi_1]\}$
$[(S, \leadsto), I \models \varphi_1 \wedge \varphi_2] = \mathsf{destutter}(\{u_1 \,\&\, u_2 \mid (u_1, u_2) \in [(S, \leadsto), I \models \varphi_1] \otimes [(S, \leadsto), I \models \varphi_2]\})$
$[(S, \leadsto), I \models \varphi_1 \mathcal{U} \varphi_2] = \mathsf{destutter}(\{u_1 \mathsf{U}^a u_2 \mid (u_1, u_2) \in [(S, \leadsto), I \models \varphi_1] \otimes [(S, \leadsto), I \models \varphi_2],$
$a \in \mathsf{first}([(S, \leadsto), I' \models \varphi_1 \mathcal{U} \varphi_2])\})$

where I' is the segment that follows I in G_S, if it exists. For completeness, for every formula φ we define $[(S, \leadsto), I' \models \varphi] = \{0\}$ when $I' \notin G_S$. When $I$is the first segment in G_S, we simply write $[(S, \leadsto) \models \varphi]$. Similarly as above, we can use the standard derived operators to compute the corresponding sets of value expressions. For a given formula and a segment, the evaluation above produces a set of value expressions encoding the formula's satisfaction within the segment.

Example 3. Recall $(S, \leadsto)$ and γ from Fig. 2. To compute $[(S, \leadsto), [5,7) \models \Diamond(x_1 \wedge x_2)]$, we first compute $[(S, \leadsto), [5,7) \models x_1 \wedge x_2]$ by taking the bitwise conjunction over the asynchronous product $\gamma(x_1, [5,7)) \otimes \gamma(x_2, [5,7))$ and destuttering. For example, since $010 \in \gamma(x_1, [5,7))$ and $01 \in \gamma(x_2, [5,7))$, the pair $(0010, 0111)$ is in the product, whose conjunction gives us 010 after destuttering. Repeating this for the rest, we obtain $[(S, \leadsto), [5,7) \models x_1 \wedge x_2] = \{0, 01, 010, 1, 10\}$. Finally, we compute $[(S, \leadsto), [5,7) \models \Diamond(x_1 \wedge x_2)]$ by applying each expression in $[\![(S, \leadsto), [5, 7) \models x_1 \wedge x_2]\!]$ the bitwise eventually operator and destuttering. The resulting set $\{0, 1, 10\}$ encodes the satisfaction signal of $\Diamond(x_1 \wedge x_2)$ in $[5, 7)$. Note that we do not need to consider the evaluation of the next segment for the eventually operator since $[\![(S, \leadsto), [7, 8) \models x_1 \wedge x_2]\!] = \{0\}$.

Timed Operations. Handling timed operations requires a closer inspection as value expressions are untimed by definition. We address this issue by considering how a given evaluation interval relates with a given segmentation. For example, take a segmentation $G_S = \{[0, 4), [4, 6), [6, 10)\}$ and an evaluation interval $J = [0, 5)$. Suppose we are interested in how a signal $x \in S$ behaves with respect to J over the first segment $I = [0, 4)$. First, to see how J relates with G_S with respect to $I = [0, 4)$, we "slide" the interval J over $I \oplus J = [0, 9)$ and consider the different ways it intersects the segments in G_S. Initially, J covers the entire segment $[0, 4)$ and the beginning of $[4, 6)$, for which the potential behaviors of x are captured by the set $\gamma(x, [0, 4)) \cdot \mathsf{prefix}(\gamma(x, [4, 6)))$. Now, if we slide the window and take $J' = [3, 7)$, the window covers the ending of $[0, 4)$, the entire $[4, 6)$, and the beginning of $[6, 10)$, for which the potential behaviors are captured by the set $\mathsf{suffix}(\gamma(x, [0, 4))) \cdot \gamma(x, [4, 6)) \cdot \mathsf{prefix}(\gamma(x, [6, 9)))$. We call these sets the *profiles* of J and J' with respect to $(S, \leadsto)$, x, and I.

We first present the definitions, and then demonstrate them in Examples 4 and 5 and Fig. 3. Let $(S, \leadsto)$ be a distributed signal, $I \in G_S$ be a segment, and φ be an STL formula. Let us introduce some notation. First, we abbreviate the set $[\![(S, \leadsto), I \models \varphi]\!]$ of value expressions as $\tau_{\varphi, I}$. Second, given an interval K, we respectively denote by l_K and r_K its left and right end points. Third, recall that we denote by F the set of end points of G_S (see Sect. 4). Given an interval J, we define the *profile* of J with respect to $(S, \leadsto)$, φ, and I as follows:

$$\mathsf{profile}((S, \leadsto), \varphi, I, J) = \begin{cases} \mathsf{prefix}(\tau_{\varphi, I}) & \text{if } l_I = l_J \wedge r_I > r_J \\ \mathsf{infix}(\tau_{\varphi, I}) & \text{if } l_I < l_J \wedge r_I > r_J \\ \tau_{\varphi, I} \cdot \kappa(\varphi, I, J) & \text{if } l_I = l_J \wedge r_I \leq r_J \wedge r_J \in F \setminus J \\ \tau_{\varphi, I} \cdot \kappa(\varphi, I, J) \cdot \mathsf{first}(\tau_{\varphi, I'}) & \text{if } l_I = l_J \wedge r_I \leq r_J \wedge r_J \in F \cap J \\ \tau_{\varphi, I} \cdot \kappa(\varphi, I, J) \cdot \mathsf{prefix}(\tau_{\varphi, I'}) & \text{if } l_I = l_J \wedge r_I \leq r_J \wedge r_J \notin F \\ \mathsf{suffix}(\tau_{\varphi, I}) \cdot \kappa(\varphi, I, J) & \text{if } l_I < l_J < r_I \leq r_J \wedge r_J \in F \setminus J \\ \mathsf{suffix}(\tau_{\varphi, I}) \cdot \kappa(\varphi, I, J) \cdot \mathsf{first}(\tau_{\varphi, I'}) & \text{if } l_I < l_J < r_I \leq r_J \wedge r_J \in F \cap J \\ \mathsf{suffix}(\tau_{\varphi, I}) \cdot \kappa(\varphi, I, J) \cdot \mathsf{prefix}(\tau_{\varphi, I'}) & \text{if } l_I < l_J < r_I \leq r_J \wedge r_J \notin F \\ \{\epsilon\} & \text{otherwise} \end{cases}$$

where we assume J is trimmed to fit the temporal domain of S and $I' \in G_S$ is such that $r_J \in I'$. Moreover, $\kappa(\varphi, I, J)$ is the concatenation $\tau_{\varphi, I_1} \cdot \ldots \cdot \tau_{\varphi, I_m}$ such that $I, I_1, \ldots, I_m, I'$ are consecutive segments in G_S. If $I_1, \ldots, I_m$ do not exist, we let $\kappa(\varphi, I, J) = \{\epsilon\}$. Note that the last case happens when $I \cap J$ is empty. We now formalize the intuitive approach of "sliding" J over the segmentation to obtain the various profiles it produces as follows:

$$\mathsf{pfs}((S, \rightsquigarrow), \varphi, I, J) = \{\mathsf{destutter}(\mathsf{profile}((S, \rightsquigarrow), \varphi, I, J')) \mid J' \subseteq I \oplus J, J' \sim J\}$$

where $J' \sim J$ holds when $|J'| = |J|$ and J' contains an end point (left or right) iff J does so. Note that although infinitely many intervals J' satisfy the conditions given above (due to denseness of time), the set defined by pfs is finite. We demonstrate this and the computation of pfs in Example 4 and Fig. 3.

Example 4. Recall $(S, \rightsquigarrow)$ and γ from Fig. 2. We describe the computation of $\mathsf{pfs}((S, \rightsquigarrow), x_1, [1, 3), [0, 1))$. Sliding the interval $[0, 1)$ over the window $[1, 3) \oplus [0, 1)$ (see Fig. 3) gives us the following sets: $P_1 = \mathsf{destutter}(\mathsf{prefix}(\gamma(x_1, [1, 3))))$, $P_2 = \mathsf{destutter}(\mathsf{infix}(\gamma(x_1, [1, 3))))$, and $P_3 = \mathsf{destutter}(\mathsf{suffix}(\gamma(x_1, [1, 3))))$ where all equal to $\{0, 01, 1\}$. Moreover, we have $P_4 = \mathsf{destutter}(\mathsf{suffix}(\gamma(x_1, [1, 3))) \cdot \mathsf{prefix}(\gamma(x_1, [3, 4)))) = \{0, 01, 010, 0101, 01010, 1, 10, 101, 1010\}$. We obtain that $\mathsf{pfs}((S, \rightsquigarrow), x_1, [1, 3), [0, 1)) = \{P_1, P_2, P_3, P_4\}$. This set overapproximates the potential behaviors of x_1, for all $t \in [1, 3)$, in the interval $t \oplus [0, 1)$.

Let φ_1 and φ_2 be two STL formulas. Intuitively, once we have the profiles of a given interval J with respect to φ_1 and φ_2, we can evaluate the corresponding untimed formulas on the product of these profiles and concatenate them. Formally, we handle the evaluation of timed formulas as follows:

$$[\![(S, \rightsquigarrow), I \models \varphi_1 \mathcal{U}_J \varphi_2]\!] = \mathsf{destutter}(\{u_1 \mathsf{U}^0 u_2 \mid (u_1, u_2) \in P_1 \otimes Q_1\} \cdots$$
$$\cdots \{u_1 \mathsf{U}^0 u_2 \mid (u_1, u_2) \in P_k \otimes Q_k\})$$

where $\mathsf{pfs}((S, \rightsquigarrow), \varphi_1, I, J) = \{P_1, \ldots, P_k\}$ and $\mathsf{pfs}((S, \rightsquigarrow), \varphi_2, I, J) = \{Q_1, \ldots, Q_k\}$ such that the intervals producing P_i and Q_i respectively start before those producing P_{i+1} and Q_{i+1} for all $1 \leq i < k$.

Example 5. Let $(S, \rightsquigarrow)$ and γ be as in Fig. 2. We demonstrate the evaluation of the timed formula $\Diamond_{[0,1)} x_1$ over the segment $[1, 3)$. Recall from Example 4 the set $\mathsf{pfs}((S, \rightsquigarrow), x_1, [1, 3), [0, 1)) = \{P_1, P_2, P_3, P_4\}$ of profiles. First, we apply the bitwise eventually operator to each value expression in each of these profiles separately: $\{\mathsf{E}u \mid u \in P_1\} = \{\mathsf{E}u \mid u \in P_2\} = \{\mathsf{E}u \mid u \in P_3\} = \{0, 1\}$, and $\{\mathsf{E}u \mid u \in P_4\} = \{0, 10, 1\}$. We then concatenate these and destutter to obtain $[\![(S, \rightsquigarrow), [1, 3) \models \Diamond_{[0,1)} x_1]\!] = \{0, 01, 010, 0101, 01010, 1, 10, 101, 1010\}$.

Computing the Semantics of STL$^+$. Putting it all together, given a distributed signal $(S, \rightsquigarrow)$ and an STL$^+$ formula φ, we can compute $[(S, \rightsquigarrow) \models \varphi]_+$ thanks to the following theorem.

Theorem 2. *For every distributed signal $(S, \rightsquigarrow)$ and STL formula φ we have $[(S, \rightsquigarrow) \models \varphi]_+ = \top$ (resp. $\bot$, ?) iff $\mathsf{first}([\![(S, \rightsquigarrow) \models \varphi]\!]) = \{1\}$ (resp. $\{0\}$, $\{0, 1\}$).*

Sets of Boolean Value Expressions as Bit Vectors. Asynchronous products are expensive to compute. Our implementation relies on the observation that sets of boolean value expressions and their operations can be efficiently implemented through bit vectors. Intuitively, to represent such a set, we encode each element using its first bit and its length since value expressions are boolean and always destuttered. Moreover, to evaluate untimed operations on such sets, we only need to know the maximal lengths of the four possible types of expressions ($0\ldots0$, $0\ldots1$, $1\ldots0$, and $1\ldots1$) and whether the set contains 0 or 1 (to handle some edge cases). This is because value expressions within the same segments are completely asynchronous and the possible interleavings obtained from shorter expressions can be also obtained from longer ones.

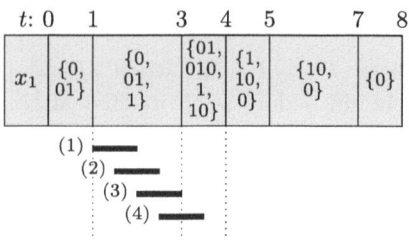

Fig. 3. The profiles of $J = [0,1)$ with respect to $x_1 \in S$ of Fig. 2. A representative interval for each profile is shown with solid black lines below the table.

Generalization to Real-Valued Signals. Our approximate distributed monitoring method, denoted ADM, can be extended to real-valued signals and numerical predicates. The key is that finite-length piecewise-constant signals take finitely many values. By defining Σ as a finite alphabet of these values, we can compute atomic propositions as above. For example, if the asynchronous product of two signals x_1 and x_2 yields $(2 \cdot 2 \cdot 3, 1 \cdot 0 \cdot 1)$, adding these letter-by-letter results in $3 \cdot 2 \cdot 4$, and comparing with > 2 gives 101.

We can avoid explicit computation of asynchronous products for some formulas and numerical predicates. Since signals are asynchronous within segments, we can compute potential value sets instead of sequences. This approach is called *Fine*, denoted by ADM-F. Assuming $x_1 + x_2$ is constant within this segment, we can avoid explicit interleaving computations. Note that ADM-F overapproximates traces when order matters. The approach *Coarse*, denoted ADM-C, abstracts *Fine* by only considering extreme values, which is useful for monotonic operations where the extreme values of outputs derive from inputs.

We assumed so far that the central monitor runs on a process independent of the observed agents. Lastly, we also consider a setting where the monitor runs on one of the observed agents. This approach reduces asynchrony by using the agent's local clock as a reference point for the monitor. We call this *Relative*, denoted ADM-FR or ADM-CR depending on the approach it is paired with. We evaluate these in Sect. 6.

Combining Exact and Approximate Monitoring. We propose a method that combines approximate distributed monitors (ADM) with their exact counterparts (EDM) with the aim to achieve better computational performance while remaining precise. The approach works as follows: Given a distributed signal $(S, \leadsto)$ and a formula φ, compute the approximate verdict $v \leftarrow [(S, \leadsto) \models \varphi]_+$.

If the verdict is inconclusive, i.e., $v =\ ?$, then compute and return the exact verdict $[(S, \rightsquigarrow) \models \varphi]$, else return v. We evaluate this approach in Sect. 6.

6 Experimental Evaluation

6.1 Research Questions

We seek answers to the following research questions (RQs):

RQ1. *What is the tradeoff between the efficiency and the accuracy of approximate distributed monitors?* The approximate distributed monitoring comes with a price in terms of the loss of accuracy. We want to understand the tradeoff between the potential speedups that an approximate distributed monitor can achieve when compared to its exact counterpart and the consequent loss in accuracy due to the approximations. We would also like to identify the classes of signals and properties for which this tradeoff is effective.

RQ2. *Can the combination of approximate and exact distributed monitors increase efficiency while preserving accuracy?* We are interested in evaluating whether a smart, combined use of approximate and exact distributed monitors can still bring improvements in monitoring efficiency while guaranteeing the accuracy of the monitoring verdicts.

6.2 Experimental Setup

Distributed Monitors. In our study, we compare our approximate distributed monitoring (ADM) approach and its variants to an exact distributed monitoring approach (EDM).[1] For EDM, we take a variant of the distributed monitoring procedure from [18] that allows to evaluate STL specifications over distributed traces using SMT-solving. Originally, that procedure assumes that input signals are polynomial continuous functions. We adapt the SMT-based approach to consider input signals as piecewise-constant signals to make a consistent comparison with ADM. We note that the passage from the polynomial continuous to piecewise-constant input signals reduces the efficiency of the SMT-based monitors. We also observe that the SMT-based monitors from [18] can split the input trace into multiple segments and evaluate the specification incrementally, segment-by-segment, allowing early termination of the monitor in some cases. Since the focus of this paper is purely on the offline monitoring, we also use the exact monitors without their incremental mode.

Experimental Subjects. To answer our research questions, we use (1) a *random generator (RG)* of distributed traces, (2) a *water tank (WT)* case study, and (3) a *swarm of drones (SD)* case study. *The random generator (RG)* uses uniform distribution to generate distributed traces, in which the user can control the duration d of the trace, as well as the ε bound on the uncertainty at which the events happen. *Water tank (WT)* model is a SimuLink model of a hybrid

---
[1] The code is available at https://github.com/egesarac/ApxDistMon.

Table 1. STL specifications used in the experiments.

Subject	STL formula(s)
RG	$\varphi_1 = \Box(p \wedge q) \quad \varphi_2 = \Box(p \Rightarrow \Diamond q) \quad \varphi_3 = \Box(p \Rightarrow \Diamond_{[0,1)} q)$
WT	$\varphi_{\text{WT}} = \Box \left(\sum_{i=1}^{n} x_i > c \right)$
SD	$\varphi_{\text{SD}} = \bigwedge_{1 \leq i \neq j \leq n} \Box \left(\sqrt{(x_i - x_j)^2 + (y_i - y_j)^2 + (z_i - z_j)^2} > c \right)$

high pressure water distribution system consisting of two water tanks. Inlet pipes connect each water tank to an external source, and outlet pipes distribute high pressure water that is regulated by valves. Each valve is operated by a controller that samples the outflow pressure at 20 Hz using its local clock. Our model is a simplified emulation of the Refueling Water Storage Tanks (RWST) module of an Emergency Core Cooling System (ECCS) of a Pressurized Water Reactor Plant [24]. *Swarm of drones (SD)* model is generated using a path planning software, Fly-by-Logic [22]. Here, a swarm of drones perform various reach-avoid missions, while securing objectives such as reaching a goal within a deadline, avoiding obstacles and collisions. The path planner finds the most robust trajectory using a temporal logic robustness optimizer. These trajectories are sampled at 20 Hz. Note that the actual values of clock skew are less important than the fact that when clock skew exceeds the sampling interval, we encounter the problem of uncertainty.

Specifications. Table 1 shows the STL specifications that we use to evaluate our experimental subjects. Specifications φ_1, φ_2 and φ_3 are monitored against the distributed traces created by the random generator and represent different classes and fragments of Boolean-valued temporal formulas. The first specification φ_1 is an LTL formula in which both the outer temporal operator ($\Box$) and the inner Boolean operator ($\wedge$) are conjunctive. The second formula φ_2 is the common LTL response formula which combines conjunctive ($\Box$) and disjunctive ($\Diamond, \Rightarrow$) operators. Finally, φ_3 adds a bounded real-time response requirement to the previous specification. The specification φ_{WT} associated to the water tank case study is an STL formula in which a sum of signals originating from different agents is compared to a constant. Finally, the specification φ_{SD} defines a mutual separation property over a swarm of drones, requiring more sophisticated arithmetic operations on signals originating from different agents.

Computing Platform. We used a laptop with Ubuntu 24.04, an AMD Ryzen 7 4800HS CPU at 2.90 GHz clock rate, and 16GB of RAM. ADM is implemented in C++ and compiled using g++ version 13.2.0 with the optimization flag -O3 enabled, and EDM invokes the SMT-solver Z3 [20] and is based on [18].

6.3 Discussion

Random Generator. Figure 4 summarizes the results of evaluating specifications φ_1 to φ_3 against distributed traces from RG. The first column in the figure

Approximate Distributed Monitoring Under Partial Synchrony 297

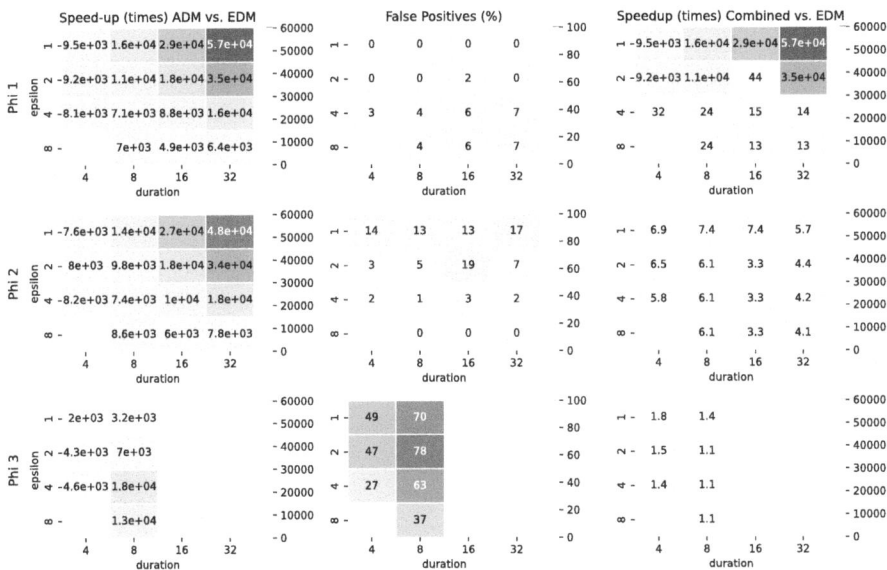

Fig. 4. Results on monitoring φ_1 to φ_3 on distributed traces created by the RG.

depicts a heatmap where cells show the speedup of ADM compared to EDM when evaluating the formula on the given distributed trace with duration d and uncertainty bound ε. The second column shows a heatmap where every cell shows the percentage of *false positives* (FP) introduced by ADM, where ADM evaluates to inconclusive when the EDM (real) verdict is true or false. Finally, the third column depicts a heatmap, where each cell estimates the achieved speedup when combining ADM with EDM, compared to using only EDM.

We see that ADM consistently achieves speedups of *several orders of magnitude* compared to the EDM approach. The speedups range from several thousands to almost 60 thousand times and are the highest for long signals with low uncertainty bounds. The price paid in terms of accuracy highly depends on the type of specification and the uncertainty bounds. For example, ADM is very accurate when monitoring the property φ_1 in which both the temporal and the combinatorial operators are conjunctive. On the other hand, having a combination of conjunctive and disjunctive operations (as in φ_2 and φ_3) increases the number of FPs. Surprisingly, we see that in these cases the introduction of FPs is higher for lower values of ε. This is because even EDM gives many inconclusive verdicts for higher values of ε. We see that adding real-time modalities to the temporal operators increases FPs. Finally, we can see (Fig. 4 right column) that by combining EDM and ADM, we consistently get better performance than by using EDM only, even in cases where ADM introduces a high percentage of FPs.

Water Tank. Speedups increase with the number of signals n and decrease with ε. The ADM-C method shows significant improvements over EDM, with

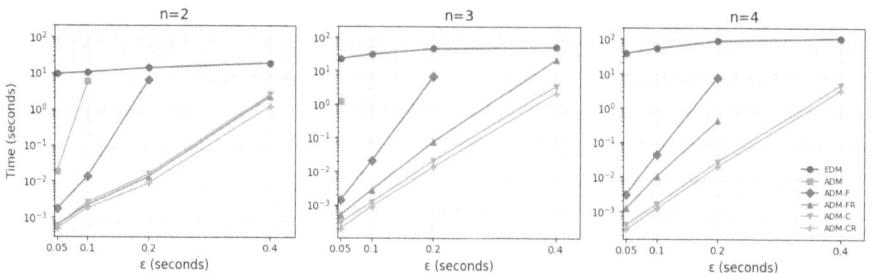

Fig. 5. Running times for monitoring φ_{WT} in log scale. Time limit is 120 s, and timed-out instances are not shown.

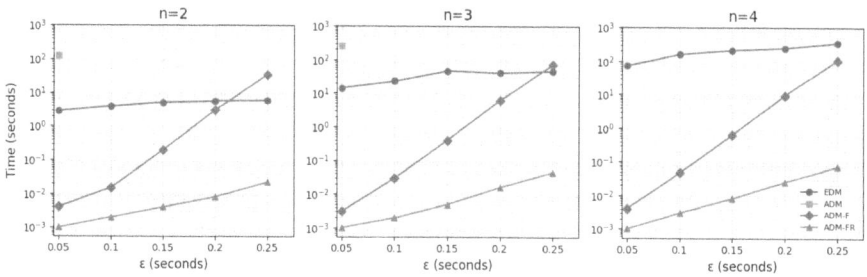

Fig. 6. Running times for monitoring φ_{SD} in log scale. Time limit is 360 s, and timed-out instances are not shown.

up to a 104000× speedup in the best-case (when $n = 4$ and $\varepsilon = 0.05$) and an 8× speedup in the worst-case (when $n = 2$ and $\varepsilon = 0.4$). Note that $\varepsilon = 0.4$ is near the realistic upper limit [18], indicating no scalability issues. The ADM-CR method adds up to a 1.63× speedup over ADM-C. The ADM-FR approach significantly improves ADM-F, bringing it below the time-out limit with up to a 476× speedup in non-time-out instances. As expected, ADM does not perform well. All methods produce the same verdict for the considered traces (Fig. 5).

Swarm of Drones. Similar to the previous case scenario, speedups in the mutual separation case increase with n and decrease with ε. The ADM-FR method achieves about a 78000× speedup in the best-case scenario (when $n = 4$ and $\varepsilon = 0.05$) and a 23× speedup in the worst-case (when $n = 2$ and $\varepsilon = 0.25$). The ADM-F method performs slower than SMT in two cases where n is small and ε is large. As in the previous case, ADM does not perform well. Additionally, ADM-C and ADM-CR are not applicable here because the arithmetic operations are not monotonic. Again, all methods yield the same verdicts (Fig. 6).

Summary. To answer RQ1, we find that ADM achieves a speedup of three to five orders of magnitude over EDM. However, the efficiency-accuracy tradeoff depends on the type of specifications, input signal duration, and maximal clock skew. Arithmetic and timed operators are particularly affected by ADM's overapproximations, reducing accuracy. Untimed temporal properties, especially those without mixed conjunctive and disjunctive operations, maintain high accuracy and offer an excellent tradeoff. Despite lower accuracy in some cases, combining ADM and EDM still results in significant gains, positively answering RQ2.

7 Conclusion

We presented an approximate, modular procedure for distributed STL monitoring that significantly improves efficiency over exact SMT-based methods. In this paper, the focus was on the offline evaluation of distributed traces. We plan to extend our monitoring approach to the online setting. We will also exploit the modular nature of our monitors to have a better control over their accuracy. More specifically, for every operator, we can either generate the exact or the approximate evaluation algorithm.

References

1. Aceto, L., Achilleos, A., Francalanza, A., Ingólfsdóttir, A., Lehtinen, K.: The best a monitor can do. In: Baier, C., Goubault-Larrecq, J. (eds.) 29th EACSL Annual Conference on Computer Science Logic, CSL 2021, 25–28 January 2021, Ljubljana, Slovenia (Virtual Conference). LIPIcs, vol. 183, pp. 7:1–7:23. Schloss Dagstuhl - Leibniz-Zentrum für Informatik (2021). https://doi.org/10.4230/LIPICS.CSL.2021.7
2. Aceto, L., Attard, D.P., Francalanza, A., Ingólfsdóttir, A.: On benchmarking for concurrent runtime verification. In: FASE 2021. LNCS, vol. 12649, pp. 3–23. Springer, Cham (2021). https://doi.org/10.1007/978-3-030-71500-7_1
3. Alechina, N., Dastani, M., Logan, B.: Norm approximation for imperfect monitors. In: Bazzan, A.L.C., Huhns, M.N., Lomuscio, A., Scerri, P. (eds.) International conference on Autonomous Agents and Multi-Agent Systems, AAMAS 2014, Paris, France, 5–9 May 2014, pp. 117–124. IFAAMAS/ACM (2014). http://dl.acm.org/citation.cfm?id=2615753
4. Bartocci, E., Grosu, R.: Monitoring with uncertainty. In: Bortolussi, L., Bujorianu, M., Pola, G. (eds.) Proceedings Third International Workshop on Hybrid Autonomous Systems, HAS 2013, Rome, Italy, 17th March 2013. EPTCS, vol. 124, pp. 1–4 (2013). https://doi.org/10.4204/EPTCS.124.1
5. Bauer, A., Falcone, Y.: Decentralised LTL monitoring. Formal Methods Syst. Design **48**(1–2), 46–93 (2016)
6. Bonakdarpour, B., Fraigniaud, P., Rajsbaum, S., Rosenblueth, D.A., Travers, C.: Decentralized asynchronous crash-resilient runtime verification. J. ACM **69**(5), 34:1–34:31 (2022)
7. Chauhan, H., Garg, V.K., Natarajan, A., Mittal, N.: A distributed abstraction algorithm for online predicate detection. In: Proceedings of the 32nd IEEE Symposium on Reliable Distributed Systems (SRDS), pp. 101–110 (2013)

8. Colombo, C., Falcone, Y.: Organising LTL monitors over distributed systems with a global clock. Formal Methods Syst. Design **49**(1–2), 109–158 (2016)
9. El-Hokayem, A., Falcone, Y.: On the monitoring of decentralized specifications: semantics, properties, analysis, and simulation. ACM Trans. Softw. Eng. Methodol. **29**(1), 1:1–1:57 (2020)
10. Ganguly, R., Momtaz, A., Bonakdarpour, B.: Runtime verification of partially-synchronous distributed system. Formal Methods Syst. Design (FMSD) (2024, to appear)
11. Ganguly, R., Momtaz, A., Bonakdarpour, B.: Distributed runtime verification under partial synchrony. In: Bramas, Q., Oshman, R., Romano, P. (eds.) 24th International Conference on Principles of Distributed Systems, OPODIS 2020, 14–16 December 2020, Strasbourg, France (Virtual Conference). LIPIcs, vol. 184, pp. 20:1–20:17. Schloss Dagstuhl - Leibniz-Zentrum für Informatik (2020)https://doi.org/10.4230/LIPIcs.OPODIS.2020.20
12. Garg, V.K.: Predicate detection to solve combinatorial optimization problems. In: Proceedings of the 32nd ACM Symposium on Parallelism in Algorithms and Architectures (SPAA), pp. 235–245. ACM (2020)
13. Henzinger, T.A., Mazzocchi, N., Saraç, N.E.: Abstract monitors for quantitative specifications. In: Dang, T., Stolz, V. (eds.) RV 2022. LNCS, vol. 13498, pp. 200–220. Springer, Cham (2022). https://doi.org/10.1007/978-3-031-17196-3_11
14. Henzinger, T.A., Mazzocchi, N., Saraç, N.E.: Quantitative safety and liveness. In: Kupferman, O., Sobocinski, P. (eds.) FoSSaCS 2023. LNCS, vol. 13992, pp. 349–370. Springer, Cham (2023). https://doi.org/10.1007/978-3-031-30829-1_17
15. Henzinger, T.A., Saraç, N.E.: Quantitative and approximate monitoring. In: 36th Annual ACM/IEEE Symposium on Logic in Computer Science, LICS 2021, Rome, Italy, 29 June–2 July 2021, pp. 1–14. IEEE (2021). https://doi.org/10.1109/LICS52264.2021.9470547
16. Maler, O., Nickovic, D.: Monitoring properties of analog and mixed-signal circuits. Int. J. Softw. Tools Technol. Transf. **15**(3), 247–268 (2013). https://doi.org/10.1007/s10009-012-0247-9
17. Mittal, N., Garg, V.K.: Techniques and applications of computation slicing. Distrib. Comput. **17**(3), 251–277 (2005)
18. Momtaz, A., Abbas, H., Bonakdarpour, B.: Monitoring signal temporal logic in distributed cyber-physical systems. In: Mitra, S., Venkatasubramanian, N., Dubey, A., Feng, L., Ghasemi, M., Sprinkle, J. (eds.) Proceedings of the ACM/IEEE 14th International Conference on Cyber-Physical Systems, ICCPS 2023, (with CPS-IoT Week 2023), San Antonio, TX, USA, 9–12 May 2023, pp. 154–165. ACM (2023). https://doi.org/10.1145/3576841.3585937
19. Mostafa, M., Bonakdarpour, B.: Decentralized runtime verification of LTL specifications in distributed systems. In: Proceedings of the 29th IEEE International Parallel and Distributed Processing Symposium (IPDPS), pp. 494–503 (2015)
20. de Moura, L., Bjørner, N.: Z3: an efficient SMT solver. In: Ramakrishnan, C.R., Rehof, J. (eds.) TACAS 2008. LNCS, vol. 4963, pp. 337–340. Springer, Heidelberg (2008). https://doi.org/10.1007/978-3-540-78800-3_24
21. Ogale, V.A., Garg, V.K.: Detecting temporal logic predicates on distributed computations. In: Pelc, A. (ed.) DISC 2007. LNCS, vol. 4731, pp. 420–434. Springer, Heidelberg (2007). https://doi.org/10.1007/978-3-540-75142-7_32
22. Pant, Y.V., Abbas, H., Mangharam, R.: Smooth operator: control using the smooth robustness of temporal logic. In: 2017 IEEE Conference on Control Technology and Applications (CCTA), pp. 1235–1240. IEEE (2017)

23. Stoller, S.D., et al.: Runtime verification with state estimation. In: Khurshid, S., Sen, K. (eds.) RV 2011. LNCS, vol. 7186, pp. 193–207. Springer, Heidelberg (2012). https://doi.org/10.1007/978-3-642-29860-8_15
24. USNRC: Pressurized water reactor systems (2021). https://www.nrc.gov/reading-rm/basic-ref/students/for-educators/04.pdf

Open Access This chapter is licensed under the terms of the Creative Commons Attribution 4.0 International License (http://creativecommons.org/licenses/by/4.0/), which permits use, sharing, adaptation, distribution and reproduction in any medium or format, as long as you give appropriate credit to the original author(s) and the source, provide a link to the Creative Commons license and indicate if changes were made.

The images or other third party material in this chapter are included in the chapter's Creative Commons license, unless indicated otherwise in a credit line to the material. If material is not included in the chapter's Creative Commons license and your intended use is not permitted by statutory regulation or exceeds the permitted use, you will need to obtain permission directly from the copyright holder.

Author Index

A
Allen, Nathan 3

B
Banno, Ryotaro 59
Baumeister, Jan 192
Benny, Amrutha 109
Bensalem, Saddek 229
Bian, Song 59
Bonakdarpour, Borzoo 282
Budnik, Christof 70

C
Caldeira, Manuel 163
Castañeda, Armando 262
Chandran, Sandeep 109
Chang, Kevin Kai-Chun 40

D
Deshmukh, Jyotirmoy V. 70

F
Finkbeiner, Bernd 22, 192
Fränzle, Martin 22

G
Guldstrand Larsen, Kim 174

H
Hashemi, Navid 70
Hashemi, Vahid 218
He, Weicheng 229
Henry, Léo 243
Huang, Chao 205

J
Jéron, Thierry 243

K
Kalayappan, Rajshekar 109
Kallwies, Hannes 163
Kauffman, Sean 174
Kautenburger, Jan 192
Khandait, Tanmay 89
Kim, Edward 40
Kohn, Florian 22
Křetínský, Jan 218
Kröger, Paul 22
Kudalkar, Vidisha 70
Kurur, Piyush P. 109

L
Leucker, Martin 163

M
Mallick, Swapnil 70
Mamouras, Konstantinos 128
Markey, Nicolas 243
Matsumoto, Naoki 59
Matsuoka, Kotaro 59
Momtaz, Anik 282
Mukhopadhyay, Shilpa 70

N
Nagaraja, Parinitha 70
Ničković, Dejan 282

P
Pedrielli, Giulia 89
Phawade, Ramchandra 109
Pinisetty, Srinivas 3

R
Reese, Lennard 150
Rieder, Sabine 218
Rodríguez, Gilde Valeria 262
Roop, Partha 3

Roussanaly, Victor 243
Rubeck, Clara 192

S

Sangiovanni-Vincentelli, Alberto 40
Saraç, N. Ege 282
Schön, Torsten 218
Seshia, Sanjit A. 40
Silva, Rafael Castro G. 150
Suenaga, Kohei 59
Suwa, Takashi 59

T

Thoma, Daniel 163
Traytel, Dmitriy 150

V

Vorhoff, Jan 218
Vuppala, Sai Rohan Harshavardhan 3

W

Waga, Masaki 59
Wang, Yixuan 205
Wu, Changshun 229

X

Xu, Kaifei 40

Y

Yang, Frank 205

Z

Zhan, Sinong Simon 205
Zhu, Qi 205
Zimmermann, Martin 174

SPRINGER NATURE

GPSR Compliance

The European Union's (EU) General Product Safety Regulation (GPSR) is a set of rules that requires consumer products to be safe and our obligations to ensure this.

If you have any concerns about our products, you can contact us on ProductSafety@springernature.com

In case Publisher is established outside the EU, the EU authorized representative is:

Springer Nature Customer Service Center GmbH
Europaplatz 3
69115 Heidelberg, Germany

The manufacturer's authorised representative in the EU is Springer Nature Customer Service Centre GmbH, Europaplatz 3, 69115 Heidelberg, Germany. If you have any concerns regarding our products, please contact ProductSafety@springernature.com

Printed and bound by CPI Group (UK) Ltd, Croydon, CR0 4YY

26/03/2026

02078933-0015